Dell
Delta Airlines
Deltona Corporation
Deutsche Post
DHL
Diesel
Digital
Disney
DKB
Dombroff & Gillmore
Domino's Pizza
Dow Chemicals
Dow Corning
Dr Pepper
Dreamworks SKG
Dun & Bradstreet
DuPont
Dutch Post Office
DVD Express

Eastman Kodak
eBay
Eccentric
EDS
EG+G
Electrolux
Electronic Arts
Eli Lilly
EMC
Emerson Electric
EMI
Enron
Exxon

Federal Express
Ferre
Filene's Basement
Fingerhut
Ford Motor Company
Fox
Frito-Lay
Fujita & Company
Fuso

Gaultier
GE Capital Corporation
Genentech
General Electric
General Foods
General Instrument
General Mills
General Motors
Genetics Institute
Genzyme
Giant
Gillette
Glaxo (Glaxo/Wellcome)
Gloria Jean

GM
Goldsmith
Goldstar Electron
Gulf and Western

H.J. Heinz
Hales Design Group
Hanson
Harley-Davidson
Harvard Graphics
Heinz
Henry Ford Clinic
Hewlett-Packard
Hilton Hotels
Hit de Venezuela
Hollywood Video
Home Depot
Honda
Hudepohl
Hyundai
Hyundai Electronics

IBM
Icahn
ICI
Illinois Department of Children and
    Family Services
Inland Steel
InteCom
Intel
International Harvester
International Nickel Topps
International Systems
ITT
Ittierre SpA

Jacobs
Jagram
Jewel
Jiffy Lube
John Fairfax and Sons
Johnson & Johnson
Johnson Controls
JVC

Kaiser Aluminum
Kasper Instruments
Kellogg
Kellogg Graduate School of
    Management
Kentucky Fried Chicken
Kerr-McGee
Kimberly-Clark
Kiri
Kiwi
KLM
Kmart
Kodak

Kraft Foods
Kubota

Laker Airlines
Lear
Leo Burnett
Levi Strauss
LG
Liggett Group
Linz-Donawitz
Lionel Corporation
Little Caesar's
Litton
Liz Claiborne
Lloyd's of London
Loblaw's
Lockheed
LucasVarity

Macy's Department Stores
Marmon Group
Marzotto SpA
Matsushita
Mattel
Maytag
Mazda
MCC
McCormick Spices
McDonald's
McDonald's-Japan
McGaw Cellular Communications
McGaw/Microsoft Teledesic
McIlhenny
McKinsey
Mead Corp
MedPartners
Mercedes-Benz
Merck
MGM
Michael Reese Hospital
Microsoft
Midas Muffler
MidCon
Midway Airlines
Minute Maid
Miroglio
Missoni
Mitsubishi
Mitsui
Mobil
Moschino
Motorola
Muse Electronics
Musicland
Myers

N.V. of Netherlands
Nan Ya Plastics

(continued)

National Basketball Association
National, The
Nationsbank
Navistar
NEC
Nestlé
Netscape
New York and Erie Railroad
New York Times
Nike
Nine West
Nissan
Nordstrom
North Star
Northern Telecom
Northwest Airlines
Nucor

Ocean Spray
Oki Electric
Omnicom Group
Outback Steakhouse

Pacific Telesis
Panasonic
Paramount
Patek Philippe
Penn Central
People's Express
Pepsi-Cola
Perrigo
Peugot
Pharmacia
Philip Morris
Philips
PhyrCor
Pickens
Pickwick International
Piggly Wiggly
Pillsbury
Pizza Hut
Polar
Post
Premium Standard Farms
Primerica
Printer's Row
Prochnik
Procter and Gamble

Qantas
Quaker Oats

Random House
Raytheon
RCA
Reel.com

Renault
Republic Steel
RJR
Roanoke Electric
Rockwell
Rohm
Rolm
Royal Crown
Ryder

Safeway
Sainsbury's
Sainsbury's Bank
Sam's Club
Samsung
Sanwa
SAP AG
Sapporo
Saturn
Schlitz
Scott Paper
Sears
Security Pacific Corporation
Sequent
Servicemaster
7-Up
SGI
Shaefer Electronics
Shell
Siemans
Silicon Graphics
Smith Barney
Smith Cogeneration
SmithKline-Beecham
SMS Schloemann-Siemag
Sony
Southwest Airlines
Springs Industries
Square Co.
Standard Oil
Starbucks
Stratus
Sumitomo
Sun MicroSystems
Suntory
Sutter Home
Swift

Taco Bell
Tandem
Target
Tatra Iron and Steel Company
TCA Cable TV
Tesco
Texas Instruments

Textron
Thompson
Thorn-EMI
3M
Times-Mirror
TJMaxx
Topco
Toshiba
Toyota
Toys "R" Us
Trans Union
Travelers
Trek
Tricon
TRW
TWA
Tyson Foods

Unifi
Union Carbide
United Airlines
United Parcel Service
United States Steel
United Technologies
Universal
University of Chicago Graduate School
    of Business
University of Chicago Hospital
Upjohn
USAirways
Usiminas
USX (United States Steel)

Value Jet
Vestron
Victor Corporation of Japan (JVC)

W.R. Grace
W.R. Wrigley
Wal-Mart
Walt Disney & Co.
Wang Laboratories
Warner Bros.
Warner-Lambert
Washington Post
Waste Management
Wendy's
Westinghouse
White Motors
Wisconsin Central

Xerox

Yahoo

Zenith

ECONOMICS OF STRATEGY

ECONOMICS
OF STRATEGY
Second Edition

David Besanko / *Northwestern University*

David Dranove / *Northwestern University*

Mark Shanley / *Purdue University*

JOHN WILEY & SONS, INC.

NEW YORK / CHICHESTER / WEINHEIM / BRISBANE / SINGAPORE / TORONTO

ACQUISITIONS EDITOR   Marissa Ryan
MARKETING MANAGER   Rebecca Hope
SENIOR PRODUCTION EDITOR   Christine Cervoni
COVER AND TEXT DESIGNER   Kevin Murphy
ILLUSTRATION EDITOR   Anna Melhorn
COVER ART   Claude Monet, Waterloo Bridge, Sunlight Effect, 1903, photograph © 1998
The Art Institute of Chicago

This book was set in 10/12 Janson Text by UG Division of GGS Information Services and
printed and bound by R.R. Donnelly. The cover was printed by
Brady Palmer Printing Co.

This book is printed on acid free paper.   ∞

Library of Congress Cataloging-in-Publication Data:
Economics of strategy / David Besanko, David Dranove, Mark Shanley.—
    2nd ed.
        p.   cm.
        Includes index.
        ISBN 0-471-25454-1 (cloth : alk. paper)
        1. Strategic planning—Economic aspects.   2. Managerial economics.
    I. Besanko, David.   II. Dranove, David.   III. Shanley, Mark (Mark T.)
    HD30.28.E25   2000
    658.4′012—dc21   98-20331
                                                                              CIP

Printed in the United States of America

10 9 8 7 6 5 4 3 2

PREFACE

*I*n the preface to his classic work, *Competitive Strategy*, Michael Porter argued that the field of business strategy lacked an analytical base and contained few generalizable or robust insights. He also noted that economists, whose work on industries and competition might serve as the basis for the development of such insights, were by and large insensitive to the needs of practicing managers. Porter's book provides an important illustration of how economic reasoning can inform and develop useful insights for practicing managers, particularly with regard to strategies for dealing with a firm's external environment.

This insight could not have come at a more propitious time. Beginning in the early 1980s, top-tier business schools began to require three to five years of post-undergraduate work experience as a precondition for admission. "Graying" MBA students could readily relate classroom material to real-world managerial challenges. At the same time, they could readily identify circumstances when classroom material did not seem relevant. Freshly minted college graduates might unquestioningly compute Cournot equilibria, but a 27-year-old ex-McKinsey business analyst would demand to know why learning Cournot could possibly enhance business decision making. This development placed additional burdens on experienced teachers of strategy courses and made it increasingly difficult for new assistant professors out of traditional economics programs to begin teaching these courses.

Following on the heels of Porter, and in the face of a maturing student body, many business school economists, including us, searched for textbooks that might be used to provide an economic foundation for strategic analysis. Most of the available standard texts in strategic management lacked disciplinary grounding, and few contained discussions of the new knowledge generated in the 1980s and 1990s by researchers in economics and strategy (e.g., transactions cost economics, commitment, and the resource-based view of the firm). Moreover, most of these books were targeted at more general audiences than what one finds at a business school such as Kellogg. Discussions with colleagues around the country led us to conclude that we were not the only ones struggling to find an appropriate text for teaching business strategy. Indeed the choice of a text for the core strategy course appears to be problematic at many business schools.

One possibility was to teach business strategy using microeconomics texts. During the 1980s new texts such as Robert Pindyck and Daniel Rubinfeld's *Microeconomics*, appeared and were an improvement over earlier texts. In particular,

Pindyck and Rubinfeld offered many real-world examples to demonstrate the practical importance of economics. But this text was targeted at the intermediate microeconomics market, and from the perspective of someone teaching strategy or business economics, it represented at best a compromise between traditional microeconomics and management strategy.

In the years immediately preceding our work on *Economics of Strategy*, two important books appeared. Sharon Oster's *Modern Competitive Analysis*, which first appeared in 1989, was remarkable for its breadth, covering most of the topics that we had identified as important to teach in a management strategy class. However, we believed that our MBA students would benefit from a more detailed exploration of the theoretical and empirical underpinnings of the ideas presented in Oster's book. Paul Milgrom and John Robert's *Economics, Organization, and Management*, which appeared in 1991, was remarkable for its depth. Milgrom and Roberts provided a deep theoretical basis for understanding issues involving organization, incentives, and hierarchy. This advanced book, however, lacked the range of topics that we needed to cover in our basic management strategy class. Our objective in writing *Economics of Strategy* was, in part, to capture the breadth of Oster at a level of analysis approaching Milgrom and Roberts, while offering the kinds of illustrative examples that appear in both books.

We believe that in the first edition of *Economics of Strategy*, we largely accomplished our goals. Even so, as we taught from the first edition we realized that there was room for improvement. Readers familiar with the first edition will note a number of changes that we believe will markedly improve the book's pedagogy. We have completely reworked our discussions of a number of difficult topics, such as "make-or-buy fallacies," competitor identification, commitment, and strategic positioning. We introduce an "industry analysis checklist" that students should find very useful when performing five-forces analyses. We have eliminated a number of peripheral discussions, particularly those for which there was substantial mathematics with little insight to show for it. There are more example boxes, with an increased emphasis on global applications. We have added a glossary of terms. Finally, there are substantially more end-of-chapter questions.

The careful reader of the first edition will also notice that we have changed the ordering of some chapters and eliminated one chapter. The chapter on horizontal boundaries now precedes the chapters on vertical boundaries—the former is essential to understanding the latter. The chapter on industry analysis now finishes, rather than begins, Part Two. While the chapter still stands on its own, it also serves a useful summary of the preceding material on competition. We have eliminated the chapter on measuring cost and benefit advantage. The bulk of this material now appears in appendixes to Chapters 2 and 12.

ORGANIZATION OF THE BOOK

This book is organized in four parts. Part One focuses on the boundaries of the firm. Major topics include economies of scale and scope, the economics of the make-versus-buy decision (vertical boundaries), the transactions costs of market exchange, and diversification. Part Two covers competitive strategy from the perspective of industrial organization (IO) economies. It includes traditional IO topics such as market structure and entry and modern IO topics such as dynamic pricing rivalry. It concludes with a discussion of Porter's Five Forces, which we view as a systematic framework for assessing the IO issues presented in the preceding chapters. Part Three of the book covers strategic positioning and dynamics. The chapters in this section provide an economic foundation for understanding what competitive advantage is, how it might be diagnosed, the conditions under which it might be sustained, and how it might be acquired in the first place. This portion of the book draws from modern literature in both economics and strategy. Part Four covers topics associated with internal organization, including the economics of agency relationships; the economics of organizational design; and politics, power, and culture. A key innovation in this section of the book is the attempt to integrate insights from economics with those from organization theory.

The book is liberally interspersed with real-world examples that bring the economic models to life. There are an average of six "example boxes" per chapter that discuss a wide variety of organizations and industries in detail. Many of these examples involve businesses outside the United States. This international focus demonstrates that the principles in this book are relevant to business worldwide. The business world is ever changing, and by the time this book hits the market, some of our references to organizations and individuals might be obsolete. We hope that the lessons learned from them will endure.

We believe that this book can either be used as a text in a core strategy course or in a business economics course that focuses on the economics of industry and the economics of the firm. For a strategy or strategic management course for MBA students, we recommend use of the chapters in Parts One, Three, and Four. In our 10-week Fall quarter strategy course for first-year MBA students at Kellogg, we typically assign the following chapters:

Chapter 1 The Evolution of the Modern Firm
Chapter 2 The Horizontal Boundaries of the Firm: Economies of Scale and Scope
Chapter 3 The Vertical Boundaries of the Firm
Chapter 4 The Transactions Costs of Market Exchange
Chapter 5 Organizing Vertical Boundaries: Vertical Integration and Its Alternatives
Chapter 11 Industry Analysis
Chapter 12 Strategic Positioning for Competitive Advantage
Chapter 13 Sustaining Competitive Advantage
Chapter 16 Strategy and Structure
Chapter 17 Power and Culture

We exclude Chapter 6 on diversification in teaching our course because that topic is covered in depth in a later course. If diversification is covered in a basic strategy course, then that chapter should be included in the preceding list. If we had an entire semester for our strategy course, we would add Chapter 7 (Competitors and Competition), Chapter 14 (Origins of Competitive Advantage: Innovation, Evolution, and the Environment), Chapter 15 (Incentives and Agency), and Chapter 17 (Power and Culture).

Our placement of the boundaries of the firm chapters (2–6) before the strategy chapters (11–14) may strike some as atypical. However, it is not essential that instructors follow this ordering. As long as students understand the material in the Economics Primer and the material on economies of scale and scope in Chapter 2, the strategy chapters (11–14) can be taught before the chapters on the boundaries of the firm (3–6).

The set of chapters 8–10 relating to commitment, dynamic competition, and entry/exit are the ones that are most closely tied to modern industrial organization economics and are thus the most "game theoretic" of the chapters in the book. This set of chapters is the most demanding one for students with weaker economic backgrounds (though the introduction to game theory in the primer coupled with material in Chapter 7 should be sufficient for students to understand this material). Because students in our basic strategy course at Kellogg have not yet taken economics, we do not cover these chapters. The material in Chapters 12 and beyond does not depend on the material in the Chapters 8–10, so these chapters can be easily skipped without any loss in continuity.

The book can also be used in a strategy or managerial economics course that emphasizes competitive strategy and modern industrial organization. For a one-quarter course, we recommend use of these chapters:

Chapter 2 The Horizontal Boundaries of the Firm
Chapter 7 Competitors and Competition
Chapter 8 Strategic Commitment
Chapter 9 The Dynamics of Pricing Rivalry
Chapter 10 Entry and Exit
Chapter 11 Industry Analysis
Chapter 12 Strategic Positioning for Competitive Advantage
Chapter 13 Sustaining Competitive Advantage
Chapter 14 The Origins of Competitive Advantage: Innovation, Evolution, and the Environment

For a one-semester course, one could add Chapter 6 to the preceding list and supplement the material from all the chapters with advanced readings on competitive strategy, industrial organization, and game theory.

ACKNOWLEDGMENTS

Many individuals helped make the second edition of *The Economics of Strategy* possible. We are especially grateful to Marissa Ryan of Wiley for the substantial work she did in coordinating the development of the book. She was an effective and enthusiastic catalyst for the many didactical changes that emerged. She also arranged for the copyediting, found reviewers, and coordinated the marketing of the book. We want to thank Fred Courtright for the work that he did in securing copyright permissions for the various figures, tables, and quotations taken from other sources and we want to thank Christine Cervoni of Wiley for so ably keeping the production of this book on track. We greatly appreciate Gerald Lombardi's developmental editing. Having painstakingly read and suggested improvements to every chapter of both the first and second editions, Gerald probably knows this material better than we do!

Many of the improvements in the second edition are the result of comments received by instructors who used the first edition. Thanks to our colleagues who so kindly pointed out the problem areas and suggested ways to improve them. In this regard, we are especially grateful to our Kellogg colleagues James Dana, Anne Gron, and Sonia Marciano. Considerable gratitude also goes to Dean Donald Jacobs and to (former) Associate Dean Mark Satterthwaite and (current) Associate Dean Dipak Jain of the Kellogg School for giving us the opportunity to develop Kellogg's basic strategy course and for the enthusiasm and support they showed for us in writing the first and second editions of this book.

We are also grateful for the comments we received from those who reviewed the book, including Sheryl Ball, Virginia Tech; Robert Becker, Indiana University; Tim Campbell, University of Southern California; Darral Clarke, Brigham Young University; Gary Fournier, Florida State University; Kenneth Marino, San Diego State University; John Stevens, University of Minnesota; and Josefina Tranfa, Florida State University. We were pleased by the many substantive suggestions they offered to a book that had already been through several revisions.

A number of Kellogg Masters of Management students provided valuable assistance for specific parts of the book. We want to thank Christopher Meyer for writing Example 3.4 (Jagram) in Chapter 3. Ana Dutra helped research and write Example 6.2 in Chapter 6 on the merger between Continental Bank and Bank of America. Jack Pardee developed the expanded Cambridge Zoo in Chapter 8. Andrew Cherry is responsible for Example 9.1 (Philip Morris versus B.A.T.) in Chapter 9. Fuminori Takemura, Edward Arnstein, Tod Salzman, Rory Altman, and Masahiro Murakami suggested the Panasonic-Epson example in Chapter 9. Sanjay Malkani, David Pereira, Robert Kennedy, Katarzyna Pitula, and Mitsunari Okamoto are responsible for Example 9.2 (Dow Chemical in the market for reverse osmosis membranes) in Chapter 9. Diane Kityama, Jon Passman, Craig Safir, Todd Reichman, and Philip Yau contributed material for Example 9.4 in Chapter 9 on the cigarette industry. Andrew Calderwood wrote Example 10.3 on the Australian Airline industry in Chapter 10. James Carr, Nina Case, Kathleen Fabsits, Robert Musson, Chet Richardson, Andrew Schwartz, and Scott Swanson wrote the first draft of the Kona coffee example in Chapter 11. Joseph Baumann helped research and write Example 15.3 in Chapter 15 on the Illinois Department of Children and Family Services. Suresh Krishna helped research and write Example 16.2 in Chapter 16 on ABB. Michael Lounsbury helped research and write Example 16.5 in Chapter 16 on Samsung.

Finally, we want to thank all of the Kellogg students during the 1996–1997, 1997–1998, and 1998–1999 academic years who took Management and Strategy D31 (Management of Organizations) or Managerial Economics D41 (Competitive Strategy) and thus used the first edition of the book. They faithfully identified typographical and factual errors, while suggesting ideas for new examples. In these and many other ways, they left their mark on the second edition. The origin of this book lay in our desire to develop a challenging, principle-based strategy course for students at Kellogg. As was the case with the first edition, we are pleased to say that our students have had a significant impact on the final product!

David Besanko

David Dranove

Mark Shanley

Evanston, Illinois   January 1999

Contents

Part Four: Internal Organization

Introduction:
Strategy
and Economics

Why Study Strategy? ◆ ◆ ◆ ◆ ◆

To answer this question, we first have to understand what strategy is. Consider how three leading contributors to the field define the concept of strategy:

> . . . the determination of the basic long-term goals and objectives of an enterprise, and the adoption of courses of action and the allocation of resources necessary for carrying out these goals.—Alfred Chandler.[1]
> . . . the pattern of objectives, purposes or goals, and the major policies and plans for achieving these goals, stated in such a way as to define what business the company is in or should be in and the kind of company it is or should be.—Kenneth Andrews.[2]
> . . . what determines the framework of a firm's business activities and provides guidelines for coordinating activities so that the firm can cope with and influence the changing environment. Strategy articulates the firm's preferred environment and the type of organization it is striving to become.—Hiroyuki Itami.[3]

These definitions have much in common. Phrases such as "long-term goals" and "major policies" suggest that strategy has to do with the "big" decisions a business organization faces, the decisions that ultimately determine its success or failure. The emphasis on "patterns of objectives" and "the framework of a firm's business" suggests that strategy is revealed in terms of consistent behavior, which in turn implies that strategy, once set, is not easy to reverse. Finally, the idea that strategy "defines . . . what kind of company it is or should be" suggests that strategic deci-

---

[1]Chandler, A, *Strategy and Structure: Chapters in the History of the American Industrial Enterprise*, Cambridge, MA: MIT Press, 1962, p. 13.

[2]Andrews, K., *The Concept of Corporate Strategy*, Homewood, IL: Irwin, 1971.

[3]Itami, H., *Mobilizing Invisible Assets*, Cambridge, MA: Harvard University Press, 1987.

sions shape the firm's competitive persona, its collective understanding of how it is going to succeed within its competitive environment.

Strategy is, in short, fundamental to an organization's success, which is why the study of strategy can be both profitable and intellectually engaging. The objective of this book is to study and analyze strategy primarily (though not exclusively) from the perspective of economics. Our central theme is that much can be learned by uncovering durable principles that are applicable to many different strategic situations. This value shows up in two fundamental ways: one, by gaining a better understanding of how firms compete and organize themselves (knowledge that we think is virtuous in its own right), and two, by developing a more secure foundation for making good strategic decisions. Having said this, we need to add that this is not intended to be a book of "strategic recipes." The situational complexity of real industries and real firms makes memorizing buzzwords or following fads risky business indeed. The successful application of the concepts and principles that are discussed in this book depends on the institutional, organizational, and economic complexity that occurs when a particular company faces a particular situation. We cannot guarantee that this book will make you a more skillful strategic decision maker. What studying this book can help you do is make much better sense of messy and ambiguous strategic situations, and that is an essential step toward skillful strategic decision making.

◆ ◆ ◆ ◆ ◆ WHY ECONOMICS?

One can approach the study of strategy in many ways. One could study strategy from the perspective of mathematical game theory, seeking to discover the logic of choice in situations that involve rivalry. Strategy could also be studied from the perspective of psychology, focusing on how the motivations and behaviors of individual decision makers shape the direction and the performance of their organizations and on how competitive or strategic decisions can be understood as reflecting the biases of individual decision makers. One could study strategy-related questions from an organizational perspective, drawing from either the discipline of sociology, which stresses the role of social structures, peer networks, and organizational routines in determining the decisions made by complex organizations, or political science, which emphasizes the importance of governance structures and coalitions.

There is much to be said for viewing strategy from the perspective of multiple models and multiple disciplinary lenses. But depth of strategic knowledge is as important as breadth of strategic knowledge. In other words, there is much to be gained from detailed application of economics. Deep knowledge of economics permits the formulation of more subtle and powerful hypotheses and the development of richer strategies. Borrowing from concepts to be introduced in this book, we believe that there are deep "economies of scale" that justify a "focus" on economics.

An advantage of economics, and one reason for its widespread use for analyzing individual and institutional decision making, is that it requires the analyst to be explicit about the key elements of the process under consideration. Economic models must carefully identify each of the following:

- *Decision makers.* Who are the active players? Whose decisions are taken as "fixed" in the situation at hand? (For example, are the capacity choices of certain firms fixed during one particular firm's planning horizon?)

- *Goals.* What are the decision makers trying to accomplish? Are they profit maximizing? Do they have nonpecuniary interests? How do decision makers trade off these conflicting goals?

- *Choices.* What actions are under consideration? What are the strategic variables? (For example, can manufacturers select different levels of quality or is quality fixed?) What is the time horizon over which decisions can be made?

- *Relationship between choices and outcomes.* What is the mechanism by which specific decisions translate into specific outcomes? Is there a functional relationship between certain choices, such as price, and certain outcomes, such as market share? (For example, will a firm lose market share if a particular rival lowers its price?) Is the relationship complicated by uncertainty about such factors as taste, technology, or the choices of other decision makers?

While political scientists, sociologists, and psychologists sometimes have to ask the same questions, economic theory is distinctive, we think, in that the answers to these questions are usually specified explicitly as part of the development of the theory. The advantage to this is that there is clear linkage between the conclusions one draws from the application of economic reasoning and the assumptions that the scholar is making in studying the situation at hand. This leaves what Garth Saloner has called an "audit trail" that allows one to be able to distinguish between unsupported conjectures or claims and logically derived propositions.[4] We will not in general provide detailed audit trails, because this will require countless pages and advanced mathematics. But we will provide the intuition behind each of the propositions that we advance.

The explicit nature of economic models permits the application of economics to a wide variety of problems. Economics has been used to study Supreme Court decisions, suicide, and drug addiction, for example. Moreover, economics offers a wide range of perspectives, from an almost exclusive focus on the interaction of firms within an industry to views of individual interactions within the context of an organization. We believe that this book demonstrates that economics provides significant insights into the major themes of strategy that we describe below.

On the other hand, economic modeling, by its very nature, abstracts from the situational complexity that individuals and firms face. Thus, the application of economic insights to specific situations to gain insight often requires creativity and a deft touch. It also often requires explicit recognition of the constraints imposed on firms by mistakes, history, and organizational and political factors. Nor does economics fully address the *process* by which choices are made and translated into actions and outcomes. The process of managing the implementation of a competitive strategy decision or a change in the nature of internal organization is often fundamental to their success. Our emphasis on economics in this book is not intended to downgrade the importance of process; it is simply beyond the scope of our expertise to say much about it.

---

[4]Saloner, G., "Modeling, Game Theory, and Strategic Management," *Strategic Management Journal*, 12, Winter 1991: pp. 119–136.

◆ ◆ ◆ ◆ ◆ THE NEED FOR PRINCIPLES

There is a keen interest among serious observers of business to understand the reasons for profitability and market success. This is understandable, since profit is the fundamental motive for business activity. However, observers of business often uncritically leap to the conclusion that the keys to success can be identified by watching and imitating the behaviors of successful firms. (This is sometimes known as "benchmarking.") A host of management prescriptions by consultants and in the popular business press is buttressed by allusions to the practices of high-performing firms and their managers. These recommendations carry all the more weight if the firms in question, and their industries, are new. The examples of biotechnology firms, such as Amgen, and software firms, such as Yahoo, easily come to mind.

However, uncritically using currently successful firms as a standard for action assumes that successful outcomes are associated with identifiable key success factors, and by imitating these factors, other firms can achieve similar successful results. While we do not believe that firms succeed randomly, we are convinced that using a given firm's experiences to understand what would make all firms successful is extremely difficult.

There are several dangers in jumping too quickly to the conclusion that the observable practices of successful firms provide lessons that observers can apply to their own firms. The reasons for success are often unclear, even to the executives of the successful firms, and also are likely to be complex. Many factors may contribute to a firm's performance, including some that are not apparent to observers. For example, the internal management systems of a firm may spur product innovation particularly well and not be apparent to individuals who are unfamiliar with how the firm operates.

The industry and market conditions in which successful firms operate may differ greatly from the conditions faced by would-be imitators. In past merger waves, for example, many firms sought to expand to gain the advantages of scale and market power. Many of these firms found out, to their dismay, that the technological conditions in their industries had to be just right before large firms can gain such advantages. We suspect that the same will occur during the present merger wave. Success may also be due in part to a host of idiosyncratic factors, including luck, that will be difficult to identify and impossible to imitate.

Finally, there may be a bias resulting from trying to understand success solely by examining the strategies of successful firms. Strategies associated with many successful firms may have been tried by an equally large number of unsuccessful firms. For example, one may find that among a sample of 50 successful firms, 35 engaged in aggressive acquisition programs, and from this one might be tempted to conclude that acquisitions are a hallmark of successful firms. However, without studying unsuccessful firms, this conclusion would be invalid. For example, if a well-matched sample of 50 unsuccessful firms revealed that 38 of them also engaged in aggressive acquisition programs, the correct (and possibly uninteresting) conclusion is that acquisition programs are a general characteristic of the 100 firms studied and not a particularly strong determinant of success.

Further biases may emerge from the failure to disentangle cause and effect. Suppose that only 10 of the unsuccessful firms engaged in acquisition programs. There would appear to be a correlation between acquisition activity and success.

But do acquisitions lead to success, or do firms that were successful for reasons that had nothing to do with acquisitions (e.g., they possessed valuable patents) use their cash surpluses to acquire other firms? Without the answer to these questions, one may again be led down a primrose path by mimicking the actions of successful firms.

We do believe that it is useful to study the behaviors of firms. The value of this study, however, lies in helping us identify the general principles behind why firms behave as they do, not in trying to develop lists of characteristics that lead to automatic success. Success or failure will be the result of firms pursuing their goals in a specific way and in a specific business context. The results of a firm's activities will be determined by the principles guiding its actions and how those principles match the conditions the firm faces. A strategy textbook can provide the general principles that underlie strategic decisions. It is not an exhaustive cookbook of uniformly effective recipes for business success. Success depends on the manager who must match principles with conditions.

To see this point, consider the variety that a serious observer of business in the late 1990s who attempted to identify success strategies would face. He or she would encounter a broad range of management practices among firms. Take, for example, three highly regarded and successful firms: Nike, Usiminas, and Wal-Mart.[5] Each of them has a different organizational structure and corporate strategy. Nike performs few of the functions traditionally associated with large industrial firms and instead uses independent contractors for much of its initial production work and to distribute its products. Nike's success is built largely on marketing campaigns involving well-known athletes. Usiminas is a traditional vertically integrated steel firm best known for its operational excellence in manufacturing. That excellence, coupled with its access to Brazil's low-cost labor and abundant energy supplies, has made Usiminas one of the lowest-cost producers of steel in the world. Unlike the first two, Wal-Mart is a distributor and retailer. It relies on the initiative of its local store managers, combined with sophisticated purchasing and inventory management, to keep its retailing costs below those of its rivals.

Making sense of this variety of strategies can be frustrating, especially because, within most industries, we see poorly performing firms employing the same strategies and management practices as industry exemplars. For every Nike, there is an L.A. Gear. For every Usiminas, there is a Bethlehem Steel. For every Wal-Mart, there is a Kmart.

If we find this variety of management practices bewildering, imagine the reactions of a manager from 1910, or even 1960, who was transported ahead in time. The large hierarchical firm that dominated the corporate landscape until the 1970s seems out of place today. General Motors received its share of criticism in the wake of the oil shortages and Japanese invasion of the 1970s, but its structure and strategy were models for manufacturing from the 1920s through the 1960s. United States Steel (now USX), the first firm in the world to achieve annual sales of $1 billion at the time of its inception in 1901, has greatly declined in relative size and now must rely on selling oil to remain one of the 25 largest U.S. industrial firms. The list of once-admired firms that today are struggling to survive is a long one.

---

[5] The full name of Usiminas is Usinas Siderurgicas de Minas Gerais.

There are two ways to interpret this bewildering variety and evolution of management practice. The first is to believe that the development of successful strategies is so complicated as to be essentially a matter of luck. If this is true, then a manager does not need to systematically study strategy except to track current trends and absorb the advice of management "gurus."

The second interpretation presumes that successful firms succeeded because the strategies their managers chose best allowed them to exploit the potential profit opportunities that existed at the time or to adapt to changing circumstances. We believe in this second interpretation. While there is no doubt that luck, both good and bad, plays a role in determining the success of firms, we believe that success is often no accident. We believe that we can better understand why firms succeed or fail when we analyze decision making in terms of consistent principles of market economics and strategic action. And we believe that the odds of competitive success increase when managers try to apply these principles to the varying conditions and opportunities they face. Throughout this book we identify what we believe are general principles of firm behavior, industry structure, and market performance that are as applicable today as they were at any other time in business history. While these principles do not uniquely explain why firms succeed, they should be the basis for any systematic examination of strategy.

Note that this interpretation does not necessarily imply that the managers of successful firms were conscious of the link between their choices and the profit opportunities that existed. Nor, conversely, does it imply that the failure of a particular strategy or management practice means that the decision to undertake it was inconsistent with principled decision making. What it does imply, it seems to us, is that it should be possible to identify underlying principles of strategy that reveal for us the conditions under which some practices are likely to be more successful than others. If this is so, then the study of strategy is indispensable to the manager who must confront change and uncertainty.

◆ ◆ ◆ ◆ ◆ A FRAMEWORK FOR STRATEGY

In our opening discussion of what strategy is, we asserted that strategy is concerned with the "big" issues that firms face. But what specifically does this mean? What are these "big" issues? Put another way, to formulate and implement a successful strategy, what does the firm have to pay attention to? We would argue that to successfully formulate and implement strategy, a firm must confront four broad classes of issues:

- *Boundaries of the firm*—What should the firm do, how large should it be, and what businesses should it be in?

- *Market and competitive analysis*—What is the nature of the markets in which the firm competes and the nature of competitive interactions between firms in those markets?

- *Position and dynamics*—How should the firm position itself to compete, what should be the basis of its competitive advantage, and how should it adjust over time?

- *Internal organization*—How should the firm organize its structure and systems internally?

Boundaries of the Firm

The firm's boundaries define what the firm does. Boundaries can extend in three different directions: horizontal, vertical, and corporate. The firm's horizontal boundaries refer to how much of the product market the firm serves, or essentially how big it is. The firm's vertical boundaries refer to the set of activities that the firm performs itself and those that it purchases from market specialty firms. The firm's corporate boundaries refer to the set of distinct businesses the firm competes in. All three boundaries have received differing amounts of emphasis at different times in the strategy literature. The Boston Consulting Group's emphasis on the learning curve and market growth in the 1960s gave prominence to the firm's horizontal boundaries. Formal planning models organized around tools, such as growth-share matrices, gave prominence to the firm's corporate boundaries. More recently, such concepts as "network organizations" and the "virtual corporation" have given prominence to the firm's vertical boundaries. Our view is that all are important and can be fruitfully analyzed through the perspectives offered by economics.

Market and Competitive Analysis

To formulate and execute successful strategies, firms must understand the nature of the markets in which they compete. As Michael Porter points out in his classic work *Competitive Strategy*, performance across industries is not a matter of chance or accident.[6] There are reasons why, for example, even mediocre firms in an industry such as pharmaceuticals have, by economywide standards, impressive profitability performance, while the top firms in the airline industry seem to achieve low rates of profitability even in the best of times. While the relative importance of industry- versus firm-specific effects is still under debate, the nature of industry structure cannot be ignored either in attempting to understand why firms follow the strategies they do or in attempting to formulate strategies for competing in an industry.

Position and Dynamics

Position and dynamics are shorthand for how and on what basis a firm competes. Position is a static concept. At a given moment in time, is the firm competing on the basis of low costs or because it is differentiated in key dimensions and can thus charge a premium over the prices charged by the other firms with which it competes? Position, as we discuss it, also concerns the resources and capabilities that underlie any cost or differentiation advantages that a firm might have. Dynamics refers to how the firm accumulates resources and capabilities, as well as to how it adjusts over time to changing circumstances. Fundamentally, dynamics has to do with the process emphasized so eloquently by the economist Joseph Schumpeter, who argued that "the impulse of alluring profit," even though inherently temporary, will induce firms and entrepreneurs to create new bases of competitive advantage that redefine industries and undermine the ways of achieving advantage.

---

[6]Porter, M., *Competitive Strategy*, New York: Free Press, 1980.

Internal Organization

Given that the firm has chosen what to do and has figured out the nature of its market, so that it can decide how and on what basis it should compete, it still needs to organize itself internally to carry out its strategies. Organization sets the terms by which resources will be deployed and information will flow through the firm. It will also determine how well aligned the goals of individual actors within the firm are with the overall goals of the firm. How the firm organizes itself—for example, how it structures its organization, the extent to which it relies on formal incentive systems as opposed to informal influences—embodies a key set of strategic decisions in their own right.

The remainder of this book is organized along the lines of this framework. Chapters 1 through 6 have to do with the firm's boundaries. Chapters 7 through 11 deal with industry structure and market analysis. Chapters 12 through 14 address position and dynamics. Chapters 15 through 18 deal with internal organization.

Primer: Economic Concepts for Strategy

$\mathcal{I}$n 1931 conditions at the Pepsi-Cola Company were desperate.[1] The company had entered bankruptcy for the second time in 12 years, and in the words of a Delaware court, was "a mere shell of a corporation." The president of Pepsi, Charles G. Guth, even attempted to sell Pepsi to its rival Coca-Cola, but Coke wanted no part of a seemingly doomed enterprise. During this period, Pepsi and Coke sold cola in 6-ounce bottles. To reduce costs, Guth purchased a large supply of recycled 12-ounce beer bottles. Initially, Pepsi priced the 12-ounce bottles at 10 cents, twice the price of 6-ounce Cokes. However, this strategy failed to boost sales. But, then, Guth had an idea: why not sell 12-ounce Pepsis for the same price as 6-ounce Cokes? In the Depression, this was a brilliant marketing ploy. Pepsi's sales shot upward. By 1934 Pepsi was out of bankruptcy. Its profit rose to $2.1 million by 1936, and to $4.2 million by 1938. Guth's decision to undercut Coca-Cola saved the company.

This example illustrates an important point. Clearly, in 1931 Pepsi's chief objective was to increase profits so it could survive. But merely deciding to pursue this objective could not make it happen. Charles Guth could not just order his subordinates to increase Pepsi's profits. Like any company, Pepsi's management had no direct control over its profit, market share, or any of the other markers of business success. What Pepsi's management did control were marketing, production, and the administrative decisions that determined its competitive position and ultimate profitability.

The link between the decisions managers control and a firm's profitability is mediated by a host of economic relationships. The success of any strategy depends on whether the firm's decisions are compatible with these relationships. Pepsi's suc-

---

[1]This example is drawn from Richard Tedlow's history of the soft drink industry in his book, *New and Improved: The Story of Mass Marketing in America*, New York: Basic Books, 1990.

9

cess in the 1930s can be understood in terms of a few key economic relationships. The most basic of these is the law of demand. The law of demand says that, all other things being the same, the lower the price of a product, the more of it consumers will purchase. Whether the increase in the number of units sold translates into higher sales revenues depends on the strength of the relationship between price and the quantity purchased. This is measured by the price elasticity of demand. As long as Coke did not respond to Pepsi's price cut with one of its own, we would expect that the demand for Pepsi would have been relatively sensitive to price, or in the language of economics, price elastic. As we will see later in this chapter, price-elastic demand implies that a price cut not only translates into higher unit sales, but also into higher sales revenue. Whether Coke is better off responding to Pepsi's price cut depends on another relationship, that between the size of a competitor and the profitability of price matching. Because Coke had such a large share of the market, it was more profitable to keep its price high (letting Pepsi steal some of its market) than to respond with a price cut of its own.[2] Finally, whether Pepsi's higher sales revenue translates into higher profit depends on the economic relationship between the additional sales revenue that Pepsi's price cut generated and the additional cost of producing more Pepsi-Cola. That profits rose rapidly after the price reduction suggests that the additional sales revenue far exceeded the additional costs of production.

The importance of economic relationships for strategy is a central theme of this book. Most of the important contributions to the literature on strategy in the past 20 years, such as Michael Porter's "Five Forces" framework or C. K. Prahalad and Gary Hamel's concept of "core competences," are based on well-developed ideas from economics. As we argue throughout this book, understanding robust economic relationships can help us understand why some strategies are well-suited to one set of conditions but not to others. The judicious application of economic principles to a firm's circumstances can increase the odds of formulating and executing a successful business strategy.

This chapter lays out the basic economic tools that we will use to develop the principles you will study in this book. We focus here on those parts of intermediate microeconomics that are relevant for understanding business strategy. Most of the elements that contributed to Pepsi's successful price-cutting strategy in the 1930s will be on display here. An understanding of the language and concepts in this chapter will, we believe, "level the playing field," so that students with little or no background in microeconomics can navigate most of this book just as well as students with extensive economics training.

This chapter has five main parts: (1) costs; (2) demand, prices, and revenues; (3) the theory of price and output determination by a profit-maximizing firm; (4) the theory of perfectly competitive markets; and (5) game theory.[3]

◆ ◆ ◆ ◆ ◆ COSTS

A firm's profit equals its revenues minus its costs. We begin our economics primer by focusing on the cost side of this equation. We discuss four specific concepts in

---

[2]We will discuss this relationship in Chapter 9.

[3]The third, fourth, and fifth sections of this chapter are the most "technical." Instructors not planning to cover Chapters 7–10 can skip this material.

this section: cost functions; economic versus accounting costs; long-run versus short-run costs; and sunk costs.

Cost Functions

Total Cost Functions

Managers are most familiar with costs when they are presented as in Tables P.1 and P.2, which show an income statement and a statement of costs of goods manufactured for a hypothetical producer during the year 2001.[4] The information in these tables is essentially retrospective. It tells managers what happened during the past year. But what if management is interested in determining whether a price reduction will increase profits, as with Pepsi? The price drop will probably stimulate additional sales, so a firm needs to know how its total costs would change if it increased production above the previous year's level.

This is what a total cost function tells us. It represents the relationship between a firm's total costs, denoted by TC, and the total amount of output it produces in a given time period, denoted by Q. Figure P.1 shows a graph of a total cost function. For each level of output the firm might produce, the graph associates a unique level of total cost. Why is the association between output and total cost unique? A firm may currently be producing 100 units of output per year at a total cost of $5,000,000, but if it were to streamline its operations, it might be able to lower costs, so that those 100 units can be produced for only $4,500,000. We

TABLE P.1
INCOME STATEMENT: 2001

(1) Sales Revenue		$35,600
(2) Cost of Goods Sold		
Cost of Goods Manufactured	$13,740	
Add: Finished Goods Inventory 12/31/00	$3,300	
Less: Finished Goods Inventory 12/31/01	$2,950	
		$14,090
(3) Gross Profit: (1) minus (2)		$21,510
(4) Selling and General Administrative Expenses		$8,540
(5) Income from Operations: (3) minus (4)		$12,970
Interest Expenses		$1,210
Net Income Before Taxes		$11,760
Income Taxes		$4,100
Net Income		$7,660

All amounts in thousands.

---

[4]The first part of this section closely follows the presentation of cost functions on pp. 42–45 of Dorfman, R., *Prices and Markets*, 2nd ed., Englewood Cliffs, NJ: Prentice-Hall, 1972.

TABLE P.2
STATEMENT OF COST OF GOODS MANUFACTURED: 2001

Materials:		
Materials Purchases	$8,700	
Add: Materials Inventory 12/31/00	$1,400	
Less: Materials Inventory 12/31/01	$1,200	
(1) Cost of Materials Used		$8,900
(2) Direct Labor		$2,300
Manufacturing Overhead		
Indirect Labor	$700	
Heat, Light, and Power	$400	
Repairs and Maintenance	$200	
Depreciation	$1,100	
Insurance	$50	
Property Taxes	$80	
Miscellaneous Factory Expenses	$140	
(3) Total Manufacturing Overhead		$2,670
Total Cost of Manufacturing: (1) + (2) + (3)		$13,870
Add: Work-in-Process Inventory 12/31/00		$2,100
Less: Work-in-Process Inventory 12/31/01		$2,230
Cost of Goods Manufactured		$13,740

All amounts in thousands.

resolve this ambiguity by defining the total cost function as an efficiency relationship. It represents the relationship between total cost and output, assuming that the firm produces in the most efficient manner possible given its current technological capabilities. Of course, firms do not always produce as efficiently as they theoretically could. The substantial literature on Total Quality Management and re-engineering attests to the attention managers give to improving efficiency. This is why we stress that the total cost function reflects the current capabilities of the

FIGURE P.1
TOTAL COST FUNCTION.

The total cost function *TC(Q)* shows the total costs that the firm would incur for a level of output *Q*. The total cost function is an efficiency relationship in that it shows the lowest possible total cost the firm would incur to produce a level of output, given the firm's technological capabilities and the prices of factors of production, such as labor and capital.

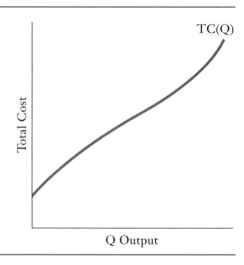

firm. If the firm is producing as efficiently as it knows how, then the total cost function must slope upward: The only way to achieve more output is to use more factors of production (labor, machinery, materials), which will raise total costs.[5]

Fixed and Variable Costs

The information contained in the accounting statements in Tables P.1 and P.2 allows us to identify the total cost for one particular level of annual output. To map out the total cost function more completely, we must distinguish between fixed costs and variable costs. Variable costs, such as direct labor and commissions to salespeople, increase as output increases. Fixed costs, such as general and administrative expenses and property taxes, remain constant as output increases.

Three important points should be stressed when discussing fixed and variable costs. First, the line dividing fixed and variable costs is often fuzzy. Some costs, such as maintenance or advertising and promotional expenses, may have both fixed and variable components. Other costs may be *semifixed*: fixed over certain ranges of output but variable over other ranges.[6] For example, a beer distributor may be able to deliver up to 5,000 barrels of beer a week using a single truck. But when it must deliver between 5,000 and 10,000 barrels, it needs two trucks, between 10,000 and 15,000, three trucks, and so forth. The cost of trucks is fixed within the intervals (0,5000), (5,000, 10,000), (10,000, 15,0000), and so forth, but is variable between these intervals. Second, when we say that a cost is fixed, we mean that it is invariant to the firm's output. It does not mean that it cannot be affected by other dimensions of the firm's operations or decisions the firm might make. For example, for an electric utility, the cost of stringing wires to hook up houses to the local grid depends primarily on the number of subscribers to the system, and not on the total amount of kilowatt-hours of electricity the utility generates. Other fixed costs, such as the money spent on marketing promotions or advertising campaigns, arise from management decisions and can be eliminated should management so desire.[7] Third, whether costs are fixed or variable depends on the time period in which decisions regarding output are contemplated. Consider, for example, an airline that is contemplating a one-week-long fare cut. Its workers have already been hired, its schedule has been set, and its fleet has been purchased. Within a one-week period, none of these decisions can be reversed. For this particular decision, then, the airline should regard a significant fraction of its costs as fixed. By contrast, if the airline contemplates committing to a year-long reduction in fares, with the expectation that ticket sales will increase accordingly, schedules can be altered, planes can be leased or purchased, and workers can be hired. In this case, the airline should re-

---

[5]Students sometimes confuse total costs with average (i.e., per unit) costs, and note that for many real-world firms "costs" seem to go down as output goes up. As we will see, average costs could indeed go down as output goes up. The total cost function, however, always increases with output.

[6]This term was coined by Thomas Nagle in *The Strategy and Tactics of Pricing*, Englewook Cliffs, NJ: Prentice-Hall, 1987.

[7]Some authors call these *programmed costs*. See, for example, Rados, D. L., *Pushing the Numbers in Marketing: A Real-world Guide to Essential Financial Analysis*, Westport, CT: Quorum Books, 1992.

gard most of its expenses as variable. Whether the firm has the freedom to alter its physical capital or other elements of its operations has important implications for its cost structure and the nature of its decision making. This will be covered in more detail below when we analyze the distinction between long-run and short-run costs.

Average and Marginal Cost Functions

Associated with the total cost function are two other cost functions: the average cost function, *AC(Q)*, and the marginal cost function, *MC(Q)*. The average cost function describes how the firm's average or per-unit-of output costs vary with the amount of output it produces. It is given by the formula:

$$AC(Q) = \frac{TC(Q)}{Q}$$

If total costs were directly proportional to output—for example, if they were given by a formula, such as $TC(Q) = 5Q$ or $TC(Q) = 37,000Q$, or more generally, by $TC(Q) = cQ$, where c is a constant—then average cost would be a constant. This is because:

$$AC(Q) = \frac{cQ}{Q} = c$$

Often, however, average cost will vary with output. As Figure P.2 shows, average cost may rise, fall, or remain constant as output goes up. When average cost decreases as output increases, there are economies of scale. When average cost increases as output increases, there are diseconomies of scale. When average cost remains unchanged with respect to output, we have constant returns to scale. A production process may exhibit economies of scale over one range of output and diseconomies of scale over another. Figure P.3 shows an average cost function that exhibits economies of scale, diseconomies of scale, and constant returns to scale.

FIGURE P.2
AVERAGE COST FUNCTION.

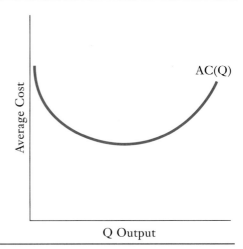

The average cost function *AC(Q)* shows the firm's average, or per-unit, cost for any level of output *Q*. Average costs are not necessarily the same at each level of output.

FIGURE P.3
ECONOMIES OF SCALE AND MINIMUM EFFICIENT SCALE.

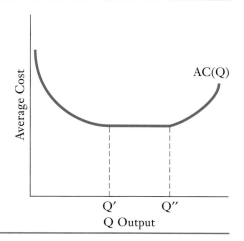

This average cost function exhibits economies of scale at output levels up to Q'. It exhibits constant returns to scale between Q' and Q''. It exhibits diseconomies of scale at output levels above Q''. The smallest output level at which economies of scale are exhausted is Q'. It is thus known as the minimum efficient scale.

Output level Q' is the smallest level of output at which economies of scale are exhausted and is thus known as the minimum efficient scale. The concepts of economies of scale and minimum efficient scale are extremely important for understanding the size and scope of firms and the structure of industries. We devote all of Chapter 2 to analyzing economies of scale.

Marginal cost refers to the rate of change of total cost with respect to output. Marginal cost may be thought of as the incremental cost of producing exactly one more unit of output. When output is initially Q and changes by ΔQ units and one knows the total cost at each output level, marginal cost may be calculated as follows:

$$MC(Q) = \frac{TC(Q + \Delta Q) - TC(Q)}{\Delta Q}$$

For example, suppose when $Q = 100$ units, $TC = \$400,000$, and when $Q = 150$ units, $TC = \$500,000$. Then $\Delta Q = 50$, and $MC = (\$500,000 - \$400,000)/50 = \$2,000$. Thus, total cost increases at a rate of $\$2,000$ per unit of output when output increases over the range 100 to 150 units.

Marginal cost often depends on the total volume of output. Figure P.4 shows the marginal cost function associated with a particular total cost function. At low levels of output, such as Q'', increasing output by 1 unit does not change total cost much, as reflected by the low marginal cost. At higher levels of output, such as Q', a 1-unit increase in output has a greater impact on total cost, and the corresponding marginal cost is higher.

Businesses often use information about average cost to estimate the marginal cost of a change in output. But average cost is generally different from marginal cost. The exception is when total costs vary in direct proportion to output, $TC(Q) = cQ$. In that case:

$$MC(Q) = \frac{c(Q + \Delta Q) - cQ}{\Delta Q} = c,$$

FIGURE P.4
RELATIONSHIP BETWEEN TOTAL COST AND MARGINAL COST.

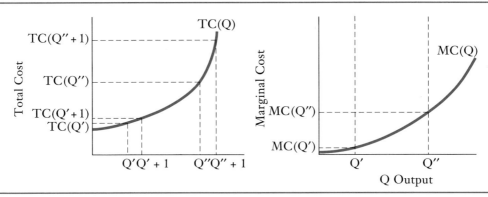

The marginal cost function *MC(Q)* on the right graph is based on the total cost function *TC(Q)* shown in the left graph. At output level *Q'*, a one-unit increase in output changes costs by *TC(Q' + 1) − TC(Q')*, which equals the marginal cost at *Q'*, *MC(Q')*. Since this change is not large, the marginal cost is small (i.e., the height of the marginal cost curve from the horizontal axis is small). At output level *Q''*, a one-unit increase in output changes costs by *TC(Q'' + 1) − TC(Q'')*, which equals the marginal cost at *Q''*. This change is larger than the one-unit change from *Q'*, so *MC(Q'') > MC(Q')*. Because the total cost function becomes steeper as *Q* gets larger, the marginal cost curve must increase in output.

which, of course, is also average cost. This result reflects a more general relationship between marginal and average cost (illustrated in Figure P.5):

- When average cost is a decreasing function of output, marginal cost is less than average cost.

- When average cost neither increases nor decreases in output—either because it is constant (independent of output) or is at a minimum point—marginal cost is equal to average cost.

FIGURE P.5
RELATIONSHIP BETWEEN MARGINAL COST AND AVERAGE COST.

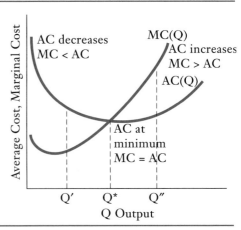

When average cost is decreasing (e.g., at output *Q'*), *AC > MC*, that is, the average cost curve lies above the marginal cost curve. When average cost is increasing (e.g., at output *Q''*), *AC < MC*, (i.e., the average cost curve lies below the marginal cost curve). When average cost is at a minimum, *AC = MC*, so the two curves must intersect.

- When average cost is an increasing function of output, marginal cost is greater than average cost.

These relationships follow from the mathematical properties of average and marginal cost, but they are also intuitive. If the average of a group of things (costs, test scores, or whatever) increases when one more thing is added to the group, then it must be because the value of the most recently added thing—the "marginal"—is greater than the average. Conversely, if the average falls, it must be because the marginal is less than the average.

The Importance of the Time Period: Long-Run versus Short-Run Cost Functions

We emphasized the importance of the time horizon when discussing fixed versus variable costs. In this section, we develop this point further and consider some of its implications.

Figure P.6 illustrates the case of a firm whose production can take place in a facility that comes in three different sizes: small, medium, and large. Once the firm commits to a production facility of a particular size, it can vary output only by varying the quantities of inputs other than the plant size (e.g., by hiring another shift of workers). The period of time in which the firm cannot adjust the size of its production facilities is known as the short run. For each plant size, there is an associated short-run average cost function, denoted by *SAC*. These average cost functions include the annual costs of all relevant variable inputs

FIGURE P.6
SHORT-RUN AND LONG-RUN AVERAGE COST FUNCTIONS.

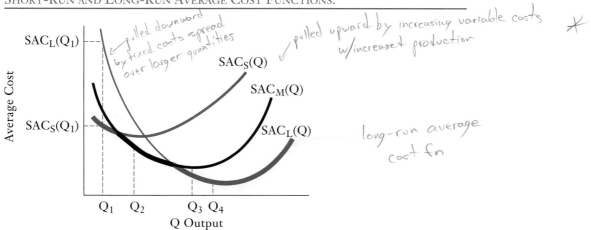

The curves labeled $SAC_S(Q)$, $SAC_M(Q)$, and $SAC_L(Q)$ are the short-run average cost functions associated with small, medium, and large plants, respectively. For any level of output, the optimal plant size is the one with the lowest average cost. For example, at output Q_1, the small plant is best. At output Q_2, the medium plant is best. At output Q_3, the large plant is best. The long-run average cost function is the "lower envelope" of the short-run average cost functions, represented by the bold line. This curve shows the lowest attainable average cost for any output when the firm is free to adjust its plant size optimally.

(labor, materials) as well as the fixed cost (appropriately annualized) of the plant itself.

If the firm knows how much output it plans to produce before building a plant, then to minimize its costs, it should choose the plant size that results in the lowest short-run average cost for that desired output level. For example, for output Q_1, the optimal plant is a small one; for output Q_2, the optimal plant is a medium one; for output Q_3, the optimal plant is a large one. Figure P.6 illustrates that for larger outputs, the larger plant is best; for medium output levels, the medium plant is best; and for small output levels, the small plant is best. For example, when output is Q_1, the reduction in average cost that results from switching from a large plant to a small plant is $SAC_L(Q_1) - SAC_S(Q_1)$. This saving not only arises from reductions in the fixed costs of the plant, but also because the firm can more efficiently tailor the rest of its operations to its plant size. When the firm produces Q_1 in the large plant, it may need to utilize more labor to assure steady materials flows within the large facility. The small plant may allow flows to be streamlined, making such labor unnecessary.

The long-run average cost function is the lower envelope of the short-run average cost functions, and is depicted by the bold line in Figure P.6. It shows the lowest attainable average cost for any particular level of output when the firm can adjust its plant size optimally. This is the average cost function the firm faces before it has committed to a particular plant size.

In this example, the long-run average cost function exhibits economies of scale. By operating with larger plant sizes, the firm can lower its average costs. This raises a deceptively simple but extremely significant point. To realize the lower average costs, the firm must not only build a large plant but must also achieve sufficient output, so that the large plant is indeed the optimal one. It would be disastrous for the firm to build a large plant if it only achieved an output of, say, Q_1. The firm would be saddled with an expensive underutilized facility. If we were to observe a firm in this situation, we might be tempted to conclude that the scale economies inherent in the production process were limited or nonexistent. This would be incorrect. Scale economies exist, but the firm is not selling enough output needed to exploit them.

It is often useful to express short-run average costs as the sum of average fixed costs (AFC) and average variable costs (AVC):

$$SAC(Q) = AFC(Q) + AVC(Q)$$

Average fixed costs are the firm's fixed costs (i.e., the annualized cost of the firm's plant plus expenses, such as insurance and property taxes, that do not vary with the volume of output) expressed on a per-unit-of-output basis. Average variable costs are the firm's variable costs (e.g., labor and materials) expressed on a per-unit-of-output basis. For example, suppose the firm's plant has an annualized cost of $9 million and other annual fixed expenses total $1 million. Moreover, suppose the firm's variable costs vary with output according to the formula $4Q^2$. Then we would have:

$$AFC(Q) = \frac{10}{Q}$$

$$AVC(Q) = 4Q$$

$$SAC(Q) = \frac{10}{Q} + 4Q$$

Note that as the volume of output increases, average fixed costs become smaller, which tends to pull down *SAC*. Average fixed costs decline because total fixed costs are being spread over an ever-larger production volume. Offsetting this (in this example) is the fact that average variable costs rise with output, which pulls *SAC* upward. The net effect of these offsetting forces creates the U-shaped *SAC* curves in Figure P.6.

Sunk versus Avoidable Costs

When assessing the costs of a decision, the manager should consider only those costs that the decision actually affects. Some costs must be incurred no matter what the decision is and thus cannot be avoided. These are called sunk costs. The opposite of sunk costs is avoidable costs. These costs can be avoided if certain choices are made. When weighing the costs of a decision, the decision maker should ignore sunk costs and consider only avoidable costs.

To illustrate the concept of sunk costs, take the case of a mail order merchandiser of laser printers. The merchandiser traditionally purchased large quantities of printers from the manufacturer, so that it could satisfy rush orders. Increasingly, though, the merchandiser was carrying high inventories, including some lines that the manufacturer no longer produced and would not repurchase. A natural response to this problem would be to put the discontinued lines on sale and reduce inventory. However, the firm's managers were reluctant to do this. They felt that even in the best of times the margins on their products barely covered their overhead, and by cutting the price, they would be unable to cover their cost of the goods they sold.

This argument is wrong. The cost incurred to purchase the laser printers is a sunk cost as far as pricing is concerned. Whether the merchandiser cuts price or not, it cannot avoid these costs. If it believes that a seller should never price below average cost, the merchandiser will end up with large losses. Instead, it should accept that it cannot undo past decisions (and their associated sunk costs) and strive to minimize its losses.

It is important to emphasize that whether a cost is sunk depends on the decision being made and the options at hand. In the example above, the cost of the discontinued lines of printers is a sunk cost with respect to the pricing decision today. But before the printers were ordered, their cost would not have been sunk. By not ordering them, the merchandiser would have avoided the purchase and storage costs.

Students often confuse sunk costs with fixed costs. The two concepts are not the same. In particular, some fixed costs need not be sunk. For example, a railroad serving Chicago to Cleveland needs a locomotive and a crew whether it hauls one carload of freight or 20. The cost of the locomotive is thus a fixed cost. However, it is not necessarily sunk. If the railroad abandons its Chicago-to-Cleveland line, it can sell the locomotive to another railroad, or redeploy it to another route.

Sunk costs are important for the study of strategy, particularly in analyzing rivalry among firms, entry and exit decisions from markets, and decisions to adopt new technologies. For example, the concept of sunk costs helps explain why an established American steel firm would be unwilling to invest in a new technology, such as continuous casting, while a new Japanese firm building a "greenfield" facility from scratch would adopt the new technology. The new technology has higher fixed costs, but lower variable operating costs. For the established American firm, the fixed cost of its old technology is sunk. This firm will adopt the new technology only if the savings in operating costs exceed the fixed cost of the new technology. Starting from scratch, the Japanese firm can avoid the fixed cost of the old technology by adopting the new technology. Thus, this firm will adopt the new technology if the savings in operating costs exceed the *difference* between the fixed costs of the new and old technologies. The American firm thus requires larger cost savings than the Japanese firm to induce it to adopt the new technology. We will return to the concept of sunk costs in our discussions of commitment in Chapter 8, entry and exit in Chapter 11, sustainable advantage in Chapter 13, and innovation in Chapter 14.

◆ ◆ ◆ ◆ ◆ ECONOMIC COSTS AND PROFITABILITY

Economic versus Accounting Costs

The costs in Tables P.1 and P.2 reflect the accountant's concept of costs. This concept is grounded in the principles of accrual accounting, which emphasize historical costs. Accounting statements—in particular, income statements and balance sheets—are designed to serve an audience outside the firm—for example, lenders and equity investors. The accounting numbers must thus be objective and verifiable, principles that are well served by historical costs.

However, the costs that appear in accounting statements are not necessarily appropriate for decision making inside a firm. Business decisions require the measurement of economic costs, which are based on the concept of opportunity cost. This concept says that the economic cost of deploying resources in a particular activity is the value of the best forgone alternative use of those resources. Economic cost may not correspond to the historical costs represented in Tables P.1 and P.2. Suppose, for example, that the firm purchased its raw materials at a price below their current market price. Would the costs of goods manufactured in Table P.2 represent the economic cost to the firm of using these resources? The answer is no. When the firm uses them to produce finished goods, it forsakes the alternative of reselling the materials at the market price. The economic cost of the firm's production activities reflects this forgone opportunity.

At a broader level, consider the resources (plant, equipment, land, and so forth) that have been purchased with funds that stockholders provide to the firm. To attract these funds, the firm must offer the stockholders a return on their investment that is at least as large as the return that they could have received from investing in activities of comparable risk. To illustrate, suppose that at the beginning of 2002, a firm's assets could have been liquidated for $100 million. By tying their funds up in the firm, investors lose the opportunity to invest the $100 million in an activity providing an 8 percent return. Moreover, suppose because of wear and tear and creeping obsolescence of plant and equipment, the value of the assets declines by 1 percent over the year 2002. The annualized cost of the firm's assets for 2002 is then $(.08 + .01) \times \$100$ million $= \$9$ million per year. This is an economic cost, but it would not appear in the firm's income statement.

In studying strategy, we are interested in analyzing why firms make their decisions and what distinguishes good decisions from poor ones, given the opportunities and the constraints firms face. In our formal theories of firm behavior, we thus emphasize economic costs rather than historical accounting costs. This is not to say that accounting costs have no place in the study of business strategy. Quite the contrary: In assessing the past performance of the firm, in comparing one firm in an industry to another, or in evaluating the financial strength of a firm, the informed use of accounting statements and accounting ratio analysis can be illuminating. However, the concept of opportunity cost provides the best basis for good economic decisions when the firm must choose among competing alternatives. A firm that consistently deviated from this idea of cost would miss opportunities for earning higher profits. In the end, it might be driven out of business by firms that are better at seizing profit-enhancing opportunities, or it may find itself starved for capital as investors bid down its stock price. Whenever we depict a cost function or discuss cost throughout this book, we have in mind the idea of costs as including all relevant opportunity costs.

Economic Profit versus Accounting Profit

Having distinguished between economic cost and accounting cost, we can now distinguish between economic profit and accounting profit:

- Accounting Profit = Sales Revenue − Accounting Cost.

- Economic Profit = Sales Revenue − Economic Cost
  = Accounting Profit −
    (Economic Cost − Accounting Cost).

To illustrate the distinction between the two concepts, consider a small software development firm that is owner operated. In 2000, the firm earned revenue of $1,000,000 and incurred expenses on supplies and hired labor of $850,000. The owner's best outside employment opportunity would be to earn a salary of $200,000 working for Microsoft. The software firm's accounting profit is $1,000,000 − $850,000 = $150,000. The software firm's economic profit deducts the opportunity cost of the owner's labor services and is thus $1,000,000 − $850,000 − $200,000 = −$50,000. This means that the owner made $50,000 less in income by operating this business than she could have made in her best outside alternative. The software business "destroyed" $50,000 of the owner's wealth in that, by operating the software business, she earned $50,000 less income than she might have otherwise.

As discussed earlier, an important cost excluded from a firm's accounting costs is the opportunity cost of its capital assets, such as its plant and equipment. When a firm's accounting earnings do not cover this opportunity cost, the firm will earn a positive accounting profit but a negative economic profit. For example, in 1995 IBM had positive accounting income of more than $10 billion, but according to one investment analyst's calculations, it had a negative economic profit of $252 million.[8] (Table P.3 shows IBM's economic profit, and that for other firms in the computer industry, between 1990 and 1995.) What does this negative $252 million

---

[8]These estimates come from Milunovich, S. and A. Tusuei, "EVA in the Computer Industry," Morgan Stanley U.S. Investment Research (April 23, 1996). The specific measure of accounting profit used is operating profit before taxes. The specific measure of economic profit use is called Economic Value Added or EVA, a term developed and trademarked by the financial consulting firm Stern Stewart & Company. This reference describes how EVA was calculated for firms in the computer industry.

TABLE P.3
ECONOMIC PROFIT IN THE U.S. COMPUTER INDUSTRY, 1990–1995

Company	1990	1991	1992	1993	1994	1995
Auspex	–	–	–	8	1	4
Data General	(280)	(164)	(230)	(219)	(222)	(187)
Digital	(878)	(1,683)	(3,184)	(2,280)	(2,546)	(1,868)
HP	(346)	(916)	(465)	(168)	526	888
IBM	(5,280)	(3,684)	(3,753)	(10,188)	(7,650)	(252)
Sequent	14	(65)	(23)	(31)	(20)	(30)
Silicon Graphics	16	0	(18)	2	55	88
Stratus	36	29	20	10	(2)	(60)
Sun Micro.	162	95	(73)	(181)	(130)	25
Tandem	(50)	(221)	(73)	(325)	(180)	(207)

All amounts are in millions of dollars.

mean? Just as with the owner of our software firm, a negative economic profit indicates that IBM's assets, when liquidated and deployed elsewhere, would have earned $252 million more in income for its owners than IBM earned in the computer business. In this sense, in 1995 IBM "destroyed" $252 million of its owners' wealth because its owners could have earned $252 million more that year by deploying the funds they had invested in IBM in their best alternative use. Not all firms, of course, make a negative economic profit. In 1995, Hewlett-Packard (HP) earned an accounting profit of slightly over $3 billion and a positive economic profit of $888 million. This positive economic profit means that HP created $888 million more in income for its owners than its sources would have created for themselves if they liquidated HP's assets and invested them in their best alternative use. In this sense, in 1995 HP "created" an additional $888 million in wealth for its owners that they could not have gotten elsewhere.

Economic Profit and Net Present Value

Economic profit is closely related to the concept of net present value from finance. We will use an example to illustrate net present value and the relationship between it and economic profit.

Consider a firm that contemplates constructing of a plant with a capacity to produce 100,000 units per year. The firm's production expenses when it produces at capacity are $5 per unit of output. The cost of building the plant is $15 million. To make the example as simple as possible, assume that the plant has an infinitely long life, (i.e., it does not depreciate). Suppose, finally, that the firm's cost of capital is 10 percent. This rate reflects what the firm's investors could make from alternative investments and thus reflects the appropriate opportunity cost for evaluating the investment in the plant.

Now suppose that the market price is currently $25 per unit and is expected to remain at that level for the foreseeable future. Should the firm build the plant? We can look at this decision in two seemingly different, but (as it turns out) equivalent, ways. First, we could calculate an annual economic profit in the way we just discussed. Total revenues would be $2.5 million per year. Total production costs that would show up on the firm's accounting statements would be $500,000 per year. The annualized opportunity cost of the plant would be the 10 percent cost of funds times the investment of $15 million, or $1.5 million per year. Economic profit would thus be $2.5 - .5 - 1.5 = \$.5$ million per year. Since the investment in the plant is expected to yield a positive economic profit year after year, the firm should build it. Put another way, by investing in the plant, the firm delivers to its owners $500,000 per year above and beyond what they could earn from their best alternative investment.

The second way to analyze this decision is to use net present value analysis. To explain this approach, we must first introduce the concept of present value. The present value of a cash flow C received in t years at an interest rate i is equal to the amount of money that must be invested today at the interest rate i, so that in t years the principal plus interest equals C.[9] Mathematically, present value would be given by

$$PV = \frac{C}{(1 + i)^t}$$

The present value of a stream of cash flows received over a period of years is the sum of the present values of the individual sums. Thus, the present value of cash flows $C_1, C_2, \ldots C_T$ received one year from now, two years from now, $\ldots$, T years from now, is

$$PV = \frac{C_1}{(1 + i)} + \frac{C_2}{(1 + i)^2} + \ldots + \frac{C_T}{(1 + i)^T},$$

which can be written more compactly as

$$PV = \sum_{t=1}^{T} \frac{C_t}{(1 + i)^t}$$

The net present value (NPV) of an investment is simply the present value of the cash flows the investment generates minus the cost of the investment.

Given the assumptions that the investment has an infinite life and that the price and revenues are expected to remain the same over the foreseeable future, the NPV of the investment in the plant is given by

$$NPV = \sum_{t=1}^{\infty} \frac{2,000,000}{(1.10)^t} - 15,000,000$$

This looks intimidating, but fortunately the term in the summation is the present value of a perpetuity. A perpetuity is a level cash flow C received each year forever. The present value of a perpetuity has a convenient formula: It is equal to the cash flow divided by the interest rate, C/i. With this formula, we can rewrite NPV as

$$NPV = \frac{2,000,000}{.10} - 15,000,000 = \$5,000,000$$

Since the net present value is positive, the firm should undertake the investment.

Note that the calculations of NPV and economic profit are similar. Indeed, with a constant annual cash flow and an infinitely lived investment, economic profit is simply equal to the NPV times the cost of capital, or put another way, NPV is equal to the present value of economic profit generated by the investment over its (infinite) lifetime. When cash flows are not constant and/or when the investment has a finite life, these relationships between NPV and economic profit

[9]For a good introduction to the basic concepts of present value, see Brealey, R. A. and S. C. Myers, *Principles of Corporate Finance*, 3rd ed., New York: McGraw-Hill, 1988.

are more complicated to illustrate, but they still hold. In particular, it can be shown that the collective *NPV* of the firm's investments is equal to the present value of the economic profit those investments generate over their useful lives. Given this, economic profit can be thought of as an annualized *NPV* calculation. The concept of zero economic profit thus begins to make more sense. It does not mean that the firm's net cash flows are zero. Instead it means that the present value of these cash flows just covers the cost of the firm's investments, or equivalently the net present value of the firm's investments are zero.

◆ ◆ ◆ ◆ ◆ DEMAND AND REVENUES

The second component of profit is sales revenue, which is intimately related to the firm's pricing decision. To understand how a firm's sales revenue depends on its pricing decision, we will explore the concept of a demand function and the price elasticity of demand.

Demand Function

The demand function describes the relationship between the quantity of product that the firm is able to sell and all the variables that influence that quantity. These variables include: the price of the product, the prices of related products, the incomes and tastes of consumers, the quality of the product, advertising, product promotion, and many other variables commonly thought to make up the firm's marketing mix.

Of special interest is the relationship between quantity and price. To focus on this important relationship, imagine that all the other variables that influence the quantity demanded remain fixed, and consider how the quantity demanded would change as the price changes. We would expect this to be an inverse relationship, as shown in Figure P.7: the lower the price, the greater the quantity demanded; the

FIGURE P.7
DEMAND CURVE.

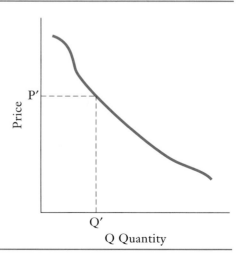

The demand curve shows the quantity of a product that consumers will purchase at different prices. For example, at price *P′* consumers purchase *Q′* units of the product. We would expect an inverse relationship between quantity and price, so this curve is downward sloping.

higher the price, the smaller the quantity demanded. This inverse relationship is called the law of demand.

The law of demand may not hold if high prices confer prestige or enhance a product's image. If a seller of fine Scotch or crystal lowered its price, it might diminish its prestige value, and thus sell less rather than more. A related phenomenon would occur when consumers cannot objectively assess the potential performance of a product and use price to infer quality. A lower price might signal low quality, reducing rather than increasing sales. Both prestige and signaling effects could result in demand curves that slope upward for some range of prices. Even so, personal experience and countless studies from economics and marketing confirm that the law of demand applies to most products.

As Figure P.7 shows, the demand curve is typically drawn with price on the vertical axis and quantity on the horizontal axis. This may seem strange because we think that price determines the quantity demanded, not the other way around. However, this representation emphasizes a useful alternative interpretation for a demand curve. Not only does the demand curve tell us the quantity consumers will purchase at any given price, it also tells us the highest possible price that the market will bear for a given quantity or supply of output. Thus, in Figure P.7, if the firm sets a target of selling output level Q' (which might be what it can produce by running at full capacity), the demand curve tells us that the highest price the firm can charge is P'.

The Price Elasticity of Demand

Look at a firm that is considering a price increase. The firm understands that according to the law of demand, the increase in price will result in the loss of some sales. This may be acceptable if the loss in sales is not "too large." If sales do not suffer much, the firm may actually increase its sales revenue when it raises its price. If sales drop substantially, however, sales revenues may decline, and the firm could be worse off.

Figure P.8 illustrates the implications of the firm's pricing decision when its demand curve has one of two alternative shapes, D_A and D_B. Suppose the firm is currently charging P_0 and selling Q_0, and is considering an increase in price to P_1.

FIGURE P.8
PRICE SENSITIVITY AND THE SHAPE OF THE DEMAND CURVE.

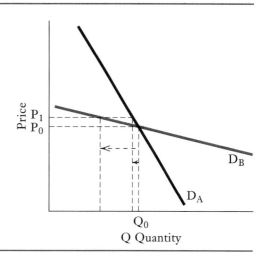

When the demand curve is D_A, a change in price from P_0 to P_1 has only a small effect on the quantity demanded. However, when the demand curve is D_B, the same change in price results in a large drop in quantity demanded. When D_A is the demand curve, we would conjecture that the increase in price would increase sales revenues but when D_B is the demand curve, the price increase would reduce sales revenues.

If the firm's demand curve is D_A, the price increase would cause only a small drop in sales. In this case, the quantity demanded is not very sensitive to price. We would suspect that the increase in price would increase sales revenue because the price increase swamps the quantity decrease. By contrast, if the firm's demand curve is D_B, the increase in price would cause a large drop in sales. Here, the quantity demanded is very sensitive to price. We would expect that the price increase would decrease sales revenues.

As this analysis shows, the shape of the demand curve can strongly affect the success of the firm's pricing strategy. The concept of the price elasticity of demand summarizes this effect by measuring the sensitivity of quantity demanded to price. The price elasticity of demand, commonly denoted by η, is the percentage change in quantity brought about by a 1 percent change in price. Letting subscript "0" represent the initial situation and "1" represent the situation after the price changes, the formula for elasticity is:

$$\eta = -\frac{\frac{\Delta Q}{Q_0}}{\frac{\Delta P}{P_0}}$$

where $\Delta P = P_1 - P_0$ is the change in price, and $\Delta Q = Q_1 - Q_0$ is the resulting change in quantity.[10] To illustrate this formula, suppose price is initially \$5, and the corresponding quantity demanded is 1,000 units. If the price rises to \$5.75, though, the quantity demanded would fall to 800 units. Then

$$\eta = -\frac{\frac{800 - 1000}{1000}}{\frac{5.75 - 5}{5}} = -\frac{-.20}{.15} = 1.33.$$

Thus over the range of prices between \$5.00 and \$5.75, quantity demanded falls at a rate of 1.33 percent for every 1 percent increase in price. The price elasticity η might be less than 1 or greater than 1.

- If η is less than 1, we say that demand is *inelastic*, which is the situation along demand curve D_A for the price change being considered.

- If η is greater than 1, we say that demand is *elastic*, which is the situation along demand curve D_B for the price change being considered.

Given an estimate of the price elasticity of demand, a manager could calculate the expected percentage change in quantity demanded resulting from a given change in price by multiplying the percentage change in price by the estimated elasticity. To illustrate, suppose management believed $\eta = .75$. If it contemplated a 3 percent increase in price, then it should expect a $3 \times .75 = 2.25$ percent drop in the quantity demanded as a result of the price increase. One complication should be noted: A given product's price elasticity of demand is not the same at all price levels.[11] This means that an elasticity that is estimated at a price level of, say, \$10

---

[10]It is customary to put the minus sign in front, so that we convert what would ordinarily be a negative number (because ΔQ and ΔP have opposite signs) into a positive one.

[11]This is due to the properties of percentages, which require dividing by base amounts. If the price is so high that the quantity demanded is close to zero, even small absolute increases in quantity can translate into huge precentage increases.

would be useful in predicting the impact of an increase in price to $11, but would accurately predict the impact of an increase to $20.

Price elasticities can be estimated using statistical techniques, and economists and marketers have estimated price elasticities for many products. But in most practical situations, managers will not have the benefit of a precise numerical estimate of elasticity based on statistical techniques. Consequently, the manager must rely on his or her knowledge of the product and the nature of the market to estimate price sensitivity. Among the factors that tend to make demand for the firm's product more sensitive to price are:

- The product has few unique features that differentiate it from rival products, and buyers are aware of the prices and features of rival products. Airline service is a good example of a product that is hard to differentiate and where consumers can easily inform themselves of the range of prices that exist in a particular market.

- Buyers' expenditures on the product are a large fraction of their total expenditures. In this case, the savings from finding a comparable item at a lower price are large, so consumers tend to shop more than when making small purchases. Refrigerators and washing machines are products whose demand is fairly price sensitive because consumers are motivated to shop around before purchasing.

- The product is an input that buyers use to produce a final good whose demand is itself sensitive to price. In this case, if buyers tried to pass through to their customers even small changes in the price of the input, demand for the finished good could decrease dramatically. The input buyers will thus be very sensitive to price. For example, a personal computer manufacturer's demand for components and materials is likely to be highly price elastic because consumer demand for personal computers is highly price elastic.

Among the factors that tend to make demand less sensitive to price are the following:

- Comparisons among substitute products are difficult. This could be because the product is complex and has many performance dimensions, because consumers have little or no experience with substitute products and thus would face a risk if they purchased them; or because comparison shopping is costly. Items sold door-to-door, such as Avon cosmetics, have traditionally been price inelastic because, at the time of sale, most consumers lack good information about the prices of alternatives.

- Because of tax deductions or insurance, buyers pay only a fraction of the full price of the product. Health care is an excellent example.

- A buyer would incur significant costs if it switched to a substitute product. Switching costs could arise if the use of a product requires specialized training or expertise that is not fully transferable across different varieties of the product. For example, to the extent that a consumer develops expertise in using a particular word processing package that is incompatible with available alternatives, switching costs will be high, and price sensitivity for upgrades will be low.

- The product is used in conjunction with another product that buyers have committed themselves to. For example, an owner of a copying machine is likely to be fairly insensitive to the price of toner, because the toner is an essential input in running the copier.

Brand-Level versus Industry-Level Elasticities

Students often mistakenly suppose that just because the demand for a product is inelastic, the demand facing each seller of that product is also inelastic. Consider, for example, cigarettes. Many studies have documented that the demand for cigarettes is price inelastic, with elasticities well below 1. This suggests that a general increase in the price of all brands of cigarettes would only modestly affect overall cigarette demand. However, if the price of only one brand of cigarettes increases, the demand for that brand would probably drop substantially because consumers would switch to the now lower-priced brands. Thus, while demand can be inelastic at the industry level, it can be highly elastic at the brand level. Research by Frank Irvine nicely illustrates this difference for the automobile industry.[12] While estimates of the industry-level price elasticity for automobiles are on the order of 1 to 1.5, Irvine found that the average price elasticity for individual makes of automobiles ranged from 6 to 10.

Brand-level elasticities are higher than industry-level elasticities because consumers can purchase other brands when only one brand raises its price. Brand-level elasticities should also increase as more firms enter the market and more brands are offered. A study of the personal computer industry by Joanna Stavins illustrates this point.[13] She finds that the average brand-level elasticity rose over time from 5.0 in 1977 to 12.4 in 1988 as new firms entered the market. These elasticity estimates highlight an important reason for the increasing price competitiveness in that industry.

Should a firm use an industry-level elasticity or a brand-level elasticity in assessing the impact of a price change? The answer depends on what the firm expects its rivals to do. If a firm expects that rivals will quickly match its price change, then the industry-level elasticity is appropriate. If, by contrast, a firm expects that rivals will not match its price change (or will do so only after a long lag), then the brand-level elasticity is appropriate. For example, Pepsi's price cut succeeded because Coke did not retaliate. Had Coke cut its price, the outcome of Pepsi's strategy would have been different. Making educated conjectures about how rivals will respond to pricing moves is a fascinating subject. We will encounter this subject again in Chapter 7, and we will study it in detail in Chapter 9.

Total Revenue and Marginal Revenue Functions

A firm's total revenue function, denoted by *TR(Q)*, indicates how the firm's sales revenues vary as a function of how much product it sells. Recalling our interpretation of the demand curve as showing the highest price *P(Q)* that the firm can charge and sell exactly *Q* units of output, we can express total revenue as

$$TR(Q) = P(Q)Q$$

Just as a firm is interested in the impact of a change in output on its costs, it is also interested in how a change in output will affect its revenues. A firm's marginal rev-

---

[12]Irvine, F. O., "Demand Equations for Individual New Car Models Estimated Using Transactions Prices with Implications for Regulatory Issues," *Southern Economic Journal*, 49, January 1983: pp. 764–782.

[13]Stavins, J., "Estimating Demand Elasticities in a Differentiated Product Industry: The Personal Computer Market," *Journal of Economics and Business* 49, July-August 1997, pp. 347–367.

enue, *MR(Q)*, is analogous to its marginal cost. It represents the rate of change in total revenue that results from the sale of ΔQ additional units of output:

$$MR(Q) = \frac{TR(Q + \Delta Q) - TR(Q)}{\Delta Q}$$

It seems plausible that total revenue would go up as the firm sells more output, and thus *MR* would always be positive. But with a downward-sloping demand curve, this is not necessarily true. To sell more, the firm must lower its price. Thus, while it generates revenue on the extra units of output it sells at the lower price, it loses revenue on all the units it would have sold at the higher price. For example, a compact disc store may sell 110 compact discs per day at a price of $11 per disc, and 120 discs at $9 per disc. It gains additional revenue of $90 per day on the extra 10 discs sold at the lower price of $9, but it sacrifices $220 per day on the 110 discs that it could have sold for $2 more. The marginal revenue in this case would equal −$130/10 or −$13; the store loses sales revenue of $13 for each additional disc it sells when it drops its price from $11 to $9.

In general, whether marginal revenue is positive or negative depends on the price elasticity of demand. The formal relationship (whose derivation is not important for our purposes) is

$$MR = P\left(1 - \frac{1}{\eta}\right)$$

For example, if η =.75, and the current price P = $15, then marginal revenue *MR* = 15(1 − 1/.75) = − $5. More generally,

- When demand is elastic, so that $\eta > 1$, it follows that *MR* > 0. In this case, the increase in output brought about by a reduction in price will raise total sales revenues.

- When demand is inelastic, so that $\eta < 1$, it follows that *MR* < 0. Here, the increase in output brought about by a reduction in price will lower total sales revenue.

FIGURE P.9
THE MARGINAL REVENUE CURVE AND THE DEMAND CURVE.

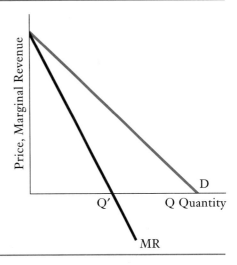

MR represents the marginal revenue curve associated with the demand curve *D*. Because *MR* < *P*, the marginal revenue curve must lie everywhere below the demand curve except at a quantity of 0. Marginal revenue is negative for quantities in excess of *Q*′.

Note that this formula implies that $MR < P$. This makes sense in light of what we just discussed. The price P is the additional revenue the firm gets from each additional unit it sells, but the overall change in revenues from selling an additional unit must factor in the reduction in revenue earned on all of the units that would have sold at the higher price, but are now being sold at a lower price.

Figure P.9 shows the graph of a demand function and its associated marginal revenue function. Because $MR < P$, the marginal revenue curve must lie everywhere below the demand curve, except at a quantity of zero. For most demand curves, the marginal revenue curve is everywhere downward sloping and at some point will shift from being positive to negative. (This occurs at output Q' in the figure.)

◆ ◆ ◆ ◆ ◆ THEORY OF THE FIRM: PRICING AND OUTPUT DECISIONS

Part II of this book studies the structure of markets and competitive rivalry within industries. To set the stage for this analysis, we need to explore the theory of the firm, a theory of how firms choose their prices and quantities. This theory has both explanatory power and prescriptive usefulness. That is, it sheds light on how prices are established in markets, and it also provides tools to aid managers in making pricing decisions.

The theory of the firm assumes that the firm's ultimate objective is to make as large a profit as possible. The theory is therefore appropriate to managers whose goal is to maximize profits. Some analysts argue that not all managers seek to maximize profits, so that the theory of the firm is less useful for describing actual firm behavior. An extensive discussion of the descriptive validity of the profit-maximization hypothesis would take us beyond this primer. Suffice it to say that a powerful "evolutionary" argument supports the profit-maximization hypothesis: If, over the long haul, a firm's managers did not strive to achieve the largest amount of profit consistent with industry economics and its own particular resources, the firm would either disappear or its management would be replaced by one that better served the owners' interests.

Ideally, for any given amount of output the firm might want to sell, it would prefer to set price as high as it could. As we have seen, though, the firm's demand curve limits what that price can be. Thus, when determining the amount it wants to sell, the firm simultaneously determines the price it can charge from its demand curve.

How, then, is the optimal output determined? This is where the concepts of marginal revenue and marginal cost become useful. Recalling that "marginals" are rates of change (change in cost or revenue per one-unit change in output), the change in revenue, cost, and profit from changing output by ΔQ units (where ΔQ can either represent an increase in output, in which case it is a positive amount, or a decrease in output, in which case it is a negative amount) is:

$$\text{Change in Total Revenue} = MR \times \Delta Q.$$
$$\text{Change in Total Cost} = MC \times \Delta Q.$$
$$\text{Change in Profit} = (MR - MC) \times \Delta Q.$$

The firm clearly would like to increase profit. Here's how:

• If $MR > MC$, the firm can increase profit by selling more ($\Delta Q > 0$), and to do so, it should *lower* its price.

- If $MR < MC$, the firm can increase profit by selling less ($\Delta Q < 0$), and to do so, it should *raise* its price.

- If $MR = MC$, the firm cannot increase profits either by increasing or decreasing output. It follows that output and price must be at their optimal levels.

Figure P.10 shows a firm whose output and price are at their optimal levels. The curve D is the firm's demand curve, MR is the marginal revenue curve, and MC is the marginal cost curve. The optimal output occurs where $MR = MC$, that is, where the MR and MC curves intersect. This is output Q^* in the diagram. The optimal price P^* is the associated price on the demand curve.

An alternative and perhaps more managerially relevant way of thinking about these principles is to express MR in terms of the price elasticity of demand. Then the term $MR = MC$ can be written as:

$$P\left(1 - \frac{1}{\eta}\right) = MC$$

Let us now suppose, that as a first approximation, the firm's total variable costs are directly proportional to output, so that $MC = c$, where c is the firm's average variable cost. The percentage contribution margin or PCM on additional units sold is the ratio of profit per unit to revenue per unit, or $PCM = (P - c)/P$. Algebra establishes that:

$$MR - MC > 0 \text{ as } \eta > 1/PCM$$
$$MR - MC < 0 \text{ as } \eta < 1/PCM$$

This implies:

- A firm should lower its price whenever the price elasticity of demand exceeds the reciprocal of the percentage contribution margin on the additional units it would sell.

FIGURE P.10
OPTIMAL QUANTITY AND PRICE FOR A PROFIT-MAXIMIZING FIRM.

The firm's optimal quantity occurs at Q^*, where $MR = MC$. The optimal price P^* is the price the firm must charge to sell Q^* units. It is found from the demand curve.

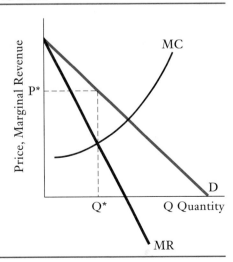

- A firm should raise its price when the price elasticity of demand is less than the reciprocal of the percentage contribution margin of the units it would not sell by raising its price.

These principles can guide pricing decisions even though managers do not know the firm's demand curve or marginal cost function. Managers have only to make educated conjectures about the relative magnitude of elasticities and contribution margins.[14] An example may help cement these concepts. Suppose $P = \$10$ and $c = \$5$, so $PCM = .50$. Then the firm can increase profits by lowering its price if its price elasticity of demand η exceeds $1/.5 = 2$. If, instead, $P = \$10$, and $c = \$8$, so that $PCM = .2$, the firm should cut its price if $\eta > 5$. As this example shows, the lower a firm's PCM (e.g., because its marginal cost is high), the greater its price elasticity of demand must be for a price-cutting strategy to raise profits.

◆ ◆ ◆ ◆ ◆ PERFECT COMPETITION

A special case of the theory of the firm is the theory of perfect competition. This theory highlights how market forces shape and constrain a firm's behavior and interact with the firm's decisions to determine profitability. The theory deals with a stark competitive environment: an industry with many firms producing identical products (so that consumers choose among firms solely on the basis of price) and where firms can enter or exit the industry at will. This is a caricature of any real market, but it does approximate an industry, such as personal computers, in which many firms produce nearly identical products and compete primarily on the basis of price.

Because firms in a perfectly competitive industry produce identical products, each firm must charge the same price. This market price is beyond the control of any individual firm; it must take the market price as given. For a firm to offer to sell at a price above the market price would be folly because it would make no sales. Offering to sell below the market price would also be folly because the firm would needlessly sacrifice revenue. As shown in Figure P.11, then, a perfectly competitive firm's demand curve is perfectly horizontal at the market price, even though the industry demand curve is downward sloping. Put another way, the firm-level price elasticity of demand facing a perfect competitor is infinite, even though the industry-level price elasticity is finite.

Given any particular market price, each firm must decide how much to produce. Applying the insights from the theory of the firm, the firm should produce at the point where marginal revenue equals marginal cost. When the firm's demand curve is horizontal, each additional unit it sells adds sales revenue equal to the market price. Thus, the firm's marginal revenue equals the market price, and the optimal output, shown in Figure P.11, is where marginal cost equals the market price. If we were to graph how a firm's optimal output changed as the market price changed, we would trace out a curve that is identical to the firm's

---

[14]The use of this formula is subject to the caveat expressed earlier about the use of elasticities. It is useful for contemplating the effects of "incremental" price changes rather than dramatic price changes.

FIGURE P.11
DEMAND AND SUPPLY CURVES FOR A PERFECTLY COMPETITIVE FIRM.

A perfectly competitive firm takes the market price as given and thus faces a horizontal demand curve at the market price. This horizontal line also represents the firm's marginal revenue curve *MR*. The firm's optimal output occurs where its marginal revenue equals marginal cost. When the market price is P_0, the optimal output is Q_0. If the market price were to change, the firm's optimal quantity would also change. At price P_1, the optimal output is Q_1. At price P_2, the optimal output is Q_2. The firm's supply curve traces out the relationship between the market price and the firm's optimal quantity of output. This curve is identical to the firm's marginal cost curve.

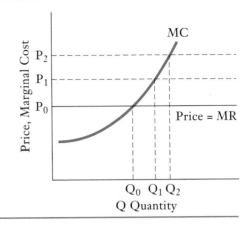

marginal cost function. This is known as the firm's supply curve. It shows the amount of output the perfectly competitive firm would sell at various market prices. Thus, the supply curve of a perfectly competitive firm is identical to its marginal cost function.

If we aggregate over the firm supply curves of all active producers in the industry, we get the industry supply curve, depicted in Figure P.12 as *SS*. This figure shows an industry with 1,000 identical active firms. At any price, the industry supply is 1,000 times the supply of an individual firm. Given the industry supply

FIGURE P.12
FIRM AND INDUSTRY SUPPLY CURVES UNDER PERFECT COMPETITION.

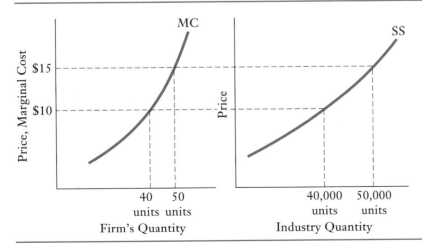

A single firm's supply curve is shown in the graph on the left. The industry's supply curve *SS* is shown in the graph on the right. These graphs depict an industry of 1,000 identical firms. Thus, at any price the industry supply is 1,000 times the amount that a single firm would supply.

FIGURE P.13
PERFECTLY COMPETITIVE INDUSTRY PRIOR TO NEW ENTRY.

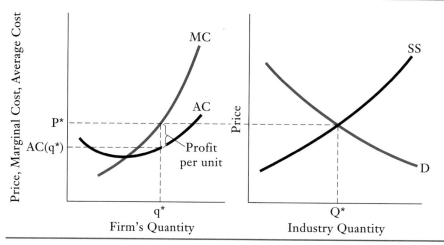

At the price P^*, each firm is producing its optimal amount of output q^*. Moreover, the quantity demanded equals the quantity Q^* supplied by all firms in the industry. However, each firm is earning a positive profit because at q^*, the price P^* exceeds average cost $AC(q^*)$, resulting in a profit on every unit sold. New firms would thus want to enter this industry.

curve, we can now see how the market price is determined. For the market to be in equilibrium, the market price must be such that the quantity demanded equals the quantity supplied by firms in the industry. This situation is depicted in Figure P.13, where P^* denotes the price that "clears" the market. If the market price was higher than P^*, then more of the product would be offered for sale than consumers would like to buy. The excess supply would then place downward pressure on the market price. If the market price was lower than P^*, then there would be less of the product offered for sale than consumers would like to buy. Here, the excess demand would exert upward pressure on the market price. Only when the quantities demanded and supplied are equal—when price equals P^*—is there no pressure on price to change.

The situation shown in Figure P.13 would be the end of the story if additional firms could not enter the industry. However, in a perfectly competitive industry, firms can enter and exit at will. The situation in Figure P.13 is thus unstable because firms in the industry are making a profit (price exceeds average cost at the quantity q^* that each firm supplies). Thus, it will be attractive for additional firms to enter and begin selling. Figure P.14 shows the adjustment that occurs. As more firms enter, the supply curve SS shifts outward to SS'. As this happens, the quantity supplied exceeds the quantity demanded, and there is pressure on price to fall. It will continue to fall until no additional entry occurs. This is when the market price just equals a typical firm's average cost. As we have seen, to optimize output, firms produce where market price equals marginal cost. Thus, in the long-run equilibrium depicted in Figure P.14, firms are producing at minimum efficient scale (recall, this is the quantity corresponding to the minimum point on the average cost curve), and the equilibrium market price P^{**} equals the minimum level of average cost.

FIGURE P.14
PERFECTLY COMPETITIVE INDUSTRY AT LONG-EUN EQUILIBRIUM.

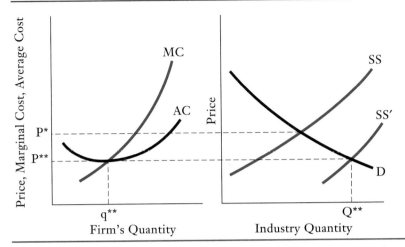

At price P^*, new entrants are attracted to the industry. As they come in, the industry's supply curve shifts to the right, from SS to SS', resulting in a reduction in market price. Entry ceases to occur when firms are earning as much inside the industry as they can earn outside it. Each firm thus earns zero economic profit, or equivalently, price equals average cost. Firms are choosing the optimal output and earning zero economic profit when they produce at the point at which market price equals both marginal cost and average cost. This occurs when the price is P^{**} and firms produce q^{**}. Firms are thus at the minimum point on their average cost function.

Suppose, now, that market demand suddenly falls. Figure P.15 shows what happens. The fall in market demand is represented by a shift from demand curve D_0 to D_1. Initially, market price would fall to P', and firms' revenues would not cover their costs. The industry "shakeout" then begins. Firms begin to exit the industry. As this occurs, the industry supply curve shifts to the left, and price begins to rise. Once the "shakeout" fully unfolds, the industry supply curve will have shifted to SS', and the market price will once again reach P^{**}. Firms are then again optimizing on output and earning zero profit. Thus, no matter what the level of industry demand is, the industry will eventually supply output at the price P^{**}.[15]

This theory implies that the free entry exhausts all opportunities for making profit. This implication sometimes troubles management students because it seems to suggest that firms in perfectly competitive industries would then earn zero net income. But remember the distinction between economic costs and accounting costs. Economic costs reflect the relevant opportunity costs of the financial capital that the owners have provided to the firm. Zero profits thus means zero economic profit, not zero accounting profit. Zero economic profit simply means

---

[15]This result is subject to the following qualification. If certain key inputs are scarce, the entry of additional firms bids up the prices of these inputs. The firm's average and marginal cost functions then shift upward, and in the long run, the market price will settle down at a higher level. An industry in which this happens is known as an increasing-cost industry. The case we focus on in the text is known as a constant-cost industry.

FIGURE P.15
EFFECT OF A REDUCTION IN DEMAND ON THE LONG-RUN PERFECTLY
COMPETITIVE EQUILIBRIUM.

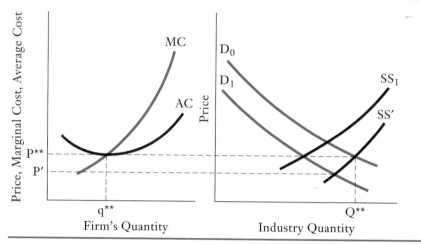

When demand falls, the demand curve shifts from D_0 to D_1, and price would initially fall to
P'. Firms would earn less than they could elsewhere and would eventually begin to leave
the industry. As this happens, the supply curve shifts to the left from SS' to SS_1. The
industry shakeout ends when price is again P^{**}.

that investors are earning returns on their investments that are commensurate
with what they could earn from their next best opportunity.

That free entry dissipates economic profit is one of the most powerful insights
in economics, and it has profound implications for strategy. Firms that base their
strategies on products that can be easily imitated or skills and resources that can be
easily acquired put themselves at risk to the forces that are highlighted by the theory of perfect competition. To attain a competitive advantage, a firm must secure a
position in the market that protects itself from imitation and entry. How firms
might do this is the subject of Chapters 11 through 14.

◆ ◆ ◆ ◆ ◆ GAME THEORY

The perfectly competitive firm faces many competitors, but in making its output
decision, it does not consider the likely reactions of its rivals. This is because the
decisions of any single firm have a negligible impact on market price. The key
strategic challenge of a perfectly competitive firm is to anticipate the future path of
prices in the industry and maximize against it.

In many strategic situations, however, there are few players. For example, four
producers—Kellogg, General Mills, Post (owned by Philip Morris' Kraft Foods),
and Quaker Oats—account for more than 90 percent of sales in the ready-to-eat
breakfast cereal market. In the market for commercial airframes, there are just two
producers: Boeing and Airbus. In these "small numbers" situations, a key part of
making strategic decisions—pricing, investment in new facilities, and so forth—is
anticipating how rivals may react.

A natural way to incorporate the reactions of rivals into your analysis of strategic options is to assign probabilities to their likely actions or reactions and then choose the decision that maximizes the expected value of your profit, given this probability distribution. But this approach has an important drawback: How do you assign probabilities to the range of choices your rivals might make? You may end up assigning positive probabilities to decisions that, from the perspective of your competitors, would be foolish. If so, then the quality of your "decision analysis" would be seriously compromised.

A more penetrating approach would be to attempt to "get inside the minds" of your competitors, figure out what is in their self-interest, and then maximize accordingly. However, your rivals' optimal choices will often depend on their expectations of what you intend to do, which, in turn, depend on their assessments of your assessments about them. How can one sensibly analyze decision making with this circularity?

Game theory is most valuable in precisely such contexts. Game theory is the branch of economics concerned with the analysis of optimal decision making when all decision makers are presumed to be rational, and each is attempting to anticipate the actions and reactions of its competitors. Much of the material in Section II on industry analysis and competitive strategy draws on basic game theory. In this section, we introduce these basic ideas. In particular, we discuss games in matrix and game tree form, and the concepts of a Nash equilibrium and subgame perfection.

Games in Matrix Form and the Concept of Nash Equilibrium

The easiest way to introduce the basic elements of game theory is through a simple example. Consider an industry that consists of two firms, Alpha and Beta, that produce identical products. Each must decide whether to increase its production capacity in the upcoming year. We will assume that each firm always produces at full capacity. Thus, expansion of capacity entails a tradeoff. The firm may achieve a larger share of the market, but it may also put downward pressure on the market price. The consequences of each firms' choices are described in Table P.4. The first entry is Alpha's annual economic profit; the second entry is Beta's annual economic profit.

Each firm will make its capacity decision simultaneously and independently of the other firm. To identify the "likely outcome" of games like the one shown in Table P.4, game theorists use the concept of a Nash equilibrium. At a Nash equilibrium outcome, each player is doing the best it can, given the strategies of the

TABLE P.4
CAPACITY GAME BETWEEN ALPHA AND BETA

| | | Beta | |
		Do not Expand	*Expand*
Alpha	DO NOT EXPAND	$18, $18	$15, $20
	EXPAND	$20, $15	$16, $16

All amounts are in millions per year. Alpha's payoff is first; Beta's is second.

other players. In the context of the capacity expansion game, the Nash equilibrium is that pair of strategies (one for Alpha, one for Beta) such that

- Alpha's strategy maximizes its profit, given Beta's strategy.

- Beta's strategy maximizes its profit, given Alpha's strategy.

In the capacity expansion game, the Nash equilibrium is (EXPAND, EXPAND), that is, each firm expands its capacity. Given that Alpha expands its capacity, Beta's best choice is to expand its capacity (yielding profit of 16 rather than 15). Given that Beta expands its capacity, Alpha's best choice is to expand its capacity.

In this example, the determination of the Nash equilibrium is fairly easy because for each firm, the strategy EXPAND maximizes profit no matter what decision its competitor makes. In this situation, we say that EXPAND is a dominant strategy. When a player has a dominant strategy, it follows (from the definition of the Nash equilibrium) that that strategy must also be the player's Nash equilibrium strategy. However, dominant strategies are not inevitable; in many games players do not possess dominant strategies (e.g., the game in Table P.5).

Why does the Nash equilibrium represent a plausible outcome of a game? Probably its most compelling property is that it is a self-enforcing focal point: If each party expects the other party to choose its Nash equilibrium strategy, then both parties will, in fact, choose their Nash equilibrium strategies. At the Nash equilibrium, then, expectation equals outcome—expected behavior and actual behavior converge. This would not be true at non-Nash equilibrium outcomes, as the game in Table P.4 illustrates. Suppose Alpha (perhaps foolishly) expects Beta not to expand capacity and refrains from expanding its own capacity to prevent a drop in the industry price level. Beta—pursuing its own self-interest—would confound Alpha's expectations, expand its capacity, and make Alpha worse off than it expected to be.

The "capacity expansion" game illustrates a noteworthy aspect of a Nash equilibrium. The Nash equilibrium does not necessarily correspond to the outcome that maximizes the aggregate profit of the players. Alpha and Beta would be collectively better off by refraining from the expansion of their capacities. However, the rational pursuit of self-interest leads each party to take an action that is ultimately detrimental to their collective interest.

This conflict between the collective interest and self-interest is often referred to as the prisoners' dilemma. The prisoners' dilemma arises because in pursuing its self-interest, each party imposes a cost on the other that it does not take into account. In the capacity expansion game, Alpha's addition of extra capacity hurts Beta because it drives down the market price. As we will see in Chapters 7 and 9, the prisoners' dilemma is a key feature of equilibrium pricing and output decisions in oligopolistic industries.

Game Trees and Subgame Perfection

The matrix form is particularly convenient for representing games in which each party moves simultaneously. In many situations, however, decision making is sequential rather than simultaneous, and it is often more convenient to represent the game with a game tree instead of a game matrix.

To illustrate such a situation, let us modify the capacity expansion game to allow the firm to choose among three options: no expansion of current capacity, a

TABLE P.5
MODIFIED CAPACITY GAME BETWEEN ALPHA AND BETA

			Beta	
		Do not Expand	*Small*	*Expand*
	DO NOT EXPAND	$18, $18	$15, $20	$9, $18
Alpha	SMALL	$20, $15	$16, $16	$8, $12
	LARGE	$18, $9	$12, $8	$0, $0

All amounts are in millions per year. Alpha's payoff is first; Beta's is second.

small expansion, or a large expansion. For contrast, let us first examine what happens when both firms decide simultaneously. This game is represented by the 3 by 3 matrix in Table P.5. We leave it to the reader to verify that the Nash equilibrium in this game is (SMALL,SMALL).

But now suppose that Alpha seeks to preempt Beta by making its capacity decision a year before Beta's. Thus, by the time Beta makes its decision, it will have observed Alpha's choice and must adjust its decision making accordingly.[16] We can represent the dynamics of this decision-making process by the game tree in Figure P.16.

FIGURE P.16
GAME TREE FOR SEQUENTIAL CAPACITY EXPANSION GAME.

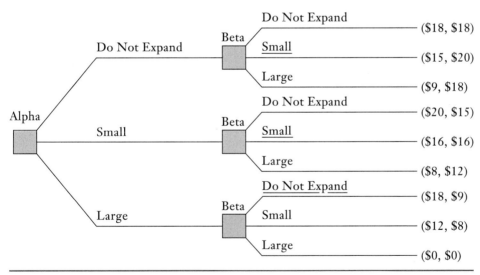

Alpha has three choices: DO NOT EXPAND, SMALL, and LARGE. Given Alpha's choice, Beta must then choose among DO NOT EXPAND, SMALL, LARGE. For whatever choice Alpha makes, Beta will make the choice that maximizes its profit. (These are underlined.) Given Beta's expected choices, Alpha's optimal choice is LARGE.

---

[16]To keep the example as simple as possible, we will assume only two stages of decision making: Alpha makes its choice first, and then Beta responds. We do not consider the possibility that Alpha might respond to the capacity decision that Beta makes.

In analyzing this game tree, we seek what is known as a subgame perfect Nash equilibrium (SPNE). In an SPNE, each player chooses an optimal action at each stage in the game that it might conceivably reach and believes that all other players will behave in the same way.

To derive the SPNE, we use the so-called fold-back method: We start at the end of the tree, and for each decision "node" (represented by squares), we find the optimal decision for the firm situated at that node. In this example, we must find Beta's optimal decision for each of the three choices Alpha might make: DO NOT EXPAND, SMALL, and LARGE:

- If Alpha chooses DO NOT EXPAND, Beta's optimal choice is SMALL.

- If Alpha chooses SMALL, Beta's optimal choice is SMALL.

- If Alpha chooses LARGE, Beta's optimal choice is DO NOT EXPAND.

(Beta's optimal choices are underlined.)

By folding back the tree in this fashion, we assume that Alpha anticipates that Beta will choose a profit-maximizing response to any strategic move Alpha might make. Given these expectations, we can then determine Alpha's optimal strategy. We do so by mapping out the profit that Alpha gets as a result of each option it might choose, given that Beta responds optimally. The fold-back analysis tells us:

- If Alpha chooses DO NOT EXPAND, then given Beta's optimal reaction, Alpha's profit will be $15 million.

- If Alpha chooses SMALL, then given Beta's optimal reaction, Alpha's profit will be $16 million.

- If Alpha chooses LARGE, then given Beta's optimal reaction, Alpha's profit will be $18 million.

The SPNE is thus for Alpha to choose LARGE. Beta responds by choosing DO NOT EXPAND.

Note that the outcome of the sequential-move game differs significantly from the outcome of the simultaneous-move game. Indeed, the outcome involves a strategy for Alpha (LARGE) that would be dominated if Alpha and Beta made their capacity choices simultaneously. Why is Alpha's behavior so different when it can move first? Because in the sequential game, the firm's decision problems are linked through time: Beta can see what Alpha has done, and Alpha can thus count on a rational response by Beta to whatever action it chooses. In the sequential-move game, Alpha's capacity choice has commitment value; it forces Beta into a corner. By committing to a large capacity expansion, Alpha forces Beta into a position where Beta's best response yields the outcome that is most favorable to Alpha. By contrast, in the simultaneous-move game, Beta cannot observe Alpha's decision, so the capacity decision no longer has commitment value for Alpha. Because of this, the choice of LARGE by Alpha is not nearly as compelling as it is in the sequential game. We discuss commitment in detail in Chapter 8.

PART ONE

FIRM BOUNDARIES

THE EVOLUTION OF
THE MODERN FIRM

1

*T*his book identifies general economic principles of strategy. Because these are general principles, they should be useful to managers who face a wide range of business conditions. This is of obvious benefit to any manager trying to improve the performance of a business that is less successful than desired. Managers can make immediate improvements by matching the firm's strategy to its business environment. This also benefits the managers of even the most successful firms. As any manager should recognize, conditions change over time, so that strategies that are appropriate to today's business environment may be inappropriate in the future. Sometimes conditions that influence the business environment change gradually, as with the growth of the suburbs in the last half of the twentieth century. Sometimes changes come quickly, such as with the rapid improvements in information processing technology during the 1990s. Some changes seem to occur overnight, as with the fall of Communism and the privatization of businesses in Eastern Europe and the former Soviet Union. Armed with a set of general principles, the manager can successfully adjust his or her firm's business strategy to its ever changing environment.

To demonstrate the applicability of economic principles to widely disparate business conditions, we will conduct a brief historical analysis. This chapter examines the evolution of the modern business firm by focusing on economic activity and business organization at three points in time: 1840, 1910, and today. For each period, we will discuss the infrastructure of business and market conditions that firms faced, how those conditions affected the size and scope of the activities of the firm, and how business organizations responded to changes. We concentrate on developments in the U.S. economy, although parallel lines of development occurred in other industrializing nations, such as Great Britain, France, and Germany.[1] We conclude by considering modern business conditions in developing nations.

The dates we study were not chosen randomly. The period before 1840 was one in which conditions constrained firms to operate in small localized markets. Changes in infrastructure between 1840 and 1910 encouraged the growth of corporate giants, such as Standard Oil, U.S. Steel, and DuPont. Even the largest and best managed firms of that time were still constrained by problems of coordination and control—how to gain sufficient information on a timely basis to manage large-scale operations efficiently and adapt to changes in their markets. Since 1910, and particularly in the last 30 years, changes in telecommunication and data processing have revolutionized firms' abilities to process information and control their operations. As a result, increasingly diverse organizations can respond more effectively to their business environments. The environment has continued to change, however, perhaps even more quickly than before. This has increased the pressures to which firms must respond.

◆ ◆ ◆ ◆ ◆ THE WORLD IN 1840

Doing Business in 1840

Before 1840, businessmen[2] largely managed their own firms in ways that their counterparts today would find unfamiliar. The experience of John Burrows was typical of the era.[3] Burrows was an Iowa merchant who bought potatoes from nearby farmers and cleaned and packaged them. Hearing that potatoes were fetching $2 a bushel in New Orleans, he loaded an Illinois River flatboat and floated downstream. On the trip, he was offered 50 cents a bushel for his potatoes but rejected it in hope of getting a better price at New Orleans. While floating south, he was joined by other potato merchants seeking the same high prices. Soon, the New Orleans market was glutted. Supply and demand dictated that potato prices would plummet. After a six-week journey, Burrows sold his potatoes to a Bermuda ship captain for 8 cents a bushel.

Burrows was a merchant known as a "factor." Farmers in the United States sold their output to factors like Burrows, who brought the goods to major markets, such as New Orleans or New York, in search of buyers. Some of these buyers were local merchants, looking to stock their grocery stores. Most buyers, however, were

---

[1]For comparisons of Europe and America on these issues see, Chandler, A. D. and H. Daems (eds.), *Managerial Hierarchies: Comparative Perspectives on the Rise of the Modern Industrial Enterprise*, Cambridge, MA: Harvard University Press, 1980. For issues concerning industrialization within Europe, see Pollard, S., "Industrialization and the European Economy," *Economic History Review*, 26, November 1973: pp. 636–648. For international comparisons on the development of ideas about the organizations and management, see Guillen, M. F., *Models of Management: Work, Authority, and Organization in a Comparative Perspective*, Chicago: University of Chicago Press, 1994.

[2]We use the term *businessmen* literally. Few, if any, women were involved in business in 1840. This had not changed much by 1910.

[3]This example comes from William Cronon's excellent history of the city of Chicago, *Nature's Metropolis*, New York: Norton, 1991.

"agents," representing out-of-town merchants, including some from Europe. Factors and agents rarely dealt directly with each other. Instead, they enlisted the help of "brokers." Brokers served as matchmakers between factors and agents. Brokers possessed specialized knowledge of market conditions (knowledge that individual factors and agents lacked), including the names of factors and agents, the availability of supplies, and the magnitude of demands.

Selling was informal. Factors and agents sought out brokers with whom they had done business before. Terms were rarely set in advance or specified in a contract. Instead, the brokers tried to arrange a price that best balanced supply and demand. This was how most business was transacted in 1840. The brokerage arrangement no longer dominates the American business landscape, but it does survive in various forms, such as real estate. An important modern example of the broker is the "market maker" in securities transactions. Market makers in the New York Stock Exchange (NYSE) match the buy and sell orders of parties who do not know each other, facilitating transactions that would otherwise be difficult to conduct.

Buy and sell orders for shares traded on the NYSE are filled almost immediately, so that both parties to a given transaction can be reasonably certain about the price at which the exchange will occur. John Burrows' experience shows that this was not the case in 1840. Factors and agents faced considerable price risk—that is, the price that they received when the transaction took place may have been different from what they expected when they began doing business (e.g., when John Burrows started floating downstream). This risk obviously increased with the distance between the site of production and its final destination. Thus, European merchants trading with the United States ran even larger risks than those Mr. Burrows faced.

The lack of knowledge about prices, buyers, and sellers, and the associated risks, dramatically shaped the nature of business. Farmers faced the most risk, and they relied on factors like Burrows to assume some of it, by selling different farm products at different times of the year, and by selling specific products at various times on the way to market. Presumably, Burrows was more willing to bear risk than most farmers, which may have been why he became a factor rather than a farmer. Once Burrows reached the market, he relied on brokers to find buyers for his goods, a task that he could not easily perform himself.

The nature of information and risk had other implications for the size and structure of business. With few exceptions, such as in the textiles, clockmaking, and firearms industries, goods were produced by small, family operated "firms." This stands in stark contrast to today, where a firm employing 100 workers is considered small, and there is often a clear distinction between owners (shareholders) and managers. Given the tremendous uncertainty about the market value of output, it is not surprising that individuals were reluctant to use their own resources to expand the productive capabilities of their businesses. For similar reasons, banks were also unwilling to finance business expansion. Because of the problems with transportation and communication, which we describe below, family-operated firms could not justify investing in acquiring raw materials or the distribution of final products, even though such investments might have allowed them to better coordinate the production process and become more efficient. Production and distribution involved many individual firms, simply because market conditions made any other system impossible.

Conditions of Business in 1840: Life Without a Modern Infrastructure

The dominance of the family-run small business in 1840 was a direct consequence of the *infrastructure* that was then in place. Infrastructure includes those assets that assist in the production or distribution of goods and services that the firm itself cannot easily provide. Infrastructure facilitates transportation, communication, and financing. It includes basic research, which can enable firms to find better production techniques. The government also has a key role, both because it affects the conditions under which firms do business (e.g., by regulating telecommunications), and because it supplies infrastructure (e.g., the interstate highways).

By modern standards, the infrastructure of 1840 in Europe and America was poorly developed. Limitations in transportation, communications, and finance created the business environment with which John Burrows and others of his time had to cope. While we discuss the situation in America in this and subsequent sections, European businessmen faced similar limitations, often made worse by political factors. Given these limitations, which we detail below, it is apparent that the ways in which business was conducted in 1840, though alien to us today, were appropriate for the time.

Transportation   Transportation was undergoing a revolution in the first half of the nineteenth century, due to the harnessing of steam power. Although the Romans had made attempts to develop roadbeds by means of rails of different sorts, the modern railroad did not add value to commerce until the introduction of the steam engine and the use of iron and steel rails. By 1840, the railroads began to replace the horse and wagon for the shipment of raw materials and consumer goods.[4] Rails in the United States took time to develop, however. As late as 1836, only 175 miles of railroad track were laid in one year.[5] As late as 1850, U.S. railway systems were still too fragmented to foster the growth of national markets.[6] Few rails ran west of the Appalachian Mountains, "connecting" lines often had different gauges, and schedules were seldom coordinated. The development of an integrated transportation infrastructure through railroads in the United States would not be complete until after 1870.[7]

---

[4]Chandler, A. D. and R. S. Tedlow, *The Coming of Managerial Capitalism*, Homewood, IL: Irwin, 1985, p. 179.

[5]Cochran, T. C. and W. Miller, *The Age of Enterprise: A Social History of Industrial America*, New York: Harper & Row, 1961, p. 45.

[6]Chandler, A. D., *The Visible Hand*, Cambridge, MA: Belknap, 1977; *Scale and Scope: The Dynamics of Industrial Capitalism*, Cambridge, MA: Belknap, 1990.

[7]Completed railroad mileage in the United States grew from 2,808 in 1840 to 52,922 in 1870 to 163,597 in 1890, with a peak of 254,000 miles in 1916 (Beniger, J. R. *The Control Revolution*, Cambridge, MA: Harvard University Press, 1986, p. 213). Railroad development in Germany paralleled developments in the United States (Chandler, 1990, p. 411). In France, the government played a major role in construction through the railroad laws of 1842 and 1857. The French rail system expanded from 3,627 kilometers in 1851 to 16,207 kilometers in 1858. The rail system in Italy developed later and to a lesser degree than in France (1,758 kilometers in 1860 to 7,438 kilometers in 1876). (Langer, W. L. *An Encyclopedia of World History*, New York: Houghton Mifflin, 1980, pp. 684, 708, 835, 929).

Until the railroads developed, manufacturers used the waterways to transport goods over long distances, though transportation by water often left much to be desired. For example, while the new steamships plied major American rivers and the Great Lakes as early as 1813, no direct route connected the major cities in the east to the Great Lakes until the completion of the Erie Canal in 1825. Furthermore, steamships could not unload in Chicago until the 1840s. The trip from New York to Chicago was both lengthy and risky, especially during bad weather. Possible routes for waterways were limited, and constructing and maintaining canals was expensive.[8] Nonetheless, the opening of the Erie Canal led to startling growth. For example, between 1830 and 1840, the population of Illinois tripled, from 157,000 to 476,000, and the population of Chicago grew eight times, from 500 to more than 4,000.[9]

While canals and railroads spurred growth, in 1840 they were still in their initial stages of development. Without safe and reliable means of transporting large volumes of goods, producers were reluctant to make the investments needed to expand their production capabilities or to acquire raw materials. An industrial economy centered on large industrial firms would have to wait for the completion of the railroad system and the development of effective communications.

Communications The primary mode of long-distance communication in 1840 was the public mail. Postal service predated the Industrial Revolution. The United States Federal Postal Service was chartered in 1791. As is often still claimed today, however, the postal service may have served everyone, but it was slow and relatively expensive. As late as 1840, it depended almost exclusively on the horse, and had difficulty adjusting to the expanded volume of communication that followed the western expansion of the United States and the gradual development of a mass-production economy.

The first modern form of communications was the telegraph, which required laying wires between points of service. In 1830, Samuel Morse linked Baltimore and Washington by telegraph. Telegraph lines soon flourished. By 1852, telegraph lines paralleled most train lines. By 1870, Western Union was one of the largest firms in the United States, and the telegraph provided the communication infrastructure for the growth of an industrial economy.[10]

The local scale of business activities in 1840 was partially attributable to the lack of a modern communication infrastructure. A businessman transacting with distant trading partners needed to be able to respond if market conditions changed. Without adequate communication, businessmen preferred to delegate responsibility for the transaction to agents or factors, such as Mr. Burrows, rather than assume the risk themselves. If a businessman did establish separate facilities in different locations, he would need to communicate with each facility and coordinate their activities. Again, inadequate communication made this impossible. Similarly, railroads could not schedule trains reliably and safely. This interfered

---

[8]Chandler, A. D. and R. S. Tedlow, *The Coming of Managerial Capitalism*, Homewood, IL: Irwin, 1985, p. 176.

[9]Cochran, T. C. and W. Miller, *The Age of Enterprise: A Social History of Industrial America*, New York: Harper & Row, 1961, p. 42.

[10]Beniger, James R., *The Control Revolution*, Boston: Harvard University Press, 1986; Chandler, Alfred D., *The Visible Hand*, Cambridge, MA: Belknap, 1977.

with the flow of goods over long distances and made large-scale production more risky.

Even when modern communication capabilities became available, firms did not always adopt them, since their potential value was unclear at first while their costs were high. Firms initially used the telegraph for its value in bridging distances with agents over matters such as pricing. Although using the telegraph was expensive, important time-sensitive messages justified the cost. Railroads used the telegraph for these reasons, but they were still slow to adopt it for regular scheduling. The New York and Erie Railroad was the first to do this in the United States in 1851, following the example of British railroads.[11]

Mail service was at first unpredictable and expensive. For example, correspondence from the Waterbury, Connecticut, headquarters of the Scovill company in the 1840s took one day to reach New York City and two days to reach Philadelphia in good weather. In bad weather, it could easily take a week. To send a one-sheet letter from Waterbury cost 12.5 cents to New York and 18.5 cents to Philadelphia. The absence of postmarks on some surviving letters from this time suggests that high postage rates encouraged Scovill owners and their agents to hand carry items when possible. Business mail volume increased after the U.S. Postal Service significantly lowered its rates twice, in 1845 and 1851.[12]

Finance   Few individuals could afford to build and operate a complex firm themselves. Financial markets bring together providers and users of capital. Financial markets also enable buyers and sellers to smooth out cash flows and reduce the risk of price fluctuation. Most businesses in the first half of the 19th century were partnerships and found it difficult to obtain long-term debt. Stocks were not easily traded, which diluted their value and increased the cost of equity capital. The lack of a developed financial infrastructure inhibited firms from raising capital for the larger projects that a mass-production economy required. It also limited the extent to which investors could protect themselves against the increased risks of larger capital projects.

The major role of private banks at this time was the issuance of credit. By 1820, there were more than 300 banks in the United States. By 1837, there were 788. By offering short-term credit, banks smoothed the cash flows of buyers and sellers and facilitated reliable transactions, although there remained considerable risk from speculation and inflation throughout the 19th century. There was a recurring pattern of boom and bust, with periodic depressions, such as the Panic of 1837.[13]

Many smaller firms had difficulty getting credit, however, and if it was available at all, credit was often granted informally on the basis of personal relationships. This limited the potential of smaller firms. Government or private consortia—groups of private individuals brought together to finance a specific project—primarily funded larger projects, such as the Erie Canal. As the scale of capital projects increased after 1840, government support or larger public debt or equity offerings by investment banks increasingly replaced financing by private individuals and small groups of investors.

---

[11]Yates, J., *Control Through Communication: The Rise of System in American Management*, Baltimore, MD: Johns Hopkins University Press, 1989, pp. 22–23.

[12]Yates, *Control Through Communication: The Rise of System in American Management*, 22, pp. 160–161.

[13]Cochran, T. C. and W. Miller, *The Age of Enterprise*, pp. 43–49.

Financial institutions also reduce business risks. The mechanism for reducing the risk of price fluctuation is the futures market, in which individuals purchase the right to buy and/or sell goods on a specified date for a predetermined price. Futures markets require verification of the characteristics of the product being transacted. They also require that one party to the transaction is willing to bear the risk that the "spot" (i.e., current) price on the date the futures transaction is completed may differ from the transacted price. In 1840, no institutional mechanisms reduced the risk of price fluctuation. The first futures market was created by the Chicago Board of Trade in 1858 and profoundly affected the farming industry, as we discuss in Example 1.1.

◆ ◆

Example 1.1

The Emergence of Chicago[14]

The emergence of Chicago as a major commercial center in the 1800s illustrates the core concepts that we have discussed, albeit for a city rather than a business. In the 1840s, growing cities in the Midwest, including Cincinnati, Toledo, Peoria, St. Louis, and Chicago, were all competing, as vigorously as firms in any other markets might compete, to become the region's center of commerce. Their success would ultimately be decided by the same conditions that determined the horizontal and vertical boundaries of business firms. Significant changes in *infrastructure* and *technology* enabled Chicago's business organizations, and with them the city's financial fortunes, to outstrip other cities. For example, by 1860, the Chicago Board of Trade bought and sold nearly all the grain produced in the Midwest. Similarly, two Chicago meatpackers, Armour and Swift, dominated their industry.

Chicago prospered because it conducted business in different ways from competing commercial centers. Chicago businesses were the first to take advantage of new technologies that reduced costs and risks. For example, Swift and Armour simultaneously adopted the refrigerated train car, which had first been used by Illinois fruit growers. (Lining a standard freight car with ice from Lake Michigan produced the refrigerator car.) This allowed cattle and hogs to be butchered in Chicago, before they lost weight (and value) on the way to market. Cyrus McCormick and others took advantage of the recently invented grain elevator to inexpensively sort, store, and ship grain bought from Midwest farmers. They reduced the risk of dealing with large quantities of grain by buying and selling grain futures at the Chicago Board of Trade.

The businesses run by Swift, Armour, McCormick, and other Chicago entrepreneurs required substantial investments in rail lines, icing facilities, grain elevators, the futures market, and so forth. These businessmen recognized that they could not recoup their investments without high volumes of business. This would require *throughput*: the movement of inputs and outputs through a production process. The meat packing and grain businesses of Chicago required

---

[14]This example draws from Cronon, W., *Nature's Metropolis*, New York: Norton, 1991.

FIGURE 1.1
GROWTH OF AMERICAN RAILROADS FROM 1840 TO 1890.

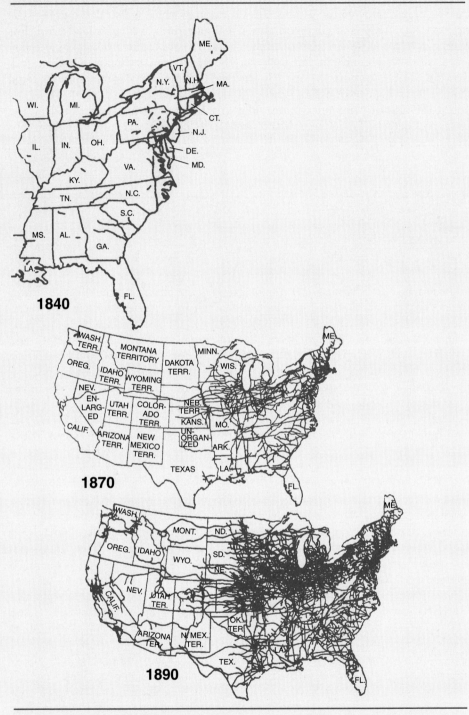

1840

1870

1890

Chicago became the hub of significant East/West and North/South rail lines. This was in part due to the efforts of local business leaders to promote the city's growth. Once Chicago started to appear as a hub, however, it was increasingly reasonable to have further railroad lines pass through the city, making it an even larger transportation center. *Source:* Association of American Railroads. Reprinted from Beniger, J. R., *The Control Revolution*, Cambridge, MA: Harvard University Press, 1986, p. 212.

large supplies of ice, large assured movements of grain and livestock from the farmlands, and large assured movements of grain and butchered meat to eastern markets. The need for throughput explains why Chicago, rather than any other city, emerged as the business center of the Midwest. Only Chicago, with its unique location as the terminus of rail and water routes from the East and West, had the transportation infrastructure necessary to assure throughput. Chicago thus emerged during the mid-1800s and remains today the "market leader" among midwestern cities.

Figure 1.1 shows the American railroad system in 1840, 1870, and 1890. As the figure shows, Chicago became the hub of significant East/West and North/South rail lines. This was in part due to the efforts of local business leaders to promote the city's growth. Once Chicago started to appear as a hub, however, it became reasonable for other railroad lines pass to through the city, making it an even larger transportation center. Only St. Louis could have competed in terms of rail throughput. But St. Louis lacked quick access to the Great Lakes—the preferred shipping route for grain during summer and fall and the principal source of ice for meat packers.

Production Technology   Production technology means the application of scientific or technical knowledge to production processes. Firms often direct resources toward internal innovation and toward stimulating the demand for new products from the market, both of which help spur technological development. However, a single firm or group of firms has only limited ability to change general levels of production technology and the current state of technology inevitably constrains the expansion of business activity. Technological constraints were substantial in 1840.

Technology was relatively undeveloped in 1840, compared to what it would become in the next half century. Most factories produced goods the same way they had been produced in the previous century, and even the most advanced factories could not produce standardized goods at the high volumes that would become common by 1910. Even though textile plants had begun to be mechanized before 1820 and standardization was common in the manufacture of clocks and firearms, the "American System" of manufacturing through the use of interchangeable parts was only just beginning. Until the 1870s, factories operated on the basis of internal contracting, in which their facilities were leased to a supervisor who in turn hired workers and produced goods. Even those factories that produced more standardized items with interchangeable parts produced small amounts of goods and made little use of inanimate sources of power, which would have accelerated production and required new forms of factory organization and coordination.[15]

Government   Government resolves commercial disputes and sets the rules under which business operates. It also participates directly in economic activity

---

[15]Best, M., *The New Competition: Institutions of Industrial Restructuring*, Cambridge, MA: Harvard University Press, 1990, chap. 1; Robinson, R. V. and C. M. Briggs, "The Rise of Factories in Nineteenth-Century Indianapolis," *American Journal of Sociology*, 97, November 1991: pp. 622–656.

through the provision or purchase of goods and services, through tax policies, or through regulation. Historically, most infrastructure investments are left to the public sector. Private investors are reluctant to invest in infrastructure because while they would bear the cost, their competitors would share in the benefits. Government agencies do not compete with private firms, so they are better suited to develop the infrastructure, such as canals and railroads, that serve the common good. For example, from 1820 until 1838, 18 states advanced credit of $60 million for canals, $43 million for railroads, and $4.5 million for turnpikes.[16] Apart from the development of these large, fixed-cost resources, the government was not much involved in the U.S. economy in 1840, especially when compared with what government would spend by the 1930s. Given the limited state of local markets at the time, this lack of involvement probably inhibited economic expansion.

Summary

The lack of a modern infrastructure limited economic activity in 1840. Firms were small and informally organized, which was a direct result of conditions that made modern business institutions impractical. Technology prevented production from expanding much beyond traditional levels. Even if such a technology had been available, the limited transportation infrastructure, coupled with difficulties in obtaining accurate and timely information, would have made investments in large production and distribution capabilities too risky for businessmen in 1840. There were no professional managers as we think of them today; owners ran their own enterprises. Market demand and technological development would have to increase before high-speed and high-volume production and distribution could develop. This required an expanded economic infrastructure.

There were forces in play, however, that would change the conditions in which business operated and greatly increase its scale of operations. The full effect of these changes could not be felt until a transportation and communications infrastructure had developed to permit increased volumes of activity over a broader area. The growth of large projects would also await the development of techniques for assuring management control and reducing the organizing costs for owners of large capital projects and the firms that developed to manage them.

THE WORLD IN 1910

Doing Business in 1910

Business changed greatly from 1840 to 1910, and the business practices and organizations of 1910 would seem much more familiar to the modern businessperson than those of 1840. In some sectors, such as farming and textiles, small firms still predominated, but they faced a well-developed set of buyers and suppliers and of service providers to facilitate commerce and circulate information. In other sectors, such as chemicals, steel, and transportation, business was increasingly dominated by large firms that not only produced finished goods, but acquired raw materials and distributed end products. Because these firms were too large for their owners to be involved in everyday decision making, a new class of "professional" managers emerged with no ownership interest in the firms they guided.

---

[16]Cochran, T. C. and W. Miller, *The Age of Enterprise*, p. 42.

These firms had internal hierarchies in which lower-level managers supervised day-to-day activities, and reported to upper management, which attempted to shape the various departments and divisions into a cohesive whole.

The evolution of the hierarchical firm was the direct consequence of changes in infrastructure and technology. No change was more important than the development of mass production technologies, such as the Bessemer process for making steel, or the continuous-process tank furnace that facilitated the mass production of many products, such as plate glass. These new technologies enabled goods to be produced at costs far below anything that firms using older technologies could achieve. To fully exploit these production opportunities, firms needed reliable supplies of inputs, as well as access to widespread distribution and retail outlets. The fixed investments required to develop these outlets were justified only when large volumes of goods flowed through them. In short, firms needed to assure a sufficiently large throughput to make the expansion of productive capacity economical. The needed throughput was assured by the development of the infrastructure: railroads for shipping inputs and finished goods; telegraph and telephone for communication, control, and coordination of materials over expanded areas; and banking and accounting practices to provide the investment capital needed to finance production and distribution facilities.

Businessmen quickly appreciated the potential benefits of reorganizing production to reach many customers at lower costs per customer. Historian Alfred Chandler has noted how businessmen reorganized their firms to take advantage of new production technologies.[17] The owner-operator who invested in a new technology found that he needed to increase production substantially to recoup his investment. This required a tremendous increase in throughput. This increased the owner-operator's responsibilities in functional areas of business, such as purchasing, sales, distribution, and finance. These all needed to be coordinated by a central office to assure that production runs went smoothly and finished goods found their way to market.

Product line and volume expansion altered relationships among manufacturers, their suppliers, and their distributors. Manufacturing firms increasingly chose to *vertically integrate*, that is, they chose to produce raw materials and/or distribute finished goods themselves, rather than rely on independent suppliers, factors, and agents. Chapters 3 through 5 discuss the benefits of vertical integration, but briefly, manufacturing firms in 1910 found it desirable to vertically integrate because the high volume of production made them more vulnerable to gaps in the chain of supply and distribution. This explains why vertical integration occurred in some industries, such as steel, chemicals, and machinery, but not in others, such as textiles and furniture. Vertical integration only made sense when firms could exploit new technologies to achieve cost savings from high-volume production. In industries like furniture and textiles, few technological breakthroughs occurred. High-volume firms in these industries had no advantages over low-volume firms, so vertical integration to assure throughput did not occur in them.

New production technologies also allowed firms to produce a wider range of products at lower costs than if they were produced separately. In the years immediately following 1910, many firms, such as DuPont, General Motors, and Alcoa,

---

[17]Chandler, A. D., *Scale and Scope: The Dynamics of Industrial Capitalism*, Cambridge, MA: Belknap, 1990.

expanded horizontally by offering a wider variety of products. They found that the increased size and complexity of multiproduct operations necessitated a further re-organization into semiautonomous divisions. Each division in these firms made the principal operating decisions for their own businesses, while a separate corporate office made decisions that affected the entire corporation. For example, the divisions of General Motors made operating decisions for each car line, while corporate management controlled corporate finance, research and development, and new model development. This organizational form, known as the multidivisional or *M-form*, became characteristic of the largest industrial firms until the 1960s.

The growth of vertically and horizontally integrated firms often reduced the number of firms in an industry and increased the potential for collusion to restrict competition and increase profits. Mergers and informal associations of firms to restrict competition were common in such industries as tobacco, steel, aluminum, and oil. During the period around 1910, the U.S. government directed antitrust activities toward breaking up firms that appeared to be national monopolies. Among the major cases during this time were those involving Standard Oil (1911), American Tobacco (1911), DuPont (1912), International Harvester (1918), and Eastman Kodak (1920).[18]

Integrated firms employed more individuals in more complex and interrelated tasks than had earlier firms, both in production and distribution.[19] They also implemented systematic approaches to managing employees to standardize jobs and tasks, monitor worker compliance with management directives, appraise worker performance, test and train employees, and conduct the other functions that have come to be associated with personnel administration. These approaches spread widely among large firms, under the influence of a new type of specialist, the management consultant.[20] Perhaps the best known of these approaches was "Scientific Management," developed by Frederick W. Taylor, which sought to identify the most efficient ways of performing tasks through "time and motion" studies and then compel workers to adopt these ways through the judicious use of incentives, rewards, and sanctions.[21]

Besides vertical and horizontal integration, large firms needed to develop managerial hierarchies. As Alfred Chandler describes, the managerial hierarchy substituted the *visible* hand of management for the *invisible* hand of the market.[22] That is, it coordinated across the various functions that had been brought inside the firm. Hierarchy was needed because of the greater volume of goods to coordinate, the larger workforce needed for mass production and distribution, and the enlarged markets integrated firms served.

---

[18]Fligstein, N., *The Transformation of Corporate Control*, Cambridge, MA: Harvard University Press, 1990, chaps. 2 and 3.

[19]O'Brien, A. P., "Factory Size, Economies of Scale and the Great Merger Wave of 1898–1902," *Journal of Economic History*, 48, 1988: p. 648.

[20]Nelson, D., "Industrial Engineering and the Industrial Enterprise, 1890–1940," in Lamoreaux, N. R. and Raff, D.M.G. (eds.) *Coordination and Information: Historical Perspectives and the Organization of Enterprise*, Chicago: University of Chicago Press, 1995, pp. 35–53.

[21]Kanigel, R. *The One Best Way: Frederick Winslow Taylor and the Enigma of Efficiency*, New York: Viking, 1997.

[22]Chandler, A. D., *The Visible Hand*, Cambridge, MA: Belknap, 1977.

The growth of managerial hierarchies fostered the emergence of a class of professional managers, many of whom owned little or no share of the business. These individuals tended not to have worked their way up in a particular business, but rather had been trained as engineers or in newly founded schools of business. On behalf of the owners, managers applied their expertise in control and coordination to the firm and its business units. In doing so, they pioneered the standardized collection of data on a firm's operations, and with it the beginnings of cost accounting.

These changes in the business world caused problems and conflicts. Expansion into new markets easily led to overexpansion and overcapacity. The development of internal control techniques easily led to excessive bureaucracy and red tape. Newly expanded workforces resisted the controls on their work habits needed to facilitate greater and more predictable throughput. The growth of large integrated firms was paralleled by the growth of unions, with occasionally violent confrontations. Finally, the skill that new professional managers exhibited raised the problem of ensuring that managers worked in the best interests of owners rather than for their own ends.

Business Conditions in 1910: A "Modern" Infrastructure

A substantially new infrastructure for business had emerged by 1910, notably in transportation and communications. These developments fostered the growth of national markets by enabling firms to count on the fast and reliable movements of goods, along with instantaneous and accurate communication over vast areas.

Production Technology Technology developed greatly between 1840 and 1910, which promoted the growth of mass production. Mass production processes permitted high-volume, low-cost manufacturing of many products, including steel, aluminum, automobiles, and chemicals, to name only a few.

Transportation For mass production to be viable, producers needed assured throughput. The continued growth of the railroads made this possible. By 1910, railroads dominated passenger and freight transportation. Travel became faster, safer, and more reliable. Manufacturers could obtain raw materials from distant sources, and swiftly ship their product to customers hundreds or even thousands of miles away. Smaller manufacturers often sold to the new mass distribution firms, such as Sears, which could efficiently distribute via the rails vast arrays of consumer goods to widely scattered customers.[23]

Communications The infrastructure in 1910 enabled businesses to communicate more accurately and quickly than ever before and allowed managers of growing firms to feel more confident in expanding their volume of transactions well beyond traditional levels. The principal components of the communications infrastructure in 1840—the postal system and the telegraph—were still important in 1910 and were becoming increasingly part of the management systems of large firms. During this time, however, the telephone was growing in importance, rela-

---

[23]The automobile was emerging as a competitor for passenger transport. Trucks, however, did not seriously compete with rails for freight transport until the 1950s.

tive to other means of communications. A few phone calls to suppliers and distributors instantly assured managers that large production runs were feasible, and that there were markets for their output.

The growth of the largest telephone firm, American Telephone and Telegraph (AT&T), illustrates how the development of large firms during this period depended on market and technological conditions. When the telephone was invented in 1876, its technological potential (and hence its profitability) was uncertain because some devices essential for telephone service as we know it, such as the switchboard, were unknown. The market conditions facing the telephone were also uncertain because of patent conflicts, and as a result, there was competition to provide local telephone service. By the 1880s, patent conflicts had been resolved, and new technology made consolidation possible. In 1883, AT&T adopted a strategy of merging local telephone companies into a national system. The resulting network greatly reduced the costs of interconnecting large numbers of users, and the telephone quickly replaced the telegraph as the communications technology of choice.[24]

Finance In 1910, active security markets publicly traded the shares of the largest industrial firms. Since the 1860s, the large investment banking houses had been underwriting most stock transactions that were essential for the financing needs of large firms. Investment bankers like J. P. Morgan were among the most powerful businessmen in the world in 1910.[25] The development of a financial infrastructure was further aided during this period by the systematization and circulation of information about credit (credit bureaus), the availability of installment financing, and the development of the communications infrastructure.

Between 1840 and 1910, owners, managers, and investors also realized that the growing scope of business activity required new ways of keeping track of a firm's activity and reporting its results. New accounting techniques were developed, and mandatory reporting standards for public firms became law. The new large firms developed these techniques to solve record-keeping problems occasioned by the size and scope of their activities. For example, the railroads produced major innovations in cost accounting to manage their requirements of operating efficiencies. The newly formed mass marketing firms, such as Sears, developed new accounting concepts, such as inventory turnover, to link profits to fluctuations in sales volume, while large industrial firms, such as DuPont, pioneered cost accounting.

Accounting developments also focused around the idea of public accounting—the public disclosure of details of a firm's operations to insure that investors were not being cheated by managers and that capital was being maintained. In England, for example, laws enacted between 1844 and 1900 required: the presentation of a "full and fair" balance sheet at shareholders meetings; the payment of dividends

---

[24]For details, see Garnet, R. W., *The Telephone Enterprise: The Evolution of the Bell System's Horizontal Structure, 1876–1909*, Baltimore, MD: Johns Hopkins University Press, 1985. Also see, Smith, G. D., *The Anatomy of a Business Strategy: Bell, Western Electric, and the Origins of the American Telephone Industry*, Baltimore, MD: Johns Hopkins University Press, 1985.

[25]Chernow, R., *The House of Morgan: An American Dynasty and the Rise of Modern Finance*, New York: Simon & Schuster, 1990.

out of profits; the maintenance of a firm's capital stock; and the conduct of compulsory and uniform audits of all registered firms. Similar developments occurred in the United States. For example, by the 1860s, the railroads employed more accountants than the U.S. government. The first U.S. independent accounting firm was founded in New York in 1883, and the American Association of Public Accountants was formed in 1886.[26]

Government Government regulation of the conditions under which business was conducted, in such areas as corporate law and governance, antitrust, provisions for disability insurance and worker safety, and insurance for widows and children increased during this period. (Securities markets and labor relations were not fully regulated until the 1930s.) This increased regulation not only affected how firms behaved toward competitors and employees, but also how they were managed, since government forced managers to collect detailed data on their operations that had not been gathered before and that were useful to professional managers. Finally, nearly universal, mandatory secondary school education also became the norm for industrialized nations in the first half of the 20th century. This produced a workforce able to meet the specialized needs of large integrated and bureaucratic firms.

Summary

The expanded business infrastructure in 1910 made it cost effective for firms to expand their markets, product lines, and production quantities. It is thus not surprising that the capital stock of the United States grew at a faster rate than the gross national product in the second half of the 19th century as businessmen invested in the new technologies.[27] New technologies permitted the higher volume of standardized production, while the growth of the rail system permitted the reliable distribution of manufactured goods to a national market. The telegraph enabled large firms to monitor and control geographically separate suppliers, factories, and distributors. The growth of futures markets, capital markets, insurance companies, investment banks, and other financial institutions enabled business to be transacted on a scale that would have been impossible in 1840. By one estimate, the "transaction-processing sector," which included transportation, communication, and financial institutions, had become one-third of the U.S. economy by 1910.[28]

To take best advantage of the cost savings afforded by mass production, many firms reorganized. This growth of vertically and horizontally integrated firms defined the period between 1840 and 1910. Increasingly, managers, a new class of professionals that developed during this period, made critical decisions for firms. These managers became expert in functions that had not previously been handled

---

[26]Carruthers, B. G. and W. N. Espeland, "Double Entry Bookkeeping and the Rhetoric of Economic Rationality," *American Journal of Sociology*, 97, July 1991: pp. 31–70.

[27]See Gallman, R. E., "The United States Capital Stock in the Nineteenth Century," chap. 4 in Engerman, S. L. and R. E. Gallman (eds.), *Long-Term Factors in American Economic Growth*, Chicago: University of Chicago Press, 1986: pp. 165–214.

[28]Wallis, J. J. and D. C. North, "Measuring the Transaction Sector in the American Economy, 1870–1970," chap. 3 in Engerman, S. L. and R. E. Gallman (eds.), *Long-Term Factors in American Economic Growth*, Chicago: University of Chicago Press, 1986: pp. 95–161.

by individual owners and entrepreneurs, and their new skills became a source of competitive advantage for M-form firms and a key to success in industries that could benefit from expansion.

◆ ◆ ◆ ◆ ◆ ◆ THE WORLD TODAY

Doing Business Today

Since 1910, and particularly in the last 30 years, the ways of doing business have changed profoundly. Strategies that were effective when American firms competed mostly with each other no longer seem to work in an era of global competition. In many industries, firms that relied on cost advantages associated with high volume production have been slow to adapt to changes that allow specialized niche firms to offer tailor-made products at low cost. Business practices that evolved in an era of political and economic stability can no longer be taken for granted when change is rapid and unpredictable. Business–government relations now fundamentally affect a firm's strategy and operations.

Compared with 1910, the scope of product market activities carried out within firms today has changed. While some firms had begun to diversify beyond traditional product lines as early as 1890, the pace of diversification increased significantly after World War II. Some of this diversification may have been the result of antitrust pressures that prevented large firms from growing even larger by acquiring rivals in the same industry. It also occurred because new opportunities opened in related markets and distribution channels. For example, consumer products companies like Philip Morris and Quaker Oats realized that they could distribute a much wider range of products through their distribution channels than they had previously considered. Technology-oriented companies, such as United Technologies or 3M, realized that they could apply skills mastered in an underlying technology, such as jet engines or adhesive chemistry, to a group of related business units.

Other firms, such as ITT and Textron, acquired portfolios of unrelated businesses. The corporate management of these conglomerates took little interest in making decisions regarding research and development, advertising, and major capital projects. Instead, these managers ran their firms as holding companies and delegated most strategic and operating decisions to the individual business units. Movements toward conglomeration eased in the 1970s, and the trend of subsequent mergers has been to focus on core markets and enhance linkages among business units.

Firms have also taken a fresh look at their internal structure and the organization of the vertical chain of production. Until the 1960s, most large diversified firms followed the General Motors model and employed the M-form. But as these firms diversified into less related businesses, the role of corporate management changed. Highly diversified conglomerates eliminated layers of hierarchy and reduced corporate staffs. Even within firms with related product lines, the M-form has become increasingly outdated. Some firms, such as Dow Corning, Amoco, and Citibank, have had difficulty coordinating complicated production processes across different customer groups and market areas using traditional multidivisional structures. These firms have enhanced the extent of control and the complexity of the internal hierarchy through matrix structures, in which two or more overlapping hierarchies are

EXAMPLE 1.2

RESPONDING TO THE BUSINESS ENVIRONMENT: THE CASE OF AMERICAN WHALING

Historical accounts, such as Chandler's, have featured large manufacturing and distribution firms that took advantage of new technologies to lower costs. However, small firms also had to respond to changing conditions. The American whaling industry in the 19th century provides an example.[29]

In the middle of the 19th century, whaling was a competitive industry that consisted of many relatively small firms. There were no appreciable cost advantages to large firms, because whales had to be caught one at a time, and the whaling ships had to go to the whaling grounds to hunt. The technology for hunting whales did improve in productivity during the century, with such innovations as whale guns and more effective lances. But these developments did not change the basic processes by which whales were caught, and they certainly did not improve productivity to the same degree that the introduction of mass production and distribution techniques did for other industries. Whaling ships at this time also were not able to use the advances in steam power that were revolutionizing passenger and freight transport, due to the amount of space that steam engines occupied (space that was needed for the whales). New sailing vessals were specifically designed for the needs of whalers, but their effects on productivity were largely incremental.

The principal whaling products at the time, spermaceti, sperm oil, and whale oil, were used as illuminants and lubricants. By 1850, whale oils were facing increasing competition from coal, oil, coal gas, and kerosene. Demand for lubricants for machinery was also increasing from manufacturing facilities, such as textile mills. The growth in demand offset increases in competition, so that the real price of sperm oil (i.e., the price after adjusting for inflation) doubled between 1820 and 1850, while the real value of industry output rose tenfold.

Whalers responded to the rapid increase in demand by finding new whaling grounds in the Pacific, Indian, and Arctic Oceans. Exploiting these grounds required longer voyages, often lasting up to four years. This led to the use of larger ships which were more difficult to provision. The longer voyages to new grounds made whaling riskier and increased the chance of losing the entire ship to one in ten. When these problems grew, the geographic center of the American whaling industry shifted from New Bedford, Massachusetts, to San Francisco, California. These changes in the whaling business, along with the incremental technological adjustments mentioned previously, were the only reasonable responses available to an industry that could not adopt high-volume production and distribution techniques.

---

[29]This discussion is based on Davis, L. E., R. E. Gallman, and T. D. Hutchins, "Productivity in American Whaling: The New Bedford Fleet in the Nineteenth Century," Chapter 3 in Galenson, D. W., ed., *Markets in History: Economic Studies of the Past*, Cambridge: Cambridge University Press, 1989.

These changes adversely affected the industry's performance. On the whole, they made whaling less attractive to qualified seamen, a serious problem in a labor-intensive industry. This problem was especially severe after 1850, when industrialization increased opportunities in commercial shipping and on land. To respond to this problem, whalers either had to increase experienced seamen's rewards, which were based on the size of the catch, or attract less experienced hands, who could be paid less and who were less aware of the rigors of the longer voyages. As the 19th century progressed, whalers chose to hire inexperienced seamen, which reduced the productivity of whaling voyages. The American whaling industry declined after 1870 and had all but disappeared by 1914.

used simultaneously to coordinate staff. Other firms, including Benetton, Nike, and Harley-Davidson have simple internal hierarchies. These firms control product design and brand image but leave most other key organizational functions, including manufacturing, distribution, and retailing to independent market specialists.

As firms increasingly focus on core businesses, market specialists are performing more and more activities in the vertical chain. Firms like EDS and Servicemaster, for example, perform management functions that were previously done by large hierarchical firms. Those managerial functions that are not returning to the market are increasingly being automated, so that managers can focus on a mix of highly technical, specialized, coordinative tasks and broader, general-management duties.[30]

Changes in industry conditions, organizational structure, and the balance of activities done inside the firm have fundamentally changed the job of the general manager. In the large hierarchical firm that dominated the industrial landscape through the 1970s, a manager's power came from the vertical chain of command. The manager's career path was usually within a particular functional department, and evaluations were based on the manager's contribution to departmental objectives. The organization was controlled through highly structured administrative systems, highly circumscribed job descriptions, and hierarchical relationships involving "bosses" and "subordinates." In many firms today, however, traditional hierarchies are weakening. Increased competition in many industries has placed a premium on anticipating shifts in market demand and quickly transforming ideas into marketable products.[31] Such skills necessitate much more coordination across functional areas, both within and outside the firm, than in the traditional hierarchical firm, resulting in changes in where power resides in the organization, changes in career paths, and changes in how performance is evaluated.

The Infrastructure Today

Infrastructure today is marked by communications, transportation, and computing technologies that can insure coordination of extensive activities on a global scale. This, in turn, increases the interdependence of what had been separate geographic

---

[30]Kotter, J. P., *The General Managers*, New York: Free Press, 1982.

[31]See Stalk, G., P. Evans, and L. Shulman, "Competing on Capabilities: The New Rules for Corporate Strategy," *Harvard Business Review*, March–April 1992.

markets and has magnified the costs of infrastructure failure. The financial markets in New York and Chicago, for example, are so thoroughly linked with those in Tokyo, Hong Kong, and London, that businesspeople need to consider more information from a wider area than ever before.

Transportation Automobile and air travel have transformed the transportation infrastructure since 1910. The enormous increase in the number of motor vehicles, greatly aided by national highway systems, also created a major industry in its own right. Interstate trucking has become a major competitor to the railroads. Fast, reliable transportation of both passengers and freight by air has also profoundly changed the nature of business.

Air, rail, and ground travel have become better coordinated. Increasing demands from shippers of large volumes of goods for efficient and reliable transportation over long distances, coupled with more sophisticated communications and data processing technology, allowed goods to be shipped in containers that move from ships to railroads to trucks. The widespread use of air travel for both freight and passengers has reduced the need for cities and firms to be close to railroads and waterways. Some cities, such as Atlanta, have thriving airports that have spurred growth despite relatively poor rail and water connections.

Communications Telecommunications technologies, such as the fax or the modem, have made possible the nearly instantaneous transmission and reception of information over long distances, creating global markets for a wide range of products and services. This technology, coupled with data processing technology, has also drastically changed the abilities of individuals to do their work and of firms to coordinate workers. In particular, communications and computing advances have made the paper-based coordination and control of older integrated firms obsolete. Although fundamental developments in computer technology occurred before World War II, many observers have argued that the growth of data processing, telecommunications, and computer-based production technologies has defined the economic infrastructure in the late 20th century.

Finance The failure of financial markets in 1929, followed by worldwide recession in the 1930s, led to the creation of the modern financial infrastructure, through the separation of commercial and investment banking, the enhanced role of central banks, and the increased regulation of securities markets. The result was a stable financial services sector that supplied firms with equity and debt funding that the firms themselves could not provide through their retained earnings.[32]

Deregulation of financial services in the 1970s and 1980s changed the role of the financial sector in the economic infrastructure. Since 1980, capital markets have more actively evaluated firm performance. The ready availability of large funds through so-called junk bonds allowed mergers and acquisitions to multiply in number and dollar amount per deal. Globalization of financial markets facilitated many notable mergers and acquisitions such as Chrysler's merger with Daimler-Benz, Sony's acquisition of Columbia Studios, and German publisher Bertelsmann's acquisitions of Random House and Bantam Doubleday Dell. The

---

[32]Donaldson, G. and J. Lorsch, *Decision Making at the Top*, New York: Harper & Row, 1983.

dizzying pace of mergers in the late 1990s has elevated finance from a support service to a central focus of many large firms.

Financial accounting developed to cope with the increased complexity of multidivisional firms, a process that began with the consolidation of General Motors in the 1920s and has continued with the creation of accounting procedures for mergers and acquisitions, restructuring, and hostile takeovers. Cost or managerial accounting also provides managers with timely and accurate information on which to base their decisions. These developments were often made in conjunction with advances in data processing and statistical quality control. The most recent manifestation of this is the growth of activity-based accounting.

Production Technology Computerization and other innovations have increased the sophistication of production technology. The economic implications of new technology are complex. Changes in production technology, such as the development of computer-aided design and manufacturing (CAD/CAM), have changed traditional ideas of price/quality tradeoffs and allowed the production of high-quality, tailor-made goods at low cost. In using new technologies, managers in the 2000s must choose between reorganizing around new information/production technologies or using these technologies incrementally, to reinforce traditional modes of production and organization. These are some of the issues behind the debate on corporate "reengineering."[33]

Government Between 1910 and 1990, the role of government in the economic infrastructure became much more complex. Government bureaucracy and regulation of economic activities greatly increased in the first half of the 20th century, in response to two world wars and the Great Depression.[34] The government spent vast sums on the military and public works. The government's needs during World War II spread knowledge of bureaucratic and differentiated personnel practices across many industries.[35] Federal antitrust developed after World War II and regulated potential competition by limiting horizontal mergers. Specific regulations loomed large in several industries (telephones, railroads, airlines, communications, financial services).

Since the 1960s, the government has relaxed many of the traditional regulations on some industries while increasing them on others. The breakup of the Bell System, the deregulation of the airline, trucking, and financial service industries, and the weakening of banking regulations have been major influences in the economy since 1980. Intergovernmental treaties and agreements on the development of regional free trade zones, such as with NAFTA or the European Community, have greatly affected how firms compete in an increasingly global marketplace. Regulation of health care, workplace safety, discrimination, and the environment became common in the 1960s and 1970s.

---

[33]Hammer, M., "Reengineering Work: Don't Automate, Obliterate," *Harvard Business Review*, 69, 1990: pp. 104–113.

[34]Higgs, R., *Crisis and Leviathan: Critical Episodes in the Growth of American Government*, Oxford: Oxford University Press, 1987.

[35]Baron, J. N., F. R. Dobbin, and P. D. Jennings, "War and Peace: The Evolution of Modern Personnel Administration in U.S. Industry, *American Journal of Sociology*, 92, September 1986: pp. 350–383.

EXAMPLE 1.3

EVOLUTION OF THE STEEL INDUSTRY

Nowhere has change had more effect than in the American steel industry. In the first half of the 20th century, success in the steel industry required both horizontal and vertical integration. Traditionally, the leading firms, such as U.S. Steel, Bethlehem Steel, and Republic Steel, produced a wide array of high-volume steel products and controlled the production process, from the mining of ore through the production of the finished steel products to marketing and distribution. But in the early 1950s, changes in market demand and technology transformed the industry.

The most significant change in market demand was driven by shifts in the economy. In the 1950s, "lighter" products, such as strips and sheets used to produce appliances, automobiles, and computers, became relatively more important than "heavier" products, such as rails and plates used for railroad and ship building. But the large steel producers, particularly U.S. Steel, were committed to the "heavy" products. Much of the steel makers' capacity was also poorly located to meet the new demands for lighter products. These factors allowed foreign producers to penetrate American markets.

The most notable technological advances were the basic oxygen furnace, the continuous casting process, and scrap metal processing with the electric arc furnace. The basic oxygen furnace, which was commercialized in 1950 by an Austrian firm, Linz-Donawitz, replaced the open-hearth process as the fastest way to convert iron into raw steel. Continuous casting, a German invention that was perfected in the early 1960s by a small American company, Roanoke Electric, allowed steel producers to bypass the costly process of pouring molten steel into ingots and reheating them for milling and finishing. The electric arc furnace was available before World War II, but was little used before 1960. However, the increasing availability of scrap steel from discarded automobiles changed that, and by 1970, the electric arc furnace had become a viable way of producing nonalloy steel.

These technological advances had two profound effects. First, in postwar Japan and Germany, and later in Brazil and South Korea, startup steel firms quickly adopted the basic oxygen furnace and continuous casting. By contrast, in the United States, the established integrated mills had made nonrecoverable investments in the older technologies, both in terms of physical capital and expertise. These firms were therefore reluctant to shift to the new technologies. As late as 1988, 93 percent of all Japanese firms and 88 percent of South Korean steel firms had adopted continuous casting, while only 60 percent of American firms had done so, and nearly half of these U.S. firms had only made the changes in the 1980s.[36] (U.S. Steel still does not have continuous casting at two of its major steel producing plants.[37]) This allowed foreign producers to become com-

---

[36]Adams, W. and H. Mueller, "The Steel Industry," in W. Adams, ed., *The Structure of American Industry*, 8th ed., New York: Macmillan, 1988, p. 90.

[37]Barnett, D. F. and R. W. Crandall, "Steel: Decline and Renewal," in L. L. Duetsch, ed., *Industry Studies*, Englewood Cliffs, NJ: Prentice-Hall, 1993.

petitive threats to the large integrated American producers. Second, the new technology spurred the development of *minimills*, small nonintegrated producers that convert scrap metal into finished steel products. The success of minimill producers, such as Nucor, Chapparal, and North Star, is emblematic of the significance of this new way of producing steel. Minimills have eliminated the advantages of high-volume manufacturing in product lines, such as steel bars, structural shapes, and wire rods, and with Nucor's recent breakthrough in thin-slab casting, they may also take away the advantages of scale in the production of hot- and cold-rolled sheet. While the large integrated producers have not disappeared, their importance has clearly diminished. From 1970 to 1990, American integrated producers retired nearly 40 percent of their capacity (55 million tons), while in the same period minimills increased their capacity from 4.5 million tons to 29 million tons[38]

Faced with strong competition from abroad and at home, the older, integrated steel makers have been forced to become more efficient, but they are still barely profitable. Not surprisingly, they have turned to government trade regulations for relief.

Infrastructure in Emerging Markets

The technologies that have revolutionized modern infrastructure are widely accessible, yet infrastructure hinders economic development in many emerging markets. The quality of transportation systems varies from nation to nation. Central Africa, for example, has few highways and its rails have deteriorated since colonial days. South Korea, on the other hand, boasts ultramodern rail lines and seaports. Transportation within urban business centers of developing nations can be particularly difficult. Example 1.4 describes the worst-case scenario—the near complete gridlock that plagues Bangkok.

Developing nations may also lack other forms of infrastructure. Their businesses and consumers have limited access to the Internet, particularly through high-speed ISDN connections. Their finance infrastructure is especially limited. In the past two decades, there have been substantial loans to businesses throughout Southeast Asia without the usual checks and balances provided by a diligent independent banking sector. Many believe that this precipitated the Asian economic collapse. Finally, many developing nations have been crippled by their own governments. Businesses have been reluctant to invest in central and east Africa, for example, because of government corruption, cronyism, and civil war. Similar concerns arose just before President Suharno's government in Indonesia fell in May 1998.

Summary

While the first half of the 20th century was the era of the large hierarchical firm, changes in market conditions and infrastructure in the last 30 years have made smaller and flatter business organizations the preferred structure in many industries. This has come about for many reasons. The globalization of markets, facilitated by improvements in transportation, communications, and financial

---

[38]Barnett and Crandall, p. 143.

EXAMPLE 1.4

ECONOMIC GYRATIONS AND TRAFFIC GRIDLOCK IN THAILAND

Thailand's economic growth during the last 25 years demonstrates the power of the big push. Thailand's growth began after its government liberalized investment and export policies and promoted a laissez-faire mentality. Many investors expected Thailand to become an economic tiger, and those expectations fed upon themselves. Banks granted credit which fueled economic growth which encouraged even more liberal credit. Industrial plants proliferated, producing textiles, chemicals, oil, and plastics for export to developed nations. Between 1975 and 1995, Thailand's economy grew at an annual rate of 8 percent.

As the western experience illustrates, economic growth must be accompanied by a well-developed infrastructure and managers able to handle the complex transactions that growth requires. Thailand lacks both, and the results have been dire. By 1996, Thailand's economic growth had faltered. Investment credit dried up, recently constructed office towers stood empty, and thousands of workers were laid off. In 1997 the government devalued the Baht (the Thai unit of currency) to maintain the competitiveness of manufacturing plants, whose costs were higher than in nations such as China and Vietnam.

The Thai bubble seemed to have burst. The reasons why are a lesson in the importance of infrastructure. While the Thai economy was growing, its government adopted a laissez-faire approach. This encouraged foreign investment, but discouraged investment needed for infrastructure. The main infrastructure problem in Thailand—especially in Bangkok—is one that we often take for granted in the West—traffic. Bangkok's roads are based on a traditional Asian pattern in which many small roads feed into a few large arteries that flow through the central city. During Thailand's boom, high-rise office buildings replaced the small dwellings that lined Bangkok's feeder roads. Construction was so dense that existing roads could not be widened. To add to traffic problems, Bangkok does not have a subway. The result has been traffic gridlock in Bangkok beyond anything imaginable (even for New Yorkers). It can take more than an hour to drive less than one kilometer. Individuals who live outside of Bangkok and work or attend school in the city must allow six hours for the round-trip commute. About 300 women a year give birth in Bangkok taxis and rickshaws. Gas stations sell portable toilets. Traffic is so bad that in 1997 international business leaders cited it as the major reason why they were reluctant to continue doing business in Bangkok.

Traffic is not the only infrastructure problem. Bangkok also suffers from periodic flooding during monsoon season due to unlimited development on the floodplains of the Zhao Phaya River. Pollution is also rampant, in part because the government does not regulate emissions. Finally, the absence of financial oversight for business loans has destabilized Thailand's banks and its currency. This combination of problems has soured overseas investors on Thailand. With many investment alternatives available across Asia, it is not surprising that the Thai bubble economy burst.

There may be light at the end of the gridlocked tunnel. With the downturn in the Thai economy, many people can no longer afford their new cars, which are being repossessed. This may ease the traffic problem a bit.

infrastructure, has increased competition in many industries, which in turn has placed a premium on quickness and flexibility in responding to shifts in market demand. Changes in technology have reduced the advantages of large-scale production in many production processes. Advances in communications and computing have enabled independent market specialists to coordinate complex activities over great distances, thus reducing the need for vertical integration. These changes have already begun to alter the role of the manager and will continue to do so.

Changes in market conditions, infrastructure, and ways of doing business in the last 30 years have created both opportunities and constraints. For example, the growth of global markets has increased the potential sales of key products, but has also produced powerful foreign competition. Similarly, changes in capital markets have made huge resources available to firms that could not have previously obtained them. Technological innovation and computerization have given firms more control over production processes than ever before, but also allow smaller firms to compete on even or better terms with larger firms, which had previously been the primary beneficiaries of production improvements. Finally, at a time when management skills are becoming more important for firms, competitive pressures to outsource and downsize are thinning management ranks and making the jobs of managers who remain more complex.

◆ ◆ ◆ ◆ ◆ THREE DIFFERENT WORLDS: CONSISTENT PRINCIPLES, CHANGING CONDITIONS, AND ADAPTIVE STRATEGIES

The enormous differences in business practices and infrastructure among the three periods we surveyed illustrate a key premise of this book: *Successful strategy results from applying consistent principles to constantly changing business conditions.* Strategies are—and should be—the adaptive, but principled, responses of firms to their surroundings. The infrastructure and market conditions of business do not uniquely determine the strategies that firms choose. In all three of our periods, there was considerable experimentation by firms, and various types of firms succeeded and failed. But market conditions and infrastructure do constrain how business can be conducted and the strategic choices that managers can make. For example, the railroad, telegraph, and telephone by 1910 doomed most of the factors, agents, and brokers who facilitated trade in the 1840s.

Because circumstances change, one might conclude that no business strategy endures. Whatever one learns is bound to be obsolete as markets change or infrastructure evolves. This is true if one is looking for recipes for success under *any* conditions. If the historical survey in this chapter suggests nothing else, it is that recipes that purport to work under any market conditions or within any infrastructure (e.g., "divest any business that does not have the largest or second largest share in its market") are bound to fail eventually. Principles, however, are different from recipes. Principles are economic and behavioral relationships that apply to wide classes of circumstances. Because principles are robust, organizing the study of strategy around principles allows us to understand why certain strategies, business practices, and organizational arrangements are appropriate under one set of conditions but not others. To illustrate, consider a simple, yet important, principle that has helped firms decide throughout business history whether to produce some

EXAMPLE 1.5

INFRASTRUCTURE AND EMERGING MARKETS: THE RUSSIAN PRIVATIZATION PROGRAM[39]

Infrastructure generally develops over an extended time and in a largely incremental manner. That need not always be the case, however. In times of great change, an infrastructure may become obsolete overnight. The situation in Russia after 1989 provides an opportunity to see how decisionmakers developed a property rights infrastructure for a market economy.

Ideally, in an efficient property rights regime the owners of productive assets will have the rights to control those assets and enjoy the gains (or suffer the losses) from their business decisions. This does not always occur, of course, in market economies: for example, when the owners of large public corporations (shareholders) are not the individuals (managers) who control those corporations. Even arrangements that are less than ideal can still be fairly efficient, however, if the parties involved in transactions can contract around imperfect arrangements and use incentives and sanctions. These conditions prevail in Western economies.

In the Soviet system before Gorbachev, there were three nominal holders of property rights in firms: politicians, managers, and the public. Most control rights were shared by a wide array of politicians, Communist Party officials, and enterprise managers. The public, via the Treasury, held cash flow rights (rights to capture gains and losses). The total control exercised by the Communist Party kept bureaucrats and managers from claiming cash flows for themselves (i.e., from profiting from the enterprise they regulated or managed). This system gave decision makers few incentives to make efficient decisions and forced the Soviet people to bear the costs of inefficiency.

Gorbachev and others recognized the inefficiency of the system and initiated reforms in 1986 that reallocated control rights from the Communist Party to the heads of government agencies and public enterprises, while maintaining public control over cash flows (i.e., profits and losses). This meant that managers could now decide how their enterprises would be run but would still not earn profits or suffer losses. By failing to link cash flow rights with control rights, however, Gorbachev's reforms, though well-intended, increased inefficiencies by removing the constraints that kept politicians from appropriating cash flows from enterprises for themselves in pursuit of inefficient and politically based objectives. This exacerbated theft and bribery without solving to the fundamental problem of the separation of control and cash flow rights.

Following the dissolution of the Soviet Union and the election of Boris Yeltsin as president of Russia in 1991, reformers pursued a privatization program

[39]This example is adapted from Boycko, M., A. Shleifer, and R. Vishny, *Privatizing Russia*, Cambridge, MA: MIT Press, 1996, chaps. 2, 3, and 4. For additional details on the Russian program, see Blasi, J. R., M. Kroumova and D. Kruse, *Kremlin Capitalism: Privatizing the Russian Economy*, Ithaca, NY: ILR Press/Cornell, 1997. For details on the Polish privatization program, see Sachs, J., *Poland's Jump to the Market Economy*, Cambridge, MA: MIT Press, 1994.

that attempted to align cash flow rights and control rights in firms. They thus sought to resolve the fundamental property rights problem that had plagued the Soviet system.

The privatization program had three parts. The first involved taking control rights away from the politicians and managers. The second involved transferring these rights to shareholders, who could exercise their control the way stockholders in Western economies do. Third, cash flow rights over privatized firms were granted directly to the public in the form of vouchers that were distributed to all citizens for a nominal fee. These vouchers could then be traded on an open market or used to purchase shares in privatized firms.

The program was implemented quickly and on a large scale. Speed and scope were seen as necessary to minimize political interference with the program that would have perpetuated economic stagnation. By the end of 1994, over 16,000 mid-sized and large firms and nearly 100,000 small firms (including many local retail shops) had been privatized. In addition, over 750,000 new small businesses had been started. The ultimate results of the program are unclear, and the program did not escape political interference and its associated corruption. Advocates, however, claim that rapid privatization programs like those in Russia and Poland will eventually outperform more gradual programs, such as occurred in Hungary, as well as liberalization programs that the central government controls, and strong control, such as is being tried in China.

---

good or service themselves or purchase it from another firm (the so-called make-or-buy decision):

> A production technology that involves a large upfront investment in facilities and equipment will have a cost advantage over a technology that involves a small upfront investment only if the firm can achieve a sufficiently large level of throughput.

This principle is as valid today as it was in 1840 or 1910. Applying this principle to the different conditions that existed in 1840, 1910, and today explains why large, vertically integrated firms were appropriate in 1910 but not in 1840 or, perhaps, today. In 1910, firms in industries such as steel, farm machinery, chemicals, and cigarettes could make their investments in new capital-intensive production techniques pay only if they could achieve sufficiently large throughput. These firms could have relied on independent market specialists to produce key inputs and components and bring their finished products to market. But the rudimentary communications and transportation infrastructure, although vastly more developed than those of the 1840s, would have prevented independent firms from coordinating the procurement, production, distribution, and marketing functions to achieve the needed throughput. In many industries, it was better to bring all of these critical functions inside a single vertically integrated firm and build a managerial hierarchy to coordinate them.

Vertical integration was not needed in 1840, because many of the technologies offering efficiencies from mass production did not exist. Even if they had existed, the undeveloped transportation and communications infrastructure would have limited the size of markets, constraining firms from achieving the throughput needed to take advantage of the new technologies. Vertical integration is less beneficial in today's business environment for a different reason. Modern communications and computing technologies have reduced the costs of coordinating complex transactions. Independent suppliers and purchasers can work together to plan production runs and set delivery schedules more easily than they could have in 1910. As a result, transactions that in 1910 were most efficiently guided by the "visible hand" of internal hierarchy can be carried out in the marketplace between independent specialists.

This book is about principles, not recipes. In the remaining chapters, we develop principles that pertain to the boundaries of the firm, the nature of industry structure and competition, the firm's strategic positions within an industry, and the internal organization and management of the firm. Through the study of these principles, we believe that students of management can understand why firms and industries are organized the way they are and operate the way they do. We also believe that by judiciously applying these principles, managers can enhance the odds of successfully adapting their firms' strategies to the environment in which they compete.

CHAPTER SUMMARY

◆ A historical perspective demonstrates that while the nature of business has changed dramatically since 1840, successful businesses have always applied consistent principles to their business conditions.

◆ In 1840, communications and transportation infrastructures were poor. This increased the risk of business and mitigated against large-scale production. Business in 1840 was dominated by small, family-operated firms that relied on specialists in distribution as well as market makers who matched the needs of buyers and suppliers.

◆ By 1910, innovations in production technology made it possible to greatly reduce unit costs through large-scale production.

◆ Businessmen in 1910 who invested in these new technologies needed to assure a sufficient throughput to keep production levels high. As a result, manufacturing firms vertically integrated into raw materials acquisition, distribution, and retailing.

◆ Manufacturing firms also expanded their product offerings, creating new divisions that were managed within an "M-form" organization.

◆ These large hierarchical organizations required a professional managerial class. Unlike managers in 1840, professional managers in 1910 generally had little or no ownership interest in their firm.

◆ Continued improvements in communications and transportation have made the modern marketplace global. New technologies have reduced the advantages of large-scale production and vertical integration.

◆ In many industries, small manufacturers can meet the changing needs of their clients better than large hierarchical firms. In other industries, market specialists use computers, facsimile machines, and modems to coordinate activities that used to require a single integrated firm.

◆ Limited infrastructure hinders growth in many developing economies.

QUESTIONS

1. Why is infrastructure essential to economic development?
2. What is throughput? Is throughput a necessary condition for the success of modern business?

3. In light of recent downsizing and restructuring of Corporate America, was Chandler's explanation of benefits of size incorrect?

4. The technology to create a modern infrastructure is more widely available today than at any time in history. Do you think that this will make it easier for developing nations to create modern economies that can compete with the economies of developed nations?

5. Two features of developing nations are an absence of strong contract law and limited transportation networks. How might these factors affect the vertical and horizontal boundaries of firms within these nations?

6. Many analysts say that the infrastructure of Eastern Europe today resembles that of the United States at the start of the 20th century. If this is true, then what patterns of industrial growth might you expect in the next decade in the context of contemporary competitive forces?

7. How might U.S. industry have evolved differently if strong antitrust laws had been in place as of 1900?

8. In the past half-century, several American cities have been identified with specific industries: Akron/tires; Macon/carpets; Sunnyvale/computer chips; Orlando/tourism. Why do such centers emerge? Given evolving technology, what is their future?

THE HORIZONTAL BOUNDARIES OF THE FIRM: ECONOMIES OF SCALE AND SCOPE

2

A firm's *horizontal boundaries* identify the quantities and varieties of products and services that it produces. Horizontal boundaries differ markedly across industries, and across the firms within them. In some industries, such as frozen foods, aluminum production, and airframe manufacturing, a few large firms (e.g., General Foods, Alcoa, and Boeing) account for an extremely large share of industry sales, and there are virtually no viable small firms. In other industries, such as apparel design and management consulting, small firms predominate. Even the largest firms in these industries (e.g., Liz Claiborne, Andersen Consulting) are small by most conventional measures of business size, such as sales revenue and number of employees. In still other industries, such as beer and computer software, small firms (Boston Brewing Company, Electronic Arts) and corporate giants (Anheuser-Busch, Microsoft) coexist successfully.

Why do giants dominate some industries and not others? Why do firms in some industries, such as hospitals and pharmaceuticals, catch "merger fever," in the belief that bigger is suddenly better? The optimal horizontal boundaries of firms depend critically on economies of scale and scope. Economies of scale and scope are present whenever large-scale production, distribution, or retail processes have a cost advantage over smaller processes. According to Alfred Chandler, it was the ability of giant firms, such as DuPont and General Motors, to exploit economies of scale and scope that allowed them to succeed while their smaller rivals failed.[1] Economies of scale and scope are not always available, however. Many activities, such as farming, tailoring, management consulting, and the preparation of gourmet food, do not appear to enjoy substantial scale economies. These activities are typically performed by individuals or relatively small firms.

---

[1]Chandler, A., *Scale and Scope: The Dynamics of Industrial Capitalism*, Cambridge, MA: Belknap, 1990.

By offering cost advantages to large-scale producers, economies of scale and scope not only affect the sizes of firms and the structure of markets, but they also shape critical business strategy decisions, such as whether independent firms should merge, and whether a firm can achieve a longterm cost advantage in its market through expansion. Thus, an understanding of the sources of economies of scale and scope is critical for formulating competitive strategy. This chapter identifies the key sources of economies of scale and scope and provides approaches for assessing their importance.

◆ ◆ ◆ ◆ ◆ FORMAL DEFINITIONS OF ECONOMIES OF SCALE AND SCOPE

Informally, when there are economies of scale and scope, "bigger is better." To facilitate identification and measurement, it is useful to define economies of scale and scope more precisely.

Definition of Economies of Scale

The production process for a specific good or service exhibits *economies of scale* over a range of output when average cost (i.e., cost per unit of output) declines over that range. For average cost *(AC)* to decline as output increases, the marginal cost *(MC)* (i.e., the cost of the last unit produced) must be less than the overall average cost.[2] If average cost is increasing, then marginal cost must exceed average cost, and we say that production exhibits *diseconomies of scale*.

An *average cost curve* captures the relationship between average costs and out-

FIGURE 2.1
A **U**-SHAPED AVERAGE COST CURVE.

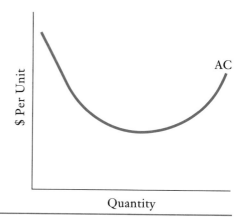

Average costs decline initially as fixed costs are spread over additional units of output. Average costs eventually rise as production runs up against capacity constraints.

[2]If you do not understand why this must be so, consider this numerical example. Suppose that the total cost of producing five bicycles is $500. The *AC* is therefore $100. If the *MC* of the sixth bicycle is $70, then total cost for six bicycles is $570 and *AC* is $95. If the *MC* of the sixth bicycle is $130, then total cost is $630 and *AC* is $105. In this example (and as a general rule), when *MC < AC*, *AC* falls as production increases, and when *MC > AC*, *AC* rises as production increases.

FIGURE 2.2
AN L-SHAPED AVERAGE COST CURVE.

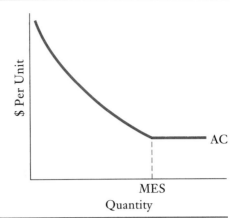

When capacity does not prove to be constraining, average costs may not rise as they do in a "U-shaped" cost curve. Output equal to or exceeding minimum efficient scale (*MES*) is efficient from a cost perspective.

put. Average cost curves are often U-*shaped*, as shown in Figure 2.1, so that average costs decline over low levels of output, but increase at higher levels of output. Economists identify a combination of factors that cause many cost curves to be U-shaped. A common explanation for the initial decline in average costs is the spreading of fixed costs over increasing output. *Fixed costs* are insensitive to volume; they must be expended regardless of the total output. Examples of such volume insensitive costs are manufacturing overhead expenses, such as insurance, maintenance, and property taxes. As output increases, these costs are averaged over greater volumes, tending to drive down average costs. A common explanation for the eventual upturn in average costs is that as output increases, capacity constraints may result in bottlenecks, and there may be bureaucratic and agency problems. We will develop these ideas more fully in this chapter.

The standard textbook usually depicts average cost curves as U-shaped, so that the smallest and largest firms have equally high costs relative to medium-sized firms. In reality, very large firms rarely seem to be at a substantial cost disadvantage relative to smaller rivals. Indeed, the noted econometrician John Johnston once examined production costs for a number of industries and determined that the corresponding cost curves were closer to L-shaped than U-shaped. Figure 2.2 depicts an L-shaped cost curve. When average cost curves are L-shaped, average costs decline up to the *minimum efficient scale* (MES) of production. Beyond the MES, average costs are flat or slightly increasing. When average cost curves are L-shaped, all firms operating at or beyond MES have similar average costs. To the extent that there are any diseconomies of scale, the firms producing exactly at MES may have a slight cost advantage over larger rivals.

Definition of Economies of Scope

Economies of scale are related to economies of scope, and the two terms are sometimes used interchangeably. Economies of scale exist if the firm achieves unit-cost savings as it increases the production of a given good or service. *Economies of scope* exist if the firm achieves savings as it increases the variety of goods and services it produces. Whereas economies of scale are usually defined in terms of declining average cost functions, economies of scope are usually defined in terms of the relative total cost of producing a variety of goods and services together in one firm versus separately in two or more firms.

Because it is difficult to show scope economies graphically, we will instead introduce a simple mathematical formulation. Formally, let $TC(Q_x, Q_y)$ denote the total cost to a single firm producing Q_x units of good X and Q_y units of good Y. Then a production process exhibits scope economies if

$$TC(Q_x, Q_y) < TC(Q_x, 0) + TC(0, Q_y)$$

This formula captures the idea that it is cheaper for a single firm to produce both goods X and Y than for one firm to produce X and another to produce Y. To provide another interpretation of the definition, note that a firm's total costs are zero if it produces zero quantities of both products, so $TC(0, 0) = 0$. Then, rearrange the proceding formula to read:

$$TC(Q_x, Q_y) - TC(0, Q_y) < TC(Q_x, 0) - TC(0, 0).$$

This says that the incremental cost of producing Q_x units of good X, as opposed to none at all, is lower when the firm is producing a positive quantity Q_y of good Y.

The cost implications of economies of scope are shown in Table 2.1, which shows the production costs of a hypothetical manufacturer of adhesive message notes (good X) and tape (good Y). To produce tape, the firm must spend $100 million to perfect the process of working with chemical adhesives, attaching these adhesives to cellophane, and manufacturing and packaging tape. Once this setup cost is incurred, each roll of tape can be produced at a cost of $.20 each. Thus, we can write $TC(0, Q_y) = \$100m + .20Q_y$. For example, if $Q_y = 600$ million rolls of tape, total cost is $220 million.

Now, given that the firm has made the investment in developing the know-how for manufacturing tape, much of that know-how can be applied to producing related products, such as adhesive message notes. Suppose that the additional investment needed to ramp up production of message notes, given that the up-front setup costs in tape production have already been incurred, is $20m. Suppose also that the cost per ream of message notes is $.05. Then $TC(Q_x, Q_y) = \$120m + .05Q_x + .20Q_y$. For example, if $Q_y = 600$ million and $Q_x = 100$ million, then total cost is $245m. The cost to the firm of adding message notes to its production line is only $245m - $220m = $25m.

By contrast, if the firm did not produce tape, much of the up-front investment in developing the know-how for working with chemical adhesives would have to be made just to get the expertise needed to make message notes. If developing this know-how requires an investment of $50m, then with a per ream cost of $.05,

TABLE 2.1
COSTS TO PRINT MESSAGE NOTES AND TAPE

Q_x	Q_y	$TC(Q_x, Q_y)$
100m	0	$55m
0	600m	$220m
100m	600m	$245m
200m	0	$60m
0	1200m	$340m
200m	1200m	$370m

$TC(Q_x,0) = \$50m + .05Q_x$. Thus, if $Q_x = 100m$, total cost would equal \$55m. This more than doubles the additional cost to the tape manufacturer to add message notes to its production line.

This example illustrates the economic logic of exploiting economies of scope. This logic is often known as "leveraging core competences," "competing on capabilities," or "mobilizing invisible assets."[3] In this example it makes much more sense for the tape manufacturer to diversify into the production of message notes than it would for a firm producing unrelated products, such as a prepared-food manufacturer.

Economies of scale and scope may arise at any point in the production process, from acquisition and use of raw inputs to distribution and retailing. Although business managers often cite scale and scope economies as justifications for growth activities and mergers, they do not always exist. In some cases, bigger may be worse! Thus, it is important to identify specific sources of scale economies and, if possible, measure their magnitude. The rest of this chapter shows how to do this.

WHERE DO ECONOMIES OF SCALE COME FROM?   ◆ ◆ ◆ ◆ ◆

There are four major sources of scale and scope economies:

- Indivisibilities and the spreading of fixed costs

- Increased productivity of variable inputs (mainly having to do with specialization)

- Inventories

- The cube-square rule

We discuss each in detail.

Indivisibilities and the Spreading of Fixed Costs

The most common source of economies of scale is the spreading of fixed costs over an ever greater volume of output. Fixed costs arise when there are *indivisibilities* in the production process. Indivisibility simply means that an input cannot be scaled down below a certain minimum size, even when the level of output is very, very small. For example, imagine that a railroad is shipping a boxcar of merchandise from Chicago to New York. Among the required inputs are 840 miles of railroad track, a locomotive and boxcar, and an engineer. Shipping half the amount would require the same inputs. Thus, the track, cars, and engineer are indivisible, and the railroad must bear the associated costs no matter how little is shipped. By the same token, these costs do not increase as output increases. Shipping twice the amount of freight does not require additional track or a second engineer. Indivisibilities may give rise to fixed costs, and hence scale and scope economies, at several

[3]Prahalad, C. K. and G. Hamel, "The Core Competence of the Corporation," *Harvard Business Review*, May–June, 1990; Stalk, G., P. Evans, and L. Shulman, "Competing on Capabilities: The New Rules of Corporate Strategy," *Harvard Business Review*, March–April, 1992: pp. 57–69; Itami, H., *Mobilizing Indivisible Assets*, Cambridge, MA: Harvard University Press, 1987.

different levels: the product level, the plant level, and the multiplant level. The next few subsections discuss the link between fixed costs and economies of scale at each of these levels.

Economies of Scale Due to Spreading of Product-Specific Fixed Costs

The production of a specific product often involves fixed costs. Product-specific fixed costs may include special equipment, such as tools and dies (e.g., the cost to manufacture a special die used to make an aircraft fuselage). Fixed costs may also include research and development expenses—for example, the estimated $150 million to $300 million required to develop a new pharmaceutical product. Fixed costs may include training expenses—for example, a one-week training program preceding the implementation of a total quality management initiative. Fixed costs may also include the costs necessary to set up a production process—for example, the time and expense required to set up a newspaper before printing it.

Even a simple production process, such as that for an aluminum can, may require substantial fixed costs. The production of an aluminum can involves only a few steps. Aluminum sheets are cut to size, formed into a rounded shape, and then punched into the familiar cylindrical can shape. A lid with an opener is then soldered on top. Though the process is simple, a single line for producing aluminum cans costs about $50 million. If the opportunity cost of tying up funds is 10 percent, the fixed costs expressed on an annualized basis would amount to about $5 million per year.[4]

The average fixed cost of producing aluminum cans will fall as output increases. To illustrate, suppose that the peak capacity of an aluminum can plant is 500 million cans annually, or about 1 percent of the total U.S market. The average fixed cost of operating a fully automated plant operating at full capacity for one year is determined by dividing the annual cost ($5,000,000) by total output (500,000,000). This works out to one cent per can. On the other hand, if the plant only operates at 25 percent of capacity, for total annual production of 125 million cans, then average fixed costs equal four cents per can. The underutilized plant is operating at a three-cent cost differential per can. In a price-competitive industry, such as aluminum can manufacturing, such a cost differential is likely to make the difference between profit and loss.

Economies of Scale Due to Tradeoffs Among Alternative Technologies

Suppose that a firm is considering entering the can manufacturing business, but does not anticipate being able to sell more than 125 million cans annually. Is it doomed to a three-cent cost differential and eventual bankruptcy? The answer depends on the nature of the alternative production technologies. The fully automated technology described previously may yield the greatest cost savings when used to capacity, but it may not be the best choice at lower production levels because there may be an alternative to the fully-automated plant that requires less initial investment, albeit with a greater reliance on ongoing expenses. A firm choosing this "partially automated" technology may be able to enjoy fairly low average costs even if it produces 125 million cans annually.

---

[4]The opportunity cost is the best return that the investor could obtain if he or she invested a comparable amount of money in some other similarly risky investment. In this example, we have assumed, for simplicity, that the production line never depreciates and thus lasts forever. See the Economics Primer for further discussion.

TABLE 2.2
COSTS OF PRODUCING ALUMINUM CANS

	500 million cans per year	*125 million cans per year*
Fully Automated	Average fixed costs = .01 Average labor costs = .00 Average materials costs = .03 Average total costs = .04	Average fixed costs = .04 Average labor costs = .00 Average materials costs = .03 Average total costs = .07
Partially Automated	Average fixed costs = .0025 Average labor costs = .01 Average materials costs = .03 Average total costs = .0425	Average fixed costs = .01 Average labor costs = .01 Average materials costs = .03 Average total costs = .05

Suppose that the fixed costs of setting up a partially automated plant are $12.5 million, annualized to $1.25 million per year. The shortcoming of this plant is that it requires additional labor costs of one cent per can, compared with the fully automated plant. To simplify matters, assume that the fully automated plant has zero labor costs. With this assumption, the cost comparison between the two plants is shown in Table 2.2.

Table 2.2 shows that while the fully automated technology is superior for high production levels, it is markedly inferior at lower production levels. This is seen in Figure 2.3, which depicts average cost curves for both the fully and partially automated technologies. The curve labeled SAC_1 is the average cost curve for a plant that has adopted the fully automated technology; the curve labeled SAC_2 is the average cost curve for a plant that has adopted the partially automated technology. At output levels above 375 million, the fully automated technology has lower average total costs. At lower output levels, the partially automated technology is cheaper.

The aluminum can example illustrates the distinction between economies of scale that arise because of fuller or more efficient capacity utilization, and

FIGURE 2.3
AVERAGE COST CURVES FOR CAN PRODUCTION.

SAC_1 represents a high fixed/low variable cost technology. SAC_2 represents a low fixed cost/high variable cost technology. At low levels of output, it is cheaper to use the latter technology. At high outputs, it is cheaper to use the former.

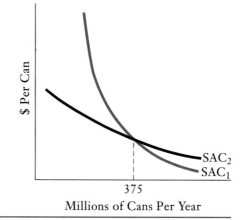

FIGURE 2.4
SHORT-RUN VERSUS LONG-RUN AVERAGE COST.

In the long run, firms may choose their production technology as well as their output. Firms planning to produce beyond point X will choose the technology represented by SAC_1. Firms planning to produce less than point X will choose the technology represented by SAC_2. The heavy "lower envelope" of the two cost curves represents the lowest possible cost for each level of production, and is called the *long-run average cost curve*.

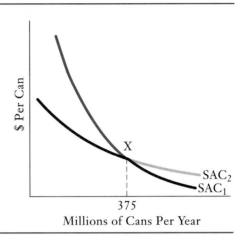

economies of scale that arise because of tradeoffs between technologies with low fixed costs and higher variable costs, on the one hand, and high fixed costs and lower variable costs, on the other. Reductions in average costs due to increases in capacity utilization are *short-run* economies of scale in that they occur within a plant of a given size. Reductions due to adoption of a technology or larger plant size that have high fixed costs but lower variable costs are *long-run* economies of scale. Given time to build a plant from scratch, a firm can choose the plant that best meets its production needs, avoiding excessive fixed costs if production is expected to be low, and excessive capacity costs if production is expected to be high.

Figure 2.4 illustrates the distinction between short-run and long-run economies of scale. (The primer discusses this distinction at length.) SAC_1 and SAC_2, which duplicate the cost curves in Figure 2.3, are the short-run average cost curves for the partially automated and fully automated plants, respectively. Each decreases because as output within each plant grows, fixed costs are spread over more and more units. If we trace out the lower regions of each curve, the so-called lower envelope of the curves, we see the long-run average cost curve. The long-run average cost curve is everywhere on or below each short-run average cost curve. This reflects the flexibility that firms have to adopt the technology that is most appropriate for their forecasted output.

Indivisibilities Are More Likely When Production Is Capital Intensive

When fixed capital costs are a significant percentage of total costs, we say that production is *capital intensive*. Much productive capital, such as factories and assembly lines, is indivisible. Thus, when production is capital intensive, the average total cost of production contains a substantial fixed component. Output may be increased by increasing the utilization of existing production facilities, often at little additional expense. As a result, average costs fall. Conversely, cutbacks in production may not reduce total costs by much. As a result, average costs rise. When most production expenses go to raw materials or labor, we say that production is *materials* or *labor intensive*. In such a production process, the average total cost of production depends mainly on the amount of materials and labor that goes into

XAMPLE 2.1

HUB-AND-SPOKE NETWORKS AND ECONOMIES OF SCOPE IN THE AIRLINE INDUSTRY

An important example of multiplant economies of scope arises in a number of industries in which goods and services are routed to and from several markets. In these industries, which include airlines, railroads, and telecommunications, distribution is organized around "hub-and-spoke" networks. In an airline hub-and-spoke network, an airline flies passengers from a set of "spoke" cities through a central "hub," where passengers then change planes and fly from the hub to their outbound destinations. Thus, a passenger flying from, say, Omaha to Louisville on American Airlines would board an American flight from Omaha to Chicago, change planes, and then fly from Chicago to Louisville.

Recall that economies of scope occur when a multiproduct firm can produce given quantities of products at a lower total cost than the total cost of producing these quantities in separate firms. If the quantity of a firm's products can be aggregated into a common measure of output, this definition is equivalent to saying that a firm producing many products will have a lower average cost than a firm producing just a few products. In the airline industry, it makes economic sense to think about individual origin-destination pairs (e.g., St. Louis to New Orleans, St. Louis to Houston, etc.) as distinct products. Viewed in this way, economies of scope would exist if an airline's average cost is lower the more origin-destination pairs it serves.

To understand how hub-and-spoke networks give rise to economies of *scope*, it is first necessary to explain *economies of density*. Economies of density are essentially economies of scale along a given route, that is, reductions in average cost as traffic volume on the route increases. (In the airline industry, traffic volume is measured as revenue-passenger miles [RPM], which is the number of passengers on the route multiplied by the number of miles, and average cost is the cost per revenue passenger mile.) Economies of density occur because of spreading flight-specific fixed costs (e.g., costs of the flight and cabin crew, fuel, aircraft servicing) and because of the economies of aircraft size. In the airline industry, traffic-sensitive costs (e.g., food, ticket handling) are small in relation to flight-specific fixed costs. Thus, as its traffic volume increases, an airline can fill a larger fraction of its seats on a given type of aircraft (in airline industry lingo, it increases its *load factor*—the ratio of passengers to available seats), and because the airline's total costs increase only slightly, its cost per RPM falls as it spreads the flight-specific fixed costs over more traffic volume. As traffic volume on the route gets even larger, it becomes worthwhile to substitute larger aircraft (e.g., 300-seat Boeing 767s) for smaller aircraft (e.g., 150-seat Boeing 737s). A key aspect of this substitution is that the 300-seat aircraft flown a given distance at a given load factor is less than twice as costly as the 150-seat aircraft flown the same distance at the same load factor. The reason for this is that doubling the number of seats and passengers on a plane does not require doubling the sizes of flight and cabin crews or the amount of fuel used, and that the 300-seat aircraft is less than twice as costly to build as the 150-seat aircraft, owing to the cube-square rule, which will be discussed below.

Economies of scope emerge from the interplay of economies of density and the properties of a hub-and-spoke network. To see how, consider an origin-destination pair—say, Indianapolis to Chicago—with a modest amount of daily traffic. An airline serving only this route would use small planes, and even then, would probably operate with a relatively low load factor. But now consider an airline serving a hub-and-spoke network, with the hub at Chicago. If this airline offered daily flights between Indianapolis and Chicago, it would not only draw passengers who want to travel from Indianapolis to Chicago, but it would also draw passengers traveling from Indianapolis to all other points accessible from Chicago in the network (e.g., Los Angeles or San Francisco). An airline that includes the Indianapolis-Chicago route as part of a larger hub-and-spoke network can operate larger aircraft at higher load factors than can an airline serving only Indianapolis-Chicago and as a result, can benefit from economies of density to achieve a lower cost per RPM along this route. (It can also justify offering more frequent service, making it more convenient for Indianapolis travelers.) Moreover, because there will now be passengers traveling between Chicago and other spoke cities in this network, the airline's load factors on these other spokes will increase somewhat, thereby lowering the costs per RPM on these routes as well. The overall effect is that an airline that serves Indianapolis-Chicago as part of a larger hub-and-spoke network will have a lower average cost overall than an airline that only serves Indianapolis-Chicago. This is precisely what is meant by economies of scope.

Many of the same principles of economies of scale are exhibited by the new LEO (low earth orbit) technology. Several firms or consortia of firms, including the Iridium consortium led by Motorola and the McGaw/Microsoft Teledesic group, are in the midst of launching hundreds of satellites into orbit a few hundred miles above the earth. Combined with land-based switching technology, these satellite networks will permit digital communications anywhere on the globe. At this time, each consortium is negotiating with nations around the world to obtain signal transmission rights. As each consortium must incur several billions of dollars of fixed costs to establish their networks, the advantage will clearly accrue to the sellers who can sign up the most users, in the most nations.

each unit of output. Because materials and labor are divisible, they can change in proportion to changes in output, with the result that average costs do not vary with output. It follows that substantial product-specific economies of scale are more likely when production is capital intensive, and minimal product specific economies of scale are more likely when production is materials or labor intensive.

Endogenous Fixed Costs

Ordinarily, one thinks of the source of fixed setup costs as being technological; for example a steel firm must incur the cost of blast furnaces and ingot casters before it can efficiently produce steel on a large scale, or an airline must invest millions of dollars in airport hub operations before it can efficiently transport passengers between many cities. Such fixed costs may be thought of as *exogenous*—any firm wishing to produce a large amount of output at low costs must incur these expenses. Traditionally, when economists emphasize the importance of fixed costs for determining market structure, they are usually referring to exogenous fixed costs. However, John Sutton points out that many fixed expenditures are not necessitated by production considerations.[5] Good examples are research and development aimed at product improvement, and advertising expenses aimed at increasing consumer awareness of one's product. These may be thought of as *endogenous* fixed costs because the firm can continue to produce any level of output it chooses without incurring them. The firm will choose to make these expenditures as long as the additional benefits in terms of increased sales revenue exceed the additional costs.

Inventories

Economies of scale may arise when firms must carry inventories. This may include "traditional" inventory, such as parts at an auto repair shop, and nontraditional inventories, such as grocery clerks at a supermarket. Firms carry inventory to minimize the chances of a "stock-out" (i.e., running out of stock). A stock-out can cost a retailer lost sales, and drive away potential customers who seek more reliable sources of supply. For a manufacturer, a stock-out for a single part may delay an entire production process. Of course, there are costs to carrying inventory, including interest on the expenses borne in producing the inventory and the risk that it will depreciate in value while waiting to be used or sold, perhaps due to changes in fashion or technological obsolescence.

Inventory costs drive up the average costs of goods that are actually sold. Suppose, for example, that a firm needs to hold inventories equal to 10 percent of its sales to maintain a tolerable level of expected stock-outs. This will increase its average cost of goods sold by as much as 10 percent. (The increase will be smaller if, at the end of the selling season, the firm can sell its inventories at some fraction of original cost.) In general, inventory costs are proportional to the ratio of inventory holdings to sales. The ability to manage its inventories so that they are lower (relative to sales) than its competitors has been cited as contributing to Wal-Mart's success in the mass merchandising business.

The need to carry inventories creates economies of scale because firms doing a high volume of business can usually maintain a lower ratio of inventory to sales while achieving a similar level of stock-outs. This reduces their average cost of goods sold. *Queuing theory* explains why large firms can carry smaller inventories as a percentage of sales than can small firms. Queuing theory shows that as the arrival rate (the rate at which people enter the queue) increases, the seller need carry a smaller excess inventory in percentage terms to maintain a fixed rate of stock outages. The corollary to this result is that if one fixes excess inventory in percentage terms, then higher arrival rates are associated with lower rates of stock outages.

To understand why, consider two equal-sized hospitals stocking a blood substitute that must be discarded after one month. Although each expects to use 20 liters per month, they each hold 50 liters, to insure that there is only a 5 percent chance of running out. If one hospital does run out, the other will probably not be out of the blood substitute at exactly the same time. Hence, if they combined their inventories, the probability of both having an outage would be less than 5 percent. It follows that if the two hospitals merged their inventories, they could keep the same level of inventories (100 liters combined) and achieve superior performance (fewer than 5 percent outages) Alternatively, they can reduce their inventories slightly, to roughly 80 liters, while maintaining a 5 percent outage rate. In this way, the larger

---

[5]Sutton, J., *Sunk Costs and Market Structure*, Cambridge, MA.: MIT Press, 1992.

"merged" hospital has a lower inventory cost than does each smaller, independent hospital. William Lynk (1995) has estimated the potential economies from hospitals sharing supplies and equipment in this way, and thereby reducing inventory costs.[6] The potential savings is as large as 10 percent in some departments.

The Cube-Square Rule and the Physical Properties of Production

Economies of scale also arise because of the physical properties of processing units. An excellent example of this is the *cube-square rule*, well-known to engineers.[7] It states that as we increase the volume of the vessel (e.g., a tank or a pipe) by a given proportion (e.g. we double it) the surface area increases by less than this proportion (e.g., it less than doubles).

What does the cube-square rule have to do with economies of scale? In many production processes, production capacity is proportional to the *volume* of the production vessel, whereas the total cost of producing at capacity is proportional to the *surface area* of the vessel. This implies that as capacity increases, the average cost of producing at capacity decreases because the ratio of surface area to volume decreases. More generally, the physical properties of production often allow firms to expand capacity without comparable increases in costs.

Oil pipelines are an excellent example of this phenomenon. The cost of transporting oil is an increasing function of the friction between the oil and the pipe. Because the friction increases as the pipe's surface area increases, transportation costs are proportional to the pipe's surface area. By contrast, the amount of oil that can be pumped through the pipe depends on its volume.[8] Thus, the average cost of a pipeline declines as desired throughput increases. Other processes that exhibit scale economies owing to the cube-square rule or related properties include warehousing (the cost of making the warehouse is largely determined by its surface area) and brewing beer (the volume of the brewing tanks determine output).

◆ ◆ ◆ ◆ ◆ SPECIAL SOURCES OF ECONOMIES OF SCALE AND SCOPE

The sources of economies of scale in the previous chapter related mainly to the engineering properties of production. This section describes three special sources of economies of scale and scope having to do with areas other than production:

- Economies of scale and scope in purchasing

- Economies of scale and scope in advertising

- Economies of scale and scope in research and development

---

[6]Lynk, W. 1995. "The Creation of Economic Efficiency in Hospital Mergers" *Journal of Health Economic.* 14(6), pp. 507–530.

[7]The name comes from the fact that the volume of a cube is proportional to the cube of the length of its side, whereas the surface area is proportional to the square of that length.

[8]See L. Cockenboo, "Production Functions and Cost Functions: A Case Study," in E. Mansfield, ed., *Managerial Economics and Operations Research, 5th ed.* New York: Norton, 1987.

EXAMPLE 2.2

THE ACE HARDWARE CORPORATION

With the recent growth of national hardware "superstore" chains such as Home Depot and Builder's Square, it might seem that "neighborhood" hardware stores will be unable to stay in business. After all, the chains enjoy economies of scale that local, independently owned stores could not hope to match. In fact, thousands of independently owned hardware stores do enjoy many of the same scale economies realized by national giants, by virtue of membership in hardware purchasing groups. Thanks to these groups, independent hardware stores continue to thrive.

One of the two largest purchasing groups is the Ace Hardware Corporation. Ace began as a hardware wholesaler and distributor based in the Midwest. A dealer buyout in 1974 led to a national expansion. Today, the Ace cooperative is jointly owned by its 5,200 member stores. (The members of the other large cooperative, Cotter and Co., operate under the True Value name.) Ace purchases in bulk from more than over 4,000 suppliers, including Stanley Tools, Toro (lawnmowers), and Weber (grills). This gives individual store owners access to the same distribution channels as Home Depot and Builder's Square. Ace employs its own buyers, who obtain quantity discounts that are then passed on to individual stores. Ace provides its members with other benefits as well. It places national advertising and coordinates national marketing campaigns. It provides information about local marketing practices and new products. It developed and supervised the installation of electronic systems for store owners, allowing them to rapidly check on inventories and prices (this is especially helpful for products such as lumber which experience volatile price movements), place special orders, and communicate by e-mail with other stores. Finally, Ace used its clout to push suppliers to adopt bar codes to facilitate pricing and inventory maintenance.

Individual Ace hardware stores can match the purchasing and marketing economies of national chains. At the same time, they enjoy the benefits of independence. Store owners face hard-edged market incentives that limit their ability to shirk in areas such as customer service. (Market analysts often comment about how Home Depot and Builder's Square employees are working hard to develop the same "small town" friendliness that is often the norm at Ace and True Value.) Stores can tailor their prices and supplies to local needs, and the typical Ace store obtains only half its merchandise from the purchasing group. Indeed, whereas some Ace stores resemble indoor flea markets, others look more like department stores *sans* clothing, stocked with appliances, televisions, cutlery, bicycles, bedding, and the occasional hammer.

The cooperative concept has disadvantages, though. Absent direction from a central office, individual stores may cannibalize each other through aggressive pricing and marketing practices. Store locations are not chosen with a mind toward inventory management. Key decisions regarding inventories, purchasing, and marketing can be delayed due to the democratic nature of the cooperative. And Ace lacks the standardization that assures a Home Depot customer of consistent selection and service at all stores.

Economies of Scale and Scope in Purchasing

Most of us have experienced the benefits of purchasing in bulk. Whether we are buying gallon containers of milk or six packs of soda, the price per unit of many items falls as the amount we purchase increases. Purchasers all along the vertical chain may be able to realize discounts for volume purchasing, giving large purchasers an inherent cost advantage over small purchasers.

Why do firms offer discounts for volume purchasers? After all, why should a firm care whether its sales of X units come from a single buyer or from X different buyers? There are three possibilities:

- It may be less costly for a seller to sell to a single buyer. If each sale requires some fixed cost, say in writing a contract, setting up a production run, or delivering the product, then it truly is less costly to sell in bulk.

- A bulk purchaser may be more price sensitive. For example, someone making weekly grocery purchases is more likely to consider the price of soda than someone purchasing a can of soda at the beach. That is, unit-price differences mean more to purchasers when they buy more units. This may encourage large purchasers to shop more aggressively for the best prices.

- Sellers may fear a costly disruption to operations, or in the extreme case, bankruptcy, if they fail to do business with a large purchaser. Thus, they offer a discount to the large purchaser so as to assure a steady flow of business.

It is not necessary for independent firms to merge to obtain the benefits of bulk purchasing. Independent firms may form purchasing alliances that buy in bulk in order to obtain quantity discounts, but otherwise remain independent. Example 2.2 describes one retail industry that is largely organized around purchasing groups—hardware. Nor is it always the case that the largest purchasers will obtain discounts, as exemplified by wholesale pricing of prescription drugs. Some smaller pharmacies such as mail-order pharmacies, have been more price sensitive than certain larger pharmacies, including some national pharmacy chains. In particular, mail-order pharmacies often do not stock drugs for which they are unable to obtain favorable wholesale prices, whereas some pharmacy chains stock and sell drugs with little regard to their wholesale prices. As a result, drug manufacturers sometimes extend favorable pricing terms to smaller pharmacies that they do not extend to larger ones.

Economies of Scale and Scope in Advertising

The advertising cost per consumer of a product may be expressed by the following formula:

$$\frac{\text{Cost of sending a message}}{\text{Number of potential consumers receiving the message}} \div \frac{\text{Number of actual consumers as a result of message}}{\text{Number of potential consumers receiving the message}}$$

Larger firms may enjoy lower advertising costs per consumers either because they have lower costs of sending messages per potential consumer (the first term) or because they have higher advertising *reach* (the second term).

Costs of Sending Messages per Potential Consumer

Larger firms often enjoy lower advertising costs per potential consumer. This is because there are important fixed costs associated with placing an ad, including preparation of the ad and negotiation with the broadcaster. If ad preparation costs and the costs of negotiating a single national and local advertising "buy" are about the same, the national advertiser will have a lower cost per potential consumer because these fixed costs get spread over a larger base of potential consumers.

To illustrate, suppose that Anheuser-Busch places an ad in *USA Today* and pays Gannett (the publisher of *USA Today*) $10 per thousand papers sold to run this ad. Because *USA Today* has a daily circulation of about two million, the direct costs of this ad to Anheuser-Busch would be $10 × (2,000,000/1000) or $20,000. The same day, Hudepohl, a local brewery in Cincinnati, Ohio, places an ad in the *Cincinnati Enquirer* (the local paper) and, let's say, pays the same rate of $10 per thousand papers sold. The *Enquirer* has a daily circulation of about 250,000, so the direct cost to Hudepohl would be $10*(250,000/1000) or $2,500. Finally, suppose that for both companies the time to prepare the ad and negotiate the buy is $4,000.

Let us now look at the advertising cost per potential consume for Anheuser-Busch and Hudepohl.

- Anheuser-Busch Advertising Cost per Potential Consumer = ($20,000 + $4,000)/2,000,000 = $.012 per potential consumer, or $12.00 per 1,000 potential consumers.

- Hudepohl Advertising Cost per Potential Consumer = ($2,500 + $4,000)/250,000 = $.026 per potential consumer, or $26.00 per 1,000 potential consumers.

This example, though fictitious, illustrates the approximate difference in the cost per potential consumer between national and local advertising.

The logic underlying this example illustrates why national firms, such as Border's Books in book merchandising, enjoy an advertising cost advantage over their local counterparts, (e.g., Barbara's Books in Chicago). Advertising by national sellers can even have a local flavor. At one time sellers of national advertising, such as television networks, could not easily vary an advertising message from one market to another. Today, the major networks permit advertisers to run different ad copy in different markets. Thus, Border's Book ads can feature different books that may be popular in different parts of the nation.

Advertising Reach and Umbrella Branding

Even when two firms have national presences, the larger one may still enjoy an advantage. Suppose that Wendy's and McDonald's both place advertisements on rival television networks to air at the same time. The ads are seen by audiences of equal sizes and cost the same to place. Both ads are equally persuasive—20,000 viewers of the McDonald's ad have an urge to visit McDonald's; 20,000 viewers of the Wendy's ad are motivated to visit Wendy's. Despite these similarities, the cost per effective message is much lower for McDonald's. The reason is that there are about three times as many McDonald's in the United States as there are Wendy's. Almost all of the 20,000 viewers craving McDonald's can find one nearby, but many of the 20,000 who crave Wendy's cannot. They will go elsewhere or go unsatisfied.

The effectiveness of a firm's ad may be higher if that firm offers a broad product line under a single brand name. For example, an advertisement for a Sony big screen television may encourage customers to consider other products made by Sony, such as DVD players. This is known as *umbrella branding*. Umbrella branding is effective when consumers use the information in an advertisement about one product to make inferences about other products with the same brand name, thereby reducing advertising costs per effective image. When Sony advertises its big-screen television, consumers may infer that Sony is on the cutting edge of technology, and therefore that its other high tech products are also good.

Umbrella branding may also reduce the riskiness of new product introductions. Consumers are often reluctant to try new products because they are unsure about their quality. If consumers infer product quality from the brand name, firms may leverage the reputation of an existing brand name to help launch a new product. It seems likely that Sony high definition televisions will gain instant market acceptance, in large part due to the consumer's favorable opinion of other Sony products. Umbrella branding also explains why diet Coke and Cherry Coke are more successful than products Coke introduced at earlier times, Tab and Mr. Pibb, which did not share the Coke image and reputation for flavor.

Umbrella branding has some risks. Some conglomerates have been unable to create a corporate brand identity despite extensive advertising. One example is Beatrice, which attempted but failed during the 1980s to create a corporate brand identity for an array of products that included Levelor blinds, Danskin exercise clothes, and Butterball turkeys. Sometimes firms prefer to keep brand identities separate, such as when Kraft Foods acquired the Seven Seas brand name, so that it could use it to introduce a line of zestier salad dressings rather than do so under the Kraft name. Some firms fail to recognize potential diseconomies of scope associated with conflicting brand images. This occurred when British conglomerate EMI initially signed and then bought out of its recording contract with punk pioneers the Sex Pistols in the mid-1970s. EMI feared that the band's violent and anarchic reputation might harm the company's image, particularly among hospitals and physicians considering the purchase of EMI's new CT scanner medical diagnostic equipment. Although EMI salvaged its CT sales, it suffered in the music market. It was unable to sign any significant "new wave" performers for many years thereafter.

Economies of Scale in Research and Development

Manufacturers must often make substantial investments in R&D to develop new products, or to improve existing products or production processes. R&D expenditures exceed 5 percent of total sales revenues at many companies in a variety of industries, including Samsung, Microsoft, Glaxo, and Siemans. R&D involves significant indivisibilities. The nature of engineering and scientific research implies that there is a minimum feasible size to an R&D project as well as an R&D department. For example, researchers at Tufts University have carefully measured the costs of developing new pharmaceutical products for the U.S. market.[9] They found that drug companies spent approximately $200 million on R&D for each

---

[9]DiMasi, J. et al., "Cost of Innovation in the Pharmaceutical Industry," *Journal of Health Economics* 10(2), 1991: pp. 107–142.

drug the Food and Drug Administration approved for marketing in the United States. This implies that the average fixed costs of prescription drugs can vary widely, depending on sales volume.

R&D may also entail economies of scope. Economies of scope may result from R&D spillovers when ideas developed in one research project are of help in another project. A firm with a diversified research portfolio may be better positioned to determine the general applicability of new ideas than a firm with a narrower portfolio of projects. Using detailed R&D data, Rebecca Henderson and Iain Cockburn documented the magnitude of spillovers in pharmaceutical firms.[10] They measured productivity as the number of patents per dollar of R&D. They found that for an average firm with 19 research programs, the addition of 2 research programs increased the productivity of existing programs by 4.5 percent.

As discussed in Chapter 1, economies of scale and scope in R&D are important enough to materially affect market structure in some industries. One such industry may be pharmaceuticals. Lacy Glenn Thomas argues that high R&D costs have favored large pharmaceutical firms.[11] Thomas believes that larger companies are better able to manage the complexities of the FDA approval process by virtue of their experience. They also have the production and sales organizations to assure the throughput and high sales volumes necessary to expand output and drive down average fixed costs. Thomas might be right. A glimpse of the leading pharmaceutical manufacturers in the 1990s reveals few newcomers since the 1960s and several significant mergers in the industry have further contributed to consolidation. Providing the "exceptions that prove the rule," when smaller pharmaceutical firms successfully innovate, they frequently sell their innovations to larger drug houses that then shepherd the drugs through the regulatory process and market them.

Despite the presence of economies of scale in R&D, there is no clear relationship between size and innovativeness. On the one hand, large firms can reduce the average costs of innovation by virtue of their size. On the other hand, as discussed below, small firms may be better able to motivate researchers. Firms of different sizes may also face different incentives to innovate. We elaborate on these ideas in Chapter 14. Suffice it to say that economic theory and empirical evidence is ambiguous about whether big firms are more innovative than small firms.

SOURCES OF DISECONOMIES OF SCALE ◆ ◆ ◆ ◆ ◆

Given that there are so many potential sources of scale and scope economies, it may be surprising that there is not some colossal "mega-firm" dominating production across all industries. Perhaps no firm has ever tried. More likely, though, firms understand that there are limits to economies of scale, so that beyond a certain size, bigger is no longer better. Firms may have even experienced diseconomies of scale, so that bigger is worse. Diseconomies of scale may arise for a number of reasons, including those discussed in this section.

---

[10]Henderson, R. and I. Cockburn, "Scale, Scope, and Spillovers: Determinants of Research Productivity in the Pharmaceutical Industry," *RAND Journal of Economics*, 1996.

[11]Thomas, L. G., "Regulation and Firm Size: FDA Impacts on Innovation," *RAND Journal of Economics*, 1990.

Labor Costs and Firm Size

Larger firms generally pay higher wages. Evidence from as early as the 1890s pointed to the wage premium paid to workers in large manufacturing firms compared with smaller firms.[12] The wage premium persists. U.S. government census data reveal that companies with 500 or more employees pay their workers 35 percent more, on average, than do smaller firms, even after controlling for key determinants of productivity such as job tenure. The wage gap cuts across all manufacturing and service industries. Even if one controls for other determinants of wages, such as work experience and job type, a wage gap of 10 percent or more still persists.

One reason for the wage gap is that large firms are more likely to be unionized than small firms. H. Gregg Lewis summarized 40 studies of wage differentials between unionized and non-unionized firms.[13] After controlling for a variety of other possible sources of wage differentials (such as sex, race, and experience) he found that unionized workers earn about 10 to 18 percent more than comparable non-unionized workers. Another possible reason is that workers in smaller firms may enjoy their work more than workers in large firms, so that large firms must pay a *compensating differential* to attract workers. One final reason is that large firms may need to draw workers from greater distances. Again the large firms may need to pay a compensating differential to offset transportation costs.

Offsetting the wage gap is that worker turnover at larger firms is generally lower than at small firms. Since it can cost thousands of dollars to recruit and train new employees, this may offset some of the added costs due to higher wages.

Incentive and Bureaucracy Effects

In the next chapter, we describe a number of incentive and bureaucracy effects that make it difficult for firms to expand their vertical boundaries. The same problems emerge as firms expand their horizontal boundaries. In larger firms, worker pay is much less likely to be tied to the contribution that the worker makes toward firm profit. Larger firms may also have a more difficult time monitoring and communicating with workers, further leading to difficulties in promoting effective worker performance. On the other hand, large firms may provide incentives to their workers by offering opportunities for advancement up the corporate ladder. One solution adopted by many large firms is the adoption of work rules to ensure that workers do not slack off. While these rules may lead workers to perform specific tasks as desired, they may also stifle creativity and lead workers to feel detached from the organization. Chapters 15 and 16 address these issues in more detail.

Spreading Specialized Resources Too Thin

Many talented individuals believe that having achieved success in one venue, they can duplicate it elsewhere. Some succeed. But others fail because they lack the

---

[12]For a comprehensive discussion of size effects on workers, see Brown, C., J. Hamilton, and J. Medoff, *Employers Large and Small*, Cambridge, MA: Harvard University Press, 1990.

[13]See *Handbook of Labor Economics*, Ashenfelter, O. and R. Layard, eds., New York: North Holland, 1986.

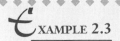

EXAMPLE 2.3

THE BEST LAID PLANS: THE STRUGGLES OF PHARMACIA & UPJOHN[14]

During the mid-1990s, pharmaceutical companies faced an unprecedented strategic challenge. The growth of managed care in the United States, and the tightening of government health care budgets in other nations, forced manufacturers to lower prices on many drugs. It appeared that only a small percentage of new products would generate enough revenue to cover the costs of research and development. Partly in response to these pressures, there were a number of mergers and acquisitions including Glaxo's acquisition of Burroughs-Wellcome, Rhone Poulenc's merger with Rorer, and Bristol-Myer's merger with Squibb. The managers who engineered these mergers cited a number of potential synergies. For example, a merged firm offering a broad enough product line could reduce purchasing costs for managed care companies seeking to obtain the bulk of their pharmaceuticals from a single supplier. As another example of synergies, firms with complementary research portfolios could pool knowledge to increase overall research productivity.

Although it is inevitable for managers to tout merger synergies, they often fail to account for a variety of less tangible inefficiencies that can imperil mergers. The merger between Pharmacia and Upjohn offers a prime example. At the time of their merger in 1995, Pharmacia and Upjohn were both medium-size drug makers facing different problems. Upjohn, whose primary offices were located in Kalamazoo, Michigan, had a number of successful products such as Rogaine but an anemic research pipeline. Pharmacia, with primary operations in Stockholm and Milan, had a number of successful drugs in less competitive categories such as allergy medication and human growth hormone, but lacked strong U.S. distribution. Facing tightening markets at home and abroad, both firms sought solutions to their strategic dilemmas.

Upjohn and Pharmacia anticipated that their merger would create a number of synergies. They expected to lay off redundant workers in a number of areas, including sales and distribution. In fact, they were able to trim their combined labor force by about 10 percent after just two years. More important, they anticipated having the financial clout to maintain large-scale integrated research operations. The firms believed that in the face of declining demand, the minimum efficient scale for research had increased.

Two years after the merger, Pharmacia & Upjohn was in trouble. The main culprit was something that was largely unmentioned amid the discussion of synergies—the problem of combining starkly different cultures. John Zabriskie, Upjohn's CEO prior to the merger, became the CEO of the combined firm. He tried to implement many of Upjohn's policies, but met with resistance. Some of these policies appeared to be relatively minor, such as those regarding smoking,

---

[14]Much of the information in this example is drawn from Frank, R. and T. Burton, "Culture Clash Causes Anxiety for Pharmacia & Upjohn Inc.," *Wall Street Journal*, February 4, 1997, p. 1.

vacations, and drug testing. But the policies that Zabriskie imposed were much stricter than what the Europeans were accustomed to, and they reacted with resentment. Zabriskie also tried to introduce a tightly controlled hierarchy, with frequent reports and updates, and decisions emanating from the corporate office. Decision making at Pharmacia had been more decentralized, with less paperwork and fewer directives from the corporate office. Many Pharmacia researchers, frustrated by the reporting requirements, quit.

By mid-1997, many of the merger goals had not been met. Most significantly, the research enterprise had not been integrated. Instead, the three geographic centers engaged in frequent turf battles. American managers sent to streamline European operations found it difficult to implement the strategies that worked for them back home. As a result, the Pharmacia & Upjohn market value languished, dropping 25 percent during 1996–1997, even as other pharmaceutical companies posted substantial increases.

Pharmacia Upjohn should have questioned the motives behind their merger. Even the combined company is not large enough to offer one-stop shopping. Besides, Pharmacia could have improved its U.S. distribution by licensing distribution to Upjohn. This would have facilitated layoffs in sales and distribution without the need to merge managers and researchers. Finally, the minimum efficient scale of R&D is not normally dependent on the riskiness of R&D. The merger may increase the probability that the combined firm generates some new products, but does little to increase overall research productivity (and thereby create shareholder value). In fact, there was relatively little overlap in the research portfolios prior to the merger, suggesting that the potential gains from cross-fertilization of research teams would be modest at best.

The merger may yet work out. In mid-1997, Fred Hassan (previously at American Home Products) became CEO. Hassan brought in a new top management team, thus ending fractious debates between previous Pharmacia and Upjohn managers. He moved the corporate headquarters from Windsor, England (a "compromise" between the previous Swedish and Michigan headquarters) to New Jersey, home to several other American pharmaceutical firms. Finally, he consolidated marketing and research programs. He was especially effective at getting researchers to prioritize their programs, rather than fight over every research dollar.

Pharmacia & Upjohn's recent upswing may merely be due to the introduction of successful new drugs. But Hassan has changed the culture, eliminating many of the conflicts that nearly crippled the merger.

skills necessary to translate their success to a new situation or they spread themselves too thin. A good example is provided by chefs, such as Chicago's Michael Foley. Foley achieved acclaim for his first restaurant, Printer's Row. He opened two other restaurants while continuing to operate Printer's Row. Not only did the new restaurants fail, the reviews for Printer's Row became negative as well. The reviews improved and business at Printer's Row picked up only after Foley returned full time to its kitchen. Michael Foley could not easily replicate himself. Thus, he could not easily replicate the success of his first restaurant. (Ultimately, Foley did find an outstanding replacement in the kitchen at Printer's Row, and he now is a consultant to other restauranteurs.) Other professionals share the same difficulties. When the key to a professional's success is the dedication of many hours to a single activity, performance may suffer across the board if he or she tries to devote time to several activities.

The same lessons also apply to specialized capital inputs, such as computers, tools and dies, or assembly lines. If a specialized input is a source of advantage for a firm, and that firm attempts to expand its operations without duplicating the input, the expansion may overburden the specialized input.

"Conflicting Out"

With the continued growth and consolidation of professional services firms in fields such as marketing, accounting, consulting, and law, it is important to consider another source of diseconomies of scale—*conflicting out*. When a potential client approaches a professional services firm with new business, it may be concerned about whether the firm is already doing business with one or more of its competitors. The potential client might be concerned about conflicts of interest that could arise in the professional services firm. Sensitive competitor information might leak out. The professional service firm might not take its interests fully to heart. Faced with these concerns, the potential client may take its business elsewhere. The professional services firm will have been conflicted out.

Obviously, as professional services firms grow internally and/or through merger, the possibilities for such conflicts increase. This places a natural limit on the market share that any one professional services firm can achieve. For example, the marketing firm Chiat/Day lost the Coke account in 1995 when it was acquired by the Omnicom Group. Omnicom already owned BBDO, which was the main ad agency for Pepsi. (The Omnicom Group was the ill-fated holding company formed when Saatchi and Saatchi attempted to become the largest marketing firm in the world. It failed, partly because of problems with conflicts such as these.)

THE LEARNING CURVE   ◆ ◆ ◆ ◆ ◆

Medical students are encouraged to learn by the axiom "See one, do one, teach one." This axiom belies the importance of experience in producing skilled physicians. Experience is an important determinant of ability in many professions, and strategists have discovered in the past three decades the significance of experience for firms. The importance of experience is conveyed by the idea of the learning curve.

The Concept of the Learning Curve

Economies of scale refer to the cost advantages that flow from producing a larger output at a given point in time. The *learning curve* (or experience curve) refers to cost advantages that flow from accumulating experience and know-how. While practice may not always make perfect, it generally helps. Workers often improve their performance of specific tasks as they gain experience. Organizations can also learn. A manufacturer can learn the appropriate tolerances for design attributes.

A retailer can learn about community tastes. An accounting firm can learn the idiosyncrasies of its clients' inventory management. The benefits of learning manifest themselves in lower costs, higher quality, and more effective pricing and marketing.

The magnitude of learning benefits is expressed in terms of a *slope*. The slope for a given production process is calculated by examining how far average costs decline as cumulative production output doubles. It is important to use cumulative output rather than output during a given time period to distinguish between learning effects and other scale effects. As shown in Figure 2.5, suppose that a firm has cumulative output of Q_x with average cost of production of AC_1. Suppose next that the firm's cumulative output doubles to $2Q_x$ with average cost of AC_2. Then the slope equals AC_2/AC_1.[15]

Slopes have been estimated for hundreds of products.[16] The median slope appears to be about .80, implying that for the typical firm, doubling cumulative output reduces unit costs by about 20 percent. Slopes vary from firm to firm and industry to industry, however, so that the actual slope enjoyed by any one firm for any given production process generally falls between .70 and .90 and may be as low as .6 or as high as 1.0 (e.g., no learning). Note that although an industry may have a slope of, say, .75, this does not imply that continual doubling of output inexorably leads to further and further 25 percent cost reductions. Estimated slopes usually represent averages over a range of outputs and do not indicate if and when learning economies may be fully exploited.

While the slope concept has been applied mainly to cost measurement, it applies equally well to quality. For example, Harold Luft, John Bunker, and Alain

FIGURE 2.5
THE LEARNING CURVE.

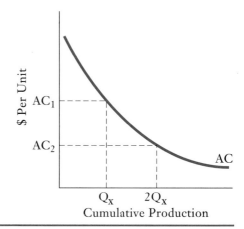

When there is learning, average costs fall with cumulative production. Here, as cumulative production increases from Q_x to $2Q_x$, the average cost of a batch of output falls from AC_1 to AC_2.

---

[15]This is sometimes referred to as the slope of the learning curve.

[16]See, for example, *Perspectives on Experience*, Boston: Boston Consulting Group, 1970, for estimates of progress ratios for over 20 industries. See Lieberman, M., "The Learning Curve and Pricing in the Chemical Processing Industries," *RAND Journal of Economics*, 1984, 15(2): pp. 213–228, for learning curve estimates for 37 chemical products.

Enthoven found that more experienced medical providers enjoyed significantly lower surgical mortality rates for a number of common surgical procedures.[17] This may explain why patients requiring complex medical procedures strongly prefer experienced providers.[18] Findings such as these bolster efforts to develop regional referral centers for the provision of highly specialized medical care. These regional centers would perform many specific surgical procedures (e.g., heart surgery), replacing local facilities with lower volumes and presumably higher mortality rates.

Expanding Output to Obtain a Cost Advantage

Some firms pursue "learning curve strategies" whereby they seemingly produce more than is optimal in the short run, to reap the benefits of experience. This strategy might make sense because the expectation that learning will reduce costs in the future effectively reduces the marginal cost of current production. To see why this is so, consider the following example:

Suppose that a manufacturer of DRAM chips has cumulative production of 10,000 chips. It currently costs $2.50 to manufacture one additional chip. Based on experience, the firm believes that once it has produced 20,000 chips its unit costs will fall to $2.00, with no further learning benefits. The company has orders to produce an additional 200,000 chips when it unexpectedly receives an offer to bid on an order for 10,000 chips to be filled immediately. What is the lowest price it would be willing to accept for this order?

Assuming that filling the new order does not create delays that jeopardize other business, the firm must compare the price that the new buyer is willing to pay with the cost of producing additional chips. If the firm myopically ignored learning effects, it would accept the order only if the price was at least $2.50 per chip. This would be wrong.

To determine an acceptable price for the new order, the chip maker must consider how its accumulated experience will affect future costs. Before it received the new order, the chip maker had planned to produce 200,000 chips. The first 10,000 would cost $2.50 per chip, and the remaining 190,000 would cost $2.00 per chip, for a total of $405,000 for 200,000 chips. The new order enables the chip maker to fully exploit available learning economies before producing the previously ordered 200,000 chips. Once the new order is filled, the cost of producing the next 200,000 chips is only $400,000.

By filling the new order, the DRAM manufacturer reduces its future production costs by $5,000. In effect, the incremental cost of filling the additional order is only $20,000 (current costs of $25,000 less the $5,000 future cost savings), or $2.00 per chip. The firm should be willing to accept any price over this amount, even though a price between $2.00 and $2.50 per chip does not cover current production costs.

---

[17]Luft, H., J. Bunker, and A. Enthoven, "Should Operations Be Regionalized? The Empirical Relation Between Surgical Volume and Mortality," *New England Journal of Medicine* 301, 1979: pp. 1364–1369.

[18]Capps, C., "Measuring the returns to innovation: Evidence from the diffusion of AICD and cochlear implants in California" Northwestern University, Department of Economics, 1998, Mimeo.

EXAMPLE 2.4

THE BOSTON CONSULTING GROUP GROWTH/SHARE PARADIGM

The Boston Consulting Group (BCG) had a major impact on corporate strategy beginning in the 1970s when it introduced the *growth/share matrix*, an outgrowth of its success advocating learning curve strategies.[19] Figure 2.6 depicts a typical BCG matrix. The matrix allows firms to distinguish their product lines on two dimensions: growth of the market in which the product is situated, and the product's market share relative to the share of its next largest competitors. A product line was classified into one of four categories. A rising star is a product in a growing market with a high relative share. A cash cow is a product in a stable or declining market with a high relative share. A problem child is a product in a growing market with a low relative share. A dog is a product in a stable or declining market with a low relative share.

The BCG strategy for successfully managing a portfolio of products was based on taking advantage of learning curves and the *product life cycle*. BCG had observed that learning curves offered significant cost advantages in many markets. They also felt that most products had a characteristic life cycle, as shown in Figure 2.7.[20] According to this product life cycle model, demand for the product is initially low just after it is introduced. The product then enters a phase in which demand grows rapidly. As demand becomes increasingly driven by replacement sales rather than sales to new customers, demand growth levels off, and the product reaches its maturity stage. Finally, as superior substitute products eventually emerge, demand for the product will begin to decline.

FIGURE 2.6
THE BCG GROWTH/SHARE MATRIX.

The Growth/Share Matrix divides products into four categories according to their potential for growth and relative market share. Some strategists recommended that firms use the profits earned from "Cash Cows" to ramp up production of "Rising Stars" and "Problem Children." As the latter products move down their learning curves, they become "Cash Cows" in the next investment cycle.

		Relative Market Share	
		High	Low
Relative Market Growth	High	Rising Star	Problem Child
	Low	Cash Cow	Dog

---

[19]For a discussion of their treatment of the learning curve, see Boston Consulting Group, *Perspectives on Experience*, Boston: Boston Consulting Group, 1970.

[20]The product life-cycle model has its origins in the marketing literature. See, for example, Levitt, T., "Exploit the Product Life Cycle," *Harvard Business Review*, November–December 1965; pp. 81–94.

FIGURE 2.7
THE PRODUCT LIFE CYCLE.

Product demand is thought to move through four stages. When the product is first introduced, sales and growth are low. Product demand then grows rapidly, but sales level off, and the industry enters a maturity phase. Eventually, demand declines as other superior products or technologies supplant it. It can be difficult to predict when each stage will begin.

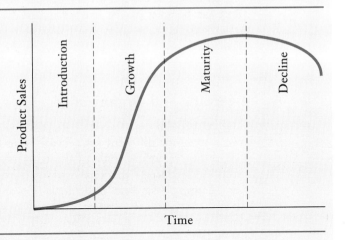

BCG felt that its clients could secure long-term cost advantages in each of its markets by increasing production in the early stages of the product's life cycle to secure learning economies. BCG recommended that firms use the profits from cash cow products to fund increased production of problem child and rising star products. In other words, the firm served as a "banker," using retained earnings to fund new ventures. Learning economies would cement the advantages of rising stars while enabling some problem children to become more competitive. As their markets matured and demand slackened, these products would then become cash cows to support learning strategies in new emerging markets.

BCG deserves credit for recognizing the strategic importance of learning curves, and many firms have prospered by utilizing the growth/share matrix framework. BCG also deserves credit for offering a rationale for maintaining a portfolio of products within a single diversified firm. However, it would be a mistake to apply the BCG framework without considering its underlying principles. As we have discussed, learning curves are by no means ubiquitous or uniform where they do occur. Increasing production runs will not by themselves necessarily generate learning economies, and knowledge gained from learning may rapidly depreciate. At the same time, product life cycles are easier to identify after they have been completed than during the planning process. Many products ranging from nylon to dedicated word processors that were forecast to have tremendous potential for growth did not meet expectations. Firms that invested heavily in them to secure learning advantages were losers. We conclude that one needs to do careful research about the learning curves and markets for the specific products in question before applying a learning curve strategy. Finally, the role of the firm as banker is questionable. As we discuss in Chapter 6, diversified firms have not demonstrated consistent success across diversified business lines. Moreover, the emergence of venture capitalists has enabled independent firms with potential stars of their own to obtain financing without being dependent on corporate authority.

Firms that pursue a learning curve strategy may earn negative accounting profits in the short run even as they prosper in the long run. For this reason, managers who are rewarded on the basis of short run profits may be reluctant to exploit the benefits of the learning curve. This may explain why U.S. electronics firms were reluctant to exploit the learning curve during the 1950s and 1960s, and ultimately ceded the market to Asian firms. One solution to this problem is to directly account for learning curve benefits when assessing profits and losses.

Learning and Organization

The variation in slopes across firms and products shows that learning occurs at different rates for different organizations and different processes. While there has been little systematic study of the determinants of learning, some common sense helps us to identify situations in which learning is likely to be important.

Learning rests with individuals. Complex tasks, such as the design and production of statistical software, offer great opportunities for individuals to learn on their own and from their coworkers. Firms can facilitate the adoption and use of newly learned ideas by encouraging the sharing of information, establishing work rules that include the new ideas, and reducing turnover. Lanier Benkard (1998) argues that labor policies at Lockheed prevented the airframe manufacturer from fully exploiting learning opportunities in the production of the L-1011 TriStar.[21] Its union contract required Lockheed to promote experienced line workers to management, while simultaneously upgrading workers at lower levels. This produced a domino effect whereby as many as 10 workers changed jobs when one was moved to a management position. As a result, workers were forced to relearn tasks that their higher ranking coworkers had already mastered. Benkard estimates that this and related policies reduced labor productivity at Lockheed by as much as 40 to 50 percent annually.

While codifying work rules and reducing job turnover facilitates retention of knowledge, it may stifle creativity. At the same time, there are instances where worker-specific learning is too complex to transmit across the firm. Examples include many professional services, in which individual knowledge of how to combine skills in functional areas with specific and detailed knowledge of particular clients or markets may give individuals advantages that they cannot easily pass along to others. Clearly, an important skill of managers is to find the correct balance between stability and change so as to maximize the benefits of learning.

The Learning Curve versus Economies of Scale

Economies of learning differ from economies of scale. Economies of scale refer to the ability to perform an activity at a lower unit cost when it is performed on a larger scale at a particular point in time. Learning economies refer to reductions in unit costs due to accumulating experience over time. Economies of scale may be substantial even when learning economies are minimal. This is likely to be the case

---

[21]Benkard, C. L., "Learning and Forgetting: The Dynamics of Aircraft Production," New Haven: Yale University, 1998, Mimeo.

in simple capital-intensive activities, such as two-piece aluminum can manufacturing. Similarly, learning economies may be substantial even when economies of scale are minimal. This is likely to be the case in complex labor-intensive activities, such as the practice of antitrust law.

Figure 2.8 illustrates how one can have learning economies without economies of scale. The left side of the figure shows a typical learning curve, with average costs declining with cumulative experience. The right side shows two average cost curves, for different experience levels. Both average cost curves are perfectly flat, indicating that there are no economies of scale. Suppose that the firm under consideration enters a given year of production with cumulative experience of Q_1. According to the learning curve, this gives it an average cost level of AC_1. This remains constant regardless of current output because of constant returns to scale. Entering the next year of production the firm has cumulative output of Q_2. Its experiences in the previous year enable the firm to revamp its production techniques. In thus moving down the learning curve, it can enjoy an average cost level of AC_2 in the next year of production.

Managers who do not correctly distinguish between economies of scale and learning may draw incorrect inferences about the benefits of size in a market. For example, if a large firm has lower unit costs because of economies of scale, then any cutbacks in production volume will raise unit costs. If the lower unit costs are the result of learning, the firm may be able to cut current volume without necessarily raising its unit costs. To take another example, if a firm enjoys a cost advantage due to a capital-intensive production process and resultant scale economies, then it may be less concerned about labor turnover than a competitor that enjoys low costs due to learning a complex labor-intensive production process.

FIGURE 2.8
LEARNING ECONOMIES WHEN SCALE ECONOMIES ARE ABSENT.

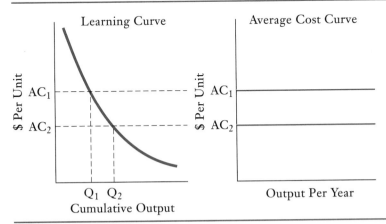

It is not necessary to have economies of scale to realize learning economies. The production process depicted here shows constant returns to scale, as evidenced by the flat average cost curves, which show output *within a given year*. The level of average cost falls with cumulative experience *across several years*, however, as shown by the learning curve.

◆ ◆ ◆ ◆ ◆ SCALE AND SCOPE ECONOMIES, FIRM SIZE, AND PROFITABILITY

Economies of scale and scope provide large firms with an inherent cost advantage. Not only does this encourage small firms to explore ways to grow in order to take advantage of scale economies themselves, it also limits the number of firms that can successfully compete in the market. This section explores these ideas.

Scale, Scope, and Firm Size

Scale and scope economies give large firms a cost advantage over small firms. In markets where consumers are price sensitive, large firms can pass along some of their cost advantage to consumers. This will drive small firms out of business or into niches not served by the large firms. If small firms are to match the production costs achieved by large firms, they must grow. A study by Timothy Dunne, Mark Roberts, and Larry Samuelson demonstrates the link between survival and growth.[22] They examined the growth of U.S. manufacturing plants from 1963 to 1982 and found that most plants opened during this time had closed within 10 years. However, of those that remained open, most had grown significantly. While new plants tended to be only about one-third the size of existing plants at the time they opened, they roughly doubled in size within 5 years and tripled in size within 10 years.

Firms can expand output in a number of ways. Expansion strategies may be internal, relying on retained earnings, equity, and debt, or external, relying on formalizing relationships with other firms. Internal expansion strategies include product portfolio management, such as the Boston Consulting Group Growth/Share Matrix strategy discussed earlier in this chapter; new product development, or geographic diversification. External strategies for growth typically involve mergers. Announcements about corporate mergers frequently refer to "synergies" that exist between the merging firms. Synergies are economies of scale waiting to be exploited. The efficiencies can be so large that the Department of Justice and the Federal Trade Commission, which enforce U.S. antitrust laws, will permit a merger between large firms that may create some monopoly power if the merger allows the firms to achieve substantial efficiencies through economies of scale. Mergers in the airlines (Republic/Northwest), soft drink (7-Up/Dr Pepper), and hospital sectors (two hospitals in Roanoke, Virginia) have been approved on these grounds.

The Relationship Between Market Share and Profitability

When economies of scale or scope exist, but only some firms have been able to exploit them, one would expect to find a positive correlation between a firm's market share and profitability. Robert Buzzell, Bradley Gale, and Ralph Sultan analyzed the PIMS (Profit Impact of Market Strategies) data collected by the Strategic

---

[22]Dunne, T., M. Roberts, and L. Samuelson, "Patterns of Firm Entry and Exit in U.S. Manufacturing Industries," *RAND Journal of Economics* 19(4), 1988: pp. 495–515.

Planning Institute and found that among the firms in that sample, market share and profitability are positively correlated.[23] (This finding is summarized in Table 2.3.) Robert Jacobson and David Aaker also found a positive relationship between market share and profitability, though the correlation they estimated was weaker than that found by Buzzell, Gale, and Sultan.[24]

Some management gurus use evidence such as that presented in Table 2.3 to support the recommendation that raising market share should be the primary strategic objective of any business. For example, the quest for "global market leadership" was central to the concept of "strategic intent" that was popularized by Gary Hamel and C. K. Prahalad in the early 1990s.[25] But the observed correlation between market share and profitability should not be taken to imply that any strategy designed to boost market share will increase a firm's profitability. The economic mechanism underlying the correlation is likely to be more subtle than merely "increases in share lead to increases in profit." It may be that a firm was able to succeed in capturing a high market share over time because its product created superior benefits for customers. A competitor that attempts to "buy" market share (e.g., by cutting its price or increasing advertising) may find that it is unable to achieve the same profitability as the market leader, either because its products do not offer a comparable level of quality to consumers or because it is unable to catch up to the initial advantage of the leader.[26] This may explain why most of the firms that Hamel and Prahalad profile as having the correct strategic intent to be market share leaders actually underperformed their competitors.[27] There is no

TABLE 2.3
RELATIONSHIP BETWEEN A FIRM'S MARKET SHARE RANK
AND PRE-TAX PROFIT AS A PERCENT OF SALES

Firm's Market Share Rank in Industry	*Average Pre-Tax Profit as a Percent of Sales for Firms with this Market Share Ran*
#1	12.7%
#2	9.1%
#3	7.1%
#4	5.5%
#5 or worse	4.5%

Source: Exhibit 5.2 in Buzzell, R. D. and B. T. Gale, *The PIMS* (Profit Impact of Market Strategy) Principles: Linking Strategy to Performance*, New York: Free Press, 1987.

---

[23]Buzzell, R. D., B. T. Gale, and R.G.M. Sultan, "Market Share: A Key to Profitability," *Harvard Business Review*, January–February 1975: pp. 97–106.

[24]Jacobson, R. and D. Aaker, "Is Market Share All that Its Cracked Up to Be?" *Journal of Marketing*, 49, Fall 1985: pp. 11–22.

[25]Hamel, G. and C. K. Prahalad, "Strategic Intent," *Harvard Business Review*, May–June 1989: pp. 63–76.

[26]Chapter 13 discusses the dynamics of early mover advantages.

[27]"The Dangers of Strategic Intent," Marketing Associates Commentary, April 1992. They use return on assets as their measure of performance.

causal mechanism whereby market share leadership automatically translates to profits.

Note, too, that market shares in an industry must, by definition, add up to 100 percent. Thus, it would be impossible for all firms in an industry to increase market share simultaneously. If firms attempted to do so, either through cutting prices, raising advertising levels, or even enhancing the quality of their products, the result would most likely be diminished, rather than increased, profitability for all firms. The key point is that a strategy designed to exploit the positive relationship between market share and profitability has no hope of succeeding unless the linkage between market share and profitability is imperfectly understood by participants in an industry. But this undermines the general value of advice that *all* firms should "go for share."

CHAPTER SUMMARY

◆ A production process exhibits economies of scale if the average cost per unit of output falls as the volume of output increases. A production process exhibits economies of scope if the total cost of producing two different products or services is lower when they are produced by a single firm instead of two separate firms.

◆ An important source of economies of scale and scope is the spreading of indivisible fixed costs. Fixed costs do not vary as the level of production varies.

◆ In general, capital-intensive production processes are more likely to display economies of scale and scope than are labor or materials intensive processes.

◆ In some industries, such as food retailing, firms may make expenditures to create scale economies that previously did not exist, such as expenditures to create and reinforce brand image.

◆ There are economies of scale in inventory management, so that processes with large volumes need to carry less inventory on a percentage-of-output basis than similar processes with small volumes.

◆ The physical property known as the cube-square rule confers scale economies on processes, such as warehousing, where costs are related to the geometric volume of the production "vessel."

◆ There are often economies of scale associated with marketing expense, research and development, and purchasing. Large-scale marketing efforts often have lower costs per message received than do smaller-scale efforts. The costs of large research ventures may be spread over greater output, although big size may be inimicable to innovation. Small firms may obtain purchasing discounts comparable to those obtained by large firms by forming purchasing groups.

◆ Sometimes, large size can create inefficiencies. These may result from higher labor costs, bureaucracy, or dilution of specialized resources.

◆ Individuals and firms often improve their production processes with experience. This is known as learning. In processes with substantial learning benefits, firms that can accumulate and protect the knowledge gained by experience can achieve superior cost and quality positions in the market.

◆ There is a statistical positive relationship between size and profits. However, this relationship is more subtle than merely "growth assures increasing profits" and growth strategies must be based on the presence of economies of scale.

◆ (Appendix) Economies of scale may be estimated by examining accounting data. Due diligence analysis of costs, based on activity based cost accounting, can generate useful estimates of the magnitude of scale economies.

◆ (Appendix) Regression analysis and frontier analysis that compares costs and outputs of firms of varying sizes and experience may be used to identify scale economies and the learning curve.

QUESTIONS

1. A firm produces two products, X and Y. The production technology displays the following costs, where $C(i, j)$ represents the cost of producing i units of X and j units of Y:

   $C(0,50) = 100$ $C(5,0) = 150$
   $C(0,100) = 210$ $C(10,0) = 320$
   $C(5,50) = 240$ $C(10,100) = 500$

   Does this production technology display economies of scale? Of scope?

2. Economies of scale are usually associated with the spreading of fixed costs, such as when a manufacturer builds a factory. But the spreading of fixed costs is also important for economies of scale associated with marketing, R&D, and purchasing. Explain.

3. What is the difference between economies of scale and learning economies?

4. A firm contemplating entering the market would need to invest $100 million in a production plant (or about $10 million annually on an amortized basis). Such a plant could produce about 100 million pounds of cereal per year. What would be the average fixed costs of this plant if it ran at capacity? Each year, U.S. breakfast cereal makers sell about 3 billion pounds of cereal. What would be the average fixed costs if the cereal maker captured a 2 percent market share? What would be its cost disadvantage if it only achieved a 1 percent share?

5. Historically, product markets were dominated by large firms and service markets by small firms. This seems to have reversed itself somewhat in recent years. What factors might be at work?

6. Most trade barriers among European nations have fallen. Many experts believe that this will allow businesses in different parts of Europe to merge. What effect, if any, will this have on competition with U.S. and Japanese firms in Europe and elsewhere? Does your answer depend on the industry under consideration?

7. Explain why the advent of ATMs has contributed to bank consolidation. Note: An important fact about ATMs is that it is costly for someone with an account at bank A to use an ATM that is owned by bank B.

8. During the 1980s, several American firms opened "hypermarts," enormous stores that sold groceries, household goods, hardware, and other products under one roof. What are the possible economies of scale that might be enjoyed by hypermarts? What are the potential diseconomies of scale?

9. Many international consumer products companies, such as Procter and Gamble and McDonald's, sell different products in different nations. For example, McDonald's sells different food products, and Procter and Gamble sells products with different brand names. How might these products differences affect the ability of these firms to achieve global marketing economies of scale?

10. During the 1980s, firms in the Silicon Valley of northern California experienced high rates of turnover as top employees moved from one firm to another. What effect do you think this turnover had on learning-by-doing at individual firms? What effect do you think it had on learning by the industry as a whole?

APPENDIX: ESTIMATING THE MAGNITUDE OF SCALE AND LEARNING ECONOMIES

*I*t is one thing to claim that a production process displays economies of scale. It is another to provide a theoretical justification for this claim. It is better still to provide hard evidence. After all, when firms merge with other firms or invest for growth, they often tout the cost reductions they will realize through scale economies or learning. These claims may or may not be based on a serious estimate of the magnitude of the cost savings that the firms expect to achieve. Given the inevitable costs associated with mergers and growth, such estimates are clearly desirable.

This section discusses two broad approaches for estimating the magnitude of scale economies: analyses that rely on managerial accounting data and analyses based on statistical techniques, such as *regression analysis* and *frontier analysis*. These estimation approaches differ in the comparison group used for analysis. An approach using accounting data focuses on the behavior of a limited group of firms for which detailed information is available. Future costs are projected on the basis of past costs of the same or similar firms. Regression and frontier analysis, on the other hand, emphasize comparisons across a broader sample of firms, using data that are comparable across the sample. The section concludes with a discussion of estimating learning economies.

Using Accounting Data to Estimate the Magnitude of Scale Economies

Accounting data are often used to assess the magnitude of scale economies when firms contemplate mergers or growth. For example, when merging to seek funding from lenders, they are usually required to perform a *due diligence* examination. This is a detailed analysis of the financial and managerial consequences of a merger and relies primarily on accounting data provided by the merging firms. Accounting data include the data from balance sheets and income statements, which are generated for external reporting purposes (e.g., to allow investors and analysts to assess the overall financial health of an enterprise). It also includes managerial accounting data, such as the internal costing of departments, that allow lenders to identify the fixed and variable costs of operations and estimate the average cost curve.

The use of managerial accounting data for assessing scale economies need not be limited to due diligence. They can also aid managerial decision making. For example, if the partners in a merger anticipated that they could consolidate their purchasing functions, they could estimate the reductions in staff, order-processing costs, space, and so forth and use cost accounting data to put a dollar value on these savings. Managerial accounting data can also serve as the cornerstone of activity-cost analyses of scale economies. Consider a specific activity, such as marketing. By estimating the increase in labor, advertising time, promotional effort, and so forth needed to achieve a given increase in sales and using internal accounting data to determine the incremental costs of these inputs, the firm can more accurately assess the benefit/cost ratio of increased marketing activity.

Using Regression Analysis to Estimate the Shapes of Cost Curves

Suppose that you had the following cost and output data for three chain saw manufacturing plants:

Plant	Annual Output	Average Cost
1	10,000	$50
2	20,000	$47
3	30,000	$45

Average costs apparently fall as output increases. It would be natural to conclude from this pattern that there are economies of scale in chain saw production. We can even estimate its magnitude—it appears that a plant producing 30,000 saws annually has average costs that are $5 lower than those at a plant producing 10,000 saws annually. One might be tempted to recommend to the managers of plants 1 and 2 that they expand output (perhaps by building larger plants) so as to lower their average costs.

Just how confident should we be about the magnitude of scale economies in this instance? After all, the differences in costs at the three plants might have nothing to do with scale economies. For example, plant 3 may be located in a region where labor costs are unusually low. If this is the case, then the cost advantage at plant 3 may have nothing at all to do with scale economies, and the other plants may have nothing to gain by expanding. To be confident that the cost/output relationship truly reflects scale economies, alternative explanations need to be ruled out.

These are the ideas underlying *regression analysis* of *cost functions*. Regression analysis is a statistical technique for estimating how one or more factors affect some variable of interest. For cost functions, the variable of interest is average cost, and the factors may include output, wage rates, and other input prices.

To illustrate, suppose that we suspect that the average cost function is a quadratic function of the volume of output:

$$AC = \beta_0 + \beta_1 Q + \beta_2 Q^2 + \beta_3 w + noise,$$

where Q denotes production volume (e.g., number of standard-size chain saws produced per year), w denotes the local wage rate, and *noise* represents all of the other factors that affect the level of cost that cannot be measured and which are not explicitly included in the analysis.

We can interpret the cost function as follows: The average cost at any particular plant is equal to some function of plant output, plus a function of wage rates, plus "noise." We expect β_3 to be positive as higher wages contribute to higher costs. We expect β_1 to be negative, suggesting that as output rises, average costs fall. We expect β_2 to be small and positive. Thus, at large levels of output (and therefore at very large levels of output^2), average costs may start to level off or even increase, as the positive effect of $\beta_2 Q^2$ offsets or dominates the negative effect of $\beta_1 Q$. It is the combination of β_1, whose negative slope indicates economies of scale and β_2, whose positive slope indicates diseconomies of scale, that produces the characteristic parabolic or U shape of the average cost function.

Finally, the noise term represents variation in costs due to factors other than size and wage rates. If we had good information about sources of that variation, we could directly include additional variables in the cost function. Otherwise, we are forced to accept that our cost function is necessarily imprecise. Regression analysis "fits" the cost function to actual cost/output data. In other words, regression provides estimates of the parameters β_1, β_2, and β_3. Regression analysis then infers from the magnitude of the remaining noise just how confident we should be about the accuracy of the parameter estimates.

For example, consider the data in Figures 2.9 and 2.10. These figures plot average costs and output pairs at several plants in two hypothetical industries. Suppose that local wage rates are the same at all plants, so that the only sources of variation in costs are output and noise. We can use regression analysis to fit cost functions of the following form:

$$AC = \beta_0 + \beta_1 Q + \beta_2 Q^2 + noise$$

to each set of data (yielding two different average cost curves). If, as expected, β_1 is negative and β_2 is positive, the average cost curve will be U-shaped, and the output at which average cost is minimized will equal $-\beta_1/2\beta_2$. The regression finds the values of β_0, β_1, and β_2 that best fit the actual data. The best fit is achieved when the sum of the squared distances between the actual cost values and the values on the fitted parabola is minimized. Best fitting parabolas are drawn through the scatterplots in Figures 2.9 and 2.10.

Given the cost/output pairs that we chose, the best fitting parabolas are identical. In both cases $\beta_0 = 70$, $\beta_1 = -1$, and $\beta_2 = .01$. Thus, minimum average cost is achieved at output 50, with average cost $= 45$. In both figures this output is near the upper end of the range of outputs, suggesting that most firms still have unexploited economies of scale. An important difference between Figures 2.9 and 2.10 is that the parabola in Figure 2.9 appears to come much closer to fitting the data than the parabola in Figure 2.10. In other words, actual costs depart significantly from the fitted curve much more often in Figure 2.10. Even though regressions report the same parameter estimates for both figures, they will report much lower

FIGURE 2.9
"PRECISELY"-FIT COST FUNCTION.

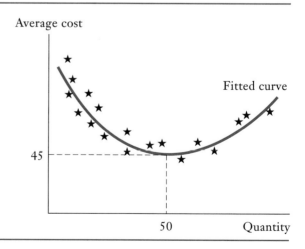

The cost/quantity pairs for each firm generally lie close to the curve that best fits the data.

ECONOMIES OF SCALE IN HOSPITALS

The 1990s saw an unprecedented number of hospital mergers in the United States. Health care policy makers generally welcomed this consolidation, believing that there has been excess hospital capacity, and that through mergers hospitals might achieve economies of scale. Most merging hospitals perform due diligence analysis, using accounting data to identify potential cost savings. Most of these analyses find potential for savings from even very large hospital mergers, suggesting that most hospitals are operating below minimum efficient scale. However, systematic regression analyses with hospitals of different sizes offer mixed evidence on economies of scale. Most researchers find that there are scale economies at small sizes, but differ about the presence and magnitude of scale economies at larger hospitals.

Both accounting and regression analyses of scale economies in hospitals are problematic. Recall that accounting studies attempt to disentangle fixed and variable costs. Unfortunately, most hospital cost accounting is primitive when compared to cost accounting in other industries (e.g., activity-based cost accounting is essentially nonexistent). As a result, roughly 50 percent of all hospital costs are classified as indirect, and are often incorrectly treated as fixed costs for purposes of estimating scale economies. This may explain why hospital CEOs have reported in several surveys that they were disappointed by the magnitude of savings that they actually achieved after mergers.

Regression analyses are problematic because it is difficult to make an "apples to apples" comparison among hospitals. Hospitals sell highly differentiated products, where the cost per patient depends not just on the efficiency of the hospital, but also on the severity of the patients' illnesses and on the quality of care delivered. It may be difficult to control for differences in severity and quality, and this can introduce noise and bias to studies of scale economies.

In one recent regression study that avoids some of these problems, Dranove (1998) measures scale economies in nonrevenue producing hospital cost centers.[28] These include administrative, fiscal, and hotel services, for which costs are less likely to be related to either severity of illness or quality of care. Using "semi-parametric" regression analysis, which does not impose a specific functional form for the average cost curve, Dranove finds that the minimum efficient scale for most cost centers is about 12,000 patients annually (about 250 beds). A hospital admitting only 2,500 patients annually has costs that are roughly 20 to 30 percent higher than the minimum efficient scale hospital. The average cost curve is essentially flat beyond the minimum efficient scale.

---

[28]Dranove D., "Economies of Scale in Non-revenue Producing Cost Centers: Implications for Hospital Mergers." *Journal of Health Economics* 17(1); pp. 69–83, 1992.

FIGURE 2.10

"IMPRECISELY"-FIT COST FUNCTION.

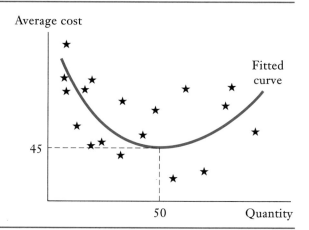

The cost/quantity pairs for each firm generally lie far from the curve that best fits the data.

confidence levels for the parameter estimates for Figure 2.10.[29] In fact, the poor fit of the curve in Figure 2.10 might make it difficult to statistically determine whether a parabolic or linear average cost function best fits the data, and therefore whether smaller firms really are at a cost disadvantage.

There is a large literature on the estimation of cost functions. Cost functions have been estimated for various industries, including airlines, telecommunications, electric utilities, trucking, railroads, and hospitals.[30] Most of these studies estimate functional forms for the average cost function that are more complicated than the simple quadratic functions discussed here. Nevertheless the basic ideas underlying these more sophisticated analyses are those described here, and these studies can be used to derive estimates of minimum efficient scale.

Frontier Analysis

Regression techniques for determining the shape of the cost curve are based on fitting a curve roughly through the middle of a range of cost/quantity pairs achieved by different firms at different times. As Figures 2.9 and 2.10 show, some firms' cost and quantity pairs will be above the fitted curve and others will be below it. If we interpret the fitted curve as representing the expected production cost for various levels of output, then a natural interpretation of the variation of cost/quantity pairs above and below the fitted curve is that some firms are more efficient than others. Using this interpretation, firms whose cost/quantity pairs are below the fitted curve are more efficient than average because their costs are less than expected

---

[29]A confidence level states the probability with which a true parameter value lies within a particular range.

[30]John Panzar's review article "Determinants of Firm and Industry Structure," in Schmalensee, R. and R. D. Willig, eds., *Handbook of Industrial Organization*, Amsterdam: North Holland, 1989, pp. 3–59, reviews some of the work on estimation of cost functions and provides many references to the literature.

for a firm producing that level of output. Similarly, firms whose cost/quantity pairs are above the fitted curve are less efficient than average.

Frontier analysis is based on this interpretation of regression analysis. The intuition behind frontier analysis is simple. Instead of fitting a curve that passes through the middle of a distribution of cost/quantity pairs, imagine fitting a curve that just touches the lowest cost/quantity pair. This curve, which is depicted in Figure 2.11, is the *efficiency frontier*. Except for firms right on the frontier, all other firms are "less efficient" because their costs exceed the theoretically achievable frontier cost levels. The farther away from the frontier a firm finds itself, the less efficient it is. A firm inside the frontier might conclude that it is not operating at maximum efficiency, and therefore it should be able to lower its costs and maintain or even increase its quantity. This is closely related to the concept of Total Quality Management (TQM), which teaches that firms can lower their costs and maintain or increase *quality* by improving the efficiency of their production processes.

Most frontier analyses use data on productive inputs and outputs, rather than costs and outputs. They also use sophisticated empirical techniques that account for complicated production technologies, as well as the effects of random chance on production levels. Richard Caves and David Barton present an excellent overview of frontier analysis techniques for the interested reader.[31]

Some economists challenge the argument that firms that lie above the frontier are not fully efficient. The apparent inefficiency may stem as much from the failure of the economist to correctly model the firm as from actual inefficiencies in the firm's operations. For example, the allegedly inefficient firm may be producing a good that is slightly differentiated from those produced by its competitors, necessitating higher costs. Or the firm may use a different mix of inputs not adequately handled by the economist's model relating inputs and costs to output.

However, these challenges do not negate the value of the frontier analysis approach. Frontier analysis requires that firms compare themselves to their competi-

FIGURE 2.11
THE EFFICIENCY FRONTIER.

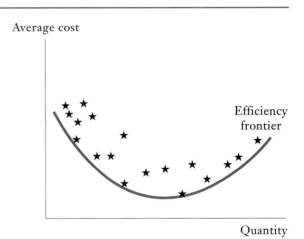

The efficiency frontier fits a curve to the lowest cost/quantity pair. Firms whose cost/quantity pairs are above the frontier are "less efficient" because their costs exceed the theoretically achievable frontier cost levels.

[31]Caves, R. and D. Barton, *Efficiency in U.S. Manufacturing Industries*, Cambridge, MA: MIT Press, 1990.

tors. A firm identified as lying inside the frontier may eventually explain its alleged inefficiencies. But in the process it will be forced to reexamine its production techniques and will often find that its production is less efficient than its competitors.

Estimating Learning Curves

Regression analysis may also be used to estimate learning curves. To do this, it is often convenient to estimate an equation with the following functional form:

$$logAC = \alpha + \epsilon log E + \gamma_1 log X_1 + \ldots + \gamma_N log X_N, + noise$$

where "log" represents the natural logarithm, E denotes cumulative production volume, $X_1, \ldots, X_n$ denote the levels of cost drivers other than cumulative production volume that affect average cost (e.g., scale, capacity utilization, input prices, and so forth), and *noise* denotes the impact of factors that cannot be measured and are thus not included in the analysis. These other cost drivers are included in the equation to distinguish between cost reductions that are due to learning and cost reductions that are due to economies of scale or favorable positions on other cost drivers. The parameter ϵ is the percentage change in average cost per 1 percent change in cumulative experience, and γ_i is the percentage change in average cost per 1 percent change in cost driver X_i. Logarithms are used in the preceding equation, so that the estimated coefficients really are elasticities.

THE VERTICAL BOUNDARIES OF THE FIRM

3

𝒯he production of any good or service usually requires many activities. The process that begins with the acquisition of raw materials and ends with the distribution and sale of finished goods and services is known as the *vertical chain*. A central issue in business strategy is how to organize the vertical chain. In Chapter 1 we saw that in the 1840s, the vertical chain featured many intermediaries, or factors. By 1910, production was dominated by large *vertically integrated firms*, (i.e., hierarchical firms that performed many of the steps in the vertical chain themselves). The modern business landscape still features many vertically integrated firms, such as Scott Paper, which cuts its own timber, mills it, makes paper products, and distributes them to the market. Other well-known firms, such as Nike, Benetton, and even Chrysler, are vertically "disintegrated": They outsource most of the tasks in the vertical chain to independent contractors. Former Hewlett-Packard CEO John Young described outsourcing by his firm as follows: "We used to bend all the sheet metal, mold every plastic part that went into our products. We don't do those things anymore, but somebody else is doing it for us."[1] The *vertical boundaries* of a firm define the activities that the firm performs itself as opposed to purchases from independent firms in the market. Chapters 3 through 5 examine a firm's choice of its vertical boundaries and how they affect the efficiency of production.

MAKE VERSUS BUY

The decision of a firm to perform an activity itself or purchase it from an independent firm is called a *make-or-buy* decision. Typical make-or-buy decisions for a manufacturer include whether to develop its own source of raw materials, provide

---

[1]From *Chicago Tribune* February 21, 1993, section 1, p. 15.

its own shipping services, or operate its own warehouses and retail stores, rather than rely on outside suppliers and merchants. Firms at other points in the vertical chain must also come to grips with make-or-buy decisions. Raw materials suppliers can integrate forward into production, as when Alcoa began manufacturing aluminum foil in the 1920s. Retailers can integrate backward into production, as when Circuit City formed a joint venture to develop and promote the DIVX home video technology. Distributors can also integrate backward, as when Vestron, a video distributor, produced its own movie, *Dirty Dancing*, in 1987, or forward, as when John Rockefeller, who owned oil pipelines, bought refineries in the 1870s.

Upstream, Downstream

Economists often refer to one firm being "upstream" or "downstream" from another. The terms are relative—a firm may be upstream from some firms and downstream from others. In general, goods in an economy "flow" along a vertical chain from raw materials and component parts to manufacturing, through distribution and retailing. Economists say that early steps in the vertical chain are upstream in the production process, and later steps are downstream, much as lumber flows from upstream timber forests to downstream mills. Thus, Ford Motor Company is downstream from U.S. Steel but upstream to local Ford dealerships.

Figure 3.1 depicts a vertical chain for the production and sale of furniture. The vertical chain includes activities directly associated with the processing and handling of materials from raw inputs (e.g., wood) through the finished product. Processing activities include raw materials acquisition, goods processing, and assembly. Handling activities include all associated transportation and warehousing. When we discuss activities that are upstream or downstream in a production process, we are usually referring to these processing and handling activities.

The vertical chain within the modern industrial enterprise also involves a large variety of specialized support activities, such as accounting, finance, human resources management, and strategic planning. We place these services outside the vertical chain in Figure 3.1 to indicate that they support each step along the chain. As described in Chapter 1, large hierarchical enterprises in the early 1900s performed these support activities themselves to coordinate the flow of production through the vertical chain. Sometimes, these support activities became principal sources of value creation, so that many manufacturing firms today are well-known for their expertise in tasks not directly related to the production of consumer goods and services: Baxter and General Electric in strategic planning, Pepsi and Philip Morris in marketing, EG+G and Dow Corning in financial planning, United Technologies in human resource management, and Inland Steel in logistics. In entire industries, such as soft drinks and athletic footwear, support activities are the lifeblood of the major players.

While many firms have succeeded by producing their own processing, handling, and support activities, others obtain them from specialists in the market, or what we call *market firms*. (When a firm buys activities or inputs from market firms, we say that it is *using the market*; when a firm provides the activity or makes the input itself, we say that it is *vertically integrated* in that activity or input.) It is no wonder that many firms prefer to use the market for processing, handling, and support activities. The firms specializing in these activities include many recognized leaders in their fields, and they perform them as well or better than the firms they supply them to could. Examples of leading specialists in supporting functions

FIGURE 3.1
THE VERTICAL CHAIN OF PRODUCTION FOR FURNITURE.

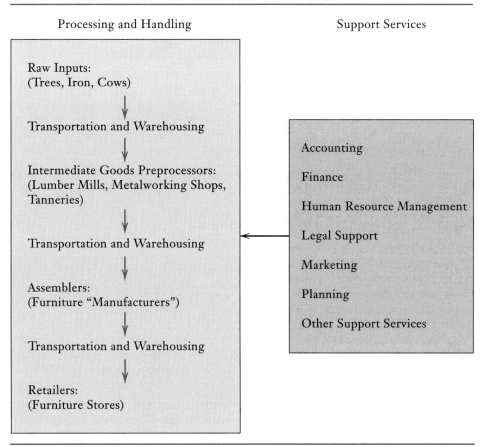

The materials necessary to make furniture are processed and handled through each step of the vertical chain. Professional support services are provided all along the chain.

include: Leo Burnett, which provides market research and creates advertisements for large industrial enterprises, such as Oldsmobile; Servicemaster, which supervises janitorial personnel for hospitals, schools, and industrial concerns; United Parcel Service, which distributes products to customers of many manufacturers and retailers; and EDS, which provides software solutions for manufacturing, distribution, and warehousing problems. Because of firms such as these, a manufacturer can obtain a superior marketing program, improve the efficiency of its housekeeping, secure rapid, low-cost distribution, and obtain accurate reports about payroll, sales, and inventories, without having to perform any of these tasks itself.

It is not always desirable to use the market, however. A firm must address certain issues before it can determine how best to coordinate the activities of its suppliers and distributors. To illustrate the key economic tradeoffs associated with make-or-buy decisions, we will present "make" and "buy" as extreme alternatives that each firm must choose for each activity in the vertical chain. In fact, there are many "intermediate" solutions to the make-or-buy problem. For example, a supplier may enter into a joint venture with a manufacturer to develop a critical component. In this way, the firms can coordinate the production of that input under a single organizational umbrella while retaining their independence for other activities. Other intermediate solutions include strategic alliances and long-term contracts. In a recent survey that we conducted in conjunction with KPMG Peat Marwick, large manufacturers reported that they relied on such intermediate solutions for 20 to 40 percent of their supply chain activities, including manufacturing and distribution. These solutions can capture some of the benefits and costs of both the make-and-buy extremes. We discuss them in greater detail in Chapter 5.

Defining Boundaries

Regardless of a firm's position along the vertical chain, it needs to define its boundaries. To resolve the associated make-or-buy decisions, the firm must compare the benefits and costs of using the market as opposed to performing the activity in-house. Table 3.1 summarizes the key benefits and costs of using market firms. These are discussed in detail in the remainder of this chapter.

Some Make-or-Buy Fallacies

Before detailing the critical determinants of make-or-buy decisions, we need to dispense with three common, but *incorrect* arguments.

1. Firms should generally buy, rather than make, to avoid the costs of making the product. This fallacy is often expressed this way: "By outsourcing an activity, we will eliminate the cost of that activity, and thereby increase earnings."
2. Firms should generally make, rather than buy, to avoid paying a profit margin to independent firms. This fallacy is often expressed this way: "Our firm should backward integrate to capture the profit of our suppliers for ourselves."
3. Firms should make, rather than buy, because a vertically integrated producer will be able to avoid paying high market prices for the input during periods of peak demand or scarce supply. This fallacy is often expressed this way: "By

TABLE 3.1
BENEFITS AND COSTS OF USING THE MARKET

Benefits
- Market firms can achieve economies of scale that in-house departments producing only for their own needs cannot.
- Market firms are subject to the discipline of the market and must be efficient and innovative to survive. Overall corporate success may hide the inefficiencies and lack of innovativeness of in-house departments.

Costs
- Coordination of production flows through the vertical chain may be compromised when an activity is purchased from an independent market firm rather than performed in-house.
- Private information may be leaked when an activity is performed by an independent market firm.
- There may be costs of transacting with independent market firms that can be avoided by performing the activity in-house.

vertically integrating, we obtain the input 'at cost,' thereby insuring ourselves against the risk of high input prices.

The first argument is easy to reject. Consider an activity on the vertical chain, say, the distribution of finished goods from a manufacturer to retailers. The manufacturer could distribute the goods itself, or use an independent distributor. While it is true that if it uses an independent distributor, the manufacturer will not have to purchase trucks, hire drivers, and so forth, this does not imply that it is less costly to use the independent distributor. The independent distributor will have to purchase the trucks and hire the drivers and will then charge the manufacturer to cover the associated expenses. Choosing to buy, rather than make, does not eliminate the expenses of the associated activity. Make-or-buy choices can, however, affect the efficiency with which the activity is carried out, which is the central argument of this chapter.

To see the flaw in the second argument, consider a manufacturer that requires a plastic part. A supplier will sell the part for $2.50. The unit cost of the part is only $2.00. It appears that the supplier of this part realizes a "profit margin" of 25 percent (i.e., $(2.50-2.00)/2.00 = .25$). The manufacturer might be tempted to backward integrate into the manufacturing of this plastic part, rather than pay such an "exorbitant" profit margin.

This could be a bad decision for several reasons. First, the profit margin of 25 percent may mask a substantial amount of variation that occurs over time. Demand for this part could slacken, for example, and the market price could therefore decline. Faced with variable prices, the investment that parts suppliers make in the plant and equipment used to produce this part is risky. The 25 percent "profit margin" may be necessary to entice their investors to supply the capital for these investments.

This points out the critical difference between *accounting profit* and *economic profit* discussed in the Economics Primer. Accounting profit is the simple difference between revenues and expenses. In this case, the plastics supplier earns an accounting profit of $0.50. Economic profit, by contrast, represents the difference between the profits earned by investing resources in a particular activity, and the profits that could have been earned by investing the same resources in the most lucrative alternative activity. Because economic profit speaks to the relative profitability of different investment decisions, it is more useful than accounting profit when making business decisions. If, in this example, a part supplier must purchase, say, $5.00 worth of plant and equipment for each part it makes, and if the best alternative use of this $5.00 per part investment yields a rate of return of 10 percent, then each part supplier earns zero economic profit per part produced: $.50 - .10(5.00) = 0$. If the manufacturer must similarly invest $5.00 in plant and equipment to make the part, and its best alternative use of funds yields a return of 10 percent, it too would earn zero economic profit should it choose to make the part itself.

The 25 percent margin may exceed the amount necessary to satisfy investors. This would be true if, for example, the necessary investment in plant and equipment is less than $5.00 per part. Then, the manufacturer might believe that it could make the part for less than it pays to its supplier. Before doing so, however, the manufacturer should ask itself the following: "If the manufacture of the plastic part is so profitable, why don't other firms compete with my supplier and drive the price down?" The answer to this question will often dissuade the manufacturer from choosing to vertically integrate. Perhaps it is difficult to obtain the expertise needed to make the desired plastic part, or maybe the existing supplier is the only one large enough to reap economies of scale. In these circumstances, the manufacturer would likely find it cheaper to pay the "exorbitant" price demanded by its supplier rather than make the part itself.

To illustrate the subtle issues raised by the third fallacy, we consider a fictitious manufacturer of log homes, Rustic Homes. Rustic Homes sells log cabins that it assembles from specially milled lumber. The market price of this lumber varies from year to year, and for this reason, Rustic's managers are contemplating backward integration into the raising and milling of trees to avoid the potentially high market prices for milled lumber. This is a tempting but fallacious reason for vertical integration.

To see why, suppose that Rustic sells its log cabins for $10,000 each. Besides the costs of milled lumber, it incurs $4,000 in labor costs for every cabin it assembles. During the next year, Rustic has 100 confirmed orders for log cabins. It contemplates two options for its raw materials needs:

1. It can purchase lumber in the open market. Rustic believes that there is a ⅓ chance that the price of the lumber needed to build one cabin will be $7,000, a ⅓ chance that the price will be $5,000, and a ⅓ chance that the price will be $3,000.
2. It can backward integrate by purchasing forest land and a lumber mill, which it will use to produce lumber for current and future needs. To finance the purchase of the land and the mill, Rustic can obtain a bank loan that entails an annual payment of $350,000. In addition, the cost of harvesting timber and milling it to produce the finished lumber for one cabin is $1,500.

Table 3.2 illustrates Rustic's annual income under these options. Under the vertical integration option, Rustic has an assured annual profit of $100,000. Under the non-integration option, Rustic's net income is uncertain: it could be $300,000, it could be $100,000, or it could be -$100,000. The expected value of this uncertain income is $100,000.[2]

TABLE 3.2
RUSTIC LOG HOMES

	Vertical Integration	Non-integration and Lumber Price Is . . .		
		$3,000	$5,000	$7,000
Revenue	$1,000,000	$1,000,000	$1,000,000	$1,000,000
Cost of Goods Sold				
Lumber	$150,000	$300,000	$500,000	$700,000
Assembly	$400,000	$400,000	$400,000	$400,000
Total	$550,000	$700,000	$900,000	$1,000,000
Interest Expense	$350,000	—	—	—
Profit	$100,000	$300,000	$100,000	($100,000)

---

[2]Expected value is found by multiplying the probability of an event by the payoff associated with that event. In this case, the expected value is (⅓) × (−100,000) + (⅓) × 100,000 + (⅓) × 300,000. = 100,000.

Even though the vertical integration and non-integration options entail the same expected profit, it is tempting to argue in favor of the vertical integration because it eliminates the firm's risk of income fluctuations. This is an especially tempting argument if management is concerned that Rustic may be liquidity constrained—that is, if it is concerned that, when lumber prices are high ($7,000), Rustic will not have enough cash to cover its loss and thus will go bankrupt. If Rustic is committed to being an ongoing business concern, according to this argument, it should vertically integrate to eliminate the risk of being unable to pay its bills.

However, these arguments are flawed. Rustic does not need to vertically integrate to eliminate its income risk. It could counteract price fluctuations by entering into long-term (i.e., futures contracts) with lumber suppliers. This is a practice known as hedging, and businesses whose products depend on raw materials that are subject to price fluctuations employ it all the time. For example, a key input in the production of margarine is soybean oil (it represents 80 percent of total materials costs), and manufacturers of margarine, such as Nabisco (producer of Blue Bonnet and Fleischmann's) and Unilever (producer of Shedd's) hedge against price fluctuations by purchasing soybean oil through futures contracts.

Even if Rustic could not hedge, the argument for vertical integration is still flawed. After all, if Rustic could raise the capital to purchase the forest land, it could instead create a capital reserve to weather short-term fluctuations in lumber prices (e.g., perhaps through a line of credit from the same bank that was willing to loan it the money to buy the land and the lumber mill). Moreover, any income risk associated with fluctuating timber prices would only be exacerbated by the purchase of timberland. Thus, concerns about risk argue *against* vertical integration.

Another possible justification for purchasing the forest is that Rustic expects the price of lumber to go up. In this case, Rustic is speculating in lumber. It is not obvious why Rustic would have an advantage over a non-integrated speculator. An exception would be if Rustic had inside knowledge of the future demand for lumber, perhaps because of private market research on the demand for log homes. But even then it should be made clear that the sole economic rationale for integration was speculation.

REASONS TO "BUY" ◆ ◆ ◆ ◆ ◆

Reasons to use the market, or "reasons to buy," are derived from a simple concept—market firms are often more efficient (i.e., they can perform the activity at lower cost or higher quality than the purchaser could if it performed the activity itself). Sometimes these efficiencies are tangible, in that they can be estimated from accounting data. Sometimes they are intangible, having more to do with incentives and "bureaucracy effects" than with anything easily tracked by accountants.

Tangible Benefits of Using the Market: Exploiting Scale and Learning Economies

In a recent survey of consumer products firms that we conducted with KPMG Peat Marwick, more than two-thirds of the respondents stated that they outsource manufacturing, transportation, or warehousing, because their independent outsourcing partners are more efficient. Market firms might be more efficient than integrated firms for several reasons. They might be able to aggregate the needs of many firms, thereby enjoying economies of scale. They might exploit their experience producing for many firms to obtain learning economies. Or, they may possess proprietary information or patents that enable them to produce at lower cost.

Chapter 2 discussed the ways in which firms can benefit from increased volume. To keep things simple here, we will assume that there are economies of scale and/or learning economies and examine their implications for vertical integration. Recall that when economies of scale or learning economies are present, firms with low production levels or little experience in production may be at a severe cost disadvantage relative to their larger, more experienced rivals. Market firms—firms that specialize in the production of an input—can often achieve greater scale, and thus lower unit costs, than can the downstream firms that use the input. The reason is that a market firm can aggregate the demands of many potential buyers, whereas a vertically integrated firm typically produces only for its own needs.

To illustrate this point, consider automobile production. An automobile manufacturer requires a vast variety of upstream inputs: steel, tires, anti-lock brakes, stereos, computer equipment, and so forth. A manufacturer, such as Chrysler, could backward integrate and produce inputs such as anti-lock brakes itself, or it could obtain them from an independent supplier, such as LucasVarity or Robert Bosch Corp.

Figure 3.2 illustrates an average cost function for anti-lock brakes. According to the figure, the production of anti-lock brakes displays declining and then constant average costs, indicating that there are economies of scale in production. In this example, the minimum efficient scale of production—the smallest level of output at which average cost is minimized—is output level A^*, with resulting average cost C^*.

Suppose that Chrysler expects to sell A'' automobiles with anti-lock brakes, where $A'' > A^*$. Thus, Chrysler expects to sell enough automobiles to achieve minimum efficient scale in the production of anti-lock brakes by producing for its own needs alone. This is seen in Figure 3.2, where the average cost of output A'' roughly equals C^*. From a cost perspective, Chrysler gets no advantage by using the market.

FIGURE 3.2
PRODUCTION COSTS AND THE MAKE-OR-BUY DECISION.

Firms need to produce quantity A^* to reach minimum efficient scale and achieve average costs of C^*. A firm that requires only A' units to meet its own needs will incur average costs of C', well above C^*. A firm that requires output in excess of A^*, such as A'', will have costs equal to C^* and will not be at a competitive disadvantage.

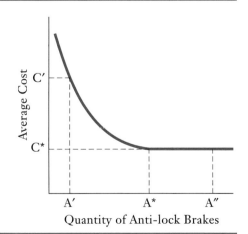

Suppose instead that Chrysler expects to sell A' automobiles with anti-lock brakes, where $A' < A^*$. In this case, Chrysler cannot achieve minimum efficient scale by producing only for its own needs. This is seen in Figure 3.2, where the average cost associated with output A', denoted C', exceeds the minimum average cost C^*. Chrysler could try to expand anti-lock brake output to A^*, thereby achieving scale economies. However, Chrysler would be producing more brakes than cars; it would have to convince other car markers to buy some of its brakes.

Other car makers might be reluctant to buy their anti-lock brakes from Chrysler when alternative sources of supply exist. (Competitors sometimes do buy inputs from each other. For example, the Taiwanese firm Giant makes frames for its own bicycles, as well as for competitors, such as Trek.) Chrysler's competitors may fear that it would use its power in the anti-lock brake market to put them at a disadvantage, either by charging higher prices or by withholding supplies during periods of peak demand. They may also fear that Chrysler would gain a strategic edge from information it obtains from sales of anti-lock brakes. While Chrysler's competitors are unwilling to buy its anti-lock brakes, Chrysler may feel that a major expansion into anti-lock brake manufacturing would distract it from its focus on automotive design and assembly. As we discuss in Chapter 6, many firms are reluctant to diversify in this manner. Thus, Chrysler may be unable and unwilling to reach minimum efficient scale in anti-lock brake production.

Alternatively, Chrysler could purchase anti-lock brakes from an independent manufacturer. There are currently four major manufacturers of anti-lock brakes, including LucasVarity. LucasVarity would reach production of A' in Figure 3.2 just from its sales to Chrysler. Because there are many more car manufacturers than there are car makers, LucasVarity will probably sell its anti-lock brakes to other car makers. This will allow it to expand output beyond A', thereby exploiting scale economies. If it passes some of these cost savings along to Chrysler, then Chrysler will prefer to buy rather than make anti-lock brakes.

Under what circumstances will LucasVarity pass along its cost savings to the downstream buyer? A basic tenet in microeconomics is that if markets are competitive, prices in those markets will approach average cost.[3] Thus, if the anti-lock brake market is competitive, market forces will drive price down toward average cost. If it is not competitive, then anti-lock brake makers may charge a price well in excess of average cost. With four major competitors, the anti-brake market probably falls somewhere between perfect competition and monopoly. LucasVarity may be able to charge a price in excess of C^*, but it could not charge a price above C'. If it did so, Chrysler could produce the anti-lock brakes itself at a lower cost. It is likely that Chrysler would be able to negotiate a price somewhere between C^* and C', so that LucasVarity earned positive profits while Chrysler enjoyed some of the benefits of using an efficient market supplier. If the other anti-lock brake manufacturers are willing to compete vigorously for Chrysler's business, Chrysler could drive a hard bargain and obtain a price at or near C^*.

"The Division of Labor Is Limited by the Extent of the Market"

When firms such as Chrysler outsource production, they usually turn to market specialists to handle the work. To become specialists, individuals or firms must often make substantial investments to develop special expertise or to achieve scale

---

[3]See the Economics Primer for a discussion of perfectly competitive markets.

SELF-INSURANCE BY BRITISH PETROLEUM

Many firms face potentially large financial losses due to events beyond their control, such as workplace accidents or acts of God. Most firms can easily bear the expense of small losses and thus "self-insure" against them. By self-insure we mean that the firm might take steps to reduce the probability or size of an adverse event, but that it bears the expense out of its operating revenues should an event occur. If the expense is large enough, it can threaten the viability of the firm. For this reason, most firms purchase insurance to hedge against large potential losses.

Insurance sellers, such as Lloyd's of London, are famous for covering the costs of catastrophic events such as the *Exxon Valdez* oil spill. It is more efficient for firms to purchase insurance against large losses from Lloyd's, rather than self-insure. Lloyd's can exploit economies of scale by (a) pooling insurance purchases from many firms, thereby spreading the risk, and (b) accessing capital from its many wealthy investors. Given the economic rationale for self-insuring small losses and outsourcing insurance against large losses, it was surprising when, in the early 1990s, British Petroleum purchased insurance to protect against losses under $10 million and self-insured against larger losses. In an interesting case study, Neil Doherty and Clifford Smith used a make-or-buy framework to explain this contrarian strategy.[4]

British Petroleum (BP) is one of the largest industrial firms in the world. Doherty and Smith observe that BP's size enables it to bear most risks without jeopardizing its viability. BP also has sufficient assets to obtain a line of credit to pay off large one-time expenses. Thus, the two main rationales for buying insurance against large losses—risk sharing and access to capital—do not apply to BP. But why does BP buy insurance against smaller losses?

Insurers do more than bear risk and provide capital; they also process and service claims, design and implement loss prevention programs, and challenge questionable claims in court. Most insurers have large databases that enable them to efficiently assess risk and evaluate loss prevention strategies. They also have experienced legal teams to challenge questionable claims. Insurance purchasers, even those as large as BP, lack these capabilities.

Insurers will have a cost advantage over BP if they have experience in the kinds of small losses that BP is likely to incur. BP may experience relatively minor losses (under $10 million) due to vehicle accidents, small fires, and industrial injuries, for example. BP estimates that it experiences nearly 2,000 such events each year, with the average event costing $30,000. Because these events occur with great frequency, and because firms in the petroleum and other industries are likely to experience similar events, independent insurers can develop expertise in dealing with them. Thus, it makes sense for BP to purchase insurance against minor risks from independent market experts.

---

[4]Doherty, N. and C. Smith, "Corporate Insurance Strategy: The Case of British Petroleum," *Journal of Applied Corporate Finance*, Fall 1993.

BP may also experience large financial losses (above $10 million) due to refinery explosions, oil spills, or tanker accidents. BP estimates that it will experience fewer than two such accidents annually and that each accident will be unique. The infrequency and uniqueness of large accidents suggests that independent insurers will not develop expertise in handling major claims.

Doherty and Smith point out two additional reasons why BP self-insures large losses. First, few insurers are willing to cover large losses, and pricing appears to be noncompetitive. As evidence, Doherty and Smith point out that during the 1980s, BP paid more than $1 billion and recovered only $250 million in claims. This suggests that insurers maintained high markups (although BP may have had unexpectedly few claims during this period). Second, insurers may be unwilling to cover large losses due to concerns that firms seeking such coverage expect the risks to be relatively high. This is known as the *adverse selection* problem and is discussed in Chapter 15.

---

economies. They will not make such investments unless demand justifies it, however, for if demand is inadequate they will not recover the cost of the investment. This is the logic underlying Adam Smith's famous theorem, "The division of labor is limited by the extent of the market." (Adam Smith is the father of laissez-faire economics. His best-known work, *Wealth of Nations*, was published in 1776.) The *division of labor* refers to the specialization of productive activities, such as when a financial analyst specializes in the analysis of startup biotech companies. The *extent of the market* refers to the magnitude of demand for these activities, in this case the demand for financial advice about startup biotech companies. Although Smith referred mainly to specialization by individuals, his ideas apply equally well to specialization by firms.

Smith's theorem implies that an individual must make up-front investments of time and/or money to develop special skills. For example, the financial analyst may need to spend a year researching the biotech industry before having the credibility to compete for clients, or a computer programmer may need to spend six months learning Java language before landing a job. These investments may also involve fixed capital, such as when a jeweler purchases a high-temperature furnace necessary to work with platinum, or a graphics designer purchases a computer work station. These investments cannot be scaled down if market demand is low. For example, the financial analyst must spend several months obtaining basic factual knowledge about the biotech industry, whether he or she subsequently serves 1 client or 100 clients. The computer programmer must learn the basics of Java to write 1 program or 100 programs. By their nature, these investments cannot be recouped unless subsequent demand is large enough, implying that individuals will not make them unless demand is high. Hence, the division of labor is limited by the extent of the market.

Smith's theorem also implies that the growth in the demand for activities over time (e.g., due to population or income growth) ought to be accompanied by increasing specialization in the provision of those activities. Much casual evidence supports this implication. Financial analysts once studied entire industries; now, many specialize in individual companies. Full-service automobile service stations have been replaced by self-service gasoline retailers, specialty muffler shops, and 10-

XAMPLE 3.2

THE DIVISION OF LABOR IN MEDICAL MARKETS

An interesting application of Smith's theorem involves the specialization of medical care. In the United States, physicians may practice general medicine or specialty medicine. "Generalists" and "specialists" differ in both the amount of training they receive and the skill with which they practice. Take the case of surgery. To become general surgeons, medical school graduates spend three to four years in a surgical residency. They are then qualified to perform a wide variety of surgical procedures. Because their training is broad, general surgeons do all kinds of surgery with good, but not necessarily great, skill.

Contrast this with the training and skills of a thoracic surgeon. Thoracic surgeons specialize in the thoracic region, between the neck and the abdomen. To become a thoracic surgeon, a medical school graduate must complete a residency in general surgery, and then an additional three-year residency in thoracic surgery. Figure 3.3 depicts average "cost" curves for thoracic surgery performed by a general surgeon and a thoracic surgeon. We use "cost" in quotes because it represents the full cost of care, which is lower if a more effective cure is achieved. The average cost curves are downward sloping to reflect the spreading out of the initial investments in training. The cost curve for the thoracic surgeon starts off much higher than the cost curve for the general surgeon because of the greater investment in time. However, the thoracic surgeon's cost curve eventually falls below the cost curve of a general surgeon because the thoracic surgeon will perform thoracic surgery more effectively than most general surgeons will. The result could be fewer complications, shorter hospital stays, and greater overall success.

FIGURE 3.3
COST CURVES FOR GENERAL AND THORACIC SURGEONS.

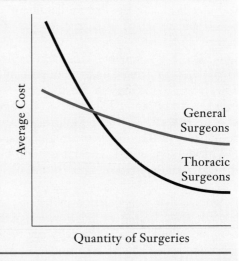

General surgeons incur lower training costs than do thoracic surgeons, but usually are less efficient in performing thoracic surgery. Thus, the general surgeon's average cost curve is below the thoracic surgeon's for low volumes (reflecting lower average fixed costs) but above the thoracic surgeon's for high volumes (reflecting higher average variable costs).

FIGURE 3.4
COST AND DEMAND FOR THORACIC SURGERY.

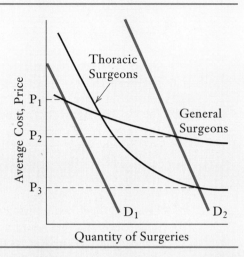

At low demands (D_1) general surgeons may be able to cover their average costs but thoracic surgeons may not. At high demands (D_2) thoracic surgeons may be able to offer lower effective prices than can general surgeons (where the effective price to the consumer includes the costs associated with ineffective surgery).

According to Smith's theorem, when the demand for thoracic surgery in a market is low, then the market will not support a specialized surgeon. Instead, thoracic surgery will be performed by a general surgeon, who may also perform other kinds of surgery. This may be seen in Figure 3.4, which superimposes demand curves over cost curves. For low levels of demand, such as at D_1, the market can support a general surgeon. As long as the general surgeon charges a price for thoracic surgery above P, he or she can more than cover average costs. When demand is D_1, the market cannot support a thoracic surgeon. There is no price high enough to enable thoracic surgeons to recoup their initial investment in time.

When demand increases to D_2, the market can support a thoracic surgeon. As long as the thoracic surgeon charges a price above P_3, he or she can cover average costs. Moreover, at prices between P_2 and P_3, the thoracic surgeon can make a profit, but the general surgeon cannot. Thus, at this high level of demand, the thoracic surgeon can drive the general surgeon from the market for thoracic surgery. At the same time that the demand for thoracic surgery has increased sufficiently to support a thoracic surgeon, we might expect the demand for other specialized surgeons to increase also. Thus, in large markets, we may expect to see a range of specialized surgeons, and few or no general surgeons.

Researchers at the RAND Corporation documented this pattern of the division of labor in medical markets.[5] They found that general practitioners are disproportionately located in smaller towns—they do not appear to fare well in larger markets, which have a wider assortment of specialists. James Baumgardner also found that physicians who practice in small towns treat a wider range of illnesses than their big city counterparts do.[6]

[5]Newhouse, J. et al., "Does the Geographic Distribution of Physicians Reflect Market Failure?" *Bell Journal of Economics* 13(2), 1982: 493–505.

[6]Baumgardner, J., "What Is a Specialist Anyway?" Duke University, Mimeo, 1991.

minute oil change shops. Internal forecasting and planning departments in hierarchical firms have yielded to specialty firms in marketing and consulting. Pet stores have given way to dog grooming salons and aquarium shops. Smith's theorem also predicts that larger markets will support a more specialized array of activities than smaller markets can. This, too, is consistent with what we observe. For example, while the finest restaurants in many small cities offer "Continental cuisine" and those in medium-sized cities offer French cuisine, restaurants in larger markets are highly specialized—one Chicago restaurant focuses exclusively on the cooking of Alsace, a region of eastern France. Although specialization is no guarantee of quality, the associated investments of time and resources frequently do pay off—the Alsatian restaurant is regarded as one of the finest restaurants in the nation.

Smith's theorem also sheds light on the growth of the hierarchical firm described in Chapter 1. In a small market, the entrepreneurial firm must perform all of the tasks in the vertical chain because the market cannot support specialists in accounting, marketing, distribution, and such. Specialists emerge in larger markets, and the growing firm can use them for many activities. When the market gets even larger, the demand for the firm's product may become so great that the firm can produce enough of its inputs in-house to fully exploit available economies of scale. The firm makes the necessary investments to develop human and physical capital, thereby adding to its corporate hierarchy. For example, the volume of demand for processing the paperwork created by its Discover Card is so great that Sears could not find a market firm large enough to handle the job. Sears handles payment processing, statement mailing, and even statement embossing itself.

Intangible Benefits of Using the Market: Agency and Influence Effects

Market firms enjoy a number of benefits related to incentives. Though difficult to quantify, these intangible benefits can give market firms an advantage over their integrated rivals.

Agency Costs

Managers and workers make many decisions that contribute to the profitability of a firm. Examples include how hard to work, how much to invest in innovation, and how many employees to keep on the payroll. When managers and workers knowingly do not act in the best interests of their firm, we say that they are *slacking*. *Agency costs* are the costs associated with slack effort and with the administrative controls to deter slack effort. A vivid example of agency costs is provided by the case of Crown, Cork, and Seal, a producer of metal cans. When John Connelly became an outside director of Crown, Cork and Seal in 1956, he found an organization full of slack. According to one story, Connelly was escorted through a Crown manufacturing plant by a foreman who sang as they walked. The singing alerted workers, who were all hard at work when Connelly greeted them. Connelly asked the foreman to stop singing and continued the tour alone. He found some workers asleep; those who were not, were playing cards. The next year Connelly took over the presidency of Crown, Cork and Seal, and promptly laid off nearly a fourth of the workers.[7]

---

[7]"The Unoriginal Ideas that Rebuilt Crown Cork," *Fortune* October, 1962: pp. 118–164.

Agency costs may be as simple as overstaffing or using express mail when regular mail will do. Agency costs can affect the firm's bottom line, but within divisions of a large vertically integrated firm, they may go unnoticed by top management. A division in a large firm usually has a captive market for its output. In addition, when there are common overhead or joint costs that are allocated across divisions, top management cannot easily measure an individual division's contribution to overall corporate profitability. The absence of market competition, coupled with difficulties in measuring divisional performance, make it hard for top management to know just how well an internal division is doing relative to its best achievable performance. This, in turn, gives division managers the latitude to engage in behavior that cuts into corporate profits.

Agency costs can be especially problematic when the in-house division performing an activity is a *cost center*. A cost center is a department or division that performs an activity solely for the firm of which it is a part. That is, a cost center generates no revenue from outside the firm. An example of a cost center would be the laundry service in a hospital or the data processing department in a bank. It is often difficult to evaluate the efficiency of cost centers within firms because there is often no obvious market test based on profitability for judging their performance. In addition, it is often hard to obtain the data needed for "benchmarking" the efficiency of the cost center against the performance of similar cost centers in other firms.

Even when it is aware of agency costs, management may find it less costly to ignore them than to eliminate them. For example, many firms are unwilling to endure the ill-will generated by firing a nonproductive worker who is near retirement age. The unwillingness of top management to eliminate agency costs farther down in the organization is itself an agency cost. This is particularly likely if the vertically integrated firm possesses some inherent advantages in the market that insulates it from competition and relieves top management from the pressure of controlling agency costs. The famous economist Frederick von Hayek pointed out, "How easy it is for an inefficient manager to dissipate the differentials on which profitability rests."[8]

In principle, one could replicate internally the incentives of market firms by judiciously designing contracts that tie employees' pay and/or department budgets to specific measures of performance or effort. Chapter 15 explores the role of incentives contracts in eliminating slack. Incentive-based pay has become increasingly common in U.S. firms. In the mid-1990s, a divisional manager in a typical large U.S. firm received bonuses and long-term incentives (e.g., stock options) that totaled more than 45 percent of annual total compensation.[9] (The CEO of such a firm received bonuses and long-term incentives that totaled 65 percent of total compensation.) The goal of incentive-based pay is to present the managers of an internal division with approximately the same "high-power" profit incentives that they would face if they were the owners of a market firm that performed the same activity. As we will see in Chapter 15, however, a limitation of incentive-based pay is that managers (like most people) are risk-averse, that is, they do not like the

---

[8] "The Use of Knowledge in Society," *American Economic Review*, 35, September 1945: pp. 519–530.

[9] *The Hay Report: Compensation Strategies for 1995 and Beyond*, Philadelphia, PA; Hay Consulting, 1996.

fluctuations in year-to-year income that incentive pay can produce. Thus, in exchange for facing "higher-power" incentives, risk averse managers may also demand higher-base-level compensation, and may resist efforts to fully tie pay to performance.

One activity for which firms have worked hard to "replicate" the high-power incentives of the market is innovation. Large companies, such as 3M, Merck, and SGI, often rely on judiciously designed incentives to promote innovation. For example, Cray Research, a division of SGI, provided the seed money for Circuit Tools, a firm jointly owned by a Cray employee who developed an application of the Cray supercomputer for testing other high-tech equipment. This encouraged other Cray employees to develop supercomputer applications. On the other hand, Cray could not come to terms with Stephen Chen, the developer of the first parallel processing supercomputer, when Chen demanded $50 million in development funds for a new generation of supercomputers. Ironically, Chen was lured away by IBM, which provided more than $100 million in funding. Chen never developed a marketable product for them.

Internal mechanisms for promoting innovation can break down for a number of reasons. As IBM's experience with Chen demonstrates, it can be difficult to determine the scientific merits of proposals to do innovative work. It may also be difficult to assign specific responsibility for ideas or efforts that lead to breakthroughs. The firm may decide to base its reward systems on easy-to-measure dimensions, such as the number of new products brought to market per year. But this may bias innovation efforts toward short-term but low-reward activities (e.g., incremental improvements on existing products) and away from riskier ventures with longer-term and more lucrative profits. Some critics of the U.S. pharmaceutical industry claim that during the 1980s it shifted its research in exactly this way. If this is true (and it is hard to document), it could be traced to regulations in the 1960s to 1980s that made it easier to obtain marketing approval for generic drugs and more costly to get approval for truly novel drugs. Regulations in the 1990s have sought to reverse this undesirable trend by reducing the costs of obtaining approval for novel drugs, and the industry has responded with several breakthroughs.

Without special mechanisms to reward innovation, such as seed money, firms may choose to raise the salaries of innovative employees to spur innovation. For example, research universities normally pay higher salaries to the most productive research faculty. It may be difficult, however, to implement salary schedules that fully reflect differences in productivity. It has been estimated that researchers within the same scientific discipline can differ in their productivity, as measured by the number of publications, by a factor of 50 or more.[10] Salary schedules within most organizations, especially in the public sector, are unlikely to reflect such differences, whether for political or social reasons. Indeed, one study found that to win a 10 percent raise, research workers must increase their publications by 30 to 50 percent. This compression of the salary structure is a disincentive to the most innovative workers to continue working their hardest. As a result, they may leave for smaller firms, where the financial rewards may be greater.

---

[10]Schockley, W., "Variations of Individual Productivity in Research Laboratories," *IEEE*, December 1957: pp. 279–280.

Influence Costs

Another class of costs that arise when transactions are organized internally is what Paul Milgrom and John Roberts have called *influence costs*.[11] Milgrom and Roberts observe that firms allocate financial and human resources to internal divisions and departments through "internal capital markets." If internal capital is scarce, then when resources are allocated to one division or department, fewer resources are available to be allocated to others. Influence costs are the costs of activities to influence internal capital markets. Influence costs not only include the direct costs of influence activities (e.g., the time consumed by a division manager lobbying central management to overturn a decision that is unfavorable to his or her division), they also include the costs of bad decisions that arise from influence activities (e.g., resources that are misallocated because an inefficient division knows how to lobby for scarce resources). As with agency costs, a large vertically integrated firm may be prone to influence costs that a smaller, independent firm, might avoid.

◆ ◆

MAKE VERSUS BUY: PEPSI-COLA AND ITS BOTTLERS

When the cola industry began, the two major suppliers were Coca-Cola and Pepsi-Cola. Coke and Pepsi were primarily syrup manufacturers. They obtained raw materials, such as caramel and sugar, from independent suppliers and relied on independent bottlers to distribute and market their products. This allowed Coke and Pepsi to protect the source of their advantage in the market—their syrup formulas—while using independent firms to perform all other tasks. This division of labor made sense. Upstream inputs like caramel and sugar can be obtained from competitive markets at prices at or near minimum average cost. Downstream bottlers knew their local consumers better than did the Pepsi and Coke corporate offices, and could better judge the need for price discounts and other marketing ploys.

As the market for cola has grown, Coke and Pepsi have continued to obtain raw inputs from the market. However, both of them, especially Pepsi, have increasingly consolidated distribution and marketing. Whereas Pepsi at one time relied exclusively on independent bottlers, it now owns over 60 percent of its bottling operations.[12]

---

[11]Milgrom, P. and J. Roberts, "Bargaining Costs, Influence Costs, and the Organization of Economic Activity," in *Perspectives on Positive Political Economy*, J. Alt and K. Shepsle, eds., Cambridge: Cambridge University Press, 1990.

[12]Coke is the largest shareholder of Coca-Cola Enterprises, its largest bottler, and is part owner of many other "independent" bottlers.

Timothy Muris, David Scheffman, and Pablo Spiller have identified several important reasons for the consolidation of ownership of cola bottlers.[13] Changes in the technology of bottling have created economies of scale that have reduced the number of bottling plants by 85 percent. Roughly 5 percent of existing bottling plants continue to close each year, their output taken up by expanding existing facilities. The remaining independent bottlers are larger and more strongly committed to their own marketing philosophies. This became a large problem for cola makers, who found that in the 1980s they needed to substantially increase the coordination of their retailing activities across the different regions served by bottlers.

The need for increased coordination of retailing activities can be traced to several changes in marketing. First, the 1970s and 1980s saw the emergence of regional and national purchasers of cola products, including major grocery chains, discount retailers, and fast-food outlets. Retailers, such as Wal-Mart, purchase soft drinks through a national office and use sophisticated sales information to design their own marketing plans. Coke and Pepsi need to be equally centralized and sophisticated to service these customers. Second, Coke and Pepsi increasingly use sophisticated advertising and promotions—the "Pepsi Challenge" is a good example—as a major competitive weapon. These require a strong national marketing campaign and the cooperation of bottlers in implementing the promotions across different territories.

Coke and Pepsi must determine how to coordinate the marketing and distribution functions when there are important national and local components. Pepsi found that its national marketing themes and campaigns often conflicted with those of local bottlers. In one instance, Pepsi distributors promoted a "real fruit" display for Pepsi Slice while Pepsi's national marketing division was pushing an end-of-aisle display by offering VCRs to store managers. Neither promotion was fully implemented, and Pepsi was left with a surplus of VCRs. The solution to the coordination problem has been simple—Pepsi has bought out many of its bottlers and centralized its marketing activities.

As the following excerpt shows, supply relationships within General Motors nicely illustrate how influence activity can harm a vertically integrated firm:

> Let's take the example of one of GM's in-house suppliers. We'll imagine the program manager for a new GM product is unhappy with the in-house supplier's bid—it's too high and in the past the supplier had quality and delivery problems. However, no sooner does the manager identify an alternative bidder outside the company than the in-house supplier goes to corporate headquarters and explains the loss of business on his part will require an increase in the costs of similar parts already being supplied by other GM products. Why? Because economies of scale will be lost and the in-house supplier will have excess capacity.
>
> Headquarters, always respectful of scale-economy and capacity-utilization justifications in a mass production firm such as GM, then has a talk with the program

---

[13]Muris, T., D. Scheffman, and P. Spiller, "Strategy and Transaction Costs: The Organization of Distribution in the Carbonated Soft Drink Industry," *Journal of Economics and Management Strategy*, 1, Summer 1992: pp. 83–128.

manager. The in-house supplier makes solemn promises to try harder to reduce costs in the future while improving quality and delivery reliability—and gets the business. In this way, the internal market, which supposedly keeps the in-house supply divisions honest, is gradually diluted. This process explains how GM managed to have both the world's highest production volume and the world's highest costs in many of its components supply divisions through much of the last decade.[14]

COSTS OF USING THE MARKET ◆ ◆ ◆ ◆ ◆

The three major costs associated with using the market include the costs of poor coordination between steps in the vertical chain, the reluctance of trading partners to develop and share valuable information, and transactions costs. Each of these problems can be traced to costs associated with writing and enforcing contracts. We discuss the coordination and information issues in this chapter, and explain why firms may be unable to solve these problems using contracts. Chapter 4 describes the contracting problem in more detail and the transactions costs of doing business when contracts are costly.

Coordination of Production Flows Through the Vertical Chain

A key to exploiting of economies of scale is the coordination of production flows throughout the vertical chain, from raw materials acquisition, through production, to finished goods distribution. For coordination to succeed, players must make decisions that depend, in part, on the decisions of others. Suppliers must plan for and produce adequate supplies of the right quality and design. Distributors must be able to transport and warehouse the goods. Retailers must have appropriate space and the right marketing concept. Without good coordination, bottlenecks may arise. The failure of one supplier to deliver parts on schedule can shut down a factory. A failure to coordinate advertising images across local markets can undermine a brand's image and dampen sales.

To protect against coordination problems, firms often rely on contracts. Contracts may specify delivery dates, design tolerances, or other performance targets. If a supplier fails to meet the specified targets, it might have to pay a penalty. Alternatively, if they exceed expectations, they might receive a bonus. For example, construction firms often receive a bonus if they finish their work ahead of schedule. Firms may also assure coordination in the vertical chain by relying on *merchant coordinators*, independent firms that specialize in linking suppliers, manufacturers, and retailers. Example 3.4 discusses a successful Polish merchant coordinator of furniture manufacturing.

The use of contracts and middlemen clauses is widespread, yet in some circumstances the protections afforded by contracts and middlemen may be inadequate. Paul Milgrom and John Roberts explain that coordination is especially important in processes with "design attributes," which are attributes that need to relate to each

---

[14]Womack, J., D. Jones, and D. Roos, *The Machine that Changed the World: The Story of Lean Production*, New York: HarperCollins, 1990, p. 143.

Example 3.4

Jagram[15]

Though the need for tight coordination across stages in the vertical chain can be an important motivation for vertical integration, coordination can sometimes be facilitated by market firms. An example of such a firm is Jagram, a Polish seller of wooden garden furniture. In Poland's chaotic macroeconomic and business environment, Jagram's success is based on its ability to coordinate the stages of the vertical chain.

Prior to 1990, the wood processing and furniture industry in Poland consisted of a small number of vertically integrated state-owned enterprises (SOEs). These SOEs comprised hundreds of small factories which performed all tasks on the vertical chain, from acquisition of timber to distribution of final product to stores. The collapse of communism created an opportunity for new types of market-oriented firms to arise in the wood products sector. Jagram has been one of the most successful of these firms. Founded by two multilingual Polish entrepreneurs, Jagram is primarily a marketing and sales company. Jagram's chosen niche is wooden garden furniture, which includes everything from picnic tables to grape arbors. The firm's customers are the Western European "DIY" (Do-it-Yourself) stores. The business is highly seasonal, with nearly all production occurring during the winter months so that the chains can have their merchandise on display by the spring. Timing is thus an essential success factor for firms that seek to supply products to these chains.

Jagram owns almost no physical assets except for one small factory that accounts for less than 10 percent of its total revenues. Instead, Jagram signs supply contracts with dozens of formerly state-owned wood processing factories. Due to the collapse of traditional Soviet-era markets, tremendous overcapacity exists in the Polish wood processing sector, and managers are eager for contracts which keep their factories afloat. Because these managers are generally unaccustomed to production to Western standards, Jagram often plays an important quality assurance role. To ensure that necessary equipment is on hand, Jagram will sometimes lease its own name machinery, which it installs on its suppliers' premises. Jagram is able to achieve economies of scale by combining the production of several factories to attain full truckloads. Because Jagram ships so much, it is able to negotiate better contracts with shipping companies than any of its suppliers could acting alone.

In response to requests from its manufacturer/suppliers, Jagram also started a wood-trading division of the company, which searches Eastern Europe and Russia for the best prices on freshly cut timber. Due to its suppliers' poor cash position, Jagram will often finance the purchase of wood, the initial sawmill cutting and the transport to the manufacturer, for which it takes a generous share of the producer's margin.

---

[15]We are grateful to Christopher Meyer for researching and writing this example.

Jagram has profited from its deep understanding of its customers' requirements and the limitations faced by its upstream suppliers. Jagram's founders note that whenever either their DIY customers or Polish suppliers have tried to circumvent Jagram, the attempt has never succeeded for more than one transaction. Jagram is able to coordinate the vertical chain so effectively because its products are relatively simple to make, rarely requiring the involvement of more than one production facility, and because product quality is not supremely important in garden furniture. For more complicated products with higher quality thresholds, the Jagram model may not be feasible. Western indoor furniture manufacturers, for instance, have for quality control reasons found it necessary to acquire and integrate their Polish factories into their existing network.

other in a precise fashion, otherwise they lose a significant portion of their economic value.[16] Table 3.3 lists activities that are, and are not, design attributes. What the former have in common but the latter lack is that small errors can be exceptionally costly. For example, a slight delay in delivering a critical component can shut down a manufacturing plant. On the other hand, a slight delay in completing a construction project may be inconvenient, but is unlikely to be critical.

With design attributes, the downstream firm often understands how the various inputs and outputs should relate to each other, but the various input suppliers may not adequately coordinate with each other. The failure to achieve the proper relationship among inputs can be costly. As a result, it often makes sense to integrate all critical upstream and downstream activities and rely on administrative control to achieve the appropriate coordination, rather than rely on independent firms and hope that coordination emerges automatically through the market mechanism. These issues may be illustrated more thoroughly by considering a problem that arises each year at many business schools—the production of photocopies in advance of the first day of class.

TABLE 3.3
EXAMPLES OF DESIGN ATTRIBUTES

Are Design Attributes	Are Not Design Attributes
Timely delivery of part necessary for manufacturing process to begin	Timely completion of building construction
Sequencing of courses in MBA curriculum	Sequencing of sports activities in summer camp
Fit of automobile sunroof glass in opening of auto roof.	Fit of bicycle handlebar covers on handlebars.
Matching colors of sportswear ensembles within narrow tolerances	Matching sizes of sportswear ensembles within narrow tolerance

[16]Milgrom, P. and J. Roberts, *Economics, Organization and Management*, Englewood Cliffs, NJ: Prentice-Hall, 1992.

The timing of delivery of photocopies is often crucial in business education. Weeks before the beginning of classes, dozens of professors at each major business school assemble reading packets for their courses. Each packet may contain dozens of articles, each of which must be photocopied for every student in the class. A single business school may require millions of pages to be photocopied, collated, and assembled into course packets.

Business schools can prepare reading packets on their own photocopying equipment, or outsource production to a photocopying specialist. One advantage of outsourcing is that the independent specialist can achieve the scale economies needed to support low cost–high volume copiers. Another advantage is that the school can play one copying service against another, obtaining competitive prices. Outsourcing production creates a potentially severe coordination problem, however, because the reading packets must be available when classes begin. If packets are late, students and professors may lack necessary materials for lectures and case discussions. This can permanently disrupt the course curriculum.

The coordination problem is represented by Figure 3.5. The X-axis depicts a time line, beginning well before the first day of class and ending after classes are underway. The Y-axis measures benefits and costs of delaying production, in dollar terms. The curve labeled MC^1 represents the marginal cost to the school of each additional day of delay in reading packet production. This is initially zero—as

FIGURE 3.5
THE COORDINATION PROBLEM IN THE PRODUCTION OF READING PACKETS.

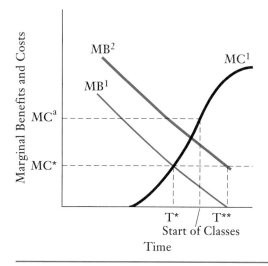

The curve labeled MC^1 represents the marginal cost to the school of delaying case packet production by an additional day. It is initially 0 well before the start of classes, but it rises rapidly as the start of school approaches. For example, if the readings packets have not yet arrived by the start of classes, the cost of an additional day of delay is MC^a. The curve labeled MB^1 is the marginal benefit to the copying service of delaying production. The optimal time of delivery occurs at date T^*, where MC^1 equals MB^1. If the school offers the copy service a flat fee for copy services, independent of the delivery date, the copy service will maximize profits by setting MB^1 equal to zero, and delivering the readings packets on date T^{**}. If the school offers the copy service a contract that imposes a late fee of MC^* for each day of delay, but the actual marginal benefit curve for the copy service is MB^2, then the copy service would deliver the packets by date T^{**} as well.

long as copies are available well before the start of classes, there is no cost of an additional day's delay. As the start of school approaches, marginal costs rise rapidly. For example, if the reading packets have not arrived by the day that classes start, the cost of an additional day's delay is MC^a. Eventually, the school will begin copying itself, limiting further costs. The sharply rising portion of the MC curve indicates a design attribute—a small departure from desired performance creates a large cost.

The curve labeled MB^1 represents the marginal benefit to the copying service of delaying the completion of reading packets. The copying service, like most firms and individuals, would rather put off the copying job than do it immediately. It benefits from delay for at least two reasons. First, it can spread out production over several days or weeks, thereby taking advantage of idle capacity (both idle machines and idle workers). This lowers the effective cost of production. Second, it can squeeze in additional business from customers who are under even greater time pressure. The benefits of delay often show up directly in price—the copying service may charge a premium if the work must be completed right away, and will reduce price if it can do the work as time permits. In Figure 3.5, MB^1 is downward sloping. This indicates that the incremental benefits of delay are high when the delay is short, but diminish as the work is pushed back further. Eventually MB^1 might even be negative, since the copying service wastes time and energy responding to irate students and faculty.

An efficient contract would equate the marginal cost of delay to the school and the marginal benefit of delay to the copying service.[17] This occurs at time T^* in Figure 3.5. Although the school bears some cost of delay, it prefers this time to earlier times because the copy service can pass on the considerable benefits of delay to the school in the form of a lower price. But can the school be sure that the copies will be ready by time T^*? Probably not. If the school offered a fixed fee for completing the job, the copying service would not finish the job until T^{**}, the time at which MB^1 equals zero.[18] The school could instead set a stiff fine for any delivery after time T^*. But this would punish the copying service even if the late delivery were not its fault. For example, a dispute over permission to copy a copyrighted article might delay reproduction through no fault of the copying service. The copying service may be unwilling to assume such risk, and the service and the school may be unwilling to bear the legal costs needed to resolve disputes.

Another solution is to impose a fixed per diem late fee. If the late fee is set equal to the marginal benefit of delay at time T^*, or MC^* in Figure 3.5, then the copying service will find it optimal to aim for completion by that time, because penalty for additional delay, MC^*, would exceed the marginal benefit. Many delivery contracts, such as those for highway construction and seasonal retail merchandise, have such late fees. The late fee may not be very effective for the business school, however. To see why not, suppose that the business school slightly miscal-

---

[17]If the marginal benefit of delay exceeded the marginal cost of delay, the school would benefit by an increase in the delay period. If the marginal benefit of delay was less than the marginal cost of delay, the school would benefit by a decrease in the delay time.

[18]This is because under a fixed fee, the marginal cost of delay, *as perceived by the copying service*, is zero. The copying service maximizes its profits by choosing the delivery date at which its marginal benefit from delay equals its marginal cost of delay.

culates the MB curve for the copying service. That is, suppose that the school believes that the marginal benefit curve is MB^1, but that the actual curve is MB^2. If the contract imposes a late penalty of MC^*, then the copying service will aim for completion by time T^{**}. But this is too late for the school, whose students and faculty suffer substantially from even a short delay.

There is a critical difference between highway construction and seasonal merchandise, on the one hand, and reading packet preparation, on the other. In the former cases, each additional day of delay is about as costly as the previous day's delay. Thus, the failure of the outsourcing firm to comply perfectly with the contract does not create substantial costs. Not so for reading packet preparation, where delays around the start of class are much more costly than delays just a week or two prior. Thus, contract failure can lead to very costly delays.

The decision to make or buy copying services is a balancing act. On the one hand, independent copying centers can exploit economies of scale and must be efficient to survive. On the other hand, coordination costs of using an independent service can be high. If the school believes that by producing packets internally it can do a better job of assuring completion by T^*, then it might prefer to "make" packets. (We discuss why internal decision making may solve such contracting problems in Chapter 5.) Some schools, such as the University of Chicago Graduate School of Business, handle reading packet preparation internally, whereas others, such as the Kellogg Graduate School of Management, use the market. Interestingly, both schools obtain copyright permissions internally. This necessary task for reading packet production also presents coordination problems, but it does not involve significant scale economies. Hence, it makes sense to perform it internally.

A high marginal cost curve, which indicates that total costs rise rapidly as performance deviates from desired levels, is the hallmark of a potential coordination problem. As in the photocopying example, the marginal cost curve may describe the marginal cost associated with delayed delivery of an input. Another example is the development of applications software for CareMark, which provides home intravenous drug infusion therapy for patients with AIDS, cancer, and other illnesses. Software development time often determines time-to-market for new drug therapies, and delays can be costly. The marginal cost curve may describe other critical determinants of success. For example, it may describe the cost of failing to achieve a precise fit of a silicon wafer or a desired style. This could be extremely costly for matching the desired colors for fabrics used by Benetton, for example. When small errors in a component or task can lead to large costs, the manufacturer may abandon the market price system and make the component or perform the task itself. Each of the firms in these examples makes the critical inputs or performs the critical tasks itself.

Leakage of Private Information

A firm's *private information* is information that no one else knows. Private information often gives a firm an advantage in the market. It may pertain to production know-how, product design, or consumer information. When firms use the market to obtain supplies or distribute products, they risk losing control of valuable private information. Speaking about relying on outside Japanese suppliers, a vice president of technology and market development for Xerox stated, "It's not a

Example 3.5

Made in Italy?[19]

When it comes to clothing, the label "Made in Italy" conjures up unrivaled quality and fashion. Traditionally, clothing from well-known design houses, such as Armani, Versace, and Gaultier, are designed and manufactured exclusively in Italy. But faced with rising cost pressures due to high domestic wages and declining margins due to global tariffs and a strong lire, many Italian clothing manufacturers have begun outsourcing production to firms in other nations. These manufacturers send production designs, fabrics, buttons, and so forth, to "cut-make-trim" (CMT) firms to assemble the garments. In 1997, roughly one-sixth of all Italian clothing was produced by CMT firms elsewhere, and that figure was expected to increase.

The advantage of outsourcing clothing manufacturing is readily apparent by considering that the average Italian apparel worker makes more than $15 per hour, second globally only to Germany. Workers in North Africa, the Mideast, Eastern Europe, and Asia earn just a fraction of that. That is why Miroglio, a leading manufacturer of bridge collections, and Diesel, a designer of trendy "urban" clothes, outsource roughly half their production to other nations.

But not all Italian manufacturers are convinced that the cost savings from outsourcing are worth it. Ittierre SpA, which produces sportswear for several top design labels including Versace and Ferre, keeps everything domestic. Managing director Giancarlo Di Risio explained it this way: "It would be unthinkable for a Versace dress not to be made in Italy . . . If the dress were made in Hong Kong it wouldn't have a soul."[20] Other Italian manufacturers have offered more concrete reasons for maintaining domestic production. Diesel produces all of its top-selling, five-pocket jeans in Italy. Diesel principal Renzo Rosso explains that this gives Diesel control over sizes, styles, and colors, thereby assuring retailers that they will always have the necessary stock of this fast-moving product. Aeffe, which manufactures for Moschino and Gaultier, among others, remains 100 percent Italian. Its chairman, Massimo Ferritti, echoes Rosso's concerns about logistics and delivery times as reasons for not outsourcing. He adds, "The issue isn't only a question of sewing a garment. It has to do with the full range of work that the Italian (manufacturing) companies offer, from the interpretation of a designer's sketch to the support and know-how and the follow-up." Silvano Storer, executive at Marzotto SpA (which manufacturers for Ferre and Missoni), puts it differently, "It is those that manage the brands that are successful, not so much the production process."

It is simplistic to frame the outsourcing question as a tradeoff between labor costs and logistics and fashion. Miroglio actually owns its foreign factories. It be-

---

[19]Most of the information for this example is from Forden, S. G., "Pride versus profits: Italian makers confront offshare production," *WWD*, March 18, 1997.

[20]Forden, S., "Pride versus profits: Italian makers confront offshore production," *WWD*, March 18, 1997.

lieves that it can obtain lower-cost labor while retaining greater control over scheduling and other coordination issues. Benetton remains 100 percent Italian, but has controlled labor costs by investing in a capital intensive manufacturing and distribution system. One additional issue: Those firms that outsource production to developing nations today may gain earlier access to these nations' retail markets in the future.

game for the naive player. It demands careful study. If you bungle a relationship with the Japanese, you can lose your technology, your business."[21]

Benetton and Hewlett-Packard (HP) have used the market judiciously because of their concern over leakage of valuable private information. While Benetton contracts out many production and distribution activities, it selects dyes and designs and does the actual dyeing of fabrics in-house. These activities are generally regarded as the source of its advantage in the market. By keeping them in-house, Benetton has limited competitors' ability to discover and master its secrets. Until 1995, HP relied on Canon to produce the engines for its laser printers. When HP and Canon reached this agreement, HP denied Canon access to the PCL software that differentiates HP printers from those of competitors. Without this access, Canon has been unable to clone HP's laser printers and has a relatively small presence in the laser printer market.

As with the coordination problem, firms sometimes rely on contracts to protect themselves against leakage of critical information. A good example is "non-compete clauses." Many professionals must sign non-compete clauses when they join a firm. These clauses state that should the individual leave the firm, he or she may not directly compete with it for several years. Protected by the non-compete clause, the firm is can reveal important competitive information to its new employees, such as client lists or expert contacts. Although non-compete clauses are generally effective, in other cases contracts do not provide much protection.

Transactions Costs

The concept of transactions costs was first described by Ronald Coase in his famous paper "The Nature of the Firm."[22] Coase raised the following question: In light of the efficiencies of the competitive market mechanism emphasized in economic theory, why does so much economic activity take place outside the price system (i.e., within firms in which market transactions are replaced by centralized direction)? Coase concluded that there must be costs to using the market that can be eliminated by using the firm. These costs have come to be known as transactions costs.

Transactions costs include the time and expense of negotiating, writing, and enforcing contracts. They arise when one or more parties to a transaction can act opportunistically (i.e., seek private gain at the expense of the greater good). Transactions costs include the adverse consequences of opportunistic behavior, as well as the costs of trying to prevent it. Contracting costs are certainly one component

---

[21]Excerpted from *The Wall Street Journal*, July 29, 1992, p. A5.

[22]Coase, R. "The Nature of the Firm," *Economica*, 4, 1937: pp. 386–405.

of transactions costs. After all, a key purpose of contracts (and of the lawyers paid to ensure their enforcement) is to protect each party's interests in an exchange relationship. But transactions costs can be more subtle. To grasp these subtleties, we explore *transactions costs economics* in greater depth in Chapter 4.

TECHNOLOGICAL CHANGE AND EVOLVING FIRM BOUNDARIES

◆ ◆ ◆ ◆ ◆

As discussed in Chapter 1, business history shows that the boundaries of firms are largely determined by the infrastructure around them. This is as true today as it was in the 1840s when John Burrows made his ill-fated trip to New Orleans. Indeed, firm boundaries today resemble those in 1840 more than those in 1910. Increasingly, firms have become less vertically integrated, focusing instead on core business activities, or gaining market share by expanding horizontally.

The shrinking of firm boundaries in the vertical chain accelerated during the recession of the early 1990s. This recession was characterized by unusually large permanent layoffs at some of America's biggest companies, including General Motors, General Electric, Sears, and Westinghouse. While many bemoaned the apparent decline of these firms, others saw these moves as sensible responses to a changing calculus of make-or-buy decisions.

The 1980s saw the emergence of the computer and telecommunications as management and production tools. Thanks to the fax and modem, independent firms can communicate their intentions and coordinate their production activities far more easily than ever before. At the same time, computer-aided design and manufacturing (CAD-CAM) minimizes setup costs associated with frequent changes in product designs and manufacturing runs. This reduces the cost advantages of large production runs, making smaller firms, which may perform only a few steps along the vertical chain, more competitive with vertically integrated industrial giants. Computer and telecommunication advances also facilitated innovations in inventory management permitting firms to replace their own internal inventory with just-in-time inventory held by independent firms.

New technology has thus reduced many of the advantages of "make" decisions. As firms buy more from the market, they reduce the size of their own staffs. This does not imply that the level of economic activity or overall level of employment has declined. Instead, employment has shifted to firms that are experts in their particular part of the vertical chain. In fact, while the early to mid-1990s were notable for layoffs at large firms, overall employment in the United States rose considerably. Hewlett-Packard's John Young put it this way: "The Fortune 500 is not growing, but what nobody looks at is how much they have rationalized and created a whole bunch of new jobs in other places."[23] Indeed, while employment among manufacturing firms has stagnated, employment among firms performing specialized tasks in the vertical chain, including telecommunications, information processing, distribution, and sales, has grown. Moreover, many of the employees in the latter firms perform tasks that vertically integrated manufacturing firms used to do.

---

[23]*Chicago Tribune*, February 2, 1993, section 1, p. 15.

◆ ◆

*E*XAMPLE 3.6

AN APPLICATION OF THE MAKE-OR-BUY FRAMEWORK TO CHILDREN'S MEMORIAL HOSPITAL

Although the trend in most industries is to "buy" rather than "make," there has been substantial vertical integration in the health care industry. Integrated health care systems like the Henry Ford Clinic in Michigan or the Sutter system in California have consolidated the vertical chain, placing hospitals, physician offices, home health care, pharmacies, health insurance, and diagnostic imaging facilities in a single corporate entity. Increasingly, however, health care systems recognize that full integration is not always optimal, and many are evaluating each link in the vertical chain to determine which activities to "make" and which to "buy." An interesting example of a make-or-buy decision occurred in 1993 when the Children's Memorial Hospital in Chicago chose to retain ownership of its pediatric home care subsidiary. The framework developed in this chapter can be used to analyze the economics of this decision.

Home health care includes nursing, therapy, homemaker, and other services delivered to patients in their homes. Industry experts believe that home health care is a cost-effective alternative to institutional care. There were dozens of home care agencies in Chicago in 1993, including CM Health Care Resources (CMHR), which was wholly owned by Children's Memorial Medical Center (CMMC), the owner of Children's Memorial Hospital (CMH). Most CMH patients who received home care got it from CMHR. On the other hand, CMHR received more than half of its patients from hospitals other than CMH. An important strategic question faced by CMH's owners in 1993 was whether to make CMHR a fully independent firm or to keep it as a wholly-owned subsidiary. By spinning off CMHR, CMH would have more flexibility to refer patients to other independent home care agencies. This would, in effect, be a decision to "buy" or "use the market." By retaining ownership of CMHR, CMH would continue to rely almost exclusively on it for home care services. This, in effect, would be a decision to "make."

What are the potential benefits to CMH from using the market? Since home care is labor intensive, economies of scale in the provision of home care services are probably minimal. The only potentially significant source of scale economies stems from transportation costs. As a tertiary care children's hospital, CMH gets patients from throughout the Chicago area. The labor costs of a home care agency increase when nurses must travel great distances between patients. Thus, it might make sense for CMH to use independent home care agencies rather than CMHR to service distant communities. These agenices could combine patients from hospitals in their local areas with CMH patients to reduce transportation costs. CMHR could then redeploy its nurses more efficiently to serve nearby communities with an adequate patient density.

Using the market would also be attractive if the market provided discipline and sharp incentives for efficiency that CMH cannot instill in an integrated CMHR. CMHR was at best an average cost supplier in the market, as indicated by the fact that several insurers directed CMH to discharge patients to less costly home care agencies. This suggests that CMHR either was less efficient than other home care agencies in the Chicago area, or at least, that it had selected a cost/quality position that was not suited to all consumers. CMHR did have reason to feel complacent: Many CMH physicians felt loyal to CMHR and referred patients to them without considering alternatives. Thus, CMHR had some guaranteed sales regardless of its efficiency.

Still, CMHR was probably not grossly inefficient. Most of its business came from other hospitals. This could not occur if CMHR did not provide a reasonable cost/quality mix. CMH encouraged CMHR to compete for non-CMH patients, and CMHR's continued success at doing so is powerful evidence that it was not terribly less efficient than competing home care agencies.

Despite the potential for scale economies based on transportation cost savings and concerns over operating efficiency, CMHR probably did not suffer too much compared to market firms. The advantages to CMH from using the market were probably not overwhelming. Still, unless there were offsetting advantages to keeping CMH and CMHR vertically integrated, a case could be made to spin CMHR off. What were the advantages to "making" rather than "buying" in this case?

One benefit to "make" comes from enhanced coordination in the vertical chain of health care delivery for home care patients. Decisions about nurse training, drug use, and therapy must be coordinated between the hospital and home care agency. CMHR works with CMH to develop protocols to improve these areas of care. Families that use CMH and CMHR benefit from using the same supplies and equipment in the inpatient and home settings. There are also critical timing decisions involved in discharging a patient from the hospital. Poor coordination between CMHR and an independent home care agency delays a patient's discharge from the hospital and drives up costs. Close coordination between CMH and CMHR prevents these bottlenecks.

The fact that CMH and CMHR are under common ownership also helps to align their incentives. A critical factor is the relatively low payments made by Medicaid to CMH. CMH would like to discharge Medicaid patients as soon as it is safe to do so. This will allow CMH to treat more privately insured patients, and earn more revenues. Many independent home care agencies are reluctant to accept Medicaid patients, because payments are so low. But CMHR accepts them from CMH. This reduces CMHR's profits, but increases CMH's. We estimated that CMHR's policy of accepting Medicaid patients from CMH boosts the overall financial performance of CMH's owner, Children's Memorial Medical Center, by more than $1,000 per patient.

One might wonder whether vertical integration really has an advantage here. Why couldn't CMH and an independent home care agency similarly resolve the Medicaid problem through an arm's-length contract? For example, CMH might pay an independent agency $500 to accept Medicaid patients to free hospital beds for more remunerative patients. However, a contract like this risks violating federal anti-kickback statutes. In particular, if the home care agency ever recommended that one of its patients receive hospital care at CMH, the $500 could be considered a fee to generate future referrals, and could therefore be illegal. Joint ownership eliminates concerns about the anti-kickback laws.

Joint ownership of CMH and CMHR may also encourage investments in *relationship-specific assets*, a concept that will be discussed at length in Chapter 4.

Relationship-specific assets are investments in physical capital or know-how that are made to support a specific transaction. The value of a relationship-specific asset is greatest when it is deployed in the transaction for which it was created; it is less valuable when it is redeployed to another transaction or put to another use. A key relationship-specific asset in this case is nurses' training. CMHR trains nurses who work full-time at CMH. This improves the discharge process and training of home caregivers. However, the profitability of this training depends on the fact that CMHR receives most of the patients that CMH discharges to home care. CMHR would be reluctant to make these investments if it could not count on receiving the bulk of CMH's business.

To summarize, vertical integration of CMH and CMHR reduced CMH's flexibility to use other home care agencies, which may raise the cost of delivering home care because it sacrificed scale economies. It may also have partially shielded CMHR from market forces, making it somewhat less efficient than competing home care agencies. However, CMH and CMHR probably gained significantly from being vertically integrated. These gains are attributable to the benefits from coordinated discharge and treatment protocols and from CMHR's willingness to accept Medicaid patients. Vertical integration has probably also created stronger incentives for CMHR to train nurses at CMH. On balance, we conclude that CMH and CMHR should remain vertically integrated. If Medicaid payment rules change, however, so that many other agencies will accept CMH discharges, then integration becomes less attractive, and Children's Memorial Medical Center should revisit the issue of spinning off CMHR.

CHAPTER SUMMARY

◆ The production of any good or service usually requires a range of activities organized in a vertical chain. Production activities flow from upstream suppliers of raw inputs to downstream manufacturers, distributors, and retailers.

◆ The vertical chain includes processing and handling activities associated directly with the processing and distribution of inputs and outputs, and professional support activities, such as accounting and planning.

◆ A fundamental question is which activities in the vertical chain a firm should perform itself, and which it should leave to independent firms in the market. This is known as the "make-or-buy" problem.

◆ A fallacious make-or-buy argument is that firms should buy to avoid incurring the associated costs. The firm it buys from will have to incur these costs, and will charge accordingly.

◆ A second fallacy is that firms should make, rather than buy, to keep for themselves the profits earned by independent firms. These profits usually represent the returns necessary to attract investment, and would be required of the firm that "makes" just as they are required of independent firms.

◆ A third fallacy is that vertically integrated firms can produce an input at cost and thus have an advantage over nonintegrated firms that must buy inputs at market prices. This argument ignores a hidden opportunity cost to the vertically integrated firm: by using the input to produce its final output, it forgoes outside sales in the open market.

◆ The solution to the make-or-buy decision depends on which decision leads to the most efficient production. This is determined by assessing the benefits and costs of using the market.

◆ Market firms can often achieve economies of scale in production of an input that firms that choose to make the input themselves cannot.

◆ Market firms offer other advantages. While a division within a hierarchical firm may hide its inefficiencies behind complex monitoring and reward systems, independent firms must survive market competition. This encourages efficiency and innovation.

◆ Vertically integrated firms can try to replicate market incentives but may encounter problems associated with motivation (agency costs) and internal lobbying for resources (influence costs).

◆ Use of market firms often presents coordination problems. This is especially problematic for inputs with design attributes that require a careful fit between different components.

◆ Firms may be reluctant to use the market when they risk losing control of valuable private information.

◆ Use of market firms may entail transactions costs.

QUESTIONS

1. Describe the vertical chain for the production of automobiles.

2. A manufacturer of pencils contemplates backward integration into the production of rape seed oil, a key ingredient in manufacturing the rubberlike material (called factice) that forms the eraser. Rape seed oil is traded in world commodity markets and its price fluctuates as supply and demand conditions change. The argument that has been made in favor of vertical integration is this: "Pencil production is very utilization-sensitive (i.e., a plant that operates at full capacity can produce pencils at much lower cost per unit than a plant that operates at less than full capacity). Owning our own source of supply of rape seed oil insulates us from short-run supply–demand imbalances and therefore will give us a competitive advantage over rival producers." Explain why this argument is wrong.

3. Dixieland Bottlers, by virtue of a lifetime contract, has exclusive rights to distribute Big Dog products in South City, AL. Big Dog has a 7 percent share of the South City market, similar to its nationwide share. Dixieland uses its monopsony power to pay a lower price for Big Dog products than does any other distributor in the United States. Is this sufficient justification for Big Dog to buy out Dixieland Bottlers?

4. In each of the following situations why are firms likely to benefit from vertical integration?

   (a) A *grain elevator* is located at the terminus of a *rail line*.
   (b) A *manufacturer* of a product with a national brand name reputation uses *distributors* that arrange for advertising and promotional activities in local markets.
   (c) A *biotech firm* develops a new product that will be produced, tested, and distributed by an established *pharmaceutical company*.

5. Consider the following pairs of situations. In each pair, which situation is more likely to be susceptible to *coordination* problems?

   (a) Maintenance of a *homeowner's lawn* by a gardening company versus maintenance of a *football or soccer stadium's grass turf* by a gardening company.
   (b) Design of a *toolbox* to hold *tools* versus design of a *wafer* to hold the wires of a microscopic *silicon chip*.

6. Universities tend to be highly integrated—many departments all belong to the same organization. There is no technical reason why a university could not consist of free-standing departments linked together by contract, much in the same way that a network organization links freestanding businesses. Why do you suppose that universities are not organized in this way?

7. Several years ago, Disney purchased Capitol Cities/ABC, parent of the ABC network television. Some analysts praised the deal because it assured Disney a channel to distribute its programming. Do you think that this was a good motive for the acquisition? Can you think of other possible motives for the deal?

The Transactions Costs of Market Exchange

4

*B*efore a good or service reaches the consumer, many transactions may be conducted along the vertical chain. Raw materials must be procured, productive technology must be developed and implemented, labor must be hired and trained, and so forth. The standard textbook model of microeconomics views these transactions as occurring through market exchange, that is, between independent parties in the market.

In the textbook model, market exchange is simple and powerful. Large numbers of buyers and sellers engage in straightforward transactions. Each possesses perfect information about market prices and exchange opportunities. Market prices emerge to clear the market, that is, equate supply with demand. In this context, market exchange has many desirable features. Buyers and sellers exhaust all mutually beneficial trading opportunities without having to communicate their preferences or technologies to each other or to a central authority. Sellers face strong pressures to improve production processes and innovate new products. And since competition tends to drive inefficient agents from the market, market exchange allows buyers and sellers to measure their actual performance against optimal performance.

In some real-life markets, this representation of market exchange is accurate. Markets for fuels, agricultural commodities, and financial instruments usually operate smoothly and efficiently. In many other settings, however, market exchange can entail significant costs. Consider the following examples in which market transactions proved to be costly:

- The production of aluminum requires several stages.[1] The first two are mining bauxite ore and refining the ore into alumina, the chief chemical ingredient of semifinished aluminum. The chemical properties of bauxite vary

---

[1]The following discussion draws heavily from John Stuckey's *Vertical Integration and Joint Ventures in the Aluminum Industry*, Cambridge, MA: Harvard University Press, 1983.

considerably across deposits, and the refinery for a particular deposit cannot accept ore from another deposit without incurring substantial expense to reengineer the plant. As a result, a particular bauxite supplier and its designated alumina refiner are strongly dependent on each other. They agree to a contract that guarantees exclusivity and specifies that the refiner pay the market price for bauxite.

This dependency can create problems. Suppose the supplier and refiner are surprised by an unexpected surge in the demand for finished aluminum. The refiner would like to process more bauxite to reap additional profits. The bauxite supplier recognizes the tremendous profit that the refiner stands to reap, and tries to force it to pay more than the market price in exchange for accelerated production. The two sides hire lawyers, and the negotiations consume the time of top management. Eventually production is increased, but only after costly delays.

- When the New York crime syndicate headed by "Lucky" Luciano decided to open the first gambling casino in a barren section of Nevada that was eventually to become Las Vegas, it initially assigned all responsibility to "Bugsy" Siegal, who, with his girlfriend, had responsibility for a vast array of entrepreneurial tasks, such as site selection and marketing campaigns. Siegal repeatedly requested additional funding from Luciano, who had no alternative but to support Siegal or stop construction. After sinking over $50 million into the Flamingo casino, Luciano discovered that Siegal's girlfriend had embezzled most of the funds.

- In 1970 IBM needed to obtain a family of specialized integrated circuits for a new product that it was planning to market two years later.[2] While similar circuits were available commercially, none had ever been produced with the tight quality tolerances IBM required. IBM turned to a small electronics firm, International Systems, which agreed to build a production line dedicated to the IBM circuits. All went well initially, but in mid-1974, IBM began to detect serious quality problems with one specific circuit, the BR1. Reports from the field indicated that the BR1 was experiencing abnormally high failure rates, with serious consequences for the new product. IBM managers suspected that International Systems had not carefully managed the dedicated line by, for example, inappropriately rotating labor, and not keeping the air in the facility clean enough. International Systems countered by challenging the validity of IBM's quality testing procedures and claiming that the defects were not its fault. Despite time-consuming negotiations involving top managers on both sides, nothing was resolved. IBM managers had to admit that because the process of making these circuits involved "black magic," the problem may have been due to circumstances beyond International System's control.

All three examples illustrate the difficulties that can arise in market transactions. At the heart of each example is the absence of a sufficiently powerful contract to assure efficient performance. In the first example, the bauxite miner and alumina refiner failed to account for a sharp and sustained increase in the demand

---

[2]This example is from Corey, R. E., *Procurement Management: Strategy, Organization, and Decision-Making*, Boston: CBI Publishing, 1978.

for aluminum. Given their complete reliance on each other, they ended up in a costly battle over how to divide profits. The firms might be advised to do what nearly all alumina refiners and bauxite miners have done—merge into a single firm. In the second example, the New York crime syndicate could have asked Siegal to sign a contract that specified performance criteria and penalties in the event of cost overruns. Of course, the syndicate would not want to enforce such a contract in court. After implementing its own enforcement—Siegal was murdered— the New York syndicate took more direct responsibility for its Las Vegas actions. In the third example, IBM could not directly observe how careful International Systems had been in producing the BR1, so a contract that penalized International Systems for sloppy production was impossible. IBM and International Systems did agree on quality standards, but when those standards were not met, IBM could not tell whether International Systems had been careless. Because no other outside vendor knew how to produce this component, IBM simply had to accept International System's word and hope that quality would improve. Quality did improve for a while, but in 1975, after its own engineers had figured out how to produce the circuit, IBM terminated its contract with International Systems and produced the BR1 itself.

The transactions in these examples share key similarities: a strong mutual reliance by each party on the other once the deal had been struck; efforts by one or both parties to sweeten its end of the deal; and an inability to write enforceable contracts that cover important contingencies and penalize shirking. Each transaction also gave rise to significant costs. These included extra negotiations; delays and disruptions in production; and efforts by both parties to safeguard their positions once they entered into the contract (e.g., Bugsy Siegal took elaborate precautions to protect himself against a mob hit; IBM had to develop internal production capabilities to avoid dependence on a sole supplier). Costs like these occur in many market transactions. Economists refer to the costs of organizing and transacting exchanges as transactions costs. These costs are considered so important that an entire branch of economics—transactions costs economics—is devoted to their study.

Chapter 3 provided an overview of the benefits and costs of using independent market firms to perform activities in the vertical chain but only briefly discussed transactions costs. This chapter develops the concept of transactions costs in much greater detail and discusses how they determine the vertical boundaries of the firm.[3] The main emphasis here is on the costs of arm's-length market transactions. An arm's-length market transaction is one in which autonomous parties exchange goods or services with no formal agreement that the relationship will continue into the future. Purchases of computer equipment, office supplies, or the construction of an office building are examples of arm's-length transactions. Arm's-length transactions are governed by contract law, and serious disputes about whether one party has fulfilled its obligations are often resolved through litigation. Of course, arm's-length transactions are not the only way that a firm might "use the market." A firm might enter into a long-term relationship with an input supplier, through a

---

[3]The chapter draws heavily on the work of Ronald Coase, Oliver Williamson, and others who have made pivotal contributions to transactions cost economics. Seminal works include Coase's article, "The Nature of the Firm," *Economica*, 4, 1937: pp. 386–405, and Oliver Williamson's book *Markets and Hierarchies: Analysis and Antitrust Implications*, New York: Free Press, 1975 and *The Economic Institutions of Capitalism*, New York: Free Press, 1985.

long-term (e.g., 20-year) contract or strategic alliance. But these arrangements are likely to be different from an arm's-length transaction. Each party's obligation to the other would be less precisely defined, and disputes are less likely to be resolved through litigation. We defer discussion of these alternative modes of organizing exchange to Chapter 5.

This chapter is organized in three main sections. The first section discusses the role of contracts and contract law in market exchange and introduces the important concept of an *incomplete contract*. The second section develops three important concepts that are needed to understand why market exchange can entail transactions costs: *relationship-specific assets*, *quasi-rents*, and the *holdup problem*. The third section discusses why vertical integration might be a good alternative to market contracting when the exchange involves incomplete contracting and relationship-specific assets.

◆ ◆ ◆ ◆ ◆ CONTRACTS AND MARKET EXCHANGE

The Economic Foundations of Contracts

Any analysis of the costs of arm's-length market exchange must begin with a discussion of contracts.

Contracts define the conditions of exchange. They may take standardized forms, such as the "Conditions of Contract" on the back of an airline ticket or the terms and conditions of purchase printed on the back of a company's purchase order. Or they may be lengthy and complicated because they are carefully tailored to a specific transaction. For example, the contract for the sale of the Empire State Building in the 1960s involved more than 100 attorneys and was over 400 pages long.[4]

Contracts are a key element of a private-ownership economy. Their philosophical foundations include important social values, such as the sanctity of promises, the right of individuals to enter into autonomous transactions, and economic efficiency. Our focus is on economic efficiency.

To understand how contracts promote economic efficiency, it is useful to highlight an obvious but nevertheless significant characteristic of market transactions: In most exchanges, parties perform their obligations sequentially rather than simultaneously. For example, a firm might ship steel to a customer, who pays for it after taking delivery. Contracts prevent trading partners from taking advantage of one another in sequential exchanges as, for example, when the customer refuses to pay for the delivered steel. The fact that parties bear the expense of writing and enforcing contracts is evidence of their concern about such selfishness.

Without contracts, exchange activities would be biased toward those in which performance occurs simultaneously with payment. For instance, the steel firm would refuse to sell steel unless customers paid cash immediately, and customers would refuse to pay cash unless the firm could fill the order immediately. An insistence on simultaneous performance would clearly raise the costs of transacting business. In our example, the customer would have to carry enough cash to complete all its transactions, and the steel firm would have to have enough steel on hand

---

[4]Macauley, S., "Non-Contractual Relations in Business: A Preliminary Study," *American Sociological Review*, 28, 1963: pp. 55–67.

to fill all its orders as they arise. In addition, in an economy without contracts, parties would invest in private safeguards to prevent themselves from being exploited. In the extreme case, a seller might purchase a gun and threaten to shoot its customers if they do not pay for delivery of a good. This is what often happens in illegal transactions, such as drugs or smuggling. This mode of transacting exchange would not only be costly, but it would also have an insidious effect on the legitimacy of private ownership and government institutions that are built around it.

Contracts, then, protect parties to a transaction from opportunistic behavior. By so doing, they allow transactions to be organized in more economical ways. However, contracts are not equally effective in all circumstances. Their ability to facilitate exchange depends on (1) the "completeness" of the contract, and (2) the available body of contract law. We discuss each of these factors in turn.

Complete versus Incomplete Contracting

A *complete contract* eliminates opportunistic behavior. A complete contract stipulates each party's responsibilities and rights for each and every contingency that could conceivably arise during the transaction. A complete contract would bind the parties to particular courses of action as the transaction unfolded. Neither party could exploit weaknesses in the other's position while the transaction was in progress.

The requirements of complete contracting are severe. Parties to the contract must be able to contemplate all relevant contingencies and agree on a "mapping" that specifies for each possible contingency a set of actions that each party must take. The parties must also be able to stipulate what constitutes satisfactory performance and must be able to measure performance. Finally, the contract must be enforceable. This means that parties cannot unilaterally renege on the contract. It also implies that an outside party, such as a judge or an arbitrator, must be able to observe which contingencies occurred and whether each party took the actions that were required for those contingencies. For example, a contract in which the price of an item is tied to the seller's production costs might not be enforceable without an independent auditing mechanism that could verify those costs.

An incomplete contract does not fully specify the "mapping" from possible contingencies to rights, responsibilities, and actions. This might be because some of the relevant contingencies cannot be contemplated, or because performance obligations cannot be articulated in those that can be contemplated. As might be imagined, virtually all real-world contracts are incomplete. Incomplete contracts involve some degree of open-endedness or ambiguity; there are circumstances under which neither party's rights and responsibilities are clearly spelled out. Consider, for example, the case, *Cook v. Deltona Corp.*[5] In 1971 Deltona Corporation, a land developer, sold Cook a piece of property in Marco Shores, Florida. The land was underwater at the time of the sale. The title to the land was to be delivered in 1980, by which time Deltona was to have dredged and filled the land. However, during the 1970s changes in federal policy toward wetlands made it difficult for developers to obtain dredge and fill permits from the Army Corps of Engineers. In 1976, after failing to obtain permits on nearby land, Deltona gave up trying to ob-

---

[5]*Cook v. Deltona Corp.*, 753 F2d 1552 (1985) United States Court of Appeals, Eleventh Circuit.

tain a permit for Marco Shores. The sale contract did not specify the buyer's rights and the developer's responsibilities under these circumstances, so the contract was incomplete. Because the contract was silent on this unanticipated turn of events, it was not clear whether Deltona had breached the contract by not delivering the land in the condition promised. The outcome was a lawsuit that took nine years to resolve. (Cook won.)

Three factors prevent complete contracting:

* Bounded rationality

* Difficulties specifying or measuring performance

* Asymmetric information

We will discuss each in turn.

Bounded Rationality Bounded rationality refers to limits on the capacity of individuals to process information, deal with complexity, and pursue rational aims. Boundedly rational parties cannot contemplate or enumerate every contingency that might arise during a transaction. As a result, they cannot write complete contracts. In *Cook v. Deltona Corp.*, Deltona essentially offered a defense based on bounded rationality. It argued that changes in regulatory requirements by the Army Corps of Engineers seemed so unlikely when the contract was written as to be unforeseeable. The court acknowledged that, in principle, this could be a valid defense, but held that evidence that the Army Corps of Engineers had begun to toughen its policy meant that Deltona should have accounted for this risk in the contract.

Difficulties Specifying or Measuring Performance When performance under a contract is complex or subtle, not even the most accomplished wordsmiths may be able to spell out each party's rights and responsibilities. Language in contracts is thus often left so vague and open-ended that it may not be clear what constitutes fulfillment of the contract. For example, a standard clause in lease contracts for new cars allows the company to bill the lessee for "excess wear and tear." However, the contract does not specify what "wear and tear" or "excess" means. Some leasing companies have used this clause to charge customers who return the car in less than showroom condition.

A related problem is that performance may be ambiguous or hard to measure. For example, in relationships between airframe manufacturers and engine suppliers, engine thrust is the subject of much contention. Thrust cannot be measured exactly, and each engine supplier uses a different methodology. John Newhouse, in *The Sporty Game*, writes of Boeing engineers who "speak astringently about a Hartford pound of thrust [Pratt & Whitney], a Cincinnati pound of thrust [GE], and a Derby pound of thrust [Rolls-Royce]."[6]

Asymmetric Information Even if the parties can foresee the contingencies and the relevant performance dimensions can be specified and measured, a contract may still be incomplete because the parties do not have equal access to all contract-relevant information, that is, *asymmetric information* exists. If one party knows

---

[6]Newhouse, J., *The Sporty Game*, New York: Knopf, 1982, pp. 53–54.

something that the other does not, that party may distort or misrepresent that information. For example, suppose a contract stipulates that a manufacturer is to receive a bonus if it maintains stringent quality control to assure the durability of its product. Because the manufacturer is responsible for quality control, it is the only one that can verify that appropriate quality control measures have been taken. The manufacturer would want to claim that it took the required steps to assure durability, even when it did not. Understanding the manufacturer's self-interest, the buyer might protest these claims. To enforce this contract, a court would have to look at evidence (e.g., an independent quality audit or testimony from each party) to ascertain whether the contract was fulfilled. But if the item being produced is complex or unique, this evidence may well be inconclusive, and the court would have little basis on which to resolve the dispute. Under these circumstances, contracting for "quality control" would not be attractive to the two parties.

The Role of Contract Law

A well-developed body of contract law makes it possible for transactions to occur smoothly when contracts are incomplete. In the United States, contract law is embodied in both common law and the *Uniform Commercial Code* (UCC), the law governing contracts in all states except Louisiana. The doctrines of contract law specify a set of "standard" provisions applicable to wide classes of transactions. These doctrines eliminate the need for parties to specify these provisions in every single transaction.

For example, the UCC contains general rules known as *gap fillers* that the courts must apply in setting specific terms of exchange (e.g., delivery time, location, price, or quantity) when the contract is silent on them. Section 2–309(1) of the UCC, for instance, provides that, unless otherwise specified in the contract, delivery must occur within a "reasonable time," with "reasonable" being determined by such factors as the nature and uses of the goods purchased and transportation conditions. As another example, Section 2–305 of the UCC directs the courts to determine a "reasonable price" when the contract is silent on the price or contains a price-setting formula that cannot be applied because of a change in circumstances. In the case *North Central Airlines, Inc. v. Continental Oil Co.*, the parties agreed to a contract for aviation fuel in which the price would be determined by a formula based on the market price of crude oil produced in the United States.[7] But this formula became inapplicable when the U.S. government instituted a complex system of price controls on crude oil in 1973. The court resorted to the "reasonable price" standard in the UCC to complete this contract.

However, contract law is not a perfect substitute for complete contracting for two important reasons. First, the doctrines of contract law are phrased in broad language ("reasonable time," "reasonable price") that is open to differing interpretations when applied to specific transactions. For complicated or novel exchanges, the relevant law may be unclear. Ambiguities in doctrines and uncertainty about how particular doctrines will be applied raise the costs of transacting the exchange relative to an ideal world in which complete contracting is possible.

Second, litigation can be a costly way of "completing" contracts. A vivid illustration of this occurred in the mid-1970s when Westinghouse invoked the doc-

---

[7]*North Central Airlines, Inc. v. Continental Oil Co.*, 574 F2d 582 (1978), D.C. Circuit.

trine of *commercial impracticability* to justify reneging on contracts to deliver 70 million pounds of uranium.[8] This doctrine excuses a seller from performing its obligations under a sales contract if "performance has been made impracticable by the occurrence of a contingency the nonoccurrence of which was a basic assumption on which the contract was made" (UCC 2–504). In the early 1970s Westinghouse had agreed to sell uranium at $10 per pound to a group of electric utilities. Soon after signing the contracts, the price of uranium increased dramatically, to $26 per pound in 1975. Westinghouse argued that the price increase was the result of unforeseeable events (the Arab oil embargo and the subsequent runup of oil prices), and that it could not deliver the uranium without incurring serious financial harm—losses of more than $1 billion on the contracts. The subsequent breach-of-contract litigation took over three years to resolve. Eventually, most of the cases were settled out of court, but the utilities accepted payments that were smaller than the value of the uranium they would have received under the original contracts.

Litigation can also weaken or destroy business relationships. As Stewart Macauley writes, "A breach of contract suit may settle a particular dispute, but such action often results in 'divorce,' ending the 'marriage' between two businesses, since a contract action is likely to carry charges with at least overtones of bad faith."[9] The termination of longstanding business relationships as a result of a breach of contract suit can be especially costly if the parties have invested in the relationship and become mutually dependent on one another. Establishing new relationships that are equally beneficial to both parties may be difficult or even impossible.

◆ ◆ ◆ ◆ ◆ TRANSACTIONS WITH RELATIONSHIP-SPECIFIC ASSETS

Contract law might ameliorate the opportunism that can arise under incomplete contracting, but it is unlikely to eliminate it. Thus, incomplete contracting will inevitably entail some transactions costs. To help explain more precisely the nature of these transactions costs and how they might bias economic decision making, this section introduces three important theoretical concepts from transactions-cost economics: *relationship-specific assets*, *quasi-rents*, and the *holdup* problem. The following subsections define these concepts and explain their significance.

Relationship-Specific Assets

A relationship-specific asset is an investment made to support a given transaction. Relationship-specific assets are often essential for the efficiency of a particular transaction. However, a relationship-specific asset cannot be redeployed to another transaction without some sacrifice in the productivity of the asset or some

---

[8]Joskow, P., "Commercial Impossibility, the Uranium Market, and the Westinghouse Case," *Journal of Legal Studies*, 6, 1977: pp. 119–176.

[9]Macauley, S., "Non-contractual Relations in Business: A Preliminary Study," *American Sociological Review*, 28, 1963: pp. 55–67.

cost in adapting the asset to the new transaction. When a transaction involves relationship-specific assets, parties to the transaction cannot costlessly switch trading partners. This is because the assets involved in the original exchange would have to be reconfigured to be valuable in the new relationship or the investments would have to be made all over again in the new relationship. This implies that investments in relationship-specific assets lock the parties into the relationship to a some degree.

Each of the examples in the introduction to this chapter involved relationship-specific assets:

- An alumina refiner makes a relationship-specific investment when it builds a refinery to accommodate a particular grade of bauxite ore. It is efficient to do this because the costs of refining are lower when the plant is configured to handle one specific grade of bauxite than many different grades. Once the refinery is set up in this way, however, the refinery cannot be reconfigured to handle other grades of bauxite without significant expenditures to redesign the facility. This investment makes both parties in the transaction strongly dependent on one another. The alumina refiner could not replace the bauxite supplier without incurring significant costs in reconfiguring its plant. The bauxite miner may have no other possible customers because no other refinery could process its particular grade of bauxite.

- The New York crime syndicate made a relationship-specific investment when it hired Bugsy Siegal to develop Las Vegas. Once the syndicate had committed funds to Siegal, he was able to develop transaction-specific knowledge and skills that made him, for a time, indispensable. Replacing Siegal with another mobster would have delayed the development of their gambling empire and thus entailed significant costs.

- International Systems made relationship-specific investments in production facilities and the development of production know-how in its contract with IBM to deliver integrated circuits (ICs). These investments enhanced the development of ICs, but they also bound International Systems and IBM together in a mutually dependent relationship. International Systems was strongly dependent on IBM because its dedicated facilities could not be easily adapted to produce other products, and the know-how it developed in producing the specialized ICs for IBM had limited usefulness in producing other products. IBM was strongly dependent on International Systems because no other suppliers had the facilities or the know-how to produce ICs with the tolerances IBM required.

The Fundamental Transformation

The need to create relationship-specific assets transforms the relationship as the transaction unfolds. Before the relationship-specific investments are made, a party may have many alternative trading partners, for example, a buyer may be able to choose among many possible sellers. This allows competitive bidding. But after the relationship-specific investments have been sunk, the parties to a transaction have few, if any, alternative trading partners. Competitive bidding is no longer possible. Instead, bilateral bargaining between the parties to the transaction determines the terms of the exchange. In short, once the parties invest in relationship-

XAMPLE 4.1

THE FUNDAMENTAL TRANSFORMATION IN THE U.S. AUTOMOBILE INDUSTRY[10]

A real-life example of the fundamental transformation is the relationship between U.S. automobile assemblers and their component suppliers. Assemblers usually use competitive bidding for outside suppliers. The assembler solicits bids for short-term (usually one-year) supply contracts. These contracts specify price, quality (e.g., no fewer than two bad parts per thousand), and a delivery schedule. Before the contract, there are many potential bidders. Once the contract is let, however, specific investments on both sides bind the assembler and supplier in a mutually dependent relationship. For some components, the assembler must invest in specific production tooling. The supplier must invest in equipment that is tailored to the assembler's specifications. Because of asset specificity, suppliers and assemblers understand that suppliers are often bidding not just for a one-year contract, but for a long-term business relationship.

The fundamental transformation makes the relationship between assemblers and suppliers contentious. Because suppliers often hope to enter a long-term relationship with an assembler, they will sometimes bid below cost to win the contract, a strategy known as "buy-in." A supplier knows from experience that it might be able to renegotiate with the assembler based on claims that unanticipated events (e.g., poorer than expected qualities of key materials) have raised costs. Because changing suppliers at this stage is costly, the assembler may acquiesce. On the other hand, the assembler's procurement managers are under tremendous pressure to hold costs down. At the competitive bidding stage, assemblers will routinely share production drawings with several potential suppliers. Thus, although it may be costly for an assembler to replace a supplier once the component goes into production, it can still do so. Assemblers do threaten to replace suppliers to hold component prices down. Because a supplier makes investments that are specific to its relationship with an assembler, termination of a supply contract can harm it severely. The supplier thus cannot take these threats lightly. The upshot is that once the fundamental transformation occurs, the relationship between the assembler and its suppliers often becomes one of distrust and noncooperation. Suppliers are reluctant to share information on their production operations or their production costs with the assembler for fear that the assembler will use this information to bargain down the contract price in subsequent negotiations. As Womack, Jones, and Roos express it, a supplier's attitude is "what goes on in my factory is my own business."[11] This greatly impedes the ability of the assembler and a supplier to work together to enhance production efficiencies and develop new production technologies.

---

[10]This discussion draws from Chapter 6 of Womack, J., D. Jones, and D. Ross, *The Machine that Changed the World: The Story of Lean Production*, Cambridge, MA: MIT Press, 1991.

[11]Womack, J., D. Jones, and D. Roos, op cit., p. 144.

specific assets, the relationship changes from a "large numbers" bidding situation to a "small numbers" bargaining situation. Oliver Williamson refers to this change as the *fundamental transformation*.[12]

Forms of Asset Specificity

Asset specificity can take at least four forms:

- Site specificity
- Physical asset specificity
- Dedicated assets
- Human asset specificity

Site Specificity   Site specificity refers to assets that are located side-by-side to economize on transportation or inventory costs or to take advantage of processing efficiencies. Traditional steel manufacturing offers a good example of site specificity. Side-by-side location of blast furnaces, steelmaking furnaces, casting units, and mills saves fuel costs. The pig iron, molten steel, and semifinished steel do not have to be reheated before being moved to the next process in the production chain. In the beverage industry, a standard arrangement locates can-producing plants next to can-filling plants to economize on inventory and transportation costs that arise from the bulkiness of metal cans.

Physical Asset Specificity   Physical asset specificity refers to assets whose physical or engineering properties are specifically tailored to a particular transaction. For example, glass container production requires molds that are custom tailored to particular container shapes and glass-making machines. Physical asset specificity inhibits customers from switching suppliers.

Dedicated Assets   A dedicated asset is an investment in plant and equipment made to satisfy a particular buyer. Without the promise of that particular buyer's business, the investment would not be profitable. International Systems' investment in an assembly line to manufacture integrated circuits for IBM was a dedicated asset.

Human Asset Specificity   Human asset specificity refers to cases in which a worker, or group of workers, has acquired skills, know-how, and information that are more valuable inside a particular relationship than outside it. Human asset specificity not only includes tangible skills, such as expertise with a company-specific computer operating system, but it also encompasses intangible assets. For example, every organization has unwritten "routines" and "standard operating procedures." A manager who has become a skillful administrator within the context of one organization's routines may be less effective in an organization with completely different routines. Consider also a defense contractor that is attempting to convert its production to commercial markets. Human asset specificity makes conversion difficult.

---

[12]Chapter 2 of Williamson, O., *The Economic Institutions of Capitalism*, New York: Free Press, 1985.

XAMPLE 4.2

FLOATING POWER PLANTS

How do you deal with trading partners who are reluctant to make investments that have a high degree of site-specificity? This is the problem that many developing nations face in convincing foreign corporations to construct power plants. Power plants are usually highly specialized assets. Once a firm builds a power plant in a developing nation, the associated investment undergoes the "fundamental transformation" and becomes a site-specific asset. If the purchasing government defaults on its payments, the manufacturer has few options for recovering its investment. (The firm could route the power to consumers in other nations, but the defaulting government can easily prevent this.) Even though no manufacturer has had to repossess a plant, the fear of default has scared them off. As a result, growing economies in developing nations may be slowed by power shortages.

The solution to the problem is ingenious. Manufacturers have eliminated the geographic asset specificity associated with power generation! They do this by building power plants on floating barges. During the 1990s, companies, such as Raytheon, Westinghouse, Smith Cogeneration, and Amfel, have built floating power plants (which can generate upwards of 500 megawatts of power and cost as much as $500 million) for countries including Bangladesh, Ghana, Haiti, Kenya, and Malaysia. These countries purchase the plants, which are moored on one or more barges in safe harbors and "plugged into" land-based transformers that send electricity to domestic consumers. If the purchaser defaults, the manufacturer can tow the barge(s) away and sell the plant to another customer.

Floating power plants are not new. Since the 1930s, U.S. Navy battleships have used their turboelectric motors to provide emergency power to utilities. Consolidated Edison operates a gas-turbine generator that is housed on a barge in the Gowanis Canal in Brooklyn. Recent innovations have reduced the size and increased the reliability of gas turbines, making it possible to house large-capacity generators on a small number of barges. This is especially attractive to nations such as Ghana that have their own natural gas reserves. (Some floating power plants use oil or geothermal energy.)

Floating power plants can also be assembled off-site and then towed to the purchasing nation. This lowers labor costs, because the manufacturers do not have to pay their skilled workers to go to a distant site for a long time. One final incentive for floating power plants: A recent amendment to the 1936 U.S. Merchant Marine Act provides substantial financing advantages for constructing vessels in the United States but documented under the laws of another nation. Floating barges fit this description, and enjoy favorable financing.

Successful marketing in defense contracting requires managers who have specialized expertise in government budgetary and procurement processes and are skilled at lobbying Congress and the executive branch. These skills are nearly worthless in the commercial market. Rockwell's unsuccessful experience in electronic calculators and digital watches illustrates the difficulty of transferring skills from defense contracting to commercial ventures.[13] Rockwell did not lack the technological expertise to compete; benefiting from its experience in miniaturization for the space program, its watches and calculators were at the cutting edge of technology. However, its managers apparently did not understand these commercial markets. Its products were overpriced and ignored consumer fashions.

Rents and Quasi-Rents

The fundamental transformation that occurs because of asset specificity has significant consequences for the economics of bargaining between buyer and seller, which in turn affects the costs of arm's-length market exchange. To set the stage for our discussion of these costs that follows, we must first define and explain rent and quasi-rent.

These are hard concepts. To explain them we will walk through a numerical example about a hypothetical transaction. Suppose your company contemplates building a factory to produce cup holders for the Ford Taurus automobile. The factory can make up to 1 million holders per year, at an average variable cost of C dollars per unit. You finance the construction of your factory with a mortgage from a bank that requires an annual payment of I dollars. The loan payment of I dollars thus represents your (annualized) cost of investment in this plant. Note that this is an unavoidable cost: You have to make your mortgage payment, even if you do not do business with Ford.[14] Your total cost of making 1 million cup holders is thus $I + 1,000,000\,C$ dollars per year.

You will design and build the factory specifically to produce cup holders for the Ford Taurus. Your *expectation* is that Ford will purchase your holders at a profitable price (to be discussed in more detail below). But if you build the factory and *do not* end up selling cup holders to Ford, you still have a "bail-out" option: You can sell the holders to jobbers who, after suitably modifying them, so that they can be used on other automobiles besides the Ford Taurus, will resell them to other automobile manufacturers. The "market price" you can expect to get from these jobbers is P_m. If you sell your cup holders to jobbers, you would thus get total revenue of $1,000,000 P_m$.

Suppose that $P_m > C$, so the market price covers your variable cost, but that the annual investment cost I exceeds $1,000,000(P_m - C)$, that is, $I, > 1,000,000 (P_m - C)$. Thus, it *would not* make sense for you to build the cup holder factory if you *did not* expect to sell cup holders to Ford. In this sense, a portion of your investment is specific to your relationship with Ford. In particular, the difference $I - 1,000,000(P_m - C)$ represents your company's *relationship-specific investment (RSI)*:

- The RSI equals the amount of your investment that you cannot recover if your company *does not* do business with Ford.

---

[13]This example is drawn from Lundquist, J., "The False Promise of Defense Conversion," *Wall Street Journal*, March 18, 1993, p. A12.

[14]In particular, we assume that default or declaring "bankruptcy" is not an option. Once you build the factory, you have to make your mortgage payment no matter what! To justify this assumption, imagine that your company has many other profitable business activities that generate enough cash to cover your mortgage payment on his factory under all circumstances. You would thus be legally obligated to pay your mortgage no matter how unprofitable the factory proves to be.

- For example, if $I = \$8{,}500{,}000$, $C = \$3$, and $P_m = \$4$, then the RSI is $\$8{,}500{,}000 - 1{,}000{,}000(4 - 3) = \$7{,}500{,}000$. Of your $\$8{,}500{,}000$ investment cost, you lose $\$7{,}500{,}000$ of it if you do not do business with Ford and sell to jobbers instead.

We can now explain rent and quasi-rent. First, let us explain rent. Suppose that before you take out the loan to invest in the cup holder plant, Ford agreed to buy 1 million sets of cup holders per year at a price of P^* per unit, where $P^* > P_m$. Thus, your company expects to receive total revenue of $1{,}000{,}000\,P^*$ from Ford. Suppose that $1{,}000{,}000(P^* - C) > I$, so that given your expectation of the price Ford will pay, should build the plant. Then,

- Your *rent* is $1{,}000{,}000(P^* - C) - I$.

- In words: your rent is simply the profit you expect to get when you build the plant, assuming all goes as planned.[15]

Let us now explain quasi-rent. Suppose, after the factory was built, your deal with Ford fell apart. You can still sell cup holders to the jobbers. Should you do so? The answer is yes! Even though sales to jobbers do not cover your investment cost I, once you have built the factory, the cost I is unavoidable—remember, you still have to pay your mortgage! Thus, I is a sunk cost and does not affect decision making. You should sell to the jobbers because $1{,}000{,}000(P_m - C) > 0$, that is, sales to distributors cover your variable costs.

- Your quasi-rent is the difference between the profit you get from selling to Ford and the profit you get from your next best option, selling to jobbers. That is, quasi-rent is $1{,}000{,}000(P^* - C) - I - [1{,}000{,}000(P_m - C) - I] = 1{,}000{,}000(P^* - P_m)$.

- In words: your *quasi-rent* is the *extra* profit that you get if the deal goes ahead as planned, versus the profit you would get if you had to turn to your next-best alternative (in our example, selling to jobbers).

It seems clear why the concept of rent is important. Your firm—indeed any firm—must expect positive rents to induce it to invest in an asset. But why is quasi-rent important? It turns out that quasi-rent tells us about the possible magnitude of the holdup problem, a problem that can arise when there are relationship-specific assets.

The Holdup Problem

If an asset was *not* relationship-specific, the associated quasi-rent would be zero. The profit the firm could get from using the asset in its best alternative and its next-best alternative would be the same. But when a firm invests in a relationship-specific asset, the quasi-rent must be positive—it will always get more from its best alternative than from its second-best alternative. If the quasi-rent is large, a firm

---

[15]Rent is synonymous with economic profit, and we will often use the terms interchangeably. To relate this to an important concept from corporate finance, when an investment has a positive rent, it will have a positive net present value. See the Economics Primer for net present value.

stands to lose a lot if it has to turn to its second-best alternative. This opens the possibility that its trading partner could exploit this large quasi-rent, through *holdup*.[16]

- A firm *holds up* its trading partner by attempting to renegotiate the terms of a deal. A firm can profit by holding up its trading partner when contracts are incomplete (thereby permitting breach) and when the deal generates quasi-rents for its trading partner.

To see how this could happen, let's return to our example of Ford and your cup holder company. Ford could reason as follows. You have already sunk your investment in the plant. Even though Ford "promised" to pay you P^* per cup holder, it knows that you would accept any amount greater than P_m per unit and still sell to it. Thus, Ford could break the contract and offer you a price *between* P^* and P_m; if you accept this renegotiation of the deal, Ford would increase its profits.

Could Ford get away with this? After all, didn't Ford sign a contract with you? Well, if the contract is incomplete (and thus potentially ambiguous), Ford could assert that, in one way or another, circumstances have changed and that it is justified breaking the contract. It might, for example, claim that increases in the costs of producing the Taurus will force it to discontinue the model unless suppliers, such as yourself, renegotiate their contracts. Or it might claim that the quality of your cup holders fails to meet promised specifications, and that it must be compensated for this lower quality with lower prices. Unless you want to fight Ford in court for breach of contract (itself a potentially expensive move), you are better off accepting Ford's revised offer than not accepting it.

By reneging on the original contract, Ford has "held you up" and has "transferred" some of your quasi-rent to itself. To illustrate this concretely, suppose $P^* = \$12$ per unit, $P_m = \$4$ per unit, $C = \$3$ per unit, and $I = \$8,500,000$.

- At the original expected price of $12/unit, your rent is $(12 - 3)1,000,000 - 8,500,000 = \$500,000$ per year.

- Your quasi-rent is $(12 - 4)1,000,000 = \$8,000,000$ per year.

- If Ford "renegotiates" the contract down to $8 per unit, Ford will increase its profits by $4 million per year and it will have transferred half of your quasi-rents to itself.

Note that after the holdup has occurred, you realize that you are now getting a profit of $(8-3)1,000,000 - 8,500,000 = -\$3,500,000$. You thus lose money! This tells us that if, instead of trusting Ford, you had anticipated the prospect of holdup, then you would not have made the investment in the factory to begin with. This situation is especially problematic because your rent was small but your quasi-rent was large. When Ford "holds you up" and extracts a portion of your quasi-rent, you end up with losses on your investment. This example shows why we talk about the holdup problem. If you are afraid of being held up, you might be reluctant to invest in relationship-specific assets in the first place.

---

[16]The expression "holdup problem" was coined by Victor Goldberg in his article, "Regulation and Administered Contracts," *Bell Journal of Economics*, 7, Autumn 1976: pp. 426–448.

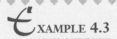XAMPLE 4.3

TACO BELL AND THE HOLDUP PROBLEM[17]

In the late 1980s and early 1990s, Taco Bell pursued a growth strategy to make its market presence comparable to McDonald's. Taco Bell significantly increased the number of its outlets all over the United States. It also introduced Taco Bell Express, concession stands that offer a limited menu of its food. Existing Taco Bell franchisees strongly opposed this strategy fearing that new outlets would cut into their business.[18]

At first glance, it is not clear why a policy that harms its franchisees would benefit Taco Bell. If Taco Bell sold franchises through an up-front franchise fee, its optimal policy would be to give each franchisee an exclusive territory (essentially making each franchise a local monopoly) and sell the franchises through a competitive auction. A potential franchisee's reservation price—the most it would pay for a franchise—would be the present value of the monopoly profits it expects to earn from the exclusive territory. In a competitive auction, the price of a franchise would be bid up to this reservation price.[19] But Taco Bell does not employ this policy. Its franchisees pay a royalty based on a percentage of their sales revenues. This drives a wedge between the *ex post* interests of Taco Bell and its franchisees. Adding outlets in a local market creates additional competition that probably hurts existing franchisees. But by giving Taco Bell greater visibility or opening at locations convenient for more consumers, the additional outlets could stimulate total market demand and increase total market revenues, which makes Taco Bell better off.[20]

Taco Bell franchisees are caught in a classic holdup situation. Their contracts give them exclusive rights to their own restaurants but not to their territories. Taco Bell is free to open other outlets in the same local market. Taco Bell is not even required to study the market impact of new outlets on existing franchisees. Of course, in principle, a franchisee could terminate its relationship with Taco Bell. But many franchisees have undoubtedly built up relationship-specific human capital. For many, the "next best" outside opportunity is probably less attractive than running a Taco Bell franchise, even taking into account the reduction in profits from the new outlets in their market. In short, franchisees have quasi-rents in their relationship with Taco Bell, and Taco Bell's growth strategy has probably redistributed a portion of those quasi-rents from the franchisees to itself.

---

[17]This example draws from "Indigestion at Taco Bell," *Business Week*, December 14, 1992, pp. 66–67.

[18]The president of the Taco Bell franchise organization claims to have documented 70 instances in which new franchises have stolen business from existing outlets. See "Indigestion at Taco Bell," p. 67.

[19]That exclusive territories and up-front franchise fees constitute an optimal franchising contract is proven in Mathewson, G. F. and R. A. Winter. "An Economic Theory of Vertical Restraints," *RAND Journal of Economics*, 15, Spring 1984: pp. 27–38.

[20]Total revenues could also go up if additional competition within a local market intensifies pricing rivalry and market demand is elastic. (See the Economics Primer for a review of demand elasticity.) In that case, the lower prices due to greater competition would increase overall revenues.

The Holdup Problem and Transactions Costs

The holdup problem raises the cost of transacting arm's-length market exchanges in four ways. It can lead to:

- More difficult contract negotiations and more frequent renegotiations

- Investments to improve ex post bargaining positions

- Distrust

- Reduced investment in relationship-specific investments

Contract Negotiation and Renegotiation   The most obvious way in which the holdup problem raises the costs of market transactions is by increasing the difficulty of contract negotiations and the frequency of contract renegotiations. When each side anticipates the possibility of holdup, the initial contract negotiations are likely to be time consuming and costly as each party attempts to protect itself against being held up later on. But if the relationship is sufficiently complex, the ability to write complete contracts that safeguard each party is limited, and as circumstances change in unanticipated ways, the temptation for a party to hold up its trading partner is likely to lead to frequent renegotiations of contracts. This, too, raises the direct costs of carrying out the transaction. In addition, more frequent renegotiations are likely to be associated with more frequent delays or disruptions in the exchange, raising production costs and impeding delivery of products to customers. This problem can be particularly serious when the exchange is part of a sequential production process in which precise synchronization among different stages of production is key. For example, in traditional steel production, heating economies make it desirable to locate the stages of production next to each other. In principle, each stage could be independently owned and operated, and exchanges between separate processes (e.g., production of pig iron) could be mediated by arm's-length contracts. However, given the significant site-specific investments involved and the inefficiencies that would result from the interruptions in product flows that would arise from contractual holdup, arm's-length contracting is inferior to other arrangements, such as common ownership of the site-specific facilities.

Investments to Improve *Ex Post* Bargaining Positions   The possibility of holdup may also lead parties to make investments that improve their postcontractual bargaining positions. This can take several forms. For example, a manufacturer may acquire a standby production facility for a key input as a hedge against contractual holdup by the input supplier. A firm might also seek a second source for an input to reduce the risk of holdup by a sole supplier. For example, in the early 1980s, its customers (including IBM) pressured Intel to provide second sources for its 8088 and 80286 microprocessors. Although standby facilities and second sources can reduce the possibility of holdup, they are not without cost. A standby facility that duplicates the production facility of the input supplier may stand idle much of the time, thus representing costly excess capacity. Diverting volume to a second source will reduce the primary source's scale of production, and when there are economies of scale, this will raise production costs.

Distrust   A less tangible, but real, cost of holdup is the distrust that can arise between parties in the relationship. Distrust raises the costs of contracting in two ways. First, it raises the direct costs of contract negotiation as parties insist that more formal safeguards be written into the contract. For instance, some communities have begun writing detailed contracts with any business that receives tax breaks and specific infrastructure improvements.[21] When the village of Hoffman Estates, Illinois, provided tax incentives to support Sears' new corporate headquarters, its officials negotiated an extensive agreement with Sears that, among other things, obligates Sears to pay $70 million in village expenses for 20 years, support a public transportation project, and refrain from protesting real estate taxes or assessed valuations.[22] While formal contracting of this sort creates stronger safeguards than handshake agreements, it is also costly. Sears' negotiations with Hoffman Estates took 18 months and involved executives at the highest levels.

Second, distrust impedes sharing information or ideas to achieve production efficiencies or quality improvements. As discussed in Example 4.1, distrust characterizes the relationship between U.S. auto assemblers and their suppliers. Industry experts cite it as a reason for high production costs and the less-than-satisfactory quality of components.[23]

EXAMPLE 4.4

UNDERINVESTMENT IN RELATIONSHIP-SPECIFIC ASSETS BY BRITISH SUBCONTRACTORS[24]

Bruce Lyons recently studied investments in relationship-specific assets by British subcontractors. Lyons' study focused on small firms (ones employing 110 or fewer workers) that produced components for British manufacturers. The firms studied by Lyons included both "low-tech" firms making products such as metal casings, and "high-tech" firms producing items such as microprocessors and computer software. In all cases, the firms manufactured products that were customized to individual buyers.

Many of the subcontractors in Lyon's sample did not use formal contracts in their transactions with their principal customers. The subcontractors who did employ formal contracts were those whose principal buyer accounted for a large fraction of the subcontractors' sales revenues, who produced a highly customized product, and who made significant relationship-specific investments. These subcontractors faced the greatest risks of holdup and, perhaps not surprisingly, sought to protect themselves through formal contracts.

However, resorting to formal contracts was not the only way, or even the main way, that the subcontractors studied by Lyons protected themselves against

---

[21]See "Firms Finding it More Difficult to Leave Town," *Wall Street Journal*, March 3, 1993, p. B8.

[22]"It's All in Writing in the Sears Move" (letter to the editor), *Chicago Tribune*, April 10, 1993.

[23]Womack, J., D. Jones, and D. Roos, op. cit.

[24]Lyons, B., "Contracts and Specific Investment: An Empirical Test of Transaction Cost Theory," *Journal of Economics and Management Strategy*, 3, Summer 1994: pp. 257–278.

potential holdup. Many underinvested in relationship-specific assets. Half of the subcontractors in Lyons'sample indicated that an "ideal" relationship-specific production technology was available to support its transactions with its primary customer. However, only 40 percent of this group said they were using this technology or planning to do so. The subcontractors who were most likely to avoid investing in the relationship-specific technology saw themselves as vulnerable to opportunistic behavior by their principal customer and characterized their relationship with that customer as involving a high degree of distrust. These subcontractors refrained from investing in the ideal production technology because they were afraid that they would be held up.

XAMPLE 4.5

HOSTILE TAKEOVERS AND RELATIONSHIP-SPECIFIC INVESTMENTS AT TRANS UNION

Andre Shleifer and Lawrence Summers use transactions-cost economics to explore possible adverse consequences of hostile takeovers.[25] They suggest that hostile takeovers are often motivated by shareholders' desire to renege on implicit contracts (i.e., unwritten but mutually understood agreements) with employees who have made relationship-specific investments in the firms they work for. A serious consequence of this—and why, according to Shleifer and Summers, hostile takeovers could hurt the economy—is that in a climate of hostile takeovers, employees will refrain from investing in relationship-specific skills in their firms. This will reduce productivity and raise production costs.

To support their argument, Shleifer and Summers quote from William Owen's book, *Autopsy of a Merger*, about the merger between Trans Union and the Pritzker family's Marmon Group.[26] Most of the employees at Trans Union's corporate headquarters lost their jobs after the merger, in violation of what many of them felt was an implicit promise of guaranteed employment by the management of Trans Union. Owens asked former employees what they had learned from the experience. One said that in the future he would be much less willing to invest in his relationship with his employer: "I learned that I should cover my butt the next time around . . . and have my foot out the door immediately the next time it happens. . . . All of a sudden, you find the rug pulled out from under you—and there is nothing you can do about it. . . . You've worked hard for many, many years, tried to do the best job you could for the company—I loved that company—but what do you have to show for it? How can you go to another company and give 100% of your effort?"[27]

[25]Shleifer, A. and L. Summers, "Breach of Trust in Hostile Takeovers," in Auerbach, A., (ed.), *Corporate Takeovers: Causes and Consequences*, Chicago: University of Chicago Press, 1988.

[26]Owens, W., *Autopsy of a Merger*, Deerfield, IL: William Owen, 1986.

[27]Ibid., p. 251.

Reduced Investment   Finally, and perhaps worst of all, the possibility of holdup can reduce incentives to invest in specific assets. We saw earlier why this could occur. The anticipation of a holdup problem can turn what would otherwise be profitable investments into unprofitable ones because the investing party may not fully capture the potential profits from its investment.

Underinvestment could occur in several ways. A firm might reduce the scale of its investment in relationship-specific assets. For example, an alumina producer might build a small refinery rather than a large one. Or a firm might substitute general-purpose assets for more specific ones. For example, an alumina producer might build a refinery that can process many different grades of bauxite, instead of just one grade.

The tendency to underinvest in relationship-specific assets causes problems because relationship-specific investments usually allow firms to achieve efficiencies that they cannot achieve with general-purpose investments. For example, an alumina refinery that is set up to accommodate more than one grade of bauxite is generally more costly to operate than one that is designed to accommodate a particular type of bauxite. When the holdup problem leads to underinvestment in relationship-specific assets, the result is likely to be lower productivity and higher production costs.

Recap: From Relationship-Specific Assets to Transactions Costs

Because the ideas developed in this section are complex and subtle, let's recap the main lines of argument:

- A relationship-specific asset is an asset that supports a particular transaction. Redeploying a relationship-specific asset reduces its productivity or entails extra costs.

- A relationship-specific asset gives rise to quasi-rents. The quasi-rent in a transaction with relationship-specific assets equals the *extra profit* a firm gets when it deploys its relationship-specific assets in their intended use and the transaction goes ahead as planned, as opposed to deploying those assets in their best alternate use.

- When a party has quasi-rents, it can be held up by its trading partner. When this happens, the trading partner transfers the quasi-rents to itself. Holdup is especially tempting when contracts are highly incomplete, so that proving breach of contract is difficult.

- The potential for holdup raises the cost of market transaction by making contract negotiations more contentious, by inducing parties to invest in "safeguards" to improve postcontractual bargaining positions, by engendering distrust, and by leading to underinvestment in relationship-specific assets.

TRANSACTIONS COSTS AND VERTICAL INTEGRATION

The possibility of contractual holdup can raise the costs of negotiating and writing contracts and might also increase production costs. To avoid these inefficiencies, a natural alternative to market exchange is vertical integration.[28] But this immediately raises the question: What difference would vertical integration make? If there is a strong likelihood that an independent input-supply firm can hold up the firm that buys the input, why would there not be an equally strong likelihood of holdup when the independent input supplier becomes the selling division in a vertically integrated firm? In short, why can internal organization better resolve the holdup problem than arm's-length market contracting?

In this section, we argue that vertical integration might be preferable to market exchange for three reasons:

- Differences in governance: Vertical integration gives the parties access to more powerful governance structures than those available with arm's-length market contracting.

- Repeated relationship: Vertical integration places the transacting parties in a repeated relationship.

- Organizational influences: By placing the parties in the same organization, vertical integration may temper opportunistic behavior.

We will discuss each of these reasons in turn.

Differences in Governance

Governance mechanisms permit the adaptation of the terms of a transaction when circumstances change or when disputes arise. The governance of inside-the-firm transactions is fundamentally different from the governance of arm's-length market transactions. This difference is frequently described in terms of an employment or authority relationship, in which the employee, in exchange for a longer term of employment, predictable compensation, or other arrangements, agrees to work at the direction and discretion of a superior within general bounds (or as Chester Barnard called it, a "zone of indifference") rather than according to a thoroughly defined employment contract.[29]

Use of an authority/employment relationship, in effect, moves the dispute resolution mechanism for conflicts from the courts to administrative mechanisms inside the firm, such as managerial fiat, recourse to general rules, or informal mediation. Management has more flexibility in the choice of these mechanisms, and this flexibility will presumably lead to more efficient dispute resolution in situations where recourse to the courts would be costly, both in time lost and production disrupted.

To illustrate this point, suppose that a seller refuses to honor an arm's-length supply contract with a customer because the seller's costs have unexpectedly increased. The buyer and the seller could, in principle, renegotiate a new contract. Failing that, though, the buyer's main recourse would be a breach-of-contract lawsuit. As discussed earlier, breach-of-contract litigation is usually a costly way of resolving disputes, sometimes resulting in the termination of business relationships.

---

[28]Chapter 4 discusses alternatives to both arm's-length market exchange and vertical integration.

[29]Barnard, C., *The Function of the Executive*, Cambridge, MA: Harvard University Press, 1938.

It is also fairly inflexible in that the court would focus on assessing damages that are consistent with each party's obligations under the initial agreement. The court would not attempt to fashion an adjustment that would allow the parties to resume their relationship under the changed conditions.

By contrast, if the conflicting parties are separate divisions within a vertically integrated firm, more powerful and flexible administrative mechanisms are available. For example, top management could resolve the conflict directly by working out the issues that were caused by the differences between the initial agreements and changed conditions. This resolution can then be imposed on the parties. Management can also mediate a compromise. Management can act unilaterally in these situations because the courts give wide latitude to internal governance mechanisms. If, for example, top management imposed a solution that forced a division to accept a higher transfer price, the division could not appeal to the courts to rescind the increase.

Why internal governance mechanisms can be superior to external ones is an interesting question. In some sense, parties make the same kind of calculation in agreeing to such arrangements that they make in choosing market mechanisms. The bases of influence of management in internal governance arrangements are also similar to those in market mechanisms—withdrawal from future business and/or reductions in compensation. Furthermore, recourse to the courts would not be totally excluded from internal governance arrangements if extreme conflicts arise. Parties may also exit internal arrangements if their benefits are no longer comparable to those obtainable from the marketplace.

But one key difference between the employment/authority relationship of internal governance mechanisms and arm's-length market contracting is in the accommodation of the internal governance mechanisms to the bounded rationality of the parties and the complexity of contracting conditions—in other words, the sorts of factors that give rise to incomplete contracting in a market setting. For example, management can require the submission of detailed and standardized information from subsidiaries that would be much more costly to obtain from parties in an arm's-length relationship. This allows better information to be brought to bear in resolving disputes than would be available in court, where such information would have to be obtained through discovery procedures. Access to such information would allow higher-quality decisions to be made to resolve the disputes. It would also make the behavior of actors in the firm more observable to management and thus reduce the chances for opportunistic hidden actions.

Repeated Relationship

A second reason why vertical integration could resolve the holdup problem better than market contracting is that vertical integration binds the parties in a repeated relationship over time. Of course, vertical integration is not the only way for parties to be bound together over time. The parties could sign a long-term contract, or they might have a long-term business relationship such as exists between automobile parts suppliers and automobile assemblers in Japan. Still, vertical integration can tightly bind parties together over time.

Two divisions bound together within a given firm might have more incentive to make relationship-specific investments aimed at lowering costs than they would if they were separate firms, since the benefits of such investments can be calculated with relative certainty and the costs of the other party leaving the relationship are

XAMPLE 4.6

ASSET SPECIFICITY IN JAPANESE AND AMERICAN AUTOMOBILE MANUFACTURING

An interesting example of the importance of repeated relationships in reducing the transactions cost of exchange is the contrast between Japanese and American automobile manufacturers. Jeffrey Dyer has documented how automobile assemblers in Japan are far more willing to make relationship-specific investments than their American counterparts, and shows how these investments yield dramatic improvements in productivity.[30]

Dyer examined the relationship between two Japanese auto assemblers, Nissan and Toyota, and 96 of their direct suppliers. He compared these with the relationships between Ford, Chrysler, and General Motors and 125 of their suppliers. Perhaps the most striking of Dyer's findings is that Japanese parts suppliers make site-specific investments with the assemblers. For example, Toyota's affiliated supplier plants are, on average, only 30 miles away from assembly plants, and Toyota's independent suppliers are, on average, only 87 miles away. In contrast, the distance between U.S. suppliers and assemblers is 350 to 400 miles. Not only does proximity reduce shipping costs, it assures assemblers that necessary parts can be provided on time. As a result, inventory costs at Japanese assembly plants are 50 percent or less than those at U.S. plants.

Dyer also documents human asset specificity in auto production. Suppliers must often work from blueprints provided by the assemblers. These blueprints are often incomplete, and omitted details can frustrate well-intentioned suppliers. Suppliers with a long history of experience and communication with an assembler can usually figure out how to meet its needs without costly detailed written explanations for each aspect of the blueprint. This reduces product development times and enhances product reliability. Dyer also finds that Japanese suppliers are far more likely to customize the engineering of parts to meet the needs of a particular supplier, whereas U.S. suppliers tend to make generic parts that can be used by several manufacturers. Customized parts add to product integrity and quality.

Why can American firms not obtain the same relationship-specific investments from their suppliers as their Japanese counterparts? An important part of the answer lies in the differing traditions of vertical relationships in the two nations. Japanese firms in a vertical chain tend to remain business partners indefinitely. The relationship between an assembler and a parts supplier is a repeated one. This is partly the result of the formal and informal linkages in Keiretsu—a network of vertically related firms that we describe more fully in Chapter 5. By contrast, U.S. manufacturers often switch partners to get a better deal. This volatility discourages relationship-specific investments.

One should not necessarily conclude, however, that U.S. automobile manufacturers are short-sighted because they do not enter into long-term relation-

---

[30]Dyer, J., "Dedicated Assets: Japan's Manufacturing Edge," *Harvard Business Review*, November–December 1994: pp. 174–178.

ships with their suppliers to the same extent as the Japanese manufacturers do. Although long-term relationships of the sort documented by Dyer do facilitate specific investments, they also create many of the same problems as "make" decisions. A parts supplier in a long-term relationship with an automobile assembler, such as Nissan, might face reduced pressure to be efficient and innovative because it is assured of continued business. In addition, innovative new suppliers may be unable to break into the market because manufacturers are reluctant to end longstanding relationships with established suppliers.

The balance of these factors might argue in favor of long-term, rather than temporary, relationships between auto manufacturers and their suppliers, *at this point in time*. But this does not imply that this balance will remain unchanged, or that similar conclusions would apply in other industries. The dominance of U.S. firms in industries, such as biotechnology and software development, suggests that the flexibility of the free-wheeling U.S. production system can offer significant advantages.

---

much higher. Both divisions know that their relationship is likely to persist, and both recognize that they are more likely to recoup the fruits of their investment than if contractual holdup and termination of the relationship were probable. Moreover, the fact that both divisions are in a long-term relationship without a definite end period reduces the likelihood that one or both of the divisions will engage in opportunistic activities around the end period, after which no retaliation by the other division would be possible.

Of course, as emphasized in Chapter 3, the benefits of vertical integration are not free. A vertically integrated firm (or even two independent companies bound together in a long-term business relationship) can experience agency problems. Still, if the transactions costs due to asset specificity and the holdup problem are severe, the parties may endure these agency costs in return for eliminating opportunistic behavior and eliciting additional investment in relationship-specific assets.

Organizational Influences

The fact that two parties are in the same organization may by itself temper opportunistic behavior. Two divisions within the same organization may be more likely to behave cooperatively (e.g., in making relationship-specific investments to lower costs) because they see themselves as bound together in a common purpose to maximize the organization's welfare, rather than as adversaries in a market-mediated transaction. This raises the issue of why parties to an arm's-length transaction are less likely to take advantage of gains from cooperative behavior than parties who are participating in an identical exchange inside a common organization. Put another way, why do "organizations" create opportunities for promoting "good" behavior that arm's-length market contracting settings do not?

One reason is that firm members may be bound by ties of family or social similarity, so that they value their association with the firm, with its subunits, or with other workers in the firm in addition to monetary compensation. The commitment of the individual to the organization would thus supplement the more formal governance mechanisms inside the firm, and would make internal governance of transactions more effective than market governance. In small businesses, conflict resolution means working things out among family members.

Corporate culture may provide an analogous condition for larger firms. Organizations have histories, folklore, and other cultural elements that can powerfully influence individual behavior. For example, a culture that stresses teamwork may make the opportunities for mutual gains from cooperative behavior much more salient than they would be in an arm's-length market setting. The presence of cultural influences indicates the importance for workers of work-group acceptance, adherence to group norms, and status within the organization, and these factors can often determine the degree of cooperation within the organization. A nonpecuniary penalty, such as a loss in status within an organization for noncooperative behavior (e.g., refusing to be a "team player"), might be just as powerful for workers as would be termination of a formal contract in a market setting. In these situations, culture can complement the formal governance mechanism in the firm and make internal organization a more effective mode for organizing the transaction than the market would be. Examples of these situations are often found in Japanese firms.

Of course, nothing guarantees that two parties on the same "team" will act like "teammates." There are many examples of adversarial relationships between divisions within a single firm (e.g., the U.S. automobile assemblers' relationships with their in-house suppliers). Indeed, capital budgeting and profit center systems within firms often presume competitive rather than cooperative systems between divisions. Moreover, fashioning highly desirable career paths and highly competitive tournaments among management prospects is how firms can use individually oriented incentives, in addition to any market incentives, to promote greater efficiency.

Gary Miller argues that exercising the "political leadership" to balance incentives for competitive and cooperative behaviors among autonomous units within the firm is the single most important task of top management.[31] Our point is that the sociology of organizations opens up potential avenues for discouraging opportunistic behavior and achieving cooperative outcomes that are not available in a market contracting setting.

The preceding discussion leaves us with an important issue. While vertical integration undoubtedly has advantages over market contracting in terms of economizing on transaction costs, we have also seen from Chapter 3 that vertical integration has important drawbacks. How do the factors discussed in Chapter 3 interact with the transactions-cost considerations to determine how the vertical chain is actually organized? This is the subject of Chapter 5.

CHAPTER SUMMARY

◆ Transactions costs are the costs of using arm's-length market exchange to carry out exchanges of goods and services. The existence of significant transaction costs can explain why organizations sometimes carry out transactions internally rather than relying on market specialists.

---

[31]Miller, G., "Managerial Dilemmas: Political Leadership in Hierarchies," in Cook, K. S. and M. Levi, (eds.), *The Limits of Rationality, Chicago*: University of Chicago Press, 1990.

◆ A complete contract provides a complete and thorough specification of the responsibilities and rights of each party in the relationship, and would completely protect parties from opportunistic behavior.

◆ Most real-world contracts are incomplete. An incomplete contract involves some ambiguity about what each party to the contract is required to do and what rights each has.

◆ Contracts are incomplete due to bounded rationality, difficulties in specifying or measuring performance, and asymmetric information: hidden knowledge about contract-relevant parameters or contingencies and hidden actions that parties can take to influence contractual outcomes.

◆ Contract law reduces the costs of relying on contracts in a world of incomplete contracting. Doctrines of contract law relieve parties of the necessity of writing down low-probability contingencies in each and every transaction. But litigation is costly, so contract law is not, in general, a perfect substitute for complete contingent contracting.

◆ The problem of opportunistic behavior is particularly serious when the transaction involves relationship-specific assets. In that case, parties to the transaction cannot costlessly switch trading partners.

◆ Transacting with relationship-specific assets involves a fundamental transformation in the nature of contracting possibilities. Before the relationship-specific investment is made, the firm may have many potential trading partners. After the investment is made, however, the firm has few, if any, alternatives to its current trading partner.

◆ Asset specificity takes several forms, including physical asset specificity, site specificity, dedicated assets, and human asset specificity.

◆ Rent is the profit a firm expects to receive when a transaction goes as planned and its assets are deployed in their intended use.

◆ Quasi-rent is the extra profit a firm gets when it deploys its relationship-specific assets in their intended use and the transaction goes ahead as planned, as opposed to deploying those assets in their best alternative use.

◆ Relationship-specific assets give rise to positive quasi-rents, which, in turn, create the potential for holdup. Holdup occurs when one party in the relationship seeks to capture the quasi-rents of the other party through contract renegotiations.

◆ The holdup problem raises the costs of exchange in four ways: (1) It increases the amount of time and money parties spend in contract negotiations; (2) It can lead to distrust, resulting in lost opportunities for achieving production efficiencies; (3) It induces parties to safeguard their bargaining positions through investments in standby facilities or development of second sources. These strategies can give rise to production cost inefficiencies; (4) Parties threatened with hold-up may not invest in relationship-specific assets. When this occurs, production costs will generally be higher than they would be otherwise.

◆ Vertical integration might lower the transactions costs that stem from the incomplete contracting and the holdup problem in three ways: (1) Organizing the transaction inside the firm opens up opportunities for distinctive governance arrangements that allow more flexible and more powerful forms of dispute resolution and greater adaptability of the transaction to unforeseen circumstances; (2) Parties that transact inside the firm deal with each other in a repeated relationship that reduces uncertainty and thus makes investments in relationship-specific assets more profitable; (3) Sociological influences, such as organizational culture, enhance the willingness and ability of parties to transact in a cooperative, as opposed to adversarial, mode.

QUESTIONS

1. Why does asymmetric information lead to inefficient actions?

2. Some contracts, such as those between municipalities and highway construction firms, are extremely long with terms spelled out in minute detail. Others, such as between consulting firms and their clients, are short and fairly vague about the division of re-

sponsibilities. What factors might determine such differences in contract length and detail?

3. Explain why the "holdup problem" is only a problem when there are relationship-specific assets involved in the transaction.

4. "If the corporate governance function can not protect specific assets, then firms may as well transact at arm length." Discuss.

5. As developing countries begin to prosper, what do you expect will happen to their demand for specific assets? How will this affect the boundaries of firms doing business in these countries?

6. Historically, compensation for workers followed a "wage/tenure profile" in which a worker's wages tended to be low relative to his or her productivity when the worker was first hired, and high relative to his or her productivity after the worker had remained with the firm for many years. How might such a profile create a possibility for the firm to hold up its workers? Be sure to identify a source(s) of quasi-rents in your analysis.

7. Use transactions costs economics to explain why General Motors owns Fisher Body (which makes body panels for GM cars) but does not own any tire manufacturers.

8. Noted fashion expert Sid Sims has been asked by New World Movie Studios to design the wardrobe for the forthcoming film *Bananas and Fog*. The wardrobe will test Sims' abilities—the fashions are to be made entirely of old newspapers, dead leaves, and scrap iron. The studio offers Sims the following contract: It will pay $500,000 upon acceptance of the wardrobe by the movie studio. Sims estimates that he can get the newspapers and leaves for free, must pay $50,000 for the scrap iron, and must commit an additional $350,000 in labor to produce the wardrobe. Full of excitement, Sims signs the contract.

   (a) What is the rent that Sims hopes to realize prior to signing the contract?
   (b) After the wardrobe is complete, what is the quasi-rent? What assumptions, if any, did you make to obtain this figure?
   (c) Offer a scenario whereby the studio holds up Sims.
   (d) Can Sims hold up the studio? Explain?

9. Suppose that Arnold Schwarzenegger (AS) pays Besanko, Dranove, and Shanley (BDS) an advance of $5 million to write the script to *Incomplete Contract*, a movie version of their immensely popular text on business strategy. The movie contract includes certain script requirements, including that AS gets to play a strong, silent, business strategist with superhuman analytic powers. BDS spend $100,000 worth of their time to write a script that is tailor-made for the ex-Terminator (AS, that is). When they turn in the script to AS, he claims that it fails to live up to the contractual requirement that he has several passionate love scenes, and attempts to renegotiate. Given the ambiguity over what constitutes passion, BDS are forced to agree.

   (a) What was BDS's rent?
   (b) What is their quasi-rent? What assumptions do you have to make to compute this?

10. In many modern U.S. industries the following patterns seem to hold:

    (a) Small firms are more likely to outsource production of inputs than are large firms;
    (b) "Standard" inputs (such as a simple transistor that could be used by several electronics manufacturers) are more likely to be outsourced than "tailor-made" inputs (such as a circuit board designed for a single manufacturer's specific needs).

    What factors might explain these patterns?

Organizing Vertical Boundaries: Vertical Integration and Its Alternatives

5

*I*n Chapters 3 and 4, we argued that the organization of the vertical chain is a matter of choice. Firms can organize exchange around arm's-length market transactions, or they can organize exchange internally; that is, they can vertically integrate. Although we discussed factors that affect the relative efficiency of market exchanges versus vertical integration—scale economies, leakages of private information, incentives, and the transactions costs of market exchange—we have not yet systematically studied how these factors trade off against one another in particular circumstances. We must do this to understand why vertical integration differs across industries (e.g., firms in the aluminum industry are generally more vertically integrated than firms in the tin industry), across firms within the same industry (e.g., GM is more vertically integrated than Ford), and across different transactions within the same firm (e.g., U.S. firms tend to outsource transportation services to a much greater degree than warehousing or inventory management).

The first part of this chapter assesses the merits of vertical integration as a function of the industry, firm, and transactions characteristics. It then discusses vertical integration in specific industries including automobiles, aerospace, and electric utilities. We also examine whether other factors besides those discussed in Chapters 3 and 4, affect a firm's decision to vertically integrate. We focus in particular on how ownership of relationship-specific assets affects vertical integration. Finally, we explore other ways of organizing exchange besides arm's-length market contracting and vertical integration. We focus on four important alternatives: (1) tapered integration (i.e., making and buying); (2) joint ventures and strategic alliances; (3) Japanese *keiretsu* (tightly knit networks of independent firms); and (4) implicit contracts that rely on firms' reputations.

TECHNICAL EFFICIENCY VERSUS AGENCY EFFICIENCY

Economizing

The costs and benefits of relying on the market can be classified as relating either to technical efficiency or agency efficiency. Technical efficiency has several interpretations in economics. A narrow interpretation is that it represents the degree to which a firm produces as much as it can from a given combination of inputs.[1] As John Connelly found with Crown, Cork, and Seal (see Chapter 3), a firm whose employees sleep or play cards at work, is probably not technically efficient. A broader interpretation—the one used in this chapter—is that technical efficiency indicates whether the firm is using the least-cost production process. For example, if efficient production of a particular good required specialized engineering skills, but the firm did not invest enough to develop those skills, then the firm has not achieved full technical efficiency. The firm could achieve technical efficiency by purchasing the good in question from a market firm, or by investing to develop the skills itself.

Agency efficiency refers to the extent to which the exchange of goods and services in the vertical chain has been organized to minimize the coordination, agency, and transactions costs discussed in Chapters 3 and 4. If the exchange does not minimize these costs, then the firm has not achieved full agency efficiency. Agency efficiency concerns the process of exchange, whereas technical efficiency concerns the process of production. To the extent that the process of exchange raises the costs of production (e.g., when the threat of holdup leads to reductions in relationship-specific investments and increases in production costs), we would classify this as an agency inefficiency rather than a technical inefficiency.

The make-or-buy decision often has conflicting implications for agency and technical efficiency. For example, when a computer maker obtains memory chips from the market, the firm may improve its technical efficiency by buying from specialized chip manufacturers. But this arrangement may reduce agency efficiency by necessitating detailed contracts that specify performance and rewards. The appropriate vertical organization of production must balance technical and agency efficiencies. Oliver Williamson uses the term *economizing* to describe this balancing act.[2]

Williamson argues that the optimal vertical organization minimizes the sum of technical and agency inefficiencies. That is, parties undertaking an exchange along the vertical chain arrange their transactions to minimize the sum of production and transactions costs. To the extent that the market is superior for minimizing production costs but vertical integration is superior for minimizing transactions costs, tradeoffs between the two costs are inevitable. Even the best organized firms confront the effects of this tradeoff, in the form of higher production costs, bureaucracy, breakdowns in exchange, and litigation.

---

[1]Caves, R. and D. Barton, *Efficiency in U.S. Manufacturing Industries*, Cambridge, MA: MIT Press, 1990.

[2]See Williamson, O., "Strategizing, Economizing and Economic Organization," *Strategic Management Journal*, 12, Winter 1991: 75–94, for a complete explanation of this concept along with a brief discussion of its intellectual history.

The Technical Efficiency/Agency Efficiency Tradeoff and Vertical Integration

Figure 5.1 provides a useful way to think about the interplay of agency efficiency and technical efficiency.[3] The figure illustrates a situation in which the quantity of the good being exchanged is fixed at a particular level. The vertical axis measures cost *differences* (costs resulting from internal organization minus costs resulting from market transaction). Positive values indicate that costs from internal organization exceed costs from market transactions. The horizontal axis measures asset specificity, denoted by k. Higher values of k imply greater asset specificity.

The curve ΔT measures the differences in technical efficiency. It measures the differences in minimum production costs when the item is produced in a vertically integrated firm and when it is exchanged through an arm's-length market transaction. By "minimum production cost," we mean to exclude from this difference any increases in production costs that result from differences in incentives to control costs or to invest in cost-reducing process improvements across the two modes of organization. ΔT is positive for any level of asset specificity because outside suppliers can aggregate demands from other buyers and thus can take better advantage of economies of scale and scope to lower production costs than firms that produce those inputs themselves. The cost difference declines with asset specificity because greater asset specificity implies more specialized uses for the input and thus fewer outlets for the outside supplier. As a result, with greater asset specificity, the scale- and scope-based advantages of outside suppliers are likely to be weaker.

The curve ΔA reflects differences in agency efficiency. It measures differences in exchange costs when the item is produced internally and when it is purchased

Figure 5.1
Tradeoff Between Agency Efficiency and Technical Efficiency.

The curve ΔT represents the minimum cost of production under vertical integration minus the minimum cost of production under arm's-length market exchange; that is, it reflects differences in technical efficiency. The curve ΔA represents the transactions costs when production is vertically integrated minus the transactions costs when it is organized through an arm's-length market exchange. (This difference includes any increases in production costs over their minimum level that are due to poor incentives or investments that are not made because of the holdup problem). This curve reflects differences in agency efficiency. The curve ΔC is the vertical sum of ΔT and ΔA and represents the overall cost difference between vertical integration and market exchange. When this cost difference is negative, which occurs when asset specificity is sufficiently high, vertical integration is preferred to market exchange.

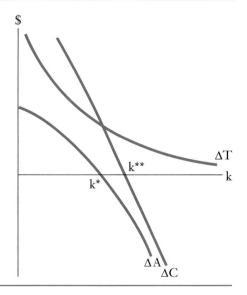

[3]This figure has been adapted from Oliver Williamson's discussion of vertical integration in *The Economic Institutions of Capitalism*, New York: Free Press, 1985, chap. 4.

from an outside supplier in an arm's-length transaction. When the item is purchased from an outside supplier, these costs comprise the direct costs of negotiating the exchange; the costs of writing and enforcing contracts; and the costs associated with holdup and underinvestments in relationship-specific assets that we discussed in Chapter 4. They also include the costs of breakdowns in coordination and leakage of private information discussed in Chapter 3. When the item is produced internally, these costs include the agency and influence costs discussed in Chapter 3. In short, the ΔA curve reflects differences in agency efficiency between the two modes of organizing transactions.

The ΔA curve is positive for low levels of asset specificity ($k < k^*$) and negative for high levels of asset specificity. When asset specificity is low, holdup is not a significant problem. In the absence of significant holdup problems, market exchange is likely to be more agency efficient than vertical integration because, as discussed in Chapter 3, independent firms often face stronger incentives to innovate and control production costs than divisions of a vertically integrated firm. As asset specificity increases, the transactions costs of market exchange also increase, and beyond a critical level, k^*, these costs are so large that vertical integration is more agency efficient than market exchange.

The curve ΔC is the vertical summation of the ΔA and ΔT curves. It represents production and exchange costs under vertical integration minus production and exchange costs under market exchange. If this curve is positive, then arm's-length market exchange is preferred to vertical integration. If the curve is negative, the exchange costs of using the market more than offset the production costs savings, and vertical integration is preferred. As shown in Figure 5.1, market exchange is preferred when asset specificity is sufficiently low ($k < k^{**}$). When asset specificity is greater than k^{**}, vertical integration is the preferred mode of organizing the transaction.

Vertical integration becomes increasingly attractive as the economies of scale in production become less pronounced. To see this, recall that the height of the ΔT curve reflects the ability of an independent producer to achieve scale economies in production by selling to other firms. Weaker economies of scale would correspond to a downward shift in ΔT, which in turn results in a smaller range in which vertical integration dominates arm's-length market contracting increases. In the extreme case, as economies of scale disappear, the ΔT curve coincides with the horizontal axis, and the choice between vertical integration and market procurement is determined entirely by agency efficiency, that is, the ΔA curve.

Figure 5.2 shows what happens to the choice between market contracting and vertical integration as the scale of the transaction increases. There are two effects. First, the vertically integrated firm could now take fuller advantage of scale economies because it produces a higher output. This reduces the production-cost disadvantage of internal organization and shifts the ΔT curve downward. Second, increasing the scale of the transaction accentuates the advantage of whichever mode of production has lower exchange costs. Thus, the ΔA curve would "twist" clockwise through the point k^*. The overall effect of these two shifts moves the intersection point of the ΔC curve to the left, from k^{**} to k^{***}. (The solid lines are the shifted curves; the dashed lines are the original curves.) This widens the range in which vertical integration is the preferred mode of organization. Put another way, as the scale of the transaction goes up, vertical integration is more likely to be the preferred mode of organizing the transaction for any given level of asset specificity.

As the scale of the transaction increases, the firm's demand for the input goes up, and a vertically integrated firm can better exploit economies of scale and scope in production. As a result, its production cost disadvantage relative to a market specialist firm will go down, so the curve Δ*T* will shift downward. (The dashed lines represent the curves at the original scale of the transaction; the solid lines represent the curves when the scale of the transaction increases.) At the same time, increased scale accentuates the advantage of the organizational mode with the lowest exchange costs. Thus, curve Δ*A* twists clockwise through point *k**. As a result, the intersection of the Δ*C* curve with the horizontal axis moves leftward, from *k*** to *k****, expanding the range in which vertical integration is the least-cost organizational mode.

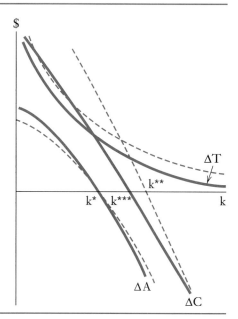

Figures 5.1 and 5.2 yield three powerful conclusions about the drivers of vertical integration:

1. *Scale and scope economies*: A firm gains less from vertical integration the greater the ability of outside market specialists to take advantage of economies of scale and scope relative to the firm itself. As we discussed in Chapter 2, a key source of economies of scale and scope is "indivisible," up-front "setup" costs, such as investments in physical capital or in the development of production know-how. From this, it follows that when production of the input involves significant, up-front setup costs, and there is likely to be a large market outside the firm for the input, vertical integration is likely to be inferior to market exchange, and the firm should purchase the input from outside market specialists. This will often be the case for routine products and services that are capital intensive or cost less to manufacture when the firm that produces them acquires experience and know-how.

2. *Product market scale and growth*: A firm gains more from vertical integration the larger is the scale of its product market activities. This is because the more the firm produces, the more its demand for the input grows and the more likely it becomes that in-house input production can take as much advantage of economies of scale and scope as an outside market specialist. This implies that a firm with a larger share of the product market will benefit more from vertical integration than a firm with a smaller share of the product market. It also implies that a firm with multiple product lines will benefit more from being vertically integrated in the production of components for those products in which it can achieve significant market scale. It will benefit less from being

vertically integrated in the production of components for "boutique" or "niche" items that it produces on a small scale.

3. *Asset specificity*: A firm gains more from vertical integration when production of inputs involves investments in relationship-specific assets. If asset specificity is significant enough, vertical integration will be more profitable than arm's-length market purchases, even when production of the input is characterized by strong scale economies or when the firm's product market scale is small.

Real-World Evidence

Do real-world firms behave according to this theory? Evidence suggests that they do. Let us look first at business history. The evolution of the hierarchical firm discussed in Chapter 1 is certainly consistent with the product market scale and the asset-specificity effects. A key step in the growth of the modern firm was forward integration by manufacturers into marketing and distribution.[4] Between 1875 and 1900, technological breakthroughs allowed for unprecedented economies of scale in manufacturing industries. This, coupled with improvements in transportation and communication that expanded the scope of markets, led to vast increases in the size of firms in capital-intensive industries, such as steel, chemicals, food processing, and light machinery.

As these firms grew, they vertically integrated. Before 1875, most manufacturers relied on independent commercial intermediaries to distribute their products. Because an intermediary could aggregate the demands of many manufacturers, it could sell and distribute at a lower cost per unit than any individual manufacturer could. However, there were limits to the economies of scale and scope in selling and distribution. As the scale of the manufacturers in the capital-intensive industries grew, independent wholesaling and marketing agents lost much of their scale- and scope-based cost advantages. As this happened, manufacturers forward integrated into marketing and distribution, a result consistent with the firm-size hypothesis. As predicted by the asset-specificity hypothesis, forward integration was most likely to occur for products that required specialized investments in human capital (e.g., George Eastman's marketing of cameras and film) or in equipment and facilities (e.g., Gustavus Swift's refrigerated warehouses and boxcars). For those industries in which manufacturers remained small (e.g., furniture or textiles) and/or marketing and distribution did not rely on specialized assets (e.g., candy), manufacturers continued to rely on independent commercial intermediaries to distribute and sell their products.

Statistical evidence on vertical integration from a variety of industries is also consistent with the theory developed earlier. Consider specific examples.

Automobiles   Kirk Monteverde and David Teece studied the choice between vertical integration and market procurement of components by General Motors and Ford.[5] Monteverde and Teece surveyed design engineers to determine the importance of applications engineering effort in the design of 133 different components.

---

[4]Chandler, A. D., Jr., *Scale and Scope: The Dynamics of Industrial Capitalism*, Cambridge, MA: Belknap, 1990.

[5]Monteverde, K. and D. Teece, "Supplier Switching Costs and Vertical Integration in the Automobile Industry," *Bell Journal of Economics*, 13, Spring 1982: pp. 206–213.

Greater applications engineering effort is likely to involve greater human asset specificity, so Monteverde and Teece hypothesized that car makers would be more likely to produce components that required significant amounts of applications engineering effort and more likely to buy components that required small amounts of applications engineering effort. Their analysis of the data confirmed this hypothesis. They also found that GM is more vertically integrated than Ford on components with the same asset specificity. This is consistent with the firm-size hypothesis.

Aerospace Industry Scott Masten studied the make-or-buy decision for nearly 2,000 components in a large aerospace system.[6] He asked procurement managers to rate the design specificity of the components, that is, the extent to which the component was used exclusively by the company or could be easily adapted for use by other aerospace firms or firms in other industries. A transistor or resistor would be an example of a nonspecific item; a circuit board designed to individual specifications would be an example of a component with high design specificity. Consistent with the asset-specificity hypothesis, Masten found that greater design specificity increased the likelihood that production of the component was vertically integrated. He also studied the effect of the complexity of the component, that is, the number of relevant performance dimensions and the difficulty in assessing satisfactory performance. He found that more complex components were more likely to be manufactured internally. This is consistent with the discussion in Chapter 4 about the hazards of incomplete contracting: When the item being purchased is complex or it is not easy to measure performance, parties in an arm's-length market transaction find it hard to protect themselves with contracts, which increases the risk of holdup.

Electric Utility Industry Paul Joskow studied the extent of backward integration by electric utilities into coal mining.[7] Coal-burning electricity-generating plants are sometimes located next to coal mines. This minimizes the costs of shipping coal and maximizes the operating efficiency of the generating plant. A utility that makes a "mine-mouth" investment will typically design its boilers with tight tolerances to accommodate the quality of coal from that particular mine. The utility may also make large investments in rail lines and transmission capacity, and the mine will often expand its capacity to supply the on-site utilities. The relationship between the utility and the mine thus involves both site and physical-asset specificity. Joskow found that mine-mouth plants are much more likely to be vertically integrated than other plants. Where mine-mouth plants were not vertically integrated, Joskow found that coal suppliers relied on long-term supply contracts containing numerous safeguards to prevent holdup. Mine-mouth plants rarely relied on short-term arm's-length contracts with the coal mine.

Electronic Components Erin Anderson and David Schmittlein studied the decision by firms in the electronic components industry to forward integrate into marketing and distribution and use an in-house sales force or to rely on indepen-

---

[6]Masten, S., "The Organization of Production: Evidence from the Aerospace Industry," *Journal of Law and Economics*, 27, October 1984: pp. 403–417.

[7]Joskow, P., "Vertical Integration and Long-Term Contracts: The Case of Coal-Burning Electric Generating Plants," *Journal of Law, Economics, and Organization*, 33, Fall 1985: pp. 32–80.

dent manufacturers' representatives.[8] Manufacturers' reps offer selling services to manufacturers in exchange for a sales commission. Manufacturers' reps operate like the sales department of a firm except that they usually represent more than one manufacturer. (Sometimes a rep will carry complementary products, for exam-

◆ ◆

XAMPLE 5.1

THE VIRTUAL CORPORATION

One of the best-selling management books of the early 1990s was *The Virtual Corporation*, by William Davidow and Michael Malone.[9] The book's basic premise is that because technological and competitive conditions are changing more rapidly than ever before, business organizations need to be far more flexible in responding to changing circumstances than they have been. Davidow and Malone argue that to enhance flexibility, firms must abandon their reliance on internal hierarchy and continually fashion relationships with independent vendors. To the traditional make-or-buy question, Davidow and Malone argue that each element in the vertical chain must remain independent; that is, buy should dominate. Indeed, the virtual corporation is even less rigidly structured than the "network organization" advocated by Tom Peters and other management gurus because the network organization presumes long-term relationships in the vertical chain.[10]

Given our discussion of vertical integration, it is tempting to dismiss Davidow and Malone's arguments as incomplete. They seem to ignore the costs of coordination and the transactions costs of market exchange, assuming that independent market experts can unite to achieve efficient production without encountering problems with coordination or holdup. What makes their arguments plausible, however, is the recognition that advances in data processing, telecommunications, and computer-assisted manufacturing have minimized coordination costs, while also reducing asset specificity in many production relationships. In terms of Figure 5.1, the ΔA curve has flattened, so that agency efficiency differences between internal and market organization have diminished. As a result, technical efficiencies achievable by using market experts now dominate vertical integration decisions.

Whether Davidow and Malone's recommendations make sense for a particular organization depends, of course, on the relevant technological and agency conditions. While the virtual corporation will be inappropriate for many firms, and no manager should adopt the model without considering the consequences for agency efficiency, it may be increasingly appropriate for some firms. Just as changes in communication and production technology between 1840 and 1910 rendered organizational structures obsolete, changes in the decades ahead could permit the virtual corporation to replace the structures that currently dominate business.

[8]Anderson, E. and D. C., Schmittlein, "Integration of the Sales Force: An Empirical Examination," *RAND Journal of Economics*, 15, Autumn 1984: pp. 385–395.

[9]Davidow, W. H. and M. S. Malone, *The Virtual Corporation*, New York: HarperBusiness, 1992.

[10]See Peters, T., *Liberation Management: Necessary Disorganization for the Nanosecond Nineties*, New York: Knopf, 1992.

ple, computers and modems, but often manufacturers' reps will carry products of competing manufacturers). Anderson and Schmittlein surveyed territory sales managers in 16 major electronics component manufacturers to determine the extent to which the manufacturers relied on manufacturers' reps or on their own sales forces in a given sales territory for a given product. The survey measured the amount of asset specificity in the selling function and the degree of difficulty in evaluating a salesperson's performance. The measure of asset specificity embraced such factors as the amount of time a salesperson would have to spend learning about the company's product; the extent to which selling the product would necessitate extra training even for a person experienced with the product class; and the importance of the personal relationship between the salesperson and the customer. Consistent with the asset-specificity hypothesis, Anderson and Schmittlein found that greater asset specificity in the selling function was associated with a greater likelihood that firms rely on their own sales forces rather than manufacturers' reps. They also found that holding asset specificity constant, larger manufacturers were more likely to use a direct sales force than smaller firms, a result consistent with the firm-size hypothesis. Finally, they found that the more difficult it was to measure performance, the more likely manufacturers were to rely on direct sales forces rather than manufacturers' reps. This is consistent with the notion that when the transaction environment is less amenable to contractual safeguards (e.g., because contracting on performance is more difficult), arm's-length market contracting becomes a relatively more costly form of organizing an exchange.

VERTICAL INTEGRATION AND ASSET OWNERSHIP ◆ ◆ ◆ ◆ ◆

The basic argument of the preceding section is that the interplay of technical and agency efficiency (which is influenced by the factors discussed in Chapters 3 and 4) determines the relative desirability of vertical integration versus arm's-length market contracting.

Sanford Grossman, Oliver Hart, and John Moore (GHM) develop a different theory for comparing vertical integration with market exchange.[11] Their theory focuses on the importance of asset ownership and control and makes the critical observation that the resolution of the make-or-buy decision determines ownership rights. The owner of an asset may grant another party the right to use it, but the owner retains all rights of control that are not explicitly stipulated in the contract. These are known as residual rights of control. When ownership is transferred—when these residual rights are purchased—they are lost by the selling party, which fundamentally changes the legal rights of that party.

To illustrate, consider the relationship between PepsiCo and its bottlers. PepsiCo has two types of bottlers: independent and company owned.[12] An independent bottler owns the physical assets of the bottling operation and the exclusive rights to the franchise territory. It can thus determine how these assets are used, for example, how frequently to restock particular stores. PepsiCo has no direct au-

---

[11]Grossman, S. and O. Hart, "The Costs and Benefits of Ownership: A Theory of Vertical and Lateral Integration," *Journal of Political Economy*, 94, 1986: pp. 619–719; Hart, O. and J. Moore, "Property Rights and the Nature of the Firm," *Journal of Political Economy*, 98, 1990: pp. 1119–1158.

[12]See Chapter 3 for additional discussion of vertical integration in soft-drink bottling.

thority over how the independent bottler manages the operations within its territory. If, for example, a bottler refuses to participate in a national campaign like the Pepsi Challenge, PepsiCo can only try to persuade the bottler to cooperate. Suppose, however, PepsiCo acquires one of its independent bottlers. The bottler is now a subsidiary of PepsiCo, so PepsiCo can specify what the bottler must do. PepsiCo could cede to the bottler specific forms of authority over the assets; for example, PepsiCo could delegate responsibility for local advertising and product promotion to the bottler. However, PepsiCo, not the bottler, has the ultimate authority over how the bottling assets are deployed and how the bottler's territory is managed. If the management of the bottling subsidiary refused to participate in a national advertising campaign, PepsiCo could replace them with a more cooperative team.

If contracts were complete (i.e., if they specified every action under every contingency), it would not matter who owned the assets. The contract would spell out exactly what actions should be taken at all times, and how all parties were to be compensated. In other words, complete contracts would render make-or-buy decisions inconsequential.[13] As discussed in Chapter 4, however, most contracts are incomplete. For example, individuals cannot contemplate all possible contingencies, performance cannot be precisely measured, and asymmetric information can make it difficult to verify that promised actions were taken.

Taking incomplete contracting as a starting point, the GHM theory analyzes how the pattern of asset ownership affects the willingness of parties to invest in relationship-specific assets. The theory considers a situation in which two units enter a transaction with each other. For simplicity, think of unit 1 being upstream from unit 2 in the vertical chain. To carry out the transaction, the parties must jointly make an array of operating decisions. The theory assumes that the parties cannot write a contract that specifies these operating decisions in advance. Instead, they must bargain over them once the transaction is underway.

We can imagine three alternative ways to organize the transaction:

1. *Nonintegration:* The two units are independent firms, each with control over its own assets.
2. *Forward integration:* Unit 1 owns the assets of unit 2 (i.e., unit 1 forward integrates into the function performed by unit 2 by purchasing control over unit 2's assets).
3. *Backward integration:* Unit 2 owns the assets of unit 1 (i.e., unit 2 backward integrates into the function performed by unit 1 by purchasing control over unit 1's assets).

GHM's theory establishes that the form of integration affects the incentives of parties to invest in relationship-specific assets. Generally speaking, by having control over the other unit's assets, a unit has a better bargaining position when it negotiates with the other unit over the operating decisions that they could not contract on. With a better bargaining position, the unit can capture more of the economic value created by the transaction, thus boosting its willingness to make relationship-specific investments. The theory implies that vertical integration is desirable when one unit's investment in relationship-specific assets has a signifi-

---

[13]Grossman and Hart point out the need to be able to enforce the contracts in a court of law. This includes the ability to collect penalties for contract breach.

EXAMPLE 5.2

VERTICAL INTEGRATION OF THE SALES FORCE IN THE INSURANCE INDUSTRY

In the insurance industry, some products (e.g., whole life insurance) are usually sold through in-house sales forces, while other products (e.g., fire and casualty insurance) are often sold through independent brokers. The GHM theory helps us understand this pattern. Relying on independent agents versus in-house sales employees is essentially a choice by the insurance firm for nonintegration versus forward integration into the selling function. This choice determines the ownership of an extremely important asset in the process of selling insurance: the list of clients. Under nonintegration the agent controls this key asset; under forward integration, the insurance firm controls it.

If the agent owns the client list, the agent controls access to its clients; they cannot be solicited without the agent's permission. A key role of an insurance agent is to search out and deliver dependable clients to the insurance company, clients who are likely to renew their insurance policies in the future. To induce an agent to do this, the commission structure must be "backloaded," for example, through a renewal commission that exceeds the costs of servicing and re-signing the client. When the insurance company owns the client list, however, this commission structure creates incentives for the company to hold up the agent. It could threaten to reduce the likelihood of renewal (e.g., by raising premiums or restricting coverage) unless the agent accepts a reduced likelihood of his or her renewal commission. Faced with the possibility of this holdup problem, the agent would presumably underinvest in searching out and selling insurance to repeat clients. By contrast, if the agent owned the client list, the potential for holdup by the insurance company would be much weaker. If the company did raise premiums or restrict coverage, the agent could invite its client to switch companies. Threats by the company to jeopardize the agent's renewal premium would thus have considerably less force, and underinvestment in the search for persistent clients would not be a problem.

In some circumstances the holdup problem could work the other way. Suppose the insurance company can engage in list-building activities such as new product development. The agent could threaten not to offer the new product to the customer unless the insurance company paid the agent a higher commission. Faced with the prospect of this holdup, the company is likely to underinvest in developing of new products. By contrast, if the insurance company owned the list, this type of holdup could not occur, and the insurance company's incentive to invest in new product development would be much stronger.

This suggests that there are tradeoffs in alternative ownership structures that are similar to those discussed above. According to the GHM theory, the choice between an in-house sales force versus independent agents should turn on the relative importance of investments in developing persistent clients by the agent versus list-building activities by the insurance firm. Given the nature of the product, a purchaser of whole life insurance is much less likely to switch insurance companies than, say, a customer of fire and casualty insurance. Thus, the insurance agent's effort in searching out persistent clients is less important for whole life insurance than it is for fire and casualty insurance. For whole life insurance, then, backloading the commission structure is not critical, which diminishes the possibility of contractual holdup when the insurance company owns the client list. The GHM theory implies that whole life insurance would typically be sold through an insurance company's in-house sales force. This is consistent with industry practice: Most companies that offer whole life insurance have their own sales forces. By contrast, for term life or substandard insurance, the agent's selling and renewal-generation efforts are relatively more important. Consistent with the GHM theory, many insurance companies rely on independent agents who own the client list to sell these products.

cantly greater impact on the value created in the vertical chain than the other's investment does. When the investments of both units are of comparable importance, nonintegration is the best arrangement.

By emphasizing asset ownership, the GHM theory identifies an important dimension of vertical integration. It also suggests that there are degrees of vertical integration depending on the extent to which one party or the other controls specialized assets. This helps us understand certain real-world arrangements that fall between vertical integration and arm's-length market contracting. For example, General Motors and Ford often own their own specialized tooling and dies even though an independent firm produces body parts and components. This is especially likely for components, such as radiators and starters, that require specialized physical assets, but do not require much specialized engineering or operational know-how.[14] Similarly, in the glass bottle industry, large buyers will often retain ownership of specialized molds even though an independent manufacturer produces the jars and bottles. The GHM theory implies that this is a form of vertical integration and is distinct from the situation in which the independent supplier carries out production and owns the physical asset.

Their emphasis on asset ownership also suggests that physical and human-asset specificity can have different implications for vertical integration. Ownership of specialized physical assets can be transferred, but ownership of specialized human capital often cannot be. Thus, we might expect that the degree of vertical integration is likely to be affected not only by the degree of asset specificity, but also by its form. Benjamin Klein, who studied the 1925 vertical merger between General Motors and Fisher Body, notes that if the only relationship-specific investments had been in physical assets (dies and stamping machines), the potential for Fisher to hold up General Motors would have been removed if General Motors had simply retained ownership of the specialized physical assets and contracted with Fisher to produce auto bodies using GM's capital.[15] That would have preserved the advantages of having Fisher Body as an independent supplier. This arrangement was not chosen because much of the asset specificity in this case came from investments in relationship-specific know-how by Fisher workers, which would have made it difficult for General Motors to find another supplier if Fisher had tried to engage in holdup.

[14]See Masten, S., J. W. Meehan, and E. A. Snyder, "Vertical Integration in the U.S. Auto Industry: A Note on the Influence of Transactions Specific Assets," *Journal of Economic Behavior and Organization*, 12, 1989: pp. 265–273.

[15]Klein, B., "Vertical Integration as Organizational Ownership," *Journal of Law, Economics, and Organization*, 1988: pp. 199–213.

PROCESS ISSUES IN VERTICAL MERGERS ◆ ◆ ◆ ◆ ◆

The principles presented in this chapter thus far are often taken as a basis for assessing the desirability of vertical mergers.[16] If the net balance of technical efficiencies and agency inefficiencies is more favorable after a merger between a buyer and a supplier than it was before the merger, then the merger is appropriate. If the net balance of expected efficiencies after the merger is negative, the merger is not appropriate. The decision whether to vertically merge is not so simple, however. Merging on the vertical chain is not a clear make-or-buy decision, but more a matter of "buying" an opportunity to "make." Whether that opportunity will be productive depends on how governance arrangements between the two merging firms develop.

Assessing whether a merger on the vertical chain will enhance efficiency must take into account the fact that the governance arrangements between the acquired and acquiring firms need further adjustment after the combination has been formally completed. After the merger, the managers of the acquired firm may have to cede much of their decision-making authority to managers of the acquiring firm.

The GHM theory discussed in the previous section suggests a criterion for judging which governance arrangements will be efficient. It addresses situations in which the specialized human capital of acquired firm managers and employees may be important for the success of a merger. Ownership rights over such assets cannot be transferred even if ownership over the physical assets associated with that capital can be transferred. If the specialized assets of these managers are not employed in the interests of the firm, the merged firm will be less profitable. A governance arrangement that does not grant acquired managers decision-making rights commensurate with their control over specialized resources thus risks being inefficient.

This suggests that decision-making rights for an activity should be given to those managers whose decisions will have the greatest impact on the performance of the activity and ultimately on the profitability of the firm. For example, if the success of a merger depends largely on synergies associated with the combined physical assets of two firms, such as through the resolution of coordination problems between a buyer and a supplier, then decision-making authority should be centralized. If, however, success depends on the specialized knowledge of acquired managers, such as their knowledge of key contacts in local markets, then decision authority should be decentralized.

Who will actually exercise decision-making authority in the combined firm? What governance arrangements will develop between formerly independent firms? It is not clear in advance which of several possible governance arrangements will develop after a merger. On the one hand, managers at the acquiring firm could delegate significant decision-making authority to unit managers and grant them an autonomy that parallels their prior independent state. On the other hand, managers at the acquiring firm may assume authority for most decisions themselves. In between are numerous arrangements in which authority is delegated on some decisions and not on others. The actual arrangements that develop may or may not be efficient, in that they will not necessarily reflect the transactions-cost requirements suggested by GHM. The process by which governance develops can

---

[16]See Williamson, O. E., *Antitrust Economics*, Oxford, UK: Basil Blackwell, 1987, chaps. 1–4, for a discussion of the role of transactions cost considerations in antitrust policy.

also exhibit *path dependence*. That is, past circumstances could exclude certain possible governance arrangements in the future. For example, if the period following a merger is marked by conflict, an efficient governance structure requiring cooperation between acquired and acquiring firm managers might not be feasible.

These same considerations will also apply to vertical disintegration. At first glance, a vertically related unit of a firm that was spun off to the market as an independent firm would appear to be a market actor. Initially, however, managers in that unit will not be used to making decisions as an autonomous market actor and may continue to rely on associations with managers in the former parent firm. This would make the relationship between the two firms after a spin-off not a market transaction, but rather a long-term informal association, which is somewhere between being part of an integrated firm and a specialized market actor.

The path-dependent nature of the processes by which firms develop can also affect vertical relationships by affecting the capacity of the firm to sell the products of a unit to other downstream buyers besides itself. In Chapter 3, we suggested that market specialists could be more efficient sources of an input for a firm than self-manufacture, since specialists could gain economies of scale by selling to multiple downstream buyers, that were not available to a firm that self-manufactured. Firms manufacturing for internal uses would typically not sell excess output to other firms. We assumed that, for firms that built their abilities to self-manufacture in order to supply their internal needs, the sale to outside firms of excess product would be both a distraction and an activity for which the firm lacked the requisite skills. If a firm acquired rather than built its supply capacity, however, the situation would be different. The acquired firm would know how to sell to multiple buyers. This marketing capacity would presumably be one of the resources acquired by the parent through the merger. In such a situation, selling product produced primarily for internal uses to outside firms would be neither a distraction nor an activity for which the firm lacked resources. The firm's opportunities for selling to other users of the product could be limited by competitive conditions, however.

◆ ◆ ◆ ◆ ◆ ALTERNATIVES TO VERTICAL INTEGRATION

This chapter poses the problem of the firm's vertical boundaries rather starkly—the firm must either make an input or purchase it from an independent firm through an arm's-length market transaction. A variety of in-between alternatives may capture the best of both worlds. In this section we consider four "hybrid" ways of organizing exchange: (1) tapered integration, in which the firm both makes and buys a given input; (2) joint ventures; (3) close-knit semiformal relationships among buyers and suppliers, best embodied by the Japanese *keiretsu*; and (4) long-term implicit contracts that are supported by reputations for honesty, cooperativeness, and trust.

Tapered Integration: Make and Buy

Tapered integration represents a mixture of vertical integration and market exchange. A manufacturer might produce some quantity of an input itself and purchase the remaining portion from independent firms. It might sell some of its product through an in-house sales force and rely on an independent manufacturers' representative to sell the rest. Examples of tapered integration include such retailers as Blockbuster Video and Wendy's, who own some of their retail outlets but award franchises for others; Coca-Cola and Pepsi, who have their own bottling subsidiaries, but also rely on independently owned bottlers to produce and distribute their soft drinks in some markets, and General Motors, which has its own market research division but also purchases market research from independent firms.

Tapered integration offers three benefits. First, it expands the firm's input and/or output channels without requiring substantial capital outlays. This is helpful to growing firms, such as fledgling retail chains. Second, the firm can use information about the cost and profitability of its internal channels to help negotiate contracts with independent channels. The firm can threaten to use the market further to motivate the performance of its internal channels, and it can use the threat of self-manufacture to discipline its external channels. Third, the firm may also develop internal input supply capabilities to protect itself against holdup by independent input suppliers.

Oil refiners provide a classic example of tapered integration. The largest refiners, such as Exxon and Shell, explore for and produce crude oil. Because they can refine twice as much oil as they internally produce, they make substantial purchases of oil in the open market. This forces their internal production divisions to stay competitive with independent oil producers.

However, if tapered integration offers the best of both the make-and-buy worlds, it may also offer the worst. Forced to share production, both the internal and external channels may not achieve sufficient scale to produce efficiently. Shared production may lead to coordination problems because the two production units must agree on product specifications and delivery times. Moreover, a firm's monitoring problems may be exacerbated. Not only must the firm duplicate contracting and monitoring efforts, it cannot be certain that its production units are producing efficiently. For example, the firm may mistakenly establish the performance of an inefficient internal supplier as the standard to be met by external suppliers. Finally, managers may maintain inefficient internal capacity rather than close facilities that had formerly been critical to the firm. An example of this is the excess capacity for internal productions that major movie studios maintain.

EXAMPLE 5.3

TAPERED INTEGRATION IN GASOLINE RETAILING

Gasoline retailing offers an interesting example of tapered integration.[17] The major oil refining companies (e.g., Exxon, Mobil) own and operate their own service stations. The refiner determines the hours of business and the retail prices at the

---

[17]This example draws heavily from Borenstein, S. and R. Gilbert, "Uncle Sam at the Gas Pump: Causes and Consequences of Regulating Gasoline Distribution," *Regulation*, 1993: pp. 63–75.

stations it operates, and station personnel are employees of the refiner.[18] Refiners also sell their gasoline through service stations that carry their brand name, but are operated by independent dealers who either own the service station outright or lease it from the refiner. At independent stations, the dealer, not the refiner, sets the retail price of gasoline and the hours of business. Company-operated stations account for roughly 16 percent of U.S. retail sales of gasoline.

Tapered integration did not always exist. In the 1920s and 1930s, most large oil companies were fully integrated at the retail level: They owned almost all the stations that sold their gasoline. In the mid-1930s, the possibility that Iowa might impose a "chain-store" tax led the major refiners to experiment with sales through independent franchised dealers. The oil companies soon found that this arrangement had significant advantages. Selling gasoline through independent dealers gave the major refiners access to many local markets without having to make substantial capital investments. Independent operation also relieves the refiner of having to monitor and evaluate the activities of the service station and instead subjects dealers to the discipline of the market forces. But sales through independent dealers also have a significant disadvantage. The refiners cannot set retail prices, and imperfect competition in downstream markets often leads independent dealers to impose high markups over the wholesale price of gasoline. The resulting decrease in volume hurts the refiner by reducing the profit from its markup over the unit cost of production.

Because vertical integration has advantages as well as disadvantages, the major oil companies continue to own and operate their own stations. What is interesting is that changes in how gasoline is sold at the retail level have changed the balance between the costs and benefits in a way that seems to favor vertical integration. Traditionally, most gasoline stations not only sold gasoline, but also automobile maintenance and repair services, such as oil changes or brake replacement. For these stations, the cost of monitoring salaried employees was likely to be substantial because many repair tasks were nonroutine and the quality of a worker's output was difficult to measure. Thus, in most cases the optimal arrangement for these stations was likely to be independent operation. Since 1980, however, the traditional service station has given way to large "pumper" stations—gasoline stations with 10 or 12 self-service pumps staffed by a single cashier—and maintenance and repair business is increasingly being done by specialized outlets such as Jiffy Lube and Midas Muffler.[19] The result has been a shift in the relative proportion of independently operated and company-operated gasoline stations. Between 1980 and 1990, the number of major-brand, independently operated stations declined from about 180,000 to 110,000, whereas the number of company-operated stations grew from about 8,000 to 11,000.

---

[18]Independent operators who lease from the refiner receive the profits (or bear the losses) from running the station. Oil companies often lease stations as a way to generate the capital to finance their construction. A local investor will put up money to construct a service station on the promise that the oil company will lease the station from the investor on a long-term basis. The oil company then leases the station to the dealer on a shorter-term basis (e.g., three years).

[19]Another increasingly common arrangement is convenience stores that sell gasoline on a self-service basis. However, the gasoline sold at these outlets is usually not produced by the major brand-name refiners.

Strategic Alliances and Joint Ventures

In the 1980s and 1990s, firms increasingly turned to strategic alliances as a way to organize complex business transactions collectively without sacrificing autonomy. To illustrate the ubiquity of alliances, Table 5.1 shows summary of alliances in a single industry and country— Japanese producers of semiconductors—that formed in 1994.

In a strategic alliance, two or more firms agree to collaborate on a project or to share information or productive resources. Alliances may be horizontal, involving collaboration between two firms in the same industry, as when United Technologies and Daimler Benz teamed up to cooperate on a range of engine development activities. They may be vertical, involving collaboration between a supplier and a buyer, as when Texas Instruments (TI) and ACER (in the late 1980s, the largest computer company in Taiwan) jointly built a plant in Taiwan to manufacture DRAM chips. Or they may involve firms that are neither in the same industry, nor related through the vertical chain, as when Toys "R" Us and McDonald's of Japan formed a venture to build Toys "R" Us stores in Japan that would include a McDonald's restaurant.

A joint venture is a particular type of strategic alliance in which two or more firms create, and jointly own, a new independent organization. The new organization may be staffed and operated by employees of one or more parent firms, or it may be staffed independently of either. Examples of joint ventures include Coca-Cola's and Cadbury Schweppes' agreement to bottle and distribute Coca-Cola in Great Britain; Merck's and Johnson and Johnson's venture to market over-the-counter medicines such as Pepcid, an anti-ulcer treatment; and Genetics Institute's (one of the largest U.S. biotech companies) and Wellcome's (the largest British pharmaceuticals company) agreement to manufacture products based on recombinant DNA.

Alliances and joint ventures fall somewhere between arm's-length market transactions and full vertical integration. As in arm's-length market transactions, the parties to the alliance remain independent. However, an alliance typically involves more cooperation, coordination, and information sharing than would occur in an arm's-length transaction. Kenichi Olmae has likened a strategic alliance to a marriage: "There may be no formal contract . . . There are few, if any, rigidly binding provisions. It is a loose, evolving kind of relationship."[20] Like a marriage, the participants in an alliance rely on norms of trust and reciprocity, rather than contracts, to govern their relationship, and they resolve disputes through negotiation, rather than litigation.

What kinds of business transactions should be organized through alliances? The most natural candidates for alliances are transactions for which, using the frameworks in Chapters 3 and 4, there are compelling reasons to both make *and* buy. Specifically, transactions that are natural candidates for alliances have all or most of the following features:

1. The transaction involves impediments to comprehensive contracting. For example, the transacting parties know that as their relationship unfolds, they will need to perform a complex set of activities. But because of uncertainty and the

---

[20]Ohmae, K., "The Global Logic of Strategic Alliances," *Harvard Business Review*, March–April 1989: pp. 143–154.

TABLE 5.1
EXAMPLES OF ALLIANCES INVOLVING JAPANESE SEMICONDUCTOR SUPPLIERS
ENTERED IN 1994

Companies	Activity
Actel—Matsushita	Joint development of next generation Field Programmable Gate Array process
Advanced Telecomm. Modules—Kawasaki Steel	Kawasaki provides foundry services for ATM's Proton telecom chip-set.
Alliance Semiconductor—Rohm	Rohm provides foundry services for 256K and 1M SRAM chips.
Altera—Mitsubishi	Co-develop a design tool for Altera's Field-Programmable Gate Array.
Altera—Sharp	Sharp provides foundry services for Altera's Field-Programmable Logic Devices.
Altera—Sharp	Joint development of Programmable Logic Devices
AMD—Fujitsu	Constructed manufacturing plant for non-volatile memories.
Atmel—Seiko Epson	Seiko provides foundry services for Atmel's Field-Programmable Logic Devices.
C-Cube Microsystems—Yamaha	Yamaha provides foundry services for C-Cube's video compression integrated circuit
IBM—Toshiba, Siemens	Joint development of 64M DRAM.
MosaidTech., Newbridge Networks—Kawasaki Steel	Joint development of application specific integrated circuit.
Motorola—Toshiba	Agreed to construct Tohuku Semiconductors plant for 16M DRAM.
Oak Technology—Rohm	Joint development of digital signal processor.
Olicom A/S—Fujitsu	Joint development of IBM-compatible 25Mbps Asynchronous Transfer Mode integrated circuit.
Opti Computer—Ricoh	Ricoh provides foundry services for Opti's chip sets.
Opti Computer—Toshiba	Toshiba provides foundry services for Opti's chip sets.
Quality Semiconductor—Seiko Epson	Seiko provides foundry services for Quality's QSFCT integrated circuits.
Quality Semiconductor—Yamaha	Yamaha provides foundry services for Quality's QSFCT integrated circuits.
Ramtron International—Hitachi	Joint feasibility study for ferro-electric RAM.
Ramtron International—Rohm	Rohm provides foundry services for RAMtron's ferro-electric RAM.
Samsung—NEC	Agreed to exchange technical information for 256M DRAM.
Sun Disk—NEC	Joint development of 256M flash memory.
Texas Instruments—Sony	Cooperation for 16-bit MPU technology.
Xilinx—Seiko Epson	Seiko Epson provides foundry services.

* Source: *Semiconductor Facts, 1995*, Electronic Industries Association of Japan, pp. 2–4, 2–6.

parties' bounded rationality, the parties cannot write a contract that specifies how decisions about these activities are supposed to be made.

2. The transaction is complex, not routine. Standard commercial and contract law could not easily "fill the gaps" of incomplete contracts.

3. The transaction involves the creation of relationship-specific assets by both parties in the relationship, and each party to the transactions could hold up the other.

4. It is excessively costly for one party to develop all of the necessary expertise to carry out all of the activities itself. This might be due to indivisibilities (developing the expertise to operate on even a small scale requires significant upfront investments in information acquisition and training) and the presence of an experience curve (the cost of developing incremental expertise becomes less costly the more expertise that is acquired). These considerations make it difficult for a single firm to organize the transaction internally.

5. The market opportunity that creates the need for the transaction is either transitory, or it is uncertain that it will continue on an ongoing basis. This makes it impractical for the independent parties to merge or even commit themselves to a long-term contract.

6. The transaction or market opportunity occurs in a contracting or regulatory environment with unique features that require a local partner who has access to relationships in that environment. For example, the strong role that the Chinese government plays in regulating foreign investment requires that nearly all foreign ventures in China are joint ventures with Chinese partners.

To illustrate some of these points, consider the alliance between McDonald's-Japan and Toys "R" Us mentioned earlier.[21] Toys "R" Us formed this alliance with McDonald's of Japan in 1990 to facilitate its entry into the Japanese market.[22] Toys "R" Us, which had expanded to Europe, Hong Kong, and Singapore in the 1980s, had long hoped to enter the Japanese market. However, Japan's Large-Scale Retail Store Law required that Toys "R" Us be approved by Japan's Ministry of International Trade and Industry (MITI) before building its stores. This law, which protected Japan's politically powerful small merchants, made it difficult even for Japanese retailers, such as supermarket operator Daiei, to open large-scale establishments. Toys "R" Us concluded that it had to find a local partner.

The alliance with McDonald's-Japan was formed to help Toys "R" Us navigate the politically charged entry process. McDonald-Japan's president, Den Fujita, was politically well-connected and understood the ordeal Toys "R" Us faced, having built McDonald's-Japan into the largest fast-food operator in the country. He also had a remarkable knowledge of Japanese real estate. "If you name a city," he bragged, "I can see the post office, train station, everything." In 1990, Toys "R" Us and McDonald's-Japan formed an alliance in which McDonald's took a 20 percent stake in the Toys "R" Us Japanese unit, Toys "R" Us Japan. As part of the alliance, 9 of the 11 Toys "R" Us stores would have a McDonald's restaurant on the premises.

This transaction was a good candidate for an alliance because it had elements that strongly argued for both "buying" and "making." Toys "R" Us needed to obtain McDonald's political know-how, site selection expertise, and business connec-

---

[21]McDonald's-Japan is a joint venture between McDonald's and Fujita & Company.

[22]See "Guess Who's Selling Barbies in Japan Now?" *Business Week*, December 9, 1991: p. 60.

tions to enter the Japanese market. It would have been extremely costly, perhaps even impossible, for Toys "R" Us to have developed this know-how on its own. These considerations argued for Toys "R" Us "buying" the political and site selection services from the market rather than "making" them itself.

Toys "R" Us could have conceivably signed a contract with McDonald's (or perhaps even a public relations or consulting firm) to lobby on its behalf, select sites, and help negotiate deals with suppliers. However, Toys "R" Us would have been contracting for difficult to measure services. For example, measuring the efficacy of behind-the-scenes help to lobby government officials is not easy. How would Toys "R" Us know that McDonald's-Japan did what it promised it would do? This was especially problematic given Toys "R" Us' inexperience with the Japanese political economy. It was also problematic because, at the time, Japan's retail store laws were in flux. By 1990 momentum was already building to overhaul them. McDonald's, or some other market firm, might have promised to perform the political services Toys "R" Us needed, but reneged by secretly shirking, and then (assuming a change in the law) claimed credit for actions it promised to take but didn't. Considerations such as these complicated the ability of Toys "R" Us to "buy" the political know-how and lobbying services it needed to attain government approval to enter the Japanese market.

By taking a stake in the success of Toy's "R" Us' Japanese venture—through both its 20 percent ownership of the venture and the colocation of the Toys "R" Us stores and McDonald's restaurants—McDonald's faced hard-edged incentives to carry out its part of the bargain. For example, McDonald's-Japan estimated that a McDonald's restaurant located inside a Toys "R" Us store would generate three times more customers than a stand-alone restaurant would. The potential payoff from this venture gave McDonald's-Japan a strong incentive to work hard on behalf of Toys "R" Us. The alliance enabled Toys "R" Us to obtain the political services and site selection know-how it needed without having to make costly investments of its own. The alliance also avoided the difficult incentive problems that might have arisen had Toys "R" Us relied on traditional market contracting to obtain the services and know-how it needed.

The alliance between McDonald's-Japan and Toys "R" Us illustrates how governance in an alliance differs from the governance or arm's-length market transactions.[23] In principle, when they formed their alliance in 1990, Toys "R" Us and McDonald's could have written a comprehensive contract to govern the operation of the colocated Toys "R" Us stores and McDonald's restaurants. They didn't do this. Such contracting would have been very impractical. The profitability of a McDonald's franchise within a Toy's "R" Us toy store depends on such operating decisions as merchandise mix, store layout, number of employees, and store maintenance and cleanliness. In light of the uncertainties involved in bringing the novel business concept of a toy "superstore" to Japan, it would have been extremely difficult to specify the full array of contingencies McDonald's and Toys "R" Us might face as the venture unfolded. And it would have been harder still to specify in advance how operating decisions would vary as a function of these contingencies.

Had the McDonald's-Toys "R" Us been organized as a traditional arm's-length transaction, the inability to write a comprehensive contract, coupled with the site specificity of the investment in the colocated toy store and restaurant

---

[23]Chapter 4 discusses governance.

would have created holdup risks. For example, since McDonald's cannot easily replicate the lucrative location inside a Toys "R" Us toy store, it is vulnerable to opportunistic behavior by Toys "R" Us. Governance based on trust and reciprocity can mitigate holdup risks and preserve needed flexibility in environments where comprehensive contracting is impractical.

Although alliances can combine the best features of buying and making, they can also suffer from the drawbacks of both buying and masking. For example, just as traditional market transactions can involve a risk of leakage of private information, independent firms that collaborate through alliances also risk losing control over proprietary information. In fact, the risk of information leakage can often be more severe in an alliance than in a traditional market transaction because the conditions that tend to make an alliance desirable (complex, ambiguous transactions that do not lend themselves to comprehensive contracting) often force the parties to exchange a considerable amount of closely-held information.

In addition, although the loose, evolving governance structure of an alliance can help the parties adapt to unforeseen events, it may also compromise coordination between the firms. Unlike an "inside-the-firm" transaction in an alliance there are often no formal mechanisms for making decisions or resolving disputes expeditiously. The "footprints" of this are delay and lack of focus, problems that plagued the highly publicized alliances between IBM and Apple in the early 1990s to develop a new operating system, a multimedia software language and the PowerPC. Indeed, by 1994 IBM's senior management had become so frustrated in its protracted negotiations with Apple over the operating system for the PowerPC, that it concluded it would have been better off acquiring Apple, rather than dealing with it through an alliance.

Finally, just as agency costs can arise within departments of firms that are not subject to market discipline, alliances can also suffer from agency and influence costs. Agency costs in alliances can arise because the fruits of the alliance's efforts are split between two or more firms. This can give rise to a *free-rider problem*. Each firm in the alliance is insufficiently vigilant in monitoring the alliance's activities because neither firm captures the full benefit of such vigilance. Influence costs can arise because the absence of a formal hierarchy and administrative system within an alliance can encourage employees to engage in influence activity, such as lobbying, to augment their resources and enhance their status.

Collaborative Relationships: Japanese Subcontracting Networks and *Keiretsu*

Japanese industrial firms are less vertically integrated than their American and European counterparts. They tend to be smaller and more specialized in their particular place in the vertical chain.[24] For example, the 10 largest Japanese automobile firms outsource about 75 percent of their components; in the United States only Chrysler has approached this degree of outsourcing. But Japanese firms do not organize the vertical chain through arm's-length contracts. Instead, they rely on a labyrinth of long-term, semiformal relationships between firms up and down the

---

[24]See Clark, R., *The Japanese Company*, New Haven: Yale University Press, 1979, or Nishiguchi, T., *Strategic Industrial Sourcing: The Japanese Advantage*, New York: Oxford University Press, 1994.

vertical chain. We consider two closely related types of relationships: subcontractor networks and *keiretsu*.

Subcontractor Networks

Many Japanese manufacturers make extensive use of networks of independent subcontractors with whom they maintain close long-term relationships. Unlike the relationships many American and European firms have with their subcontractors, in Japan these relationships typically involve a much higher degree of collaboration between the manufacturer and the subcontractors and the delegation of a more sophisticated set of responsibilities to the subcontractor. Toshihiro Nishiguchi's study of Japanese and British subcontracting in the electronics industry illustrates these differences.[25] In Great Britain, electronics manufacturers typically rely on subcontractors for specific, narrowly defined jobs. Their relationship is mediated by contractual agreements on price and performance and often does not persist beyond a few clearly defined transactions. Subcontractors are much less dedicated to the needs of particular buyers, and the customer base of a particular supplier is usually much larger than a Japanese subcontractor of comparable size. By contrast, the relationship between a Japanese electronics manufacturer and its suppliers can persist for decades. Subcontractors generally perform more sophisticated and comprehensive tasks than their British counterparts. For example, rather than just fabricating a component, a subcontractor might also be involved in its design and the testing of prototypes. In addition, subcontractors typically see their role as not just to fill the buyer's orders, but more generally, to closely integrate their operations with the buyer's, for example, by dedicating assembly lines to the buyer's product, by developing special-purpose machines that can produce to the buyer's specifications more efficiently, or by working closely with the customer to improve production. Nishiguchi concludes that the relationship between electronics manufacturers and subcontractors in Japan involves significantly more asset specificity than the corresponding relationship in Britain.

Keiretsu

Keiretsu are closely related to subcontractor networks, but they involve more formalized institutional linkages. The six largest *keiretsu*—Mitsubishi, Sumitomo, DKB, Mitsui, Fuso, and Sanwa—each have more than 80 members, with a core bank that facilitates relationships among members. Figure 5.3 depicts the complex nature of these linkages. Most of the key elements in the vertical chain are represented in a *keiretsu*, from banks to production facilities to distribution channels. The firms in a *keiretsu* exchange equity shares, and place individuals on each other's boards of directors.[26] For example, the core banks of the Mitsubishi and Mitsui *keiretsu* place nearly 200 bank representatives on the boards of other *keiretsu* members and effectively choose the CEOs of about 20 percent of the member firms.

Firms in a *keiretsu* are also linked by informal personal relationships. Top executives belong to the same clubs and socialize together. An executive who retires

---

[25]Nishiguchi, T., *Strategic Industrial Sourcing: The Japanese Advantage*, New York: Oxford University Press, 1994.

[26]This is known as an "interlocking directorate," and is prohibited under many circumstances in the United States under antitrust laws.

FIGURE 5.3
DEBT, EQUITY, AND TRADE LINKAGES IN JAPANESE *KEIRETSU*.

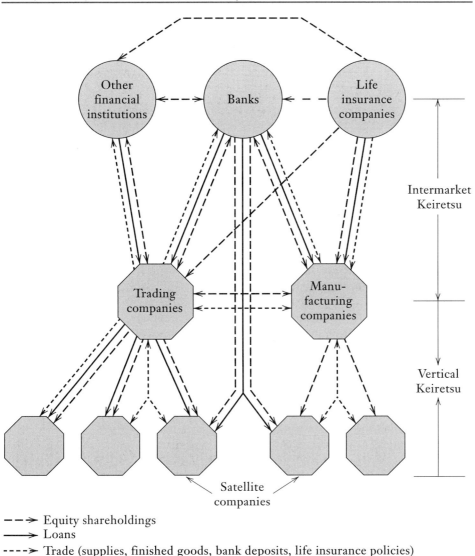

– – ▶ Equity shareholdings
——▶ Loans
- - - ▶ Trade (supplies, finished goods, bank deposits, life insurance policies)

Source: Gerlach, M. L. and J. Lincoln, "The Organization of Business Networks in the United States and Japan," in Nigria, N. and R. G. Eccles (eds.), *Networks and Organizations: Structure, Form, and Action*, Boston: Harvard Business School Press, p. 494. The dashed lines show equity holdings within a typical *keiretsu*; the solid lines show loans, and the small dashed lines show the patterns of exchange within the *keiretsu*.

from Toyota, for example, may then go to work for one of the component suppliers in the Toyota *keiretsu*. Each member of a *keiretsu* believes that it will be the first choice of another *keiretsu* member in future business dealings. As a result, each has invested in learning each of the others' businesses, inventory needs, marketing practices, and so forth. When a *keiretsu* member involved in production experiences a sharp upsurge in demand, it is understood that suppliers in the *keiretsu*

EXAMPLE 5.4

INTER-FIRM BUSINESS NETWORKS IN THE UNITED STATES: THE WOMEN'S DRESS INDUSTRY IN NEW YORK CITY[27]

Business networks based on social ties and governed by norms of trust and reciprocity exist outside Japan. As Brian Uzzi has shown, they even exist in New York City.

Uzzi recently studied business networks in the "better dress" segment of the women's apparel industry in New York City. This is a highly fragmented industry, with low barriers to entry and intense competition, both domestic and international. One might expect that in such a context, arm's-length contracting would be the norm and social ties would not count for much. Uzzi's research demonstrates that this is not the case. He shows that many business relationships in this industry are characterized by what he calls *embedded ties*: relationships characterized by trust and a willingness to exchange closely-held information and work together to solve problems.

The design and marketing of women's dresses is carried out by firms called jobbers. Working with in-house or free-lance designers, these firms design dresses and market these designs to retail buyers, who then place orders. Most jobbers do not manufacture the dresses themselves. Instead, they manage a network of subcontractors, including grading contractors, who size the dress patterns, cutting contractors, who cut the fabric, and sewing contractors, who sew the dresses. The jobbers also manage the flow of raw materials in the production process. For example, they purchase fabric from converters and send it to the cutting contractors, who cut the fabric to make the pieces of the dress.

Uzzi observed two main ways of organizing exchange in this industry: arm's length ties, or what the participants called "market relationships," and embedded ties, which they called "close or special relationships." Market relationships were characterized by a lack of reciprocity between the parties in the exchange. "It's the oppositite of a close tie," one participant reported to Uzzi, "one hand doesn't wash the other." They also lacked social content. "They're relationships that are like far away," according to one manager, "They don't consider the feeling for the human being." Many exchanges in this industry were governed by arm's-length relationships. However, for major transactions that participants considered for the company's overall success, the exchange was often governed by embedded ties.

The "close" or "special" relationships that Uzzi observed were characterized by a high degree of trust. Such trust often developed when one party voluntarily did a favor for another that was then reciprocated later. For example, a subcontractor might work overtime so a jobber could fill a rush order. Later, the jobber

---

[27]This example is based on Uzzi, B., "Social Structure and Competition in Interfirm Networks: The Paradox of Embeddedness," *Administrative Sciences Quarterly*, 42 (1997), pp. 35–67.

might place an order to help the subcontractor keep its shop running when demand was slow. According to Uzzi, trust gave the parties access to resources and information that improve efficiency, but would have been difficult to acquire through arm's length contracts. It also promoted collaborative problem solving. One manufacturer told Uzzi: "When you deal with a guy you don't have a close relationship with, it can be a big problem. Things go wrong, and there's no telling what will happen. With my guys [his key contractors], if something goes wrong, I know we'll be able to work it out. I know his business and he knows mine."

Relationships in this industry based on trust could be extremely powerful. In one instance, according to Uzzi, a jobber was moving its production to Asia and would thus be ending its relationship with its New York City subcontractors. This jobber had strong incentives *not* to inform its subcontractors that it was going to leave. By doing so, it risked provoking opportunistic behavior by its subcontractors (e.g., shirking on quality) to take advantage of what they would now regard as a temporary relationship. Yet, the CEO of this firm personally informed the subcontractors with whom he had a special relationship, and he promised to help them adapt to the loss of his business. In turn, those subcontractors continued to provide high-quality services. This firm did *not* inform the subcontractors with whom it had market relationships that it was planning to close its New York operation.

will increase their production without raising supply prices. If one *keiretsu* member requires a product change, it is understood that its suppliers will participate in the design discussions. These activities eliminate many of the coordination problems discussed in Chapter 3. They also reduce the chances for holdup, including the possibility that one firm will take advantage of another firm for short-term gains.

Implicit Contracts and Long-Term Relationships

An implicit contract is an unstated understanding between parties in a business relationship. The understandings that exist among members of the *keiretsu* are implicit contracts. But implicit contracts are generally not enforceable in court, so parties to an implicit contract must rely on alternative mechanisms to make the understanding viable. A powerful mechanism that makes implicit contracts viable is the threat of losing future business if one party breaks the implicit contract for its own gain.[28]

To see why the threat to withdraw future business can be so powerful, imagine two firms in the vertical chain that routinely transact business with each other. Their longstanding relationship has enabled them to coordinate their activities through formal planning and monitoring of product quality, and as a result, both firms have profited significantly. In particular, suppose that the upstream firm sells

---

[28]The idea that future flows provide firms with incentives to maintain ongoing relationships was initially developed by Benjamin Klein and Keith Leffler in the article "The Role of Market Forces in Assuring Contractual Performance," *Journal of Political Economy*, 89, 1981: pp. 615–641.

inputs to the downstream firm for a $1 million profit every year, and the downstream firm processes the inputs and sells a finished product to consumers for a $1 million profit of its own. Each firm has an alternative trading partner, but each would only reap profits of $900,000 per year if forced to switch.

Although it seems as if each firm has no reason to switch, in fact the relationship has a potential complication. Each firm could increase its profit at the expense of the other by performing less of the planning and monitoring that make the relationship successful. Specifically, suppose that the upstream firm estimates that by breaking its implied commitments to the downstream firm, it could boost its annual profits to $1.2 million. If it does this, however, the downstream firm will learn that it has broken its commitments, and the relationship will end. Each firm would then be forced to do business with another trading partner.

How much does the upstream firm benefit by honoring its implicit contract indefinitely? In one year, it earns $100,000 more by transacting with the downstream firm than with its alternative trading partner. If the firm's discount rate is 5 percent, the net present value of honoring the implicit contract indefinitely would be $2 million.[29] This far exceeds the short-term (i.e., one-year) increase in profit of $200,000 from breaking the contract. Indeed, to make breaking the implicit contract worthwhile, the discount rate would have to be 50 percent! This high hurdle for switching helps sustain the implicit contract.

Thomas Palay's study of rail freight contracting illustrates the power of long-term relationships in sustaining cooperative behavior.[30] He discusses a railroad that purchased specially designed auto-rack railcars to move a particular make of automobile for a major auto manufacturer. Soon after the railroad made the investment, however, the manufacturer changed the design of the car, making the auto racks obsolete. Even though it was not contractually obligated to do so, the manufacturer compensated the railroad for more than $1 million to cover the unamortized portion of the investment. The director of shipping at the automobile manufacturer alluded to the importance of maintaining a long-term relationship as the basis for this action. "We've got to keep them healthy, viable, and happy to guarantee that we'll get the equipment we need, when we need it."

CHAPTER SUMMARY

◆ The advantages and disadvantages of relying on the market versus relying on internal organization can be expressed in terms of a tradeoff between technical efficiency and agency efficiency. Technical efficiency occurs if the firm is using least-cost production techniques. Agency efficiency refers to the extent to which the firm's production and/or administrative costs are raised by the transactions and coordination costs of arm's-length market exchanges or the agency and influence costs of internal organization.

◆ Vertical integration is preferred to arm's-length market exchange when it is less costly to organize activities internally than it is to organize them through arm's-length mar-

---

[29]If the discount rate is r, then an infinite-lived stream of X dollars per year is worth X/r in today's dollars.

[30]Palay, T., "Comparative Institutional Economics: The Governance of Rail Freight Contracting," *Journal of Legal Studies*, 13, 1984: pp. 265–287.

ket exchange. This cost difference will reflect differences in both technical efficiency and agency efficiency across the two modes of organization.

◆ Vertical integration is relatively more attractive when (a) the ability of outside market specialists relative to the firm itself to achieve scale or scope economies is limited; (b) the larger the scale of the firm's product market activities; (c) the greater the extent to which the assets involved in production are relationship specific.

◆ Vertical integration changes the pattern of asset ownership and control, and thus alters the bargaining power between parties in a vertical relationship. This, in turn, affects incentives to invest in relationship-specific assets. Vertical integration will be attractive when there are large asymmetries in the importance of relationship-specific investments in achieving the full efficiencies from the exchange, and where it is important for one party to control the use of those assets.

◆ Vertical integration and arm's-length market exchange are not the only ways to organize transactions. A firm may pursue tapered integration, in which it supplies part of its input requirement itself and relies on market exchanges for the remainder.

◆ Firms may undertake strategic alliances or joint ventures. Although the transacting parties remain legally separate under these modes of organization, they typically entail much closer cooperation and coordination than an arm's-length exchange between two independent firms.

◆ Firms may also be bound together in cooperative relationships in long-lasting networks, such as the Japanese *keiretsu*. Finally, long-term, arm's-length market relationships can provide strong incentives for cooperative behavior and can thus achieve the advantages of vertical integration (e.g., avoidance of transactions costs, flexibility in governance) without incurring the disadvantages (e.g., softening incentives for innovation).

QUESTIONS

1. Why is the "technical efficiency" line in Figure 5.1 above the *x*-axis? Why does the "agency efficiency" line cross the *x*-axis?

2. Explain why the following patterns seem to hold in many industries:
   (a) Small firms more like to outsource production of inputs than are large firms.
   (b) "Standard" inputs (such as a simple transistors that could be used by several electronics manufacturers) are more likely to be outsourced than "tailor-made" inputs (such as a circuit board designed for a single manufacturer's specific needs).

3. Use the argument of Grossman, Hart, and Moore to explain why stockbrokers are permitted to keep their client lists (i.e., continue to contact and do business with clients) if they are dismissed from their jobs and find employment at another brokerage house.

4. Analysts often array strategic alliances and joint ventures on a continuum that begins with "using the market" and ends "full integration." Do you agree that these fall along a natural continuum?

5. What does the *Keiretsu* system have in common with traditional strategic alliances and joint ventures? What are some of the difference?

6. The following is an excerpt from an actual strategic plan (the company and product name have been changed to protect the innocent):

   Acme's primary raw material is PVC sheet that us produced by three major vendors within the United States. Acme, a small consumer products manufacturer, is consolidating down to a single vendor. Continued growth by this vendor assures Acme that it will be able to meet its needs in the future.

Assume that Acme's chosen vendor will grow as forecast. Offer a scenario to Acme management that might convince them that they rethink their decision to rely on a single vendor. What do you recommend Acme do to minimize the risk(s) that you have identified? Are their any drawbacks to your recommendation?

7. Shaefer Electronics is a medium-size producer (about 18 million in sales in 1993) of electronic products for the oil industry. It makes two main products—capacitors and integrated circuits. Capacitors are standardized items. Integrated circuits are more complex, highly customized items made to individual customer specifications. They are designed and made to order; require installation, and sometimes require postsale servicing. Shaefer's annual sales are shown in the table below.

Shaefer relies entirely on manufacturers' representatives (MRs) located throughout the United States to sell its products. MRs are independent contractors who sell Shaefer's products in exchange for a sales commission. The company's representatives are not exclusive—they represent manufacturers of related but noncompeting products, such as circuit breaker, small switches, or semiconductors. Often a customer will buy some of these related products along with integrated circuits or an order of capacitors. MRs have long experience within local markets, close ties to the engineers within the firms that buy control systems, and deep knowledge of their needs. In the markets in which they operate, MRs develop their own client lists and call schedules. They are fully responsible for the expenses they incur in selling their products.

Once an order for one of Shaefer's products is taken by the MR, Shaefer is then responsible for any installation or postsale servicing that is needed.

Shaefer recently hired two different marketing consultants to study its sales force strategy. Their reports contained the conclusions reported below. Please comment on the soundness of each conclusion.

(a) "Shaefer should continue to sell through MRs. Whether it uses MRs or an in-house sales force, it has to pay commissions. By relying on MRs, it avoids the variable selling expenses (e.g., travel expenses for salespeople) it would incur if it had its own sales force. As a result, Shaefer's selling expenses are lower than they would be with an in-house sales force of comparable size, talent and know-how."

(b) "Selling through MRs made sense for Shaefer's when it was first getting started and specialized in capacitors. However, given its current product mix, it would not want to see itself up the way it is now if it were designed its sales force strategy from scratch. But with what it has got, Shaefer should be extremely cautious about changing."

SHAEFER ANNUAL SALES ($000)

	1980	1985	1989	1990	1991	1992	1993
Capacitors	$5,568	$6,488	$7,131	$7,052	$7,043	$7,360	$8,109
Integrated Circuits	$678	$1,679	$4,651	$6,245	$7,363	$8,589	$9,508
Total	$6,246	$8,167	$11,782	$13,297	$14,406	$15,959	$17,617

DIVERSIFICATION

6

*B*ecause complex firms have numerous opportunities to reduce costs and improve marketing effectiveness by exploiting economies of scale and scope, most well-known firms are *diversified*—they produce in multiple output markets. For example, Philips is a diversified manufacturer of home electronics equipment, and Sears is diversified both in its product line and in the local markets its stores serve.

Since about 1950, many large firms have expanded beyond the boundaries of any particular business area. Careful readers of Chapter 2 will be puzzled trying to determine the economies of scope to be derived from combining the production of automobiles and televisions (Mitsubishi), medical equipment and popular music (EMI), and seat belts and credit rating services (TRW). In analyzing these broadly diversified firms (sometimes called *conglomerates*), it is often difficult to specify what businesses the firm is in, what its key resources are, and what services corporate management contributes to individual business units.

This chapter examines corporate diversification. After describing its history, we explore the degree to which diversification can be explained by the pursuit of scale and scope economies. In fact, many diversifications are pursued for other reasons. We explore what these goals may be, and then review the performance of diversified firms. The result is clear—successful diversification combines businesses that can exploit scope economies. Diversification for other reasons tends to be less successful.[1]

---

[1] There are several aspects to diversification, such as the structuring of diversified firms, the conduct of strategic planning, and the integration of parent and acquired firms, that are beyond the scope of this chapter. Some of these topics are considered in other chapters. For a comprehensive review of issues related to corporate diversification, see V. Ramanujam and P. Varadarajan, "Research on Corporate Diversification: A Synthesis," *Strategic Management Journal* 10, November–December 1989: pp. 523–553.

◆ ◆ ◆ ◆ ◆ ◆ THE EXTENT OF DIVERSIFICATION

We begin our discussion of diversification by showing how diversification has changed over the past century. Most historical analyses have focused on diversification in the United States, and we do too. Diversification activity seems to ebb and flow, and each new "wave" seems to have a different character, with different implications for efficiency.

A Brief History

Firms can diversify in a variety of ways, including internal development of new business areas, joint ventures with other firms, and acquisition of firms in unrelated lines of business. One can see the variety and extent of diversification by looking at periods during which the number of mergers was unusually high—the so-called merger waves. There have been five such waves in the United States within the last century.

The first merger wave began after the worldwide depression of 1883, which left many capital-intensive industries with overcapacity, and ended in the early 1900s. This wave involved roughly one-sixth of all U.S. manufacturing firms. Some combinations that arose at this time, such as Standard Oil and United States Steel, were able to monopolize their industries. A second, smaller merger wave occurred after World War I in the early 1920s. Antitrust laws, such as the Sherman Act and the Federal Trade Commission Act, discouraged grabs for monopoly power that failed to promote increased efficiency. As a result, many combinations stopped short of achieving 50 percent market share, and their industries resembled oligopolies instead of monopolies. Many other combinations involved vertical, rather than horizontal, integration. The formation and growth of General Motors during this time displayed both types of integration.

The reasons for the first two merger waves are easy to understand. Firms in the same market combined to reduce competition and achieve scale economies. The emergence of manufacturing giants tilted the calculus of the make-or-buy decision in favor of vertical integration. The Great Depression of the 1930s and American participation in World War II put a damper on merger activity until 1950. Antitrust laws, especially the Celler-Kefauver Act, were then toughened, further hindering both horizontal and vertical mergers. By the late 1950s and early 1960s, managers understood that diversified combinations were legal, while horizontal and vertical mergers were more likely to encounter antitrust problems.[2]

By 1960, the pace of merger activity had again quickened. Unlike the previous waves, this third wave featured increased levels of corporate diversification and produced large conglomerates selling extensive product lines in diverse markets. Mergers in the 1960s resulted in firms such as American Can, which sold cans, clothing, and financial services, and ITT, whose business portfolio included life insurance, car rental, hotels, and vending machines. There was scarcely a lull between this wave of conglomerate mergers and the fourth merger wave of the 1980s. The mergers of the 1980s were different from their predecessors, however. Many cash-rich firms saw in a slumping stock market the opportunity to buy up

---

[2]For an extensive discussion of these waves, see Fligstein, N., *The Transformation of Corporate Control*, Cambridge, MA: Harvard University Press, 1990.

other firms at "bargain" prices. There is no better example than Philip Morris, which, flush with cash from the tobacco business, bought 7-Up in 1978, General Foods in 1985, and Kraft in 1988. Some economists have argued that the fourth merger wave was a reaction to the poor performance of the conglomerations formed during the third wave. Many acquisitions, including Goldsmith's hostile takeover of Crown Zellerbach and Jacobs' "hostile takeover" of AMF, were made expressly to break up conglomerates.[3]

The fifth merger wave began in the mid-1990s: 1997 saw a record level of merger activity that was surpassed in 1998, which featured such deals as Exxon—Mobil ($86 billion) and Travelers—Citicorp ($73 billion). It is too early to evaluate these deals, but they seemed to be motivated by one of two factors: (1) firms desired to establish dominant market shares within specific industries; (2) firms desired access to international markets. In either case, merging firms were usually "related" businesses. The emphasis on merging with related businesses is consistent with financial economics research to which we now turn.

"Relatedness" Over Time

Financial economists have long recognized that the success of a merger may depend critically on whether the two firms can achieve economies of scale. To document how such economies might be present in diverse multibusiness firms, Richard Rumelt developed the idea of *relatedness*. He measured relatedness according to how much of a firm's revenues were attributable to product market activities that had shared, or related, technological characteristics, production characteristics, or distribution channels. He focused on three characteristics of firms: the proportion of a firm's revenues (1) from its largest business; (2) from its largest group of related businesses; and (3) from the stages of a vertically integrated production process.[4]

Rumelt's classification scheme has four general types of relatedness. A *single business* firm is one with more than 95 percent of its business in a single activity or line of business. Examples of this include W. R. Wrigley in chewing gum, De-Beers in diamonds, and KLM in airlines. A *dominant business* firm has between 70 percent and 95 percent of its annual revenues in a principal activity. Examples include Glaxo/Wellcome, 3M, and the *New York Times*. A *related business* firm derives less than 70 percent of its revenue from a primary area, but has other lines of business related to the primary area. Examples include Daewoo, Philip Morris, ICI, and Nestlé. Finally, an *unrelated business* firm derives less than 70 percent of its business from a primary area and has few related business lines. The British firm Hanson is an example, as were American firms such as ITT and Beatrice.

---

[3]A hostile takeover (or hostile tender offer) involves two parts. The first is the *tender offer*, which is a direct offer to shareholders to purchase a quantity of shares at a given price. This offer succeeds or fails independently of the approval of a firm's managers. The second part, whether the offer is hostile or not, refers to whether top management of the acquired firm approves of the offer. If top management disapproves of the initial offer, the takeover attempt is hostile, regardless of whether it approves of subsequent offers.

[4]This discussion of Rumelt's work is based on Rumelt, R., *Strategy, Structure, and Economic Performance*, Boston: Division of Research, Harvard Business School, 1974. For a review of research building on Rumelt's work, see Galbraith, J. R. and R. K. Kazanjian, *Strategy Implementation*, 2nd ed., St. Paul, MN: West Publishing, 1986.

These last type of firms are commonly called "conglomerates." Rumelt documented a trend toward diversification among U.S. businesses after World War II. In 1949, 70 percent of major firms had a single business or dominant business focus. By 1969, only 35 percent of his sample showed a similar focus. In contrast, the proportion of firms with unrelated business portfolios increased from 3.4 percent of all firms in 1949 to 19.4 percent in 1969.

Gerald Davis, Kristina Dieckman, and Catherine Tinsley updated Rumelt's findings through 1990.[5] To measure diversification, they use an "entropy" measure. Entropy equals 0 for a firm that derives all of its sales from a single four-digit SIC category. It increases as the firm's sales are spread across more categories. For Fortune 500 firms, entropy fell from an average of 1.00 in 1980 to .67 in 1990; that is, these firms had become less diversified. (As a benchmark, a firm that derives 5 percent of its sales from each of 20 different lines of business has entropy ≈ 3.)

Example 6.1

CHANGES IN DIVERSIFICATION FROM AMERICAN CAN TO PRIMERICA

Business history is filled with examples of firms that have reinvented themselves, sometimes more than once. The managers of these firms, when confronted with changes in technological and market conditions, refocused their businesses into areas less subject to environmental threats or else entered new businesses that forced them to acquire new organizational capabilities to enable their firms to compete under changed conditions.[6]

Among contemporary businesses, American Can provides one of the most interesting examples of refocusing. American had long manufactured tin cans and other metal containers for buyers that included major food and beverage companies. In Rumelt's typology, it was a single-product firm. The can industry, however, became increasingly unfavorable during the 1950s and 1960s for several reasons. First, the technology for making cans was simple, so that American Can had many competitors. Second, forward integration by aluminum producers and backward integration by food companies eroded American's market share and limited its ability to raise prices. Finally, plastic containers threatened the marketability of cans because plastics could be used in ways that cans could not.

Beginning in the 1950s, American Can diversified into businesses unrelated to can manufacturing, including paper products and printing. In 1977, the company acquired Pickwick International, a record distributor, and its retail sub-

---

[5]Davis, G. F., K. A. Dieckman, and C. H. Tinsley, "The Decline and Fall of the Conglomerate Firm in the 1980s: The De-Institutionalization of an Organizational Form," *American Sociological Review*, 59, August 1994: pp. 547–570.

[6]Best, M., *The New Competition: Institutions of Industrial Restructuring*, Cambridge: MA: Harvard University Press, 1990, chap. 1.

sidiary Musicland. In 1978, it purchased the direct mail marketer Fingerhut. By 1980, American Can was an unrelated business firm.

In 1980 American Can began to refocus its entire portfolio of businesses. The first move was to acquire Associated Madison, a life insurance company. American proceeded during the 1980s to acquire several other financial services businesses, including Barclays Bank and Smith Barney. In 1986, American Can sold off its can business, and has since sold off other businesses. The restructuring of American Can was crowned in 1987 when the firm changed its name to Primerica, which had become a financial services firm. In 1993, it merged with Travelers, adopting its partner's well-known name and umbrella logo. The evolution of the firm culminated with its 1997 acquisition of Salomon for $9.2 billion—the second largest acquisition of a securities brokerage firm to date—and its 1998 merger with Citicorp.

American Can is not the only firm to diversify away from the business around which it was built to refocus on another business. USX, formally US Steel, today derives most of its revenue from oil, and remains in steel largely because of labor considerations. International Harvester (IH), once focused on farm equipment, diversified in the 1930s and 1940s into trucks and construction equipment. Facing bankruptcy in the 1980s, IH sold its farm equipment business (and rights to the "International Harvester" name) to Tenneco and sold its construction equipment business to Dresser Industries. The firm that remained is called Navistar and is a world leader in medium and heavy truck production.

RATIONALES FOR DIVERSIFICATION ◆ ◆ ◆ ◆ ◆

Rationales for diversification range from traditional efficiency enhancement, such as the exploitation of economies of scale and scope and the disciplining of bad managers, to more troubling explanations, stemming from the use (some would say abuse) of power by top management.

Economies of Scale and Scope

Chapter 2 suggests that one motive for diversification may be to achieve economies of scale and scope. A study by Thomas Brush supports the plausibility of scale and scope economies as a starting point for understanding the performance of diversified firms.[7] He conducted a large sample longitudinal analysis of mergers in 356 manufacturing industries. His intuition was that if mergers are associated with operational synergies, then the market share of merged firms should increase following a combination. Brush studied whether mergers were more likely when there was an expectation of positive changes in market share. They were, and expected gains from mergers were substantial. He also examined whether these performance expectations, on average, were realized. Later changes in market share were, in fact, explained by expectations from mergers.

---

[7]Brush, T. H., "Predicted Change in Operational Synergy and Post-Acquisition Performance of Acquired Businesses," *Strategic Management Journal*, 17, 1996: pp. 1–24.

If firms diversify to pursue economies of scope, we might also predict that large firms would offer a related set of products to a narrow population of consumers. Historical analyses, such as the work of Daniel Nathanson and James Cassano, find that this only happens occasionally. Nathanson and Cassano classified more than 180 U.S. firms from the 1970s, according to the degree of their "product diversity" and "market diversity." Some firms, such as Schlitz, Maytag, and Zenith, were undiversified on both dimensions. They may be seen as pursuing economies of scale and scope in narrow markets with a common technology. At least as many firms, however, were highly diversified on both dimensions. Firms such as Union Carbide, Allis-Chalmers, and Gulf and Western, produced products that shared little technology and were sold to consumer groups that had little in common.

A possible explanation for this finding is that economies of scope can come from sources other than sharing technology or consumers. Edith Penrose, a founder of the "resource-based view of the firm," argues that scope economies can come from spreading a firm's underutilized managerial and organizational resources to new areas.[8] At any given time, a firm may possess specific resources that it cannot fully utilize in its current product market. Increasing the size of the firm to fully utilize those resources in the firm's home market may not be feasible, due to competitive conditions. However, those resources might be effectively applied in other product markets, and doing so would give rise to scope economies. But this possibility does not give firms a license to diversify. The farther away a business is from the firm's established businesses, the more resources the firm will have to expend to master it. This will limit the firm's possibilities for expansion.

C. K. Prahalad and Richard Bettis suggest that managers of diversified firms may spread their own scarce resources across nominally unrelated business areas. They call this a *dominant general management logic*, which comprises "the way in which managers conceptualize the business and make critical resource allocations—be it in technologies, product development, distribution, advertising, or in human resource management."[9]

This logic applies most directly when managers develop specific skills, say in information systems, and seemingly unrelated businesses rely on these skills for success. Managers sometimes mistakenly apply this logic when they develop particular skills but diversify into businesses that do not require them. For example, some wonder if Michael Eisner's ability to develop comprehensive marketing plans for Disney's animated motion pictures will be valuable in the scheduling of network television programming at Disney's ABC subsidiary. The dominant general management logic is more problematic when managers perceive themselves as possessing superior general management skills with which they can justify any diversification. Without detailed knowledge about the particular businesses involved in a diversification initiative, one cannot know at the time of the diversification whether the new business fits the "dominant logic" or whether the general manager involved is above average or not. In the absence of obvious relationships between businesses, such as those identified by Nathanson and Cassano, it is difficult

---

[8]Penrose, E., *The Theory of the Growth of the Firm*, 3rd ed., Oxford: Oxford University Press, 1995.

[9]Prahalad, C. K. and R. A. Bettis, "The Dominant Logic: A New Linkage Between Diversity and Performance," *Strategic Management Journal*, 7, 1986: pp. 485–501.

to defend claims that economies of scope derive from the dominant general management logic.

This discussion tells us that many diversified firms cannot exploit scope economies. If this is true, then why do they diversify? In addition to economies of scope, three broad rationales for diversification are frequently offered:

- Financial synergies

- Economizing on transactions costs

- The pursuit of managerial (rather than firm) objectives

We discuss each of these rationales in turn. Before we do so, however, consider a synergistic merger in the banking industry.

$\mathcal{E}$XAMPLE 6.2

ACQUIRING FOR SYNERGY: BANKAMERICA BUYS CONTINENTAL

An example of strategic diversification in the banking industry is the acquisition of the Continental Bank by BankAmerica (BAC), which was announced in January of 1994. Although both corporations are commercial banks, this acquisition represents a diversification strategy, since it enables the BAC to build a significant presence and a strong portfolio of corporate banking clients in the Midwest. When the deal was completed, the merger constituted one of the largest banking mergers ever, with BankAmerica paying approximately $1.9 billion. A premise of this chapter has been that, to create economies of scale and scope, businesses have to be related in either products or markets. The BAC/Continental combination fits into both rationales.

BAC is a San Francisco bank that has always invested heavily in its corporate banking business. It has maintained a high credit rating since its founding in 1904 and was at the time of the merger the second largest American bank in terms of total assets (Citibank was first). The geographic concentration of BAC activities on the West Coast, however, limited the bank's potential for expansion into the large commercial centers of the Midwest and East. BAC officers have frequently mentioned their intention to build a presence in the Midwest, and through its acquisition of Continental, BAC appears to have found a way to enter the Midwest corporate banking business.

Continental Bank, based in Chicago, was the second largest financial institution in the Midwest, with assets totaling $22.6 billion. Continental did business with most of the large firms headquartered in the Chicago area and generated more than a third of its revenues in Illinois. After almost going out of business in 1984, when the Federal Deposit Insurance Corporation (FDIC) temporarily took control of the bank's holding company, Continental returned to modest prosperity and was admired by its competitors for smart marketing and innovative deals. Continental recovered from near death by focusing on the commercial side of its business, which gave it strong profits in recent years. Continental has never fully recovered its credit rating, however, which limited the services that it could provide to corporate clients.

In considering the synergies that each bank brought to this transaction, most observers believed that BAC's principal strength was its strong credit rating, which was critical to winning clients in high-margin corporate financial transactions. BAC also brought billions of dollars of low-cost deposits, gathered through its multistate branch network, to fund commercial loans.

Continental brought a strong client portfolio to the deal. Continental had a wide and strong client network in the Midwest, but had been unable to fully service these clients alone because of its poor credit rating. Continental enjoyed a stable and loyal customer base of more than 2,000 long-term corporate clients. BAC, in turn, hoped to use Continental's client relationships as a channel through which additional products could be sold. BAC Chairman Richard Rosenberg hoped that the merger would boost BAC from second to first in U.S. corporate business at the time, in terms of the number of corporations that rely on BAC as their main bank. BAC's commitment to investments in corporate banking business was shown in its plans to move the bank's corporate business headquarters to Chicago in early 1995.

Observers have questioned how BAC would implement the merger. In its past mergers, BAC has emphasized the consolidation of similar businesses to realize economies of scale. For example, in a 1991 deal totaling $4.7 billion, BAC acquired Security Pacific Corporation, creating a giant West Coast bank. The lessons BAC may have taken from this deal concern the high price paid, the high levels of employee turnover, and the loss of some corporate customers due to post-merger disturbances. The fundamental difference between the Security Pacific and Continental deals was that the Continental acquisition involved both geographic expansion and product diversification into corporate business. The Security Pacific deal was neither. This suggests an effort to avoid the difficulties associated with large business consolidations.

Both BAC and Continental were already thought to have efficient operations. This, when combined with the synergistic goals of the merger, suggests that few jobs would be lost because of the combination. In terms of culture, however, BankAmerica's bureaucratic and hierarchical culture contrasts sharply with Continental's freewheeling and entrepreneurial culture. Meshing these cultures will be a major challenge in combining the banks.

Industry and financial analysts have viewed the merger as an excellent strategic fit. Continental's strong customer relationships have benefited from BAC's network, product line, and credit rating. More than that, the deal brought financial efficiencies and an infusion of new talent to BAC. For these reasons this combination was an example of productive diversification, based on plausible opportunities for scale and scope economies.

It would be instructive to follow the results of this merger over time, to see if expectations of synergy are realized. That will not be possible, however. On April 13, 1998, BankAmerica and Nationsbank agreed to merge in a deal that produced a bank (called BankAmerica) with combined assets of $570 billion and nearly 160,000 employees. At this time the results of the Continental acquisition were unclear. The size of this deal dwarfs the Continental acquisition and makes it very unlikely that synergies from it can ever be verified.

Financial Synergies

One argument for diversification is that the long-term success of a firm requires it to develop a portfolio of businesses that assures an adequate and stable cash flow with which to finance its activities. Such a portfolio strategy underlies the BCG growth/share matrix that we described in Chapter 2. The parent firm can also use profits from one business to subsidize others. Although portfolio strategies may smooth cash flows and prop up expanding or troubled businesses, they do not always create additional value for their owners. This is so for several reasons.

First, shareholders of firms can diversify their own personal portfolios and seldom need corporate managers to smooth earnings for them. For example, shareholders of Philip Morris could have purchased shares of Kraft Foods to diversify their portfolios and did not need the firm to acquire Kraft. Indeed, many shareholders may have preferred not to be diversified in this particular way, which implies that the acquisition of Kraft may have made them worse off, absent any other efficiency gains from the purchase. One might argue that a corporation may be able to diversify more extensively or more inexpensively than shareholders themselves can. But this is questionable, because it is usually less expensive for shareholders to diversify their personal portfolios through the purchase of stocks and bonds than it is for one large firm to purchase and integrate another firm. An exception to this is that investors with large ownership blocks in a firm may be unable to fully diversify their holdings themselves and thus may value a firm's risk reduction efforts.[10]

The notion that the diversified firm can create value by serving as a source of investment funds for internal divisions is also questionable. Unless the parent firm is a bank or other financial institution, it presumably performs its financial functions as a by-product of doing business in another area. While some firms are large enough and conduct enough transactions to develop a skill in banking (e.g., GE Capital Corporation), a diversification strategy based on the "firm-as-banker" rationale can only succeed if the firm can outperform banks in evaluating and servicing its investment opportunities. In other words, the "firm-as-banker" rationale can succeed if the diversifying firm is skillful at identifying firms that are undervalued by the rest of the market. This may be possible if the firm possesses special knowledge of the business being evaluated. But this is only likely to be true if the two firms are related, and therefore is not a good reason for unrelated diversification. Moreover, many firms that appear to use the "firm-as-banker" strategy contract out financial evaluation activities to independent firms, such as the Alcar Group. By relying on independent firms to perform the essential banking activity of financial evaluation, the "firm-as-banker" cannot possibly outperform the independent firms in this area.

Some potential acquirers believe that they are skillful at identifying undervalued firms. Firms under scrutiny for possible purchase are known as *target* firms. A target will often be considered for acquisition by several firms. The firm that actually acquires the target is generally the one that perceives the target to have the highest value, and is therefore willing to bid the most for it. The managers of the acquiring firm may congratulate themselves for finding a "bargain," but they might also ask why other potential acquirers bid less than they did. Perhaps the target was less valuable than they thought it was.

---

[10]See Shleifer, A. and R. W. Vishny, "Large Shareholders and Corporate Control," *Journal of Political Economy*, 1986: pp. 461–468.

This is an example of the *winner's curse*, in which the winning bidders in auctions and similar sales arrangements tend to be overly optimistic in their appraisal of the value of the item being sold. As Max Bazerman and William Samuelson point out in their article "I Won the Auction But Don't Want the Prize," unless the diversifying firm knows much more about the target than other bidders do, it will probably pay too much to "win" the bidding.[11] In addition, by bidding on the target, the diversifying firm alerts other potential bidders that the target may have unexploited profits. This may drive up the bidding, and further dissipate potential gains.

Even if financial synergies are plausible, they may still not justify a merger. Combinations that can exploit economies of scope can also get financial synergies. Thus, combinations that achieve both types of synergies will outperform comparable combinations made solely for financial synergies.

Economizing on Transactions Costs

The issue of transaction costs developed in conjunction with our discussion of vertical integration in Chapters 3 and 4 is also relevant if diversification occurs through mergers or acquisitions. A merger or acquisition is only a legal basis for combining firms. If the firms involved can exploit economies after the legal change in ownership, why couldn't they do so before the change? David Teece asked why scope economies cannot be achieved by coordinating several independent firms; that is, why must business units be brought into a firm for economies to be realized?[12]

Teece argues that the multiproduct firm is an efficient choice when transaction costs complicate coordination among independent firms. Recall from Chapters 3 and 4 that transactions costs are more likely to arise in relationships with independent firms when the production process involves specialized assets, such as human capital, organizational routines, or other forms of proprietary knowledge. In the absence of specialized assets, transaction costs are not likely to be a problem. In this case, market coordination may provide superior incentives and flexibility.

Many decisions regarding whether to diversify or operate as independent firms follow the logic of minimizing transactions costs. Consider how higher education is organized. Undergraduate universities represent the "merger" of separate schools and departments, each of which could, in principle, offer educational programs located contiguously but operated independently of each other. Undergraduate students tend to take courses in many departments, however, creating economies of scale in locating the departments near each other, and near common dormitory, library, athletic, and other facilities. The common location of these facilities means that any investments by any department are, in part, relationship-specific. In other words, the value of one department's investments depends on the actions other departments take. For example, even if the Northwestern University Department of Economics recruits several prize-winning teachers, their value in the classroom will not be fully realized if the university cannot attract high-quality students. This might happen if, say, the other departments were of low quality or

---

[11]Bazerman, M. and W. Samuelson, "I Won the Auction But Don't Want the Prize," *Journal of Conflict Resolution*, 1983: pp. 618–34.

[12]Teece, D. "Toward an Economic Theory of the Multiproduct Firm," *Journal of Economic Behavior and Organization*, 3, 1982: pp. 39–63.

refused to support actions aimed at enhancing the educational experience, such as funding for the library, student computer labs, and residence halls. Common "ownership" of Northwestern's various departments allows for a single policy regarding hiring and promotion, as well as specialized investments.

Contrast the organization of undergraduate education into "diversified firms" with the way many paraprofessional training schools, such as schools for legal assistants or medical technicians, are organized. Students interested in paraprofessional training generally do not require courses in other areas, so there is no need to assure access to them. The paraprofessional school reaps the full benefits of its investments in plant and labor, and does not have to fear holdup by other schools that share in the student population. Given the absence of transactions costs facing paraprofessional schools, it is not surprising that many of them are freestanding; they offer training in only one area and do not invest in facilities that other schools share.

Influence Costs and Incentive Effects

Influence costs are another problem associated with vertically integrated firms that can also adversely affect diversified firms. Corporate management evaluates each division to determine where to allocate resources. This is generally done during the firm's strategic planning and capital budgeting processes. The success of these processes depends on the quality of information received from division heads, and the ability of corporate management to evaluate information objectively, rather than let personal feelings affect decisions. To the extent that these decisions are affected by internal lobbying, resource allocations may be inefficient.

The capital market allocates resource for independent firms. Capital market observers regularly monitor how firms acquire and use their funds. A firm's share price and bond ratings are constantly reevaluated on the basis of monitoring results. Poor judgment by managers in using investment funds will decrease stock prices and diminish access to additional capital. We do not expect fund managers to fall prey to influence costs, especially those associated with personal lobbying. Thus, capital markets probably allocate resources more efficiently than corporate managers. This effect is attenuated for large firms that compete in stable product markets through the opportunities the managers of these firms have to control the use of retained earnings.

Corporate management of diversified firms must also use costly control systems that reward division managers on the basis of division profits and discipline managers by tying their careers to business unit objectives. This assumes, of course, that corporate management has the proper incentives to work on behalf of shareholders. Capital markets also provide incentives for managers to act in the interests of shareholders (e.g., to reward superior returns and penalize inferior returns). They do this without the need for costly internal control systems.

If one grants that diversification has to do jointly with the potential for scope economies and the transactions costs of market versus nonmarket options for exploiting those economies, then several nonmarket options are feasible to attain diversification objectives, short of integration through merger. Alternatives to merger and acquisition include internal development, joint ventures, and different types of informal or formal strategic alliances and minority participation.[13] These alternatives may enable managers to achieve scope economies without suffering

---

[13]Chapter 5 defines and discusses joint ventures and strategic alliances.

the diseconomies of scope that limit the optimal breadth of the organization. Despite attention in the popular business press to alternative diversification modes, research to date has not shown when one mode is preferable to others.

Changes in the conditions diversified firms face may affect the severity of transaction cost problems and the desirability of diversification. For example, Michael Useem argues that the restructuring of large corporations in the 1980s was a reaction to the increased influence of capital market actors that allowed for much greater stockholder control over professional managers.[14] For example, in the past decade, conglomerates have refocused their strategic positions and restructured their business portfolios. Jack Welch's strategic focusing of General Electric after 1980 is an example. Kodak's decision to divest its chemical, pharmaceutical, household products, and medical-testing device businesses in 1993 and 1994 is another. American Can's metamorphosis out of the metal can business and into financial services, which we discussed in Example 6.1, is still another.

Managerial Reasons for Diversification

The rationales discussed earlier presume some efficiency-enhancing objective for diversification, whether it is exploiting economies of scope or achieving transactions-cost economies. A third reason for diversification is what we call managerial. Managerial reasons for diversification are oriented toward maintaining or enhancing the position of executives making diversification decisions, rather than efficiency or enhancing shareholder wealth. That executives would make such decisions is not surprising. Indeed, much of the economic literature on organizations takes management's proclivity toward self-serving behavior as the basis for the corporate governance problem. If shareholders cannot judge the effectiveness of managers, then managers need not always act in the shareholders' best interest. As we discuss in Chapter 16, the potential for divergence between management action and shareholder interest is greatest in an environment of incomplete and imperfect information.

For an example of how managers can make strategic decisions to pursue their own self-interest rather than the interest of shareholders, consider the situation of managers in a firm targeted for a hostile takeover. These managers realize that if the hostile acquisition goes through, they are likely to lose their jobs. They elude this takeover by agreeing to be acquired by a third firm. In such a "friendly" deal, incumbent managers may be able to retain their positions and perquisites longer than they could under a hostile takeover. Shareholders stand to lose, however, because management will promote the tender offer of the friendly acquirer, regardless of whether other offers are higher. As long as shareholders are not fully informed about the value of the competing tender offers, managers can succeed with this plan to retain their jobs.

Another common managerial rationale for diversification is the pursuit of growth, which argues that managers diversify when it is easier to acquire new sales than to develop them internally. As Dennis Mueller has pointed out, diversifica-

---

[14]Useem, M., *Executive Defense: Shareholder Power and Corporate Reorganization*, Cambridge, MA: Harvard University Press, 1993. For an overview of research on corporate restructuring, see Bowman, E. and H. Singh, "Corporate Restructuring: Reconfiguring the Firm," *Strategic Management Journal*, 14, Special Issue, Summer 1993: pp. 5–14.

tion buys growth that cannot be achieved through internal development.[15] Growth is pursued because the pecuniary and nonpecuniary advantages to managing large growing firms are appealing to managers, although not necessarily to shareholders. Growth is not necessarily unprofitable or inefficient, although it can be. Again, as long as shareholders are not fully informed about the benefits to them of growth through diversification, managers can pursue their own objectives at shareholder expense.

If diversification is a strategy for growth, then we may expect to see greater unrelated diversification by firms with fewer opportunities for internal growth or related diversification. This is consistent with the increase in diversification that followed passage and enforcement of the Celler-Kefauver Act in 1950, which made related acquisitions more difficult. During this time there were more conglomerate mergers and fewer horizontal mergers.

Yakov Amihud and Baruch Lev suggest another reason why managers pursue unrelated acquisitions: to avoid getting fired.[16] They observe that shareholders are unlikely to replace top management unless the firm performs poorly relative to the overall economy. To reduce the risk of losing their jobs, managers must reduce the risk of poor performance. One way to do this is through unrelated acquisitions. Simple statistics tell us that the performance of a highly diversified firm is likely to mirror the performance of the overall economy, and is therefore less likely to lead shareholders to fire management. To support their point, Amihud and Lev show that manager-controlled firms engage in more conglomerate acquisitions than owner-controlled firms. While these acquisitions reduce the risk of job loss for top management, they may not benefit shareholders, who may easily reduce their own financial risk by managing their portfolio of investments (e.g., by purchasing mutual funds).

Some authors have offered rationales for unrelated diversification that support both managerial and shareholder goals. Debra Aron points out that unrelated diversification can improve incentives by reducing the cost of motivating managers under pay-for-performance schemes.[17] Gordon Donaldson and Jay Lorsch argue that managers will be reluctant to make firm-specific investments if they do not see the prospects for advancement within the firm. They view diversification as a substitute for a steeply rising wage structure as a means for promoting managerial motivation. Donaldson and Lorsch also argue that diversification offers managers opportunities for lateral movement.[18] Of course, if the divisions are unrelated, it is not clear if there is any value to lateral movement, apart from the dominant general management logic that we have already discussed.

The persistence of diversification despite vigorous antitrust enforcement, poor conglomerate performance (described in the next section), and the weak ra-

---

[15]For the principal statement of this rationale, see Mueller, D., "A Theory of Conglomerate Mergers," *Quarterly Journal of Economics*, 82, November 1969: pp. 643–659.

[16]Amihud, Y. and B. Lev, "Risk Reduction as a Managerial Motive for Conglomerate Mergers," *Bell Journal of Economics*, 12, 1981: pp. 605–617.

[17]For a detailed presentation of this point, see Aron, D. J., "Ability, Moral Hazard, Firm Size, and Diversification," *RAND Journal of Economics*, 19, Spring 1988: pp. 72–87. The use of pay-for-performance to motivate managers is discussed in detail in Chapter 14.

[18]Donaldson, G. and J. Lorsch, *Decision Making at the Top*, New York: HarperCollins, 1983.

tionales for unrelated diversification, suggest that managerial rationales help explain diversification activity. The possibility that managers may protect and expand their personal empires at the expense of shareholders is both troubling and intriguing. We believe, of course, that managers should work to enhance shareholder wealth, but circumstances have historically permitted managers to do otherwise.

If managers do entrench themselves at shareholder expense, then profit opportunities will arise for shareholders to monitor management performance more vigorously, and for outsiders to replace self-aggrandizing managers and offer shareholders a better value. One principle of economics is that when profit opportunities exist, individuals will take advantage of them. The fourth wave of corporate acquisitions that began in the mid-1970s is a testament to this principle.

The Market for Corporate Control

What limits the ability of managers to use corporate resources for their own benefit and neglect the interests of shareholders? Put a little differently, if managerial reasons for diversification are plausible, what keeps managers focused on the goals of owners and on improving efficiency within the firm? While boards of directors may provide some control, the discretion of top managers in slating boards, controlling elections, and providing board members with information can limit the ability of boards to act independently. If top managers stray too far from the interests of owners, then shareholders, or actors external to the firm, must step in to replace them.

This is the rationale expressed by the architects of hostile takeovers, including Goldsmith, Pickens, Icahn, and Jacobs. These corporate "raiders" claimed that they were replacing entrenched, inefficient management to benefit shareholders. Although their claims were hotly contested by those who thought the raiders were little more than speculators, the idea of disciplining errant managers by takeover has a long history and informed many current studies of corporate control changes.

The classic statement of this rationale for takeovers is provided by Henry Manne, who argued for the existence of a "market for corporate control" (MCC).[19] Control of corporations is a valuable asset. A market for this control exists, and according to Manne's theory, the main purpose of a merger is to replace one management team with another. If a management team fails to maximize shareholder value, this poor performance will be noticed by observers of the firm, and competing management teams will vie to displace incumbents via takeover. This threat of takeover disciplines current management to act in the interests of shareholders. In addition, the potential for competitive bidding once a tender offer has been made will ensure the highest valuation for firms and the largest returns to shareholders.

A raider who hopes to improve on the performance of existing managers will need to bring specialized knowledge and/or resources to a takeover attempt. Without such knowledge and/or resources, the expected benefits from the takeover may not be achieved due to poor implementation or may even be bid

---

[19]Manne, H., "Mergers and the Market for Corporate Control," *Journal of Political Economy*, 73, 1965: pp. 110–120.

away in the auction that follows the initial tender offer. These considerations imply that the market for corporate control argument needs to be supplemented by a scope argument. It also implies that, without specialized knowledge or resources, the winner of the auction in the market for corporate control will have overpaid and be subject to the "winner's curse."[20]

The MCC perspective has appealed both business academics and individuals involved in merger activity. It has significantly altered the rules, and even the language, of mergers and acquisition activity in the 1980s and 1990s, giving such terms as "white knights" and "shark repellents" whole new meanings.[21] It has also motivated important research on stock price valuations of corporate control transactions. The threat of takeover provides a plausible limit on opportunistic managerial behavior, and the idea of a corporate control market is especially convincing for "bust-up" hostile takeovers, in which the takeover is paid for by selling off the constituent business units of the acquired firm, in effect undoing the conglomerate.

Several studies have found characteristics of hostile takeovers that are broadly consistent with the predictions of the MCC perspective. For example, Randy Morck, Andrei Shleifer, and Robert Vishny found that targets of hostile takeovers tend to be in declining or rapidly changing industries where managers have failed to properly adjust the scale and scope of operations.[22] They argue that managers may be protecting their domain of control. Michael Jensen found that before takeovers, managers of oil industry firms continued costly explorations despite declining oil prices.[23] Shleifer and Vishny report that before takeovers, managers of airlines were unwilling to cut union wages from the high levels that had been reached under regulation. Finally, in a paper titled, "Do Bad Bidders Make Good Targets?" Mark Mitchell and Kenneth Lehn find that corporate raiders profit by acquiring and busting up firms that had previously pursued unprofitable diversification strategies.[24]

When the behavioral details of the MCC perspective have been tested, however, the results have not been as supportive. For example, James Walsh and John Ellwood tested the theory and found only limited support for it.[25] Pre-acquisition

---

[20]Shleifer, A. and R. W. Vishny, "Takeovers in the 60's and the 80's: Evidence and Implications," *Strategic Management Journal*, 12, Special Issue, 1991: pp. 51–60.

[21]A white knight is a friendly acquirer sought by a firm under threat of hostile takeover as an alternative to the hostile acquirer. A shark repellent is a measure, such as the amendment of corporate bylaws, that firms can take to make takeover less attractive. The lexicon of takeovers is too broad to repeat in detail here. Useful summaries can be found in Davidson, K. M., *Megamergers*, Cambridge, MA: Ballinger, 1985, and Commons D. L., *Tender Offer*, Berkeley, CA: University of California Press, 1985.

[22]Morck, R., A. Shleifer, A. and R. W. Vishny, "Characteristics of Targets of Hostile and Friendly Takeovers," in Auerbach, A., ed. *Takeovers: Causes and Consequences*, Chicago: University of Chicago Press, 1989.

[23]Jensen, M. C. and R. S. Ruback, "The Market for Corporate Control: The Scientific Evidence," *Journal of Financial Economics*, 1983: pp. 5–50.

[24]Mitchell, M. and K. Lehn, "Do Bad Bidders Make Good Targets?" *Journal of Political Economy*, 98, 1990: pp. 372–392.

[25]Walsh, J. P. and J. W. Ellwood, "Mergers, Acquisitions, and the Pruning of Managerial Deadwood," *Strategic Management Journal*, 12, 1991: pp. 201–217.

executive turnover in targets was not different from that of a control group, suggesting that managers were not entrenched. Post-merger managerial turnover did not vary inversely with pre-merger stock performance, as would be predicted. There was also little association between favorable market evaluation of the merger and post-merger turnover. A study by Albert Cannella and Donald Hambrick found that the turnover of executives in acquired firms was associated with diminished rather than improved performance.[26] James Walsh and Rita Kosnik found little support for the claim that corporate raiders can accurately identify and eliminate ineffective boards of directors and entrenched management teams.[27]

It is unclear whether disciplining poorly performing managers accounts for more than a small number of mergers. Even so, the threat posed by the MCC may deter many managers from blatant pursuit of self-interest. For example, recent research strongly confirms that managers who fight off hostile takeovers do not serve their shareholders' interests. Hostile acquirers usually offer shareholders of the target firm a substantial premium above the pre-tender offer market value of the firm. Several studies conclude that when management of a target firm successfully fights off a hostile takeover, the target's market value quickly falls back to the pre-tender offer level.[28] These findings belie the oft-heard claim that hostile acquirers actually undervalue the firms' assets.

Diversification, Wealth Redistribution, and Long-Run Efficiency

The MCC argument hinges on the ability of capital market observers to identify and replace inefficient management teams, so that new managers can realize efficiency gains. But the MCC argument fails to clarify who benefits and loses from efficiency gains. If the gains from replacing management teams come from improving operating economies, then shareholders, employees, and others with a stake in the firm (called *stakeholders*) can win, since the firm will be more profitable and less risky. If takeovers occur without a basis in operating synergies, however, gains may accrue largely to new owners at the expense of workers, buyers, suppliers, or local communities. This happens because gains to some parties must come at the expense of others, since no new wealth is being created. If this is the case, then takeovers redistribute rather than create wealth. This raises concerns about equity, and, as Andrei Shleifer and Lawrence Summers point out, may also raise concerns about long-run economic efficiency.[29]

Shleifer and Summers argue that wealth redistribution may adversely affect economic efficiency when the acquired wealth is in the form of quasi-rents extracted from stakeholders who have relationship-specific investments in the target firm. Recall from Chapter 4 that after making a relationship-specific investment,

[26]Cannella, A. A. and D. C. Hambrick, "Effects of Executive Departures on the Performance of Acquired Firms," *Strategic Management Journal*, 14, 1993: pp. 137–152.

[27]Walsh, J. P. and R. D. Kosnik, "Corporate Raiders and their Disciplinary Role in the Market for Corporate Control," *Academy of Management Journal*, 38, 1993: pp. 671–700.

[28]See Jarrell, G., J. Brickley, and J. Nutter, "The Market for Corporate Control: The Empirical Evidence Since 1980," *Journal of Economic Perspectives*, 2, 1988: pp. 49–68.

[29]Shleifer, A. and L. H. Summers, "Breach of Trust in Hostile Takeovers," in Auerbach, A. J. (ed.), *Corporate Takeovers: Causes and Consequences*, Chicago: University of Chicago Press, 1988, pp. 33–68.

an individual expects to receive quasi-rents that exceed the amount of the investment. These quasi-rents may take the form of wages in excess of what the worker could earn elsewhere, promotion opportunities, or perquisites, such as a company care. Once the investments are sunk, however, the person will proceed with the deal if quasi-rents are positive. Firms facilitate relationship-specific investments. A relative benefit of firms over markets is the ability of workers and managers to rely on implicit versus explicit contracts in settling disputes within the firm. Indeed, it is precisely the inability to efficiently forge sufficiently complete contracts that makes firms necessary in the first place.

Employees (or providers of other factors) who develop firm-specific assets become vulnerable to having quasi-rents taken by new owners, who are not bound to honor the implicit contracts made with former owners. This can occur because employees cannot readily sell firm-specific assets to other employers at a price comparable to what they currently receive. New owners can reduce that price substantially before the market value of the firm-specific asset is reached, and the employees consider leaving the firm.

Two examples may be useful. First, long-time employees of a single firm develop assets that are valuable chiefly to their firm, such as knowledge of how to operate the firm's specialized equipment or how best to use the firm's administrative procedures. These resources are not readily salable on the job market, since other firms have their own specialized equipment and practices. A new owner could break long-standing assurances of job security and reduce wages significantly before the employee would find it worthwhile to look for a new job.

Second, consider the relationship between a city or town and a major production facility located there that is part of a much larger concern. (The negotiations between Anaheim, California, and Walt Disney over the expansion of the original Disneyland come to mind.) In this situation, municipal administrators could easily be tempted to improve infrastructure, such as providing new sewers and roads, as incentives to keep the plant in the area or induce the owner of the plant to locate new facilities there. Once made, however, those improvements cannot be easily unmade. Roads and sewers cannot be moved. The firm, however, can move, such as when United Technologies moved its American Bosch manufacturing plant from Springfield, Massachusetts, to Columbia, South Carolina. Firms may threaten to move to seek tax abatements and other changes in the conditions under which they do business, thereby reducing the compensation that the town receives for providing infrastructure.

While takeovers motivated by redistribution may be rational for an acquirer in the short term, they may have long-term adverse consequences for firms. In the short term, the raider gains from redistribution. In the long term, employees, as well as other parties who do business with the firm, will be aware of the firm's past behavior and are unlikely to invest in firm-specific assets in the future, unless they are adequately compensated for their risk of future redistribution. If the raider had foresight, it would anticipate such problems and consider them as acceptable costs of doing the deal.

Shleifer and Summers are more concerned about the effects of takeovers on the stakeholders of firms other than the target. These stakeholders may observe the upheaval in other firms and conclude that their own jobs are in jeopardy and that it no longer pays to make firm-specific investments.[30] If this were to happen, the produc-

---

[30]Example 4.3 from Chapter 4 provides a vivid illustration of this point in the context of the acquisition of the Trans Union Corporation by the Marmon Group in 1981.

tivity of these workers would decline and the economy as a whole would suffer because of hostile takeovers. Even if the raider had foresight, it would not count these as costs of the deal because they are largely borne by firms other than the target.

Two concerns have been raised about the Shleifer and Summers' argument. The first is that firms do not have to be acquired to extract quasi-rents from stakeholders. As long as contracts do not dictate wages, promotions, and such, a firm can always renege on implicit agreements when it believes that its wages have gotten out of hand. Shleifer and Summers counter that firms that have honored commitments for many years often find it difficult to break them. Managers of firms located in a community for many years may also live there and might oppose moving the firm for personal reasons, even if it makes good business sense. This assures the community that their investments in infrastructure are secure. An outside acquirer does not have such ties to workers and community, and will be less reluctant to break implicit agreements.

The second concern is that the argument is difficult to test, and therefore, its practical implications are unclear. The claim that the activities of an acquirer are redistributing rather than creating wealth can easily be countered by the response that the actions taken (firing employees; reducing salaries) improved the efficiency of the firm and that the employees affected were overpaid or even redundant. Such a dispute is, in principle, resolvable. One could identify the standards for efficient behavior for the employees and determine if the actual employees met these standards. However, if the productivity of workers was easily ascertainable and their performance was easily monitored, the transaction cost issues at the heart of the Shleifer and Summers' argument would not pose problems.

◆ ◆ ◆ ◆ ◆ EVIDENCE ON THE PERFORMANCE OF DIVERSIFIED FIRMS

Although we have discussed why diversification is potentially profitable, many are skeptical of the ability of diversification strategies to add value. Perhaps Michael Goold and Kathleen Luchs, in their review of 40 years of diversification, best sum up the skeptic's viewpoint:

> Ultimately, diversity can only be worthwhile if corporate management adds value in some way and the test of a corporate strategy must be that the businesses in the portfolio are worth more than they would be under any other ownership.[31]

Studies of the performance of diversified firms, undertaken from a variety of disciplines and using different research methods, have consistently found that although diversification up to a point can be efficient, the sources of performance gains for diversified firms are unclear. Realizing efficiencies from diversification can also be difficult. Extensive diversification is often associated with poorer performance.

In this section we review some of the research that led Goold and Luchs and others to question the value of diversification. Unfortunately, there are no published studies that assess the performance of the most recent wave of mergers.

---

[31]Goold, M. and K. Luchs, "Why Diversify? Four Decades of Management Thinking," *Academy of Management Executive*, 7, 1993: pp. 7–25.

Studies of Diversified Firm Performance Using Accounting Data

Researchers have studied performance in terms of some measure of capital productivity, such as return on invested capital, by comparing the performance of firms in different diversification categories. They found the relationship between performance and corporate diversity to be unclear. Profits were more likely to be determined by industry profitability, coupled with how the firm related new businesses to old ones, rather than by diversification per se.[32] These results have persisted despite methodological differences associated with the measurement of diversification and performance, as well as the time frame used to assess changes in performance.

Some examples of these studies may be helpful. Richard Rumelt found several systematic relationships between diversification and firm performance. In particular, moderately diversified firms had higher capital productivity. Firms with moderate to high levels of unrelated diversification, however, had moderate or poor productivity. Cynthia Montgomery reconfirmed Rumelt's results for more recent years, using different measures of diversification.[33] Daniel Nathanson found that diversification is associated with deteriorating performance. In many cases, corporate performance never surpassed the levels obtained before the initiation of a diversification strategy. Noel Capon and his colleagues found that firms that restricted their diversification to narrow markets performed better than did broadly specialized firms, presumably due to their learning particular market demands.[34] Donald Hopkins examined unrelated diversification, as well as diversification based on shared markets or technologies. He found that market-based diversification performed the best of the three groups, but did not outperform nondiversified firms.[35] Constantinos Markides and Peter Williamson studied 136 U.S. firms and found that the relationship between diversification and performance depended on the ability of the diversifying firm to gain preferential access to critical resources and share them among business units.[36] They saw the adoption of an appropriate form of multidivisional structure (see Chapter 17) as a necessary condition for acquiring these resources.

[32]The classic study on this point is Christensen, H. K. and C. A. Montgomery, "Corporate Economic Performance: Diversification Strategy versus Market Structure," *Strategic Management Journal*, 2 1981: pp. 327–343. Also see Bettis, R. A., "Performance Differences in Related and Unrelated Diversifiers," *Strategic Management Journal*, 2, 1981: pp. 379–383.

[33]Montgomery, C. A., "The Measurement of Firm Diversification: Some New Empirical Evidence," *Academy of Management Journal*, 25, 1982: pp. 299–307.

[34]Capon, N., J. M. Hulbert, J. U. Farley, and L. E. Martin, "Corporate Diversity and Economic Performance: The Impact of Market Specialization," *Strategic Management Journal*, 9, January–February 1988: pp. 61–74.

[35]Hopkins, H. D., "Acquisition Strategy and the Market Position of Acquiring Firms," *Strategic Management Journal*, 8, November–December 1987: pp. 535–548.

[36]Markides, C. C. and P. J. Williamson, "Corporate Diversification and Organizational Structure: A Resource-Based View," *Academy of Management Journal*, 39, 1996: pp. 340–367.

Stock Price Studies of Diversified Firms

Another group of diversification studies has considered the reaction of the stock market to the announcement of diversification activities, such as mergers, acquisitions, divestments, and hostile takeovers. This research sought to assess the extent to which stock prices reflected gains upon the announcement of an action that were abnormally above or below those that would have been predicted if the action had not been announced. These studies presume some degree of efficiency in the way that markets assimilate information about firms into share prices. Thus, the market value of a firm at any point in time is assumed to reflect the best estimate of the firm's future stream of profits. If a firm's stock price increases when it announces that it intends to acquire another firm, this is assumed to reflect the value created by the acquisition that will be retained by the acquiring firm. A decrease in share value would indicate that the market believes the acquirer is probably overpaying for the target.

These stock price studies, many of which are summarized by Michael Jensen and Richard Ruback, considered the reactions of the stock market to announcements of corporate control changes.[37] Three important results about mergers that occurred before 1980 emerge:

- The combined value of parent and target firms tended to rise following the announcement of a combination, leading to the claim that mergers were efficient.

- A preponderance of abnormal returns accrue to the shareholders of target firms (as high as 30 percent, on average).

- The shareholders of acquiring firms receive small and statistically insignificant returns (4 percent or less).

These results suggest that acquisitions have the potential to create value to acquirers—either by exploiting synergies, removing ineffective managers, or redistributing wealth—but that the wealth is bid away as several firms vie for control.

Studies on mergers in the 1980s have shown generally negative returns from mergers, together with higher merger premiums. Randy Morck, Andrei Shleifer, and Robert Vishny studied 172 mergers and acquisitions between 1980 and 1987 and found negative returns to acquirers on average with little more than a third of the sample earning positive stock price returns.[38] Mark Sirower studied 168 deals between 1979 and 1990 and found significant negative returns to acquirers, with only a third of his sample reporting any positive returns.[39]

These results generated a second set of studies to identify more precisely how different types of diversification might lead to different allocations of wealth between acquirer and target. Harbir Singh and Cynthia Montgomery found that acquirers had greater returns when they targeted related firms than they did from

---

[37]Jensen, M. C. and R. S. Ruback, "The Market for Corporate Control: The Scientific Evidence," *Journal of Financial Economics*, 11, 1983: pp. 5–50.

[38]Morck, R., A. Shleifer, and R. W. Vishny, "Characteristics of Targets of Hostile and Friendly Takeovers," in Auerbach, A. (ed.), *Takeovers: Causes and Consequences*, Chicago: University of Chicago Press, 1989.

[39]Sirower, M. L., *The Synergy Trap*, New York: Free Press, 1997.

unrelated acquisitions.[40] Indeed, the gains to unrelated acquirers appeared to be completely bid away during the auction for the target. Anju Seth studied the abnormal stock price returns for 102 tender offers made between 1962 and 1979 to discover whether there were synergistic gains from acquisitions and whether returns differed between related and unrelated acquisitions. She found that mergers produce synergistic gains, but that one could not clearly associate gains with mergers.[41] Lois Shelton obtained similar results while using a more refined measure of relating acquisitions to gains.[42]

As with the research based on Rumelt's work, stock price studies of diversification have found that diversifying mergers and acquisitions can be associated with performance gains. Mergers can create value for parent firms, both in terms of increased stock returns and reduced risk. To realize performance gains, however, diversification must involve related business areas—diversification must make use of specialized and intangible resources that the parent brings to a combination. Firms that fail to diversify this way have poorer results, consistent with an inefficient and/or managerially motivated strategy. In one of the most comprehensive stock price studies of diversification, Sayan Chatterjee and Birger Wernerfelt find that firms with highly specialized resources engage in more related diversification strategies and achieve superior results over firms that use unspecialized resources, such as cash, to diversify.[43]

◆ ◆

$\mathcal{E}$XAMPLE 6.3

PEPSI'S FAST-FOOD TROIKA

The mid-1990s were not particularly kind to PepsiCo. Its flagship Pepsi product was losing ground to Coke in the United States and abroad, and Diet Pepsi had slipped to fourth among soft drinks (behind Coca-Cola's Sprite citrus soda). Even the fast-food chains that had provided Pepsi with substantial revenue growth over the prior two decades—Pizza Hut, Taco Bell, and Kentucky Fried Chicken—were experiencing declining revenues. Only the Frito-Lay snack division continued to outperform its rivals. In 1997, Pepsi spun off its fast-food operations into an independent company called Tricon.

When it acquired Pizza Hut and Taco Bell in the 1970s, Pepsi seemed intent on becoming the world's largest fast-food vendor. After Pepsi successfully digested the pizza and taco chains, it was widely expected to further expand its fast-

---

[40]Singh, H. and C. A. Montgomery, "Corporate Acquisitions and Economic Performance," *Strategic Management Journal*, 8, 1987: pp. 377–386.

[41]Seth, A., "Sources of Value Creation in Acquisitions: An Empirical Investigation," *Strategic Management Journal*, 11, 1990: pp. 431–446.

[42]Shelton, L. M., "Strategic Business Fits and Corporate Acquisition: Empirical Evidence," *Strategic Management Journal*, 9, pp. 278–287.

[43]Chatterjee, S. and B. Wernerfelt, "The Link Between Resources and Type of Diversification," *Strategic Management Journal*, 12, 1991: pp. 33–48.

food empire. By the mid-1980s, Pepsi's next target was rumored to be Wendy's. (Pepsi and Wendy's executives were seen sharing meals at numerous golf clubhouses.) But RJR Nabisco was eager to leave retailing and set an appetizing price for its Kentucky Fried Chicken unit. Pepsi eagerly gobbled it up.

Business analysts praised the deal—PepsiCo's stock price rose 5 percent when the deal was announced—citing the potential for numerous synergies. Pepsi would bring its vaunted expertise in marketing and new product development to Kentucky Fried Chicken. It would have the potential to create one-stop shopping for fast food. Finally, the deal would enhance Pepsi's share of fountain beverage sales as Kentucky Fried Chicken franchises switched from Coke to Pepsi.

Pepsi failed to deliver on many of the promised benefits of the acquisition. Kentucky Fried Chicken trailed the market when competitors, including Boston Market and grocery stores, successfully introduced healthier roasted chicken. At the same time, Pizza Hut struggled during the decade-long "pizza war" that its principal rivals—Domino's and Little Caesar's—seemed more intent on winning. (Some analysts question whether Pizza Hut has had the stomach to win the pizza war.) Pizza Hut's recent fortunes have depended entirely on the temporary success of new product launches (such as the stuffed crust pizza). Taco Bell's new product launches have also met with mixed success, and its attempt to attract price-conscious customers with 59-cent tacos failed when McDonald's and Burger King engaged in a bitter price war of their own. Overall, the profitability of Pepsi's restaurant division has substantially trailed that of the soft drink and snack food divisions.

To make matters worse, the acquisition of Kentucky Fried Chicken not only failed to enhance Pepsi's fountain beverage sales, it drove potential customers to choose Coke. Wendy's switched its fountain purchases from Pepsi to Coke only months after the Kentucky Fried Chicken acquisition, and for the past decade wherever a consumer buys fast-food hamburgers and a cola, that cola is almost surely a Coke. At the time of the Tricon spin-off, Pepsi's share of the fountain beverage market—just one-third that of Coke—was at its lowest since the Kentucky Fried Chicken acquisition.

As its woes mounted, PepsiCo CEO Roger Enrico decided to focus the company's efforts on its core businesses of soft drinks and snacks. Enrico also believed that Pepsi's fast-food businesses needed an injection of entrepreneurial spirit, even though Pepsi had allowed them to operate with near total autonomy. Ironically, the market responded to the spin-off with the same enthusiasm that it showed when Pepsi made the acquisitions—Pepsi's stock shot up 11 percent when it was announced. Tricon's first boss, David Novak, now faces many challenges in the fiercely competitive fast-food market, including helping the firm realize the synergies that eluded its parent.

Long-Term Performance of Diversified Firms

A third set of studies concerned with the performance of diversified firms has compared results of the mergers of the 1960s with those of the 1980s. The intuition of this work is that the true time horizon for assessing the results of diversification is longer than is commonly measured in research and that the longer-term performance of diversified firms has been poor.

Two major studies have shown that merger performance over time has generally been poor.[44] David Ravenscraft and F. M. Scherer studied nearly 6,000 mergers and acquisitions made between 1950 and 1977 and found that performance, whether measured by stock price changes or by accounting results, was poor. Moreover, the larger the merger, the more likely returns were to be negative. Michael Porter considered the corporate portfolios of 33 major diversified firms and found that between one-third and one-half of all acquisitions made by firms in his sample between 1950 and 1986 were eventually divested. More than half of the acquisitions into new businesses are eventually divested. Since divestiture is usually for poor performance, this indicates the failure of acquisition policies. Similar poor results were obtained for joint ventures and strategic alliances.

Andrei Shleifer and Robert Vishny summarize and compare the evidence on the merger waves of the 1960s and 1980s.[45] They conclude that the merger wave of the 1980s, which was characterized by more related acquisitions and by corporate refocusing, can best be understood as a broad correction to the conglomerate mergers of the 1960s. This implies that capital market imperfectly evaluated conglomerate mergers in the 1960s. It also highlights the importance of antitrust policy in merger activity, since the mergers of the 1980s coincided with a period of relaxed antitrust enforcement, which permitted a degree of horizontal and vertical combination that had not been possible in the 1960s. In a related study, Constantinos Markides looked at mergers in the 1980s and identified overdiversified firms. The returns to these firms from refocusing were significant and positive, consistent with Shleifer and Vishny's conclusion that the mergers of the 1980s corrected the mistakes of the 1960s and refocused overdiversified firms.[46] Robert Hoskisson and Michael Hitt echo this idea of refocusing by arguing that diversified firms need to reduce their scope of activities to reach a point where profitable diversification is possible.[47]

John Matsusaka examined the stock market responses to acquisition announcements during and immediately after the conglomerate merger wave of the 1960s and arrived at results that conflict with those of Shleifer and Vishny.[48] He found that buyers earned significant positive returns while making diversifying acquisitions. This is at odds with the view that the mergers of the 1980s were a corrective for those of the 1960s. It also refutes managerial explanations for these combinations. To explain the differences between mergers in the 1960s and 1980s, Matsusaka suggests that conditions in the world may have changed, so that diversifying acquisitions were valuable in the 1960s but not later because the antitrust climate changed. He also suggests that positive perceptions about conglomerates in the 1960s may have been reasonable when diversifying was a new activity, but were eventually shown to be incorrect, once experience with conglomerates had accumulated.

---

[44]Ravenscraft, D. J. and F. M. Scherer, *Mergers, Self-Offs, and Economic Efficiency*, Washington, D.C.: Brookings Institution, 1987: Porter, M. E. "From Competitive Advantage to Corporate Strategy," *Harvard Business Review*, May–June 1987: pp. 43–59.

[45]Shleifer, A. and R. W. Vishny, "Takeover in the '60s and the '80s: Evidence and Implications," *Strategic Management Journal*, 12, Special Issue, 1991: pp. 51–60.

[46]Markides, C. C., "Consequences of Corporate Refocusing: *Ex Ante* Evidence," *Academy of Management Journal*, 35, 1992: pp. 398–412.

[47]Hoskisson, R. E. and M. A. Hitt, *Downscoping: How to Tame the Diversified Firm*. New York: Oxford University Press, 1994.

[48]Matsusaka, J. G., "Takeover Motives During the Conglomerate Merger Wave," *Rand Journal of Economics*, 24, 1993: pp. 357–379.

Larry Lang and Rene Stultz provide further evidence that overdiversification is inefficient. They use "Tobin's q" to measure how well firms deployed their assets. (Tobin's q is the ratio of the market value of a firm to the cost of replacing its tangible assets.) They found that Tobin's q of specialized firms was 10 percent higher than for diversified firms in the same industries.[49]

The poor long-term performance of diversified firms is often attributed to their lack of investment in research and development. The failure to make and manage these investments leads diversifying firms to be unresponsive and noninnovative in the face of environmental changes and foreign competition. While there is some evidence of differences between diversifying and nondiversifying firms regarding R&D expenditures, whether diversification hampers corporate innovation has not been established.[50]

In summary, three different lines of research on the performance of diversified firms have led to similar overall conclusions. Diversification can create value, although its benefits per se relative to nondiversification are unclear, due to industry effects and other factors. Among diversifying firms, there is no clear association between simple measures of diversity within a business portfolio and overall corporate performance. However, firms that diversify according to a core set of resources, and with an eye toward integrating old and new businesses, tend to outperform those firms that do not work toward building interrelationships among their units. This is consistent with the generally accepted idea that defensible diversification will combine some basis in scope economies with transaction cost conditions that make it efficient to organize diverse businesses within a single firm, relative to joint ventures, contracts, alliances, or other governance mechanisms.

◆◆◆

XAMPLE 6.4

DIVERSIFICATION AND CORPORATE PERFORMANCE FOR PHILIP MORRIS

Performance issues for diversified firms can be made clearer by considering how they arise for specific firms. Philip Morris has engaged in a large and widely followed diversification program since the mid-1960s.[51] It has always highlighted innovation. Not a part of the tobacco cartel at the turn of the century, by 1950 it

---

[49]Lang, L. and R. Stultz, "Tobin's q, Corporate Diversification, and Firm Performance," *Journal of Political Economy*, 102, 1994: pp. 1248–1280.

[50]See Hall, B. H., "The Effect of Takeover Activity on Corporate Research and Development," in Auerbach, A. J., (ed.), *Corporate Takeovers: Causes and Consequences*, Chicago: University of Chicago Press, 1988, 69–100. Also see Hitt, M. A., R. E. Hoskisson, R. D. Ireland, and J. S. Harrison, "Effects of Acquisitions on R&D Inputs and Outputs," *Academy of Management Journal*, 34, 1991: pp. 693–706.

[51]The discussion that follows is based on public sources of information and on the case study of the tobacco industry by Robert Miles and Kim Cameron, *Coffin Nails and Corporate Strategies*, Englewood Cliffs, NJ: Prentice-Hall, 1982.

had the smallest market share among major firms in the industry. It thus had little to lose and much to gain from doing business differently. It pioneered the use of discount cigarette brands in the 1930s. It was the first to introduce filter-tip cigarettes with a brand named Marlboro initially targeted at women. Philip Morris was also a pioneer in the marketing of low-tar cigarette brands, such as Merit and Marlboro Light.

A period of significant environmental turbulence for the cigarette industry began in 1950, with the publication of the initial report linking smoking and lung cancer. This was followed in 1953 by the report from the Sloan-Kettering Institute on smoking and cancer in laboratory animals and in 1954 by a key article in *Reader's Digest* that put the link between smoking and lung cancer before the public. Further research and several reports of the Surgeon General on smoking and health have built on these initial reports.

In their industry history, *Coffin Nails and Corporate Strategies*, Robert Miles and Kim Cameron detail the response of tobacco firms to this environmental threat, both in terms of product-market diversification, lobbying to prevent government restrictions on smoking, and research support for alternative positions on the cigarette-cancer linkage. Philip Morris began diversifying in the 1950s and initially focused on small companies in a mixed set of unrelated businesses, ranging from paper products, shaving products, hospital supply, chewing gum, and real estate development.

The Philip Morris diversification changed in 1969, when it acquired the Miller Brewing Company for more than $200 million. This acquisition signaled an effort to buy firms that were large enough to become leaders in their industries and that could benefit from Philip Morris' marketing and distribution skills. Miller had traditionally occupied a small high-quality niche in the beer market (it advertised itself as the "champagne of bottled beers"). In seven years (and after early losses), Miller had been turned around in a marketing campaign that transformed industry practice and made Miller second in the industry. In 1978, Philip Morris acquired 7-Up in an apparent attempt to repeat the success obtained with Miller. It acquired General Foods in 1985 and Kraft in 1988.

How does one assess the performance of Philip Morris in light of this diversification program? Has it been successful or not? On the surface, Philip Morris would appear to be a success. Its stock has been consistently strong during this period: Philip Morris is now included in the Dow-Jones index of 30 leading industrial firms. Its sales growth has also been strong. Ranked 218th on the Fortune 500 in 1955, by 1980 it had climbed to 49th. Its nontobacco group alone would rank 111th. Philip Morris also ranked 32nd in net earnings in 1979.

The effectiveness of this diversification strategy, however, is different from the effectiveness of the firm as a whole. The 7-Up acquisition failed, and 7-Up was sold (the international portion to PepsiCo and the domestic portion spun-off to join with Dr Pepper). The food businesses have grown slowly. Even the success of Miller has to be qualified, since success took seven years and has not been sustained in recent years.

Perhaps the most interesting issue about the Philip Morris diversification, however, arises when one considers that before the Kraft deal in 1988, nearly 80 percent of its earnings came from a single cigarette brand, Marlboro (long the world's most profitable brand). Even today, approximately 60 percent of corporate profits arise from cigarettes. In what ways can the noncigarette businesses of

Philip Morris be seen as contributing to its performance? They do not contribute to profits in any way near what one would expect, given the billion-dollar size of these deals. They have not been high-growth businesses. They do not appear to benefit from association with Philip Morris. Indeed, the Kraft-General Foods group within Philip Morris does not promote its link with Philip Morris.

An alternative explanation is that this diversification involves stable businesses that produce predictable cash flows. As such, these businesses are desirable vehicles for reinvesting the substantial profits of the tobacco business of Philip Morris in an environment in which reinvestment in tobacco is unlikely to affect market share. The plausibility of this alternative story was borne out in 1993 when Philip Morris announced significant price reductions in its major cigarette brands, in response to the increasing market share of generic and discount brands. This signal of vulnerability in its base business caused a substantial drop in the price of Philip Morris shares. Even after more than two decades of major diversification, the key factors affecting the firm still concern its core tobacco business.

CHAPTER SUMMARY

◆ A firm is *diversified* if it produces in more than one output market. Most large and well-known firms are diversified to some extent. Broadly diversified firms (*conglomerates*) have portfolios of businesses that go beyond conventional ideas of scope economies. In these firms, it is often difficult to identify the core skills of the corporation.

◆ Firms can diversify in several ways, ranging from internal growth, to strategic alliances, to joint ventures, to formal combinations via merger or acquisition. Merger and acquisition have been the principal modes of diversification, although alternative modes, such as alliances and joint ventures, have become increasingly popular in the 1980s and 1990s.

◆ Diversification has increased dramatically since 1950, largely in two merger waves—the first in the 1960s highlighting the growth of conglomerates and the second in the 1980s highlighting more focused diversification and the deconglomeration of broadly diversified firms.

◆ It has been difficult to measure the extent of diversification. Most approaches have considered the similarity of businesses in a firm's portfolio according to some measure of technological or market relatedness—that is, according to how similar the businesses are in terms of the products sold or the customers served.

◆ Scope economies provide the principal rationale for why firms diversify. These economies can be based on market and technological factors, as well as on managerial synergies, due to a "dominant general management logic." Financial synergies, such as risk reduction or increased debt capacity, comprise a related rationale that emphasizes corporate management's role as a banker and financial adviser to its business units.

◆ Transaction cost economizing is another important diversification rationale. This is because the diversifier must consider the costs of a particular mode of diversification in addition to the benefits that are obtained from it. Common ownership, for example, is justified only when transaction costs problems make less formal combinations, such as strategic alliances, infeasible.

◆ Diversification may also occur for managerial reasons, such as the smoothing of a firm's performance to reduce the risk of job loss. The "market for corporate control" limits the extent to which firms can diversify for primarily managerial motives. Firms that do not pursue the interests of shareholders can become vulnerable to hostile takeover. Hostile takeovers may not be efficiency-enhancing, however, if they redistribute rather than create value for shareholders.

◆ Research on the performance of diversified firms has shown mixed results. Where diversification has been effective, it has been based on economies of scope among businesses that are related in terms of technologies or markets. More broadly diversified firms have not performed well, and many conglomerates refocused their business portfolios during the 1980s. While mergers have increased shareholder value, these increases have largely gone to the shareholders of acquired firms. Over a longer time frame, active diversifiers have divested many of their acquisitions.

QUESTIONS

1. The main reason that firms diversify is to achieve economies of scope. Discuss.
2. Is relatedness necessary for success in the market for corporate control?
3. How is expansion into new and geographically distinct markets similar to diversification? How is it different?
4. Many mangers justify diversification as a way to diversify risk. Use the ideas in Chapters 3 through 5 to explain why diversification may diversify the manager's job risk. Shareholders can, of course, diversify risk themselves, for example, by holding a diversified portfolio of stocks and bonds. Under what conditions can a diversified firm spread the risk to its shareholders to a greater extent than the shareholders can themselves?
5. With the growing number of firms that specialize in corporate acquisitions (e.g., Berkshire Hathaway, KKR), there appears to be a very active market for corporate control. As the number of specialist firms expands, will control arguments be sufficient to justify acquisitions? Do you think that relatedness will become more or less important as competition in the market for corporate control intensifies?
6. Professor Dranove's son has been shoveling snow for his neighbors at $5 per hour since last year, using his dad's shovel for the job. He hopes to save up for a bicycle. The neighbors decided to get a snow blower, leaving the boy a few dollars short and sorely disappointed. (He knows that his dad will not contribute a penny!). How is this situation different from that described by Shleifer and Summers? Is there an efficiency loss as a result of the neighbors' actions?
7. Suppose you observed an acquisition by a diversifying firm and that the aftermath of the deal included plant closings, layoffs, and reduced compensation for some remaining workers in the acquired firm. What would you need to know about this acquisition to determine whether it would be best characterized by value creation or value redistribution?
8. How would you tell if the businesses owned by a diversified firm would be better off if they were independent?

PART TWO

MARKET AND COMPETITIVE ANALYSIS

COMPETITORS AND COMPETITION

7

$\mathcal{T}$hrough the early 1990s, American breakfast cereal manufacturers, such as Kellogg and General Mills, were among the most profitable firms in America, realizing earnings before taxes of 10 to 20 percent of revenues. In this concentrated industry (the four leading firms combined accounted for well over 80 percent of sales), prices substantially exceeded costs and price wars were virtually unknown. But not all of the major players were faring well. Post was losing market share and, in April 1996, it cut prices across the board. In just two months, its market share rose by 4 percent, largely at the expense of market leader Kellogg. Kellogg matched the price reduction in June 1996, as did General Mills. The stock market greeted the price war coldly—Kellogg is one of the few firms listed on the New York Stock Exchange whose value did not increase between 1996 and 1998. Cereal prices crept back up in 1998, but analysts did not rule out future price wars.

This episode illustrates the interplay among competitors in a concentrated market. The major players had avoided price wars, but when one player was no longer satisfied with the status quo, it shook things up for everyone. The resulting price wars have scarred the industry.

Part Two of this book is concerned with competition. The first part of this chapter discusses a prerequisite for analyzing competition: identifying the competitors and defining the market. The second part considers four different ways in which firms compete: perfect competition, monopoly, monopolistic competition, and oligopoly. This chapter concludes with a brief discussion of the relationship between market structure and firm and industry performance. Chapters 8 through 10 present advanced concepts in competitive strategy, including the effect of commitments on competition, the dynamics of competition, and entry. Chapter 11 discusses how to use the material in Part Two to assess competition in specific markets.

◆ ◆ ◆ ◆ ◆ COMPETITOR IDENTIFICATION AND MARKET DEFINITION

Most managers can readily identify their competitors. Even so, it is worthwhile to develop both qualitative and quantitative methods for identifying competitors. These methods force managers to carefully identify the features that define the markets they compete in, and often reveal the nature of competition.

A given firm may compete in several input and output markets simultaneously. It is important to analyze each market separately, because the competitors and the nature of competition may be quite different in each one. For example, a coal mining operation in a small town in northern England may have little or no competition in the market for labor, an input, but may face many competitors in the market for coal, its output.

Identifying Competitors by Identifying Substitutes

Asked to identify competitors, most managers would probably name firms whose products substituted for their own. For example, a manager at Honda might name Volvo as a competitor in the family sedan market. Honda and Volvo family sedans are good examples of substitutes. In general, two products X and Y are substitutes if, when the price of X increases and the price of Y stays the same, purchases of X go down and purchases of Y go up. We can think of good X as being Honda family sedans, and good Y as being Volvos. During 1992–1993, a strong yen forced Honda to raise the price of its sedans relative to the price of Volvos. This is one of the principal reasons why Honda sales fell while the sales of non-Japanese sedans, including Volvo, increased.

As pointed out in the Economics Primer, the degree to which products substitute for each other is measured by the cross-price elasticity of demand. If the products in question are X and Y, then the cross-price elasticity measures the percentage change in demand for good Y that results from a 1 percent change in the price of good X. Formally, if η_{yx} denotes the cross-price elasticity of demand of product Y with respect to product X, Q_y the quantity of Y sold, and P_x the price of product X, then

$$\eta_{yx} = (\partial Q_y/Q_y) / (\partial Px/Px)$$

When η_{yx} is positive, it indicates that consumers increase their purchases of good Y as the price of good X increases. Goods X and Y would thus be substitutes. The appendix to this chapter presents a methodology for estimating cross-price elasticities using retail sales data.

Managers often draw a distinction between *direct competitors* and *indirect competitors*. When firms are direct competitors, the strategic choices of one directly affect the performance of the other. This would be the case for Honda and Volvo—a price reduction by Honda directly affects sales of Volvos. It follows that if the cross-price elasticity of demand between products X and Y is relatively large in magnitude, then the manufacturers of these goods are usually direct competitors.

When firms are indirect competitors, the strategic choices of one also affect the performance of the other, but only through the strategic choices of a third firm.[1] For example, product X might be Honda sedans and product Y might be Jeep Grand Cherokees. The cross-price elasticity between the two products is small in magnitude. However, if Honda reduces the prices on its sedans, Volvo may lower the price on its sedans. The latter price reduction might affect the sales of Jeep Grand Cherokees, because Volvos and Jeeps are substitutes, even though Hondas and Jeeps are not.

Products tend to be close substitutes when three conditions hold:

- They have the same or similar *product performance characteristics*.

- They have the same or similar *occasions for use*.

- They are sold in the same *geographic market*.

A product's performance characteristics describe what it does for consumers. Though highly subjective, listing product performance characteristics often clarifies whether products are substitutes. Honda and Saturn sedans have the following product performance characteristics in common:

a. Seat four comfortably

b. Good fuel economy

c. Reliability

d. Acceptable acceleration and handling

Based on this short list, we can assume that the products are in the same market. We would probably exclude Jeeps from this market, however.

A product's occasion for use describes when, where, and how it is used. Both orange juice and cola quench thirst, but because they are used in different ways (orange juice is primarily a breakfast drink and cola is consumed with or between meals), they are probably in different markets.

Products with similar characteristics and occasions for use may not be substitutes if they are in different geographic markets. In general, two products are in different geographic markets if: (a) they are sold in different locations, (b) it is costly to transport the goods, and (c) it is costly for consumers to travel to buy the goods. For example, a company that mixes and sells cement in Cleveland is not in the same geographic market as a similar company in Phoenix. The cost of transporting cement over long distances is so large relative to its price that it would not be economical for the Cleveland cement seller to ship its product to Phoenix, even if cement prices in Phoenix are higher.

Efforts to identify competitors are often limited to the type of qualitative analysis that we have described earlier. While potentially informative, it has several shortcomings. First, identifying substitutes based on product performance characteristics is subjective and imprecise (e.g., is a Lexus sedan in the same market as Honda and Saturn?). As a result, market definitions are often debatable. Second, it is difficult to calibrate the degree to which products substitute for each other (e.g., airport limo service is undoubtedly a substitute for taxi service, but

---

[1] Indirect competitors may also include firms that are not currently direct competitors but might become so. This definition forces managers to go beyond current sales data to identify potential competitors.

how close a substitute is it?). Finally, it is often difficult to assess the importance of transportation costs (e.g., how important are transportation costs in a consumer's choice of a doctor or dentist?).

This qualitative approach to competitor identification may be enhanced in several ways. One can try to obtain information on cross-price elasticities, as discussed previously. One might also observe how prices of different firms change over time—the prices of close competitors tend to be highly correlated. A popular approach is to identify firms in the same Standard Industry Classification (SIC), as defined by the U.S. Bureau of the Census. SIC codes identify products and services by a seven-digit identifier, with each digit representing a finer degree of classification. For example, within the two-digit category 35 (Industrial and Commercial Machinery and Computer Equipment) are four-digit categories 3523 (Farm Machinery and Equipment) and 3534 (Elevators and Moving Stairways). Within 3534 are six-digit categories for automobile lifts, dumbwaiters, escalators, and so forth.

One should use caution when using SIC codes to identify competitors. Although products with the same SIC code often share the same product performance characteristics and may correctly be considered competitors, this is not always so. For example, all pharmaceuticals share the same four-digit SIC code (2834), but not all drugs substitute for each other. In this case, the four-digit SIC code is too aggregated to identify meaningful competitors. In other cases, firms that probably do compete with each other may have different SIC codes. An example is variety stores (5331), department stores (5311), and general merchandise stores (5399). These SICs are too disaggregated to identify meaningful competitors. Finally, SIC codes do not consider the geographic component of competition.

◆ ◆

XAMPLE 7.1

SUBSTITUTES AND COMPETITION IN THE POSTAL SERVICE

One of the few constants about international business is that the postal service is a government-regulated or government-owned monopolist. Among the developed countries, only Holland has fully privatized its postal service. Advocates of maintaining government monopoly control of the postal service claim that it is in their nation's best interest to assure that all residents, regardless of location, have equal access to communication by post. Considering the growth of advertising ("junk") mail, on the one hand, and the growth of telephones, televisions, modems, and facsimile machines, on the other, this argument seems questionable. Postal communications seem less than vital, and access to other sources of communication continues to grow. Another justification for government-sponsored postal monopoly is that it is unnecessarily costly for two or more people to deliver mail to the same addresses. Some arguments for government control, such as some Britishers' concern that a private post office may not wish to depict the Queen on stamps, seem less compelling.

As monopolies, postal services have operated with legendary inefficiency. In the early 1990s, Chicago newspapers routinely reported bags of undelivered mail found abandoned in unlikely places, such as under highway overpasses and in workers' garages. (Fortunately for Chicagoans, the media attention brought substantial improvements in service.) But changes in technology and global competition are beginning to catch up with postal services, and their protected status is at risk.

Government regulations do not limit all forms of competition to the postal service. Businesses increasingly use private express mail service for relatively routine matters. For example, in 1998 there were an estimated 360,000 European express shipments per day. Locally, most big cities have private courier services that deliver mail between downtown office buildings in a few hours or less. Electronic mail, fax, and interactive television also threaten established postal services and have siphoned off billions of dollars of business from European postal services alone. (Following the dictum "If you can't beat 'em, join 'em," the British Post Office recently formed a partnership with Microsoft to convert letters to electronic form to be transmitted over the internet.)

Faced with these competitive pressures, national postal services are seeking to operate more like private businesses, especially in the fiercely competitive international parcel post market. Germany's largely privatized Deutsche Post, which expects to be publicly traded in the year 2000, and the Dutch Post Office have acquired ownership stakes in private international parcel post carriers such as DHL. Other national postal services have sales offices throughout Europe to compete for international parcel post, and New Zealand's postal service has sales teams that travel the world in search of business.

As the European Union liberalizes postal services, Europe's national post offices may eventually lose their protected status for local service. Already, private postal services may compete with national postal services on mail weighing more than 350 grams. Some foresee the elimination of all barriers to competition. National postal services may even have to compete head to head for local and international business.

Market Definition

Market definition identifies the market or markets in which a firm competes. George Stigler and Robert Sherwin have described a market as "that set of suppliers and demanders whose trading establishes the price of a good."[2] This suggests that two firms are in the same market if one firm's production and pricing decisions materially affect the price that the other firm can charge.[3] In other words, two firms are in the same market if they constrain each other's ability to raise price.

Market definition is a cornerstone of antitrust economics, where it is often necessary to compute market shares to establish that a firm has market power.

---

[2]Stigler, G. and R. Sherwin, "The Extent of the Market," *Journal of Law and Economics*, 28, 1985: pp. 555–585.

[3]This does not imply, however, that if one firm's decisions do not affect another firm, they are not in the same market. In particular, two firms may be in a competitive market, in which no one firm's decisions affect the market. Hence, the notion of constraints as a tool for market definition is more appropriate for oligopolistic markets than it is for competitive markets.

Naturally, one cannot compute market shares without determining the size of the market, so market definition is almost always a component of antitrust analysis. To determine if a market is well-defined for antitrust purposes, antitrust economists often conduct the following "thought experiment." Suppose that all of the firms in the candidate market were to set prices collectively so as to maximize their combined profits. Would they choose to raise prices by at least 5 percent? If so, then there must be few firms outside the candidate market to *constrain* the pricing behavior of firms within it. This implies that the market is well-defined.

For example, suppose that we wish to determine if major U.S. office supply retailers (e.g., Staples and Office Max) constitute a market. We would conduct the following thought experiment. Suppose that all major office supply retailers in the United States were permitted to collectively choose price levels. Would they choose to raise prices by 5 percent or more? If they feared losing substantial business to other retailers, such as smaller office supply retailers and mass merchandisers, then they might not raise price. If this were the case, then we would need to expand the market definition to include these other retailers. If the major office supply retailers did not fear losing substantial business to other stores, then they would be expected to raise prices. In this case, we would consider major office supply retailers to constitute a market.

The antitrust approach to market definition is closely related to the concept of the own-price elasticity of demand. Recall from the Economics Primer that the own-price elasticity of demand equals the percentage change in a firm's sales that results from a 1 percent change in price. If η_x denotes the own-price elasticity of demand facing firm X, Q_x denotes the quantity sold by firm X, and P_x the price, then

$$\eta_x = - \left(\Delta Q_x / Q_x \right) / \left(\partial P_x / P_x \right)$$

We use the negative sign to make η_x a positive number, since ∂Q and ∂P will generally have the opposite sign. We can easily extend this concept to consider the own-price elasticity of demand facing a group of firms. This would be the percentage change in the group's sales if the group were to collectively raise price by 1 percent. If this is small in magnitude, then the group of sellers faces few constraints on pricing from other firms, and may be considered a well-defined market.[4]

We would expect that individual office supply retailers, such as Staples, face a fairly large own-price elasticity. If Staples were to raise its prices, customers could go to another major retailer, such as Office Max. However, it is not obvious whether the major office supply retailers *collectively* face a large own-price elasticity. In a recent antitrust analysis, the Department of Justice (DOJ) believed that the major office supply retailers collectively faced a low own-price elasticity. This implies that if the major retailers collectively raised price, they would lose little business. Based on this view, the DOJ blocked a proposed merger between Staples and Office Max, fearing that this would lead to price increases.

The antitrust approach to market definition is closely related to competitor identification. A firm's antitrust market generally includes its direct competitors. It may also include indirect competitors, depending on whether indirect competition is sufficiently strong to constrain prices.

---

[4]The technique for computing the own-price elasticity of demand facing a group of sellers that historically have operated as independent firms is known as residual-demand curve analysis. To implement this analysis, one would need historical data on prices, quantities, and exogenous factors that cause prices to vary across firms.

EXAMPLE 7.2

DEFINING COCA-COLA'S MARKET

In 1986, the Coca-Cola Company sought to acquire the Dr Pepper Company. At the time, Coca-Cola was the nation's largest seller of carbonated soft drinks, and Dr Pepper was the fourth largest. The Federal Trade Commission (FTC) went before federal judge Gerhard Gesell seeking an injunction to block the merger on the grounds that it violated Section 7 of the Clayton Act, which prohibits any acquisition of stock or assets of a company that may substantially lessen competition. Coca-Cola apparently sought the deal to acquire, and more fully exploit, the Dr Pepper trademark. Coca-Cola's marketing skills and research ability were cited as two factors that would allow it to increase the sales of Dr Pepper. Judge Gesell also noted that Coca-Cola was motivated, in part, by a desire to match the expansion of Pepsi-Cola, which had simultaneously been seeking to acquire 7-Up. Although the threat of FTC action caused Pepsi to abandon the 7-Up acquisition, Coca-Cola pressed on.

Judge Gesell granted the injunction, and the Coca-Cola/Dr Pepper deal was never consummated. In his decision, Judge Gesell addressed the question of market definition. He wrote: "Proper market analysis directs attention to the nature of the products that the acquirer and the acquired company principally sell, the channels of distribution they primarily use, the outlets they employ to distribute their products to the ultimate consumer, and the geographic areas they mutually serve." The judge was concerned not only with the end-user market, but also intermediate markets for distribution and retailing. Reduction of competition in any of these markets could harm consumers.

Depending on how the market in which Coca-Cola and Dr Pepper competed was defined, one might conclude that the merger would either have no effect on competition or a significant effect. The FTC argued that the appropriate "line of commerce" was carbonated soft drinks. It presented data to show that under this definition, the merger of Coca-Cola and Dr Pepper would increase Coca-Cola's market share by 4.6 percent nationwide, and by 10 to 20 percent in many geographic submarkets. (Geographic submarkets were considered because of the special characteristics of soft drink distribution channels.) Given Coca-Cola's already high market share of 40 to 50 percent in many of these markets, the merger would significantly reduce competition.

In defending the merger, Coca-Cola attempted to define the relevant market as "all . . . beverages including tap water." Under this definition, the proposed merger would have a negligible effect on competition. Judge Gesell ruled: "Although other beverages could be viewed as within 'the outer boundaries' of a product market . . . determined by the reasonable interchangeability of use or the cross-elasticity of demand between carbonated soft drinks and substitutes for them, carbonated soft drinks . . . constitute a product market for antitrust purposes." In reaching this decision, he relied on factors such as the product's distinctive characteristics and uses, distinct consumers, distinct prices, and sensitivity to price changes. Judge Gesell found such indicia to be present in this case, stating that the rival firms "make pricing and marketing decisions based primarily on comparisons with rival carbonated soft drink products, with little if any concern about possible competition from other beverages." In other words, carbonated soft drink makers constrain each others' pricing decisions, but are unconstrained by other beverages. Thus, carbonated soft drinks constitute a well-defined market.

Geographic Competitor Identification

Otherwise identical products will not be good substitutes if they are sold in different geographic areas, and if the cost of transporting the product (or the consumer) from one area to another is prohibitive. To identify competitors by location, one might use census-defined areas, such as cities or states, classifying all firms within the same area as competitors. Without knowledge of actual product or consumer flows, however, this can lead to gross errors. For example, it is unlikely that all the grocery stores in Chicago compete with one another. Those on Chicago's north side could collectively raise their prices by 5 percent without losing much business to stores in other parts of Chicago.

Rather than rely on ad hoc market boundaries, it is preferable to identify competitors by directly examining the flow of goods and services across geographic regions. To illustrate this approach, consider how a hypothetical sporting goods store in the Sunset section of San Francisco—Bay City Sports—might try to identify its competitors. Bay City Sports might assume that its competitors include all sporting goods stores in San Francisco. This is mere guesswork and is probably wrong. Bay City Sports might instead survey its customers to find out where else they shop. This would certainly identify some direct competitors. But it might fail to identify other direct competitors, and would likely miss indirect competitors.

To identify all of its direct and indirect competitors, Bay City Sports should adopt a two-stage approach. First, it should ask its customers where they live. The store can then identify the contiguous area from which it draws most of its customers, sometimes called the *catchment area*. Bay City Sports could reasonably assume that people prefer to buy their sporting goods close to home. It should consider other sporting goods stores in the catchment area to be local direct competitors. Some residents of the catchment area, especially those who live on its fringes, may prefer to travel outside the area to buy their sporting goods. To identify these distant direct competitors, Bay City Sports should perform a second survey of residents of its catchment area (not just its own customers) to find out if and where they shop outside the area. Stores located near these distant direct competitors should be considered indirect competitors.

Kenneth Elzinga and Thomas Hogarty used these concepts to develop an approach for identifying geographic competitors that is frequently used in antitrust cases.[5] Elzinga and Hogarty claim that a geographic market, and the competitors within it, are properly identified if two conditions are satisfied: (1) the firms in that market draw most of their customers from that area, and (2)

---

[5]Elzinga, K. and T. Hogarty, "The Problem of Geographic Market Definition Revisited: The Case of Coal," *Antitrust Bulletin*, 23, 1978: pp. 1–18.

the customers residing in that area make most of their purchases from sellers in that market. Using this approach, if it turns out that (1) sporting goods stores in the Sunset section of San Francisco draw 80 to 90 percent of their business from residents of Sunset, and (2) residents of Sunset buy 80 to 90 percent of their sporting goods from stores in Sunset, then Sunset is a well-defined market. Bay City Sports could therefore restrict its competitor analysis to other stores in Sunset.

MEASURING MARKET STRUCTURE ◆ ◆ ◆ ◆ ◆

Markets are often described as being concentrated (having just a few sellers) or unconcentrated. As we will see, such characterizations often permit a quick and accurate assessment of the likely nature of competition in a market. These characterizations are aided by having measures of *market structure*.

Market structure refers to the number and distribution of firms in a market. A common measure of market structure is the N-firm concentration ratio. This gives the combined market share of the N largest firms in the market. For example, the four-firm concentration ratio in the soft drink industry is about .90, which indicates that the combined market share of the four largest soft drink manufacturers is about 90 percent. When calculating market share, one usually uses sales revenue, although concentration ratios based on other measures, such as production capacity, may also be used. Table 7.1 shows four-firm and eight-firm concentration ratios for selected U.S. manufacturing industries in 1992.

Another commonly used measure of market structure is the Herfindahl index.[6] The Herfindahl index equals the sum of the squared market shares of all the firms in the market, that is, letting S_i represent the market share of firm i, Herfindahl $= \Sigma_i(S_i)^2$. Thus, in a market with two firms that each have 50 percent market share, the Herfindahl index equals $.5^2+.5^2 = .5$. In general, the Herfindahl index in a market with N equal-size firms is $1/N$. Because of this property, the reciprocal of the Herfindahl index is referred to as the *numbers-equivalent of firms*. Thus, a market whose Herfindahl is .125 has a numbers-equivalent of 8. When calculating a Herfindahl, it is usually sufficient to restrict attention to firms with market shares of .01 or larger, since the squared shares of smaller firms are too small to affect the Herfindahl.

The Herfindahl conveys more information than the N-firm concentration ratio. One problem with the N-firm ratio is that it is invariant to changes in the sizes of the largest firms in the market. For example, a four-firm ratio does not change value if the largest firm gains 10 percent share at the expense of the second largest firm. The Herfindahl index does increase under such circumstances. If one believes that the relative size of the largest firms is an important determinant of conduct and performance, as economic theory suggests, then the Herfindahl is likely to be more informative.

---

[6]The index is named for Orris Herfindahl who developed it while writing a Ph.D. dissertation at Columbia University on concentration in the steel industry. The index is sometimes referred to as the Herfindahl-Hirschman index and is often abbreviated HHI.

TABLE 7.1
CONCENTRATION STATISTICS FOR SELECTED U.S. MANUFACTURING INDUSTRIES, 1992

SIC code	Industry description	Number of Firms	4-firm CR	8-firm CR	Herfindahl Index	Numbers-equivalent of Firms
2024	Ice cream and frozen desserts	411	24	40	.029	34
2033	Canned fruits and vegetables	502	27	42	.030	33
2037	Frozen fruits and vegetables	182	28	42	.031	32
2041	Flour and other grain mill products	230	56	68	.097	10
2043	Cereal breakfast foods	42	85	98	.225	4
2046	Wet corn milling	28	73	93	.152	7
2047	Dog and cat food	102	58	77	.123	8
2273	Carpets and rugs	383	40	53	.085	11
2411	Logging	12985	19	26	.016	63
2448	Wood pallets and skids	1902	5	7	.0014	714
2511	Wood household furniture	2636	20	31	.017	60
2731	Book publishing	2504	23	38	.025	40
2771	Greeting cards	157	84	88	.292	3
2812	Alkalies and chlorines	34	75	90	.199	5
2841	Soap and other detergents	635	63	77	.158	6
2911	Petroleum refining	131	30	49	.041	24
3221	Glass containers	16	84	93	.216	5
3274	Line	57	46	61	.069	14
3312	Blast furnaces and steel mills	135	37	58	.055	18
3334	Primary aluminum	30	59	82	.146	7
3411	Metal cans	132	56	74	.104	10
3491	Industrial valves	392	24	34	.028	35
3511	Turbines and turbine generators	64	79	92	.255	4
3562	Ball and roller bearings	123	51	65	.085	12
3565	Packaging machinery	590	16	25	.015	65
3571	Electronic computers	803	45	59	.068	15
3581	Automatic vending machines	105	52	73	.084	11
3632	Household refrigerators and freezers	52	82	98	.189	5
3711	Motor vehicles and car bodies	398	84	91	.268	4
3823	Process control instruments	822	27	38	.026	39
3931	Musical instruments	437	25	41	.030	33
3995	Burial caskets	195	64	72	.216	4

Source: "Concentration Ratios in Manufacturing," *1992 Census of Manufactures report MC92-S-2*, Washington, DC: U.S. Department of Commerce, Economics and Statistics Administration, Bureau of the Census, 1992.

◆ ◆ ◆ ◆ ◆ MARKET STRUCTURE AND COMPETITION

Many economic models link the structure of a market to the conduct and financial performance of its firms. The Economics Primer discussed models of price determination, showing that as a firm faces more elastic demand, the desired margin between price and marginal cost narrows. In the extreme case of a perfectly competitive market, firms face infinitely elastic demand, so that price is equated to marginal cost. With free entry and exit, all profit opportunities are eroded, so that price is also driven to minimum average cost. In contrast, the price set by a monopoly exceeds marginal cost, often by a substantial amount.

TABLE 7.2
FOUR CLASSES OF MARKET STRUCTURE AND THE INTENSITY
OF PRICE COMPETITION

Nature of Competition	Range of Herfindahls	Intensity of Price Competition
Perfect competition	Usually below .2	Fierce
Monopolistic competition	Usually below .2	May be fierce or light, depending on product differentiation
Oligopoly	.2 to .6	May be fierce or light, depending on interfirm rivalry
Monopoly	.6 and above	Usually light, unless threatened by entry

This discussion suggests that a firm may face a continuum of pricing possibilities, depending on the nature of its competition. Economists have divided this continuum into four broad categories, which are identified in Table 7.2. Associated with each category is a range of Herfindahls that is common for each kind of competition. These ranges are *only suggestive* and should not be taken as gospel, however. For example, the table suggests that if there are only two competitors in a market, they will not behave competitively. But in some instances, a market with only two firms would be characterized by fierce price competition. Additionally, as we will see in Chapter 10, some conditions might produce competitive pricing even when a market has only one firm.[7] Thus it is essential to assess the circumstances surrounding the competitive interaction of firms to make conclusions about the intensity of price competition, rather than rely solely on the Herfindahl or other measures of concentration.

We provided a mathematical treatment of perfect competition and monopoly in the Economics Primer. The ensuing discussion of these competitive conditions highlights some intuitive issues for managers. We begin with brief discussions of perfect competition and monopoly. (More detailed discussions may be found in microeconomics textbooks.) We then provide lengthier discussions of monopolistic competition and oligopoly. Because the theory of oligopoly is especially rich, we will elaborate on it in Chapters 8 and 9.

Perfect Competition

In the theory of perfect competition, there are many sellers of a homogeneous good and many well-informed consumers who can costlessly shop around for the best price. Under these conditions, there is a single market price that is determined by the interaction of all sellers and buyers, but is beyond the control of any one of them. This implies that if a firm charges even one penny more than the market price it will sell nothing, and if it sets a price below the market price, it will needlessly sacrifice revenue. In other words, each firm faces infinitely elastic demand. Its only decision, then, is how much output to produce and sell.

---

[7]This is called a contestable market. See Baumol, W., J. Panzar, and R. Willig, *Contestable Markets and the Theory of Industry Structure*, New York: Harcourt Brace Jovanavich, 1982, for a definition of contestable markets and an extensive analysis of the conditions that might give rise to contestability.

Recall from the Economics Primer that a firm maximizes profit by producing a volume of output at which marginal revenue equals marginal cost. Recall, too, that the percentage contribution margin (*PCM*) equals $(P - MC)/P$, where P = price and MC = marginal cost. The condition for profit maximization can then be written $PCM = 1/\eta$.[8] In perfect competition, $\eta = \infty$, so the optimal PCM is 0. Many markets approximate perfect competition, including those for many metals and agricultural commodities. As the model predicts, price competition in these markets is fierce. Sellers set identical prices, and prices are generally driven down to marginal costs.

Many other markets, including those for most consumer goods and professional services, do not fit the literal conditions of the model of perfect competition. Even so, some of these markets may experience fierce price competition. Chapter 9 provides a rigorous explanation of why prices in some markets are driven down toward marginal costs. Below, we present some informal explanations.

Market conditions will tend to drive down prices when two or more of the following conditions are met:

- There are many sellers.

- Consumers perceive the product to be homogeneous.

- There is excess capacity.

We discuss how each of these features may contribute to fierce pressure to reduce prices.

Many Sellers

A top airline executive once said that "the industry is led by its dumbest competitor."[9] He made this statement in conjunction with a round of price cutting by two competitors. He probably meant that the airlines could increase their profits if they would stop cutting prices in vain attempts to increase market share. Of course, if the members of an industry could collude to maintain high prices, consumers would suffer. To prevent this, the DOJ and Federal Trade Commission (FTC) and their counterparts in the European community, Canada, and Australia, vigorously enforce antitrust laws designed to prevent collusive pricing. In enforcing these laws, the antitrust authorities are seldom concerned about markets with more than a few sellers. Experience, coupled with economic theory has taught them that it is unusual for more than a handful of sellers to raise prices much above costs for a sustained period. This is true for a number of reasons.

First, when there are many sellers, there is likely to be a diversity of pricing preferences. Even if the industry *PCM* is high, a particular seller may prefer a low price, for example, if it has low costs. In the airline industry, for example, a low-cost airline, such as Southwest, will often underprice higher-cost competitors, such as Delta and United, on routes in which they directly compete.

Second, a price increase will result in fewer purchases by consumers, so some sellers will have to reduce production to support the elevated prices. But the more sellers there are, the more difficult it is to agree on who should cut production. This point is illustrated by the contrast between the historical success of cartels in

---

[8]See the Economics Primer.

[9]*Fourtune*, October 20, 1980, p. 27.

the potash and nitrogen industries.[10] The potash cartel that existed before World War II was highly concentrated and generally succeeded in restricting production and keeping prices high. The world nitrogen cartel, by contrast, consisted of many firms in the United States, Europe, and South America and was far less successful in its attempts to raise prices above competitive levels.[11]

Third, even if sellers appear willing to cut production, some may be tempted to "cheat" by lowering price and increasing production. Among the firms most tempted to lower prices are those with small market shares, of which there will be many when the market is relatively unconcentrated. A small firm may view the collusive bargain among bigger rivals as an opportunity to increase market share. Recall from Chapter 2 that together with increased market share may come learning benefits and economies of scale that will enhance a firm's competitive position. A small firm may also gamble that its larger rivals will be unable to detect its price reductions. Even if they did, they may be reluctant to slash prices further in retaliation, since they would stand to lose more (in absolute terms) from a price war than does the small firm.[12]

Homogeneous Products

When a firm lowers its price, it expects to increase its sales. The sales increase may come from three different courses:

* Increased sales to customers who were planning to buy a smaller quantity from the firm

* Sales to customers who were not planning to purchase from the firm or its competitors

* Sales to customers who were planning to buy from a competitor but switched to take advantage of the lower price

For many firms that reduce prices, customer switching represents the largest source of sales gain. A good example is automobiles. When Honda lowers its price on the Accord sedan, most of the resulting sales increase comes from car buyers who might have bought a competitor's car, as opposed to Honda owners who decide to buy another Honda because of the price reduction, or people who were not planning to buy any car before the price reduction.

Customers are more willing to switch from one seller to another when the product is homogeneous, that is, if the characteristics of the product do not vary across sellers. When products are homogeneous, customers will switch from one seller to another to obtain a better price. This intensifies price competition, because firms that lower prices can expect large increases in sales.

Some products are clearly homogeneous. A share of IBM stock sold by one trader provides the same financial rights as a share of IBM stock sold by another. One ounce of 24-karat gold is completely interchangeable with another. Other products, such as compact disc players, are slightly differentiated, and most (but

---

[10]Potash (potassium oxide) is a compound used to produce of products such as fertilizer and soap.

[11]Chapters 5 and 6 of Markham, J. *The Fertilizer Industry*, Nashville, TN: Vanderbilt University Press, 1958.

[12]This point is developed more fully in Chapter 9.

not all) consumers will switch to obtain a lower price. Yet other products, such as medical services, are highly differentiated, and most consumers are unwilling to switch just to obtain a lower price.

Excess Capacity

To understand the role of capacity in pricing problems recall the distinction between average costs and marginal costs that we made in the Economics Primer and in Chapter 2. For production processes that entail high fixed costs, marginal cost can be well below average cost over a wide range of output. Only when production nears capacity—the point at which average cost begins to rise sharply—does marginal cost begin to exceed average cost.

The numerical example in Table 7.3 illustrates the implications of excess capacity for a firm's pricing incentives. The table depicts the situation facing a diesel engine manufacturer, such as Deere & Company, whose plant has a capacity of 50,000 engines per year. Because of a recession, suppose that Deere has confirmed orders for only 10,000 engines during the upcoming year. Deere is confident, however, that it can increase sales by another 10,000 engines by stealing a major customer from one of its competitors, Navistar. To do so, Deere has to offer this customer a price of $300 per engine.[13] Should Deere offer this price?

Deere is better off offering this price and stealing the business from Navistar even though this price is well below the average cost of $700 per engine that it would cost Deere to fill the order. To see this, note that the increase in Deere's revenue is $3 million whereas while the increase in its total cost is only $1 million. It is better off selling the extra engines at $300 apiece because the sale contributes to fixed costs. Of course, Navistar may not let Deere steal its business, so the result may be a battle that drives the price for this order below $300. But as long as the order carries a price greater than the average variable cost of $100, Deere would be better off filling the order than not filling it.

In the long run, competition like this can drive price below average cost. Firms may choose to exit the industry rather than sustain long-run economic losses. But if firm capacity is industry-specific—that is, it can only be used to produce in this industry—firms will have no choice but to remain in the industry until the plant reaches the end of its useful life or until demand recovers. If demand does not recover, the industry may suffer a protracted period of excess capacity, with prices below average costs.

TABLE 7.3
CAPACITY UTILIZATION AND COSTS

Annual Output	Total Variable Cost ($millions/year)	Total Fixed Cost ($millions/year)	Total Cost ($millions/year)	Average Cost per Engine
10,000	$1	$12	$13	$1300
20,000	2	12	14	700
30,000	3	12	15	500
40,000	4	12	16	400
50,000	8	12	20	400

[13]We will assume that this offer does not require Deere to adjust the price at which it sells engines to its other customers.

Monopoly

The noted antitrust economist Frank Fisher describes monopoly power as "the ability to act in an unconstrained way," such as increasing price or reducing quality. Constraints come from competing firms. If a firm lacks monopoly power, then when it raises price or reduces quality, its customers take their business to competitors. It follows that a firm is a *monopolist* if it faces little or no competition in its output market. Competition, if it exists at all, comes from fringe firms—small firms that collectively account for no more than about 30 to 40 percent market share and do not threaten to erode the monopolist's market share.

A firm is a *monopsonist* if it faces little or no competition in one of its input markets. The analysis of monopoly and monopsony is closely related. We will discuss issues concerning monopolists, but all of these issues are equally important to monopsonists. Whereas a discussion of monopoly focuses on the ability of the firm to raise output prices, a discussion of monopsony would focus on its ability to reduce input prices.

A monopolist usually ignores fringe firms when setting its own price, since it does not believe that the decisions of the fringe firms can materially affect its profits. Instead, it considers the entire market demand for its product, and selects price, so that the marginal revenue from the last unit sold equals the marginal cost of producing it. For example, suppose that the market demand for a product is given by $P = 100 - Q$, and the constant marginal cost of production is 10 per unit. As a benchmark, note that price in a competitive market would equal marginal cost, or 10, and total output would be 90. It is straightforward to calculate the monopolist's price and quantity.

The monopolist's total revenue is price times quantity, or $100Q - Q^2$. The corresponding marginal revenue is $100 - 2Q$ (see the Economics Primer for further discussion of marginal revenue). Hence, marginal revenue and marginal cost are equal when $Q = 45$. It follows that $P = \$55$, and profits (total revenues minus total costs) equal $2,025. Note that the monopolist's price is well above its marginal cost, and its output is well below the competitive level. Limiting output to boost price well above marginal cost is an example of what Fisher described as unconstrained action.

Antitrust enforcers in the United States and the European Community are concerned about the high profits many monopolists earn. They argue that these profits come at the expense of consumers, who must pay higher prices for limited output. The economist Harold Demsetz notes that high monopoly profits do not necessarily indicate that consumers are worse off.[14] He argues that most monopolies arise when a firm discovers a more efficient way of manufacturing a product, or creates a new product that fulfills unmet consumer needs. Consumers benefit from such innovations, and monopoly profits may represent only a small percentage of the gains consumers enjoy. Moreover, firms will continue to innovate only if they can expect high profits when their innovations succeed. If Demsetz is correct, then restricting monopoly profits may hurt consumers in the long run, by choking off innovation. Microsoft has used this argument to defend itself against charges that its profits are excessive.

---

[14]Demsetz, H., "Two Systems of Belief About Monopoly," in Goldschmidt, H. et al. (eds.), *Industrial Concentration: The New Learning*, Boston: Little Brown, 1974.

XAMPLE 7.3

THE OPEC CARTEL

Sellers who agree not to cut prices are said to be in a cartel. Perhaps the best known cartel is the Organization of Petroleum Exporting Countries (OPEC). OPEC was formed in 1960 by Saudi Arabia, Venezuela, Kuwait, Iraq, and Iran in response to efforts by U.S. oil refiners, led by Standard Oil of New Jersey, to reduce the price they were paying for imported oil. (Indeed, OPEC, a cartel of oil producers desiring to raise oil prices, was a response to an effort by a cartel of oil buyers to suppress prices!) Until the 1972 oil boycott, OPEC had little impact on world markets. It was not until the early 1980s, however, that OPEC explicitly attempted to raise the price of oil. (The U.S. antitrust laws do not apply to OPEC, which consists of government-controlled businesses.)

To maintain high prices, the OPEC members must restrict their output, or they will produce more oil than the world will demand. Each member nation must therefore agree to an output quota. In 1982, OPEC set an overall output limit of 18 million barrels per day, down from 31 million barrels per day in 1979. Prices were to be maintained at $34 per barrel. Each member nation had an individual production quota, except for Saudi Arabia, the largest producer, which adjusted its output as necessary to maintain prices.

Maintaining the cartel has proven difficult. Sometimes, such as during the Iran-Iraq War (1980–1985), member nations sought to produce more than their allotment. This glutted the world market with OPEC oil. Despite Saudi Arabia's efforts to reduce output, prices plunged. Further pressure on prices came from companies that elected not to participate in OPEC, such as the British National Oil Company. When this company cut the price of its North Sea oil by $3 per barrel in 1983, the Nigerian oil minister (Nigeria is a member of OPEC) was prompted to say "We are ready for a price war." Before long, OPEC had slashed its price by 15 percent and reduced its output by 3 percent. Today, OPEC accounts for less than 30 percent of world oil production, and with world oil prices hovering well below $20 per barrel, OPEC appears to have a negligible effect on prices.

There have been efforts to cartelize many other international commodities industries, including copper, tin, coffee, tea, and cocoa. A few cartels have had short-term success, such as bauxite and uranium, and one or two, such as the De-Beers diamond cartel, appear to have enjoyed long-term success. In general, however, most international cartels are unable to substantially affect pricing for long.

Monopolistic Competition

The term *monopolistic competition* was introduced by Edward Chamberlin in 1933 to characterize markets with two main features:[15]

• There are many sellers. Each seller reasonably supposes that its actions will not materially affect others. For example, consider the retail women's clothing market in Chicago. There are many sellers in this market (there are

---

[15]Chamberlin, E. H., *The Theory of Monopolistic Competition*, Cambridge, MA: Harvard University Press, 1933.

three pages of listings in the Chicago Yellow Pages). If any one seller were to lower its prices, it is doubtful that other sellers would react. There are simply too many retailers to keep track of. Even if some sellers did notice a small drop-off in sales, they would probably not alter their prices just to respond to a single competitor.

- Each seller sells a differentiated product. Products A and B are differentiated if there is some price for each product at which some consumers prefer to purchase A and others prefer to purchase B. The notion of product differentiation captures the idea that consumers make choices among competing products on the basis of factors other than just price. Unlike under perfect competition, where products are homogeneous, a differentiated seller that raises its price will not lose all its customers.

Economists distinguish between *vertical differentiation* and *horizontal differentiation*. A product is vertically differentiated when it is unambiguously better or worse than competing products. A producer of a household cleaner, such as Colgate-Palmolive's Ajax brand, engages in vertical differentiation when it enhances the cleaning effectiveness of its product (e.g., Colgate-Palmolive might alter the formula for Ajax, so that less cleaner needs to be mixed with water to clean a given surface). This enhances the product for all prospective consumers, although consumers may disagree about how much they are willing to pay for this enhancement. A product is horizontally differentiated when some consumers prefer it to competing products (holding price equal). Colgate-Palmolive engages in horizontal differentiation when it adds a lemon scent to Ajax. This makes the cleaner more attractive to some consumers (e.g., those who associate a clean house with the aroma of fresh lemon) but perhaps less attractive to others (e.g., those who dislike lemon scent or prefer pine).

An important source of differentiation is geography, because consumers prefer stores that are convenient to reach. For example, consumers living in Brooklyn will tend to frequent stores in Brooklyn, whereas consumers in Manhattan will tend to frequent stores in Manhattan. Figure 7.1 depicts a market in which products are differentiated based on location. The figure shows the town of Linesville. The only road in Linesville—Straight Street—is depicted by the straight line in the figure, and is exactly 10 miles long. There is a video rental store at each end of Straight Street. Blockbuster Video is at the left end of town (denoted by L in the

FIGURE 7.1
VIDEO RETAILERS IN LINESVILLE.

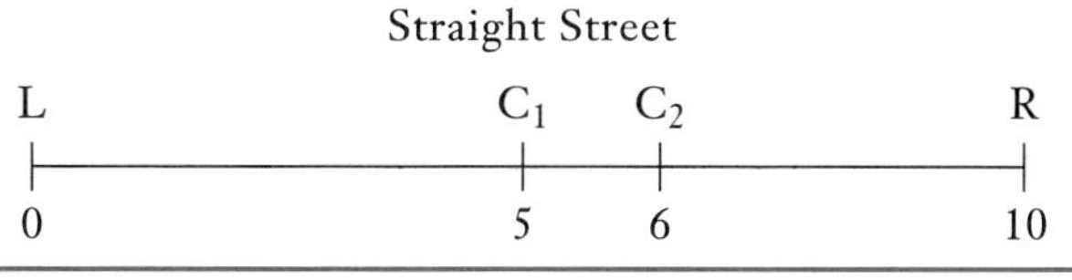

If store L and store R both charge \$3 per video, then all consumers living to the left of C_1 shop at store L and all consumers living to the right of C_1 shop at store R. If store L lowers its price to \$2 per video, then some customers living to the right of C_1 may wish to travel the extra distance to buy from store L. If travel costs \$.50 per mile, then all customers living between C_1 and C_2 will travel the extra distance to save a dollar on the rental.

figure); Hollywood Video is at the right end (denoted by R). Each store carries identical inventory. There are 100 video rental customers in Linesville, and their homes are equally spaced along Straight Street. Thus, 50 consumers live closer to Blockbuster and 50 live closer to Hollywood Video.

When consumers decide which store to visit, they take two factors into account: the prices that each store charges and the cost of traveling to each store. Transportation costs can include direct costs, such as gasoline, as well as indirect costs, such as the cost of the time required to get to the store. Let the cost of traveling one mile equal 50 cents for all consumers. Given this information, we can determine the degree to which consumers will switch from one store to another as the stores vary their prices.

Suppose first that both stores charge $3 per video rental. In this case, the two stores will split the market—each store will have 50 customers. Now suppose that Blockbuster lowers its price per video from $3 to $2, while Hollywood Video keeps its price at $3. How will this affect the sales of both stores? To answer, we need to identify the location on Straight Street at which a consumer would be indifferent between purchasing from Blockbuster and Hollywood Video. Because travel is costly, all customers living to the left of that location will visit Blockbuster and all customers living to the right will visit Hollywood Video.

A customer will be indifferent between the two stores if he or she faces identical costs of purchase, where costs include both video rental and transportation costs. Consider a customer living M miles from Blockbuster (and therefore living $10 - M$ miles from Hollywood Video) who is planning to rent just one video. For this customer, the total cost of visiting Blockbuster is $2 + .50M$. The total cost of visiting Hollywood Video is $3 + .50(10 - M)$. These costs are equal if $M = 6$. A consumer located at $M = 6$ will have total purchase costs of $5, regardless of which store he or she visits. Thus 60 consumers will visit Blockbuster, and 40 will visit Hollywood Video.

In this market, the video stores are horizontally differentiated because their locations differ and consumers bear positive transportation costs. Hollywood Video's location makes it particularly attractive for consumers located at the right end of Straight Street, even when its price is higher than Blockbuster's. Because consumers prefer not to travel, Blockbuster gains only 10 customers from Hollywood video even though it charges $1 less per rental. One would intuitively expect that as product differentiation declines in importance—in this case, as the transportation cost decreases—Blockbuster would gain even more from its price decrease. The model bears this out. If the transportation cost were only 20 cents per mile rather than 50 cents, the indifferent consumer lives at $M = 7.5$, so that Blockbuster has 75 customers. As transportation costs diminish further, Blockbuster and Hollywood Video become homogeneous—consumers have no strong preference for either store. Indeed, if the transportation cost is 1 cent, then Blockbuster need only lower its price by 10 cents to gain all the business.

The idea that differentiated products can be represented by distinct "locations" can be applied to a variety of settings. The straight line in Figure 7.1 could represent the sportiness of automobiles, the sweetness of colas, or the cut of business suits. Individuals with strong preferences for, say, conservative suits, would be "located" at one end of the line, whereas individuals who preferred more stylish suits would be at the other end. "Transportation costs" would be high if individuals were unwilling to purchase a suit that was not to their liking just to save some money.

Under what conditions might individuals be reluctant to switch sellers to save money? This might occur if preferences were highly idiosyncratic, that is, if tastes differ markedly from one person to the next. In this case, different sellers could keep loyal followings even if they raised prices. Switching may also be mitigated if consumers lack information about alternatives. If, in the preceding example, Blockbuster did not publicize its price decrease, customers who frequented Hollywood Video may not have known about it and would therefore have no reason to switch. On the other hand, if preferences are not highly idiosyncratic, and consumers are well-informed about alternatives, switching is more likely.

A Graphical Depiction of the Theory of Monopolistic Competition

The theory of monopolistic competition emphasizes the importance of consumer switching as a determinant of the demand facing individual sellers. This may be illustrated by comparing demand curves with and without switching. First, imagine a market consisting of many differentiated sellers, say, the market for furniture. To understand the role of switching in such a market, suppose initially that each seller sets exactly the same prices at all times, and that consumers are well-informed about prices. Consumers base their choice of seller on style, color, materials, and location, but not price, and will choose the seller that provides the best idiosyncratic match. If there are M customers and N sellers in the market, a typical seller would have M/N customers. Call these the sellers' "regular customers."

The demand curve facing an individual seller when each seller sets the same price at all times is depicted by the curve labeled DD in Figure 7.2. The DD curve is obtained by dividing the total demand for furniture from the M customers in the population, by the number of sellers N. It is downward sloping because as all sellers lower price in unison, total demand for furniture increases. For example, if all sellers lower price from, say, P_0 to P_1, each seller sells a bit more furniture to its regular customers. The amount by which regular customers increase their purchases is easily read off the demand curve to be $Q_1 > Q_0$.

FIGURE 7.2
DEMAND CURVE FACING AN INDIVIDUAL SELLER WHEN ALL FIRMS CHANGE PRICE IN LOCKSTEP.

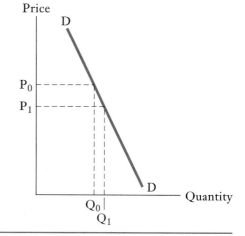

At price P_0, the firm's demand is Q_0, which is equal to the total market demand at P_0 divided by the number of firms. When all firms lower the price to P_1, the firm moves along curve DD, and its demand increases to Q_1.

FIGURE 7.3
DEMAND CURVE FACING AN INDIVIDUAL SELLER WHEN IT INDEPENDENTLY CHANGES PRICE.

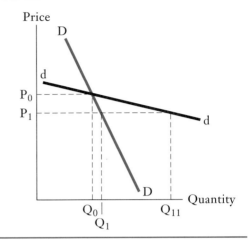

When the seller unilaterally reduces its price from P_0 to P_1 (with all other sellers holding their prices at P_0), it moves along demand curve dd, and its sales increase to Q_{11}. Part of the increase, Q_1-Q_0, is increased demand from loyal customers. The remainder, $Q_{11}-Q_1$, is from customers who have switched from other firms.

The DD curve does not reflect consumer switching. Since all prices change at the same time, consumers have no reason to switch. However, it is unreasonable to assume that all prices move in lockstep in a market like furniture, which has many sellers. It is hard to imagine that all sellers would be able or willing to coordinate their pricing so carefully. Consider, instead, what happens when only one seller changes its price, while the other sellers keep their prices unchanged. For example, suppose initially that all sellers set a price P_0. If one seller unilaterally lowers its price to P_1, it will gain sales for two reasons. First, its regular customers may increase their purchases, because the price is lower. Second, some customers who were previously planning to purchase from another seller will switch to this seller to take advantage of the lower price.

The demand curve facing a seller who independently changes price is depicted by the curve labeled dd in Figure 7.3. This curve is flatter than the DD curve due to consumer switching. As the seller lowers its price from P_0 to P_1 its sales increase from Q_0 to Q_{11}. This sales increase, which equals $Q_{11} - Q_0$, consists of two components: $(Q_{11} - Q_1)$ and $(Q_1 - Q_0)$. The first component represents the increase in demand from consumers who switch from other stores. The second component is the increase in demand from loyal customers.

The greater the willingness of consumers to switch among sellers when one seller changes its price, the flatter will be the dd curve. Put another way, when dd is relatively flat, the price elasticity of demand facing an individual seller is large in magnitude. When demand is elastic, sellers have much to gain by lowering prices, and the $PCMs$ that arise from profit-maximizing behavior will be fairly small. In contrast, if there is little switching, the dd is relatively steep, and the price elasticity of demand is small in magnitude. In this case, sellers have little to gain by undercutting their competitors, and PCMs will be large.

Entry into Monopolistically Competitive Markets

In differentiated product markets, each firm faces a demand curve with less than infinite elasticity, that is, $\eta < \infty$. The theory of optimal pricing implies that firms will set prices in excess of marginal costs. The resulting PCMs help to defray the fixed costs of doing business. If prices are high enough to exceed average costs, firms will earn positive economic profits. These profits will attract investors and entrepreneurs seeking profits of their own and will therefore invite entry. Entry will reduce prices and erode market shares, until economic profits equal zero.

These forces can be understood with a numerical example. Suppose that a market currently has 10 firms, called *incumbents*. Each of the 10 incumbents has a constant marginal cost of $10 per unit and a fixed cost of $120. Each incumbent sells a horizontally differentiated product and faces a price elasticity of demand η = 2. With this elasticity, the profit-maximizing price for each incumbent firm is $20.[16] Suppose that at this price, the total market demand is 240, which is divided evenly among all sellers in the market. Thus, each incumbent sells 24 units. It is straightforward to calculate each incumbent's profits. Each one has revenues of $480 and total costs of $360, so profits equal $120. These facts are summarized in Table 7.4 in the column labeled "Before Entry."

Profits attract entry by other firms. Suppose that entrants' and incumbents' costs are identical, and that each entrant can differentiate its product, so that all sellers have the same market share. Suppose further that differentiation is such that the price elasticity of demand facing all sellers remains constant at 2. Then each entrant will set a price of $20. If enough entrants are interested in pursuing profit opportunities, entry will continue until there are no more profits to be earned. This occurs when there are 20 firms in the market, each with sales of 12. The last column of Table 7.4 summarizes these results.

This example shows that when product differentiation enables sellers to set prices well above marginal costs, new entrants will erode the resulting profits, even if price remains unchanged. Entrants usually steal some market share from incumbents, thereby reducing each incumbent's revenue and making it increasingly difficult for incumbents to cover fixed costs. In our example, entry did not intensify price competition. If that happens (e.g., because entrant's products are not highly differentiated from incumbent's), entry will erode profits even faster.

TABLE 7.4
PROFITS AND NUMBER OF FIRMS UNDER MONOPOLISTIC COMPETITION

	Before Entry	*After Entry*
Number of Firms	10	20
Fixed Costs per Firm	$120	$120
Marginal Cost	$10	$10
Price	$20	$20
Market Demand	240 units	240 units
Sales per Firm	24 units	12 units
Profit per Firm	$120	0

---

[16]Recall that the optimal $PCM = 1/\eta$. Thus, in this case, $PCM = (P - 10)/P = .5$. Solving for P yields P = $20.

PRICING IN THE AIRLINE INDUSTRY

For the first fifteen years after deregulation in 1978, the U.S. airline industry was plagued by frequent price wars and large financial losses. U.S. airlines have enjoyed soaring profits during the economic recovery of the mid- to late 1990s. These trends may be directly tied to industry cost structure and the nature of competition among carriers.

Airline costs fall into three broad categories:

Flight-sensitive costs, which vary with the number of flights the airline offers. These include the costs associated with crews, aircraft servicing, and fuel. Once the airline sets its schedule, these costs are fixed.

Traffic-sensitive costs, which vary with the number of passengers. These include the costs associated with items such as ticketing agents and food. Airlines plan their expenditures on these items in anticipation of the level of traffic, but in the short run, these costs are also fixed.

Fixed overhead costs, which include general and administrative expenses, advertising and marketing, and interest expenses.

Once an airline has set its schedule, flight-sensitive and overhead costs are fixed. Traffic-sensitive costs, which make up only a small percentage of total costs, are the only variable costs. This means that the airline is better off selling a seat at a low price—near marginal cost but well below average total cost—than not selling the seat at all. Thus, if airlines are operating well short of capacity, they have tremendous incentives to reduce prices. Because marginal costs are so far below average costs, airlines can lose staggering sums during price wars. The airlines may cover their marginal costs, but will fail to make any contributions toward fixed costs. On the other hand, if airlines are at or near capacity, as is often the case nowadays, they can raise prices substantially above average costs without losing customers to competitors.

Many other factors affect airline pricing. In some cases, such as when a carrier dominates a hub, an airline faces little competition on certain routes and may raise price accordingly. Even when two or three carriers compete on a route, they may be able to price at or near the monopoly level. Chapter 9 discusses how firms that compete over a long time or in many markets often avoid price competition. Finally, although airlines seem to sell homogeneous products, there are a number of sources of differentiation among them. Business travelers prefer carriers that offer frequent service, which gives them flexibility to schedule meetings. Many travelers accumulate frequent-flier miles, which encourages them to use the same carrier for all their flights.

While the industry currently enjoys a respite from price competition, that may change if there is a recession or if entrants attempt to take market share from the incumbents. The Value Jet plane disasters of the mid-1990s may have helped incumbent carriers, at least for a while. Some consumers remain leery of startup carriers.

Oligopoly

In perfectly competitive and monopolistically competitive markets, sellers do not believe that their pricing or production strategies will affect the overall market price or volume of production. This makes sense in a market with many sellers. In a market with only a few sellers, however, it is more reasonable to expect that the pricing and production strategies of any one firm will affect overall industry price and production levels. A market in which the actions of individual firms materially affect the industry price level is called an oligopoly.

The economics literature has produced many models of how firms should and do behave in oligopolistic markets. A central element of many models is the careful consideration of how firms respond to each other and to opportunities in the market. This is illustrated by considering two of the oldest and most important oligopoly models—Cournot quantity competition, and Bertrand price competition. We investigate these models below, and will elaborate on oligopoly models in the next two chapters.

Cournot Quantity Competition

One of the first models of oligopoly markets was developed by Augustin Cournot in 1835.[17] Cournot initially considered a market in which there were only two firms, firm 1 and firm 2. These might be two producers of DRAM chips, such as Samsung (firm 1) and LG (firm 2). These firms produce identical goods, so that they are forced to charge the same prices. In Cournot's model, the sole strategic choice of each firm is the amount they choose to produce, Q_1 and Q_2. Once the firms are committed to production, they set whatever price is necessary to "clear the market." This is the price at which consumers are willing to buy the total production, $Q_1 + Q_2$. The intuition behind this assumption is that if either firm is unable to sell all its output, it will lower price until it is able to do so. Thus, the market price is that which enables both firms to sell all their output.

We will analyze the output decisions of Samsung and LG facing specific demand and cost functions. Suppose that both Samsung and LG have the following total costs of production:

$$TC_1 = 10Q_1$$
$$TC_2 = 10Q_2$$

In other words, both firms have constant marginal costs of $10 per unit, just as in the case of monopoly discussed earlier. Thus, if $Q_1 = Q_2 = 10$, then $TC_1 = TC_2 = 100$. As in our monopoly example, let market demand be given by $P = 100 - Q_1 - Q_2$. With this demand curve, the market price falls if either firm tries to increase the amount that it sells. For example, if Samsung and LG both produce 10 units (i.e., $Q_1 = Q_2 = 10$) then $P = \$80$. If the both produce 20 units (i.e., $Q_1 = Q_2 = 20$), then $P = \$60$.

How much will each firm produce? Each firm cares about the market price when it selects its production level. Because market price depends on the total pro-

---

[17]Cournot, A., "On the Competition of Producers," chap. 7 in *Research into the Mathematical Principles of the Theory of Wealth*, translated by N. T. Bacon, New York: Macmillan, 1897. For an excellent review of the Cournot model and other theories of oligopoly behavior, see Shapiro, C., "Theories of Oligopoly Behavior," chap. 6 in Willig, R. and R. Schmalensee (eds.), *Handbook of Industrial Organization*, Amsterdam: North Holland, 1989.

duction of both firms, the amount that, say, Samsung produces depends on how much it expects LG to produce. Cournot investigated production under a simple set of expectations: Each firm "guesses" how much the other firm will produce and believes that its rival will stick to this level of output. Each firm's optimal level of production is the *best response* to the level it expects its rival to choose. Put another way, Samsung chooses the level of production that maximizes its own profits, given the level of production it conjectures LG will choose, and LG chooses the level of production that maximizes its profits given the amount of output it conjectures Samsung will produce.

A *Cournot equilibrium* is a pair of outputs $Q_1{}^*$ and $Q_2{}^*$ and a market price P^* that satisfy three conditions:

(C1) P^* is the price that clears the market given the firms' production levels, that is, $P^* = 100 - Q_1{}^* - Q_2{}^*$.
(C2) $Q_1{}^*$ is Samsung's profit-maximizing output given that it conjectures LG will choose $Q_2{}^*$.
(C3) $Q_2{}^*$ is LG's profit-maximizing output given that it conjectures Samsung will choose $Q_1{}^*$.

Thus, in a Cournot equilibrium, each firm's conjecture about its rival's production level is "correct," that is, it corresponds to the output its rival actually chooses.

To find the market equilibrium choices of Q_1 and Q_2, consider first Samsung's choice of Q_1. According to condition (C2), for Q_1 to be an equilibrium choice, it must maximize Samsung's profits, given LG's choice of Q_2. Suppose that Samsung thinks that LG is going to produce output Q_{2g}, where the g subscript reminds us that this is a guess, rather than the actual value. Then Samsung estimates that if it produces Q_1 units of output, its profits, denoted by π_1 will be:

$$\pi_1 = \text{Revenue} - \text{Total cost} = P_1 Q_1 - TC_1 = (100 - Q_1 - Q_{2g})Q_1 - 10Q_1.$$

Samsung needs to solve for the value of Q_1 that maximizes its profits. We can use calculus to determine that the profit-maximizing value of Q_1 satisfies:[18]

$$\text{Profit-maximizing value of } Q_1 = 45 - .5Q_{2g}.$$

The profit-maximizing value of Q_1 is called Samsung's best response to LG. According to this equation, Samsung's best response is a decreasing function of Q_{2g}. This implies that if Samsung expects LG to increase output, it will reduce its own output. This makes sense. If LG increases output, then condition (C1) states that the market price must decrease. Facing a lower price, Samsung prefers to produce less itself. The line labeled R_1 in Figure 7.4 depicts Samsung's choice of Q_1 as a function of its conjecture about Q_2. Economists call this line Samsung's *reaction function*.

Similarly, we can use condition (C3) to solve for LG's best response to Samsung's choice of Q_1:

$$\text{Profit-maximizing value of } Q_2 = 45 - .5Q_{1g}$$

---

[18]Profit π_1 can be written as: $90Q_1 - Q_1{}^2 - Q_{2g}Q_1$. If we treat Q_{2g} as a constant and take the derivative of π_1 with respect to Q_1 we get $\partial \pi_1 / \partial Q_1 = 90 - 2Q_1 - Q_{2g}$. Setting this derivative equal to 0 and solving the resulting equation for Q_1, yields the profit-maximizing value of Q_1.

LG's choice of Q_2 as a function of Samsung's choice of Q_1 is shown as reaction function R_2 in Figure 7.4.

We need one more step before we can solve for the equilibrium choices of Q_1 and Q_2. Recall that in equilibrium, each firm's guess about its rival's output must be correct. If a firm guesses incorrectly, then it would have an incentive to change its output, thereby violating condition (C2) or (C3). For example, suppose that Samsung expects LG to choose $Q_2 = 50$ and, as a result, Samsung selects $Q_1 = 20$. If it turns out, though, that LG chooses $Q_2 = 30$, then Samsung's choice would not be optimal, and Samsung would want to adjust its output of chips.

Only one pair of outputs is simultaneously the best response to each other. These outputs, which we denote by Q_1^* and Q_2^*, are found by solving both firms' reaction functions simultaneously. This solution turns out to be $Q_1^* = Q_2^* = 30$. Graphically, this corresponds to the point in Figure 7.4 where the two reaction functions intersect. We can also solve for the equilibrium market price P^* and the profits each firm earns. Recall that $P = 100 - Q_1 - Q_2$. In this case, $P^* = \$40$. Substituting price and quantity into the equation for each firm's profits reveals that each firm makes $900 in profit in equilibrium.

Cournot's assumption that firms will simultaneously select the best response to each others' choices is often hard to accept as an accurate depiction of how real firms behave. It seems to impose unrealistic omniscience on each firm. Each firm somehow expects that its rival will choose its Cournot equilibrium output, and in response, each firm actually chooses its Cournot equilibrium output.[19]

In a Cournot model, however, neither Samsung nor LG need be omniscient for the equilibrium quantities to emerge. Suppose that both firms are "out of equilibrium," in the sense that at least one firm has chosen to produce a quantity other than 30. For example, suppose that $Q_1 = Q_2 = 40$. Neither firm will be happy with

FIGURE 7.4
COURNOT REACTION FUNCTIONS.

The curve R_1, is firm 1's reaction function. It shows firm 1's profit-maximizing output for any level of output Q_2 produced by firm 2. The curve R_2 is firm 2's reaction function. It shows firm 2's profit-maximizing output for any level of output Q_1 produced by firm 1. The Cournot equilibrium outputs, denoted by Q_1^* and Q_2^*, occur at the point where the two reaction functions cross. In this case, the equilibrium output of each firm is 30. At the Cournot equilibrium, each firm is choosing its profit-maximizing output, given the output produced by the other firm.

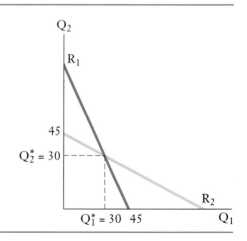

[19]Cournot's assumption is actually a special case of a modeling assumption known as the Nash equilibrium, that is used to identify likely strategies in a variety of contexts. A Nash equilibrium is discussed in the Economics Primer. We will rely heavily on it in Chapters 8 and 9.

its choice of quantity—each is producing more than it would like given its rival's production. As a result, we would expect each firm to adjust to the other firm's choices.

Table 7.5 shows an example of the adjustment process. Suppose that Samsung makes the first adjustment. It examines its profit-maximization equation and determines that if $Q_2 = 40$, it should choose $Q_1 = 25$. Suppose now that Samsung reduces its output to 25. LG will examine its own profit-maximization equation and determine that if Samsung chooses $Q_1 = 25$, then it should choose $Q_2 = 32.5$. Now it is Samsung's turn to adjust its output. If $Q_2 = 32.5$, then Samsung will prefer $Q_1 = 28.75$. Table 7.5 shows that Q_1 and Q_2 continue to converge toward the equilibrium values of $Q_1 = Q_2 = 30$.

The Cournot model implies that the equilibrium industry output does not maximize industry profit. Industry profit is maximized at a total output of 45 and a market price of $55. (This is the monopoly quantity and price computed earlier.) By independently maximizing their own profits, firms produce more output than they would if they collusively maximized industry profits. This is characteristic of oligopolistic industries: The pursuit of individual self-interest does not maximize the well-being of the group as a whole. This occurs under Cournot competition for the following reason. When one firm, say Samsung, expands its output, it reduces the market price and thus lowers the sales revenues of rival chip producers. Samsung does not care about this *revenue destruction effect* because it is maximizing its own profit, not total industry profit. Thus, Samsung expands its production volume more aggressively than it would if its objective had been to maximize industry profit. If all DRAM producers behave this way, the market price must be less than the monopoly price.

The smaller a firm's share of industry sales is, the greater the divergence between its private gain and the revenue destruction effect from output expansion. This suggests that as the number of firms in an industry exhibiting Cournot competition increases, the greater the Cournot equilibrium diverges from the collusive outcome. Table 7.6 illustrates this point by showing equilibrium prices, profits, and outputs in a Cournot industry with the same demand curve and cost function as in the preceding example. The equilibrium price and profit per firm decline as the number of firms increases. More generally, it can be shown that the average PCM of a firm in a Cournot equilibrium is given by the formula $PCM = H/\eta$, where H denotes the Herfindahl, and η is the price elasticity of market demand. Thus, the less concentrated the industry (the lower the industry's H), the smaller will be PCMs in equilibrium.

TABLE 7.5
THE COURNOT ADJUSTMENT PROCESS

Starting Q_1	Starting Q_2	Firm that Is Adjusting	Ending Q_1	Ending Q_2
40	40	Firm 1	25	40
25	40	Firm 2	25	32.5
25	32.5	Firm 1	28.75	32.5
28.75	32.5	Firm 2	28.75	30.63
28.75	30.63	Firm 1	29.69	30.63

TABLE 7.6
COURNOT EQUILIBRIA AS THE NUMBER OF FIRMS INCREASES

Number of Firms	Market Price	Market Quantity	Per-Firm Profits	Total Profits
2	$40	60	$900	$1800
3	$32.5	67.5	$506.25	$1518.75
5	$25	75	$225	$1125
10	$18.2	81.8	$66.94	$669.40
100	$10.9	89.1	$0.79	$79

◆ ◆

XAMPLE 7.5

COURNOT EQUILIBRIUM IN THE CORN WET MILLING INDUSTRY

Michael Porter and Michael Spence's case study of the corn wet milling industry is a real-world illustration of the Cournot model.[20] Firms in the corn wet milling industry convert corn into cornstarch and corn syrup. The corn syrup industry had been a fairly stable oligopoly until the 1960s, when several firms entered the market, including Archer-Daniels-Midland and Cargill. The new competitors and new capacity disrupted the old equilibrium and drove prices downward. By the early 1970s, however, competitive stability returned to the industry, as capacity utilization rates and prices rose.

In 1972, a major development hit the industry: The production of high fructose corn syrup (HFCS) became commercially viable. HFCS can be used instead of sugar to sweeten products, such as soft drinks. With sugar prices expected to rise, a significant market for HFCS beckoned. Firms in the corn wet milling industry had to decide whether and how to add capacity to accommodate the expected demand.

Porter and Spence studied this capacity expansion process. They did so through a detailed simulation of competitive behavior based on an in-depth study of the 11 major competitors in the industry. Porter and Spence postulated that each firm's expansion decision was based on a conjecture about the overall expansion of industry capacity, as well as expectations about demand and sugar prices. Their model also took into account that capacity choices coupled with demand conditions determined industry prices of cornstarch, corn syrup, and HFCS. The notion that a firm's capacity choice is based on conjectures about the capacity choices of other firms is directly analogous to the idea in the Cournot model that each firm bases its output choice on conjectures of the output choices of other firms. The notion that capacity decisions then determine a market price is also analogous to the Cournot model.

---

[20]Porter, M. and A. M. Spence, "The Capacity Expansion Decision in a Growing Oligopoly: The Case of Corn Wet Milling," in McCall, J. J. (ed.), *The Economics of Information of Uncertainty*, Chicago: University of Chicago Press, 1982: pp. 259–316.

Porter and Spence's simulation of the industry attempted to find an "equilibrium": an industry capacity expansion path that, when each firm made its optimal capacity decision based on the conjecture that that path would prevail, resulted in an actual pattern of capacity expansion that matched the assumed pattern. This is directly analogous to the notion of a Cournot equilibrium, in which each firm's expectations about the behavior of its competitors is confirmed by their actual behavior. Based on their simulation of industry decision making, Porter and Spence determined that an industry equilibrium would result in a moderate amount of additional capacity added to the industry as a result of the commercialization of HFCS. The specific predictions of their model compared with the actual pattern of capacity expansion are shown below.

Though not perfect, Porter and Spence's calculated equilibrium comes quite close to the actual pattern of capacity expansion in the industry, particularly in 1973 and 1974. The discrepancies in 1975 and 1976 mainly reflect timing. Porter and Spence's equilibrium model did not consider capacity additions in the years beyond 1976. In 1976, however, the industry had more than 4 billion pounds of HFCS capacity under construction, and that capacity did not come on line until after 1976. Including this capacity, the total HFCS capacity expansion was 9.2 billion pounds, as compared with the 9.1 billion pounds of predicted equilibrium capacity. Porter and Spence's research suggests that a Cournot-like model, when adapted to the specific conditions of the corn wet milling industry, provided predictions that came remarkably close to the actual pattern of capacity expansion decisions.

	1973	1974	1975	1976	post-1976	Total
Actual industry capacity	0.6	1.0	1.4	2.2	4	9.2 (billions of lbs.)
Predicted equilibrium capacity	0.6	1.5	3.5	3.5	0	9.1

Bertrand Price Competition

In Cournot's model, each firm selects a quantity to produce, and the resulting total output determines the market price. Alternatively, one might imagine a market in which each firm selects a price and stands ready to meet all the demand for its product at that price. This model of competition was first analyzed by Joseph Bertrand in 1883.[21] In Bertrand's model, each firm selects a price to maximize its own profits, given the price that it believes the other firm will select. Each firm also believes that its pricing practices will not affect the pricing of its rival; each firm views its rival's price as fixed.

We can use the cost and demand conditions from the Cournot model to explore the Bertrand market equilibrium, again using the (hypothetical) example of rival DRAM producers Samsung and LG. Recall that when $MC_1 = MC_2 = \$10$, and demand is given by $P = 100 - Q_1 - Q_2$, then the Cournot equilibrium is $Q_1 = Q_2 = 30$ and $P_1 = P_2 = \$40$. This is not, however, a Bertrand equilibrium. Consider, for

[21]Bertrand, J., "Book Review of Recherche sur Les Principes Mathematiques de la Theorie des Richesses," *Journal des Savants*, 67, 1883: pp. 499–508.

example, the pricing decision of Samsung. If Samsung believes that LG will charge a price of $40, then it will not wish also to charge a price of $40. Samsung would realize that if it were to slightly undercut LG's price, say by charging a price of $39, it would get all of LG's business. Thus, Samsung believes that if $P_1 = \$39$, and $P_2 = \$40$, then $Q_1 = 61$, and $Q_2 = 0$. In this case Samsung expects to earn profits of $1,769, well above the profits of $900 it would earn if it charged a price of $40.

Of course, $P_1 = \$39$ and $P_2 = \$40$ cannot be an equilibrium, because at these prices, LG will wish to undercut Samsung's price. As long as both firms set prices that exceed marginal costs, one firm will always have an incentive to corner the market by slightly undercutting its competitor. This implies that the only possible equilibrium is $P_1 = P_2 = $ marginal cost $= \$10$. At these prices, neither firm can do better by changing its price. If either firm lowers price, it will lose money on each unit sold. If either firm raises price, it would sell nothing.

In Bertrand's model, rivalry between two firms is enough to achieve the perfectly competitive outcome. Price competition is particularly fierce in this setting because the firms' products are perfect substitutes. When firms' products are differentiated (as in monopolistic competition), price competition is less intense. (Later in this chapter, we will examine Bertrand price competition when firms produce differentiated products.)

Bertrand competition can be unstable in markets where firms must make upfront investments in plant and equipment to enter. As firms cut prices to gain market share, they may fail to cover long-run costs. If one firm should exit the market, the remaining firm could try to raise its price. But this might simply attract a new entrant that will wrest away some of the remaining firm's business. Fierce price competition may also end if one or both firms run up against capacity constraints (so that the ability to steal market share is limited), or learn to stop competing on the basis of price. These ideas are covered in greater depth in Chapter 9.

Why Are Cournot and Bertrand Different?

The Cournot and Bertrand models make dramatically different predictions about the quantities, prices, and profits that will arise under oligopolistic competition. How can one reconcile these dramatic differences?

One way to reconcile the two models is to recognize that Cournot and Bertrand competition may take place over different time frames. Cournot competitors can be thought of as choosing capacities and then competing as price setters given the capacities chosen earlier. The result of this "two-stage" competition (first choose capacities and then choose prices) can be shown to be identical to the Cournot equilibrium in quantities.[22]

Another way to understand the difference between the Cournot and Bertrand models is to recognize that they make different assumptions about the expectations each firm has about its rivals' reactions to its competitive moves. The Cournot model applies most naturally to markets in which firms must make production decisions in advance and face high costs for holding inventories. In such settings, prices will adjust more quickly than quantities, and each firm will set a

---

[22]The idea that the Cournot equilibrium can (under some circumstances) emerge as the outcome of a "two-stage game" in which firms first choose capacities and then choose prices is due to Kreps, D. and J. Scheinkman, "Quantity Precommitment and Bertrand Competition Yield Cournot Outcomes," *Bell Journal of Economics*, 14, 1983: pp. 326–337.

price that lets it sell all that it produces. Under these circumstances, each firm expects that its competitors will instantaneously match any price change that the firm might make, so that competitors can keep their sales equal to their planned production volumes. Thus, if a firm lowers its price, it cannot expect to steal customers from its rivals. Because "business stealing" is not an option, Cournot competitors set prices less aggressively than Bertrand competitors. Thus, the Cournot equilibrium outcome, while not the monopoly one, nevertheless results in positive profits and a price that exceeds marginal and average cost.

The Bertrand model pertains to markets in which capacity is sufficiently flexible that firms can meet all of the demand that arises at the prices they announce. When firms' products are perfect substitutes, each Bertrand competitor believes that it can steal business from its competitors through a small cut in price. Of course, all competitors think this way, so each firm in the market attempts to steal market share from competitors through price cutting. In equilibrium, price-cost margins and profits are driven to zero.

There are many other issues to consider when assessing the likely conduct and performance of firms in an oligopoly. Competition may be based on a variety of product parameters, including quality, availability, and advertising. Firms may not know the strategic choices of their competitors. The timing of decision making can profoundly influence profits. We discuss all of these issues in Chapters 8 and 9.

Bertrand Price Competition When Products Are Horizontally Differentiated

In many oligopolistic markets, products are close, but not perfect, substitutes. The Bertrand model of price competition described earlier does not fully capture the nature of price competition in these settings. Fortunately, we can adapt the logic of the Bertrand model to deal with horizontally differentiated products.

When products are horizontally differentiated, a firm will not lose all of its business to rival firms that undercut its price. As in the theory of monopolistic competition, this implies that a firm's demand will decrease "smoothly," rather than discontinuously, with a decrease in rivals' prices. To illustrate, consider the U.S. cola market. Farid Gasini, Quang Vuong, and J. J. Lafont (GVL) have used statistical methods to estimate demand curves for Coke (denoted by 1) and Pepsi (denoted by 2):[23]

$$Q_1 = 63.42 - 3.98P_1 + 2.25P_2$$
$$Q_2 = 49.52 - 5.48P_2 + 1.40P_1$$

With these demand functions, as Coke raises its price above that of Pepsi, Coke's demand falls gradually.

GVL estimated that Coca-Cola had a constant marginal cost equal to $4.96, and Pepsi had a constant marginal cost of $3.96. What price should each firm charge? As in the preceding models, an equilibrium occurs when neither firm has an incentive to change its price, given the price the other firm sets. The logic of finding this equilibrium is similar to the logic of the Cournot model. We begin by deriving each firm's reaction function, that is, the firm's optimal price as a function

---

[23]Gasini, F., J. J. Laffont, and Q. Vuong, "Econometric Analysis of Collusive Behavior in a Soft-Drink Market," *Journal of Economics and Management Strategy*, Summer 1992: pp. 277–311.

of its conjecture about its rival's price. Coca-Cola's optimal price maximizes its profit, which can be written as its price-cost margin times the quantity it sells, which is given by its demand function.[24]

$$\pi_1 = (P_1 - 4.96)(63.49 - 3.98P_1 + 2.25P_{2g})$$

(We again use the subscript g to emphasize that Coca-Cola is making a guess about Pepsi's price.) Using calculus to solve this maximization problem yields a reaction function[25]

$$P_1 = 10.44 + .2826P_{2g}$$

Pepsi's optimal price is derived similarly. It maximizes

$$\pi_2 = (P_2 - 3.94)(49.52 - 5.48P_2 + 1.40P_{1g})$$

which yields a reaction function

$$P_2 = 6.49 + .1277P_{1g}$$

Note that these reaction functions, displayed in Figure 7.5, are upward sloping. Thus, the lower the price the firm expects its rival to charge, the lower the price it itself should charge. In this sense, "aggressive" behavior by one firm (price cutting) is met by "aggressive" behavior by rivals. Note the contrast with the Cournot model, where "aggressive" behavior by one firm (output expansion) was met by "passive" behavior by rivals (output reduction).

Solving the two reaction functions simultaneously yields the Bertrand equilibrium in prices:

$$P_1 = \$12.72$$
$$P_2 = \$8.11$$

FIGURE 7.5
BERTRAND EQUILIBRIUM WITH HORIZONTALLY DIFFERENTIATED PRODUCTS.

Firm 1's reaction function shows its profit-maximizing price for any price charged by firm 2. Firm 2's reaction function shows its profit-maximizing price for any price charged by firm 1. The Bertrand equilibrium prices occur at the intersection of these reaction functions. In this example, this is at $P_1 = \$12.72$ and $P_2 = \$8.11$. At this point, each firm is choosing a profit-maximizing price, given the price charged by the other firm.

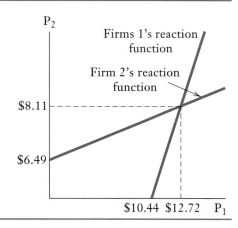

[24]These profits expressions do not deduct fixed production or marketing expenses.

[25]Differentiating total profits π_1 with respect to P_1 (treating P_{2g} as a constant), setting this expression equal to 0, and solving the resulting equation for P_1 yields firm 1's reaction function.

Interestingly, the actual average real prices over the period (1968–1986) to which GVL's analysis pertains were $12.96 for Coca-Cola and $8.16 for Pepsi. The Bertrand model does an excellent job matching the actual pricing behavior of these two firms in the U.S. market. Note that both Coke and Pepsi's equilibrium prices are well in excess of their marginal production costs. This illustrates that product differentiation softens price competition. This is because when products are differentiated, price cutting is less effective for stealing a rival's business than when products are perfect substitutes.

◆ ◆ ◆ ◆ ◆ EVIDENCE ON MARKET STRUCTURE AND PERFORMANCE

The theories examined in the previous sections suggest that market structure should be related to the level of prices and profitability that prevail in a market. Many economists have tested whether the predicted link between structure and performance actually exists.

Price and Concentration

The relationship between price and concentration could be studied by comparing differences in price-cost margins and concentration levels across different industries. As discussed earlier, economic theory suggests that price-cost margins should be higher in more concentrated markets (e.g., recall the discussion of the Cournot model). But price-cost margins may vary across markets for other reasons, such as accounting practices, regulation, product differentiation, the nature of sales transactions, and the concentration of buyers.

For these reasons, most studies of concentration and price focus on specific industries.[26] In these studies researchers compare prices for the same products in geographically separate markets that have different numbers of competitors. By comparing the same products across distinct markets, researchers can be more confident that variations in price are due to variations in competition, rather than variations in accounting, or other factors.

Leonard Weiss summarizes the results of price and concentration studies in more than 20 industries, including cement, railroad freight, supermarkets, and gasoline retailing. He finds that with few exceptions, prices tend to be higher in concentrated markets. For example, one study found that gasoline prices in local markets in which the top three gasoline retailers had a 60 percent market share were, on average, about 5 percent higher than in markets in which the top three retailers had a 50 percent market share.

Timothy Bresnahan and Peter Reiss used a novel methodology to study the relationship between concentration and prices. They asked, "How many firms must be in a market for price to approach competitive levels?"[27] They examined

---

[26]Two excellent surveys are provided by Weiss, L. (ed.), *Concentration and Price*, Cambridge, MA: MIT Press, 1989, and Schmalensee, R., "Studies of Structure and Performance," in Schmalensee R. and R. Willig (eds.), *The Handbook of Industrial Organization*, Amsterdam: North-Holland, 1989.

[27]Bresnahan, T. and P. Reiss, "Entry and Competition in Concentrated Markets," *Journal of Political Economy*, 99, 1991: pp. 997–1009.

locally provided services, such as doctors, tire dealers, and plumbers. For each service, they calculated "entry thresholds," defined as the minimum population necessary to support a given number of sellers. Let E_n denote the entry threshold for n sellers. For all services, they found that E_2 was about four times E_1. This could make sense only if prices are lower when there are two sellers than when there is one. When this happens, demand must more than double to make up for the intensified competition. They also find that $E_3 - E_2 > E_2 - E_1$, suggesting further intensification of price competition as the number of sellers increases from two to three. Finally, they find $E_4 - E_3 \approx E_3 - E_2$, suggesting that once there are three sellers in a market, price competition is as intense as it can get.

Other Studies of the Determinants of Profitability

Chapter 2 discussed the theoretical link between economies of scale and market structure, while this chapter has discussed the theoretical link among market structure, competition, and profitability. Together, these theories suggest a link between economies of scale and profits. Researchers have used a number of approaches to validate these ideas.

Many studies verify the link between economies of scale and market structure. One consistent finding is that the same industries tend to be highly concentrated in all countries. This suggests that some underlying factor, such as economies of scale, determines market structure in all markets. Studies in which researchers have attempted to measure the magnitude of scale economies are consistent with this conclusion. Industries in which the minimum efficient scale of production is large relative to the size of the market tend to be more concentrated than industries with minimal scale economies.

Researchers have had a more difficult time demonstrating the link between concentration and profitability. Richard Schmalensee has summarized this work as follows: "The relation, if any, between seller concentration and profitability is weak statistically, and the estimated concentration effect is usually small."[28] One explanation may be that different accounting practices across industries hide underlying differences in profitability. Another explanation may be that if an industry was truly profitable, we would expect to observe entry. That an industry has only a few firms may indicate that it is inherently unprofitable for reasons that the researcher cannot identify. To more accurately test the link between concentration and profits, researchers need to identify industries that are concentrated because entry is difficult even when profits are available.

A second line of research copes with this problem by examining the relationship between profits and economies of scale that might limit entry. Some researchers have examined economies of scale in production processes as reflected in large capital-to-sales ratios. Others have examined economies of scale in marketing as reflected in large advertising-to-sales ratios. In most cases, industry profits are higher when production and/or marketing displays economies of scale. This is consistent with the theory that when industries are concentrated because entry is difficult, profits are high.

---

[28]Schmalensee, R., "Interindustry Studies of Structure and Performance," in Schmalensee, R. and R. Willig (eds.), *The Handbook of Industrial Organization*, Amsterdam: North-Holland, 1989.

EXAMPLE 7.6

PRICE AND CONCENTRATION IN LOCAL HOSPITAL MARKETS

Does competition in health care markets lead to lower or higher prices? The answer is of vital importance to the larger debate about how, if at all, the U.S. health care system should be reformed. Advocates of a centralized health care delivery system, such as that in Canada, often argue that health care is unlike other goods and services, so that competitive forces do not work to benefit consumers. Advocates of market-based reforms argue that competition can contain prices.

Health economists have measured the relationship between the degree of competition and the levels of costs and prices in health care markets. Early studies tended to confirm the argument that competition does not affect health care prices in the same way that it affects prices of other goods and services. Researchers reported that during the 1970s and early 1980s, prices and cost levels appeared to be the same or higher in markets in which there were more hospitals. Studies in recent years, however, find just the opposite—competition appears to reduce hospital prices and costs.

What changed in the health care industry to reverse the relationship between structure and performance? Before the mid-1980s, the choice of a hospital in the United States was left entirely up to individual patients and their physicians. Patients and their physicians do not necessarily make for good shoppers. They have difficulty comparing the prices of different hospitals. Moreover, patients with health insurance may not care about price. Faced with such unmotivated and unskilled shoppers, hospitals during the 1970s and early 1980s did not need to maintain low prices to attract patients. Competitive pressures barely affected pricing decisions.

Today, the locus of purchasing power in hospital markets has shifted away from individual patients and physicians toward managed care organizations such as Health Maintenance Organizations. These large purchasers steer patients to hospitals perceived as offering the best value. They are motivated shoppers because they keep any cost savings they may realize from shopping around. They are also skillful shoppers, collecting data that enable them to evaluate and compare the costs of different hospitals. Hospitals increasingly find that if they do not offer low prices, they will lose market share. As researchers such as David Dranove, Mark Shanley, and William White, have shown, this has held down the rate of growth of hospitals' prices and costs, especially in markets in which there are many sellers with excess capacity.[29] It is precisely in these markets that economic theory says that employers and insurers can shop around most effectively. Indeed, managed care has grown fastest in those markets where there have historically been many hospitals and excess capacity.

---

[29]Dranove, D., M. Shanley, and W. White, "Price and Concentration in Local Hospital Markets: The Switch from Patient-Driven to Payor-Driven Competition," *Journal of Law and Economics*, 36, 1993: pp. 179–204.

CHAPTER SUMMARY

◆ The first step in analyzing competition is to identify competitors. Competitors in output markets sell products that are substitutes. Competitors in input markets buy inputs that are substitutes.

◆ Generally, two sellers are competitors in an output market if their products are close substitutes, that is, have similar product-performance characteristics. Price elasticities are useful for determining if a product has close substitutes.

◆ Competitor identification is closely related to market definition. A market consists of the buyers and sellers whose interactions determine the price and quantity of the transacted good.

◆ Once a market is well-defined, its structure may be measured using an N-firm concentration ratio or a Herfindahl index.

◆ The structure of a market is often related to the conduct of the firms within it. The spectrum of competitive interaction ranges from competition and monopolistic competition to oligopoly and monopoly.

◆ In competitive markets, consumers are extremely price sensitive, forcing sellers to set prices close to marginal costs. Markets with homogeneous products and many sellers are more likely to feature competitive pricing. Excess capacity exacerbates pricing pressures, often driving prices below average costs.

◆ Monopolists have such a substantial share of their market that they ignore the pricing and production decisions of fringe firms. They may set prices well above marginal cost without losing much business.

◆ Monopolistically competitive markets have many sellers, each with some loyal customers. Prices are set according to the willingness of consumers to switch from one seller to another—if consumers are disloyal, sellers may lower prices to steal business from their competitors. Profits may be eroded further by entrants establishing market niches—and finding loyal customers—of their own.

◆ Oligopolies have so few firms that each firm's production and pricing strategy appreciably affects the market price. Market prices can be well above marginal costs, or driven down to marginal costs, depending on the interaction among oligopolists and the degree of product differentiation among them.

◆ Studies confirm that prices are strongly related to industry structure. Price-cost margins tend to be much lower in more competitive markets.

◆ Factors that may deter entry, such as economies of scale and advertising, are associated with higher profits, This is consistent with the theoretical link between market structure and firm profits.

QUESTIONS

1. Why are the concepts of own and cross-price elasticities of demand essential to competitor identification and market definition?

2. In a recent antitrust case, it was necessary to determine whether certain "elite" schools (mainly the Ivy League schools and MIT) constituted a separate market. How would you go about identifying the market served by these schools?

3. How would you characterize the nature of competition in the restaurant industry? Are there submarkets with distinct competitive pressures? Are there important substitutes that constrain pricing? How can a restaurant be profitable?

4. How does industry-level price elasticity of demand shape the opportunities for making profit in an industry? How does the firm-level price elasticity of demand shape the opportunities for making profit in an industry?

5 What is the "revenue destruction effect"? As the number of Cournot competitors in a market increases, the price generally falls. What does this have to do with the revenue destruction effect?

6. How does the calculation of demand responsiveness in Linesville change if customers rent two videos at a time? What intuition can you draw from this about the magnitude of price competition in various types of markets?

7. Numerous studies have shown that there is usually a systematic relationship between concentration and price. What is this relationship? Offer two brief explanations for this relationship.

8. The relationship described in question 7 does not always appear to hold. What factors, besides the number of firms in the market, might affect margins?

9. The following are the approximate market shares of different brands of soft drinks during the 1980s: Coke—40% Pepsi—30% 7-Up—10% Dr Pepper—10% All other brands—10%.

    a. Compute the Herfindahl for the soft drink market. Suppose that Pepsi acquired 7-Up. Compute the post-merger Herfindahl. What assumptions did you make?

    b. Federal antitrust agencies would be concerned to see a Herfindahl increase of the magnitude you computed in (a), and might challenge the merger. Pepsi could respond by offering a different market definition. What market definition might they propose? Why would this change the Herfindahl?

10. The dancing machine industry is a duopoly. The two firms, Chuckie B Corp. and Gene Gene Dancing Machines, compete through Cournot quantity setting competition. The demand curve for the industry is $P = 100 - Q$, where Q is the total quantity produced by Chuckie B and Gene Gene. Currently, each firm has marginal cost of $40 and no fixed costs. Show that the equilibrium price is $60, with each firm producing 20 machines and earning profits of $400.

11. Consider a market with two horizontally differentiated firms, X and Y. Each has a constant marginal cost of $20. Demand functions are

$$Q_x = 100 - 2P_x + 1P_y$$
$$Q_y = 100 - 2P_y + 1P_x$$

Calculate the Bertrand equilibrium in prices in this market.

STRATEGIC COMMITMENT

8

$\mathcal{I}$n 1982, the management of Philips, N.V. of the Netherlands faced a critical choice: Should it build a disk-pressing plant to supply compact disks (CDs) to the American market, or should it delay its decision a year or so, until the commercial appeal of the CD market became more certain?[1] Philips' prototype had emerged as the industry standard for CDs, and within the next year, Philips was preparing to introduce CDs to the American market. By investing in substantial capacity in the American market in 1982, Philips might be able to discourage other firms—including its erstwhile partner Sony, who had allied itself with Philips in 1979 to promote the Philips CD standard—from investing of their own in disk-pressing capacity in the United States, an outcome that might avert overcapacity among firms in the CD market and brutal price competition. Yet in 1982, the commercial viability of the CD was very much unproven. With a cost of $25 million, a minimum efficient scale CD plant was an expensive proposition. If Philips' bet on the commercial success of the CD proved to be wrong, it would be stuck with a costly facility that had practically no alternative uses.

Whether to invest in new capacity or introduce new products are examples of strategic commitments. Strategic commitments are decisions that have long-term impacts and are difficult to reverse. Strategic commitments should be distinguished from tactical decisions—decisions that are easily reversed and whose impact persists only in the short run. What price to charge or how much output to produce in a given quarter are examples of decisions that can be easily altered or reversed. Unlike strategic commitments, tactical decisions can be adapted to whatever situation the firm currently faces.

---

[1]This discussion is based on McGahan, A. M., "The Incentive Not to Invest: Capacity Commitments in Compact Disc Introduction," *Research on Technological Innovation, Management and Policy*, 5, 1993: pp. 177–197.

Strategic commitments can significantly influence competition in an industry. A decision by a firm to expand capacity, for example, might deter new firms from entering the market, but it also could intensify pricing rivalry among firms that are already in the market. If firms are farsighted when they make their commitments, however, they will anticipate the effect their decisions will have on market competition. This implies that the details of market rivalry can influence the commitments firms make and the levels of commitment they choose.

Philips' dilemma illustrates the tensions associated with strategic commitments: When these commitments are effective, they can often shape competitors' expectations and change their behavior in ways that benefit the firm making the commitment. But because strategic commitments are hard to reverse, they are inherently risky. Firms facing commitments of the sort Philips faced must balance the benefits that come from preempting or altering competitors' behavior with the loss in flexibility that comes from making competitive moves that may be hard to undo once they have been made. This chapter discusses the economic considerations that underlie this balancing act.

◆ ◆ ◆ ◆ ◆ WHY COMMITMENT IS IMPORTANT

To illustrate the importance of commitment, consider a simple example. Two firms are competing in an oligopolistic industry. Firm 1, the dominant firm, is contemplating its capacity strategy and is considering two options, which we will broadly characterize as "aggressive" and "passive." The "aggressive" strategy involves a large and rapid increase in capacity aimed at increasing its market share, while the "passive" strategy involves no change in the firm's capacity. Firm 2, a smaller competitor, is also contemplating its capacity expansion strategy; it will also choose between an "aggressive" strategy or a "passive" strategy. Table 8.1 shows the net present value of profit associated with each pair of options the two firms can choose.

If we imagine that they choose their strategies simultaneously, there is a unique Nash equilibrium in this game: Firm 1 chooses "passive," and Firm 2 chooses "aggressive," yielding a net present value of 15 for Firm 1.[2] For Firm 1, this is not the best outcome. For example, Firm 1 is always better off if Firm 2

TABLE 8.1
PAYOFFS IN THE SIMPLE STRATEGY SELECTION GAME

		Firm 2	
		Aggressive	Passive
Firm 1	Aggressive	12.5, 4.5	16.5, 5
	Passive	15, 6.5	18, 6

Net present values are in millions of dollars. First payoff listed is Firm 1's; second is Firm 2's.

---

[2]See the Economics Primer for a formal definition and discussion of the concept of a Nash equilibrium.

chooses "passive," and it most prefers the outcome in which both firms choose "passive." Yet, without the cooperation of Firm 2, Firm 1 could probably not achieve this outcome. Can Firm 1 improve on the equilibrium that both firms actually reach?

The answer is yes, by committing to choose the aggressive strategy no matter what Firm 2 does. One way to pull this off would be for Firm 1 to make a preemptive aggressive move: accelerating its decision and expanding its capacity before Firm 2 decides what to do. Such a move would transform a *simultaneous* move game into a *sequential* game in which Firm 2 would choose its capacity strategy only after it has seen what Firm 1 has done. Firm 1 could also announce that it planned to "go for share," and that it would reward its manager on the basis of market share rather than profit. It would then be in the interest of Firm 1's managers to select the aggressive strategy even though it is seemingly less profitable than the passive strategy.

It may seem odd that Firm 1 would want to commit itself to an irreversible aggressive strategy. After all, for Firm 1 the profit from passive is greater than the profit from aggressive, no matter what strategy Firm 2 chooses. Yet, look what happens when Firm 1 commits itself to aggressive. Firm 2, realizing that Firm 1 has bound itself in this way, finds that it is better off choosing passive rather than aggressive. The resulting equilibrium (Firm 1 chooses aggressive, Firm 2 chooses passive) gives Firm 1 a higher profit (16.5 versus 15) than it would have gotten in the equilibrium that would have resulted if it had not committed itself to aggressive.

This simple example illustrates a profound point. Strategic commitments that seemingly limit options can actually make a firm better off. Inflexibility can have value because a firm's commitments can alter its competitors' expectations about how it will compete. This, in turn, will lead competitors to make decisions that benefit the already committed firm. In this example, by committing itself to choose what seems to be an inferior strategy (aggressive), Firm 1 alters Firm 2's expectations about what Firm 1 will do. Had Firm 1 not made the commitment, Firm 2 would calculate that it would have been in Firm 1's interest to "capitulate" and play passive. This would have led Firm 2 to choose aggressive. Firm 1's commitment makes aggressive an undesirable strategy for Firm 2. With Firm 1 committed to play aggressive, Firm 2 chooses passive, moving the industry to an equilibrium that makes Firm 1 better off.

Generals throughout history have understood the value of inflexibility, as the famous example of Hernán Cortés' conquest of the Aztec empire in Mexico illustrates. When he landed in Mexico in 1518, Cortés ordered his men to burn all but one of his ships. What appeared to be an act of lunacy was in fact a move that was purposeful and calculated: By eliminating their only method of retreat, Cortés forced his men to fight hard to win. According to Bernal Diaz del Castillo, who chronicled Cortés conquest of the Aztecs, "Cortés said that we could look for no help or assistance except from God for we now had no ships in which to return to Cuba. Therefore we must rely on our own good swords and stout hearts."[3]

---

[3]This quote comes from Luecke, R., *Scuttle Your Ships Before Advancing and Other Lessons from History on Leadership and Change for Today's Managers*, Oxford: Oxford University Press, 1994, p. 23.

A commitment by one firm will not generate the desired response from its competitors unless it has three characteristics:

- It must be *visible*

- It must be *understandable*

- It must be *credible*

To understand why these are necessary for successful commitment, consider the example we have been discussing. Firm 2 must understand that Firm 1 has made the commitment to the aggressive strategy. Thus, whatever tangible form the commitment takes, whether it be through preemptive capacity expansion or a change in compensation structure for Firm 1's managers, Firm 2 must observe and understand it. Otherwise, it will not affect Firm 2's decision making.

Visibility and understandability are not enough; the commitment must also be credible. Firm 2 must believe that Firm 1 intends to limit its options the way it claims it will. This is important because in our simple example, Firm 1's ideal course of action is to bluff Firm 2 into believing that it intends to choose aggressive, thereby causing Firm 2 to choose passive, but then to actually choose passive itself. For example, Firm 1 might announce that it intends to expand its capacity in the hope that Firm 2 will then abandon its own decision to expand. Once this happens, Firm 1 would then abandon its own decision to expand.[4] If Firm 1 bluffs and forces the outcome (passive, passive), it enjoys a profit of 18, as opposed to the 16.5 it would get if it carried out the aggressive strategy. Of course, Firm 2 should understand this, and discount as bluster any claims that Firm 1 makes regarding its intention to choose the aggressive strategy unless those claims can be backed up with credible actions.

A key to credibility is *irreversibility*. To be a true commitment, a competitive move must be hard or costly to stop once it is set in motion. For Firm 1 to state publicly, for example, that it intends to expand its capacity may not be enough. "Talk is cheap," and press releases can be repudiated. It may instead have to begin constructing a new plant, which is far more irrevocable than a press release.

The degree to which real firms see competitive moves as irreversible commitments or reversible tactics is an interesting question.[5] Competitive moves, such as capacity expansion, that require significant up-front expenditures and create relationship-specific assets have a high commitment value. This is because once the assets have been created, the firm's ability to redeploy them outside their intended use is limited. For example, a CD pressing plant of the sort contemplated by Philips had virtually no alternative uses. Once it was built, Philips would have few options other than to run it full out.

Contracts can also facilitate commitment. One example of this that we will discuss in greater detail in Chapter 9 is a contract provision known as a most favored

---

[4]One might wonder whether Firm 2's decision to abandon a capacity expansion decision is irreversible. Why couldn't Firm 2 reverse its decision not to build once its sees that Firm 1 has called off its plans? However, this may be difficult to do. For example, Firm 2 may have an option on the land where the plant is to be built that it may be unable to exercise later. If other sites are distinctly inferior, Firm 2's choice may be "now or never."

[5]Avinash Dixit and Barry Nalebuff's excellent book *Thinking Strategically: The Competitive Edge in Business, Politics and Everyday Life*, New York: Norton, 1991, contains a thorough discussion of credibility and the commitment value of various competitive moves.

customer clause (MFCC). If a seller includes such a clause in a sales contract with a buyer, the seller is required to extend the same price terms to the buyer that it extends to its other customers. For example, if the seller discounts below its list price to steal a customer from a competitor, the buyer with an MFCC in its contract is entitled to the same discount. The MFCC makes discounting "expensive," and thus can be considered a tool that creates a credible commitment not to compete on price.

Sometimes, even public statements of intentions to act ("We plan to introduce a new and improved version of our existing product six months from now") can have commitment value. For this to be true, however, the firm's competitors and its customers must understand that the firm or its management are putting something at risk if it fails to match words with actions; otherwise, they will discount the claims, promises, or threats the firm is making. The credibility of public announcements is enhanced when it is clear that the reputation of the firm or its senior management will suffer if the firm fails to do what it has said it will do. In the computer software industry, it is more common for established firms, such as Microsoft, to make promises about new product performance and introduction dates than it is for smaller firms or newcomers to do so. This may, in part, be related to the fact that a newcomer has far more to lose in terms of credibility with consumers and opinion setters in the various personal computer magazines (an important forum for product reviews) than an established firm has. Smaller firms may thus be more reluctant to make exaggerated claims than established firms that have a track record of success. Failure to match actions to words will result in loss of face or reputation for both the firm and its senior management.

◆ ◆

XAMPLE 8.1

COMMITMENT AND IRREVERSIBILITY IN THE AIRLINE INDUSTRY

Ming-Jer Chen and Ian MacMillan surveyed senior airline executives and industry analysts (e.g., financial analysts and professors) to study irreversibility in competitive moves in the airline business.[6] Mergers and acquisition, investment in the creation of hubs, and feeder alliances with commuter airlines had the highest perceived irreversibility. Hubs required the creation of transaction-specific assets (e.g., maintenance facilities) that could not be redeployed if the hub was abandoned. Mergers and acquisitions required cooperation with the management of other airlines and third parties, such as investment bankers and regulatory authorities. Not only does the negotiation of the merger or acquisition entail significant nonrecoverable negotiation costs, it may also entail significant transaction-specific changes in operating procedures or systems. The reputation of a firm's management would also suffer greatly (e.g., the firm would be seen as capricious or frivolous) if, after negotiating the merger or acquisition, it backed out at the last minute or tried to undo it once it was consummated. Feeder alliances with commuter airlines were seen as hard to reverse because employees and unions would oppose reversing the move.

---

[6]Chen, M. J. and I. C. MacMillan, "Nonresponse and Delayed Response to Competitive Moves: The Roles of Competitor Dependence and Action Irreversibility," *Academy of Management Journal*, 35, 1992: pp. 539–570.

Promotions, decisions to abandon a route, and increases in commission rates for travel agents were considered the easiest moves to reverse. Price cuts, while seen as having a below-average degree of irreversibility, were not considered the easiest competitive move to reverse. Evidently, airline executives and industry analysts believe that once an airline cuts its prices, the inescapable cost of advertising the change is significant enough to make the airline maintain the new prices for some time. However, because price cuts are visible and clearly affect competing airlines' profitability, they are more provocative than other moves, such as temporary ad campaigns, that might be considered more reversible. Indeed, as we show in the next section, a firm's profit-maximizing response to a price cut by a competitor is generally to cut its own price. In addition, as we point out in Example 9.3, in Chapter 9, in the airline business, prices are instantaneously known through a computerized clearinghouse, so competitors learn them and can quickly match them.

Chen and MacMillan hypothesized that competitors are less likely to match an airline's competitive move when the original move is hard to reverse. Their logic is akin to the simple example we discussed earlier. The more credible a firm's commitment to play aggressive, the more likely it is that its competitors will respond by playing soft. This logic would suggest that a preemptive move by one airline to expand its route system by acquiring another airline is less likely to provoke a matching response than is a decision to engage in a short-term promotional or advertising campaign. Chen and MacMillan test this hypothesis through an exhaustive study of competitive moves and countermoves reported over a seven-year period (1979–1986) in a leading trade publication of the airline industry, *Aviation Daily*. In general, their findings support their hypothesis: harder-to-reverse moves are less frequently matched than easier-to-reverse moves. The study also supports the hypothesis that price cuts are especially provocative and thus likely to be matched frequently and quickly. MacMillan and Chen find that rival airlines responded to price cuts more frequently than other moves the authors saw as having a similar, or even higher, degree of irreversibility.

◆ ◆ ◆ ◆ ◆ STRATEGIC COMMITMENT AND COMPETITION

In the simple game described by Table 8.1, the link between strategic commitments and tactical decisions was not explicit. To be explicit, we need to introduce some new concepts. *Strategic complements* and *strategic substitutes* are concepts that capture how competitors react when one competitor changes a tactical variable such as price or quantity. *Tough commitments* and *soft commitments* are concepts that capture whether a commitment by one firm places its rivals at a disadvantage.

Strategic Complements and Strategic Substitutes

It is easiest to introduce the concepts of strategic complements and strategic substitutes with an example. Suppose that Honda announces a massive cut in the price of its Accord family sedan. In reaction, Ford would probably conclude that its best response would be to lower the price of the Taurus. In this case, Honda's and

Ford's prices are strategic complements. Suppose instead that Honda greatly increases production of the Passport minivan, driving down minivan prices to 10 percent below current levels. Observing this capacity increase, Ford might believe that its best response would be to reduce production of Windstar minivans. In this case, Honda and Ford's production volumes are strategic substitutes.

To formalize the concepts of strategic complements and substitutes, we return to the two models of product market competition introduced in Chapter 8: the Cournot model of quantity setting and the Bertrand model of price setting. Recall that in the Cournot model it was convenient to represent the equilibrium using reaction functions. In a two-firm Cournot industry, a firm's reaction function shows its profit-maximizing quantity as a function of the quantity chosen by its competitor. In the Cournot model, reaction functions are downward sloping, as Figure 8.1*a* shows. Reaction functions in the Bertrand model with horizontally differentiated products are defined analogously.[7] In this case, however, the reaction functions are upward sloping, as in Figure 8.1*b*.

In general, when reaction functions are upward sloping, the firm's actions (e.g., prices) are strategic complements. When reaction functions are downward sloping, the actions are strategic substitutes.[8] When actions are strategic complements, the more of the action one firm chooses, the more of the action the other firm will also optimally choose. In the Bertrand model, prices are strategic complements because a reduction in price is the profit-maximizing response to a competitor's price cut. When actions are strategic substitutes, the more of the action

FIGURE 8.1
STRATEGIC SUBSTITUTES AND COMPLEMENTS.

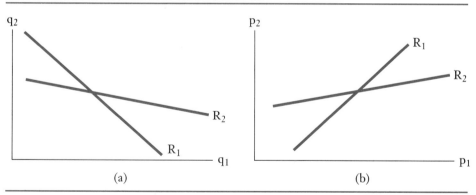

(a)   (b)

Panel (a) shows the reaction functions in a Cournot market. The reaction functions R_1 and R_2 slope downward, indicating that quantities are strategic substitutes. Panel (b) shows the reaction functions in a Bertrand market with differentiated products. The reaction functions slope upward, indicating that prices are strategic complements.

[7]Reaction functions in the Bertrand model with undifferentiated products do not concern us because a firm always wants to slightly undercut its rival's price. Hence, throughout this section, we confine our attention to Bertrand industries where firms' products exhibit some degree of horizontal differentiation.

[8]The terms *strategic complements* and *strategic substitutes* were introduced by Bulow, J., J. Geanakopolos, and P. Klemperer, "Multimarket Oligopoly: Strategic Substitutes and Complements," *Journal of Political Economy*," 93, 1985: pp. 488–511.

one firm takes, the less of the action the other firm optimally chooses. In the Cournot model, quantities are strategic substitutes because a quantity increase is the profit-maximizing response to a competitor's quantity reduction. Determining whether actions are strategic complements or substitutes involves careful consideration of the competitive interdependence among the firms. One general rule is that prices are usually strategic complements, whereas quantity and capacity decisions are usually strategic substitutes.

We will employ these concepts later in our discussion. But to see why they are important, note that these concepts tell us how a firm expects its rival to react to its tactical maneuvers. When actions are strategic complements, one firm's aggressive behavior leads its competitors to behave more aggressively as well. For example, if Honda lowers its price (an aggressive move), on the Accord, Ford will also lower the price of a Taurus (an aggressive response), because its price reaction function is upward sloping. When actions are strategic substitutes, aggressive behavior by a firm leads its rival to behave less aggressively. For example, if Honda increases its output of Passport minivans (an aggressive move), Ford will decrease its output of Windstar Minivan (a soft response), since its output reaction function is downward sloping.

Strategic Incentives to Make Commitments

Commitments have both a direct and a strategic effect on a firm's profitability. The direct effect of the commitment is its impact on the present value of the firm's profits, assuming that the firm adjusts its own tactical decisions in light of this commitment, but that its competitor's behavior does not change. For example, if Nucor invests in a process that reduces the average variable cost of producing sheet steel, the direct effect of the investment is the present value of the increase in Nucor's profit due to the reduction in its average variable costs, less the up-front cost of the investment. The increase in profit would come not only from cost savings on existing units produced but also from any benefits Nucor gets from lowering its price or increasing its output.

The strategic effect takes into account the competitive side effects of the commitment: How does the commitment alter the tactical decisions of the rival and, ultimately, the market equilibrium? For example, the strategic effect of Nucor's investment is the incremental change in the present value of its profits, as compared to the direct effect, due to the effect of the commitment on the market equilibrium for sheet steel. This strategic effect can be positive or negative; that is, it can benefit or harm the firm making the commitment. As we will show, the direction of the strategic effect depends on whether the choice variables affected by the commitment (e.g., prices) are strategic complements or strategic substitutes. If a firm takes the "long view" when making its commitment decision, as we believe it should, then it must take into account how the commitment alters the nature of the equilibrium.

Tough versus Soft Commitments

To understand the impact of a commitment on market equilibrium, it is useful to distinguish between *tough* commitments and *soft* commitments. Conceptually, a firm's tough commitment is bad for competitors, whereas a soft commitment is good for its competitors. In Cournot competition, if a firm makes a tough commitment, then no matter what output its rival produces, it is certain to produce more output than it would have done without the commitment. A soft commitment leads

EXAMPLE 8.2

STRATEGIC SUBSTITUTES IN THE WORLD MARKET FOR MEMORY CHIPS

As discussed in Chapter 7, the Cournot model of quantity setting can be thought of as pertaining to a market in which firms first choose capacities and then compete on price. This interpretation would then suggest that capacities are strategic substitutes and that a reduction in capacity by one firm would induce its competitors to increase their capacities. The $22 billion world market for memory chips illustrates this dynamic.[9]

The demand for memory chips, wafers of silicon smaller than a thumbnail, has exploded in recent years, driven by increased demand for personal computers and cellular phones as well as by the growing electronic sophistication of products, such as stereos and automobiles, that increasingly rely on memory chips. The timing of new investments is critical for doing business in this industry. New chip factories cost over $1 billion, but they become obsolete quickly, in some cases within three years.

In the early 1980s, the memory chip industry was dominated by American semiconductor firms. But in 1984, a drop in prices caused leading American chip makers, such as Intel and Texas Instruments, to postpone plans to build new chip factories. Japanese firms, such as Toshiba, NEC, and Oki Electric, responded by increasing their investments in new capacity. By the late 1980s, the Japanese had captured 80 percent of the world market, while the Americans held only 15 percent. Some American firms, such as Intel, abandoned the industry altogether.

A replay of this dynamic is occurring in the 1990s, but this time the firms that are aggressively expanding capacity are South Korean. Around 1990, in the midst of an industry downturn, major Japanese firms scaled back chip production. Then, as the Japanese economy entered a recession, Japanese chip makers began delaying investments in new chip factories, and those that did not delay found it increasingly difficult to finance new plants due to a weak Japanese stock market. By contrast, South Korean firms, such as Hyundai, Samsung, and Goldstar Electron, invested heavily in new chip-making capacity. By 1994, the South Koreans had 36 percent of the memory chip market, and Samsung had become the world's largest producer of memory chips.

the firm to produce less than it otherwise would have. In Bertrand competition, if a firm makes a tough commitment, then no matter what price its rival charges, that price will be lower than it would have been without the commitment. A soft commitment leads the firm to charge more than it otherwise would have.

Tough commitments are easier to visualize than soft commitments, because they conform to the conventional view of competition as an effort to outdo one's

---

[9]This example draws from "Silicon Duel: Koreans Move to Grab Memory-Chip Market from the Japanese," *Wall Street Journal*, March 14, 1995, pp. A1, A8.

rivals. For example, we "understand" why firms may commit to be the lowest price seller or the largest volume producer in a market. But firms should not automatically refrain from making soft commitments. A firm may benefit from a soft commitment that produces a sufficiently beneficial strategic effect.

Tough and Soft Commitments in Cournot and Bertrand Equilibria

The strategic effects of tough and soft commitments may be illustrated by considering a market with two firms. Firm 1 (but not Firm 2) is contemplating making a strategic commitment.[10] For example, the commitment might be the decision to adopt a process innovation that lowers variable production costs, such as Nucor's decision in 1987 to pioneer the thin-slab casting process in the steel industry. Or it might be a decision about how to position a new product, such as Quaker's 1994 decision to sell bagged cereals to appeal to sensitive customers. Whatever its nature, the decision has two key properties. First, the rival firm must be aware of it. Second, the decision cannot be reversed once the firm makes it. The commitment is thus credible.

The timing of decision making in this market is as follows. Firm 1 first decides whether to make the commitment. Then, the two firms compete with each other. This two-stage game corresponds roughly to the distinction between strategy and tactics: Firm 1 first makes a strategic commitment in stage 1, then both firms maneuver tactically in stage 2. We will focus on two competitive scenarios in stage 2: Cournot quantity competition and Bertrand price competition. In the Cournot model, once Firm 1 decides whether to make the commitment, both firms then simultaneously choose quantities. In the Bertrand model, once Firm 1 decides whether to make the commitment, both firms then simultaneously choose prices.

To keep the analysis simple, we assume that Firm 1 believes that the market will quickly reach the relevant equilibrium once it has made the commitment. For example, in the quantity-setting market, Firm 1 believes that the market will immediately reach a new Cournot equilibrium after it has made its commitment. In the price-setting market, Firm 1 believes that the market will quickly reach a new Bertrand equilibrium. The assumption that Firm 1 is forward looking and anticipates how its commitment will alter the market equilibrium means that we are searching for a subgame perfect Nash equilibrium (SPNE) in a two-stage game in which, at stage 1, Firm 1 makes its commitment decision, and then at stage 2, both firms simultaneously choose quantities (or prices).[11]

For firm 1 to analyze the SPNE in a two-state game, it should first consider the equilibrium in the second stage, as a function of the capacity that it selects in the first stage. This analysis varies according to whether competition in the second stage is Cournot or Bertand.

Stage 2 Competition Is Cournot

Firm 1 must anticipate how the commitment might alter the Cournot equilibrium between it and Firm 2. This depends on whether the commitment is tough or soft.

---

[10]The case in which both firms make strategic commitments is similar to the one where only one firm makes a commitment. However, the economics of this case are more difficult to describe, so we concentrate on the simpler case of a one-firm commitment to keep the discussion compact.

[11]The Economics Primer contains a full discussion of the SPNE.

If Firm 1 makes a tough commitment, then no matter what output level Firm 2 produces, it will produce more output than it would have done if it had not made the commitment. This corresponds to a rightward shift in Firm 1's reaction curve R_1, from R_1^{before} to R_1^{after}, as shown in Figure 8.2. For example, Firm 1 would be making a tough commitment if it adopted a process innovation that reduced its marginal cost of production.[12]

If Firm 1 makes a soft commitment, then no matter what output level Firm 2 produces, it will produce less output than it would have done if it had not made the commitment. This corresponds to a leftward shift in Firm 1's reaction curve R_1, as shown in Figure 8.3. To illustrate a soft commitment under Cournot competition, suppose that Firm 1, in addition to producing the good it produces in the Cournot market, has the opportunity to sell the same good as a monopolist in a second, geographically distinct, market. Suppose, further, that the marginal cost of production goes up as the firm produces more output overall. That is, the firm's technology is characterized by diseconomies of scope. This might occur because the firm would use the same factory to produce output for both markets, and as a greater volume of output is produced, the managerial resources of the firm become increasingly strained and production becomes less efficient. The decision to enter the monopoly market would be a soft commitment: By making that decision, Firm 1 would cause its marginal cost in the Cournot market to go up, and as a result, it would reduce its profit-maximizing output level for any given output expected from Firm 2. This would shift Firm 1's reaction function inward, as shown in Figure 8.3.

Figure 8.2 reveals that Firm 1 gets a beneficial competitive side effect from making the tough commitment: R_1 shifts rightward, which results in a Cournot equilibrium in which Firm 2 produces less output. Because, in the Cournot

FIGURE 8.2
COMMITMENT MAKES FIRM 1 "TOUGH" IN A COURNOT MARKET.

For any output produced by Firm 2, Firm 1 wants to produce more output than it would have before it made the commitment. This is represented by a rightward shift in its reaction function from R_1^{before} to R_1^{after}. As a result, the Cournot equilibrium moves to the southeast and involves a higher quantity for Firm 1 and a lower quantity for Firm 2.

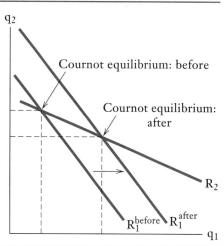

[12]Strategic incentives for investments of this kind have been analyzed by Brander, J. and B. Spencer, "Strategic Commitment with R & D: The Symmetric Case," *Bell Journal of Economics*, 14, Spring 1983: pp. 225–235.

FIGURE 8.3
COMMITMENT MAKES FIRM 1 "SOFT" IN A COURNOT MARKET.

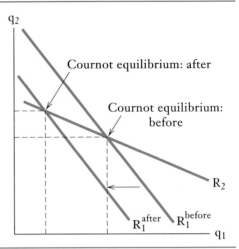

For any output produced by Firm 2, Firm 1 wants to produce less output than it would have before it made the commitment. This is represented by a leftward shift in its reaction function from R_1^{before} to R_1^{after}. As a result, the Cournot equilibrium moves to the northwest and involves a lower quantity for Firm 1 and a higher quantity for Firm 2.

model, Firm 1 is better off the less output its rival produces (because the market price will be higher), the Cournot equilibrium in which Firm 1 makes the commitment is better than the Cournot equilibrium in which Firm 1 does not make the commitment.

Taking this beneficial side effect into account can significantly affect how Firm 1 evaluates the commitment. In particular, the commitment might be valuable in this case, even though its direct effect is unfavorable. For example, suppose the commitment is an investment in a new process for which the direct effect is negative (i.e., the present value of the investment assuming no competitive reaction is less than the up-front investment cost). The beneficial strategic effect could outweigh the negative direct effect, and if so, the firm should make the investment for strategic purposes, even though its direct effect is negative.

By contrast, as shown in Figure 8.3, when the commitment makes Firm 1 soft, it has a negative strategic effect. Firm 1's reaction curve R_1 shifts leftward, resulting in a Cournot equilibrium in which Firm 2 produces more output than it would have produced had Firm 1 not made the commitment. If the direct effect of the commitment is negative, zero, or even slightly positive, Firm 1 should not make it. This analysis would suggest, for example, that entry into a new market in which the firm would be a monopolist may be undesirable if, due to diminishing marginal returns or diseconomies of scope, the firm's marginal cost in its first market goes up.

Stage 2 Competition Is Bertrand

Incentives for strategic commitment are different when stage 2 competition is Bertrand. As before, we distinguish between tough and soft commitments. If Firm 1 makes a tough commitment, then no matter what price Firm 2 charges, Firm 1 will charge a lower price than it would have if it had not made the commitment. This corresponds to a leftward shift in Firm 1's reaction curve R_1, as shown in Figure 8.4. If Firm 1 makes a soft commitment, then no matter what price Firm 2 charges, Firm 1 will charge a higher price than it would have if it had not made the commitment. This corresponds to a rightward shift in Firm 1's reaction curve R_1, as shown in Figure 8.5.

FIGURE 8.4
COMMITMENT MAKES FIRM 1 "TOUGH" IN A BERTRAND MARKET.

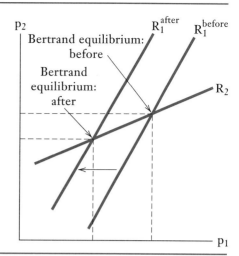

For any price charged by Firm 2, Firm 1 wants to charge a lower price than it would have before it made the commitment. This is represented by a leftward shift in its reaction function from R_1^{before} to R_1^{after}. As a result, the Bertrand equilibrium moves to the southwest and involves a lower price for Firm 1 and a lower price for Firm 2.

Consider, now, the competitive side effects of the commitment when it makes Firm 1 tough. As shown in Figure 8.4, Firm 1's reaction curve R_1 shifts leftward, moving the Bertrand equilibrium down to the southwest.[13] Firm 1 charges a lower price in equilibrium, but so does Firm 2, although its drop in price is smaller than Firm 1's. Firm 2's drop in price hurts Firm 1; the strategic effect is negative from

FIGURE 8.5
COMMITMENT MAKES FIRM 1 "SOFT" IN A BERTRAND MARKET.

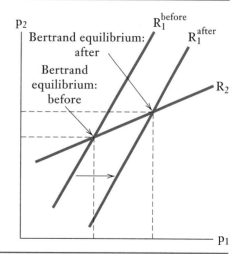

For any price charged by Firm 2, Firm 1 wants to charge a higher price than it would have before it made the commitment. This is represented by a rightward shift in its reaction function from R_1^{before} to R_1^{after}. As a result, the Bertrand equilibrium moves to the northeast and involves a higher price for Firm 1 and a higher price for Firm 2.

[13]Firm 1's commitment could also result in a shift in Firm 2's reaction function. For example, if Firm 1 made its product less differentiated than Firm 2's, Firm 2's demand function would change, which would alter its profit-maximizing pricing decisions and thus shift its reaction function. However, taking this shift into account would move the Bertrand equilibrium even farther down to the southwest in Figure 8.4.

Firm 1's perspective. If, for example, the strategic commitment is investment in a new process, and the direct effect is positive (i.e., the present value of the investment assuming no competitive reactions exceeds the up-front investment cost), it might be optimal for Firm 1 to refrain from this investment if the strategic effect is sufficiently negative.

If the net present value of a cost-reducing commitment is positive, why wouldn't Firm 1 make the investment, but keep its price constant afterward? It would then enjoy the benefits of its commitment (the cost reduction) without the negative competitive side effects. However, Firm 1 could not implement this strategy. Even though it seems appealing before the commitment is made, it runs counter to Firm 1's self-interest after the commitment is made. After Firm 1 makes the commitment, its profit-maximizing price is lower than it was before, and its reaction function shifts inward (see Figure 8.4). Thus, once the commitment has been made, Firm 1 wants to behave more aggressively in the second-stage pricing game. Since Firm 2 observes the commitment, it anticipates that Firm 1 will behave more aggressively, and it does so as well. The result is the Bertrand equilibrium in which both firms charge lower prices than they would have before Firm 1 made its commitment. Firm 1 could attempt to short circuit this dynamic by announcing in advance that it planned to cut its costs, but not its price. But such an announcement would not be credible because both parties would understand that it would require Firm 1 to go against its self-interest once the commitment is made.

Finally, let us consider the incentives to make the commitment when it makes Firm 1 soft. In that case, shown in Figure 8.5, the commitment shifts Firm 1's reaction function rightward. This, in turn, moves the Bertrand equilibrium to the northeast. The result is a higher price for both Firm 1 and Firm 2. This competitive side effect benefits Firm 1 and may make the commitment worthwhile, even if its direct effect is negative.

Consider, for example, the direct and strategic effects of repositioning Firm 1's product to appeal to a narrower segment of the market in which consumers have more specialized tastes. This move will make the products of Firm 1 and 2 more horizontally differentiated.[14] Holding prices of both firms fixed, the direct effect of this move is probably negative because Firm 1's product now appeals to fewer consumers than before, effectively shifting its demand curve inward. However, the strategic effect may be positive. The more horizontally differentiated the products of Firms 1 and 2 are, the less incentive each firm has to cut price to capture each other's customer base.

A Taxonomy of Commitment Strategies

Drew Fudenberg and Jean Tirole argued that two-stage models of commitment can be analyzed by considering the two important dimensions that we discussed earlier—whether commitments are tough or soft, and whether the stage 2 tactical variables are strategic substitutes or strategic complements. There are four ways of combining these dimensions. In two combinations, *making* the commitment generates a beneficial strategic effect, and in the other two, *refraining* from making the commitment avoids a harmful strategic effect. Fudenberg and Tirole described

---

[14]Chapter 7 discusses horizontal differentiation.

and named these four combinations. These are shown in Table 8.2, and are marked by the superscript [FT]. For completeness, we include and name in Table 8.2 those commitment actions that generate harmful strategic effects.

The four combinations described by Fudenberg and Tirole represent different strategic situations. If the stage 2 tactical variables are strategic complements—that is, the reaction curves slope upward—and the commitment makes the firm tough, then the commitment alters the stage 2 equilibrium, so that rival firms behave more aggressively (e.g., set lower prices in the Bertrand model). In this case, the commitment has a harmful strategic effect, and the firm has an incentive either to forsake the commitment altogether or to underinvest in it—to make the commitment at a lower level (e.g., spend less on a new process) than it would have had it not considered the strategic side effects. Fudenberg and Tirole call this the "puppy-dog ploy." By contrast, when the commitment makes the firm soft, it results in an equilibrium in which rivals behave less aggressively (e.g., set higher prices). The commitment thus has a beneficial strategic effect, and the firm has an incentive to overinvest in it—to make the commitment at a higher level than it would have had it not considered the competitive side effects. They call this the "fat-cat effect."

If the stage 2 tactical variables are strategic substitutes—that is, the reaction curves slope downward—and the commitment makes the firm tough, then in the second-stage equilibrium, rival firms become less aggressive (e.g., choose lower quantities). The commitment has a beneficial strategic effect, and the firm has an incentive to overinvest in the commitment. This is the "top-dog" strategy of investing to become a more aggressive competitor. The other possibility is that the commitment makes the firm soft, which has a negative strategic effect because rival firms respond by behaving more aggressively. Here the firm has an incentive to underinvest in the commitment. This is the "lean and hungry" look.

TABLE 8.2

Nature of Stage 2 Tactical Variables	Commitment Posture	Commitment Action	Strategy	Comments/Role of Actor in the Competitive Arena
• Strategic Substitutes	Tough	Make	Top-Dog Strategy[FT]	Assert dominance Force rivals to back off
• Strategic Substitutes	Tough	Refrain	Submissive Underdog	Accept follower role Avoid fighting
• Strategic Substitutes	Soft	Make	Suicidal Siberian	Invite rivals to exploit you (May indicate exit strategy)
• Strategic Substitutes	Soft	Refrain	Lean and Hungry Look[FT]	Actively submissive Posturing to avoid conflict
• Strategic Complements	Tough	Make	Mad Dog	Attack to become top dog, invite battle heedless of costs
• Strategic Complements	Tough	Refrain	Puppy-Dog Ploy[FT]	Placate the top dog Enjoy available scraps
• Strategic Complements	Soft	Make	Fat-Cat Effect[FT]	Confidently take care of self Share the wealth with rivals
• Strategic Complements	Soft	Refrain	Weak Kitten	Accept status quo out of fear Wait to follow the leader

One may occasionally see a firm pursue one of the strategies that Fudenberg and Tirole do not describe, even though they generate harmful strategic effects. For example, a firm may pursue the "mad dog" strategy of making a tough commitment when the tactical variables are strategic complements. An example is when a firm commits to low prices even though this will invite a price war. Such strategies, though seemingly counterintuitive, can make sense if the firm views price competition as a dynamic competitive process. If so, short-term strategic losses might be offset by long-term gains. Chapter 9 discusses the long-run dynamics of competition in greater detail. A "mad dog" strategy can also make sense if the firm is attempting to deter entry. By making a tough commitment, the firm intensifies price competition with existing rivals, but by driving own price-cost margins, it might deter new firms from entering the market. Chapter 10 discusses entry deterrence in more detail.

Making Sense of the Taxonomy

The taxonomy of strategic commitments in Table 8.2 has two important implications for strategic decision making and market analysis. First, and most basic, it suggests that when making hard-to-reverse investment decisions, managers ought not to look only at the effects of the investment on their own firm. They should also try to anticipate how the decision to invest or not invest will affect the evolution of market competition in the future. A recent management fad that is intended to promote this way of thinking is known as "war gaming": Elaborate computer simulations allow managers to track the likely competitive implications of pricing and investment decisions over many years.[15] For example, the consulting firm Coopers & Lybrand commissioned the creation of a war game known as TeleSim for Pacific Telesis. TeleSim allowed Pacific Telesis's managers to analyze the competitive effects of changes in regional toll rates and investments in new plant and equipment. RJR managers used a war game created by the consulting firm Booz Allen to help plot competitive reactions to Philip Morris' decision to cut the price of its Marlboro brand of cigarettes in April 1993.

Second, the details of market rivalry can profoundly influence the willingness of firms to make commitments. For example, the theory developed previously tells us that an investment in a process innovation that reduces marginal costs has a beneficial strategic effect in a Cournot industry, but has a negative strategic effect in a Bertrand industry. At one level, this implication may not seem to be terribly useful. In practice, it is often difficult to distinguish which model applies in any particular situation. Indeed, as we will argue in Chapter 9, neither the Cournot nor the Bertrand model may do an especially good job of capturing the richness of repeated interactions among firms. However, one should not take the models of product market competition so literally that they obscure the robust point that comes out of the theoretical discussion above: A commitment that induces competitors or potential entrants to behave less aggressively—for example, to refrain from price cutting, to postpone or abandon capacity expansion plans, or to reduce their advertising or promotion—is likely to have a beneficial strategic effect on the firm making the commitment. By contrast, a commitment that induces competitors or potential entrants to behave more aggressively is likely to have a harmful strategic effect.

---

[15]See "Business War Games Attract Big Warriors," *Wall Street Journal*, December 22, 1994, pp. B1, B4.

Assessing how a commitment will affect the evolution of market competition depends on industry conditions and the characteristics of the firm's competitors. Sometimes the effect of the strategic commitment on a competitor may depend on whether the competitor is currently in the industry or has not yet entered. For example, if a firm adopts a process innovation, it may price more aggressively, disrupting the industry equilibrium and leading to more aggressive pricing by existing competitors as they attempt to preserve their market shares. Yet, as discussed earlier, the expectation of intensified pricing rivalry may deter potential competitors from entering the market at all.

The strategic effects of the commitment might also depend on capacity utilization rates in the industry. For example, when these rates are low, a firm's commitment to a process innovation that lowers its marginal cost may be met by an aggressive price response from rivals who fear further losses in capacity utilization and who have the capacity to take on new business that comes their way if they cut price. In this case, the strategic effect of the commitment is likely to be negative. By contrast, when capacity utilization rates are high, competitors are less well positioned to respond aggressively unless they expand their capacities. But the expectation of more aggressive behavior by the firm making the commitment may deter its competitors from going forward with their plans to expand capacity. If so, the strategic effect is likely to be positive.

The strategic effects of the commitment may also depend on the degree of horizontal differentiation among the firm making the commitment and its competitors. For example, Figure 8.6a shows that in a Bertrand market the magnitude

FIGURE 8.6
STRATEGIC EFFECTS AND PRODUCT DIFFERENTIATION.

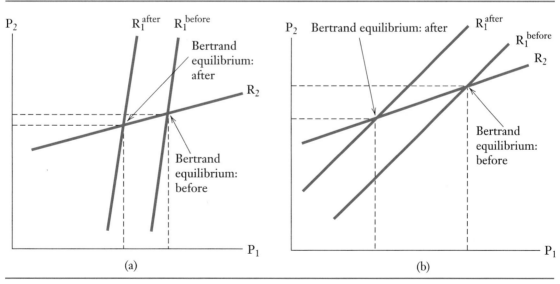

Panel (a) shows a market in which the two firms' products are highly differentiated. Firm 1's commitment to a cost-reducing investment hardly affects Firm 2's pricing decision, so the strategic effect in this case is negligible. Panel (b) shows a market in which the two firms' products are less differentiated. Firm 2's commitment to a cost-reducing investment has a relatively bigger impact on Firm 2's pricing decision, so the strategic effect is more significant than it is in the market in panel (a).

of the strategic effect depends on the degree of horizontal differentiation. When the firms' products are highly differentiated, as in panel (a), the strategic effect from an investment in cost reduction is likely to be relatively unimportant. However, when products are relatively less differentiated, as in panel (b), the strategic effect is relatively larger.

EXAMPLE 8.3

COMMITMENT AT NUCOR AND USX: THE CASE OF THIN SLAB CASTING[16]

Pankaj Ghemawat's case study of the adoption of thin slab casting by Nucor and the nonadoption by USX illustrates the relationship between commitment and product market competition, and how previous commitments can limit a firm's ability to take advantage of new commitment opportunities.

The modern production of steel relies on a process called continuous casting in which molten steel is cast into a long continuous slab, about 8 to 10 inches thick. The long slab is then cut into smaller slabs of about 20 to 40 feet that are converted into finished products, such as sheet steel. Continuous casting, which was commercialized in the 1950s, was a major technological breakthrough. However, its efficiency for producing sheet steel was limited by the need to reheat the slabs before rolling them into thin sheets. Major cost savings would result if the molten steel could be cast directly into thin sheets. Such a process, known as thin slab casting, was finally developed in the mid-1980s by a West German company, SMS Schloemann-Siemag.

In 1987, Nucor Corporation became the first American firm to adopt thin slab casting. At that time, Nucor was looking to enter the flat-rolled sheet segment of the steel business, a segment that had been unavailable to the so-called minimills, of which Nucor was the largest. Adoption of this thin slab casting was a major commitment for Nucor. All told, the up-front investment in developing the process and building a facility to use it was expected to be $340 million, close to 90 percent of Nucor's net worth at the time. Nucor's commitment was successful. By 1992, Nucor's thin slab casting mill in Crawfordsville, Indiana, had become profitable, and Nucor built a second thin slab casting plant in Arkansas.

USX, the largest American integrated steel producer, which was 60 times larger than Nucor, also showed an early interest in thin slab casting, spending over $30 million to perfect a thin slab casting technology known as the Hazelett process. Yet, USX eventually decided not to adopt thin slab casting. Ghemawat argues that this decision is anomalous in light of extant economic theory on process innovations. This theory suggests that if (1) an innovation is nondrastic

---

[16]This example is based on Ghemawat, P., "Commitment to a Process Innovation: Nucor, USX, and Thin Slab Casting," *Journal of Economics and Management Strategy*, 2, Spring 1993: pp. 133–161.

(i.e., it will not lower the first-adopter's costs so much as to make all other firms in the industry noncompetitive); (2) the innovation is likely to make the adopter tough as opposed to soft in postadoption competition; and (3) the returns from the process are not much more uncertain than returns from the existing technology, then a large incumbent firm (i.e., USX) will have a stronger incentive to adopt the technology than a new entrant (i.e., Nucor). (This is a complicated example of the top-dog strategy discussed earlier.) Ghemawat argues the case that all these conditions held for thin slab casting: It was a nondrastic innovation; capacity utilization rates in the industry were well below 100 percent, which suggested that firms in the industry competed as Bertrand price setters, which in turn would suggest that a process innovation like thin slab casting that lowered average variable costs would make the adopter tough, rather than soft. And the returns from thin slab casting were fairly predictable because the process Nucor adopted was, from the perspective of 1986–1987, considered to be incremental as opposed to pathbreaking.

So why did USX not adopt thin slab casting? Ghemawat argues that the decision stemmed from prior organizational and strategic commitments that constrained USX's opportunity to profit from thin slab casting. For example, in the mid-1980s, USX had already modernized four of its five integrated steel mills. The fifth plant, located in the Monongahela River Valley in Pennsylvania, was a vast complex in which the steel-making facility and the rolling mill were 10 miles apart. Moreover, the labor cost savings that would accrue to a non-unionized firm like Nucor would not be nearly as significant to unionized USX, which was bound by restrictive work rules. Finally, there was doubt as to whether appliance manufacturers, which were major customers of the sheet steel produced in the Monongahela Valley plant, would purchase sheet steel produced via continuous casting due to the adulteration in the surface quality of the steel that the new process might cause.

Ghemawat argues that the prior commitment by USX to modernize existing facilities—in particular the one at Monongahela Valley—as opposed to building "greenfield" plants, locked USX into a posture in which nonadoption of thin slab casting was a natural outcome. This conclusion highlights an important strategic point: In forecasting the likely reactions of competitors to major strategic commitments, a firm should recognize that prior commitments made by its competitors can constrain those firms' potential responses. In this case, Nucor's management anticipated USX's behavior. Nucor decided to enter the flat-rolled sheet steel business because it expected that integrated producers, such as USX, would not adopt thin slab casting.

FLEXIBILITY AND OPTION VALUE ◆ ◆ ◆ ◆ ◆

The strategic effect of a commitment is positive when the commitment alters competitors' behavior in ways that are advantageous to the firm making the commitment. These beneficial strategic effects are often rooted in inflexibility. For example, by preemptively investing in capacity expansion, a firm may have to price aggressively to maintain capacity utilization rates. In doing so, it may force rival firms to scale back their plans to expand capacity.[17]

However, strategic commitments are almost always made under conditions of uncertainty about market conditions, costs, or competitors' goals and resources. For example, in deciding whether to build a CD plant in the United States, Philips had to confront the risk that CDs would appeal only to the most dedicated audiophiles. When competitive moves are hard to reverse, and their outcomes are shrouded in uncertainty, the value of preserving flexibility, of keeping one's future options open, must be considered when evaluating the benefits of the commitment.

Flexibility gives the firm options.[18] A simple example of the value of options occurs when the firm can delay an investment and await new information about its profitability. To illustrate the option value of delay, consider a firm that can invest $100 million in a plant to enter a new market. Given the uncertainties about how the market will accept the new product, the firm forecasts two scenarios: a "high-acceptance" scenario in which the investment will have a present value of $300 million, and a "low-acceptance" scenario in which the present value of the investment will be $50 million. The firm believes that each scenario is equally likely. If the firm invests today, the expected net present value (NPV) of the investment is $.5(300) + .5(50) - 100 = \$75$ million. But suppose, by waiting a year, the firm can learn for certain which scenario will arise (perhaps by observing the demand for the product in another geographically distinct market). If the firm waits, and the product turns out to have a high level of market acceptance, the firm should invest and get a net present value of $200 million. But if the investment has a present value of $50 million, the firm is better off not investing in this project and putting its money in the next best alternative, which we will assume is a zero NPV investment. Assuming a 10 percent annual discount rate, if the firm waits, its expected NPV is $[.5(200) + .5(0)]/(1.1) = \$91$ million, which exceeds the $75 million NPV from investing right away.[19] The option value of delay is the difference between the expected net present value if the firm invests today and the expected net present value if the firm waits until the uncertainty resolves itself. In this case, the option value of delay is $91 - $75 = \$16$ million.

Option value arises when the firm leaves itself with options that allow it to tailor its decision making to the underlying circumstances it faces. In the preceding example, by waiting, the firm avoids investing in a bad project (i.e., one with a present value of $50 million). Of course, there are factors that limit option values. For instance, our example did not take into account the fact that by waiting the firm risks having the investment opportunity preempted by competitors. A complete analysis of the option value of delaying investments should attempt to factor in such considerations.

---

[17]This is an example of the top-dog strategy.

[18]See Dixit, A. K. and R. S. Pindyck, *Investment Under Uncertainty*, Princeton, NJ: Princeton University Press, 1994, for pioneering work on the option value of real investments.

[19]We divide by 1.1 to reflect the fact that if the firm waits, all cash flows from the investment are delayed by one year. Alternatively, we could have adjusted the present values of the investment to reflect the time value costs of delay.

ℰXAMPLE 8.4

COMMITMENT VERSUS FLEXIBILITY IN THE CD MARKET

In the introduction to this chapter and again in this section, we have referred to Philips' decision in 1983 whether to invest in a new CD pressing plant in the United States. That decision highlights the tension between the strategic effects of commitment and the option value of waiting. By building a plant in 1983, Philips might preempt Sony and other potential competitors from building their own CD plants, an example of the top-dog strategy. But because the investment in a CD plant involved a large irreversible commitment, there was an option value for Philips to wait and see whether market acceptance of CDs would be strong enough to justify an investment in a U.S. plant.

Anita McGahan studied Philips' decision in detail and derived thresholds on what the probability of market acceptance would have to have been to justify Philips deciding to delay investment.[20] To isolate the pure option effect, McGahan first analyzed what Philips' decision would have been if it had faced no competition in the CD market. She concludes that Philips would have been better off waiting and retaining flexibility if the probability that the popular market would accept the CD was .38 or lower, indicating a nontrivial, albeit not overwhelmingly large, option effect. By contrast, if Philips faced competitors that would learn about market demand at the same time it did, Philips would have been better off delaying investment only if the probability of market acceptance was .006 or lower. This substantially lower threshold indicates that had Philips faced competitors that were as well-informed as it was about market demand, Philips should have almost certainly built a plant immediately despite the demand uncertainty. This indicates that Philips' incentive to be a top dog was strong, even taking into account the option value of flexibility. But, as McGahan points out, Philips' information about demand was likely to be obtained through its experience with CD operations in Europe. Thus, it would know before the competition whether market acceptance was likely to justify investment in a CD plant in the United States. This informational advantage raises the option value of flexibility; McGahan estimates that Philips would have been better off waiting if the probability of market acceptance was .13 or lower.

Philips ultimately decided not to build the U.S. plant in 1983, suggesting that it was fairly pessimistic about the prospects of CDs in the American market. In 1984, Sony became the first CD manufacturer to produce in the United States, opening a plant in Terre Haute, Indiana. Philips initially chose to increase capacity at its pressing plant in Hanover, Germany. It decided to invest in a U.S. plant only after Sony's plant was fully operational.

---

[20]McGahan, A. M., "The Incentive Not to Invest: Capacity Commitment in the Compact Disc Introduction," *Research on Technological Innovation, Management and Policy*, 5, 1993: pp. 177–197.

◆ ◆ ◆ ◆ ◆ A FRAMEWORK FOR ANALYZING COMMITMENTS

Pankaj Ghemawat argues that major strategic decisions usually involve investments in "sticky factors": physical assets, resources, and capabilities that are durable, specialized to the particular strategy that the firm follows, and untradeable (i.e., they cannot be sold on the open market).[21] Once made, investments in such assets cannot easily be transformed or redeployed elsewhere. For example, once Wang Laboratories staked its future on dedicated word processing, it would have been extremely difficult for Wang to move into personal computer manufacturing, which required capabilities that it did not have and could not quickly acquire. Because strategic investments are durable, specialized, and untradable, after a firm has made them, it is stuck. The firm must continue with its chosen strategy for a considerable time. In this sense, according to Ghemawat, the choice of a strategy is manifested in a few commitment-intensive decisions. The essence of strategy, in his view, is getting these commitments right.

But getting these decisions right is difficult. Commitment-intensive decisions are fraught with risk and require that managers look for into the future to evaluate alternative strategic actions. To help managers make such choices, Ghemawat developed a four-step framework for analyzing commitment-intensive choices:

- Positioning analysis

- Sustainability analysis

- Flexibility analysis

- Judgment analysis

Positioning analysis can be likened to determining the direct effects of the commitment. It involves analyzing whether the firm's commitment is likely to result in a product market position in which the firm delivers superior benefits to consumers or operates with lower costs than competitors. Chapter 12 develops a set of concepts, frameworks, and tools for conducting positioning analysis.

Sustainability analysis can be likened to determining the strategic effects of the commitment. It involves analyzing potential responses to the commitment by competitors and potential entrants in light of the commitments that they have made and the impact of those responses on competition. It also involves analyzing the market imperfections that make the firm's resources scarce and immobile and the conditions that protect the firm's competitive advantages from imitation by competitors. Chapters 11, 13, and 14 develop frameworks and concepts for conducting sustainability analysis.

The culmination of positioning and sustainability analysis, in Ghemawat's view, should be a formal analysis of the net present value of alternative strategic commitments. Positioning analysis provides the basis for determining the revenues and costs associated with each alternative. Sustainability analysis provides the basis

---

[21]Ghemawat, P., Commitment: *The Dynamic of Strategy*, New York: Free Press, 1991.

for determining the time horizon beyond which the firm's rate of return on incremental investments is no greater than its cost of capital, that is, its economic profits are zero.[22]

Flexibility analysis incorporates uncertainty into positioning and sustainability analysis. As discussed earlier, flexibility gives the firm option value. Ghemawat points out that a key determinant of option value is the learn-to-burn ratio. This is the ratio of the "learn rate"—the rate at which the firm receives new information that allows it to adjust its strategic choices—and the "burn rate"—the rate at which the firm invests in the sunk assets to support the strategy. A high learn-to-burn ratio implies that a strategic choice has a high degree of flexibility. In this case, the option value of delay is low because the firm can quickly accumulate information about the prospects of its strategic choice before it is too heavily committed. Ghemawat argues that many commitment-intensive choices have the potential for high learn-to-burn ratios, but that realizing this potential requires careful management. Experimentation and pilot programs are ways that a firm can increase its learn-to-burn ratio and increase its flexibility in making commitment-intensive choices.

The final part of Ghemawat's framework is judgment analysis: taking stock of the organizational and managerial factors that might distort the firm's incentive to choose an optimal strategy. Ghemawat notes that firms can make two types of errors in making commitment-intensive choices: Type I errors—rejecting an investment that should have been made—and Type II errors—accepting an investment that should have been rejected. Theoretical work by Raaj Kumar Sah and Joseph Stiglitz suggests that decision-making systems inside the organization can influence the likelihood of both types of errors.[23] Specifically, they show that organizations in which the authority to screen and accept investment projects is decentralized will accept more investment opportunities—both good and bad—than an organization in which investment decisions are made hierarchically, that is, they are first screened at lower levels and then sent "upstairs" for final approval. This implies that decentralized decision making results in a relatively higher incidence of Type II errors, whereas hierarchical decision making results in a relatively higher incidence of Type I errors. This analysis suggests that part of the process of making commitment-intensive decisions is a choice of how to make such decisions. In working through the first three parts of this framework, managers must be cognizant of the biases imparted by the incentives of the firm's managers to send accurate information up through the hierarchy, by the structure of the organization, and by its politics and culture. We take up these issues in Chapters 16, 17, and 18.

---

[22]The concept of a time horizon beyond which the firm's investments yield a rate of return no greater than its cost of capital is a standard part of models used by financial analysts to determine the value of firms. In some models, it is called the forecasting horizon. G. Bennett Stewart refers to this horizon as "big T." See *The Quest for Value: A Guide for Senior Managers*, New York: HarperBusiness, 1991.

[23]Sah, R. K. and J. Stiglitz, "The Architecture of Economic Systems: Hierarchies and Polyarchies," *American Economic Review*, 76, September 1986: pp. 716–727.

CHAPTER SUMMARY

◆ Strategic commitments are hard-to-reverse decisions that have long-term impacts. They should be distinguished from tactical decisions that are easy to reverse and have short-term impact.

◆ Strategic commitments that seemingly limit options may make a firm better off. Inflexibility can have value because a firm's commitments can lead competitors to make decisions that are advantageous for the firm making the commitment.

◆ The impact of strategic commitments depends on the nature of product market competition. The concepts of strategic complements and strategic substitutes are useful for characterizing how commitment affects competition. When reaction functions are upward sloping, actions are strategic complements. When reaction functions are downward sloping, actions are strategic substitutes.

◆ The direct effect of a commitment is its impact on the present value of the firm's profits, assuming that competitors' actions remain unchanged after the firm has made its commitment. The strategic effect of a commitment is the impact of competitive side-effects of the commitment on the firm's profits.

◆ In a two-stage setting, in which a firm makes a commitment and then the firm and its competitors choose tactical actions, the desirability of the commitment depends on whether the actions are strategic substitutes or complements and whether the commitment makes the firm tough or soft.

◆ Flexibility gives the firm option value. A simple example of option value occurs when the firm can delay an investment and await new information that bears on the investment's profitability.

◆ Strategic choices are commitment-intensive, because they involve investments in durable, specialized, and immobile resources and capabilities. Analyzing commitment-intensive choices thus requires careful consideration of the likely sources of competitive advantage (i.e., positioning), the sustainability of the advantage, and the flexibility a firm possesses once it makes a strategic investment. An important determinant of flexibility is the learn-to-burn ratio. Managers must also carefully analyze the biases created by internal organizational factors, such as structure and culture.

QUESTIONS

1. What is the difference between a soft commitment and no commitment?
2. How are commitments related to sunk costs?
3. Explain why prices are usually strategic complements and capacities are usually strategic substitutes.
4. Why did Fuderberg and Tirole identify only four of the eight possible strategic commitment strategies? Of the four that they did not identify, which do you think firms might actually adopt?
5. Use the logic of the Cournot equilibrium to explain why it is more effective for a firm to build capacity ahead of its rival than it is for that firm to merely announce that it is going to build capacity.
6. An established firm is considering expanding its capacity to take advantage of a recent growth in demand. It can do so in one of two ways. It can purchase fungible, general purpose assets that can be resold at close to their original value if their use in the industry proves to be unprofitable. Or it can invest in highly specialized assets that, once put

in place, have no alternative uses and virtually no salvage value. Assuming that each choice results in the same production costs once installed, under what choice is the firm likely to encounter a greater likelihood that its competitors will also expand their capacities?

7. Consider a monopoly producer of a durable good, such as a supercomputer. The good does not depreciate. Once consumers purchase the good from the monopolist, they are free to sell it in the "secondhand" market. Oftentimes in markets for new durable goods, one sees the following pricing pattern: The seller starts off charging a high price but then lowers the price over time. Explain why, with a durable good, the monopolist might prefer to commit to keep its selling price constant over time. Can you think of a way that the monopolist might be able to make a credible commitment to do this?

8. Indicate whether the *strategic effects* of the following competitive moves are likely to be positive (beneficial to the firm making them) or negative (harmful to the firm making them).

   a. Two horizontally differentiated producers of diesel railroad engines—one located in the United States and the other located in Europe—compete in the European market as Bertrand price competitors. The U.S. manufacturer lobbies the U.S. government to give it an export subsidy, the amount of which is directly proportional to the amount of output the firm sells in European market.

   b. A Cournot duopolist issues new debt to repurchase shares of its stock. The new debt issue will preclude the firm raising additional debt in the foreseeable future, and is expected to constrain the firm from modernizing existing production facilities.

9. Consider two firms competing in a Cournot industry. One firm—Roomkin Enterprises—is contemplating an investment in a new production technology. This new technology will result in efficiencies that will lower its variable costs of production. Roomkin's competitor, Adams, Co., does not have the resources to undertake a similar investment. Roomkin's corporate financial planning staff has studied the proposed investment and reports that *at current output levels*, the present value of the cost savings from the investment is less than the cost of the project, but just barely so. Now, suppose that Roomkin Enterprises hires you as a consultant. You point out that a complete analysis would take into account the effect of investment on the market equilibrium between the Roomkin Enterprises and Adams Co. What would this more complete analysis say about the desirability of this investment?

10. The chapter discussed a situation in which a Cournot competitor would refrain from entering a geographically distinct market for its product, even though it would have a monopoly in that market. Under what circumstances would this incentive be reversed?

11. This question refers to information in question 10 in Chapter 7.

   Chuckie B Corp. is considering implementing a proprietary technology they have developed. The onetime sunk cost of implementing this process is $350. Once this investment is made, marginal cost will be reduced to $25. Gene Gene has no access to this, or any other cost-saving technology, and its marginal cost will remain at $40. Chuckie B's financial consultant observes that the investment should not be made, because a cost reduction of $15 on each of the 20 machines results in a savings of only $300, which is less than the cost of implementing the technology. Is the consultant's analysis accurate? Why or why not? Compute the strategic effect of the investment.

THE DYNAMICS
OF PRICING RIVALRY

9

For many years, two companies dominated the morning and afternoon newspaper markets in Sydney, Australia: John Fairfax and Sons, which published the *Sydney Morning Herald* in the morning and the *Sun* in the afternoon; and Rupert Murdoch's News Limited, which published the *Daily Telegraph* in the morning and the *Daily Mirror* in the afternoon.[1] The morning market was clearly segmented; the *Morning Herald* appealed to a more affluent readership than the *Daily Telegraph*. By contrast, the newspapers in the afternoon market competed for the same readers and were close substitutes for one another.

Throughout much of the post-World War II period, prices in the afternoon market moved in lockstep. Seven price increases occurred between 1941 and January 1974. In four of these cases, the price increase was announced by the *Sun* (acknowledged to be the price leader in the afternoon market) and was matched within days by the *Daily Mirror*. In the other three instances papers gave simultaneous notice of the price increase. In the morning market, by contrast, a price increase by one paper would often go unmatched by the other for 9 or 10 months.

But pricing behavior in the afternoon market changed in 1975. In July of that year, Fairfax increased the price of the *Sun* from 10 cents to 12 cents. Breaking with more than 30 years of tradition, Murdoch chose to keep the price of the *Daily Mirror* at 10 cents. The price war waged by Murdoch's paper lasted for three and a half years. During this time, the *Daily Mirror*'s share of the afternoon market, which had been virtually 50 percent when its price was equal to the *Sun*'s, rose to slightly over 53 percent. This allowed the *Daily Mirror* to increase its advertising revenues relative to the *Sun*. William Merrilees estimates that by underpricing the *Sun*, the *Daily Mirror* increased its annual profit by nearly $1.6 million, while the

---

[1] This example is based on Merrilees, W., "Anatomy of a Price Leadership Challenge: An Evaluation of Pricing Strategies in the Australian Newspaper Industry," *Journal of Industrial Economics*, XXXI, March 1983: pp. 291–311.

Sun's annual profit fell by approximately $1.3 million.[2] In January 1979, Fairfax finally surrendered, dropping its price back down to 10 cents. Henceforth, Murdoch's *Daily Mirror* was the price leader in Sydney's afternoon paper market.

This example raises issues about the dynamics of rivalry within a market. What conditions influence the intensity of price competition in a market? Why do firms in some markets seem to be able to coordinate their pricing behavior to avoid costly price wars, while in other markets intense price competition is the norm? Why do price wars erupt in previously tranquil markets? What is the value, if any, of policies under which the firm commits to matching the prices its competitors charge? When should a firm match its rival price, and when should it go its own way? These are some of the questions we consider in Chapter 9.

This chapter builds on Chapter 7 by introducing a set of models and analytical frameworks that can help us understand why firms compete as they do. To add realism to the analysis, we view price competition as a dynamic process, that is, one that unfolds over time. This implies that a firm's decisions made at one point in time affect how competitors, and indeed the firm itself, will behave in the future. For example, Fairfax not responding to Murdoch's decision to underprice the *Sun* made Murdoch's decision profitable. However, had Murdoch anticipated that Fairfax would have reverted to the 10-cent price quickly after it became clear that he was not going to increase the price of the *Mirror*, he might have been better off following Fairfax's lead. This suggests that Fairfax should have clearly communicated that it would match whatever price Murdoch's paper charged in the previous week, a policy known as tit-for-tat pricing.

This chapter also discusses nonprice competition, focusing in particular on competition with respect to product quality. In this part of the chapter, we explore how market structure influences a firm's incentives to choose its product quality how consumer information shapes the nature of competition with respect to quality.

◆ ◆ ◆ ◆ ◆ DYNAMIC PRICING RIVALRY

In real-world markets firms that compete with one another do so over time, again and again. This implies that competitive moves that might have short-run benefits may, in the longer run, hurt the firm once its competitors have had time to make countermoves of their own. For example, a firm that cuts its price today to steal business from rivals may find that they retaliate with their own price cuts in the future, thus nullifying the business-stealing "benefits" of the original price cut. This section develops a theory of rivalry when firms meet repeatedly over time. The next section uses these theories to illuminate the link between market structure and the intensity of price competition.

Why the Cournot and Bertrand Models Are Not Dynamic

The reader might wonder whether dynamic elements of competition haven't already been included within the context of the Cournot and Bertrand models. After all, in Chapter 7, we described the process of attaining a Cournot or Bertrand equilibrium as if it came out of a sequence of reactions and counterreactions by

---

[2]Ibid., p. 304.

each firm to its rivals' decisions. For example, in a simple Cournot industry with two firms, Firm 1 and Firm 2, the process of achieving an equilibrium is described as follows: Firm 2 makes an output decision; Firm 1 then reacts to the quantity chosen by Firm 2 by selecting the quantity along its reaction function that is associated with the quantity chosen by Firm 2 (see Figure 9.1). Firm 2 then reacts to the quantity chosen by Firm 1 by choosing the quantity along its reaction function corresponding to Firm 1's choice. This process unfolds until the equilibrium is reached.

However, this depiction of Cournot competition (and analogous depictions of Bertrand competition) is, strictly speaking, not correct. In truth, both models are static rather than dynamic. They are static because in each model all firms simultaneously make once-and-for-all quantity or price choices. The reaction–counterreaction story is only a convenient fable that reinforces the notion that a Cournot (or Bertrand) equilibrium is a point of "stability": No firm has an incentive to deviate from its equilibrium quantity (or price), given that it expects that its rivals will also choose their equilibrium quantities (or prices).

To see the inadequacy of the "dynamic" depiction of the Cournot model in Figure 9.1, note that each time a firm chooses its quantity, it bases that decision on what its rival did in its previous move. Moreover, its "reaction" is the choice that maximizes its current (i.e., single-period) profit. But presumably an intelligent firm would take the long view and choose its quantity to maximize the present value of profits over its entire time horizon. To do this, it must anticipate what its rival will do in the future, not just naively react to what it has done in the past. Figure 9.1 reveals the limitations of naively reacting to the rival firm's previous output choice. Unless the two firms are at the equilibrium point, as Firm 1 reacts to Firm 2 and Firm 2 reacts to Firm 1, what either firm did in the past is an unreliable guide to what each will do in the future.

This discussion does not imply that the Cournot or Bertrand models are wrong or useless. Both models reduce a complicated phenomenon—industry ri-

---

FIGURE 9.1
CONVERGENCE TO A COURNOT EQUILIBRIUM.

This figure shows the "story" that is sometimes told about how firms reach a Cournot equilibrium. Suppose in an initial period Firm 1 produces q_1^0. Firm 2 then reacts in the next period by producing q_2^1. Firm 1 would then react to this choice by producing q_1^1. Firm 2 would react to this choice by producing q_2^2, which would then induce Firm 1 to produce q_1^2. As the arrows show, this process of reaction and counterreaction will eventually converge to the Cournot equilibrium, q_1^* and q_2^*.

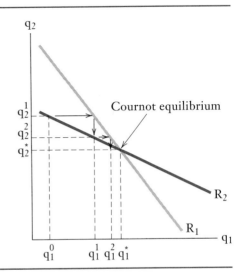

valry—to an analytically convenient form that helps answer such questions as "What impact does the number of firms have on the prevailing level of prices in the market?" or "What would be expected to happen to prices in an oligopolistic market as demand shifts outward?" These models are also useful—as Chapter 8 emphasized—for examining the interplay between strategic commitments of various kinds and tactical maneuvering. However, neither the Cournot and Bertrand models can fully explain why in certain highly concentrated oligopolies (e.g., the U.S. steel industry until the late 1960s or the U.S. cigarette industry until the early 1990s), firms can maintain prices above competitive levels without formal collusion and why in other comparably concentrated markets (e.g., regional cement markets), price competition is often fierce. Dynamic models of price competition are more useful for exploring such questions.

Dynamic Pricing Rivalry: Intuition

The starting point for our analysis is the premise that, all else equal, firms would prefer prices to be closer to their monopoly levels than to the levels reached under Bertrand or Cournot competition. For example, Figure 9.2 depicts the demand and cost conditions in the world market for a commodity chemical. Imagine that the market consists of two firms, Shell Chemical and Exxon Chemical. This is a mature business in which demand is stable (i.e., neither growing nor shrinking) and both firms have access to the same technology and factors of production and thus have equal marginal and average costs. We assume that marginal cost is constant at $20 per hundred pounds over the entire range of possible output levels. Buyers regard each firm's product as a perfect substitute for the other's, so consumers choose solely on the basis of price.

By colluding the two competitors could charge the monopoly price, which is $60 per hundred pounds, and together they would produce 40 million pounds of the chemical per year. How they divide this market cannot be deduced from monopoly theory, but given that the firms are identical, we can assume that they will split the market 50:50. If so, the monopoly outcome would give each firm an an-

FIGURE 9.2
MONOPOLY PRICE AND QUANTITY.

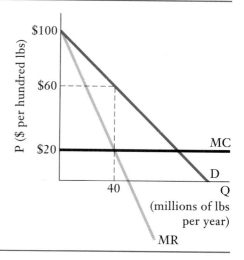

With the market demand curve shown in the figure and a constant marginal cost of $20, the monopoly quantity is 40 million pounds per year, and the monopoly price is $60 per pound.

nual profit of $8 million. By contrast, if the two firms were to compete as Bertrand competitors, they would charge $20, and their annual profit would be zero.[3]

Shell and Exxon could avoid the Bertrand result by colluding formally, that is, by discussing and jointly making their pricing decisions. This would be illegal in many countries. In the United States, for example, explicit price collusion is a felony. To emphasize that we are not focusing on formal collusion, we use the term *cooperative pricing* to refer to situations in which firms can sustain prices in excess of those that would arise in a noncooperative single-shot price or quantity-setting game, such as Cournot or Bertrand.

Is cooperative pricing achievable when firms make pricing decisions noncooperatively? Put another way, are there conditions under which a firm might not wish to undercut its rivals, either by lowering its price relative to theirs or refusing to go along when they increase their prices? Under those conditions, cooperative pricing is feasible. Without those conditions, cooperative pricing is difficult to achieve. In the remainder of this section, we describe the benefits and costs confronting a firm that contemplates undercutting the prices of its competitors. In the following section, we identify market conditions that affect these benefits and costs.

A firm that contemplates undercutting its rivals confronts a tradeoff. It stands to reap a short-term increase in profits if the price reduction translates into an increase in market share. It might also enjoy a long-term increase in profit if, once pricing stability is restored to the market, it experiences a permanent increase in market share. On the other hand, the firm's rivals might respond by lowering their own prices. Once they do, the firm that initiated the price reduction could end up with no increase in market share, but with lower price-cost margins.

The economist Edward Chamberlin identified these forces when he argued that sellers in concentrated markets would recognize that the profit they gain from cutting price below the monopoly level is likely to be fleeting:

> If each seeks his maximum profit rationally and intelligently, he will realize that when there are two or only a few sellers his own move has a considerable effect upon his competitors, and that this makes it idle to suppose that they will accept without retaliation the losses he forces upon them. Since the result of a cut by any one is inevitably to decrease his own profits, no one will cut, and although the sellers are entirely independent, the equilibrium result is the same as though there were a monopolistic agreement between them.[4]

Competitor Responses and Tit-for-Tat Pricing

To understand how Chamberlin's argument works in our example, suppose that Shell and Exxon are currently charging a price somewhere between the Bertrand price of $20 and the monopoly price of $60, say $40 per hundred pounds. Suppose that Shell has recently suffered setbacks in its other markets and is considering raising its price to the monopoly level of $60.

You might think that it would be foolish for Shell to raise its price to $60 without having enlisted Exxon's agreement to follow suit. After all, if Shell raises its price, but Exxon does not, Exxon will capture 100 percent of the market. At a price of $40, Exxon's profits will increase to $12 million per year, which exceeds

---

[3]If the firms competed as Cournot competitors, prices and profits would be $46.67 and $711.11 million, respectively.

[4]Chamberlin, E. H., *Monopolistic Competition.* Cambridge, MA: Harvard University Press, 1933, p. 48.

the $8 million annual profit Exxon would get if it follows Shell's lead and raises its price to the monopoly level. Thus, Shell and Exxon face a prisoners' dilemma similar to that described in the Economics Primer: Although it is in the collective interest of both firms to charge the monopoly price, Exxon is better off undercutting Shell's price if Shell raises its price to the monopoly level.

But now suppose that prices can be changed every week, so that if Shell can rescind its price increase, it can do so without waiting more than a week. Further, suppose that Shell can observe Exxon's pricing decision immediately, so Shell will know at once whether Exxon has followed its price increase.

Under these conditions, Shell's decision to raise price carries little risk. If Exxon refuses to follow, Shell can drop its price back to $40 after one week. At most, Shell sacrifices one week's profit at current prices (roughly $115,400 or $.1154 million).

Not only is the risk to Shell low from raising its price, but if Shell puts itself in Exxon's position, it would see that Exxon has a compelling motive to follow Shell's price increase. To see why, suppose that both firms use a 10 percent annual rate to discount future profits. On a weekly basis, this corresponds roughly to a discount rate of .2 percent (i.e., .002).[5] Shell reasons as follows:

- *If Exxon sticks with the current price of $40, we will learn this quickly, so Exxon should anticipate that we will drop our price back down to $40 after the first week if it does not follow. By keeping its price at $40, Exxon will get a one-week "bump" in profit from $.1154 million to $.2307 million per week ($.2307 = 12 million/52). However, after we rescind our price increase, Exxon's weekly profit would go back to $.1154 million. The discounted present value of Exxon's weekly profit (expressed in millions of dollars) under this scenario would be*

$$.2308 + .1154/(1.002) + .1154/(1.002)^2 + .1154/(1.002)^3 + \ldots,$$

  which equals $57.93 million.[6]

- *If Exxon follows us and raises its price to $60, we each will earn annual profits of $8 million, which translates into a weekly profit of $153,846 or $.1538 million. By following our price increase, the discounted value of Exxon's weekly profit is*

$$.1538 + .1538/(1.002) + .1538/(1.002)^2 + .1538/(1.002)^3 + \ldots,$$

  which equals $77.05 million. Clearly, Exxon is better off following our lead, even though for the first week it would be better off if it refused to raise its price to $60.

Because Exxon has much to gain by matching Shell's price, and Shell loses little if Exxon does not match, it makes sense for Shell to raise its price to $60. If Exxon behaves rationally, then it will behave the way Shell expects it to behave (as described by the preceding reasoning), and Exxon will match Shell's price increase. The outcome thus corresponds to the monopoly outcome even though neither firm colludes with each other. A simple calculation reveals that the monopoly price is sustainable as long as Exxon's weekly discount rate is less than 50 percent, which corresponds to an annual discount rate of 2,600 percent!

---

[5]The weekly discount rate is the annual discount rate divided by 52. Thus, .10/52 = .002.

[6]This calculation easily follows by using the formula for the present value of an annuity, which is discussed in the appendix to the Economics Primer. Specifically, for any amount C and discount rate i, $C/(1 + i) + C/(1 + i)^2 + \ldots = C/i$. Thus, the preceding calculation simplifies to .2308 + .1154/.002 = 57.93.

Shell would be even more confident that Exxon would match its price increase if Shell also announced to Exxon that starting next week, its price in any given week would match the price that Exxon charged in the preceding week. This *tit-for-tat strategy* is akin to a commitment by Shell to its customers that "We will not be undersold." If Shell signals to Exxon that it is following a tit-for-tat strategy, and if Exxon does not match Shell's increase to $60, then Exxon knows that Shell will drop its price back down to the original level of $40 after the first week. As it figures out its best reply, Exxon will thus go through exactly the same reasoning described earlier and will find it worthwhile to match Shell's price of $60.

By following a policy of tit-for-tat, Fairfax & Sons might have avoided the costly price war described in the introduction to this chapter. Once it became clear that Murdoch's *Daily Mirror* was not going to raise its price to 12 cents, Fairfax would have dropped its price back down to 10 cents. Had Murdoch's paper anticipated this behavior by Fairfax, it would have had a powerful incentive to match Fairfax's price.

Tit-for-Tat Pricing with Many Firms

It is straightforward to extend the logic of the Shell-Exxon example to an arbitrary number of firms and to pricing periods of arbitrary lengths (e.g., one month, one quarter, or one year). To do so, let π_0 be the per-period industry profit at the prevailing price P_0, and let π_M be the industry's profit when all firms charge the monopoly price, P_M. The industry as a whole would be better off at the monopoly price than at the prevailing price P_0, so $\pi_0 < \pi_M$. However, as in the Shell-Exxon example, imagine that each of the N firms in this industry faces a prisoner's dilemma. If an individual firm expects its competitors to raise their prices to the monopoly level, that firm gets a larger profit by sticking at P_0 (thereby undercutting its competitors and capturing the entire market at the prevailing price P_0) than it would get if it matched the price increase and captured 1/Nth of the monopoly profit. A firm's one-period profit gain from refusing to cooperate with an industry-wide move to the monopoly price is thus $\pi_0 - (1/N)\pi_M$.

Suppose that the firms compete with each other over an infinite horizon (i.e., period after period, without end), and that each firm discounts future profits using a discount rate of i per period. (In the Shell-Exxon example, where a period was a week, $i = .002$.) If each firm believes that its competitors will raise the price from P_0 to P_M in the current period and thereafter will follow a tit-for-tat strategy, then each firm will find it in its self-interest to charge the monopoly price as long as[7]

$$\frac{\frac{1}{N}[\pi_M - \pi_0]}{\pi_0 - \frac{1}{N}\pi_M} \geq i \tag{9.1}$$

---

[7]To derive equation (9.1), we used the same logic we used in the Shell-Exxon example. We first derived the present value of a firm's profit if, like its competitors, it raised its price to the monopoly level. In this case, the firm gets a per-period profit of $(1/N)\pi_M$ in all periods, and the present value of that profit stream is $(1/N)(\pi_M + \pi_M/i)$. We then derived the present value of the firm's profit if it kept its price at the current level. Under this scenario, the firm enjoys a one-period increase in its profit to π_0, but in all periods thereafter, its profit equals $(1/N)\pi_0$, as the firm's competitors follow their tit-for-tat strategies and match the firm's first-period price P_0. The present value of the profit stream in this latter scenario is thus $\pi_0 + (1/N)\pi_0/i$. To derive equation (9.1), we subtracted the two present value expressions and used algebra to rearrange the resulting equation.

If the condition in (9.1) holds, each firm will independently (i.e., without collusion) raise price to the monopoly level. Though formidable looking, this condition has a straightforward interpretation and—as we will discuss later— some powerful implications. The left-hand side of the inequality is a benefit–cost ratio. The numerator of this ratio is the single-period benefit to an individual firm from cooperating; it represents the difference in an individual firm's per-period profit when all firms set the monopoly price as opposed to P_0. The denominator is the extra profit the firm could have earned in the current period if it had refused to cooperate. This foregone profit is the cost of cooperation. The inequality in (9.1) states that cooperative pricing will be sustainable when this benefit–cost ratio exceeds the threshold level on the left side of the inequality. This threshold is equal to the per-period discount rate, i. For example, if $N = 5$, $\Pi_M = \$100,000$ per month and $\Pi_0 = \$40,000$ per month, then the benefit–cost ratio is

$$\frac{\frac{1}{5}[100,000 - 40,000]}{40,000 - \frac{1}{5}(100,000)} = \frac{12,000}{20,000} = .60$$

If the pricing period is one month long, this calculation implies that as long as the monthly discount rate is below 60 percent (or an annual rate below 720 percent), each firm has an incentive to independently raise price to the monopoly level.

XAMPLE 9.1

WHAT HAPPENS WHEN A FIRM RETALIATES QUICKLY TO A PRICE CUT: PHILIP MORRIS VERSUS B.A.T IN COSTA RICA[8]

We have seen that the tit-for-tat strategy encourages firms to raise prices toward the monopoly level. Tit-for-tat also discourages firms from cutting price to steal business from competitors. If a firm expects that its competitors will quickly reduce their prices when it cuts its price, the firm will perceive the gains from price cutting to be transitory. The firm will anticipate that the principal effect of lower prices will be lower price-cost margins with little or no change in market shares, and as a result, the firm will have no incentive to cut price.

An excellent illustration of what can happen when one firm cuts its price and its competitor immediately matches the cut occurred in the cigarette industry in Costa Rica in 1993. The most famous cigarette price war of 1993 occurred in the United States, when Philip Morris initiated its "Marlboro Friday" price cuts.[9] The lesser-known Costa Rican price war, also initiated by Philip Morris, began several months before and lasted one year longer than the Marlboro Friday price

---

[8]We would like to thank Andrew Cherry for developing this example.

[9]See Example 9.4 for a description of events leading up to Marlboro Friday.

war. From Philip Morris' perspective, its outcome was different from the price war in the United States.

At the beginning of the 1990s, two firms dominated the Costa Rican cigarette market: Philip Morris, with 30 percent of the market, and B.A.T, with 70 percent of the market. The market consisted of three segments: premium, mid-priced, and value-for-money or VFM. Philip Morris had the leading brands in the premium and mid-priced segments (Marlboro and Derby, respectively). B.A.T, by contrast, dominated the VFM segment with its Delta brand.

Throughout the 1980s, a prosperous Costa Rican economy fueled steady growth in the demand for cigarettes. Both B.A.T and Philip Morris were, as a result, able to sustain price increases that exceeded the rate of inflation. By 1989, industry price-cost margins exceeded 50 percent. However, in the late 1980s, the market began to change. Health concerns slowed the demand for cigarettes in Costa Rica, a trend that hit the premium and mid-priced segments much harder than it did the VFM segment. In 1992, B.A.T gained market share from Philip Morris for the first time since the early 1980s. Philip Morris faced the prospect of slow demand growth and a declining market share.

On Saturday, January 16, 1993, Philip Morris reduced the prices of Marlboro and Derby cigarettes by 40 percent. The timing of the price reduction was not by chance. Philip Morris reasoned that B.A.T's inventories would be low following the year-end holidays, and that B.A.T would not have sufficient product to satisfy an immediate increase in demand should it match or undercut Philip Morris' price cut. Philip Morris also initiated its price cut on a Saturday morning, expecting that B.A.T's local management would be unable to respond without first undertaking lengthy consultations with the home office in London.

However, B.A.T surprised Philip Morris with the speed of its response. B.A.T cut the price of its Delta brand by 50 percent, a price that industry observers estimated barely exceeded Delta's marginal cost. Having been alerted to Morris' move on Saturday morning, B.A.T had salespeople out selling at the new price by Saturday afternoon.

The ensuing price war lasted two years. Cigarette sales increased 17 percent as a result of the lower prices, but market shares did not change much. By the time the war ended in 1994, Philip Morris' share of the Costa Rican market was unchanged, and it was U.S. $8 million worse off than it was before the war had started. B.A.T lost even more—U.S. $20 million—but it had preserved the market share of its Delta brand and was able to maintain the same price gaps that had prevailed across segments before the war.

Why did Philip Morris act as it did? In the early 1990s, Philip Morris had increased Marlboro's market share at B.A.T's expense in other Central American countries, such as Guatamala. Perhaps it expected that it could replicate that success in Costa Rica. Still, had it anticipated B.A.T's quick response, Philip Morris should have realized that its price cut would not gain it market share. Whatever the motivation for Philip Morris' actions, this example highlights how quick retaliation by competitors can nullify the advantages of a price cut. If firms understand that and take the long view, the anticipated punishment meted out by a tit-for-tat pricing strategy can deter using price as a competitive weapon.

The "Folk Theorem"

The benefit–cost condition in (9.1) implies that if each firm is reasonably patient (i.e., if the discount rate i is not too large), then the cooperative outcome will be sustainable. This result is a special case of what game theorists have referred to as the *folk theorem* for infinitely-repeated prisoner dilemma games.[10] The folk theorem says that for sufficiently low discount rates, any price between the monopoly price P_M and marginal cost can be sustained as an equilibrium in the infinitely repeated prisoners' dilemma game being studied here.[11] Of course, strategies other than tit-for-tat would be necessary to generate these other equilibria. For example, one equilibrium would be for each firm to set a price equal to marginal cost in each period. Given that it expects its competitors to behave this way, a firm can do no better than to behave this way as well.

Coordinating on an Equilibrium

The folk theorem implies that cooperative pricing behavior is a possible equilibrium in an oligopolistic industry. There can be many other equilibria, however, and thus there is no guarantee that cooperative pricing will emerge. Achieving a particular equilibrium in a game with many equilibria, some potentially more attractive than others, is a *coordination problem*. To attain the cooperative outcome, firms in the industry must coordinate on a strategy, such as tit-for-tat, which makes it in each firm's self-interest to refrain from aggressive price cutting.

An obvious—and in most countries, illegal—way to solve this coordination problem is through a collusive agreement. Achieving coordination without an agreement or overt communication is far more difficult. Somehow, each firm in the industry must adopt a strategy, such as tit-for-tat, that moves the industry toward cooperative pricing. In short, the cooperation-inducing strategy must be a *focal point*—a strategy so compelling that a firm would to expect all other firms to adopt it.

Theories of how focal points emerge in economic or social interactions are not well-developed.[12] Focal points are highly context- or situation-specific. For example, consider a game called "Divide the Cities" concocted by David Kreps, a professor at the Stanford Graduate School of Business.[13]

> The following is a list of eleven cities in the United States: Atlanta, Boston, Chicago, Dallas, Denver, Houston, Los Angeles, New York, Philadelphia, San Francisco, and Seattle. I have assigned to each city a point value from 1 to 100 according to the city's importance and its "quality of life." You will not be told this scale until the game is over, except that I tell you now that New York has the highest score, 100, and Seattle has the

---

[10]The term *folk theorem* is used because, like a folk song, it existed in the oral tradition of economics long before anyone got credit for proving it formally.

[11]The multiplicity of potential equilibrium outcomes raises important issues in contexts other than oligopoly pricing. We will study one such application in Chapter 17 when discussing power and corporate culture.

[12]The best work on this subject remains Thomas Schelling's *The Strategy of Conflict*, Cambridge, MA: Harvard, 1960.

[13]Kreps, D. M., *A Course in Microeconomic Theory*, Princeton, NJ: Princeton University Press, 1990, pp. 392–393.

least, 1. I do think you will find my scale is fair. I am going to have you play the following game against a randomly selected student of the Harvard Graduate School of Business. Each of you will be asked to list, simultaneously and without consultation, some subset of these eleven cities. Your list must contain San Francisco and your opponent's must contain Boston. Then, I will give you $100 simply for playing the game. And I will add to/subtract from that amount as follows: For every city that appears on one list but not the other, the person who lists the city will get as many dollars as that city has points on my scale. For every city that appears on both lists, I will take from each of you twice as many dollars as the city has points. Finally, if the two of you manage to partition the cities, I will triple your winnings. Which cities will you list?

There are hundreds of possible outcomes to this game. Yet, when the game is played by American students, the outcome is nearly always the same: The Stanford student's list is Dallas, Denver, Houston, Los Angeles, Seattle, and San Francisco. The focal point is an East–West division of the United States, coupled with some elementary equity considerations to deal with the fact that there is an odd number (11) of cities to be divided. (Since Seattle is the lowest-valued city, students generally let the western list contain the extra city.) Kreps notes that the focal point of East–West geography becomes less focal when one of the students playing the game is from outside the United States. The U.S. student then often has concerns about the non-U.S. student's knowledge of geography. The game also loses its focal point when the list of cities has a less natural division, for example, if it contained eight western cities and only four eastern ones.

Coordination is likely to be especially difficult in competitive environments that are turbulent and rapidly changing. It can sometimes be facilitated by traditions and conventions that stabilize the competitive environment, that is, by making competitors' moves easier to follow or their intentions easier to interpret. For example, many industries have standard cycles for adjusting prices. Until the early 1990s, in the U.S. cigarette industry, June and December were the traditional dates for Philip Morris and RJR to announce price changes. The tacit understanding that prices will not be changed except on the traditional dates reduces suspicions that competitors may be cutting prices, making it easier for firms to coordinate on prices at or close to the monopoly level. The practice of quoting prices in terms of standard price points or increments may also create pricing focal points. For example, in the turbine generator industry in the United States in the 1960s, the two sellers, GE and Westinghouse, employed a single multiplier to determine discounts off the list price. This reduced a complicated pricing decision to a single, easy to understand number.[14]

Why Is Tit-for-Tat so Compelling?

Tit-for-tat is not the only strategy that allows firms to sustain monopoly pricing as a noncooperative equilibrium. Another strategy that, like tit-for-tat, results in the monopoly price for sufficiently low discount rates is the "grim trigger" strategy:

Starting this period, we will charge the monopoly price P_M. In each subsequent period, if any firm deviates from P_M, we will drop our price to marginal cost in the next period and keep it there forever.

---

[14]Various other "facilitating practices," such as price leadership or advance notice of price changes, are discussed below.

The grim trigger strategy relies on the threat of an infinite price war to keep firms from undercutting their competitors' prices. In light of other potentially effective strategies, such as grim trigger, why would we necessarily expect firms to adopt a tit-for-tat strategy?[15] One reason is that tit-for-tat is a simple, easy to describe, and easy to understand strategy. Through announcements, such as "We will not be undersold" or "We will match our competitors' prices, no matter how low," a firm can easily signal to its rivals that it is following tit-for-tat.

Tit-for-tat is also a robust strategy, in that a firm that adopts it will probably do well over the long run against a variety of different strategies. A compelling illustration of tit-for-tat's robustness is discussed by Robert Axelrod in his book *The Evolution of Cooperation*.[16] Axelrod conducted a computer tournament in which scholars were invited to submit strategies for playing a (finitely) repeated prisoners' dilemma game. Each of the submitted strategies was pitted against every other, and the winner was the strategy that accumulated the highest overall score of all of its "matches." Even though tit-for-tat can never beat another strategy in one-on-one competition (at best it can tie another strategy), it accumulated the highest overall score across all its matches. It was able to do so, according to Axelrod, because it combines the properties of "niceness," "provocability," and "forgiveness." It is nice in that it is never the first to defect from the cooperative outcome. It is provocable in that it immediately punishes a rival that defects from the cooperative outcome by matching the rival's defection in the next period. It is forgiving in that if the rival returns to the cooperative strategy, tit-for-tat will too.

Misreads

Despite the robustness of tit-for-tat against a wide range of strategies, it is not clear that tit-for-tat is forgiving enough that a firm can misread its competitors' pricing moves. By "misread," we mean that either: (1) a firm mistakenly believes a competitor is charging one price when it is really charging another, or (2) a firm misunderstands the reasons for a competitor's pricing decision.

Consider what might happen when two firms are playing tit-for-tat, and a cooperative move is misread as an uncooperative one. The firm that misreads the cooperative move as an uncooperative one responds by making an uncooperative move in the next period. That firm's competitor then responds in kind in the period after that. A single misreading leads to a pattern in which firms alternate between cooperative and uncooperative moves over time. If, in the midst of this dynamic, another cooperative move is misread as an uncooperative one, the resulting pattern becomes even worse: Firms become stuck in a cycle of choosing uncooperative moves each period.

Avinash Dixit and Barry Nalebuff have argued that when misreads are possible, pricing strategies that are less provocable and more forgiving than tit-for-tat are desirable.[17] It may be, they argue, desirable to ignore what appears to be an uncooperative move by one's competitor if the competitor then reverts to coopera-

---

[15]The following discussion is based on Satterwaite, M., "Pricing in Oligopolies: The Importance of the Long-Run," Northwestern University unpublished manuscript, 1988.

[16]Axelrod, R., *The Evolution of Cooperation*, New York: Basic Books, 1984.

[17]Dixit, A. and B. Nalebuff, *Thinking Strategically: The Competitive Edge in Business, Politics, and Everyday Life*, New York: Norton, 1991.

tive behavior in the next period. Forgiving pricing strategies can be especially desirable when rival firms may misread or misunderstand each others' competitive moves. McKinsey consultants Robert Garda and Michael Marn suggest that some real-world price wars are not prompted by deliberate attempts by one firm to steal business from its competitors. Instead, they stem from misreads and misunderstandings of competitors' behavior.[18]

To illustrate their point, Garda and Marn cite the example of a tire manufacturer that sold a particular tire at an invoice price of $35, but with an end-of-year volume bonus of $2 and a marketing allowance of $1.50, the manufacturer's net price was really $31.50.[19] This company received reports from its regional sales personnel that a rival firm was selling a competing tire at an invoice price of $32. In response, the manufacturer lowered its invoice price by $3, reducing its net price to $28.50. The manufacturer later learned that its competitor was not offering marketing allowances or volume discounts. By misreading its competitor's price and reacting immediately, the tire manufacturer precipitated a vicious price war that hurt both firms. Garda and Marn emphasize that to avoid overreacting to apparent price cuts by competitors, companies should carefully ascertain the details of the competitive initiative and figure out what is driving it before responding to it.

◆ ◆

XAMPLE 9.2

FORGIVENESS AND PROVOCABILITY: DOW CHEMICALS AND THE MARKET FOR REVERSE OSMOSIS MEMBRANE[20]

Achieving the right balance between provocability and forgiveness is important, but it can be difficult to do. Dow Chemicals learned this lesson in the mid-1990s in the market for reverse osmosis membranes, an expensive component used in environmental systems for waste water treatment and water purification. Dow sells this product to large industrial distributors that, in turn, resell it to end users.

Until 1989, Dow held a patent on its FilmTec membrane and had the U.S. market entirely to itself. In 1989, however, the U.S. government made Dow's patent public property on the grounds that the government had co-funded the development of the technology. Shortly thereafter, a Japanese firm entered the market with a "clone" of Dow's FilmTec membrane.

---

[18]Garda, R. A. and M. V. Marn, "Price Wars," *McKinsey Quarterly*, 3, 1993; pp. 87–100.

[19]A marketing allowance is a discount offered by a manufacturer in return for the retailer's agreement to feature the manufacturer's product in some way. Examples include advertising allowances to compensate for retail advertising or display allowances that are offered in exchange for superior shelf-space for the manufacturer's product or special displays.

[20]We would like to thank Sanjay Malkani, David Pereira, Robert Kennedy, Katarzyna Pitula, and Mitsunari Okamoto for developing this example.

In 1989, Dow's price was $1,400 per membrane. Over the next seven years, the Japanese competitor reduced its price to about $385 per unit. Dow, over this period, also reduced its price. With slight differentiation based on superior service support and perceived quality, Dow's price bottomed out at about $405 per unit.

During the downward price spiral, Dow alternated back and forth between forgiving and aggressive responses to its competitor's pricing moves as Dow sought to ascertain its rival's motives and persuade it to keep industry prices high. On three different occasions, Dow raised the price of its membrane. Its competitor never followed Dow's increases, and (consistent with tit-for-tat pricing) Dow ultimately rescinded its price increase each time.

During this period, Dow also attempted several strategic moves (in the spirit of Chapter 8) to insulate itself from price competition and soften the pricing behavior of its competitor. For example, Dow invested in product quality to improve the performance of its membranes. It also tried to remove distributors' focus on price by heavily advertising its membrane's superior performance features. These moves were only moderately successful, however, and Dow was unable to gain a price premium greater than 13 percent.

Eventually, Dow learned that its competitor manufactured its product in Mexico, giving it a cost advantage based on low-cost labor. It also learned that in 1991 the competitor had built a large plant and that its aggressive pricing moves were, in part, prompted by a desire to keep that plant operating at full capacity. Based on this information, Dow abandoned its efforts to soften price competition, either through forgiving pricing moves or strategic commitments aimed at changing the equilibrium in the pricing game. Dow's current strategy is to bypass industrial distributors and sell its product directly to end users. This move was motivated by Dow's learning that, despite the decreases in manufacturers' prices, distributors' prices to end users remained fairly constant. It is not clear that this strategy will help insulate Dow from price competition. Dow's competitor can presumably imitate this strategy and deal directly with end users as well. If it were to do so, it is hard to imagine pricing rivalry in this industry becoming less aggressive than it currently is.

◆ ◆ ◆ ◆ ◆ HOW MARKET STRUCTURE AFFECTS THE SUSTAINABILITY OF COOPERATIVE PRICING

Pricing cooperation is harder to achieve under some market structures than others, partly because under certain conditions, firms cannot coordinate on a focal equilibrium, and partly because market structure conditions systematically influence the benefit–cost ratio in equation (9.1). This section discusses market structure conditions that may facilitate or complicate the attainment of cooperative pricing and competitive stability. Specifically, we focus on:

- Market concentration

- Structural conditions that affect reaction speeds and detection lags

- Asymmetries among firms

Market Concentration and the Sustainability of Cooperative Pricing

The benefit–cost ratio in equation (9.1) goes up as the number of firms goes down. This implies that cooperative pricing is more likely to be an equilibrium in a concentrated market (few firms) than in a fragmented market (many firms). The insight that market concentration facilitates the sustainability of cooperative pricing is important for antitrust policy in the United States and the European Community. For example, in the United States, the Department of Justice and the Federal Trade Commission are unlikely to challenge mergers between two competitors when the postmerger market concentration exceeds certain thresholds.[21]

The intuition behind the relationship between concentration and the sustainability of cooperative pricing is straightforward. In a concentrated market, a typical firm's market share is larger than it would be in a fragmented market. Thus, a typical firm captures a large fraction of the overall benefit when industry-wide prices go up. Moreover, the temporary increase in profit the firm forsakes by not undercutting the rest of the market (i.e., the cost of cooperation) is smaller when the market is more concentrated. This is because a deviator gains from stealing business from rival firms. If the deviator has a large share of the market to begin with, the business it steals is smaller in proportion to the sales it gets if it goes along with the price than it would be if it was in a fragmented market with a small market share. Thus, the more concentrated the market, the larger the benefits from cooperation, and the smaller the costs of cooperation.

There is another sense in which high concentration facilitates cooperative pricing. As we just discussed, for firms to coordinate on tit-for-tat as a focal strategy, competitors must think alike. Although it is difficult to formalize this aspect theoretically, intuitively one expects that coordinating on a particular focal strategy is likely to be more difficult the more firms there are that compete against one another in the market. Established department stores have experienced this first-hand during the past two decades. For nearly a century, until the 1970s, they used simple rule-of-thumb pricing, such as setting prices equal to 200 percent of costs. As a result, they rarely worried about price competition. Entry by newcomers, such as TJ Maxx and Filene's Basement, has disrupted the cooperative pricing equilibrium. These entrants have gained market share by undercutting big department stores, which in turn have resorted to more frequent sales to compete effectively with these newcomers.

Reaction Speed, Detection Lags, and the Sustainability of Cooperative Pricing

The speed with which firms can react to their rivals' pricing moves also affects the sustainability of cooperative pricing. To see why, let's return to the benefit–cost condition in equation (9.1) and imagine initially that a "period" corresponds to one year. The profits in equation (9.1) would then be annual profit and the discount rate i would be an annual rate. If, by contrast, the pricing period were a quarter and sales were distributed uniformly through the year, all profits that go

---

[21]The thresholds in the 1992 merger guidelines are expressed in terms of changes in the Herfindahl index. See Chapter 7 for a discussion of this measure of market concentration.

into the benefit–cost ratio would be divided by 4, but the ratio itself would not change.[22] However, the threshhold on the right-hand side of equation (9.1) becomes a quarterly discount rate, which is the annual rate divided by 4. Thus, the benefit–cost condition becomes:

$$\frac{\frac{1}{N}[\pi_M - \pi_0]}{\pi_0 - \frac{1}{N}\pi_M} \geq \frac{i}{4} \tag{9.2}$$

The key difference between equations (9.1) and (9.2) is that the threshold above which it is optimal for a firm to follow the tit-for-tat strategy and raise its price to the monopoly level is now smaller. Holding the discount rate fixed, it then follows that an increase in the speed of reaction from one year to one quarter widens the set of circumstances in which the cooperative outcome is sustainable. If price cuts can be matched instantly, the effective discount rate goes to zero, and cooperative pricing will always be sustainable.

A firm may be unable to react quickly to its competitors' pricing moves because of (1) lags in detecting competitors' prices; (2) infrequent interactions with competitors (e.g., the firm competes against its rivals for business only a few times in a year); (3) ambiguities in identifying which firm among a group of firms in a market is cutting price; and (4) difficulties distinguishing drops in volume due to price cutting by rivals from drops in volume due to unanticipated decreases in market demand. All of these factors reduce the speed with which firms can respond to defections from cooperative pricing and thus also reduce the effectiveness of retaliatory price cuts aimed at punishing price-cutting firms.

Several structural conditions affect the importance of these factors:

- Lumpiness of orders

- Information about sales transactions

- The number and size of buyers

- Volatility of demand and cost conditions

We will discuss each in turn.

Lumpiness of Orders

Orders are lumpy when sales occur relatively infrequently in large batches as opposed to being smoothly distributed over the year. Lumpiness of orders is an important characteristic in such industries as airframe manufacturing, shipbuilding, and diesel locomotive production. Lumpy orders reduce the frequency of competitive interactions between firms. This makes price a more attractive competitive weapon for individual firms and intensifies price competition throughout the industry.

To illustrate the implications of lumpy orders, consider the problem faced by two manufacturers of automobile seats—Johnson Controls and Lear—that are

---

[22]For example, if $N = 5$, $\pi_M = 100,000$ per year and $\pi_0 = 40,000$ per year, the benefit–cost ratio with a period length of one year is $(1/5)(100,000 - 40,000)/(40,000 - (1/5)(100,000)) = .60$. If the period length is one quarter, then quarterly monopoly and current profit are 25,000 and 10,000, respectively. The benefit–cost ratio is then $(1/5)(25,000 - 10,000)/(10,000 - (1/5)(25,000))$, which also equals .60.

currently competing to supply seats for the new model of the Ford Taurus. The contract will apply for the life of the model, which is expected to be five years. Johnson Controls and Lear also compete for the seat contracts for other automobile models, but these are also multiyear contracts. Thus, at any one time, neither company is likely to have more than 30 contracts. This means that after competing for the Taurus contract, these companies may not face off against one another for the rest of the year. Orders in this industry are very lumpy.

Could Johnson Controls and Lear sustain cooperative pricing in this business? It would be difficult. Think about the problem from Johnson Control's perspective. The Taurus contract probably represents an important portion of its automotive seating business for the next half-decade, so securing the order is attractive. Moreover, even if Johnson Controls expected a tit-for-tat response from Lear on the next contract to come along, the relatively long lag between this contract and the next diminishes the perceived cost to Johnson Controls of such retaliation. From Johnson Control's perspective, the gain from undercutting Lear is likely to exceed the future costs. Lear is likely to think in much the same way, and if so, both companies will bid aggressively for the Taurus contract, and probably for most other contracts as well. This happens even though both companies would be collectively better off if they did not compete so aggressively on price. Although we have left out details, this describes how firms in the automobile seating business have actually competed for years.

Information About the Sales Transaction

When sales transactions are "public," deviations from cooperative pricing are easier to detect than when prices are secret. For example, a gasoline station can easily learn that a rival has cut its price because selling prices in this market are publicly posted. By contrast, in many industrial goods markets, prices are privately negotiated between buyers and sellers, so it may be difficult for a firm to learn whether a competitor has cut its price. Because retaliation can occur more quickly when prices are public than when they are secret, price cutting to steal market share from competitors is likely to be less attractive, enhancing the chances that cooperative pricing can be sustained.

Secrecy is a significant problem when transactions involve other dimensions besides a list or an invoice price, as they often do in business-to-business marketing settings. For example, a manufacturer of cookies, such as Keebler, that wants to steal business from a competitor, say Nabisco, can cut its "net price" by increasing trade allowances to retailers or by extending more favorable trade credit terms. Because it is often more difficult to monitor trade allowance deals or credit terms than list prices, competitors may find it difficult to detect business-stealing behavior, hindering their ability to retaliate. Business practices that facilitate secret price cutting create a prisoners' dilemma. Each firm individually prefers to use them, but the industry is collectively worse off when all firms do so.

Deviations from cooperative pricing are also difficult to detect when product attributes are customized to individual buyers, as in airframe manufacturing or the production of diesel locomotives, for example. When products are tailor-made to individual buyers, a seller may be able to increase its market share by altering the design of the product or by throwing in "extras," such as spare parts or a service agreement. These are typically more difficult to observe than the list price, complicating the ability of firms to monitor competitors' behavior.

Secret or complex transaction terms can intensify price competition not only because price matching becomes a less effective deterrent to price-cutting behavior, but also because misreadings become more likely. Firms are more likely to misinterpret a competitive move, such as a reduction in list prices, as an aggressive attempt to steal business, when they cannot fully observe all the other terms competitors are offering. When this happens, the odds of accidental price wars breaking out rise, as discussed earlier. To the extent that a firm's pricing behavior is forgiving, the effects of misreadings may be containable. Still, with secret and complex sales terms, even forgiving strategies may not work in environments where misreadings can occur.

The Number of Buyers

When firms normally set prices in secret, detecting deviations from cooperative pricing is easier when each firm sells to many small buyers than when each sells to a few large buyers. The reason for this is that a buyer that receives a price concession from one seller will often have an incentive to report the price cut to other sellers in an attempt to receive even more favorable concessions. This frequently occurs, for example, in the wholesale market for natural gas as industrial customers and buying groups shop around for supply contracts from various gas marketers, such as Enron and MidCon, that sell natural gas in bulk.

   The number of buyers can dramatically affect the likelihood that secret price cuts will be detected. Consider an industry in which buyers generally keep news of price cuts to themselves, so that if a seller offers a discount to a particular customer, there is only a 1 percent probability that rival sellers will learn about it. Suppose, now, that your firm, as part of an initiative to build its market share, offers "secret" discounts to attract 300 customers away from their current supplier. What is the probability that your competitors will learn about at least one of these price cuts? It equals one minus the probability that your rivals do not learn of *any* of the 300 price cuts, or $1 - (.99)^{300} = .951$, a surprisingly large probability. Thus, if there are enough buyers, chances are that your rivals will learn that you have cut your price to at least one of them, even when they have difficulty detecting that you have offered a price cut to any particular buyer. By contrast, if the number of buyers in your industry is small, and you offer discounts to just 10 customers, the probability that at least one of these discounts will get detected is just $1 - .99^{10} = .096$. Thus, price cuts are more difficult to detect in industries, such as diesel locomotives or automobile seat components, in which buyers are few. In such industries, the ability to make secret price cuts to which competitors cannot react makes price more attractive as a competitive weapon and can increase price competition.

Volatility of Demand Conditions

Price cutting is harder to detect when market demand conditions are volatile. Demand volatility is a particularly thorny problem when a firm can observe only its own price and volume and not those of its rival. If a firm's sales unexpectedly fall, is it because market demand has fallen or one of its competitors has cut price and is taking business from it?

   Demand volatility is an especially serious problem when much of a firm's costs are fixed. Then, marginal costs decline rapidly at output levels below capacity, and fluctuations in demand will ordinarily cause the monopoly price to fluctuate, too. By contrast, when costs are mainly variable, the marginal cost function will be nearly flat, and the monopoly price will not change as demand shifts back and forth. With high fixed costs and variable demand, the problem of coordinating on the monopoly equilibrium is severe because firms are chasing a moving target (the monopoly price). Moreover, at output levels even a little below capacity, marginal costs are likely to be low. Thus, during times of excess capacity, the temptation to cut price to steal business can be high.[23]

Asymmetries Among Firms

The theory on which equations (9.1) and (9.2) are based assumed that firms were identical. When firms are not identical, either because they have different costs or are vertically differentiated, achieving cooperative pricing becomes more difficult.

For one thing, when firms differ, the price a firm would charge if it were the monopolist depends on its marginal cost or product quality. When firms are identical, a single monopoly price can be a focal point. However, when firms differ, there is no single focal price, and it thus becomes more difficult for firms to coordinate their pricing strategies toward common objectives. Figure 9.3 depicts two firms with different marginal costs and shows that the firm with the lower marginal cost prefers a monopoly price lower than the one with the higher marginal cost.

Differences in costs, capacities, or product qualities also create asymmetric incentives for firms to agree to cooperative pricing, even when all firms can agree on the cooperative price. For example, small firms within a given industry often have more incentive to defect from cooperative pricing than larger firms. There are two related reasons for this. First, because industry profit rises when firms move toward the monopoly price and a large firm typically captures a larger share of industry profit than a smaller firm, a larger firm benefits more from the move toward cooperative pricing than a smaller firm does.

Second, small firms may also anticipate that large firms have weak incentives to punish a small firm that undercuts its price. To illustrate this point, consider the

FIGURE 9.3
MONOPOLY PRICES WITH ASYMMETRICAL FIRMS.

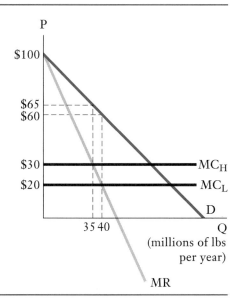

The low-cost firm's marginal cost curve is MC_L, while the high-cost firm's marginal cost curve is MC_H. If the low-cost firm was a monopolist, it would set a price of $60. If the high-cost firm was a monopolist, it would set a price of $65.

---

[23]See Scherer, F. M. and D. Ross, *Industrial Market Structure and Economic Performance*, New York: Houghton Mifflin, 1991, for an excellent graphical exposition of these points.

market for dot matrix printers in South Africa, a market that Epson dominated in the early 1990s.[24] Suppose that Panasonic recently entered this market (which it did in 1992) and offered a price 5 percent below that of Epson for printers of comparable quality. As a result, Panasonic captures a fraction α of demand that would have otherwise gone to Epson.[25] If Epson matches Panasonic's price cut, it regains its original demand.

Should Epson match? Suppose that Epson's price is Rand 1000 (the Rand is the South African unit of currency) per printer, its marginal cost is Rand 500, and its original level of demand is 1000 printers. If it matches Panasonic's price of Rand 950, Epson's profit is

$$(950 - 500)1000 = 450,000.$$

If it does not match, Epson's profit is

$$(1000 - 500)1000(1 - \alpha) = 500,000(1 - \alpha).$$

Not matching is optimal if the second expression is bigger than the first, which occurs if $\alpha < .10$ or if Epson expects to lose less than 10 percent of its business to Panasonic.

By allowing Panasonic to sell printers at a lower price than it charges, Epson would be extending a *price umbrella* to Panasonic. When should a firm do that and when should it match a price cut by a competitor or new entrant? If β represents the percentage price cut, and $PCM = (P - C)/P$ is the percentage contribution margin of the large firm, then a price umbrella is optimal when

$$\alpha < \frac{\beta}{PCM}$$

This inequality implies that a price umbrella strategy is desirable when

- β is large compared to α, that is, the price cut is relatively large, but the price cutter does not steal much market share from the larger firm.

- PCM is small, that is, margins in the industry are relatively small to begin with.

In the South African dot matrix printer market, neither of these conditions probably held. Margins for Epson's dot matrix printers were initially high. Moreover, the principal buyers of printers (wholesale distributors) were price sensitive, so the effect of Panasonic's price cuts on the demand for Epson printers was probably significant. Consistent with the predictions of theory, Epson refused to extend a price umbrella to Panasonic. However, as it turned out, Epson may have overreacted. It didn't just match Panasonic's price, it undercut it, which in turn prompted Panasonic to cut its price even more. Between 1992 and 1995, prices for dot matrix printers in South Africa spiraled downward, until they reached a point (about Rand 600) at which both companies were barely breaking even.

---

[24]We would like to thank Fuminori Takemura, Edward Arnstein, Tod Salzman, Rory Altman, and Masahiro Murakami for suggesting this example to us.

[25]Note that unlike the theory in the previous section, the undercutting firm does not steal the entire market of the high-price firm. One reason for this might be that the two firms are horizontally differentiated. For example, there may be consumers who, either because of idiosyncratic brand preferences or lack of good price information, will buy higher-priced Epson printers rather than low-priced Panasonic ones. Panasonic might also have limited capacity and cannot serve the entire market even though all consumers would prefer to buy its printers.

Smaller firms have an additional incentive to lower price on products for which buyers make repeat purchases. For such products, which include most consumer goods, consumers often purchase the same brand again and again. A small firm might lower price to induce some consumers to try its product. Once prices are restored to their initial levels, the small firm hopes that some of the consumers who sampled its product will become permanent customers. This strategy will only succeed if there is a lag between the small firm's price reduction and any response by its larger rivals. Otherwise, few if any new consumers will sample the small firm's product, and its market share will not increase.

◆ ◆

XAMPLE 9.3

FIRM ASYMMETRIES AND THE 1992 FARE WAR IN THE U.S. AIRLINE INDUSTRY[26]

When firms are different from each other—asymmetric—even the expectation that competitors will instantly match a price cut may not deter certain firms from cutting prices aggressively. Robert Gertner has argued that low-quality or low-market-share firms may make themselves better off by defecting from collusive prices even though they fully anticipate that their high-quality or high-market-share rivals will match their price cuts right away. To illustrate this argument, Gertner cites the example of Northwest Airlines.

In June 1992, Northwest Airlines triggered a fare war when it launched its promotion "Kids Fly Free." The next day, American Airlines cut coach fares on every route on which it competed with Northwest, and within hours, all major U.S. airlines had matched American's price cuts. The 1992 fare war was the most vicious price war to hit the U.S. airline industry since it was deregulated in 1978. It deepened the already record losses the airline industry was suffering in the wake of the recession that began with the Persian Gulf crisis in 1990.

It seems curious that Northwest would start a price war. After all, what did it have to gain? Airlines receive information about their competitors' fares instantaneously through a clearinghouse computer system run by the Airline Tariff Publishing Company (ATP). Northwest could hardly expect to cut fares without eliciting a competitive response. Moreover, throughout the spring of 1992, American Airlines had made it clear that it intended to defend its Value Pricing initiative that it had announced in April 1992. Indeed, earlier that spring when TWA had attempted to undercut American's fares, American quickly matched TWA's prices, by late May 1992, TWA had rescinded its price cuts. Given American's words and actions, Northwest should have known that American would match or undercut any major promotion that Northwest might announce.

But if Northwest expected that competitors would respond to its price cut, the theory we have just developed suggests that a price cut would not increase its profit: The fare cut would be matched instantly by American and Northwest's

[26]This discussion is based on Robert Gertner's Paper, "The Role of Firm Asymmetries for Tacit Collusion in Markets with Immediate Competitive Responses," working paper, University of Chicago, 1993.

other competitors. Relative market shares would not change, and with smaller margin and no increase in share, Northwest would be worse off than it would have been at higher fares. Because reduced margins are especially costly during the summer, when air travel peaks, the timing of Northwest's price cutting seems odd.

But these arguments overlook an important point: When firms are asymmetric, they will have different views about how high the price in the industry ought to be. Gertner notes that in the early 1990s, Northwest had a poor route system, an inferior frequent-flier program, and a reputation for poor service. If Northwest's principal competitors, American and United, charged the monopoly price along particular routes, and Northwest matched, Northwest would probably get less business than American and United, which had better route structures and better frequent-flier programs. Indeed, in spring 1992, suffering from excess capacity, Northwest's planes might have flown nearly empty had it matched American and United at the monopoly price.

Under these conditions, Northwest's best hope was probably to move the industry down the market demand curve through deep price cuts. Even though competitors would match these price cuts, the cuts might fit Northwest for two reasons. First, the price cuts took place during the summer, so much of the additional traffic that they would generate would consist of discretionary vacation travelers. Within this group, Northwest's competitive disadvantages were minimized because differences among airlines in terms of frequent-flier programs or on-time performance matter less to discretionary travelers' choice of carriers. Second, a disproportionate share of the additional traffic that generates the price cut will end up flying the poorer-quality airline, such as Northwest, simply because at equal prices, seats on the higher-quality carriers will sell out more quickly and cause a "spill" of traffic that only the less desirable carrier can serve. These two points explain why Northwest might have benefited from a price war and why it made sense to launch it during the summer. If Northwest could fill its planes only by stimulating market demand, its incentive was to do so when demand was most price elastic. This occurs during the summer when there are more price-elastic leisure travelers.

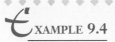

$\mathcal{E}$XAMPLE 9.4

PRICING DISCIPLINE IN THE U.S. CIGARETTE INDUSTRY[27]

An interesting example of a small undermining pricing discipline occurred in the U.S. cigarette industry in the 1980s and 1990s. As shown in Table 7.1, cigarettes are one of the most highly concentrated industries in the American economy,

[27]This example draws from "Strategic Analysis of the Marlboro Friday Price Cuts," a paper prepared by Kellogg Graduate School of Management students Diane Kitiyama, Jon Passman, Todd Reichmann, Craig Safir, and Philip Yau in March 1994. It also draws from "Tobacco Suit Exposes Ways Cigarette Firms Keep the Profits Fat," *Wall Street Journal*, March 5, 1990, pp. A1–A8.

with a four-firm concentration ratio of 93 percent in 1992 and a Herfindahl index of nearly .25. Throughout the first half of the twentieth century, the cigarette industry displayed remarkable pricing cooperation. Twice a year (generally in June and December) the dominant firms (which since the 1970s have been Philip Morris or RJR) would announce their intention to raise the list prices of their cigarettes, and within days the other cigarette manufacturers followed suit. Such pricing discipline helped the industry raise prices by 14 percent per year from 1980 through 1985, a rate far above inflation for the same period. The result was one of the most profitable businesses in the American economy, with operating profit margins (profit before interest and corporate income taxes divided by sales revenues) averaging close to 40 percent throughout the 1980s.

However, Liggett and Myers, the smallest of the six U.S. cigarette companies, did not benefit much from the industry's success in keeping prices high. Having misjudged the potential for filter cigarettes in the 1950s, Liggett saw its share of the cigarette market decline from 21 percent in 1947 to just over 2 percent by the late 1970s, when Liggett even contemplated shutting itself down.

As the smallest and least profitable of the big six cigarette producers, Liggett had the least to gain from raising prices in lockstep with its larger rivals, and it had the most to gain by undercutting their prices. When the grocery store cooperative Topco approached Liggett in 1980 with a plan to market and sell discount cigarettes at prices 30 percent below branded cigarettes, Liggett was receptive. The initial success of the discount cigarettes surprised even Liggett. By 1984, its share of overall cigarette sales had tripled, largely by virtue of its success in the discount cigarette business, which was responsible for 65 percent of Liggett's volume.

Liggett gambled that the discount market was a niche that its larger competitors would ignore. However, Liggett failed to anticipate how discount cigarettes would affect the demand for premium brands. For example, Brown and Williamson (B&W), the third largest domestic cigarette producer in the 1970s and 1980s, estimated that Liggett's discount cigarettes cost B&W $50 million in revenues in 1983. In 1984, in a variant on the tit-for-tat strategy, B&W introduced its own line of discount cigarettes called Filter Lights whose packaging was nearly identical to Liggett's Quality Lights. B&W offered its line at the same list price as Liggett's cigarettes, but it effectively undercut Liggett's price by giving trade allowances to wholesalers that stocked the B&W brand. During the mid-1980s, other manufacturers introduced their own discount brands, and by 1989, Liggett's share of the discount cigarette market had fallen from nearly 90 percent to under 15 percent.

Liggett's creation of a discount tier of the cigarette market has profoundly affected the domestic U.S. cigarette business. In the early 1990s, after the decline of its fortunes in the discount segment of the market, Liggett introduced "deep-discount" cigarettes that sell for prices 30 percent below those of the discount brands. Other manufacturers, most notably RJR, also began selling their own deep-discount brands, and by 1992, RJR and Philip Morris had over 60 percent of this segment of the market. By 1992, the domestic business could be divided into three clearly defined segments: a premium segment, in which the manufacturers' average price to the wholesale trade was $69 per thousand; a discount tier in which prices averaged $49 per thousand; and the deep-discount tier in which prices were nearly $31 per thousand.

The emergence of a segmented market has complicated pricing coordination. Competitors must now coordinate an entire structure of prices, rather than just one. With declining consumer demand, much of the growth in the discount and deep discount segments has come at the expense of the premium brands, indicating that considerable substitution takes place across segments of the market. A profit-maximizing pricing structure must take this into account.

This consideration explains Philip Morris' decision to cut the price of its flagship brand Marlboro by 20 percent on Friday, April 3, 1993. Low prices in the discount and deep-discount segments had eroded Marlboro's market share from 30 percent of the entire cigarette market in 1988 to 21 percent in 1993. Philip Morris found it difficult to induce its other competitors to raise prices in the deep-discount segment where demand was highly price elastic and retailers often absorbed increases in the wholesale price without increasing their own prices to keep theirs sales volumes high. Philip Morris' decision to cut the price of Marlboro was quickly matched by RJR and other competitors, that lowered prices on their premium brands by the same amount.

In the aftermath of "Marlboro Friday," pricing discipline seems to have returned to the cigarette business. Both Philip Morris and RJR led the industry to price increases in all segments in 1994, 1995, 1996, and 1997. As the great cigarette price war of 1993 ended, prices in the premium segment had fallen by 25 percent, but prices in the discount and deep-discount segments had risen by 8 percent and 48 percent respectively. Marlboro's share of the market, which was 21 percent in April 1993, had risen to 30 percent by mid-1995.

Market Structure and Cooperative Pricing: Summary

This section has discussed how market structure affects the sustainability of cooperative pricing. Table 9.1 summarizes the impact of the market structure characteristics discussed in this section.

◆ ◆ ◆ ◆ ◆ FACILITATING PRACTICES

As the discussion in the previous section suggests, market structure can affect firms' ability to sustain cooperative pricing. Firms themselves can also facilitate cooperative pricing by:

- Price leadership

- Advance announcement of price changes

- Most favored customer clauses

- Uniform delivered pricing

These practices either facilitate coordination among firms or diminish their incentives to cut price. We discuss each in turn.

TABLE 9.1
MARKET STRUCTURE CONDITIONS AFFECTING THE SUSTAINABILITY
OF COOPERATIVE PRICING

Market Structure Condition	How Does It Affect Cooperative Pricing?	Reasons
High Market Concentration	Facilitates	• Coordinating on the cooperative equilibrium is easier with fewer firms. • Increases the benefit–cost ratio from adhering to cooperative pricing.
Firm Asymmetries	Harms	• Disagreement over cooperative price. • Coordinating on a cooperative price is more difficult. • Possible incentive of large firms to extend price umbrella to small firms increases small firms' incentives to cut price. • Small firms may prefer to deviate from monopoly prices even if larger firms match.
High Buyer Concentration	Harms	• Reduces the probability that a defector will be discovered.
Lumpy Orders	Harms	• Decreases the frequency of interaction between competitors, increasing the lag between defection and retaliation.
Secret Price Terms	Harms	• Increases detection lags because prices of competitors are more difficult to monitor. • Increases the probability of misreads.
Volatility of Demand and Cost Conditions	Harms	• Increases the lag between defection and retaliation (perhaps even precluding retaliation) by increasing uncertainty about whether defections have occurred and about the identity of defectors.

Price Leadership

Under price leadership, one firm in an industry (the price leader) announces its price changes before all other firms, which then match the leader's price. Examples of well-known price leaders include Kellogg in breakfast cereals, Philip Morris in tobacco, and (until the mid-1960s) U.S. Steel in steel.

Price leadership is a way to overcome the problem of coordinating on a focal equilibrium. In price leadership, each firm gives up its pricing autonomy and cedes control over industry pricing to a single firm. Firms thus need not worry that rivals will secretly shade price to steal market share. Of course, as the Sydney newspaper market illustrates, systems of price leadership can break down if the price leader does not retaliate against defectors. Because of his desire to become the price leader in the afternoon paper market, Rupert Murdoch refused to follow Fairfax's price lead. When Fairfax failed to respond to Murdoch's defection, it found itself in a costly price war that eventually cost it the leadership of the afternoon market.

The kind of oligopolistic price leadership we discuss here should be distinguished from the barometric price leadership that sometimes occurs in competitive markets, such as that for prime rate loans. Under barometric price leadership, the price leader merely acts as a barometer of changes in market conditions by adjusting prices to shifts in demand or input prices. Under barometric leadership different firms are often price leaders, while under oligopolistic leadership, the same firm is the leader for years. Recent federal and state antitrust inquiries into the pricing policies of infant formula makers centered on whether the price matching strategies of Abbott Labs and Bristol Myers represented oligopolistic or barometric price leadership. The two firms alternated as price leaders during the 1980s, but the follower always matched the leader, as did a third firm, Wyeth. The firms have generally settled these inquiries out of court without admitting wrongdoing.

Advance Announcement of Price Changes

In some markets, firms will publicly announce the prices they intend to charge in the future. For example, in chemicals markets firms often announce their intention to raise prices 30 or 60 days before the price change is to take effect. Advance announcements of price changes reduce the uncertainty that firms' rivals will undercut them. The practice also allows firms to rescind or roll back proposed price increases that competitors refuse to follow.

To illustrate why advance announcements can facilitate cooperative pricing, consider a simple example in which the industry consists of two identical firms. Each firm chooses its price a month before it goes into effect. The firms can continue to adjust their prices until they are satisfied with them. The equilibrium in this market must be the monopoly price. A firm knows that its rival will always match the price that it announces. Thus each firm's market share is fixed at 50 percent, and each firm's profit is one-half of industry profit no matter what price it charges. As a result, each firm's profit-maximizing price is the monopoly price.

Most Favored Customer Clauses

A most favored customer clause is a provision in a sales contract that promises a buyer that it will pay the lowest price the seller charges. There are two basic types of most favored customer clauses: contemporaneous and retroactive.

To illustrate these, consider a simple example: Xerxes Chemical manufactures a chemical additive used to enhance the performance of jet fuel. Great Lakes Refining Company, a manufacturer of jet fuel, signs a contract with Xerxes calling for delivery of 100,000 tons of the chemical over the next three months at the "open order" price of $.50 per ton.[28] Under a contemporaneous most favored customer policy, Xerxes agrees that while this contract is in effect, if it sells the chemical at a lower price to any other buyer (perhaps to undercut a competitor), it will also lower the price to this level for Great Lakes.[29] Under a retroactive most favored customer clause, Xerxes agrees to pay a rebate to Great Lakes if during a certain period after the contract has expired (e.g., two years), it sells the chemical additive for a lower price than Great Lakes paid. For example, suppose Great Lakes' contract expired on 12/31/99, but its contract contained a two-year retroactive most favored customer clause. If sometime in 2000 Xerxes announces a general reduction in price from $.50 per ton to $.40 per ton, it would have to pay Great Lakes a rebate equal to ($.50 − $.40) × 100,000 or $10,000, the difference between what Great Lakes actually paid and what it would have paid under the new lower price.

Most favored customer clauses appear to benefit buyers. For Great Lakes, the "price protection" offered by the most favored customer clause may help keep its production costs in line with those of competitors. However, most favored customer clauses can inhibit price competition. Retroactive most favored customer clauses make it expensive for Xerxes to cut prices in the future, either selectively or across the board. Contemporaneous most favored customer clauses do not penalize the firm for making across-the-board price reductions (e.g., if Xerxes cuts prices to all its customers, it does not have to pay rebates to past customers), but they discourage firms from using selective price cutting to compete for customers with highly price-elastic demands.

Why would firms ever adopt most favored customer policies if their customers do not demand them? After all, the ideal situation from a given manufacturer's perspective is when its competitors tie their hands in the competition for customers by adopting most favored customer policies, leaving the manufacturer free to selectively or generally price cut. However, Thomas Cooper has shown that because adopting a retroactive most favored customer clause softens price competition in the future, oligopolists may have an incentive to adopt the policy unilaterally, even if rival manufacturers do not.[30]

Uniform Delivered Prices

In many industries, such as cement, steel, or soybean products, buyers and sellers are geographically separated, and transportation costs are a significant. In such contexts, the pricing method can affect competitive interactions. Broadly speaking, two different kinds of pricing policies can be identified. Under uniform FOB pric-

---

[28]An open order price is the price the manufacturer charges any buyer who orders the additive.

[29]Hence, the origin of the term "most favored customer clause." Great Lakes is extended the same price terms as the most favored customer of the manufacturer. Thus, if Xerxes offers another refiner a price of $.45, Xerxes will have to drop Great Lakes' price to $.45, too.

[30]Cooper, T. E., "Most Favored Customer Clauses and Tacit Collusion," *RAND Journal of Economics*, 17, Autumn 1986: pp. 377–388. David Besanko and Thomas Lyon prove a similar result for contemporaneous most favored customer clauses, but show that voluntary adoption is most likely in concentrated industries where a given firm internalizes much of the "competition-softening" effect of most favored customer policies. Both the Cooper model; and the Besanko-Lyon model are examples of two-stage commitment models, discussed in Chapter 8.

ing, the seller quotes a price for pickup at the seller's loading dock, and the buyer absorbs the freight charges for shipping from the seller's plant to the buyer's plant.[31] Under uniform delivered pricing, the firm quotes a single delivered price for all buyers and absorbs any freight charges itself.[32]

Uniform delivered pricing facilitates cooperative pricing by allowing firms to make a more "surgical" response to price cutting by rivals. Consider, for example, two brick producers, one located in Bombay and the other in Ahmadabad, India. These firms have been trying to maintain prices at the monopoly level, but the Bombay producer cuts its price to increase its share of the market in Surat, a city between Bombay and Ahmadabad. Under FOB pricing, the Ahmadabad producer must retaliate by cutting its mill price, which effectively reduces its price to all its customers (see Figure 9.4).[33] On the other hand, if the firms were using uniform delivered pricing, the Ahmadabad firm could cut its price selectively; it could cut the delivered price to its customers in Surat, keeping delivered prices of other customers at their original level (see Figure 9.5). By reducing the "cost" that the "victim" incurs by retaliating, retaliation becomes more likely, and enhances the credibility of policies, such as tit-for-tat, that can sustain cooperative pricing.

FIGURE 9.4
FOB PRICING.

When both firms use FOB pricing, the delivered price that a customer actually pays depends on its location. The delivered price schedules are shown by the solid lines in the figure. If the brick producer in Ahmadabad lowers its FOB price to match that of the Bombay producer, then it effectively shifts its delivered price schedule downward. (It now becomes the dashed line.) Even though the Ahmadabad firm is to retaliating against the Bombay firm's stealing business in Surat, the Ahmadabad firm ends up reducing its delivered prices to all of its customers.

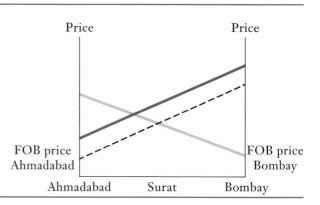

---

[31]FOB stands for "free on board," so the FOB price is the seller quotes for loading the product on the delivery vehicle. If the seller pays the transport charges, they are added to the buyer's bill, and the net price the seller receives is known as the uniform net mill price.

[32]A third type of pricing is basing point pricing: The seller designates one or more base locations and quotes FOB prices from them. The customer chooses a basing point and absorbs the freight costs between the basing point and its plant. For example, if a steel company uses Gary, Indiana, as a basing point, and a Chicago customer buys steel from the firm's Birmingham, Alabama, plant, it would pay an FOB price plus the freight charges as if the steel had been shipped from Gary to Birmingham. In a sense, basing point pricing represents a kind of intermediate case between FOB pricing and uniform delivered pricing. See Scherer, F. M. and D. Ross, *Industrial Market Structure and Economic Performance*, New York: Houghton Mifflin, 1991, for a thorough discussion of basing point pricing and of antitrust cases in the steel and cement industries that centered on the basing point system.

[33]Of course, if the firm does so, it would be using nonuniform delivered pricing rather than uniform delivered pricing.

FIGURE 9.5
DELIVERED PRICING.

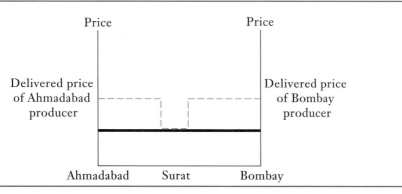

When both firms use delivered pricing, a firm's customer pays the same delivered price, no matter what its location. If the Bombay firm cuts its delivered price to steal business in Surat, the Ahmadabad producer need only cut its delivered price in Surat to retaliate.

QUALITY COMPETITION ◆ ◆ ◆ ◆ ◆

Although we have focused on price competition, price is obviously not the only factor that drives consumer decisions and firm strategies. Product attributes, such as performance and durability, also matter, and firms may compete just as fiercely on these dimensions as they do on price.

To simplify the discussion, we will lump all nonprice attributes into a single dimension called "quality"—any attribute that increases the demand for the product at a fixed price. The next section of this book emphasizes the need for firms to provide a combination of price and quality that offers superior value to what competitors offer. In this chapter, we focus on how market structure and competition influence the firm's choice of quality.

Quality Choice in Competitive Markets

In a competitive market, either all goods are identical, or they exhibit pure vertical differentiation. Recall from Chapter 7 that when products are vertically differentiated, for any set of prices, all consumers will agree about which products they most prefer. Firms may, therefore, offer different levels of quality at different prices, but the market will force all firms to charge the same price per unit of quality. This depends on a critical unstated assumption. In particular, consumers must be able to perfectly evaluate the quality of each seller. But what if consumers cannot easily do this? Then, sellers that charge more than the going price per unit of quality may still have customers.

To explore how consumer information affects quality, consider a market in which some consumers have information about product quality and others do not. Suppose that it is costly to be an informed consumer—one must invest time and effort to identify good quality sellers. In this market, uninformed consumers may be able to infer the quality of sellers merely by observing the behavior of informed consumers. For example, a prospective car buyer may be considering the purchase of a recently introduced model. If she learns sales of that model are low (e.g., she never sees anyone driving that model), she might well question the quality of the automobile even if she has no direct information about it. If no one else likes it, the car must not be very good. The car buyer can thus make an informed judgment about the quality of the car without knowing anything about cars except how many people appear to drive different models.

If there are enough well-informed buyers in a market, most buyers will be satisfied with the quality of what they buy. But if uninformed consumers cannot gauge quality by observing informed consumers, then a lemons market can emerge. The term *lemons market* is derived from the used car market, in which owners are more anxious to sell low-quality cars ("lemons") than high-quality cars.[34] A lemons market requires two ingredients: uninformed consumers, and the fact that low-quality products are cheaper to make than high-quality products.

If consumers cannot determine the quality of what they are buying, then some sellers might skimp on quality and sell only low-quality products but still charge the going price. Of course, consumers may realize that their ignorance of quality makes them susceptible to buying lemons. They may even insist on paying less for a product, figuring its quality is likely to be low. This poses a problem for sellers of high-quality products, who cannot get their money's worth from suspicious consumers. High-quality sellers may refuse to sell their product, figuring that they cannot get a price to cover their opportunity cost. If they want to get a price commensurate with quality, they must rely on money-back guarantees, reviews in independent consumer magazines, and a reputation for quality to convince buyers that their products are not lemons.

Sanford Grossman and Joseph Stiglitz point out one further problem that may arise in markets where some individuals are well-informed and others are not.[35] They consider a market in which consumers of information compete against each other, for example, the market for corporate control discussed in Chapter 6. Some consumers might spend resources gathering information, but if uninformed consumers can infer what that information is, all consumers may end up on an even footing. As a result, those who gathered the information may be worse off than those who did not, having borne the expense without realizing extra benefits. This implies that there will be underinvestment in information gathering. In the market for corporate control, for example, an investor may devote considerable effort to identifying an underperforming firm. As soon as that investor tends an offer for control of the firm, however, other investors will learn the identity of the undervalued firm because tender offers are public information. In the ensuing competition between investors to gain control of the underperforming target, profits may be bid away. This helps explain why takeover artists, such as T. Boone Pickens and the late Sir James Goldsmith, are extremely secretive in their dealings, and why there is a need for speed in effecting takeovers.

---

[34]For a formal treatment of the lemons problem and an interesting discussion of its applications, see Akerlof, G., "The Market for Lemons: Qualitative Uncertainty and the Market Mechanism," *Quarterly Journal of Economics*, 84, 1970: pp. 488–500.

[35]Grossman, S. and J. Stiglitz, "On the Impossibility of Informationally Efficient Markets," *American Economic Review*, 70, June 1980: pp. 393–408.

Quality Choices of Sellers with Market Power

Sellers with market power view quality as a critical for the demand for their product. Figure 9.6 depicts the demand facing a seller at two levels of quality. We have defined quality to include anything that increases demand, and this is reflected in the figure. When quality is high, demand is higher than when it is low. The vertical difference between the high- and low-quality demand curves represents the additional value of quality. As shown in the figure, the demand curve gets steeper as quality increases. This would occur if consumers who are willing to pay the most for a product will also pay the most to improve quality.

Suppose that a seller with market power had to select a single level of quality for all its products. This could be an appliance maker selecting a level of reliability that will be consistent across its product line, or a car maker selecting a level of safety that will be consistent across its fleet. What level of quality should the seller choose? As with other economic tradeoffs, it should choose quality so that the marginal cost of the quality increase equals the marginal revenue that results when consumers demand more of the product.[36]

The Marginal Cost of Increasing Quality

The idea that it is costly to improve quality contrasts with the literature on continuous quality improvement (CQI).[37] According to the principles of CQI, improvements in the production process can simultaneously reduce costs and increase quality. But once firms deal with inefficiencies in production, they must eventually confront tradeoffs between lowering costs and boosting quality. For example, an airplane can certainly be made more reliable by assuring that components fit properly. Beyond these assurances of productive efficiency, further improvements can be achieved by installing costly backup features, such as additional engines and brakes.

FIGURE 9.6
DEMAND CURVES ASSOCIATED WITH DIFFERENT QUALITY LEVELS.

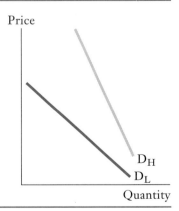

When the firm increases its quality, its demand curve shifts from D_L to D_H. Not only does the firm sell more of the product at any given price when it raises quality, its demand becomes more price inelastic, as indicated by D_H being steeper than D_L.

---

[36]To highlight the key tradeoffs, we ignore what in Chapter 8 we called strategic effects. Thus, we focus on the quality choice of a single firm in isolation and ignore the side effects of its quality choice on the intensity of price competition.

[37]See, for example, Crosby, P. B., *Quality Is Free: The Art of Making Quality Certain,* New York: McGraw-Hill, 1979.

If a firm is producing efficiently, quality is costly. Moreover, improvements tend to be incrementally more costly as quality nears "perfection." To see why, consider a university that is trying to minimize the chance of losing data in a mainframe computer crash. The university can minimize its losses by running a program to back up the system. Each run of the program is costly, both in terms of manpower and computer downtime. If the university wants to limit losses to a maximum of one week's work, it must run the backup program 52 times annually. Limiting the loss to three days' work requires running the backup program 122 times per year. Limiting the loss to one day's work requires 365 runs. It requires incrementally more and more computer runs to provide incrementally less and less additional protection.

The Marginal Benefit of Improving Quality

When a firm improves the quality of its product, more consumers will want to buy it. How much revenue this brings in depends on two factors:

• The increase in demand caused by the increase in quality.

• The incremental profit earned on each additional unit sold.

We discuss each of these factors in turn.

Michael Spence has pointed out that when contemplating an increase in quality, the firm must consider the responsiveness of its "marginal consumers"—consumers who are indifferent among buying from that firm and buying elsewhere or not buying at all.[38] Since the firm's "inframarginal" customers—those loyal to it—will continue to buy the product after the quantity increases, the financial benefit from an increase in quality stems from new customers.

Firms raise quality to attract more customers. But how can a firm determine how many more customers it will get? An increase in quality will bring in more new customers if (a) there are more marginal customers, and (b) marginal customers can determine that quality has, in fact, increased. David Dranove and Mark Satterthwaite show that these factors are determined, in turn, by (1) the degree of horizontal differentiation in the market, and (2) the precision with which consumers observe quality.[39] Recall from Chapter 7 that in a horizontally differentiated market, consumers tend to be loyal to sellers who offer a good idiosyncratic match between the product's differentiated attributes and the consumer's tastes and preferences. These loyal consumers may be reluctant to switch to another seller, even that who offers a higher overall level of quality. In a business where location matters, for example, consumers may continue to buy from the nearest seller even though there is a higher-quality seller at the other end of town. This explains why restaurants located along superhighways can survive despite providing substandard food. They have little reason to boost quality, since it is unlikely to significantly affect demand. Recently, some states have replaced independent highway restuarants with national chains, such as Wendy's, which are

---

[38]Spence, A. M., "Monopoly, Quality, and Regulation," *Bell Journal of Economics*, 1975: pp. 417–429.

[39]Dranove, D. and M. Satterthwaite, "Monopolistic Competition When Price and Quality Are Not Perfectly Observable," *RAND Journal of Economics*, Winter 1992: pp. 518–534.

concerned about brand image and thus generally maintain higher quality than the independents did.

Even if few consumers in a market are loyal to their current sellers, a seller that boosts quality will not necessarily attract new customers. Consumers must be able to determine that quality is higher than it used to be. This is why magazines like *Consumer Reports*, which provide generally unbiased product reviews, are so popular. But consumers cannot get such reviews for many goods and services—for example, many types of furniture, medical and legal services, and home repairs. Consumers would like to know the quality of these goods and services, but may be unable to do so.

When consumers have difficulty judging particular attributes of a product, they may focus on those attributes that they can easily observe and evaluate. This helps explain why retailers are so concerned about the external appearance of their shops, and why doctors and lawyers often display their diplomas, especially if they graduated from a prestigious school. Of course, this emphasis on observable attributes may mean that consumers are shortchanged on the hard-to-measure attributes that really matter.

Sellers that offer high quality on dimensions that are difficult for consumers to measure will benefit only if they can convince consumers that their goods are superior. One way to do this is to publicize objective quality measures. (Most consumers will discount subjective claims like "We have the best guacamole in town.") There are many examples of this, such as when a film advertisement cites "two thumbs up" or when a car maker boasts of being ranked number one in a J. D. Powers survey. Another way to do this is to allow consumers to sample the product, such as when food makers distribute free samples in supermarkets. Massive advertising may also help to convince consumers to sample a new product.

Conveying quality information is especially critical for goods and services whose quality is difficult to evaluate before purchase, such as stereophonic equipment, restaurant food, and medical services, all examples of *experience goods*. Sellers use various techniques to enable consumers to evaluate such products. For example, manufacturers of high-end stereo equipment, such as the Hales Design Group and Muse Electronics, rely on dealers to demonstrate the quality of their products. Dealers often build special audition rooms, attend seminars on sound technology, and learn which recordings best enhance the features of each stereo component. Though costly, these investments often convince consumers to spend thousands of dollars on components.

If two sellers can gain the same increase in sales by increasing quality, which has a stronger incentive to do so? All else being equal, the seller with the higher price-cost margin will make more money from the increase in sales and thus has a stronger incentive to boost quality. Sometimes, market structure creates conflicting incentives to boost quality. A monopolist may have a higher price-cost margin than a competitive firm, but may face few marginal consumers. Every consumer in a competitive market is a marginal consumer to a firm that is about to gain a quality edge over its rivals. Horizontal differentiation has similar offsetting implications for incentives to boost quality. On the one hand, horizontal differentiation creates loyal customers, which allows sellers to boost price-cost margins, raising the gains from attracting more customers by boosting quality. On the other hand, loyal customers are less likely to switch sellers when quality differences are low, implying that each seller faces fewer marginal customers.

CHAPTER SUMMARY

◆ If firms are sufficiently patient (i.e., they do not discount the future too much), cooperative pricing (i.e., the monopoly price) may be sustainable as an equilibrium outcome, even though firms are making decisions noncooperatively. This is a specific application of the folk theorem from game theory, which says that any outcome between marginal cost and the monopoly price is sustainable as a subgame perfect Nash equilibrium in the infinitely repeated prisoners' dilemma game.

◆ Market structure affects the sustainability of cooperative pricing. High market concentration facilitates cooperative pricing. Asymmetries among firms, lumpy orders, high buyer concentration, secret sales transactions, and volatile demand makes pricing cooperation more difficult.

◆ Practices that can facilitate cooperative pricing include price leadership, advance announcements of price changes, most favored customer clauses, and uniform delivered pricing.

◆ In competitive markets, firms will provide acceptable quality as long as there are enough informed consumers. If consumers are generally uninformed, lemons markets can develop in which owners or producers of high-quality goods may refuse to sell altogether.

◆ The quality that sellers which have market power provide depends on the marginal cost and the marginal benefit of increasing quality. The marginal benefit of increasing quality depends on the increase in demand brought on by the increase in quality and the incremental profit earned on each additional unit sold. This implies that a firm's price-cost margin is an important determinant of its incentives to raise quality.

QUESTIONS

1. "Economic theories of how price wars begin presume that firms would prefer their industry price to be high." Comment.

2. Why do misreads and misjudgments encourage firms to lower prices?

3. Firms operating at or near capacity are unlikely to instigate price wars. Briefly explain.

4. Pricing cooperation is more likely to emerge in markets where, one firm raises a price and competitors follow suit, market shares remain unchanged. It is less likely to work well in markets where price matching may not leave market shares constant." Evaluate this statement. Can you think of circumstances under which price matching behavior could alter market shares?

5. Suppose that you were an industry analyst trying to determine if the leading firms in the automobile manufacturing industry are playing a tit-for-tat pricing game. What real world data would you want to examine? What would you consider to be evidence of tit-for-tat pricing?

6. A recent article on price wars by two McKinsey consultants makes the following argument.[40]

    That the (tit-for tat) strategy is fraught with risk cannot be overemphasized. Your competitor may take an inordinately long time to realize that its actions can do it nothing but harm; rivalry across the entire industry may escalate precipitously; and as the "tit-for-tat" game plays itself out, all of a price war's detrimental effects on customers will make themselves felt.

---

[40]Garda, R. A. and M. V. Marn, "Price Wars," *McKinsey Quarterly*, 3, 1993: pp. 87–100. Quote from pp. 98–99.

How would you reconcile the views expressed in this quote with the advantages of tit-for-tat claimed in this chapter?

7. Studies of pricing in the airline industry show that carriers that dominate hub airports (Delta in Atlanta, USAir in Pittsburgh, American in Dallas) tend to charge higher fares, on average for flights in and out of the hub airport than other, nondominant carriers flying in and out of the hub. What might explain this pattern of prices?

8. It is often argued that price wars may be more likely to occur during low demand periods than high demand periods. (This chapter makes that argument.) Are there factors that might reverse this implication? That is, can you think of reasons why the attractiveness of deviating from cooperative pricing might actually be greater during booms (high-demand) than during busts (low demand)?

9. Consider a duopoly consisting of two firms, Amalgamated Electric (AE) and Carnegie-Manheim (C-M), which sell products that are somewhat differentiated. Each firm sells to customers with different price elasticities of demand, and as result, occasionally discounts below list price for the most price-elastic customers. Suppose, now, AE adopts a contemporaneous most-favored customer policy, but C-M does not. What will happen to AE's average equilibrium price? What will happen to C-M's average equilibrium price?

ENTRY AND EXIT 10

$\mathcal{I}$n early 1997, a consortium of electronics firms led by Toshiba, Sony, Matsushita, and Philips introduced a new digital video format called DVD. This format offered video resolution and sound quality that was superior to conventional videocassettes. By spring 1997, several major studios, including Warner, MGM, and Columbia, released a few movies in DVD format. The DVD hardware consortium expected "early adopters"—individuals willing to pay a premium price for new technology—to purchase DVD players at high prices, despite the shortage of movies to play on them. This would encourage the release of more movies and generate additional hardware sales. The consortium hoped to have a large installed base of DVD players in consumers' homes by Christmas 1997. Studios would then rush to release their movies on DVD, and consumers would replace their videotape players with DVD players, just as they had replaced their record players with CD players a decade earlier.

Sales of DVD players exceeded expectations through the summer of 1997, but the Christmas season was a disappointment. In the fall of 1997, electronics retailer Circuit City made a surprise announcement. They were spearheading the release of a digital video format called DIVX that was partially incompatible with DVD. Circuit City hoped to make DIVX the format of choice. Consumers, wary of previous format wars, such as that between VHS and Beta videotape, stayed on the sidelines that Christmas season, as did several major studios, such as Paramount and Fox.

Circuit City did not adequately follow through with the DIVX introduction. It finally released DIVX hardware and software in two test markets in early summer 1998. They offered only a few brands of DIVX players (initially, the only player was made by Zenith, which had entered into bankruptcy at that time), and sold only a few hundred DIVX movie titles. Circuit City was unable to persuade most other electronics retailers to sell DIVX hardware and software. Video rental outlets refused to carry DIVX software. Meanwhile, by the time of the nationwide DIVX rollout in late summer 1998, the DVD market was taking off. There were more than 1,500 movies available on DVD, all the major studios were on board, on-line DVD retailers such as DVD Express, BestBuy.com, and Reel.com were aggressively discounting software, and video rental stores such as Blockbuster and Hollywood Video were heavily promoting DVD rentals. It was a good Christmas for DVD—sales of DVD hardware in the Christmas season of 1998 topped sales in all of 1997. It was a bad Christmas for DIVX—by the week before Christmas Circuit City had begun promoting DVD alongside its promotions of DIVX, and was repositioning DIVX as a DVD product feature rather than an alternative format. Circuit City's entry strategy had failed.

This chapter is about *entry* and *exit*. Entry is the beginning of production and sales by a new firm in a market, and exit occurs when a firm ceases to produce in a market. The experience of the DVD consortium demonstrates that *incumbent* firms—firms that are already operating—should take entry into account when making their strategic decisions. *Entrants*—firms that are new to a market— threaten incumbents in two ways. First, *they take market share away from incumbent firms*, in effect reducing an incumbent's share of the "profit pie." Second, when price rivalry among incumbents is limited, entry of additional firms often *intensifies competition*. This occurs because entrants often reduce prices or even give away their product to establish a foothold in the market. In this way, entry reduces the size of the "profit pie." Exit has the opposite effect on competitors: Surviving firms increase their share, and competition diminishes.

Entry into the long-distance communications market illustrates both of these effects. After the deregulation of the market, AT&T faced entry by several firms, notably MCI and Sprint. Initially, AT&T also faced a regulatory floor on the price it could charge. Entrants to the market offered lower prices than did AT&T, so that by the mid-1990s, AT&T's market share had slipped to less than 65 percent. In the past few years, AT&T has been freed from many regulatory restraints, and has lowered its price to halt the erosion of its market share.

In this chapter we demonstrate the importance of entry and exit in most markets. We then describe structural factors (i.e., factors beyond the control of the firms in the market) that affect entry and exit decisions. We also address strategies that incumbents may employ to reduce the threat of entry and/or encourage exit by rivals.

◆ ◆ ◆ ◆ ◆ SOME FACTS ABOUT ENTRY AND EXIT

Entry is pervasive in many industries and may take many forms. An entrant may be a new firm, that is, one that did not exist before it entered a market. An entrant may be a firm diversifying its product line; that is, the firm already exists but had not previously been in that market. An entrant may also be a firm diversifying geographically, that is, the firm sells the same product in other geographic markets. The distinction between new and diversifying firms is often important, such as when we assess the costs of entry, and when we consider strategic responses to it. Recent new entrants in various markets include Dreamworks SKG (a motion picture studio founded by Stephen Spielberg, Jeffrey Katzenberg, and David Geffin), British Midlands (which provides airline service to the British Isles and several European destinations), and Amazon.com (which sells books over the internet). Recent diversifying entrants include the National Basketball Association (which opened a chain of restaurants), Microsoft (which introduced the Microsoft Explorer web browser), and Sony (which introduced the Playstation video game system).

Exit is the reverse of entry—the withdrawal of a product from a market, either by a firm that shuts down completely, or by a firm that continues to operate in other markets. In the last two decades, the Eccentric (owned by Oprah Winfrey) exited the Chicago restaurant market, Renault and Peugeot exited the U.S. automobile market, Intel stopped making DRAM chips, and Harvard Graphics fell victim to Microsoft in the graphics software market.

The best systematic analysis of entry and exit rates across industries is by Timothy Dunne, Marc Roberts, and Larry Samuelson (henceforth DRS). They examined entry and exit in U.S. manufacturing firms between 1963 and 1982. Though dated, their findings are valuable because they emphasize the importance of entry and exit in many industries, and offer insights about patterns of growth and decline.

Dunne, Roberts, and Samuelson's Evidence on Entry and Exit

DRS examined data from the U.S. Census of Manufacturing for the years 1963, 1967, 1972, 1977, and 1982. The census identifies all manufacturing firms in the United States, as well as individual manufacturing facilities. Each firm reports the products it made in each of its facilities, and then each facility is assigned a primary 2-digit S.I.C. code to indicate its principal industry. Each firm also reports the value of goods shipped from each manufacturing facility. By matching firms across different years of the census, DRS could identify entering and exiting firms, and measure postentry growth and preexit decline. Overall, DRS studied more than 250,000 firms in each census year.

To summarize the main findings of DRS, imagine an industry in the year 2000. This hypothetical industry has 100 firms, with combined annual sales of $100 million. Thus, the average incumbent has annual sales of $1 million. If patterns of entry and exit in this industry are representative of all U.S. industries in previous decades, then the following will be true:

1. *Entry and exit will be pervasive.* By the year 2005, between 30 and 40 new firms will have entered. They will have combined annual sales of $12 to $20 million (adjusted for inflation). At the same time, 30 to 40 firms that were operating in 2000 will have left the market. Their year 2000 sales would also have been $12 to $20 million. In other words, in just five years, the industry will experience a 30 to 40 percent turnover in firms, and all the entering and exiting firms will account for 12 to 20 percent of volume.

   Of the 30 to 40 new entrants, about half will be diversified firms operating in other product markets, and half will be new firms. Of the 30 to 40 exiters, 40 percent will be diversified.

2. *Entrants and exiters tend to be smaller than established firms.* A typical entrant will be only one-third the size of a typical incumbent, and will have annual sales of around $350,000. An important exception is entry by diversifying firms that build new physical plants (as opposed to switching an existing plant to making a new product). Though diversifying firms building new physical plants may represent only 5 to 10 percent of all entrants (two to four firms over five years), they tend to be three times the size of other entrants—roughly the same size as the average incumbent.

   In the year 2000, firms that will leave the industry by the year 2005 will only be about one third the size of the average firm. Diversified firms rarely close a plant permanently (such closings account for only about 2 to 3 percent of all exits), but when such exits occur the facilities that are closed are roughly twice the size of those of the typical nondiversified exiter.

3. *Most entrants do not survive 10 years, but those that do grow precipitously.* Of the 30 to 40 firms that enter the market between 2000 and 2005, roughly 60 percent will exit by 2010. The survivors will nearly double their size by 2010.

4. *Entry and exit rates vary by industry.* Not surprisingly, entry and exit are more common in some industries than in others. Some industries in which entrants are numerous and command substantial market shares include apparel, lumber, furniture, printing, and fabricated metals. Industries with high exit rates include apparel, lumber, furniture, printing, and leather. Industries with little entry include food processing, tobacco, paper, chemicals, and primary metals. Industries with little exit include tobacco, paper, chemicals, petroleum and coal, and primary metals. Clearly, entry and exit are highly related: Conditions that encourage entry in industry foster exit.

The DRS findings have four important implications for strategy:

- When planning for the future, the manager must account for an unknown competitor—the entrant. Fully one-third of a typical incumbent firm's competition five years' hence is not a competitor today.

- Not many diversifying competitors will build new plants, but the size of their plants can make them a threat to incumbents.

- Managers should expect most new ventures to fail quickly. However, survival and growth usually go hand in hand, so managers of new firms will have to find the capital to support expansion.

- Managers should know the entry and exit conditions of their industry. Entry and exit are powerful forces in some industries, but relatively unimportant in others.

EXAMPLE 10.1

McDonald's in Poland: A (Filet of) Fish Story

When Poland's first McDonald's opened in Warsaw in June 1992, the local population's appetite for hamburgers had already been whetted. Shortly after the fall of communism in Poland, thousands of entrepreneurs opened small restaurants, among them a number of burger stands (including one called Matdonald). McDonald's was already engaged in a massive global expansion, with plans to open 450 international locations in 1992 alone. It was confident that Poland would be a profitable market to enter.

McDonald's calculated that it could sell hamburgers in Poland that were identical to those found under the golden arches throughout the world, at a price comparable to that charged by independent hamburger sellers. These low prices, combined with the power of the McDonald's brand name, and the attractiveness of its relatively huge restaurants, assured early success.

McDonald's preferred to buy from local sellers to avoid transportation costs. But when it first entered the Polish market, it found few Polish vendors with the necessary abilities and technology. Thus, it purchased 75 percent of its supplies from vendors outside Poland, such as french fries imported from Russia. In some cases McDonald's could not find a low cost vendor and kept certain items off the menu. For example, McDonald's did not offer its popular fish filet because it could not find a low cost vendor of processed cod.

The absence of fish filet was particularly ironic. The Polish fishing industry was a major supplier of cod to European fish processors, including the Danish processor that supplied fish filets to McDonald's in western Europe. While it was prohibitively expensive for McDonald's in Poland to purchase Polish cod processed in Denmark, costs would be much lower if the fish was processed in Poland. So McDonald's country manager Tim Fenton suggested that the Danish firm open a processing plant in Poland. The firm entered into a joint venture with a Polish firm and the two invested $2.5 million in the plant. Further investments were made in training more than 80 workers in the special techniques needed to make McDonald's fish filets. The plant opened on February 28, 1995. The next day, McDonald's Poland began serving Fish Macs.

McDonald's expansion across Poland (there were 40 by the end of 1995) created many other entry opportunities for local vendors. A beef processing plant opened in 1993. A potato processing company opened in 1994, and farmers began growing the longer potatoes necessary for McDonald's french fries. In the same year, a bakery invested in the equipment necessary to supply all the buns McDonald's needed. By the end of 1995, McDonald's obtained 70 percent of its supplies from Polish suppliers. The investments by these suppliers clearly illustrate Adam Smith's dictum that "the division of labor is limited by the extent of the market." McDonald's entry expanded the market for locally grown food products. Local sellers responded by entering and specializing. In this way, entry begat entry.

Entry and Exit Decisions: Basic Concepts ◆ ◆ ◆ ◆ ◆

A profit-maximizing, risk-neutral firm should enter a market if the sunk costs of entry are less than the net present value of expected postentry profits.[1] There are many potential sunk costs to enter a market, ranging from the costs of specialized capital equipment, to government licenses. Later in this chapter we elaborate on these and other entry costs.

Postentry profits will vary according to demand and cost conditions, as well as the nature of *postentry competition*. Postentry competition represents the conduct and performance of firms in the market after entry has occurred. The potential entrant may use many different types of information about incumbents, including historical pricing practices, costs, and capacity, to assess what postentry competition may be like. If the potential entrant expects postentry competition to be

---

[1]A firm or individual is risk-neutral if it is indifferent between a sure thing and a gamble with an equal expected payoff. Individuals are usually risk-averse, as evidenced by purchases of auto and health insurance. Shareholders may not want their managers to avoid risk, however, since they can cheaply minimize risk by holding diversified portfolios of debt and equity instruments.

fierce, say because it expects incumbent firms to slash prices, then it is more likely to stay out. Even when the potential entrant believes that postentry competition will be relatively mild, it may not enter if there are significant barriers to entry.

Barriers to Entry

Bain's Typology of Entry Conditions

Barriers to entry are those factors that allow incumbent firms to earn positive economic profits, while making it unprofitable for newcomers to enter the industry.[2] Barriers to entry may be *structural* or *strategic*. Structural entry barriers result when the incumbent has natural cost or marketing advantages, or benefits from favorable regulations. Strategic entry barriers result when the incumbent aggressively deters entry. *Entry-deterring strategies* may include capacity expansion, limit pricing, and predatory pricing, all of which we discuss later in this chapter.

In his seminal work on entry, Joe Bain argued that markets may be characterized according to whether entry barriers are structural or strategic, and whether incumbents can profit from using entry-deterring strategies.[3] Bain described three entry conditions:

Blockaded entry Entry is blockaded if the incumbent needs to do nothing to deter entry. For example, there may be structural barriers to entry, perhaps because production in an industry requires large fixed investments or the entrant may expect postentry profits to be low, perhaps because it sells an undifferentiated product and expects price competition to be fierce. Entry by mass merchandisers into small towns that already have a Wal-Mart store, for instance, may be blockaded both because of the costs of constructing a new store and the expectation of fierce price competition.

Accommodated entry Entry is accommodated if structural entry barriers are low, and either (a) entry-deterring strategies will be ineffective, or (b) the cost to the incumbent of trying to deter entry exceeds the benefits it could gain from keeping the entrant out. Accommodated entry is typical in markets with growing demand or rapid technological improvements. Entry is then so attractive that the incumbent(s) should not waste resources trying to prevent it.

Deterred entry Entry is deterred, if not blockaded, if (a) the incumbent can keep the entrant out by employing an entry-deterring strategy, and (b) the cost of the entry deterring strategy is more than offset by the additional profits that the incumbent will enjoy in the less competitive environment. Frank Fisher calls such entry-deterring strategies *predatory acts*.[4] We describe several predatory acts later in this chapter.

---

[2] This definition is a synthesis of the definitions of entry barriers of Joe Bain in *Barriers to New Competition: Their Character and Consequences in Manufacturing Industries*, Cambridge, MA: Harvard University Press, 1956, and C. C. Von Weizsäcker in *Barriers to Entry: A Theoretical Treatment*, Berlin: Springer-Verlag, 1980.

[3] Bain, Joe, op. cit.

[4] Fisher, F., *Industrial Organization, Economics, and the Law*, Cambridge, MA: MIT Press, 1991.

Bain argued that an incumbent firm should analyze the entry conditions in its market and choose an entry-deterring strategy based on these conditions. If entry is blockaded or accommodated, the firm need do nothing more to deter entry. If entry is deterred, the firm should engage in a predatory act. To assess entry conditions, the firm must understand the magnitude of structural entry barriers, and consider the likely consequences of strategic entry barriers. We discuss the former below, and the latter in the next section.

Structural Entry Barriers

There are three main types of structural entry barriers:

- Control of essential resources
- Economies of scale and scope
- Marketing advantages of incumbency

We discuss each in turn.

Control of essential resources   An incumbent is protected from entry if it controls a resource necessary for production. DeBeers in diamonds, Alcoa in aluminum, and Ocean Spray in cranberries all maintained monopolies or cartels by controlling essential inputs. Does this imply that firms should acquire key inputs to gain monopoly status? There are several risks to this approach, some of which we discussed in Chapter 3, in the context of make-or-buy decisions. First, just when the firm thinks that it has tied up existing supplies, new input sources may emerge. For diamonds, aluminum, and cranberries, nature limits new input sources, which helps explain why these monopolies could endure. Second, owners of scarce resources may hold out for high prices before selling to the would-be monopolist.

There is also a regulatory risk associated with attaining monopoly status through acquisition. Antitrust laws in many nations forbid incumbents with dominant market shares from preventing competitors from obtaining key inputs. Under what has become known as the "essential facilities" doctrine, the U.S. Supreme Court in 1912 ordered the Terminal Railroad Association to permit competing railroads to use a bridge Terminal owned. As mentioned in Chapter 5, the bridge provided the only access into St. Louis from the east, and the Court feared that Terminal might use its control of the bridge to exclude rival railroads.[5] In 1985, the Supreme Court used similar reasoning to force the Aspen Skiing Company, which controlled three of the principle skiing mountains in Aspen, Colorado, to include in its six-day lift ticket access to a fourth facility controlled by another company.[6]

Incumbents can legally erect entry barriers by obtaining a patent to a novel and nonobvious product or production process. Patent laws vary by country, and in some countries, such as China and Brazil, they are nonexistent or extremely weak. An individual or firm that develops a marketable new product or process usually applies for a patent in its home country. In Europe and Japan, the patent rights go to the first person to apply for the patent. In the United States the first

---

[5] *United States v. Terminal R. R. Assn.*, 224 U.S. 383 (1912).

[6] *Aspen Skiing Co. v. Aspen Highlands Skiing Corp.*, 472 U.S. 585 (1985).

person to invent the idea gets the patent. As might be expected, firms seeking U.S. patents often go to considerable expense to document precedence of discovery. Once the patent is approved (it usually takes one to two years, and the invention is protected from imitation during the waiting period), anyone who wishes to use the process or make the product must obtain permission from the patent holder. Patent lives are currently 20 years in most developed nations.

Patents are not always effective entry barriers because they can often be "invented around," in part because a government patent office can sometimes not distinguish between a new product and an imitation of a protected product. As a result, some innovations, such as Rollerblades and the personal computer, seem to have had no patent protection whatsoever. Conversely, incumbents may file patent infringement lawsuits against entrants whose products are seemingly different from the incumbent's. Some observers claim that Intel used this strategy to protect its microprocessors from entry by Advanced Micro Devices.

Incumbents may not need patents to protect specialized know-how. Coca-Cola has zealously guarded its cola syrup formula for a century, and no one has learned how to duplicate the sound of a Steinway piano or the beauty of Waterford crystal. Firms may turn to the legally and ethically questionable practice of industrial espionage to steal such information.

EXAMPLE 10.2

PATENT PROTECTION IN THE PHARMACEUTICAL INDUSTRY

Patent protection is critical to success or failure in the pharmaceutical industry. For example, in the late 1960s, Eli Lilly introduced Keflin, the first of a new class of drugs called cephalosporins (a "magic bullet" antibiotic). Lilly introduced the first "second generation" cephalosporin, Keflex, in 1971. Though belonging to the same chemical class and having similar biological properties, Keflex and Keflin had sufficiently different structures to warrant separate patents. These drugs quickly became Lilly's top two sellers—one or both ranked among the top 10 selling prescription drugs in the United States every year between 1968 and 1985. The drugs would have sold even better if Lilly's patents had provided full protection. Differences in chemical structure enabled several competitors to introduce new cephalosporins by the late 1970s. A few, such as Merck's Mefoxin, also became top sellers.

Patents proved to be more enduring in the market for H2 antagonists (anti-ulcer medications). Tagamet, the first effective medication, was introduced by Smith, Kline, and French (later SmithKline) in 1978. By 1980, it was the top-selling prescription drug in the United States. In 1984, Glaxo's anti-ulcer drug Zantac was introduced, and a year later replaced Tagamet as the best-selling drug, with Tagamet running second. The substantial profits earned by SmithKline and Glaxo encouraged other companies to develop H2 antagonists. But Zantac and Tagamet sales held firm until their patents expired in the mid- to late-1990s. Faced with competition from generic drugs, SmithKline and Glaxo obtained approval to market their drugs for sale without prescription in the hope that consumers would purchase the drugs based on brand name (much the way that many consumers purchase branded aspirin).

Drug makers can reap enormous returns on their research investments for those handful of drugs, like Tagamet and Zantac, that treat common diseases yet have few substitutes. Those returns fall rapidly when patents expire. Drug makers thus became extremely concerned when the Food and Drug Administration (FDA) required lengthy testing for new drugs before marketing. These tests reduced the *effective patent lives* of new drugs (i.e., the time between FDA approval and the expiration of the patent) to as little as three years. In 1984, Congress enacted the Patent Term Restoration Act, which gives new drugs a minimum effective patent life of seven years. The act also simplified the testing requirements for generic manufacturers, thus intensifying postentry competition.

Economies of scale and scope When economies of scale are significant, established firms operating at or beyond the minimum efficient scale (MES) will have a substantial cost advantage over smaller entrants. The average cost curve in Figure 10.1 illustrates the problem facing a potential entrant in an industry where the MES is 1,000 units, and total industry sales are 10,000 units. An incumbent with a market share of 10 percent or higher is reaching the MES, and has average cost of AC_{MES}. If the entrant only achieves a market share of, say, 2 percent, it will have a much higher average cost of AC_E. The market price would have to be at least as high as AC_E for entry to be profitable.

The entrant might try to overcome the incumbent's cost advantage by spending to boost its market share. For example, it could advertise heavily or form a large sales force. While this strategy may allow the entrant to achieve a market share greater than 2 percent and average production costs below AC_E in Figure 10.1, it involves two important costs. The first is the direct cost of advertising and

FIGURE 10.1
ECONOMIES OF SCALE MAY BE A BARRIER TO ENTRY.

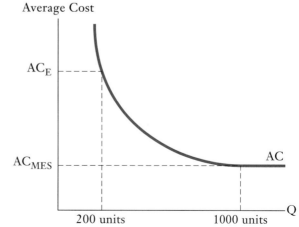

The incumbent firm producing at minimum efficient scale of 1,000 units per year has average costs AC_{MES}. If the potential entrant can only hope to produce a volume of output equal to 200 units per year, its average costs will equal AC_E. Market price must be at least this high for the potential entrant to realize profits from entry.

creating the sales force. The second is the indirect cost associated with a strategic reaction by the incumbent. For example, if the incumbent responds to a decline in its market share by reducing its price, this will cut into the entrants profits.[7] The entrant thus faces a dilemma: To overcome its cost disadvantage, it must increase its market share. But if its share increases, price competition may intensify.

Fierce price competition frequently results from large-scale entry into capital-intensive industries. Sometimes, this represents the results of intensified rivalry resulting from an increase in the number of firms competing in a market. Sometimes, this represents blatant efforts by incumbents to drive entrants out of business by pricing below marginal costs. This strategy, known as predatory pricing, is described below. The U.S. gunpowder industry in the nineteenth century offers an example of intense postentry rivalry. In 1889, eight firms, including the industry leader DuPont, formed a "gunpowder pool" to fix price and output. In the early 1890s, three new firms entered the industry. Their growth challenged the continued success of the pool. DuPont's response to one entrant was to "put the Chattanooga Powder Company out of business by selling at lower prices."[8] In this way, the gunpowder pool survived until antitrust enforcers broke it up. In the 1980s, entry into the airline business by Laker Airlines and People's Express led to price wars that eventually drove them from the market. The introduction of off-brand cigarettes by the Liggett Group in the early 1980s eventually led to hefty price reductions that eroded the profits of the entire tobacco industry. The off-price brands survived, perhaps because price-cost margins in the cigarette industry had been extremely high.

Incumbents may also derive a cost advantage from economies of scope. The ready-to-eat breakfast cereal industry provides a good example.[9] For several decades,

◆ ◆

XAMPLE 10.3

BARRIERS TO ENTRY IN THE AUSTRALIAN AIRLINE INDUSTRY

In 1992, a second attempt was made to start Australia's third airline, under the name Compass II. Compass' first startup effort, described in Chapter 9, came two years earlier, when there was considerable public support for a cut price domestic carrier. To leverage this public goodwill, the decision was made to use the name Compass II. To counter negative sentiment created when many "vacationers" were left stranded with worthless tickets when the original Compass went bankrupt, Compass II would honor the tickets issued by the original Compass airlines for a $20 fee. The new airline was forced to issue 100,000 of these $20 tickets. At the same time, Qantas and Ansett (the two incumbent airlines) both

---

[7]Such a pricing response is likely in this example, because when the entrant steals business from the incumbents, their marginal costs decrease.

[8]Fligstein, N., *The Transformation of Corporate Control*, Cambridge, MA: Harvard University Press, 1990.

[9]For a detailed discussion see Schmalensee, R., "Entry deterrence in the ready-to-eat breakfast cereal industry," *Bell Journal of Economics* 9 (2), 1978: pp. 305–27.

restarted an airfare price war with the new airline. These factors put major financial strains on an already under capitalized airline.

The biggest problem facing Compass II was the leasing of terminal space. Both Ansett and Qantas had been granted long leases on land at all Australia's major airports, and both airlines had invested considerable money in building terminal facilities. The government forced Qantas to lease terminal space to Compass II airlines. Compass II had to negotiate with Qantas for airport gates and boarding areas in their terminal. Not surprisingly, the boarding gates allocated to the new airline were all at least a half mile from the terminal entrance and the farthest gates from the terminal hub.

Compass II encountered many other obstacles. Qantas was responsible for baggage handling for Compass flights. The CEO of Compass II claimed that Qantas was committing "corporate sabotage" by delaying baggage handling for Compass flights, resulting in major delays for the new startup airline. Compass II lacked the terminal space to offer flight lounges for business travelers. This business service was critical, because several large companies offered to transfer large quantities of business travel to support airline competition, if Compass II could offer business class facilities. Another critical factor in attracting business travelers is flight frequency. Compass II could not compete with the incumbent airlines, both of whom were offering hourly flights between major Australian airports.

Compass II fell into bankruptcy less than 12 months after its incorporation, even faster than its predecessor. Incensed with the failure of its efforts to create a more competitive airline industry, the Australian government considered building a third "common use" terminal at all major Australian airports, for any airline wishing to lease terminal gates. The previous chairman of Compass announced an attempt to start a third discount airline, "Aussie Airlines." However, the two major airlines, Qantas and Ansett, both publicly committed to matching any airfares a future discount airline may offer. This commitment had the effect of scaring any investors from backing another startup airline. At the same time, the Australian government will not build any new "common use" terminal space until there are new airlines to lease these facilities, and potential investors see terminal space as a major requirement for any startup airline. It seems that the public's desire for a third carrier will not be satisfied anytime soon.

---

the industry has been dominated by a few firms, including Kellogg, General Mills, General Foods, and Quaker Oats, and there has been virtually no new entry since World War II. There are significant economies of scope in producing and marketing cereal. Economies of scope in production stem from the flexibility in materials handling and scheduling that arises from having multiple production lines within the same plant. Economies of scope in marketing are due to substantial up-front expenditures on advertising that are needed for a new entrant to establish a minimum acceptable level of brand awareness. It has been estimated that for entry to be worthwhile, a newcomer would need to introduce 6 to 12 successful brands.[10] Thus, capital requirements for entry are substantial, making entry a risky proposition.

---

[10]Scherer, F. M., "The Breakfast Cereal Industry," in *The Structure of American Industry* 7th ed., Adams, W. (ed.), New York: Macmillan, 1986.

An incumbent launching a new cereal would not face the same up-front costs as a new entrant. The incumbent has already established brand name awareness and may be able to use existing facilities to manufacture its new cereal. This explains why new products are profitable for incumbents but unprofitable for new entrants. Indeed, despite the near total absence of entry by outsiders, incumbents increased the number of cereals offered for sale from 88 in 1980 to over 200 in 1995. Successful newcomers have chosen niche markets, such as granola-based cereals, in which they may try to offset their cost disadvantage by charging premium prices.

Economies of scale and scope create barriers to entry because they force potential entrants to enter on a large scale or with many products to achieve unit cost parity with incumbent firms. Strictly speaking, though, entering at a large scale or scope is disadvantageous only to the extent that the entrant cannot recover its up-front entry costs if it subsequently decides to exit (i.e., only if the up-front entry costs are sunk costs). An entrant whose up-front entry costs were not sunk could come in at a large scale, undercut incumbent firms' prices, and exit the market and recover its entry costs if the incumbent firms retaliate. This strategy, known as *hit-and-run entry*, would leave incumbents vulnerable to entry even if economies of scale were so significant in comparison to market demand that the market could support only one firm. For this reason, as Daniel Spulber has pointed out, sunk costs, not economies of scale or scope per se, represent the underlying structural barrier to entry.[11] Still, in most markets entrants can only achieve scale and scope economies in production or marketing by making significant nonrecoverable up-front costs.

Marketing advantages of incumbency   Chapter 2 discussed umbrella branding, whereby a firm sells different products under the same brand name. This is a special case of economies of scope, but an extremely important one in many consumer product markets. An incumbent can exploit the umbrella effect to offset uncertainty about the quality of a new product that it is introducing. Consumers who are satisfied with the incumbent's old products are inclined to believe that its new product will also be satisfactory. The brand umbrella makes the incumbent's sunk cost of introducing a new product less than that of a new entrant because the entrant must spend additional amounts of money on advertising and product promotion to develop credibility in the eyes of consumers, retailers, and distributors.

A brand umbrella will not protect an incumbent if its new product turns out to be unsatisfactory. Would-be repeat purchasers will turn to other sellers' products, and word-of-mouth and poor reviews in consumer magazines may deter first-time purchasers. The incumbent may suffer even more if consumers' dissatisfaction with the new product leads them to doubt the quality of the rest of the incumbent's product line, or if managers of competing firms view the failure as a signal that the incumbent may be a less formidable competitor than they had thought. Thus, although the brand umbrella can give incumbents an advantage over entrants, the exploitation of brand name credibility or reputation is not risk free.

The umbrella effect may also help the incumbent negotiate the vertical chain. If an incumbent's other products have sold well in the past, distributors and retailers are more likely to devote scarce warehousing and shelf space to its new products. For example, Coke and Pepsi have launched new products with the confidence that retailers will allocate scarce shelf space to them. At the same

---

[11]Spulber, D. F., *Regulation and Markets*, Cambridge, MA: MIT Press, 1989.

time, suppliers may be more willing to sell on credit or extend favorable prices to successful incumbents. Physician management companies, such as PhyCor, have obtained purchasing discounts for physicians partly because suppliers trust these organizations to make good on their accounts payable.

EXAMPLE 10.4

ENTRY BARRIERS AND PROFITABILITY IN THE JAPANESE BREWING INDUSTRY

The Japanese brewing industry has enjoyed several decades of financial prosperity. The Japanese market for beer is enormous, with per capita consumption approaching 16 gallons per year. Four firms—Kirin, Asahi, Sapporo, and Suntory—account for almost 100 percent of the market. The market leader, Kirin, has a nearly 45 percent market share, and its annual sales rival those of Anheiser-Busch, the leading U.S. brewery. The industry after tax return on assets ranges from 3 to 4 percent, which is good in Japan where inflation is low. Moreover, these firms have been profitable for decades.

Normally, a profitable industry attracts entrants seeking to share the pie. Even so, Suntory is the only brewery to gain significant market share in Japan in the last 15 years, and its market share is only about 5 percent. Profitable incumbents combined with minimal entry usually indicate the presence of entry barriers. In the United States, profitable breweries are protected by strong brand identities. Would-be competitors must invest tens of millions of dollars or more to achieve the brand recognition and strength of image enjoyed by Budweiser and Miller. This deters serious competition from newcomers. Japanese brewers also enjoy brand identity, and brands like Kirin's Ichibanshibori, and Asahi's Super Dry have loyal followings. But Japanese brewers also enjoy two entry barriers not shared by U.S. firms. Entry has historically been restricted by the Japanese government, and the dominance of "Ma and Pa" retail stores complicates access to distribution channels.

Breweries in Japan must have a license from the Ministry of Finance (MOF). Before 1994, the MOF would not issue a license to any brewery producing fewer than 2 million liters annually. Although this is a relatively small percentage of the total market of 7 billion liters, it represents an imposing hurdle to a startup firm without an established brand name. It is not clear whether the MOF maintained this hurdle to protect the big four breweries, or to reduce the number of firms it needed to tax and regulate. As part of an overall liberalization of marketplace restrictions, the MOF has reduced the license threshold to 60,000 liters. In the wake of this change, existing small brewers formed a Small Brewers Association, and many new microbreweries opened.

The four incumbents responded by offering their own "gourmet" brews such as Kirin's Heartland and Sapporo's Edelpils. They have also expanded into malt liquors. This has earned them the continued loyalty of restaurant and bar owners, who are responsible for 50 percent of all retail beer sales in Japan. By combining clever marketing strategies (e.g., Heartland has a distinctive bottle and is not widely available in retail stores; Edilpils is positioned as a German-style beer) with the cost advantages of well-established distribution channels, the major breweries have maintained their stranglehold on the beer market.

Changes in Japanese retailing practices may eventually threaten the major breweries. After restaurants and bars, the second largest category of beer retailers are "Ma and Pa" liquor stores. These stores have had little purchasing power and have not aggressively sought to stock low-cost beers. In recent years, however, Japanese consumers have begun to turn to discount liquor stores offering savings of 25 percent or more on the same beers sold at family run stores. These discount stores (and, to a lesser extent, the supermarkets that are slowly replacing neighborhood groceries) are willing to sell imported beers. Imports cost two-thirds as much as domestic beers. Entry by imports, facilitated by the growth of new retail channels, could eventually force the big four breweries to lower prices to match the competition, lose market share, or both.

Barriers to Exit

Exit is the opposite of entry. To exit a market, a firm stops production and either redeploys or sells off its assets. A change in ownership that does not entail stopping production is not considered an exit. A risk-neutral, profit-maximizing firm will exit if the value of its assets in their best alternative use exceeds the present value from remaining in the market. However, exit barriers can limit the incentives for the firm to stop producing even when the prevailing conditions are such that the firm, had it known with certainty that these conditions would prevail, would not have entered in the first place.

Figure 10.2 illustrates the effect of exit barriers. The price P_{entry} is the *entry price*—the price at which the firm is indifferent between entering the industry and staying out. The price P_{exit} is the price below which the firm would either liquidate its assets or redeploy them to another market. Exit barriers drive a wedge between P_{exit} and P_{entry}.[12]

Exit barriers commonly arise when firms have obligations that they must meet whether or not they cease operations. Examples of such obligations include labor agreements and commitments to purchase raw materials. If a firm has to pay off its suppliers even if it stops production, the effective marginal cost of remaining in operation is low, and exit is less attractive. Obligations to input suppliers are a more significant exit barrier for diversified firms contemplating exit from a single market, since the suppliers to a faltering division are assured payment out of the

---

[12]In many industries there is an intermediate option short of full exit: the firm can "mothball" its production facilities and restart them when demand or cost conditions improve. Also, when there is demand uncertainty, the price that triggers entry will generally increase, and the price that triggers exit will generally decrease. This is because firms may defer entry or exit decisions to see how the uncertainty is resolved. See Dixit, A. K. and R. S. Pindyck, *Investment Under Uncertainty*, Princeton, NJ: Princeton University Press, 1994, for a lucid development of the theory of entry, exit, and mothballing under demand uncertainty.

FIGURE 10.2
THE PRICES THAT INDUCE ENTRY AND EXIT MAY DIFFER.

Firms will enter the industry as long as the market price exceeds P_{ENTRY}, the minimum level of average total costs. Firms will exit the industry only if price falls below P_{EXIT}, the minimum level of average variable costs.

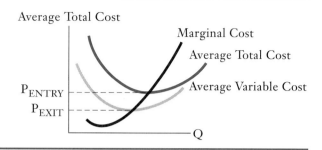

resources of the rest of the firm. Relationship-specific productive assets will have a low resale value, and are thus a second exit barrier.[13] Government restrictions are often a third exit barrier. For example, some states forbid hospitals to close without regulatory approval.

ENTRY-DETERRING STRATEGIES ◆ ◆ ◆ ◆ ◆

Under what conditions does it pay for incumbent firms to raise the barriers to entry into their market? At the most general level, entry-deterring strategies will succeed only if two conditions are met:

1. The incumbent earns higher profits as a monopolist than it does as a duopolist.
2. The strategy changes entrants' expectations about the nature of postentry competition.

The need for the first condition is obvious. The second condition is necessary because the entrant will ignore any strategy that does not change its expectations about postentry competition, rendering the strategy useless.

It seems as if a firm would always earn higher profits if it is a monopolist than if it has to share the market, because it can charge higher prices. If a monopolist cannot raise price above competitive levels, the market is said to be *perfectly contestable*, a concept developed by William Baumol, John Panzar, and Robert Willig.[14] The key requirement for contestability is hit-and-run entry, discussed earlier. When a monopolist raises price in a contestable market, a hit-and-run entrant rapidly enters the market, undercuts the price, reaps short-term profits, and exits the market just as rapidly if the incumbent retaliates. The hit-and-run entrant prospers as long as it can set a price high enough, and for a long enough time, to recover its sunk entry costs. If its sunk entry costs are zero, then hit-and-run entry will always be profitable. In that case, the market price can never be higher than average cost, even if only one firm is currently producing. If the incumbent raised price above average cost, there would be immediate entry, and price would fall.

---

[13]Asset specificity is discussed in Chapter 4.

[14]Baumol, W. J. Panzar, and R. Willig, *Contestable Markets and the Theory of Industrial Structure*, New York: Harcourt Brace Jovanovich, 1982.

The incumbent has to charge a price that yields zero profits, even when it is an apparent monopolist.

Contestability theory shows how the threat of entry can keep monopolists from raising prices. However, finding contestable markets has proven difficult. When the theory was first developed, it was felt that it might apply to the airline industry. Entry into the industry is fairly easy, especially by established carriers entering new routes. A carrier can redeploy aircraft almost overnight, and can secure gates and ground personnel almost as quickly (provided the airports involved are not at capacity.) New carriers can enter almost as fast, by leasing aircraft and gates. Even so, Severin Borenstein showed that airline markets are not perfectly contestable.[15] If they were, then fares should be independent of market concentration. However, Borenstein found that monopoly routes have higher fares than duopoly routes of comparable lengths. He also found that fares on monopoly routes are reduced when another carrier is already operating at one or both ends of the route. This makes sense. If fares on the monopoly route were high enough, such a carrier could quickly redeploy its aircraft there. Borenstein concluded that the threat of potential competition causes the monopolist carrier to moderate its prices, but not to competitive levels.

It would be surprising if airline markets were perfectly contestable. The hit-and-run entrant must be able to capture business before the incumbent can respond. But with computerized reservation systems linked to computerized tariff clearinghouses, such as the Airline Tariff Publishers, an incumbent airline can adjust its fares instantaneously in response to new entry. Faced with the prospects of duopoly pricing, the potential entrant may feel that the market is not large enough to support two firms, and will not enter. Incumbents in most markets can probably adjust prices rapidly when threatened by entry, so that the applications of the contestability theory are probably limited.[16]

Assuming that the incumbent monopolist's market is not perfectly contestable, it may expect to reap additional profits if it can keep out entrants. We now discuss three ways in which it might do so.

- Limit pricing

- Predatory pricing

- Capacity expansion

Limit Pricing

Limit pricing refers to the practice whereby an incumbent firm can discourage entry by charging a low price *before entry occurs*.[17] The entrant, observing the low price set by the incumbent, infers that the postentry price would be as low or even lower, and that entry into the market would therefore be unprofitable.

---

[15]Borenstein, S. "Hubs and High Fares: Dominance and Market Power in the U.S. Airline Industry," *RAND Journal of Economics*, 20, 1989: pp. 344–365.

[16]For a further discussion and critique of contestability, see Tirole, J. *The Theory of Industrial Organization*, Cambridge, MA: MIT Press, 1989.

[17]Bain, J. S., "A Note on Pricing in Monopoly and Oligopoly," *American Economic Review*, 39, March 1949: pp. 448–464.

To illustrate how a firm might deter entry by limit pricing, consider a market that will last for two years. Demand in each year is given by $P = 100 - Q$, where P denotes price and Q denotes quantity. The production technology has nonrecoverable fixed costs of $800 per year, and constant marginal costs of $10. In the first year, there is a single firm with the technological know-how to compete in this market. We call this firm N. Another firm that we call E has developed the technology to enter the market in year 2. Table 10.1 summarizes useful pricing and profit information about this market. This information can be confirmed by solving for the appropriate profit-maximizing prices and quantities.

If there were no danger of entry, N would select the monopoly price of $55 in each year, earning two-year total profits of $2,450. (For simplicity, we ignore the effect of discounting second-year profit.) Firm N is less fortunate, because firm E might enter in year 2. To determine if it should enter, E must anticipate the nature of postentry competition. Suppose that when E observes N charging $55 in the first year, it concludes that N will not be an aggressive competitor. Specifically, it expects the Cournot equilibrium to prevail in the second year, with both firms sharing the market equally.[18] Based on this expectation, E calculates that it will earn profits of $100 if it enters. If N shares E's belief that competition will be Cournot, then conditional on entry, firm N would also expect to earn $100 in the second year. This would give it a combined two-year profit of $1,325, which is far below its two-year monopoly profit of $2,450. Entry would be costly to firm N.

Firm N may wonder if it can deter entry. It could reason as follows:

> If I set a low first-year price, perhaps E will expect the postentry price also to be low. If E expects the postentry price to be sufficiently low, then it will not enter, and I can earn monopoly profits in the second year.

Following this logic, suppose that firm N selects a first-year price of $30. E may see this price and reason as follows:

> If firm N charges a price of $30 when it is a monopolist, then surely its price in the face of competition will be even lower. Suppose we enter and, optimistically, the price remains at $30, so that total market demand is 70. If we can achieve a 50 percent market share, we will sell 35 units, and realize profits of $\{(30 - 10) \times 35\} - 800 = -\$100$. If the price is below $30, we will fare even worse. We should not enter.

If both firms follow this logic, then N should set a limit price of $30. By doing so, it will earn $\{(30 - 10) \times 70\} - 800 = \$600$ in the first year and full monopoly profits of $1,225 in the second year, for total profits of $1,825. This exceeds the profits

TABLE 10.1

PRICE AND PROFITS UNDER DIFFERENT COMPETITIVE CONDITIONS

Market Structure	Price	Annual Profit per Firm
Monopoly	$55	$1225
Cournot Duopoly	$40	$100

---

[18]Recall from Chapter 7 that in a Cournot equilibrium, each firm makes a guess about the other's output, and the guesses prove to be correct.

it would have earned had it set the monopoly price of $55 in the first period and then shared the market in the second year.

The Flawed Logic of Limit Pricing

The previous argument is appealing, but flawed. The first flaw is the artificiality of a two-year model. In a more realistic setting of more than two years, firm N might have to limit price every year to constantly deter entry. It would never get to raise price to reap the monopoly profits that it forsook when it initially set the limit price. Limit pricing would be attractive only if the incumbent does not need to lower its price too much to deter entry. This could occur if N enjoys a substantial cost advantage over E and sets its price equal to or just below E's minimum average cost. By virtue of N's cost advantage, it could reap large profits indefinitely. Edwin Blackstone uses this argument in his analysis of Xerox's pricing of plain paper copiers in the 1960s, which we describe in Example 10.5.[19]

A second flaw is that the limit pricing argument relies on an equilibrium that is not *subgame perfect*.[20] In particular, E's expectations about N's postentry pricing are irrational. To see where the logic of limit pricing breaks down, we depict the limit pricing game in game tree form in Figure 10.3. The payoffs to N and E are calculated by using the demand and cost data from the previous example.

Figure 10.3 shows that in year one, the incumbent's strategic choices are (P_m, P_l), where P_m refers to the monopoly price of $55, and P_l refers to the limit price of $30. The entrant observes N's selection, and then chooses from (In, Out).

FIGURE 10.3
LIMIT PRICING: EXTENSIVE FORM GAME.

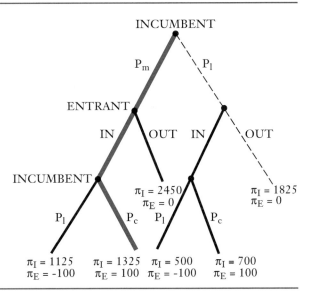

The limit pricing equilibrium is shown by the dashed line. The incumbent selects P_l, and the potential entrant stays out. This is not a subgame perfect Nash equilibrium, because if the potential entrant goes in, the incumbent will select the accommodating price P_c in the second period. The subgame perfect Nash equilibrium is depicted by the heavy line. The incumbent knows that it cannot credibly prevent entry, so it sets P_m in the first period.

[19]Blackstone, E. "Limit Pricing in the Copying Machine Industry," *Quarterly Review of Economics and Business*, 12, 1972: pp. 57–65.

[20]See the Economics Primer for a discussion of the concept of a subgame perfect equilibrium.

If E selects "Out," then N selects P_m in year two. If E selects "In," then competition is played out in year two. We suppose that N can control the nature of year-two competition. In particular, N can maintain the price at $P_l = 30$, or it can "acquiesce" and permit Cournot competition, in which case the price will be $P_c = 40$. Two-year payoffs are reported at the end node for each branch of the game tree.

The limit pricing outcome is shown by the dashed line in Figure 10.3. Under this outcome, firm N earns total profits of $1,825, and firm E earns $0. This is not a subgame perfect equilibrium, however. To see why not, we must analyze the game using the "fold-back" method.[21] First consider the branch of the game tree in which E ignores the limit price and chooses to enter. According to the limit-pricing argument, E stays out because it expects that *after entry has occurred*, N will select P_l. But examination of the game tree shows that it is not rational for N to select P_l. Conditional on entry having already occurred, N should select P_c. N would earn total profits of $700, which exceeds the profits of $500 it earns if it selects P_l. Thus, E's expectation of N's postentry behavior is flawed.

E should anticipate that if it enters, N will select P_c. E should calculate its profits from entry to be $100, which exceeds the profits of 0 that it earns if it stays out. Thus, E will choose to enter, even if N has selected P_l in the first stage of the game. Continuing to work backward, N should anticipate that it cannot prevent entry even if it selects P_l. It should calculate that if it does select P_l, it will earn profits of $700. By selecting P_m in the first stage and P_c in the second stage, N could have earned $1,325.

Our analysis of the game tree is now complete. N will select P_m in the first stage. E will select "In." Second-year competition will be Cournot. This subgame perfect Nash equilibrium is shown by the heavy solid line in Figure 10.3.

This analysis suggests that incumbent firms should not limit price. Potential entrants will recognize that any price reductions before entry are artificial, and do not commit the incumbent to maintain low prices subsequent to entry. Once entry occurs, it would make no sense for the incumbent to continue to suppress price. The lost profit opportunities from having previously set the limit price are sunk. Now that the entrant is already in the market, the incumbent should acquiesce and maximize future profits.

◆ ◆

XAMPLE 10.5

LIMIT PRICING BY XEROX

In 1960, Xerox introduced the 914 plain paper copier, the first mass-marketed product to take advantage of the innovative copying technology called xerography. A competing technology being developed at the time, electrofax, had several disadvantages. It required a paper coating that added $.01 to the cost of each copy, and the quality of its reproductions was inferior. When electrofax finally reached the market, copying centers had to charge $.005 less per electrofax page

---

[21]See the Economics Primer for a discussion of the use of the "fold-back" method to determine subgame perfect equilibria.

to induce customers to use electrofax instead of Xerox. This gave Xerox an effective $.015 advantage per copy. Xerox machines had higher manufacturing costs, however. This translated into a higher retail price, which somewhat offset the lower effective cost per copy.

Xerox usually leased copiers, charging a sliding fee per copy depending on the number of copies made per month. Xerox sought a fee schedule that would deter entry. Edwin Blackstone carefully examined Xerox's prices and costs, as well as the prices and costs of the rival electrofax process to determine if Xerox did, in fact, limit price.

Blackstone estimated that Xerox's monopoly price was about $.10 per page, which was well above the average cost of electrofax copies. If Xerox set this price, electrofax manufacturers might be tempted to enter the market. Blackstone reported that for small customers, who made approximately 1,000 copies per month, Xerox charged close to the monopoly price. But for medium and large customers, who made over 2,000 copies per month, Xerox charged only about $.05 per page.

Blackstone argued that these prices were consistent with a limit pricing strategy. The 914 had a high manufacturing cost, so that for a small user, the electrofax actually had a smaller effective cost per page. Xerox felt that it could not forestall entry into the small customer segment, and did not artificially reduce its price. As a result, about 25 electrofax firms entered this end of the market by 1968. Xerox had a significant cost advantage among medium and large users, however. It could afford to reduce prices to medium and large customers and still cover average costs. Xerox hoped that this would limit entry. The strategy appeared to succeed; by 1968, only 10 electrofax firms competed in the medium and large customer segments.

Xerox continued to prosper in the plain paper copier market until the government forced it to share its technology (even before its patents expired) in the early 1970s. Many companies, including IBM and Litton, then entered the market. By 1978, Xerox's market share of new copiers fell from 100 percent to about 40 percent, and prices fell by 30 percent. The price reductions suggest that Xerox was making substantial profits even when it was limit pricing.

Rescuing Limit Pricing—When Might It Make Sense?

This critique of the logic of limit pricing seems to suggest that no rational firm would ever limit price. Yet anecdotal examples, and a few systematic analyses (such as Blackstone's analysis of Xerox) indicate that limit pricing does occur. One possible explanation is that firms set prices irrationally. If this is correct (and we doubt that it often is), then this analysis should warn firms that limit price: Don't do it! Another explanation is that limit pricing is rational, but that the analysis thus far fails to capture important elements of the strategic interaction.

Game theorists have identified key conditions under which limit pricing may be profitable. In general, entering firms must be *uncertain* about some characteristic of the incumbent firm or the level of market demand. Reexamination of the extensive form game shows why uncertainty is important. The incumbent wants the entrant to believe that postentry prices will be low. If the entrant is not uncertain about what determines postentry pricing, the entrant can calculate the incumbent's payoffs from all possible postentry pricing scenarios and correctly forecast the postentry price. If the incumbent is best off selecting a high postentry price, the entrant will know this, and will not be deterred from entering.

If the entrant is uncertain about the postentry price, however, then the incumbent's pricing strategy could affect the entrant's expectations. Two types of uncertainty may confound the entrant's forecast. The first is uncertainty about the incumbent's objectives. The analysis of *predatory pricing* discussed in the next section illustrates how this type of uncertainty can promote behaviors that seem irrational in a world of certainty. The second is uncertainty about the incumbent's costs or the level of market demand, which we now discuss.

In a paper that explored the rationality of limit pricing, Paul Milgrom and John Roberts argued that an entrant is likely to know less about the incumbent's costs than the incumbent itself does.[22] If so, by engaging in limit pricing the incumbent may influence the entrant's estimate of its costs, and thus shape its expectations of postentry profitability. To illustrate this argument, suppose that the entrant believes that the incumbent's marginal cost is either $5 or $10. It expects that postentry competition will be Cournot. If it knew for certain that the incumbent's marginal cost is $10, then, as before, the entrant will expect profits of $100 in the second year and would want to enter. If it knew for certain that the incumbent's marginal cost is $5, however, then the entrant would expect profits of − $56 and would not enter.

If the incumbent did not think strategically, it would set its first-year price according to its marginal cost and the demand curve. If its marginal cost was $10, then its first-year price would be $55. If its marginal cost was $5, then its first year-price would be $52.50. If the entrant knew that the incumbent was not thinking strategically, then it could observe the incumbent's first-year price and immediately infer its marginal cost. For example, if the incumbent set a first-year price of $55, the entrant could infer that the incumbent's marginal cost was $10, and therefore that entry would be profitable. If the incumbent thinks strategically, however, then if it has marginal costs of $10, it may reason as follows:

> I should try to convince the entrant that my marginal cost is $5, because it will not want to compete against me if it thinks I have such low costs. I should set a price of $52.50, which is what the entrant would expect from a low-cost incumbent. Then, the entrant would not know if it was facing a low-cost or high-cost incumbent, and might decide not to enter.

In their analysis, Milgrom and Roberts recognized that because a high-cost incumbent could lower its price to disguise its costs, a low-cost incumbent would try to make sure that the entrant would recognize its cost advantage. To do so, a low-cost incumbent would lower its price by a sufficiently large amount below $52.50, so that the potential entrant is convinced that *only* a low-cost producer would price that low. In effect, a low price becomes a credible *signal* that the incumbent's cost is low. Thus, a low-cost incumbent would price below $52.50. Ironically, though, since the low-cost incumbent charges a price that a rational high-cost incumbent would not charge, the entrant could infer the incumbent's true marginal costs from the first-year price. The high-cost incumbent's limit price would not deter entry.

---

[22]Milgrom, P. and J. Roberts, "Limit Pricing and Entry Under Incomplete Information," *Econometrica*, 50, 1982: pp. 443–460.

Garth Saloner has pointed out that for limit pricing to deter entry, the entrant must be unable to perfectly infer the incumbent's cost from its limit price.[23] Saloner supposed that the entrant may be uncertain about the level of demand as well as the incumbent's cost. These two types of uncertainty support an equilibrium in which (a) the incumbent prices below its single-year monopoly price regardless of its cost, and (b) the lower the incumbent's cost, the lower the price that it sets. The low price signals to the entrant that the incumbent's costs may be low and/or market demand may be low. Either signal may deter entry.

Generalizing from Saloner's model, we conclude that the entrant must be uncertain about postentry competition for limit pricing to be effective. Experienced entrants who have competed in many markets and are well-informed about incumbent's costs and the level of market demand are unlikely to be fooled by limit pricing. The limit-pricing incumbent sacrifices short-term profits without affecting long-term competition.

Predatory Pricing

Predatory pricing refers to the practice of setting a price in order to drive other firms out of business. The difference between predatory pricing and limit pricing is that limit pricing is directed at firms that have not yet entered the market, whereas predatory pricing is aimed at firms that have already entered. All definitions of predatory pricing involve the idea that the predatory firm sets its price below cost (e.g., average variable cost or short-run marginal cost) with the expectation that it will recover whatever losses it incurs after entrants or competitors have been driven from the market, and it can exercise market power.[24]

The Chain-Store Paradox

It seems intuitive that an incumbent that prices below cost in one market may be able to deter entry in other markets in the future. The intuitive argument, however, is not always valid. To see why, imagine that an incumbent firm operates in 12 markets, and faces entry in each. In January, it faces entry in market 1; in February, it faces entry in market 2; and so on. Should the incumbent slash prices in January?

We can answer this question by working backward from December, to see how earlier pricing decisions affect later entry. Regardless of the course of action before December, the incumbent will find it optimal not to engage in predatory pricing in market 12. The reason is that there is no further entry to deter. *The entrant in the twelfth market knows this*, and counting on the rationality of the incumbent, will enter regardless of previous price cuts. But knowing that it cannot deter entry in the twelfth market, the incumbent has no reason to slash prices in November in the eleventh market either. The potential entrant in the eleventh market can anticipate that the incumbent will not slash prices against it, and so enters

[23]Saloner, G. "Dynamic Equilibrium Limit Pricing in an Uncertain Environment," mimeo, Graduate School of Business, Stanford University. See also Matthews, S. and L. Mirman, "Equilibrium Limit Pricing: The Effects of Stochastic Demand," *Econometrica*, 51, 1983: pp. 981–996.

[24]See Martin, S., *Industrial Economics*, New York: Macmillan, 1988, for a good review of the various legal tests for predatory pricing that have been proposed.

without fear of retaliation. In October, the incumbent realizes that come November, it will certainly face entry in the market 11. Thus, it calculates that there is no deterrent value to slashing prices in market 10. The potential entrant in the tenth market can figure this out too, and so enters. In this way, the problem completely unravels, so that the incumbent realizes that it has nothing to gain from predatory pricing in January in the first market! The striking conclusion is this: In a world in which all entrants could accurately predict the future course of pricing, predatory pricing would not deter entry, and therefore would be irrational.

To test this conclusion, R. Mark Isaac and Vernon Smith conducted an experiment in which students played a predation "game." They found that student subjects behaved in accordance with this theory. In their experiment, a student played the role of an incumbent for several periods, setting prices in competition with different students in each period. Students had complete information about payoffs. Isaac and Smith found that "incumbent" students did not slash prices.[25]

This result that predation is seemingly irrational is associated with a puzzle in economics known as the *chain-store paradox*.[26] The paradox is that, despite the conclusion that predatory pricing to deter entry is irrational, many firms are commonly perceived as slashing prices to deter entry. The gunpowder pool cited earlier is one example. Standard Oil, whose pricing policies in the 19th century are described in Example 10.7, is another. The paradox is resolved by considering the role of uncertainty.

Predatory pricing in the chain-store paradox is irrational because potential entrants can perfectly predict incumbent behavior in every market and are certain that predatory pricing in the "last" market is irrational, no matter what has happened up to that point. If entrants lack such certainty, then price cutting by an incumbent may affect their expectations of the incumbent's future pricing strategy. For example, suppose that the entrant stands to make profits of π_a if the incumbent is an "easy" competitor and incur losses of π_p if the incumbent is a "tough competitor," where $\pi_a > 0 > \pi_p$. In other words, a tough incumbent's single-period profit maximizing price is so low that the entrant would lose money. This might occur if the tough incumbent has substantially lower variable costs than does the entrant. Suppose also that the entrant believes that the probability that the incumbent is tough is ρ, and the probability that the incumbent is easy is $1 - \rho$. If S equals the sunk costs of entry, then the expected profitability of entry is $(1 - \rho)\pi_a + \rho\pi_p - S$.

Clearly, the potential entrant would like to know something about ρ. Suppose that it is certain that the incumbent is easy, that is, $\rho = 0$. Then it will enter as long as $\pi_a > S$, that is, as long as the profits from postentry competition when the incumbent cooperates exceed the sunk cost of entry. However, if the potential entrant believes that the incumbent is tough (i.e., ρ is close to 1), it will forecast that it is unlikely to generate sufficient profits to offset the costs of entry, and will stay out.

Obviously, the incumbent wants the entrant to believe that ρ is high. The incumbent could influence the entrant's perceptions by setting a low price in its established markets. Following the logic of the Milgrom-Roberts and Saloner

[25]Isaac, R. M. and V. Smith, "In Search of Predatory Pricing," *Journal of Political Economy*, 93, 1985: pp. 320–345.

[26]This term was coined by the game theorist Reinhard Selten in his article, "The Chain Store Paradox," *Theory and Decision*, 9, 1978: pp. 127–159.

limit-pricing analyses, the entrant might infer that an incumbent that sets extremely low prices in its established markets probably has low variable costs, and therefore that ρ is big and entry is likely to be unprofitable. If the incumbent instead sets high prices in its established markets, the entrant may feel that ρ is small and that entry is profitable. Thus, predation may deter entry.

Even if the potential entrant is certain of the incumbent's costs, predation may still deter entry. Suppose that the entrant believes that some firms simply dislike competition and will go to great lengths to protect their market share, even by sacrificing profits. If a firm can develop a *reputation for toughness*, entrants may be reluctant to challenge it. In an experiment, Yun Joo Jung, John Kagel, and Dan Levin found that when students playing a predation game were unsure about the incumbent's tendencies, incumbents did slash prices to deter entry.[27]

Some well-known firms, including Wal-Mart and American Airlines, enjoy a reputation for toughness earned after fierce price competition led to the demise of rivals. Aggressiveness is also a natural outgrowth of strategies to increase market share. Some firms announce a mission to achieve dominant market shares, such as Black and Decker and McCormick Spices. These announcements may effectively signal to rivals that these firms will do whatever is necessary, even sustain price wars, to secure their share of the market. Along these lines, firms may promote toughness by rewarding workers for aggressiveness in the market. Chaim Fershtman and Kenneth Judd suggest that a firm might want to reward managers based on market share rather than profits.[28] This will encourage them to price aggressively, thereby enhancing the firm's reputation for toughness, and could ultimately lead to higher profits than if managers were focusing on the bottom line.

EXAMPLE 10.6

COFFEE WARS[29]

In 1970, General Food's Maxwell House was the best selling brand of coffee east of the Mississippi. Procter and Gamble's (P&G's) Folgers brand was the best seller to the west. In 1971, P&G started selling Folger's in parts of the Midwest and East where it had not sold before. P&G first introduced Folger's in Cleveland in 1971. P&G followed this with introductions in Pennsylvania in 1973, and

[27]Jung, Y. J., J. Kagel, and D. Levin, "On the Existence of Predatory Pricing: An Experimental Study of Reputation and Entry Deterrence in the Chain-store Game," *The Rand Journal of Economics*, 25(1), 1994: pp. 72–93.

[28]Fershtman, C. and K. Judd, "Equilibrium Incentives in Oligopoly," *American Economic Review*, 77, 1984: pp. 927–940.

[29]This example draws on the Federal Trade Commission's opinion in General Food Corp., reprinted in *Antitrust and Trade Regulation Report*, May 3, 1984, pp. 888–905; and Hilke, J. and P. Nelson, "Strategic Behavior and Attempted Monopolization: The Coffee (General Foods) Case," in Kwoka, J. and L. J. White (eds.), *The Antitrust Revolution*, Glenview, IL: Scott Foresman, 1989, pp. 208–240.

Syracuse, New York, in 1974, before expanding throughout the East in 1979. To promote Folger's in Cleveland, P&G used a combination of television advertising, retailer's promotions, coupons, in-pack gifts, and free samples in the mail. General Foods responded with mailed and in-pack coupons as well as promotional incentives for retailers to sell Maxwell House. Even so, Folgers claimed 15 percent of the Cleveland market in its first year.

By 1972, executives in General Foods' Maxwell House division were concerned about Folger's "disturbingly successful" entry into Cleveland and feared similar successes throughout the East. At that point, General Foods adopted what came to be known as its "defend now" strategy, which attempted to limit Folger's share in the East to 10 percent. This strategy involved heavy price discounting, although General Foods instructed its Maxwell House executives not to sell the coffee below average variable costs. Regardless of these instructions, evidence presented during the Federal Trade Commission's investigation of this case suggest that Maxwell House *was* sold below average variable cost in Cleveland (from 1973 to 1974), Pittsburgh (from 1973 to 1975), and Syracuse (from 1974 to 1976). Maxwell House also introduced a so-called fighting brand (Horizon) explicitly to disrupt Folger's launch in Philadelphia and Syracuse. The evidence suggests that Horizon was also priced below its average variable cost.

It certainly appears that General Foods was signaling to P&G that it intended to fight aggressively to defend its dominant position in eastern markets. Internal General Foods' documents seem to confirm this. They spoke of a desire to "delay Folger expansion," "force them to carefully consider the financial wisdom of further eastern expansion," and to engage in "eye for eye" retaliation.[30]

In 1976, the staff of the Federal Trade Commission charged General Foods with attempted monopolization, unfair competition, and price discrimination in the ground coffee market. In 1984, the full Commission exonerated General Foods. The commission reasoned that the relevant coffee market was the United States as a whole (as opposed to individual, geographically-based markets) and that within this broader market General Foods did not possess the market power to raise prices above competitive levels should other competitors exit. As a result, the Commission concluded, " . . . Maxwell House did not come dangerously close to gaining monopoly power as a result of any of its challenged conduct in any of the alleged markets. As a result, its actions were output-enhancing and procompetitive—the kind of conduct the antitrust laws seek to promote."[31]

Excess Capacity

Many firms carry excess capacity. To measure capacity utilization, every year the U.S. Census of Manufacturers asks plant managers to state the levels of current and desired production. The resulting ratio, called *capacity use*, is typically about 80 percent. Firms hold more capacity than they use for several reasons. In some industries, it is economical to add capacity only in large increments. If firms build capacity ahead of demand, then such industries may be characterized by periods in

---

[30]Hilke and Nelson, op, cit, pp. 235–236.

[31]Re *General Foods Corp.*, 901.

which firms carry excess capacity. Downturns in the general economic business cycle, or a decline in demand for a single firm can also create excess capacity. Firms in imperfectly competitive industries may be profitable when operating at capacity. Other firms may then enter seeking a share of those profits, creating excess capacity. In these examples, excess capacity results from market forces.

Firms may also hold excess capacity for strategic purposes. By holding excess capacity, an incumbent may affect how potential entrants view postentry competition, and thereby blockade entry. For example, an incumbent that holds excess capacity may signal its intention to cut prices if entry occurs. The models of predatory pricing and limit pricing suggest that such a signal can be effective if the entrant is uncertain about the incumbent's intentions, and it believes that aggressive incumbents are more likely to hold excess capacity than are accommodating incumbents.

Unlike predatory pricing and limit pricing, excess capacity may deter entry even when the entrant possesses complete information about the incumbent's strategic intentions. The reason is that when an incumbent builds excess capacity, it can expand output at a relatively low cost. Facing competition, the incumbent may find it desirable to expand its output considerably, regardless of the impact on the entrant's profits. This will have the effect, intended or not, of substantially reducing the entrant's postentry profits. If postentry profits are less than the sunk costs of entry, the entrant will stay out. The monopolist incumbent may even decide not to utilize all of its capacity, with the idle capacity serving as a *credible commitment* that the incumbent will expand output should entry occur.

"Judo Economics" and the "Puppy Dog-Ploy"

In this chapter, we have provided examples in which an incumbent firm has used its size and reputation to put smaller rivals at a disadvantage. Sometimes, however, smaller firms and potential entrants can use the incumbent's size to their own advantage. This is known as "judo economics."[32] Consider that when an incumbent slashes prices to drive an entrant from the market, it sacrifices its own short-run profits. The larger is the incumbent, the greater the loss. If an entrant can convince the incumbent that it does not pose a significant long-term threat to the incumbent's profitability, the incumbent might think twice about incurring large losses to drive the entrant from the market. This example of judo economics is closely related to the "puppy dog ploy" described in Chapter 9.

An example is provided by Braniff Airlines. Restaurateur and doll company owner Jeffrey Chodorow and real estate developer Arthur Cohen purchased a struggling Braniff in 1988. Braniff went bankrupt the next year. In settling the Braniff assets, Chodorow and Cohen bought the rights to the Braniff trademark for $313,000, took over bankrupt Emerald Airlines, and combined the two into a new Braniff. Braniff publicly announced in the spring of 1991 that it intended to limit its flights from Dallas to Los Angeles, New York, Florida, and the Caribbean. Braniff started flying scheduled trips in June 1991. It had some immediate setbacks, including flying a banned Boeing 727 into Los Angeles International Airport (the plane violated local noise pollution ordinances). But Braniff's fate was sealed even before its first scheduled flight took off. In a move that many believe was prompted by Braniff's reentry into its home market of Dallas, Ameri-

---

[32]Gelman, J. and S. Salop, "Judo Economics: Capacity Limitation and Coupon Competition," *Bell Journal of Economics*, 14, 1983: pp. 315–325.

can Airlines introduced "value pricing" on May 27, 1991, triggering a price war that drove Braniff from the market for good two months later.

If it had stayed true to its word, Braniff would only have carried 3 percent as many passengers as American. So why did American respond aggressively to Braniff's puppy-dog ploy? Perhaps American feared that other airlines might enter (i.e., American may have set a predatory price to deter later entry). Unless resource constraints or patents deter future entrants, the puppy-dog may meet with an aggressive response. Even if American was unconcerned about future entry, it might not have believed Braniff's promise to stay small. In general, there are few ways that a firm can credibly commit not to grow.

Netscape's announcement in January 1998 that it would make the source code of its new browser, Communicator 5.0, freely available on the internet provides another example of judo economics. This move enabled sophisticated programmers to customize the Communicator browser to their own idiosyncratic needs. Many firms would be expected to prefer such a customized product to Microsoft's Internet Explorer. Given that Microsoft seemed on the verge of dominating the browser market, why would Microsoft not limit the impact of Netscape's move by permitting customization of its own Internet Explorer browser? As explained by Carl Shapiro and Hal Varian, Microsoft would be unlikely to do this because its success had been driven by uniformity—all users of Internet Explorer have identical software (just as all users of Microsoft operating systems have identical software).[33] Consumers benefited from the resulting compatibility and this is central to Microsoft's strategic vision. By facilitating customization, Netscape anticipated that Microsoft's past successes would prevent it from pursuing the same strategy. Shapiro and Varian concluded that this strategy might earn Netscape a black belt!

EXIT-PROMOTING STRATEGIES ◆ ◆ ◆ ◆ ◆

Firms occasionally contend that their rivals are slashing prices to drive them from the market. The complaining firm argues that consumers should object to low prices, because eventually the price slasher will have monopoly power, raise prices, and more than recoup its losses. As detailed in Example 10.7, oil refiners advanced these arguments when they attempted to break up the Standard Oil Trust 100 years ago. In 1993, three drugstores in Conway, Arkansas, made a similar claim about the local Wal-Mart store. They sued Wal-Mart under state antitrust statutes, and won a $300,000 award, plus a court order forcing Wal-Mart to increase its drug prices. Complaints about unfairly low prices are common during trade disputes. In 1991, the U.S. Department of Commerce ruled that Toyota and Mazda were *dumping* minivans into the U.S. market—by pricing below cost—although the International Trade Commission ruled a year later that American automakers were not harmed by such practices and were not entitled to compensation (begging the question of why Toyota and Mazda would sell below cost in the first place). In 1993, 37 nations accused Chinese firms of dumping products ranging from electronics to textiles, and in 1994, the United States accused the Canadian Wheat Board of dumping wheat. The international General Agreement on Tariffs and Taxation (GATT) is frequently renegotiated to deal with complex dumping issues.

[33] Shapiro, C. and H. Varian, "A Judo Blow Against Microsoft," *Wall Street Journal*, February 2, 1998, section I, p. 22.

◆ ◆

ℰXAMPLE 10.7

HOW STANDARD OIL DROVE OUT ITS COMPETITORS[34]

In 1865, John D. Rockefeller, the senior partner in a Cleveland oil refinery, bought the failing company at auction. Rockefeller's company grew and changed its name to Standard Oil. When the U.S. Supreme Court ordered its breakup in 1911, Standard Oil was the largest business in the world. Rockefeller built his giant by exploiting scale and scope economies in refining, distribution, and purchasing, careful organization of the vertical chain, and by destroying rivals that stood in his way.

Demand for oil boomed following the Civil War, and Rockefeller reinvested all of his profits into expanding Standard Oil's refining capacity. Because of its size, Standard could obtain discounts when shipping oil by rail. But Standard did more than obtain discounts. It instituted the practice of "drawbacks," whereby for every barrel sent to New York by a competitor, the rails paid Standard Oil a fee. Naturally, the rails passed this fee along to their other customers, so in effect Standard Oil was subsidized by its competitors.

Standard soon had near monopsony power in the refining and distribution of oil. As Standard prospered, oil producers were finding rich sources of new supply, so that the price of oil in the 1870s fell precipitously. While Rockefeller felt that enormous profits could be realized in the vertical chain of oil production, he recognized that producers had grown too poor and fragmented to achieve them. He would reap all the profits that oil had to offer by gaining a stranglehold over refining.

It is generally accepted that Standard came to dominate refining through predatory pricing. (It has also been alleged that Standard occasionally blew up competing pipelines.) Rockefeller would often offer to acquire a local refiner. When rebuffed, Standard would cut prices, until the refiner was driven from business. Often, Standard employed "shadow" companies—companies operating under different names, but owned by Standard. Standard thus tried to avoid bad publicity. By 1879, Standard Oil had captured 90 percent of America's oil refining capacity, and owned all the pipelines of the oil regions. Standard then raised prices to oil producers, squeezing all of the profits out of the vertical chain.

Oil producers, fragmented though they were, responded to Standard's monopsony power by building the first long-distance pipeline, connecting the Pennsylvania oil fields with the Pennsylvania and Reading Railroad. This pipeline—a technological marvel at the time—took Rockefeller by surprise. Standard responded by immediately building long distance pipelines from the oil regions to all of the major oil refining markets. This foreclosed further forward integration. While oil producers could build competing pipelines, they could not count on each other to avoid using Standard Oil's. This made further pipeline development too risky.

Almost immediately after the construction of the long-distance pipelines, oil producers sought to destroy Standard Oil's power by challenging its practices

---

[34]The description of Standard Oil's practices is taken from Yergin, D., *The Prize*, New York: Simon & Schuster, 1991.

under state anticompetitive statutes. But during the early 1880s, Rockefeller carefully set Standard up as a trust, so Standard did not actually own the companies it had acquired; rather, it held the shares of those companies "in trust" for the shareholders of Standard Oil. This enabled Standard to avoid antitrust problems until it was prosecuted, and eventually broken up in 1911, by federal "trustbusters" using the powers of the Sherman Antitrust Act of 1890.

Not everyone agrees that Standard's pricing policies amounted to predation. John McGee observes that Standard eventually acquired almost all of the refiners that it allegedly preyed on.[35] He argues that it made no sense for Standard Oil to conduct costly price wars if its intention was acquisition. Yamey provided two rebuttals to McGee.[36] First, he pointed out that Standard may have used predation to frighten future opposition as well as to soften up existing competition. Second, Standard may have been able to buy at a more favorable price if its rivals feared an all-out war of attrition. The latter possibility is buttressed by Malcolm Burns, who found that the American Tobacco Trust reduced acquisition costs by preying on its targets.[37]

As discussed, Standard's practices would not have made sense if its rivals could have correctly assessed the future of competition. McGee argues that many refinery owners were knowledgeable about Standard's cost position, and some were willing to play hardball with Standard. McGee quotes one owner whose response to a "sell or else" offer from Standard was to threaten even deeper price cuts! McGee feels that Standard would not have wasted resources in a costly price war when faced with such tough adversaries. Of course, Standard's deep pockets would have eventually destroyed even the most formidable opponent, if that opponent had been willing to fight it out. If the price war had the desired deterrent effect on other firms, it might have been worth the cost.

McGee's analysis makes the critical point that a successful predation strategy can be extremely costly. Perhaps Standard would have been better off exploiting economies of scale less aggressively. Economists will continue to debate both Standard's strategy and the Supreme Court decision to dissolve it.

Wars of Attrition

Standard Oil, Toyota, and Wal-Mart's rivals accused them of slashing prices to eliminate competition. Rivals claimed that any losses the incumbent incurs during the price-cutting war would be more than made up by monopoly profits once they had been forced to exit. This presumes, of course, that the rivals would exit before the incumbent abandoned its strategy. It is not obvious why this should happen. A price war harms all firms in the market regardless of who started it. If, as one might expect, a larger incumbent can sustain losses better than its smaller rivals (e.g., because of more favorable access to lines of credit), then it should be able to outlast

---

[35]McGee, J., "Predatory Pricing Revisited," *Journal of Law and Economics*, 23, 1980: pp. 289–330.

[36]Yamey, B., "Predatory Price Cutting: Notes and Comments," *Journal of Law and Economics*, 15, 1972: pp. 129–142.

[37]Burns, M., "Predatory Pricing and the Acquisition Costs of Competitors," *Journal of Political Economy*, 94, 1986: pp. 266–296.

them. In this case, the large firm is said to have "deep pockets" from which it can finance the price war. On the other hand, a large firm may also suffer greater losses during the price war, especially if it had higher sales before the war began, and did not have a cost advantage over smaller rivals. In this case, the large firm may seek to stop the price war to stem its losses. (This is another variant of judo economics.)

Price wars are examples of *wars of attrition*. In a war of attrition, two or more parties expend resources battling with each other. Eventually, the survivor claims its reward, while the loser gets nothing and regrets ever participating in the war. If the war lasts long enough, even the winner may be worse off than when the war began, because the resources it expended to win the war may exceed its ultimate reward. Many other types of interactions are wars of attrition. The U.S./Soviet nuclear arms buildup between 1945 and the late 1980s is a classic example. Both countries spent huge sums to increase their nuclear arsenals, hoping that the other country would be the first to make concessions. Eventually, the Soviet Union fell apart, and Russia acknowledged that it could not afford to carry on the buildup.

Virtually all firms are worse off during a prolonged price war. If the price war drives some firms from the market, however, the survivors can raise prices above the pre-price war levels. If a firm were certain that it would lose a price war, it would prefer to exit the market as soon as the price war began. By exiting immediately, it would avoid the costly battle that it expected to lose anyway. If no firms exit in the early stages of a price war, the war may last so long that all firms, including the survivors, lose in the end. This may have occurred in the price wars among "Warehouse Club" stores during the early to mid-1990s.[38] After exit by several rivals, Sam's Club ultimately emerged with the largest share of this market. But it suffered such major losses during the price war that it might never recover.

The more that a firm believes it can outlast its rivals, the more willing it will be to enter and sustain a price war. Firms may even try to convince their rivals that they are better positioned to survive the price war. For example, firms may claim that they are actually making money during the price war, or that they care more about winning the war than about making money. Either message may cause a rival to rethink its ability to outlast its opposition, and encourage it to exit the market early. (An analogy in the arms race is Ronald Reagan's pronouncement that the United States could survive and win a nuclear war.)

Firms that face exit barriers are also well-positioned to win a war of attrition. For example, a firm that is committed to pay its workers and other suppliers regardless of production levels may be indifferent about producing at a loss during the price war or ceasing production altogether. This firm has less to lose during a price war than a firm that can adjust its input costs.

◆ ◆ ◆ ◆ ◆ **EVIDENCE ON ENTRY-DETERRING BEHAVIOR**

Although theorists have devoted considerable attention to entry deterrence, there is little systematic evidence regarding whether firms pursue entry-deterring strategies and, if they do, whether those strategies are successful. Most of our evidence comes from antitrust cases, where discovery requirements often provide re-

---

[38]Warehouse clubs are less luxurious versions of mass merchandisers such as Target and Wal-Mart. They offer substantial savings on bulk purchases. They are called clubs because shoppers must pay a nominal fee to become members.

searchers with detailed cost, market, and strategic information. Pankaj Ghemawat used such evidence to analyze many of the entry-deterring strategies DuPont used in the market for titanium dioxide, which we detail in Example 10.8.

There may be little evidence on entry deterrence from sources other than antitrust cases for several reasons. First, firms are naturally reluctant to report that they deter entry, because this may be sensitive, competitive information and might also violate antitrust statutes. Second, many entry-deterring strategies involve pricing below the short-term monopoly price. To assess whether a firm was engaging in such a practice, the researcher would need to know the firm's marginal costs, its demand curve, the degree of industry competition, and the availability of substitutes. Outside of antitrust cases, such information is difficult for researchers to obtain. Last, to measure the success of an entry-deterring strategy, a researcher would need to determine what the rate of entry would have been without the predatory act. This, too, is a difficult question to answer.

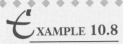

EXAMPLE 10.8

DuPont's Use of Excess Capacity to Control the Market for Titanium Dioxide

Pankaj Ghemawat analyzed DuPont's capacity expansion in the titanium dioxide industry in the 1970s.[39] Titanium dioxide is a whitener used in paints, paper, and plastics. There are a number of ways of making titanium dioxide, all of which involve substantial economies of scale and learning economies. Until the mid-1960s, virtually every firm used the "sulfate process." The lone exception was DuPont, which relied on the "chloride process" that it developed in the 1940s. DuPont's chief raw material in this process was ilmenite. The discovery of low-cost rutile ore—a substitute for ilmenite—gave a decided cost advantage to the chloride process, and all new chloride units, including those built by DuPont, used rutile. Marginal costs for existing sulfate producers (mainly American Cyanamid and Glidden) were still low enough, however, that it was not economical for them to switch processes. In the early 1970s, pollution control legislation rendered the sulfate process unworkable and increased the costs of using rutile ore. The cost of using ilmenite was unaffected.

DuPont recognized that its competitors would soon lose 160,000 tons of sulfate process capacity. DuPont also forecast that demand for titanium dioxide would grow by 377,000 tons in 13 years. Thus, DuPont expected that the industry would need 537,000 tons of additional capacity. In 1972, DuPont elected to "preempt" the market by adding 500,000 tons of capacity. It targeted a market share of 65 percent by 1985. DuPont felt that it could expand faster than its competitors because (a) its competitors had to spend money on cleanup that DuPont, using ilmenite in most of its plants, did not; and (b) it had lower costs of using ilmenite, due to scale and learning economies. Overall, DuPont believed that its costs were about 22 percent lower than its competitors, so that they would be reluctant to compete head to head.

[39]Ghemawat, P., "Capacity Expansion in the Titanium Dioxide Industry," *Journal of Industrial Economics*, 33 (2), 1984: pp. 145–163.

Of course, there is a lag between planning to add capacity and having capacity in place. During this lag, DuPont was vulnerable to expansion by competitors. In 1974, Kerr-McGee responded to a shortage of titanium dioxide by starting construction of a 50,000-ton plant. DuPont tried to forestall additional entry. It let its competitors know the magnitude of its planned expansion of existing facilities, and falsely announced that it had begun constructing a new 130,000-ton facility. DuPont also appears to have limit priced—setting prices just under the average total costs of production in the new plants. DuPont's competitors, holding out for higher prices, refused to match. While market forces had historically forced all sellers to charge the same price, this two-tiered pricing structure persisted because DuPont lacked capacity to handle the whole market. When demand slackened in early 1975, DuPont's competitors lost substantial sales, and were forced to meet DuPont's price.

When demand remained soft through 1975, DuPont reexamined its preemption strategy. It recognized that the costs of adding capacity would be substantial, since it could never hope to ramp up production as originally planned. It also realized that competitors were moving down the learning curve and would be at less of a cost disadvantage. DuPont was prepared to expand capacity as originally planned—on a faster timetable—but only if demand recovered. When demand did not recover in 1976, DuPont scaled back its capacity expansion.

Survey Data on Entry Deterrence

Despite concerns about the willingness of firms to provide frank responses, Robert Smiley asked major consumer product makers if they pursued a variety of entry-deterring strategies.[40] Smiley surveyed product managers at nearly 300 firms. To encourage frankness, Smiley promised complete anonymity. Even so, managers may have been reluctant to reveal their strategies. Many other possible biases can emerge with survey data (e.g., respondents may want to sound like good strategists, and so overreport their use of various strategies), so the results should be interpreted with caution.

Smiley asked managers whether they used several strategies discussed in this chapter, including:

- Aggressive price reductions to move down the learning curve, giving the firm a cost advantage that later entrants could only match by investing in learning themselves

- Intensive advertising to create brand loyalty

- Acquiring patents for all variants of a protect

- Enhancing firm's reputation for predation though announcements or some other vehicle

- Limit pricing

- Holding excess capacity

---

[40]Smiley, R., "Empirical Evidence on Strategic Entry Deterrence," *International Journal of Industrial Organization*, 6, 1988: pp. 167–180.

TABLE 10.2
REPORTED USE OF ENTRY-DETERRING STRATEGIES

	Learning Curve	Advertising	R&D/ Patents	Reputation	Limit Pricing	Excess Capacity
New Products						
Frequently	26%	62%	56%	27%	8%	22%
Occasionally	29	16	15	27	19	20
Seldom	45	22	29	47	73	48
Existing Products						
Frequently		52%	31%	27%	21%	21%
Occasionally		26	16	22	21	17
Seldom		21	54	52	58	62

The first three strategies create high entry costs. The last three change the entrant's expectations of postentry competition.

Table 10.2 reports the percentage of product managers who report that their firms frequently, occasionally, or seldom use each of the preceding strategies for new products and existing products. Note that managers were asked about exploiting the learning curve for new products only.

More than half of all product managers surveyed report frequent use of at least one entry-deterring strategy, and virtually all report occasional use of one or more entry-deterring strategies. Product managers report that they rely much more extensively on strategies that increase entry costs, rather than on strategies that affect the entrant's perception about postentry competition. Perhaps managers do not think about postentry competition. Or perhaps they believe that entrants have strongly held beliefs about the nature of such competition that predatory acts cannot sway. Managers also report that they are more likely to pursue entry-deterring strategies for new products than for existing products, especially for strategies that affect entry costs. Smiley reported that product managers often felt that competition among existing products was so intense that no entry-deterring strategies were needed (i.e., entry was blockaded).

SUMMARY

◆ Entry and exit are pervasive. In a typical industry, one-third of the firms are less than five years old, and one-third of firms will exit within the next five years.

◆ A firm will enter a market if it expects postentry profits to exceed the sunk costs of entry. Factors that reduce the likelihood of entry are called entry barriers.

◆ A firm will exit a market if it expects future losses to exceed the sunk costs of exit.

◆ Structural entry barriers result from exogenous market forces. Low demand, high capital requirements, and limited access to resources are all examples of structural entry barriers. Exit barriers arise when firms must meet obligations whether they produce or not.

♦ An incumbent firm can use predatory acts to deter entry or hasten exit by competitors. Limit pricing, predatory pricing, and capacity expansion change entrants' forecasts of the profitability of postentry competition.

♦ Limit pricing and predatory pricing can succeed only if the entrant is uncertain about the nature of postentry competition. Either of these strategies may convince the entrant that postentry competition will be fierce.

♦ Firms can engage in predatory practices to promote exit by rivals. Once a firm realizes that it cannot survive a price war, it exits, permitting the survivors to raise price and increase share. A firm may try to convince its rivals that it is more likely to survive a price war to hasten the rival's exit.

♦ Managers report that they frequently engage in entry-deterring strategies, especially to protect new products.

QUESTIONS

1. Dunne, Roberts, and Samuelson found that industries with high entry rates tended to also have high exit rates. Can you explain this finding? What does this imply for pricing strategies of incumbent firms?

2. Dunne, Roberts, and Samuelson examined manufacturing industries in the 1960s to 1980s. Do you think that entry and exit rates have changed in the past decade? Do you think that entry and exit rates are systematically different for service and retail industries?

3. "All else equal, an incumbent would prefer blockaded entry to deterable entry." Comment.

4. How a firm behaves toward existing competitors is a major determinant of whether it will face entry by new competitors. Explain.

5. Why is uncertainty a key to the success of entry deterrence?

6. An incumbent firm is considering expanding its capacity. It can do so in one of two ways. It can purchase fungible, general purpose equipment and machinery that can be resold at close to its original value. Or it can invest in highly specialized machinery which, once it is put in place, has virtually no salvage value. Assuming that each choice results in the same production costs once installed, under which choice is the incumbent likely to encounter a greater likelihood of entry and why?

7. In most models of entry deterrence, the incumbent engages in predatory practices that harm a potential entrant. Can these models be reversed, so that the entrant engages in predatory practices? If so, then what are the practical differences between incumbents and entrants?

8. Recall the discussion of monopolistic competition in Chapter 7. Suppose that an entrepreneur considered opening a video store along Straight Street in Linesville. Where should the entrepreneur position the store? Does your answer depend on whether additional entry is expected?

9. Consider a firm selling two products, A and B, that substitute for each other. Suppose that an entrant introduces a product that is identical to product A. What factors do you think will affect (a) whether a price war is initiated, and (b) who wins the price war?

INDUSTRY ANALYSIS

11

*I*n Parts One and Two of this text, we explored the economics of the firm's relationships with its upstream and downstream trading partners as well as with its competitors. Because these chapters introduce so many potentially important concepts, the student could lose sight of the key insights. *Industry analysis* frameworks, such as Michael Porter's *Five Forces* and Brandenberger and Nalebuff's *Value Net*, provide a structure that enables us to systematically work through these wide ranging and often complex economic issues. An industry analysis based on such frameworks facilitates the following important tasks:

- Assessment of industry and firm performance

- Identification of key factors affecting performance

- Determination of how changes in the business environment may affect performance

Most important, industry analysis is invaluable for assessing the generic business strategies that we introduce in Part Three.

Parts One and Two are rooted in microeconomics, particularly the economics of the firm and the economics of industrial organization. Although the roots of these fields can be traced to the 1930s or earlier, they had little impact on business strategy until Michael Porter published a series of articles in the 1970s that culminated in his pathbreaking book *Competitive Strategy*. Porter presented a convenient framework for exploring the economic factors that affect the profits of an industry. Porter's main innovation is to classify these factors into five major forces that encompass the vertical chain and market competition. Although it is two decades old, the five-forces approach is flexible enough to accommodate new economic concepts as they emerge.

In their book *Coopetition*, Adam Brandenberger and Barry Nalebuff propose a significant improvement to the five-forces framework. They describe the firm's "Value Net," which includes suppliers, distributors, and competitors. Whereas

Porter describes how suppliers, distributors, and competitors might detract from a firm's profits, Brandenberger and Nalebuff's key insight is that these firms often *enhance* firm profits.

This chapter shows how to perform a five-forces industry analysis that accounts for the economic principles in Parts One and Two. It also shows how to expand Porter's ideas to accommodate the "Value Net" principles introduced by Brandenberger and Nalebuff. We illustrate these ideas by examining three industries, Hospitals, Banking, and Hawaiian Coffee.

The five-forces framework has several limitations. First, it pays limited attention to factors that might affect demand other than the availability and prices of substitute and complementary products. It ignores changes in consumer income, tastes, and firm strategies for boosting demand, such as advertising. Second, it focuses on a whole industry, rather than on that industry's individual firms. Third, the framework does not explicitly account for the role of the government, except when the government is a supplier or buyer. The government as a regulator can profoundly affect industry profitability, and could be considered a sixth force. Fourth, the five-forces analysis is qualitative. For example, an analysis of industry structure may suggest that the threat of entry is high, but the framework does not show how to estimate the probability of entry. Because it is qualitative, the framework is especially useful for assessing trends—that is, for determining whether industry profitability is likely to increase or decrease.

◆ ◆ ◆ ◆ ◆ PERFORMING A FIVE-FORCES ANALYSIS

When performing a five forces analysis, you must remember that it is not a set of principles per se. The relevant principles have been developed in preceding chapters. Instead, the five-forces framework is a tool for assuring that you systematically use these principles to assess the current status and likely evolution of an industry.

As you work through the five-forces, you should appeal to the economic principles that are relevant to each force. For example, when assessing the power of suppliers to affect industry and firm performance, you should determine if firms in the industry have made relationship-specific investments with their suppliers (or vice versa) and whether they are protected from potential holdup either by contracts or market forces. In the following discussion, we will identify those principles that are most relevant to each of the forces.

The five forces, as represented in Figure 11.1, include: Internal rivalry, Entry, Substitute and Complementary products, Supplier power, and Buyer power. Internal rivalry is in the center because it may be affected by each of the other forces. One assesses each force by asking "Is it sufficiently strong to reduce or eliminate industry profits?" To answer this question, it is essential to refer to the economic principles that apply for each force. In this section, we review these principles. The appendix offers a template for doing industry analysis.

Internal Rivalry

Internal rivalry refers to the jockeying for share by firms within a market. Thus, an analysis of internal rivalry must begin by defining the market. Be sure to include all firms that constrain each other's strategic decision making, as described in

FIGURE 11.1
THE FIVE-FORCES FRAMEWORK.

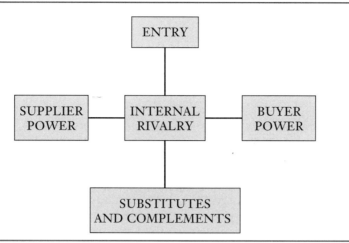

Chapter 7, and pay attention to both the product market and geographic market definitions. For example, if you are performing a five-forces assessment of hotels, note that most consumers have specific geographic preferences when selecting a hotel. This implies that competition is local, and your five-forces analysis should reflect this. If you are unsure whether to include a firm in the relevant market, remember that you can always exclude it from your consideration of internal rivalry and still consider it when you assess substitutes and complements.

As we discussed in Chapters 7 through 9, firms may compete on a number of price and nonprice dimensions. Price competition erodes profits by driving down price-cost margins. Nonprice competition erodes profits by driving up fixed costs (e.g., new product development) and marginal costs (e.g., improving product quality). To the extent that firms can pass cost increases along to consumers in the form of higher prices, nonprice competition is less likely to erode profits than is price competition.

Industry prices do not fall by themselves—one or more firms must reduce prices. A firm reduces prices if it believes it can gain market share by doing so. Hence, the incentives for a firm to reduce price are related to the degree to which it expects its market share to increase.

Each of the following conditions tends to heat up price competition:

- **There are many sellers in the market** The structure/conduct/performance paradigm introduced in Chapter 7 predicts that prices are lower when there are more firms in the market. There are several reasons for this. When there are many competitors, there is a good chance that at least one is dissatisfied with the status quo, and will want to lower price to improve its market position. At the same time, a firm with a low market share might conclude that its rivals will not respond if it lowers price.

- **The industry is stagnant or declining** Firms cannot easily expand their own output without stealing from competitors. This often elicits a competitive response that tends to intensify competition.

- **Firms have different costs** Low-cost firms may be unhappy with a high price, reasoning that if price falls their high-cost rivals may exit.

- **Excess capacity** Firms with excess capacity may be under pressure to boost sales, and often can rapidly expand output to steal business from rivals.

- **Products are undifferentiated/buyers have low switching costs** When products are undifferentiated and switching costs are low, firms are tempted to undercut their rivals prices because this can generate a substantial increase in market share.

- **Prices and terms of sales are unobservable/prices cannot be adjusted quickly** This increases the response time of rivals, enabling the price cutter to potentially gain substantial market share before its rivals match the price cut.

- **Large/infrequent sales orders** A firm may be tempted to undercut its rivals to secure a particularly large order, believing that the substantial gains may more than offset any losses from future rounds of price cutting. This is especially true if different managers are responsible for different bids, and each is rewarded on the basis of his or her own sales.

- **Industry does not use "facilitating practices" or have a history of cooperative pricing** In the absence of price leadership, price announcements, or other facilitating practices, firms may be unable to "agree" upon a suitable industry price, and some may lower price to gain an advantage. A history of cooperative pricing may assure industry participants that each is striving to find a price that works to everyone's collective benefit.

- **Strong exit barriers** This can prolong price wars as firms struggle to survive instead of exiting.

Entry

Entry erodes incumbents' profits in two ways. First, entrants steal incumbents' business, essentially dividing up market demand among more sellers. Second, entrants decrease market concentration, thereby heating up internal rivalry and reducing price-cost margins. Although most entry barriers are structural (i.e., they result from the technological requirements for successful competition), some are strategic (i.e., they result from strategic choices made by incumbents). Each of the following tends to affect the threat of entry:

- **Production entails significant economies of sales—minimum efficient scale is large relative to the size of the market** The entrant must achieve a substantial market share to reach minimum efficient scale, and if it does not, it may be at a significant cost disadvantage. This increases the risk of entry and the likelihood that the incumbent firms respond with price reductions if entry is successful.

- **Consumers highly value reputation/consumers are brand loyal** Entrants must invest heavily to establish a strong reputation and brand awareness. Diversifying entrants using a brand umbrella may be more successful than entirely new entrants.

- **Access of entrants to key inputs, including technological know-how, raw materials, distribution, and locations** Patents, unique locations, and so forth can all be natural barriers to entry. Incumbent must avoid overpaying to tic up unique inputs.

- **Experience curve** A steep experience curve puts entrants at a cost disadvantage.

- **Network externalities** This gives an advantage to incumbents with a large installed base. If incumbents are slow to establish an installed base, an entrant may do so through a large-scale product launch.

- **Government protection of incumbents** Laws may favor some firms over others.

- **Expectations about postentry competition** Historical evidence is invaluable to predicting postentry competition. Does the incumbent have a reputation for predatory pricing in the face of entry? Do incumbents have a history of persevering through price wars? Do incumbents have sufficient excess capacity to flood the market, and if necessary, to drive the entrant from the market.

Substitutes and Complements

Although the five-forces analysis does not directly consider demand, it does consider two important factors that influence demand—substitutes and complements. Substitutes erode profits in the same way as entrants by stealing business and intensifying internal rivalry. Complements boost the demand for the product in question, thereby enhancing profit opportunities for the industry. Bear in mind, however, that changes in demand can affect internal rivalry, entry, and exit. Be sure to consider these indirect effects of substitutes and complements. Factors to consider when assessing substitutes and complements include:

- **Availability of close substitutes and/or complements** Consider product performance characteristics when identifying substitutes and complements.

- **Price-value characteristics of substitutes/complements** Seemingly close substitutes may pose little threat if they are priced too high. Similarly, complements may fail to boost demand if priced too high. Many new products may be weak substitutes or complements, but gain in importance as manufacturers move down the learning curve and prices fall.

- **Price elasticity of industry demand** This is a useful measure of the pressure substitutes place on an industry. When the industry-level price elasticity is large, rising industry prices tend to drive consumers to purchase substitutes products. Elasticities have been computed for many industries.[1]

Supplier Power and Buyer Power

An assessment of supplier power takes the point of view of a downstream industry and examines the ability of that industry's upstream input suppliers to negotiate prices that extract industry profits. Recall from Chapters 3 through 5 that upstream suppliers can erode industry profits if (a) they are concentrated, or (b) their customers are

---

[1]See, for example, Pagoulatos, E. and R. Sorenson, "What Determines the Elasticity of Industry Demand?" *International Journal of Industrial Organization*, 4, 1986: pp. 237–250.

locked into relationships with them because of relationship-specific investments. An input supplier with monopoly power can raise prices when its target industrial market is faring well, thereby extracting a share of the industry's profits. The converse also applies—a powerful supplier may lower prices when its target market is doing poorly. Consistent application of both pricing strategies will permit the supplier to extract much of its target market's profits without destroying that market. Historically, unions have used this strategy to increase workers' wages. Similarly, an input supplier with a relationship-specific investment in an industry can squeeze profits from a successful industry and ease the burden on an industry in trouble.

Supplier power should not be taken as synonymous with the "importance" of an input to a firm or an industry. For example, jet fuel is an important input in the airline industry, constituting about 20 percent of the operating costs of a typical airline. However, jet fuel is purchased in a competitive market in which suppliers act much like price takers. Jet fuel is best considered in the analysis of complements.

Buyer power is analogous to supplier power. It refers to the ability of individual customers to negotiate purchase prices that extract profits from sellers. Buyer power is obviously related to internal rivalry, but the two competitive forces are conceptually distinct. In many markets, individual buyers have little power to negotiate with sellers, but the markets are nevertheless price competitive. This is true of many retail markets and commodities spot markets. Price-cost margins are low in these markets because sellers compete for price-sensitive consumers. The willingness of consumers to shop for the best price is a source of internal rivalry, not buyer power.

The following factors must be considered when assessing supplier power and buyer power. We state each in terms of supplier power relative to the downstream industry that it sells to. An analogous factor must be assessed when considering buyer power.

- **The relative concentration of the industry in question, its upstream, and its downstream industries** Firms in the more concentrated industry may have greater bargaining power, and may be able to achieve a cooperative price that puts firms in the less concentrated industry (due to internal rivalry in that industry) at a disadvantage.

- **Purchase volume of downstream firms** Suppliers may give better service and lower prices to larger purchasers.

- **Availability of substitute inputs** The availability of substitutes limits the price that suppliers can charge.

- **Relationship-specific investments by the industry and its suppliers** The threat of hold-up may determine the allocation of rents between the industry and its suppliers.

- **Threat of forward integration by suppliers** If credible, firms in an industry may be forced to accept the high supply price or risk direct competition by forward-integrating suppliers.

- **Ability of suppliers to price discriminate** If suppliers can price discriminate, they can raise the prices they charge more profitable firms.

Strategies for Coping with the Five Forces

A five-forces analysis identifies the threats to industry profits that all firms in the industry must cope with. Firms may pursue several strategies to do this. First, firms may position themselves to outperform their rivals, by developing a cost or differentiation advantage that somewhat insulates them from the five forces. Chapter 12 and 13 discuss positioning strategies in detail. Second, firms may identify an industry segment in which the five forces are less severe. For example, in the 1970s, Crown Cork and Seal served manufacturers of "hard-to-hold" liquids, a niche market that was far less competitive than the metal can segments served by industry leaders American Can and Continental Can. Through this and similar strategies, Crown earned significantly higher rates of return. (Chapter 13 discusses focus strategies of this kind.) Third, a firm may try to change the five forces, although this is difficult to do. Firms may try to reduce internal rivalry by creating switching costs, such as when a manufacturer requires consumers to use its parts to keep its warranty in force. This creates a cost—in the form of a voided warranty—to consumers who purchase parts from another supplier. Firms may reduce the threat of entry by pursuing entry-deterring strategies. Firms may try to reduce buyer or supplier power by tapered integration. In the examples that follow, we will see how firms in a variety of industries have attempted to cope, with varying degrees of success, with the five forces.

COOPETITION AND THE VALUE NET   ◆ ◆ ◆ ◆ ◆

Porter's five forces is an enduring framework that remains widely used for industry analysis. In their book *Coopetition*, Adam Brandenberger and Barry Nalebuff identify an important weakness of the framework. From the viewpoint of any one firm, Porter tends to view all other firms, be they competitors, suppliers, or buyers, as threats to profitability. Brandenberger and Nalebuff point out that firm interactions may be positive as well as negative, and emphasize the many positive interactions that Porter generally ignores. Examples of positive interactions include:

- Efforts by "competitors" to set technology standards that facilitate industry growth, such as when consumer electronics firms cooperated to establish a single format for high definition television, or when Sony and Toshiba formed an alliance to establish a compatible standard for digital video disks.

- Efforts by competitors to promote favorable regulations or legislation, such as when domestic U.S. automakers worked together to get the U.S. Environmental Protection Agency to relax CAFE fuel economy standards.

- Cooperation among firms and their suppliers to improve product quality to boost demand, such as when GM extracted work rule concessions from the workers at its Saturn plant.

- Cooperation among firms and their suppliers to improve productive efficiency, such as when Toshiba worked closely through the years with Frito-Lay to design hand-held computers to meet Frito-Lay's specific distribution needs. In fact, Frito-Lay has participated actively in Toshiba's new products steering committee.

- Cooperation among firms and their buyers that reduces inventory costs, such as when Baxter worked with American hospitals to develop just-in-time inventory programs that enabled them to survive cutbacks in federal reimbursements, permitting higher profit margins and greater profitability for both sets of firms.

In support of these ideas, Bradenberger and Nalebuff introduce the concept of the "Value Net" as a counterpart to Porter's five forces. The Value Net, which consists of suppliers, customers, competitors, and complementors (firms producing complementary goods and services), is similar to the five forces. Brandenberger and Nalebuff's admonition to perform a comprehensive analysis of the Value Net to prevent blind spots is also reminiscent of Porter. But whereas a five-forces analysis mainly assesses threats to profits, a Value Net analysis assesses threats and opportunities. This important addition does not nullify the five-forces approach so much as complement it. A complete five-forces analysis should, therefore, consider both the threats and opportunities each force poses.

To illustrate this point, contrast a traditional five-forces industry analysis of the DVD player market in 1997–1998 (the first two years of introduction) with an analysis that accounts for the Value Net. In a traditional analysis, DVD manufacturers would be somewhat pessimistic. Manufacturers would have concluded that the main source of differentiation was brand—the players are otherwise fairly homogeneous. This could have led to intensive internal rivalry. On the other hand, there were modest technological and physical capital requirements limiting entry. Satellite TV and high definition TV posed clear threats as substitutes. Powerful studios such as Disney and producers such as George Lucas and Stephen Spielberg could have demanded substantial payments to supply their movies in DVD format. The biggest threat would be from the alternative DIVX format.

This analysis fails to account for the Value Net, and, as a result, fails to identify opportunities for industry growth and profitability. The participants in the Value Net—manufacturers, studios, and retailers needed to recognize that their fortunes were intertwined. If they could generate sufficient interest in DVD, then demand would grow fast enough to make everyone profitable while thwarting DIVX.

Manufacturers had many options for boosting demand. The most obvious would be to set low prices. This would encourage hardware sales which would, in turn, encourage studios to release more movies in DVD, thereby further boosting demand for hardware. They could also heavily promote DVD so as to boost product awareness while blunting the threat from DIVX. In the first year, hardware makers did none of this. They kept prices high so as to profit from early adopters (players sold for $500–$1,000), rather than to stimulate mass market acceptance. They ran few advertisements or promotions, electing to "free ride" off of the product awareness generated by each other's advertising and promotional activities. As a result, manufacturers sold about 300,000 players, well short of expectations. In the second year, manufacturers lowered prices on some players to less than $300 and spent heavily on advertising and promotions. Other participants in the Value Net also pitched in. MGM released specially remastered editions of classic films such as *Gone With the Wind, 2001: A Space Odyssey*, and *Casablanca*. Warner slashed prices on dozens of popular titles. Columbia and Universal studios accelerated the release of popular action titles such as *Godzilla, The Mask of Zorro*, and *Mercury Rising*. Meanwhile, electronics retailers, especially Best Buy, heavily promoted DVD hardware and software, including a much publicized half-price software sale for internet purchases.

DVD succeeded when all the players in the Value Net did their part to promote the overall success of the product. Some members of the Value Net, such as Warner and Best Buy, were even willing to take a temporary loss (by setting prices below costs) so as to contribute to the future success of the format. The DVD market finally took off when firms worked to increase the size of the DVD "pie," rather than fight for their share of a given "pie." Through their complementary actions, the participants in the DVD Value Net secured its future and reaped the benefits.

APPLYING THE FIVE FORCES: SOME INDUSTRY ANALYSES

◆ ◆ ◆ ◆ ◆

The best way to illustrate the five-forces framework is by example. In this section we perform three detailed industry analyses. For each industry, we present background information, proceed with market definition, and identify the most salient economic principles from each of the five forces.

Hospital Markets Then and Now

Hospitals have experienced some financial difficulties in recent years. Hospital bankruptcies were once rare. Since the mid-1980s, however, an average of 75 hospitals a year has gone bankrupt (about 1.5 percent of the nation's total each year), and many others struggle to stay solvent. At the same time, some hospitals have been very successful financially. A comparison of the five forces at two points in time, 1980 and today, demonstrates the problems that hospitals have grown accustomed to and identifies profit opportunities that some hospitals have exploited.

Market Definition

As discussed in Chapter 7, market definition requires identification of both a product market and a geographic market. We consider the product market to be acute medical services. These services include maternity and surgical care and complex diagnostic services. While other sellers offer many of these services—outpatient surgery centers are a good example—we will treat offerings of other sellers as substitutes in this analysis. This decision is not essential to our conclusions and illustrates the flexibility of the five-forces framework. (We would be remiss, of course, if we did not consider outpatient surgery at all.)

Hospital services tend to be bought and sold locally. Residents of a metropolitan area tend to visit hospitals in the same vicinity, and most of the patients in area hospitals reside in that area. Thus, each metropolitan area might be thought of as a distinct geographic market.[2] We will assess internal rivalry in the Chicago metropolitan area.

Internal Rivalry

There are about 70 community hospitals in the Chicago market.[3] Virtually all of them were independent in 1980, so that the market Herfindahl index was below 0.05. Today, many hospitals belong to systems. Some systems, such as Advocate,

---

[2]This is overly broad. A large metropolitan area might have several smaller markets, and nearby geographic areas might be part of a single, larger market. Geographic market definition for small towns and rural areas can be difficult.

[3]Community hospitals treat a variety of patients on a short-term basis. Another type of hospital not considered here is the psychiatric hospital.

own all of their member hospitals. Other systems, such as Northwestern Healthcare Network, contract with insurers in behalf of independent members. There are several systems in Chicago, but hospitals in some of the systems are free to set their own prices, even if that results in their stealing business from sister hospitals. A small number of hospitals remain independent. Thus, even if we treat each system as a single entity to compute market shares, the market Herfindahl index is still below 0.20.

If we examine the five-forces checklist in the appendix, we see that the Chicago hospital market meets several criteria for fierce internal rivalry. There are many competitors. Production costs vary across hospitals. There is substantial excess capacity; occupancy rates at many hospitals have been below 70 percent for decades. Finally, demand for admissions has been stagnant or declining for decades.

Despite these factors, internal rivalry in 1980 was benign. At that time, hospitals were selected by patients and their admitting physicians. Most patients had insurance that paid for the bulk of the hospital bill. This meant that price was not important to many patients, implying that cross-price elasticities of demand were low. Patients also tended to be loyal to particular hospitals, largely because it was costly for their physicians to switch case loads from one hospital to another. The combination of price-insensitive patients and physician-dominated admission decisions limited the incentives of hospitals to use price as a strategic weapon. As a result, internal rivalry in 1980 was low, and most hospitals in Chicago enjoyed healthy price-cost margins.

Facing a threat to their own profitability, Chicago-area health insurers in the 1980s imposed some market discipline on hospitals.[4] Through what has become known as managed care, insurers began selectively contracting with those hospitals that offered the most favorable rates. They then offered financial inducements (in the form of lower copayments) to encourage patients to select the contracting hospitals. By steering patients to the lowest priced hospitals, insurers effectively increase price elasticities of demand. Insurers are also less "brand loyal" than are individual patients. Horizontal differentiation based on the hospital's location, or the preferences of individual admitting physicians, is muted when insurers aggregate the preferences of thousands of patients. Two additional factors contribute to internal rivalry. Price negotiations between insurers and hospitals are secret, encouraging hospitals to lower prices to win contracts. Finally, "sales" are infrequent (i.e., a contract lasts one to three years) and "lumpy" (i.e., one insurer may represent 5 percent or more of a hospital's business). This intensifies the pressure on hospitals to lower prices to win each individual contract without considering future price rivalry.

Price rivalry under selective contracting is fairly intense. Hospitals have lowered prices by 20 percent or more to stay competitive in the managed-cared marketplace. Profit margins declined through the early 1990s, and many Chicago-area hospitals closed. Some have remained profitable by establishing a strong brand identity, thus enhancing their bargaining power with managed care companies. Others diversified into related products, such as skilled nursing services (for which insurers still provide generous reimbursements), and reduced costs of services for which price is regulated (such as services to Medicare patients). Even so, the Chicago hospital market remains threatened by internal rivalry, and many analysts

---

[4]Indeed, insurers throughout the United States also practiced selective contracting.

expect further consolidation and exit. If this occurs, internal rivalry will diminish, and prices may creep back up.

Entry

Few hospitals have been built in Chicago in the past two decades. One reason is severe state regulatory restrictions on new hospital construction. Another reason is that the market has become too risky to attract much new investment, although several investors have acquired existing facilities. But suppose the market were to rebound and regulations were relaxed. Would incumbents see their anticipated profits threatened by entrants?

There are several barriers to opening a new hospital. Hospitals are capital intensive. A new 300-bed hospital can easily cost $300 million to build. A new hospital would need to establish a brand identity, since patients may be reluctant to trust their health to an unknown entity. A new hospital would also need access to distribution "channels"—the medical staff that admits patients. It might have difficulty finding a favorable location, because it would have to battle other retail establishments for large, convenient locations.

The combination of regulatory and structural entry barriers suggests that the threat of entry was low in 1980. Although regulatory barriers are lower today, structural barriers remain, and a new hospital might face a price war if it did not choose its location wisely. This suggests that the threat of entry is largely unchanged since 1980. Technological change may further lower entry barriers. Innovations in medicine might make it possible to open smaller, cost-competitive, inpatient facilities that focus on specific treatments, such as heart surgery. This will reduce the capital and number of physicians required for successful entry.

Substitutes and Complements

In 1980, few inpatient services could be performed outside the hospital. Thus, the threat from substitutes was low. Since then, hospitals have faced a growing number of substitutes. Thanks to improvements in surgical technique, anesthetics, and antibiotics, many types of surgery can now be performed outside the hospital. Other substitutes for hospital services include outpatient diagnostic facilities, which provide state-of-the-art technologies, such as magnetic resonance imaging, and home health care, which enables nurses and physicians to monitor patients and provide some treatments at home rather than in the hospital.

At the same time that substitutes have emerged, insurers have implemented reimbursement rules that encourage patients to purchase services from outpatient providers. Thus, both the availability and price of outpatient services threaten inpatient providers.

Hospitals have turned out to be the dominant sellers of outpatient services in many markets. Hospitals already possessed the technology and manpower to offer outpatient care, and were often first to do so. Economies of scope have enabled hospitals to endure even as their core inpatient business shrinks.

New medical technologies will continue to emerge. Some, such as laparoscopic surgery, will facilitate even more outpatient treatment. But some technologies, such as advances in respiratory medicine that sustain the lives of low birthweight babies, complement and boost the demand for inpatient care. An important generation of new technologies will emerge from genetic research, and it is difficult to predict whether these will substitute for or complement inpatient care.

Supplier Power

The main suppliers to hospitals include labor (nurses, technicians, etc.), medical equipment companies, and drug houses. We consider admitting physicians to be buyers because they often determine which hospitals patients will purchase services from. Hospital-based physicians, such as radiologists, anesthesiologists, and pathologists (RAP physicians), are better regarded as suppliers. There are few substitutes for any of these professionals, both because of their specialized skills and because licensing regulations limit the flexibility of hospitals to use nonprofessionals. When the supply of specialized medical personnel is tight their wages increase, and hospitals have to bear the expense. This occurred in the nursing market during the latter 1980s, but nurses' wages have since stabilized because the higher wages attracted more people into the profession (including many who had left nursing to pursue other opportunities). Suppliers of commodity products, such as surgical gloves, have less power; there is no asset specificity. For more complex supplies or equipment, where the number of suppliers is limited because of patent protection or a single firm's specialized technical know-how, supplier power can be substantial.

Hospitals and their suppliers make few relationship-specific investments. Personnel learn to work in teams, but seem to adjust rapidly to new settings. Hospitals can usually replace them at the market wage, and some hospitals routinely use "nursing pools" to handle short-term needs. A national recruiting market usually makes RAP physicians easy to replace, although hospital bylaws and staffing policies can create exit barriers. Medical suppliers without monopoly power cannot credibly threaten to hold up hospitals to obtain higher prices.

The magnitude of supplier power has not changed much over time. A much discussed national physician union movement could greatly increase the power of RAP physicians. They could demand higher wages with little fear of being replaced (except by "scab" physicians).

Buyer Power

Buyers include patients, physicians, and insurers, who decide which hospitals will get business and how they will be paid. Patients and their physicians did not wield purchasing power in 1980, and generally do not wield it today. Insurers in 1980 were also passive. Most of them reimbursed whatever the hospital charged, and did not shop around for the best value. Indeed, state regulations generally prevented such price shopping by insurers, though large state Blue Cross plans did obtain discounts because of their size. The two major government insurers, Medicaid and Medicare, also had generous reimbursement rules. Buyer power in 1980 was low.

Today, insurers wield substantial power. Managed care is largely a response to the cost concerns of employers, who may pay 10 percent or more of their total payroll costs in the form of health insurance. While all managed care purchasers appear to be able to obtain discounts from hospitals, the largest insurers in Chicago, Blue Cross in the private sector and Medicare in the public sector, use their size to negotiate significant price discounts. Medicare, which insures the elderly and disabled, has forced all hospitals to accept fixed price contracts, so that hospitals must bear the risks of excessive treatment costs. Medicaid in Illinois may be the toughest payer of all. Medicaid negotiates a separate price with every hospital willing to accept its patients. These prices are often 25 to 50 percent less than

TABLE 11.1
FIVE-FORCES ANALYSIS OF THE CHICAGO HOSPITAL MARKET

Force	Threat to Profits: 1980	Threat to Profits: Today
Internal Rivalry	Low	High
Entry	Low	Medium
Substitutes and Complements	Medium	High
Supplier Power	Medium	Medium
Buyer Power	Low	High

those paid by other insurers for comparable services. Medicaid knows each hospital's cost-and-profit position, and can use this information to minimize what it offers to pay each hospital.

Physicians may also wield significant power, especially those charismatic and highly skilled physicians who can attract patients regardless of where they practice. A classic example is the local physician who pioneered the use of the "neural knife" surgical technique. He switched hospitals after a bidding war drove up his wages, and thereby extracted from the winning hospital a significant percentage of the profits that his services generate. To the extent that managed care payers are less likely to demonstrate loyalty to individual physicians, this power has diminished since 1980. While there are no relationship-specific investments to speak of, buyer power in the Chicago market is considerable. If managed care purchasers consolidate, as many expect, then their power will increase.

Hospitals have attempted to combat buyer power. Some have sought to differentiate their services by developing "centers of excellence" in clinical areas, such as cancer care and heart surgery. They hope that insurers will tolerate higher prices to obtain superior quality. Thus far, there is no systematic evidence that this strategy has succeeded. Others have forward integrated by offering an insurance-like product such as a "physician-hospital organization." These new structures must keep the internal payments to hospitals low to stay competitive with other insurance products, and so do not really solve the problem of buyer power.

Table 11.1 summarizes the five-forces analysis of the Chicago hospital market in 1980 and today. Virtually every factor that affects industry profitability has changed for the worse since 1980. Hospital managers face dilemmas, and many hospitals are in financial disarray.

Tobacco

Tobacco firms include some of the largest and most profitable companies in the world. Philip Morris and RJR Nabisco rank in the top 75 firms in the Fortune Global 500. Though highly diversified, these giants earn a disproportionate amount of their income from tobacco. Even though Philip Morris, for example, owns Kraft, General Foods, Miller Beer, and Oscar Mayer Foods, it obtains 40 percent of its sales and 60 percent of its profits from tobacco. RJR Nabisco is also highly diversified, selling products such as Nabisco cookies, Life Savers candy, A.1 sauce, and Milk-Bone dog biscuits. Yet it received 55 percent of its sales and 75 percent of its profits from tobacco. Tobacco sales are so critical to these firms that when a cigarette price war erupted in 1993, tobacco stocks lost

20 to 30 percent of their value. A five-forces analysis helps explain why the tobacco industry has been so profitable, and why it has recently become less stable.

Market Definition

We will assess the retail cigarette market in the United States. Many of the considerations that we raise below apply to markets in other parts of the world, although the actual competitors may vary (regional variations within the United States are minor and can be ignored). As discussed in the following section, cigarettes have few if any close substitutes. Manufacturers of substitutes, such as cigars, can be safely excluded from any discussion of internal rivalry. Product niches within the broader cigarette market (such as extra long cigarettes) are not sufficiently differentiated from other types of cigarettes to warrant special consideration.

Internal Rivalry

The cigarette is a technically simple product that can be made in large quantities at low cost. Smokers often disagree about whether there are discernible differences in the way that cigarettes taste. In the early days of the industry, so many smokers were willing to switch brands that price wars were common. In fact, Philip Morris, originally a British brand, first became prominent in the United States by selling discount brands, while the established firms were raising prices. Price competition has diminished since the 1930s, however. Elie Applebaum estimated that before the most recent price wars, the price-cost margin for the industry was .65, extremely high when compared with other industries.[5]

Several factors contribute to the historically low internal rivalry. The major producers grew out of the Tobacco Trust, which was the target of two famous antitrust cases. Thus, a history of cooperative pricing facilitates "friendly" price competition. The major players continue to dominate the industry—the industry four-firm concentration ratio has exceeded 80 percent since 1950.[6]

Beginning in the 1950s, several factors reduced cross-price elasticities of demand. First and foremost, the industry introduced marketing practices that attached an image to specific brands. One of the first efforts, and by far the most successful, was Philip Morris' promotion of Marlboro as a rugged "man's" cigarette. Image-conscious smokers became reluctant to switch brands. In addition, as Americans grew wealthier after World War II, tobacco became a less significant part of their budgets, again reducing the desire to shop around. Finally, growing tobacco taxes meant that a given price increase by a tobacco firm represented a smaller percentage increase in the retail price.

Without price competition, firms have sought to increase their share by new product introductions, innovations (e.g., the 100-millimeter cigarette), and new brand identities. These activities are relatively inexpensive, and costs have historically been passed along to consumers.

Demographic changes in the smoking population have intensified internal rivalry. Today's smoker is younger and less affluent than previously. These smokers have not established strong loyalties to particular brands and are more price con-

---

[5]Miles, R. H., *Coffin Nails and Corporate Strategies*, Englewood Cliffs, NJ: Prentice-Hall, 1982, pp. 33–34; 102–103.

[6]Miles, R. H., *Coffin Nails and Corporate Strategies*, pp. 33–34.

scious. Even so, internal rivalry would not have heated up as intensely as it did were it not for entry by "off-price" brands. We discuss this below.

Entry

Although technology to manufacture cigarettes is well-known, tobacco has been an industry with traditionally high entry and exit barriers. All of the major U.S. firms today had been established in the industry by 1932. Cigarette production has significant economies of scale in production—it has been estimated that a minimum efficient scale facility could meet as much as 10 percent of the total world demand. The emphasis on brand further raises the stakes for new entrants, which must spend $10 million or more to establish a new brand. These factors make entry into the branded cigarette market a risky proposition. Established manufacturers may also have favorable access to distribution and retail channels, such as vending machines, bars, and gas stations.

Although manufacturers of "off-price" brands have had difficulty gaining access to traditional distribution channels, they have gained access to mass merchandisers, such as Wal-Mart stores. This is an ideal combination, since Wal-Mart shoppers tend to be more price conscious than average. Many believe that the tobacco price wars of the mid-1990s were a direct response by the major manufacturers to the inroads made by off-price brands. Whether this is true or not, prices have crept back up, with little additional entry.

Substitutes and Complements

Any discussion of substitutes in the cigarette business must consider that cigarette smoking is generally habit forming (to the point of being addictive). The habit-forming nature of smoking has become one of the critical aspects of the debate about the dangers of smoking that colors consideration of advertising policies, promotional programs, and governmental regulation. It also turns the search for substitutes into a choice for the consumer of whether to change brands of cigarette or quit smoking altogether.

There are two types of plausible economic substitutes for tobacco products, especially cigarettes. Neither of these has been strong enough to challenge the high profitability of the industry. The first is some other type of product that satisfies the addiction to nicotine, such as a low-tar cigarette, chewing tobacco, or a nicotine patch. The proliferation of new brands suggests that smokers might switch to an alternative, such as a low-tar cigarette, rather than quit. The second type of substitute is some nontobacco product that is consumed in place of cigarettes, such as snack food or gum. Substitutes clearly pose a negligible threat to the industry.

Buyer and Supplier Power

Supplier power is weak. Most cigarette manufacturers purchase tobacco through tobacco brokers, who obtain it from tobacco farmers. Tobacco brokers have consolidated in recent years, so that three brokers handle 80 percent of volume for the industry. However, this consolidation has not translated into increased pricing power for brokers. Other inputs, including labor and paper, are obtained from competitive markets.

Buyer power is also low. Distributors and retailers are largely fragmented. Vending machines represent one of the only relationship-specific investments, and manufacturers are in a better position to exploit the relationship than are the vendors, owing to the manufacturers' wide choice of retail outlets.

TABLE 11.2
FIVE-FORCES ANALYSIS OF THE TOBACCO INDUSTRY

Force	Threat to Profits
Internal Rivalry	Low
Entry	Low
Substitutes and Complements	Low
Supplier Power	Low
Buyer Power	Low

Table 11.2 summarizes the five forces of the tobacco industry. Despite the continued profitability of the industry, it is haunted by two major issues. First, will regulations continue to limit demand, or will smokers always find somewhere to smoke? Second, will consumers continue to be brand loyal, or will off-price entrants continue to attract new customers, driving down price-cost margins?

Hawaiian Coffee

Market definition is a cornerstone of industry analysis. Often, an industry, such as the coffee industry, has submarkets with distinctive competitive features. In such cases, it is reasonable to perform a five-forces analysis of that submarket. This analysis of the Hawaiian coffee submarket, developed by seven of our students, demonstrates the value of examining a submarket.[7]

Industry Facts

Specialty coffee is strictly of the Arabica cultivar (type of bean), identified by country of origin, high in quality and price, and generally sold by growers to wholesalers or brokers.[8] Specialty coffee wholesalers and brokers purchase green beans, roast them or sell them to roasters. Roasted beans are sold to specialty coffee retailers (e.g., Starbucks and Gloria Jean's) or directly to end consumers. Hawaii specialty coffee is mild to medium in body and strength (because of agronomic conditions) and occupies the medium to upper range in quality and price within the specialty coffee market. The Kona coffees—grown on the "big island"—have been in production for more than 60 years, are in greatest demand, and command the highest prices. The other Hawaii coffees—grown on the islands of Kauai, Molokai, and Maui—have been in business for 5 to 15 years and, to some extent, have been able to achieve premium prices by leveraging off the established Kona brand equity and the general mystique of Hawaii.[9] The Kona growers are small and numerous (10 to 20 acre farms numbering over 500) and market their crops through cooperatives. The other major Hawaii growers are large, corporate-owned plantations with Kauai being the low-cost/lower-quality producer.

---

[7]The students who prepared the analysis are James Carr, Nina Case, Kathleen Fabsits, Robert Musson, Chet Richardson, Andrew Schwartz, and Scott Swanson.

[8]Examples of countries of origin for specialty coffees are Hawaii, Costa Rica, Guatemala, Kenya, Jamaica, and New Guinea.

[9]For example, for a similar quality bean from Costa Rica, Hawaii growers can command 2 to 3 times the price per pound. See *Coffee Rating & Review*, April 1998.

Market Definition

Specialty coffee is distinct because it provides the appeal of fine taste and a unique, pleasurable experience (akin to drinking fine wines). While the occasions for use of specialty coffee are similar to those of low-quality, inexpensive coffees, the specialty coffee experience is substantially different. Once introduced to the fine taste of specialty coffee, the consumer often finds low-quality coffees unpalatable. Most Kona coffee is purchased in the United States, which is most familiar with it due to tourism and marketing.[10] In addition, the geographic isolation of Hawaii places its growers in the same submarket—with commonalities in agronomics, buyers, suppliers, marketing factors, shipping requirements, and government regulations.

Internal Rivalry

Most Kona growers are small-acreage, second- or third-generation farmers. They have well-established brand equity—producing the highest quality/priced coffee in Hawaii. The non-Kona growers are former sugar or pineapple plantations owners on Kauai, Molokai, and Maui. The non-Kona growers know each other well, having interacted in other businesses for most of the century. In addition, there is a strong bond among all growers because of the geographic separation of Hawaii, the closeness of the communities (where growers frequently join in legislative efforts), and the general "aloha" spirit of the people. All of the growers, including the individual Kona growers, freely share agronomic information. There are two statewide associations: the "Hawaii Growers Association" and the "Hawaii Coffee Association." The goal of both associations is to establish a "Hawaii" coffee identity worldwide.

Historically, there has been little evidence of direct price competition among the growers. The long-established Kona growers generally sell through cooperatives (out of 500 growers, no more than 10 farms sell directly to customers and those usually have negotiated long-term contracts for their entire crop) and work diligently to preserve the brand equity of "Kona" coffee. They are positioned at the high-quality/high-price segment of the market and have no incentive to cut prices because of steadily rising demand.

The non-Kona growers have also avoided direct price competition. Instead, they have filled gaps in the price/quality continuum. The Kauai plantation has secured the low-price/lower-quality position, whereas the Molokai and Maui growers have more recently filled the large gap between Kona and Kauai.

Although there are many giant coffee retailers, most wholesale brokers are small and unable to exert much price pressure on the growers. Brokers generally do not want to carry more than one or two types of "Hawaii" coffee, and this could lead to intensified price competition in the future. Coffee trees on Molokai and Maui continue to mature. As they do, output will increase. Growers may have to reduce prices to get brokers to purchase their beans.

Hawaii growers should also expect increased price rivalry from specialty coffee growers in other countries. Knowledgeable coffee brokers, who can capably judge quality of beans, question why they should pay two or three times as much for Hawaii beans than for similar quality beans from other countries. Fortunately for the Hawaii growers, consumers are captivated by the romance of Hawaii. Fine

---

[10]Asia and Europe are developing markets for Hawaii coffee, especially Kona, but are dwarfed in comparison to the U.S. market.

Hawaii coffees have distinct tastes and should be able to sustain higher prices. Consumers desiring Hawaii coffees are largely price insensitive, very brand loyal, and usually have some "Hawaii experience" to which they relate their coffee purchases. With the growth potential for specialty coffee, there should be a healthy-size niche for Hawaii coffees well into the foreseeable future.

Entry

The right soil, altitude, water, and sun are all essential for coffee trees. Due to the unique history of Hawaii land ownership, large corporations or nonprofit organizations (e.g., Bishop Estate) own most of the agricultural land. Except for Kona, most Hawaii coffee is grown on former sugar or pineapple lands, where the companies have owned the land for a century and have historical access rights to water. Little high altitude land and even less water are available to newcomers. In Kona, most of the desirable land is already under cultivation and the small farms tend to be family owned. The Kona farmers generally rely solely on rainfall for water, and droughts can be harmful. New entrants in the Kona region would more likely buy out an incumbent than find new land to cultivate.[11]

Overall, the structural barriers of land and water—along with the required fixed investment in planting, harvesting, and processing equipment—lead to the conclusion that entry is unlikely (except on a very small scale).[12] Because of the time and expense to develop mature trees, exit of major growers is not likely either. If any growers were to exit, it is likely that someone else would acquire the planted acres so that production levels would not vary much.

Substitutes and Complements

Brokers and roasters use only specialty coffee in their "straight" lines (i.e., pure country of origin coffees such as Kenyan, Guatemalan, etc.), but many purchase the cheaper commodity coffees to put in "blends" along with small quantities of specialty coffees (e.g., "Kona Blend"). In addition, the three major commodity coffee producers have all expanded their regular lines of coffee to include new "specialty blends" for sale in grocery stores. Producers may vary the mix of specialty and commodity coffee beans as prices vary.

Complements to specialty coffee include breakfast pastries in the morning and desserts in the evening. The proliferation of coffee carts and coffee stores, such as Starbucks, exposes many consumers to specialty coffee. Also, people tend to eat out more often and, after an expensive meal, they do not want to ruin the evening with mediocre coffee. They expect and demand more. Another fad that may last and provide a new niche of customers is the home roaster. As consumers discover the joys of great-tasting coffee, more are home roasting coffee beans. If the home roaster remains popular, it will create a new market for *retail* specialty green (unroasted) beans.

Hawaiian vacations, which are growing in popularity, are another complement. When in Hawaii, many tourists drink the local coffee for the first time. Even those on tight budgets can purchase small bags of Hawaii coffee to bring

---

[11]Hawaii growers are relatively open and friendly, and would not explicitly act to deter entry unless the newcomer was perceived as trying to lower the quality level of coffee or impugn the Kona brand.

[12]A new entrant on the island of Oahu has begun on former sugarcane land; however, the 200 acres planted are low altitude and will not likely yield high-quality coffee.

home as luxury gifts for friends. Once exposed, tourists and their friends may become loyal customers.

Supplier Power

The key marketable inputs are land, labor, and water. For the large, non-Kona growers, ownership of land and access to water sources are not problems. The local government encourages large landowners to keep land in agriculture use by turning down other (higher use) development plans. Labor for the large landowners is unionized, consisting mostly of former sugar workers. While the unions could strike and demand higher wages, this will probably not happen for two reasons. First, their members are already the highest paid agricultural workers in the world. Second, the unions are so beaten down by many sugar plantation closures that they are grateful for any operation that can dutifully employ their members and, to date, have been agreeable to keep labor rates constant.

In Kona, all of the farms are small and many family-run, so the workers are not unionized. However, the supplier of land wields a big stick. Bishop Estate is the largest landowner in the state and leases much of its land to tenants of all types (agricultural, commercial, and residential). Many Kona farmers are on Bishop-leased land and periodically face mandatory rent renegotiations, which recently resulted in six-fold increases in rent. Few farmers have choices other than to pay the rent, because of their investment in trees and equipment and their desire to maintain rural lifestyles.

Buyer Power

Coffees are sold primarily wholesale green to brokers, roasters, or roaster-retailers. For newer growers trying to establish a brand identity, the wholesalers, brokers, and roasters can force some price breaks. The buyers do not run roughshod over the growers, because they want to maintain relationships for access to quality Hawaii beans when demand is high and supply low. This is especially true with Kona growers. Sold through cooperatives, the Kona beans are highly desired and full production sells out regularly. Coffee brokers try to tie up the Kona supply whenever possible.

Not all specialty coffee buyers desire Hawaii coffee. Starbucks, the nation's largest retailer-roaster, generally buys few Hawaii beans. They favor stronger varieties grown in Africa and certain Latin American countries. The Hawaii industry would have difficulty meeting the supply requirements for a large buyer like Starbucks, in any case.

The real danger to the Hawaii growers is that some buyers may try to steer consumers to less expensive specialty coffees (where they can earn larger margins). As long as the consumer is enraptured with Hawaii, however, there will always remain a niche for high-quality Hawaii coffee. Moreover, the Hawaii growers' efforts to enter the retail roasted market (through plantation tours, retail stores, and direct mail order) may lessen some of their dependence on the middlemen buyers.

Conclusion

Table 11.3 summarizes the five forces in the Hawaii coffee submarket. The key to profitability for Hawaii specialty coffee begins and ends with consistency and quality—without which premium prices cannot be sustained. The supply of Hawaii coffee continues to increase, and there is pressure from growers in other countries. However, specialty coffee is a growing market and competition is likely to remain benign for several years.

TABLE 11.3
FIVE-FORCES ANALYSIS OF THE HAWAIIAN COFFEE
SUBMARKET

Force	Threat to Profits
Internal Rivalry	Low to Medium
Entry	Low
Substitutes/Complements	Medium
Buyer Power	Medium
Supplier Power	Low

Hawaii growers might consider creating an appellation system for Hawaii coffees (similar to the French wine appellation system) and, developing retail methods to take advantage of annual tourist flows through Hawaii. However, once an appellation system was in place, it would be self-policing among the consortium of Hawaii growers. An appellation system will grade coffees based on agronomic practices, growing conditions, and processing techniques. Such a system, together with origin certification, will provide greater assurance of bean consistency and quality, and will educate the consumer on the fine points of specialty coffee.

In addition, growers might tap into Hawaii tourism. Through plantation tours, coffee retail stores, and partnerships with restaurants, hotels, and airlines, Hawaii growers can introduce their products to receptive end users. Educating tourists, particularly with a well-planned appellation system, can only lead to greater profits. Satisfied customers will agreeably spend their dollars if they believe "Hawaii coffee no ka oi!"

CHAPTER SUMMARY

◆ An industry analysis provides an overview of the potential profitability of the average firm in an industry.

◆ A comprehensive analysis examines the five forces: internal rivalry, entry, substitutes, buyer power, and supplier power. The latter four operate independently and may also intensify internal rivalry.

◆ Internal rivalry is fierce if competition drives prices toward costs. This is more likely when there are many firms, products are perceived to be homogeneous, consumers are motivated and able to shop around, prices may be set secretly, sales orders are large and received infrequently, and the industry has excess capacity.

◆ The threat of entry is high if firms can easily enter an industry and capture market share from profitable incumbents while intensifying price competition.

◆ Substitutes also capture sales and intensify price rivalry.

◆ Buyers and suppliers exert power directly by renegotiating the terms of contracts to extract profits from profitable industries, and indirectly by shopping around for the best prices.

◆ The government can affect profitability, and should be considered either as part of the five forces or as a separate force.

◆ Profits may be threatened by any or all of the five forces. Although it is useful to construct a "five-forces scorecard" on which the forces can be rated, the exercise of assessing the five forces is more important than the actual scores. Through this exercise the analyst develops deep knowledge of key strategic issues affecting the industry in question.

◆ A sound five-forces analysis should be based on economic principles. The tools for analyzing internal rivalry, entry, and substitutes are derived from industrial organization and game theory, which are discussed in Chapters 8 through 11. The tools for analyzing buyer and supplier power are derived from the economics of vertical relationships, which were discussed in Chapters 2 through 4.

QUESTIONS

1. It has been said that Porter's five-forces analysis turns antitrust law—law intended to protect consumers from monopolies—on its head. What do you think this means?

2. Comment on the following: All of Porter's wisdom regarding the five forces is reflected in the economic identity:
$$\text{Profit} = (\text{Price} - \text{Average Cost}) \times \text{Quantity}.$$

3. How does the magnitude of scale economies affect the intensity of each of the five forces?

4. How does the magnitude of consumer switching costs affect the intensity of internal rivalry? Of entry?

5. Advances in computer-aided design have allowed small manufacturing plants to nearly match the cost advantages of larger plants. How will this affect the supplier power of the aforementioned firms in the downstream industries that they supply?

6. Consider an industry whose demand fluctuates over time. Suppose that this industry faces high supplier power. Briefly state how this high supplier power will affect the variability of profits over time.

7. What does the concept of "coopetition" add to the five-forces approach to industry analysis?

8. The following table reports the distribution of profits (on a per disc basis) for different steps in the vertical chain for music compact discs:

Artist: $.60
Record Company: $1.80
Retailer: $.60

Use the five forces to explain this pattern. (Note: There are about half a dozen major record companies, including Warner, Sony, and Polygram. They are responsible for signing up artists, handling technical aspects of recording, securing distribution, and promoting the recordings.)

APPENDIX 11.1

TEMPLATE FOR DOING A FIVE-FORCES ANALYSIS

FACTORS AFFECTING RIVALRY AMONG EXISTING COMPETITORS

To what extent does pricing rivalry or nonprice competition (e.g., advertising) erode the profitability of a typical firm in this industry?

	Characterization (Current)	Future trend
Degree of seller concentration?		
Rate of industry growth?		
Significant cost differences among firms?		
Excess capacity?		
Cost structure of firms: sensitivity of costs to capacity utilization?		
Degree of product differentiation among sellers? Brand loyalty to existing sellers? Cross-price elasticities of demand among competitors in industry?		
Buyers' costs of switching from one competitor to another?		
Are prices and terms of sales transactions observable?		
Can firms adjust prices quickly?		
Large and/or infrequent sales orders?		
Use of "facilitating practices" (price leadership, advance announcement of price changes)?		
History of "cooperative" pricing?		
Strength of exit barriers?		

FACTORS AFFECTING THE THREAT OF ENTRY

To what extent does the threat or incidence of entry work to erode the profitability of a typical firm in this industry?

	Characterization (Current)	Future trend
Significant economies of scale?		
Importance of reputation or established brand loyalties in purchase decision?		
Entrants' access to distribution channels?		
Entrants' access to raw materials?		
Entrants' access to technology/know-how?		
Entrants' access to favorable locations?		
Experience-based advantages of incumbents?		

	Characterization (Current)	Future trend
"Network externalities": demand-side advantages to incumbents from large installed base?		
Government protection of incumbents?		
Perceptions of entrants about expected retaliation of incumbents/reputations of incumbents for "toughness"?		

FACTORS AFFECTING OR REFLECTING PRESSURE FROM SUBSTITUTE PRODUCTS AND SUPPORT FROM COMPLEMENTS

To what extent does competition from substitute products outside the industry erode the profitability of a typical firm in the industry?

	Characterization (Current)	Future trend
Availability of close substitutes?		
Price-value characteristics of substitutes?		
Price elasticity of industry demand?		
Availability of close complements		
Price-value characteristics of complements?		

FACTORS AFFECTING OR REFLECTING POWER OF INPUT SUPPLIERS

To what extent do individual suppliers have the ability to negotiate high input prices with typical firms in this industry? To what extent do input prices deviate from those that would prevail in a perfectly competitive input market in which input suppliers act as price takers?

	Characterization (Current)	Future trend
Is supplier industry more concentrated than industry it sells to?		
Do firms in industry purchase relatively small volumes relative to other customers of supplier? Is typical firm's purchase volume small relative to sales of typical supplier?		
Few substitutes for suppliers' input?		
Do firms in industry make relationship-specific investments to support transactions with specific suppliers?		
Do suppliers pose credible threat of forward integration into the product market?		
Are suppliers able to price discriminate among prospective customers according to ability/willingness to pay for input?		

FACTORS AFFECTING OR REFLECTING POWER OF BUYERS

To what extent do individual *buyers have the ability to negotiate low purchase prices with typical firms in this industry? To what extent do purchase prices differ from those that would prevail in a market with a large number of fragmented buyers in which buyers act as price takers?*

	Characterization (Current)	Future trend
Is buyers' industry more concentrated than industry it purchases from?		
Do buyers purchase in large volumes? Does a buyer's purchase volume represent large fraction of typical seller's sales revenue?		
Can buyers can find substitutes for industry's product?		
Do firms in industry make relationship-specific investments to support transactions with specific buyers?		
Is price elasticity of demand of buyer's product high or low?		
Do buyers pose credible threat of backward integration?		
Does product represent significant fraction of cost in buyer's business?		
Are prices in the market negotiated between buyers and sellers on each individual transaction or do sellers "post" a "take-it-or-leave it price" that applies to all transactions?		

PART THREE

STRATEGIC POSITION AND DYNAMICS

STRATEGIC POSITIONING FOR COMPETITIVE ADVANTAGE[1]

12

$\mathcal{U}$ ntil the U.S. airline industry was deregulated in 1978, most major domestic airlines competed in the same way. With entry and prices controlled by the Civil Aeronautics Board (a regulatory agency that no longer exists), airlines competed by scheduling more frequent and convenient departures and by enhancing amenities, such as meals and movies. Deregulation of the industry led to new entry and new ways of doing business. Consider, for example, the variety of competitive strategies airlines have pursued since deregulation:

- American, the largest trunk carrier, developed a nationwide route structure organized around the hub-and-spoke concept.[2] It built traveler and travel agent loyalty through its frequent-flier programs and travel agent commission overrides (now on the decline) and attempted to maximize revenue through its sophisticated computerized reservation system, known as SABRE, and its state-of-the-art yield management capabilities.

- USAirways (formerly Allegheny and later USAir) was a regionally focused carrier before deregulation. It has tried to avoid head-to-head competition with the major airlines by serving smaller markets that the large carriers exited following deregulation. As a result, USAirways has consistently enjoyed the highest yield (dollars of revenue per passenger-mile) of any airline. But its smaller planes, lower load factors (percentage of seats filled), and generous labor contracts also give it the highest average operating costs in the industry.

- Continental engaged in bitter and protracted struggles with labor to cut wages and tighten work rules. Twice bankrupt, it is now a low-price alternative to the big trunk carriers.

---

[1]The authors would like to thank Steve Postrel and Jim Dana for valuable conversations that helped shape this chapter.

[2]See Chapter 2 for a discussion of the hub-and-spoke concept in the airline industry.

- Southwest, an intrastate carrier operating only in Texas before deregulation, expanded incrementally to selected cities in the Midwest and Southwest, and by flying into little-used airports (e.g., Chicago's Midway airport). Eschewing the hub-and-spoke concept, Southwest flies passengers from one city to another in one or two short hops. With less restrictive work rules than other major airlines, a fleet that consists only of Boeing 737s to economize on maintenance and training, and a highly motivated workforce, Southwest has enjoyed the lowest average operating costs in the industry. Its flights offer few amenities other than drinks and cheerful attendants; rather than attempting to capture traveler loyalty with frequent-flier programs, Southwest emphasizes low fares and reliable on-time service.

This example illustrates several fundamentally different ways in which firms can position themselves to compete within the same industry. With its extensive route network and its emphasis on loyalty-inducing devices, American attempts to differentiate its services from competitors to insulate itself from the effects of price-cutting by other airlines. Continental, by contrast, has sought to create a cost advantage relative to other airlines in the market. As a result, its pricing has been more aggressive than American. Like American, USAirways has sought to insulate itself from price competition. But USAirways has a narrower geographic scope than its larger rivals, and with its smaller, shorter-distance markets, it tends to have more business travelers among its fliers. Southwest's geographic scope is also narrower, and like USAirways, it has attempted to serve markets that its larger competitors have bypassed. Unlike USAirways, however, the basis of Southwest's success has been a cost advantage that allows it to offer low fares and still make a profit.

Of course, not all of these positions have been equally profitable. Moreover, the profitability of some positions has persisted, while the profitability of others was short lived. Southwest has made a profit each year since 1973. Continental consistently lost money between the mid-1980s and mid-1990s. Since then, however, it has become one of the most profitable U.S. airlines. American and USAirways were profitable throughout the 1980s, but incurred huge losses during the prolonged industry recession of the early 1990s. Since the end of that recession in the mid-1990s, American has enjoyed rates of profitability above the industry average, while USAirway's profit performance has lagged behind the rest of the industry. (Figure 12.1 shows returns on assets and sales revenues for the major U.S. airlines in 1996.) Clearly, some airlines (e.g., Southwest, American) have been better able than others (e.g., USAirways) to stake out strategic positions that are better suited to their industry environment.

This chapter develops a conceptual framework for characterizing and analyzing a firm's strategic position within an industry. This framework employs simple economic concepts to identify conditions necessary for competitive advantage in the market.

The chapter is organized in four main sections. The first defines the concept of competitive advantage and argues that to achieve it a firm must create more value than its rivals. The ability to create value is shaped by how firms position themselves to compete in an industry. The second section discusses the economic and organizational logic of two broad alternative approaches to positioning: cost advantage and benefit advantage. The third section covers market segmentation and targeting strategies. The fourth section discusses strategic groups. The appendixes to this chapter present specific tools for diagnosing a firm's cost and differentiation position in its market.

FIGURE 12.1
REVENUE AND PROFITABILITY IN THE U.S. AIRLINE INDUSTRY, 1996.

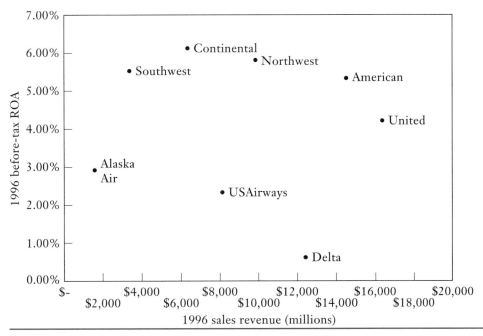

This graph shows sales revenue and profitability (as measured by return on assets) for major U.S. trunk airlines for 1996. Source: Compustat.

COMPETITIVE ADVANTAGE ◆ ◆ ◆ ◆ ◆

Competitive Advantage Defined

The five-forces framework presented in Chapter 11 is based on the idea that industry conditions are an important determinant of a firm's profitability. This premise is undoubtedly correct: Firms in some industries, such as pharmaceuticals, consistently outperform firms in other industries, such as airlines. However, profitability does not only vary across industries. It also varies within a particular industry, even over long periods of time. Some firms, such as Albertson's in grocery retailing, Amgen in biotechnology, and Kimberly-Clark in paper manufacturing have consistently earned rates of profit that exceed the average for their industries. Table 12.1 shows economic profitability (measured by the average annual spread between return on capital and cost of capital) over the years 1992–1996.[3] Within

---

[3]The data reported in Table 12.1 were obtained for the companies listed in the 1997 Performance 1000 universe collected by Stern Stewart & Company. A positive spread between return on capital and cost of capital in a particular year indicates positive economic profitability, while a negative spread indicates negative economic profitability. The earning and capital measures used by Stern Stewart to calculate returns on capital have been adjusted to eliminate accounting distortions. For example, a firm's earnings do not include book depreciation, and a firm's capital included an amortized value of R&D expenses.

TABLE 12.1
ECONOMIC PROFITABILITY WITHIN AND ACROSS INDUSTRIES, 1992–1996

Industry	High Performer		Low Performer		Industry Average
	Firm	Return on capital minus cost of capital, 1992–1996	Firm	Return on capial minus cost of capital 1992–1996	Return on capital minus cost of capital, 1992–1996
Aluminum	Alcoa	−5.77%	Kaiser Aluminum	−10.16%	−7.16%
Broadcasting	TCA Cable TV	3.36%	Cablevision Systems	−12.92%	−6.39%
Steel	Allegheny Teledyne	1.90%	Armco	−13.79%	−5.55%
Resorts and Hotels	Circus Circus	−1.51%	Hilton Hotels	−8.33%	−3.51%
Containers	Crown, Cork, & Seal	−0.04%	Corning	−2.34%	−1.63%
Paper	Kimberly Clark	2.89%	Mead Corp	−2.73%	−1.46%
Railroads	Wisconsin Central	3.16%	CSX	−3.82%	−1.08%
Publishing	Washington Post	4.30%	New York Times	−7.52%	−0.65%
Textiles	Unifi	6.34%	Springs Industries	−4.48%	−0.22%
Medical Products	Johnson & Johnson	6.03%	Bausch & Lomb	−2.98%	0.13%
Grocery Retailing	Albertson's	5.50%	American Stores	−2.10%	0.38%
Restaurant Chains	Outback Steakhouse	13.05%	Brinker Int'l	−2.08	0.83%
Personal Care	Clorox	2.93%	Alberto Culver	−0.60%	1.92%
Computer Hardware and Peripherals	EMC	15.84%	Amdahl	−22.02%	2.53%
Biotech	Amgen	36.97%	Genzyme	−10.76%	2.87%
Semiconductors	Intel	16.83%	Texas Instruments	−1.04%	5.03%
Computer Software	Cisco Systems	40.36%	Wang Laboratories	−18.65%	6.59%

each industry, the table shows the economic profitability for a representative firm (e.g., *Washington Post* in publishing) that has outperformed its industry and a representative firm (e.g., *New York Times*) that has underperformed its industry.

When a firm (or business unit within a multi-business firm) earns a higher rate of economic profit than the average rate of economic profit of other firms competing within the same market, the firm has a *competitive advantage* in that market.[4] Careful application of this definition, of course, requires an economically sensible definition of the firm's market, a topic taken up in Chapter 7. As discussed in that chapter, except for perfectly competitive markets, a group of firms are in the same market if one firm's production, pricing, and marketing decisions materially affect the prices that others in the group can charge. For example, to assess whether EMC Corporation has a competitive advantage in its core business of enterprise data storage (creation and maintenance of computer systems and software that store and exchange massive amounts of data within a large company), we would compare EMC's profitability in this business to the profitability of the business units within Compaq, IBM, and Sun, that also offer enterprise data storage systems and whose fortunes are materially affected by EMC's pricing and marketing decisions.

Figure 12.2 summarizes the framework that we develop in this chapter to explain why some firms achieve competitive advantage and others do not. According to this framework, a firm's profitability within a particular market depends both on market-level economics (as summarized, for example, by a five-forces analysis) and on the amount of economic value it creates compared to its competitors. A firm can achieve competitive advantage in a market only if it can create more economic value than its competitors. As we will see, a firm that can deliver more economic value

FIGURE 12.2
FRAMEWORK FOR COMPETITIVE ADVANTAGE.

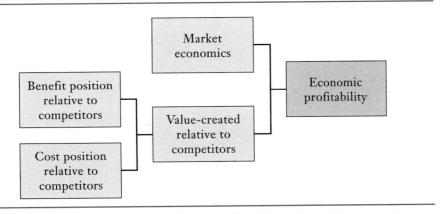

A firm's profitability depends jointly on the economics of its market and its success in creating more value than its competitors. The amount of value the firm creates compared to competitors depends on its cost and benefit positions relative to competitors.

---

[4]We continue the practice, used elsewhere in this book, of using the term *firm* to represent not only independent companies, but also autonomous business units that are subsidiaries of larger corporations. Thus, we would think of Philip Morris' Post Cereal Division as a "firm" within the cereal market.

than its competitors can simultaneously earn higher profits and deliver higher net benefits to consumers than its competitors can. The amount of value a firm creates depends on both its cost position and its benefit position relative to its competitors.

What Matters More for Profitability: The Market or the Firm?

The framework in Figure 12.2 implies that the economics of the firm's market and the firm's position in that market jointly determine the firm's profitability. But how would we determine which is more important?

To answer this question, imagine taking a broad sample of different companies or business units over many years and calculating their profitability (e.g., using standard accounting measures, such as return on assets, or more sophisticated tools, such as Economic Value Added, aimed at measuring economic profit[5]). Would you see considerable variation in profitability of business units *within industries* but little variation in profitability *across industries*? If so, the effect of the market environment on profitability (the market effect) is unimportant, but the effect of a firm or business unit's competitive position in the industry (the positioning effect) is important. Or would you see little variation in profitability of business units within industries, but lots of variation in profitability across industries? If so, the market effect is paramount, and the positioning effect is unimportant.

In fact, both market and positioning effects can explain profitability. The profitability of business units varies within the same industry and across industries. In fact, research by Anita McGahan and Michael Porter, summarized in Figure 12.3, suggests that the industry is responsible for about 18 percent of the variation in profit across firms, while competitive position accounts for about 32 percent of the variation in profit.[6] Other potential systematic influences on profitability, such as

FIGURE 12.3
INDUSTRY AND BUSINESS UNIT EFFECTS IN EXPLAINING PROFITABILITY.

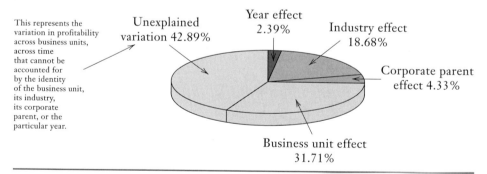

This chart shows the relative importance of business unit and industry effects in explaining variations in profitability across firms. The industry accounts for about 19 percent of profit variation across a large sample of firms and business units, while the competitive position of the business unit accounts for about 32 percent of the variation in profit.

---

[5]Economic Value Added is discussed in the Economics Primer.

[6]McGahan, A. M. and M. E. Porter, "How Much Does Industry Matter Really?" *Strategic Management Journal*, 18, Summer 1997: pp. 15–30. See also Rumelt, R. P., "How Much Does Industry Matter?" *Strategic Management Journal*, 12, 1991: pp. 167–185. Rumelt was the first to study the relative importance of business unit and industry effects, using a different data set than McGahan and Porter.

year-to-year variation in profit due to changes in macroeconomic conditions, or the business unit's corporate parentage (e.g., does it make a difference for Post Cereal's profit whether it is owned by Philip Morris or someone else), have a relatively small impact. Note that a large component (almost 43 percent) of the variation in profitability across firms is unsystematic. This component represents variation that cannot be accounted for by any systematic influence. For example, Asahi Glass' ceramic's division might earn a high profit in 1999, but a lower profit in 2000, not because of a change in its competitive position within the industrial ceramics market or poor macroeconomic circumstances, but simply because of "bad luck."

The fact that both the market and positioning effects are important drivers of profitability reinforces the need to flesh out the framework in Figure 12.2. We now proceed to do this.

COMPETITIVE ADVANTAGE AND VALUE CREATION: ANALYTICAL TOOLS AND CONCEPTUAL FOUNDATIONS

In this section, we present the analytical building blocks that we need to develop the framework in Figure 12.2 more fully. In particular, we define what we mean by value creation and show how it relates to competitive advantage. To develop the concept of value creation, we must first discuss perceived benefit and consumer surplus.

Perceived Benefit and Consumer Surplus

A particular computer software package is worth $150 to you. If its market price was $80, you would buy it because (from your perspective) its perceived benefit ($150) exceeds its cost ($80). This purchase makes you better off; you have given up $80 to receive something more valuable—a software package whose perceived benefit is worth $150. The extent by which you are better off—$70 ($150 > $80)—is known as *consumer surplus*.[7]

More formally, let B denote a product's perceived benefit to a consumer. It represents a dollar measure of what one unit of the product is worth to a particular consumer, or equivalently, the consumer's maximum willingness-to-pay for the product. To understand what maximum willingness-to-pay means, let's see how we might assess a consumer's maximum willingness to pay for a Honda Accord. Our consumer starts off with no automobile of any kind and is then given, free of charge, a Honda Accord.[8] She is certainly better off than before. Now, let's successively take money away from her. At some point, perhaps after we've taken away $26,250, she deems her situation (owning a Honda but with $26,250 less wealth)

---

[7]Marketing textbooks often use different terms to describe consumer surplus. One common synonym used in marketing is delivered value. See, for example, Kotler, P., *Marketing Management*, 7th ed., Englewood Cliffs, NJ: Prentice-Hall, 1991.

[8]This treatment is based on the construction of maximum-willingness-to-pay suggested in Brandenberger, A. M. and H. W. Stuart, Jr., "Value-Based Business Strategy," *Journal of Economics and Management Strategy*, 5, Spring 1996: pp. 5–24.

completely equivalent to her original situation (no Honda, but with her wealth intact). That dollar amount—$26,250—represents our consumer's maximum willingness-to-pay for a Honda Accord and would be her assessment of the Accord's B.

If we let P denote the product's monetary price, consumer surplus is the difference $B − P$. For example, if the price of the Honda Accord is $21,000, the consumer surplus of our hypothetical consumer would be $26,250 − $21,000 = $5,250. This example, and the preceding software example, suggest a simple model of consumer behavior: A consumer will purchase a product only if the product's consumer surplus is positive. Moreover, given a choice between two or more competing products, the consumer will purchase the one for which consumer surplus, $B − P$ is largest.[9]

The perceived benefit B should be thought of as the perceived gross benefit of the product (which depends on attributes, such as performance, reliability, durability, product aesthetics, and image) minus (1) the user cost of the product: the costs of installing, learning how to use, operating, maintaining, and (eventually) disposing of the product; and (2) any purchasing and transactions costs (excluding the purchase price itself) involved in buying the product, such as the costs of search, transportation, and (if necessary) writing contracts. Consumer surplus is then determined by simply deducting the monetary price from the product's perceived benefit (see Figure 12.4).[10]

Consumer surplus is analogous to the profit of a firm. Indeed, when the consumer is a firm, consumer surplus is identical to the increment in profit that the purchase of the good generates. To see this, imagine a firm that is considering purchasing a machine that will reduce production costs by $8,000 per year. In effect, the B of the machine is $8,000. Suppose the firm's discount rate is 5 percent, and the machine costs $100,000. The annualized purchase cost $P = .05 \times 100,000 = $5,000. "Consumer surplus" is thus $3,000 per year, which corresponds exactly to the increment in the firm's economic profit from purchasing the machine.[11]

---

[9]This is what economists refer to as the "discrete choice" model of consumer behavior. Such a model presumes that the number of units the consumer is contemplating purchasing is fixed (e.g., the consumer is only going to buy a single microwave oven), and the only issues the consumer faces are whether to purchase at all and from whom. The model of consumer choice discussed here and the concept of gross benefit can be extended to the case in which the consumer must not only decide whether and from whom to purchase, but also how many units of the product to purchase. This extension is logically straightforward, but involves introducing additional concepts, such as marginal benefit, that would distract us from the main points we are trying to develop.

[10]Marketing and strategic management textbooks often advocate adding together user costs, purchase and transactions costs, and the monetary price to obtain something that is usually called the total customer price. Consumer surplus would then be defined as gross benefit minus the total customer price. While the notion of a total customer price can be useful, we prefer instead to deduct the user and purchase and transactions costs from the perceived gross benefit to get what we call B, the perceived (net benefit). We thus distinguish between the monetary price P, which is essentially a transfer of money between consumers and the firm, and the user, purchase, and transactions costs, which entail a real resource sacrifice by society.

[11]Equivalently, we could have expressed everything on a discounted present value basis as opposed to an annualized basis. In that case, $B = $8,000/.05 = $160,000 and $P = $100,000. Consumer surplus is thus equivalent to the NPV of the project. See the appendix to the Economics Primer for a short introduction to the concept of net present value.

FIGURE 12.4
COMPONENTS OF CONSUMER SURPLUS.

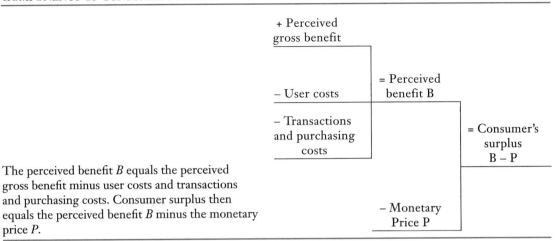

The perceived benefit B equals the perceived gross benefit minus user costs and transactions and purchasing costs. Consumer surplus then equals the perceived benefit B minus the monetary price P.

Whether its customers are firms or individuals, a seller must deliver consumer surplus to compete successfully. The value map in Figure 12.5 illustrates the competitive implications of consumer surplus. The vertical axis shows the monetary price P of the product. Each point in the value map corresponds to a particular price-quality combination. The solid upward-sloping line in Figure 12.5 is called

FIGURE 12.5
THE VALUE MAP.

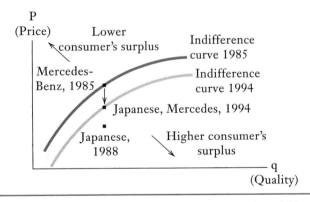

The value map illustrates the price-quality positions of firms in a market. The solid line is an indifference curve. It illustrates price-quality combinations that yield the same consumer surplus. Price-quality positions located below a given indifference curve yield a consumer surplus that is higher than that yielded by positions along the indifference curve. Price-quality positions located above an indifference curve yield consumer surplus that is lower than that yielded by positions along the indifference curve. When some products are positioned on a given indifference curve while others are positioned off the curve, consumers will flock to the firms providing the higher consumer surplus. This was apparently the case in the late 1980s when the Japanese luxury cars, such as Lexus and Infiniti, offered comparable cars at a lower price than established luxury producers, such as Mercedes-Benz.

an *indifference curve*. For a given consumer, any price-quality combination along the indifference curve yields the same consumer surplus (i.e., has the same $B - P$). A consumer choosing among products located along the indifference curve would thus be indifferent among the offerings. Products offering price-quality combinations located below a given indifference curve yield a higher consumer surplus than that yielded by products along the indifference curve. From the consumer's perspective, such products provide superior value. Products offering price-quality combinations located above a given indifference curve yield a consumer surplus lower than that yielded by products along the indifference curve. From the consumer's perspective, such products provide inferior value.

Competition among firms in a market can be thought of as a process whereby firms, through their prices and product attributes, submit consumer surplus "bids" to consumers. Consumers then choose the firm that offers the greatest amount of consumer surplus. A firm that offers a consumer less surplus than its rivals will lose the fight for that consumer's business. When firms' price-quality positions line up along the same indifference curve—that is, when firms are offering a consumer the same amount of consumer surplus—we say that the firms have achieved consumer surplus parity. If firms achieve consumer surplus parity in a market in which consumers have identical preferences (i.e., the same indifference curves), no consumer within that market has an incentive to switch from one seller to another, and market shares will thus be stable. If all firms in the market have the same quality, then consumer surplus parity means that each firm charges the same price. As discussed in the Economics Primer, a common market price is a necessary (though not sufficient) condition for a perfectly competitive market to be in equilibrium.

When a firm loses consumer surplus parity, its sales will slip, and its market share will fall. This happened to Mercedes-Benz in the luxury car market in the 1980s. Figure 12.5 depicts the indifference curve of a representative consumer in this market in 1985 and shows the position of Mercedes-Benz. When the Japanese luxury automobiles, such as Lexus, Infiniti, and Acura, were introduced in the United States in the late 1980s, they offered comparable quality to Mercedes-Benz, but at a lower price. Not surprisingly, they rapidly gained market share. Eventually, the Japanese car makers raised price, and Mercedes lowered price, moving all firms to a position of consumer surplus parity on an indifference curve to the southeast of the 1985 indifference curve.

The steepness (i.e., the slope) of an indifference curve indicates the tradeoff between price and quality a consumer is willing to make.[12] Indeed, as shown in Figure 12.6, the increase in the price along a given indifference curve corresponds exactly to the incremental benefit ΔB caused by an increase Δq in the quality delivered by the product.[13] A steeply sloped indifference curve indicates that a consumer is willing to pay considerably extra for additional quality, while a shallow indifference curve indicates that extra quality is not worth much to the customer.

Firms that overestimate the willingness of consumers to trade off price for quality risk overpricing their products and either losing market share to competitors or never becoming a viable competitor. Such was the fate of *The National*, an

---

[12]We couch our discussion in terms of the tradeoff between price and quality. More generally, though, the same discussion applies to the tradeoff between price and any benefit-enhancing or cost-reducing attribute.

[13]The logic is straightforward. Each point (E and F in Figure 12.6) yields the same consumer surplus, so $B_E - P_E = B_F - P_F$. Rearranging yields: $\Delta B = B_F - B_E = P_F - P_E$.

FIGURE 12.6

INDIFFERENCE CURVES AND THE TRADEOFF BETWEEN PRICE AND QUALITY.

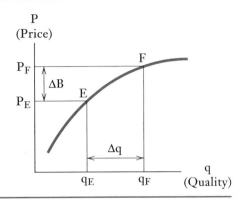

The steepness of an indifference curve indicates the tradeoff between price and quality consumers are willing to make. The increase in price from P_E to P_F along the indifference curve is equal to the change in perceived benefit, ΔB, that results from an increase, Δq, in quality from q_E to q_F.

all-sports daily newspaper launched with great fanfare in January 1990. Without question, its longer features, color photographs, detailed statistics, and columns and bylines by big-name sportswriters, such as Mike Lupica and John Feinstein, made it superior to the sports coverage provided by local newspapers. However, at a price of 75 cents per issue, most potential readers did not find it to be a good value compared to the available alternatives. *The National's* circulation remained far below projections, and the advertising revenue needed to support the highly paid staff of reporters and columnists never materialized. *The National* folded in June 1991.

Firms can also underestimate the willingness of consumers to trade off price and quality. For example, some automakers were relatively slow to introduce airbags and anti-lock braking systems (e.g., Mazda, in the MPV), while others (e.g., Ford, especially the Taurus sedan) were not and gained an advantage.

Value-Created

As goods move along the vertical chain—as raw materials are converted to components, components are assembled into finished goods, and finished goods are distributed to final consumers—economic value is created. A producer at each stage in the chain combines goods and services produced in previous stages, with labor and capital, to create a product that is worth more to its consumers than the inputs used to produce it. A product's perceived benefit B represents the value that consumers derive from the product. The cost, C, represents the value that is sacrificed when inputs are converted into a finished product. Value-created is the difference between the value that resides in the product and the value of the inputs that are sacrificed to make that product:

$$\text{Value-created} = \text{Perceived Benefit to Final Customer} - \text{Cost of Inputs}$$
$$= B - C,$$

where B and C are expressed per unit of the final product.[14]

---

[14]C thus represents the average cost of production (as opposed to the total cost), inclusive of all the inputs used in the production and sale of the good. If, for example, the finished good is a barrel of beer, C would be the cost of the labor, capital, and materials used to produce and market the beer, expressed on a per-barrel basis.

FIGURE 12.7
THE COMPONENTS OF VALUE-CREATED.

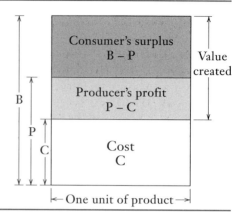

The overall area of the rectangle in the figure equals the perceived benefit B. Deducting the rectangle representing the cost C leaves the shaded region, which is value-created. Value-created can be seen to equal the sum of consumer surplus and producer profit.

The total value-created must be divided between consumers and producers. Consumer surplus, $B - P$, represents the portion of the value-created that the consumer "captures." The seller receives the price P and uses it to pay for the inputs, such as labor, capital, and materials, that are needed to manufacturer the finished product. The producer's profit $P - C$ represents the portion of the value-created that it captures. Adding together consumer surplus and the producer's profit gives us the value-created expressed as the sum of consumer surplus and profit:

$$\text{Value-created} = \text{Consumer Surplus} + \text{Producer's Profit}$$
$$= (B - P) + (P - C)$$
$$= B - C$$

Figure 12.7 depicts value-created.[15] The total area of the rectangle is the perceived benefit B. Deducting the unshaded area representing costs C leaves us with the value-created, $B - C$. The price P determines how much of the value-created sellers capture as profit and how much buyers capture as consumer surplus.

Value Creation and "Win-Win" Business Opportunities

No product can be viable without creating positive economic value. If $B - C$ was negative, there would be no price that consumers would be willing to pay for the product that would cover the costs of the resources that are sacrificed to make the product. Manufacturers of the product, along with their input suppliers, would be unable to make a profit. Vacuum tubes, rotary dial telephones, and dedicated word processing units are products that at one time created positive value, but because of changes in tastes and technology no longer create enough benefits to consumers to justify their production.

---

[15] This is based on a similar diagram in Chapter 4 of Ghemawat, P., *Commitment: The Dynamic of Strategy*, New York: Free Press, 1991.

XAMPLE 12.1

THE DIVISION OF THE VALUE-CREATED
IN THE SALE OF BEER AT A BASEBALL GAME

Assigning numbers to the areas in Figure 12.7 is usually difficult because B is hard to measure. But when the product is sold under conditions of monopoly, and no reasonable substitutes are available, B can be approximated by making some simplifying assumptions about the nature of the market demand curve. An example of a product sold under these circumstances is beer at a baseball game. Because a purchaser of beer would probably not regard soft drinks as a close substitute and since patrons are not allowed to bring in their own beer, the stadium concessionaire has as tight a monopoly on the market as one could imagine.

The first step is to estimate B. If we assume that the demand curve for beer is linear, then the relationship between per-unit consumer surplus $B - P$ and the price P is given by

$$B - P = .5P/\eta,$$

where η is the price elasticity of demand at price P.[16] The price of a 20-ounce cup of beer sold at Cincinnati's Riverfront stadium in 1988 was $2.50.[17] The stadium concessionaire, Cincinnati Sports Service, pays the distributor $.20 per cup for this beer, pays royalties to the city of Cincinnati—$.24 per cup—and the Cincinnati Reds—$.54 per cup—and an excise tax of $.14 per cup. The concessionaire's marginal cost is thus at least $1.12 per 20-ounce cup of beer. If we assume that $2.50 represents the profit-maximizing monopoly price, then the price elasticity of demand η at $2.50 must be at least 1.8.[18] Using the preceding formula, this implies that consumer surplus must (on average) be no greater than $.69 per 20-ounce cup of beer.

Table 12.2 shows the division of value in the sale of the beer using $.69 per cup as our estimate of consumer surplus. The brewer clearly captures only a

---

[16]The derivation of this relationship is not important. However, for interested readers, here goes: Total (as opposed to per-unit) consumer surplus can be shown to equal the area under the demand curve above the price. For a linear demand curve given by the formula $P = a - bQ$ (where Q is total demand), this area is given by $.5bQ^2$. Consumer surplus per unit is thus given by $.5bQ = .5P(bQ/P)$. But the term in parentheses is the reciprocal of the price elasticity of demand (i.e., $\eta = P/bQ$). Thus, per-unit consumer surplus is given by $.5P/\eta$.

[17]This and all subsequent data come from "Sports and Suds: The Beer Business and the Sports World Have Brewed Up a Potent Partnership," *Sports Illustrated*, August 8, 1988, pp. 68–82.

[18]Again, the details of this derivation are not important, but for interested readers here they are: From the Economics Primer, the optimal monopoly price is given by $(P - MC)/P = 1/\eta$. Thus, if $2.50 is the monopoly price, $(2.50 - MC)/2.50 = 1/\eta$. Since $MC = \$1.12$, straightforward algebra implies $\eta = 1.8$.

TABLE 12.2
DIVISION OF VALUE IN THE SALE OF BEER AT RIVERFRONT STADIUM

Consumer Surplus $.69
Profit to Sports Service ? ....$1.38 Sports Sevice's Costs (labor, materials, insurance, etc.) ?
Profit to Cincinnati Reds $.54
Profit to City of Cincinnati $.20
Taxes $.14
Distributor's Profit ? ....$.10 Distributor's Costs (excl. price paid to brewer) ?
Brewer's Profit $.03
Brewer's Costs $.07

small fraction of the value that is created.[19] By contrast, by controlling the access of the concessionaire to the stadium and to the event, the city of Cincinnati and the Cincinnati Reds are able to capture a significant fraction of the value that is created. They can capture value because prospective concessionaires are willing to compete for the right to monopolize this market. As a result, the city and the Reds can extract a significant portion of the monopoly profit that would otherwise flow to the concessionaire.

By contrast, when $B - C$ is positive, a firm can profitably purchase inputs from suppliers, convert them into a finished product, and sell it to consumers. When $B > C$, it will always be possible for an entrepreneur to strike "win-win" deals with input suppliers and consumers, that is, deals that leave *all* parties better off than they would be if they did not deal with each other. In economics, "win-win" trade opportunities are called *gains from trade*. When $B > C$, clever entrepreneurs can exploit potential gains from trade.

---

[19]Without knowing the production costs of Sports Service or the distributor, we cannot pin down the actual amount of value that is created through the vertical chain. Whatever it is, however, the brewer captures only a small portion of it.

Value-Creation and Competitive Advantage

Although a positive $B - C$ is *necessary* for a product to be economically viable, just because a firm sells a product whose $B - C$ is positive is no guarantee that it will make a positive economic profit. Competition in the market between producers, all offering products with identical $B - C$, can dissipate profitability. Existing firms and new entrants will compete for consumers by bidding down the product price, P. If price is competed down to cost C (so that all producers earn zero economic profit and are just earning their cost of capital), consumers will capture all the economic value that the product creates.[20]

To achieve a competitive advantage—to outperform the competitors in its market—a firm's product must not only create positive value, it must create more value than its competitors. That is, it must generate a higher $B - C$. This is a simple but powerful insight. The reason it is true follows from our earlier discussion of the competitive implications of consumer surplus. Recall that competition among firms can be envisioned as a process whereby firms "bid" for consumers on the basis of consumer surplus. The firm whose product characteristics and price offer a particular consumer the greatest amount of consumer surplus will get that consumer's business. Because value-created, $B - C$, is the sum of consumer surplus, $B - P$, and profit, $P - C$, a firm that creates more value than its competitor will be able to match the consumer surplus "bids" of its competitors and end up with a higher profit on the sale. In a market equilibrium in which all firms have attained consumer surplus parity, the firm that creates more value will be more profitable than its rivals.

◆ ◆

XAMPLE 12.2

VALUE-CREATION WITHIN A VERTICAL CHAIN: INTEGRATED DELIVERY SYSTEMS IN HEALTH CARE

Just as individual firms compete to create and deliver economic value to consumers, entire vertical chains can also be viewed as competing to create economic value. A recent development that highlights this point is the competition between integrated delivery systems (IDSs) and traditional nonintegrated delivery systems within the health care industry in the United States.

An IDS combines many elements of the health care vertical chain under common ownership. A typical IDS, such as the Henry Ford Clinic in Michigan, may own an insurance company, diagnostic facilities, physician practices, hospitals, pharmacies, ambulatory surgery centers, and home health care agencies. An IDS can provide "one-stop shopping" for virtually all a patient's health care needs.

---

[20]We have assumed that firms can obtain inputs, such as labor and land, at their relevant opportunity cost. That is, C represents the opportunity cost of the inputs used by a firm to make a product. However, firms might also compete with each other for scarce inputs. If so, the firm will incur input costs W that exceed the opportunity costs C of the inputs. In this case, the owners of the scarce inputs capture part of the economic value that the firm's product creates.

Consumers effectively select an IDS when they choose their health care plan. In the United States, individuals usually choose their plan once a year. They may choose from a variety of plans. In most traditional plans, including most Health Maintenance Organizations (HMOs) and Preferred Provider Organizations (PPOs), the vertical chain is nonintegrated. The consumer selects an insurer, who contracts with independent providers to deliver the gamut of health care goods and services. You can therefore view competition between an IDS and traditional plans as competition between a fully integrated vertical chain and several nonintegrated chains.

An IDS can succeed if it delivers greater economic value across the entire vertical chain than do the competing, nonintegrated health plans. We can use the make-or-buy framework developed in Chapter 3 to identify potential value-creation advantages of IDSs. IDSs can solve coordination problems in the vertical chain of medical delivery, sometimes by getting providers to agree to a structured medical process. IDSs can also protect relationship-specific investments made by providers who relocate their offices or change their practices to better serve the medical process. This might promote more relationship-specific investment within the IDS chain than in competing nonintegrated chains, increasing the amount of economic value that is created.

There are also disadvantages in IDSs. As described in Chapter 3, vertically integrated enterprises can suffer from incentive problems and excessive influence costs as compared to nonintegrated enterprises, which increases the C of an IDS relative to a nonintegrated delivery system. In addition, patients within an IDS often have a limited choice of providers, which reduces the B that an IDS creates. Several years ago, some health care experts predicted that IDSs would dominate the marketplace; they have not. While IDSs often generated more $B - C$ than nonintegrated systems in the health care vertical chain, they probably do not generate substantially more $B - C$ than their nonintegrated rivals, and for some types of consumers they may even deliver less $B - C$. Both systems will probably continue to compete for the forseeable future.

Understanding how a firm's product creates economic value and whether it can continue to do so is a necessary first step in diagnosing a firm's potential for achieving a competitive advantage in its market. Diagnosing the sources of value creation requires an understanding of why the firm's business exists and what its underlying economics are. This, in turn, involves understanding what drives consumer benefits (e.g., how the firm's products serve consumer needs better than potential substitutes) and what drives costs (e.g., which costs are sensitive to production volume; how costs vary with nonproduction activities, such as sales and marketing; how costs change with cumulative experience).[21]

Projecting the firm's prospects for creating value also involves critically evaluating how the fundamental economic foundations of the business are likely to

---

[21]The appendix to this chapter presents a more detailed discussion of cost drivers and benefit drivers.

evolve, an excercise that Richard Rumelt calls consonance analysis.[22] Perhaps the most basic of all is the question of whether changes in market demand or the conditions of technology are likely to threaten how the firm creates value. Although this point seems transparent, it is easily overlooked by firms in the throes of month-to-month battles for market share with their immediate rivals. Evaluating future prospects is also difficult due to the sheer complexity of predicting the future and the risks involved in acting on such predictions.

The history of an industry may also dull managers to the prospects for change. Threats to a firm's ability to create value often come from outside its immediate group of rivals and may not just threaten the firm, but the whole industry. Honda's foray into motorcycles in the early 1960s occurred within segments that the dominant producers at the time—Harley-Davidson and British Triumph—had concluded were unprofitable. IBM's initial dominance in the PC market may well have diverted its attention from the serious threat that the PC and related products, such as work stations, had for its core business of mainframes. The revolution in mass merchandising created by Wal-Mart occurred in out-of-the-way locations that companies such as Kmart and Sears had rejected as viable locations for large discount stores.

EXAMPLE 12.3

CREATING VALUE AT CEMEX[23]

It sells a commodity product that is costly to ship. It is primarily located in Mexico but it has manufacturing facilities in several other developing nations. Yet it recently made *Industry Week*'s list of 100 best-managed companies, where it ranked second in profit margin. How does Cemex, the third largest cement company in the world, do it?

When Lorenzo Sambrano took over as CEO of Cemex in 1985, the company's annual sales of $500 million went mostly to Mexican companies. Thanks to Sambrano's strategy aimed at creating value in niche markets, Cemex now operates in 22 nations, with annual revenues approaching $4 billion. Sambrano's growth strategy was simple: provide low-cost cement in developing nations where opportunities for providing value were highest; at the same time, avoid the risk inherent in doing business in small, volatile markets. Cemex has done this by taking advantage of economies of scale and utilizing state-of-the-art information technology.

---

[22]Rumelt, R., "The Evaluation of Business Strategy," in Glueck, W. F., *Business Policy and Strategic Management*, 3rd ed., New York: McGraw-Hill, 1980. A recent term for consonance analysis is the analysis of *value migration*, a concept developed by Adrian Slywotzky in his book *Value Migration: How to Think Several Moves Ahead of the Competition*, Cambridge, MA: Harvard Business School Press, 1996.

[23]Much of the information for this example is from Dombey, Daniel, "Well-Built Success" *Industry Week*, May 5, 1997.

Cemex's kiln in Tepeaca, Mexico is the largest in the Americas. Cemex sells cement made in this kiln throughout Central America. This enables Cemex to run the kiln at or near capacity, even if there is an economic downtown in one of its national markets. Running its kiln near capacity and taking advantage of numerous technological innovations (such as a conveyor system that minimizes loading and unloading, and a special chimney that reduces energy costs), Cemex produces cement at a cost of $25 per hour, which is 28 percent below the industry average.

Cemex provides its customers with more than just low-cost cement. Cemex has taken steps to minimize delivery delays to customers in other countries that can be caused by government inspections and traffic jams. These delays can dramatically drive up the costs of a construction project. Cemex trucks are equipped with dashboard computers that alert drivers of job cancellations, allowing them to reroute to another location. Cemex put its drivers through a two-year training program to make sure that they could use the computers correctly. This is just one example of how Cemex uses information technology to increase its flexibility and reduce business risk.

Cemex also supplies its operations expertise overseas. In 1992 it acquired Spain's two largest cement companies, in 1994 it acquired Venezuela's largest cement maker, and in 1996 it purchased three producers in Columbia. It has also bought controlling stakes in companies in several smaller developing nations and is exploring entering the Asian market. Each time it acquires a company Cemex reengineers the manufacturing facilities and dramatically increases the use of information technology. Invariably, this leads to an increase in profitability.

Cemex is alone among the world's largest cement makers in its focus on developing nations. By exploiting scale economies and using information technology, Cemex has maintained the low costs and flexibility necessary to markedly outperform its rivals in these markets.

◆ ◆

XAMPLE 12.4

VALUE-CREATION AT PROCHNIK[24]

Consistent value-creation is hard enough for a firm and its managers to achieve in the absence of dramatic environmental change. Competition, even under a constant set of technological and regulatory conditions, keeps most firms from earning positive economic profits on a continuing basis. When environmental conditions change dramatically, however, the value-creation problem the firm and its managers face becomes even more difficult, because the basic ways in which the firm has grown used to creating value become suspect and the firm's skills are no longer valuable. This, in turn, threatens the firm's survival.

---

[24]This example is based on materials from "Prochnik: Privatization of a Polish Clothing Manufacturer," Harvard Business School case 9-394-038.

Radical environmental change was what the Polish clothing firm, Prochnik, faced in 1990, as it became one of the first five state enterprises to be privatized by the Polish government and to be listed in 1991 on the newly formed Polish stock exchange. While Prochnik had been a star performer and a strong exporter to the West under communism, most of the firm's strengths disappeared in the post-Communist era and its managers were forced to develop new skills and find new market bases for value-creation.

Prochnik began operations in 1945 as a supplier of army uniforms to the Polish army. By 1949, the firm's line included consumer products. By 1960, Prochnik was specializing in producing men's raincoats and had begun exporting them to Western Europe, the United States, and the USSR. By the 1980s, the firm had greatly expanded its productive capacity and exported approximately 70 percent of its output to the United States and Europe and 15 percent to the USSR. Prochnik had gained a reputation as Poland's leading producer of men's coats.

Prochnik's success made it a natural candidate for privatization. Since success was expected to continue after communism, the first management team of the newly independent firm was made up of former managers of the firm from the Communist era and was headed by Longin Barski, who had been Prochnik's general director since 1980. Prochnik's initial stock offering sold quickly to domestic and foreign investors.

With the fall of communism, however, the basis of Prochnik's export success collapsed. The market in the former USSR dried up, while the firm lost sales in the West when the Polish government discontinued export subsidies. The cost of Prochnik's raw material also rose sharply. None of the firm's Communist-era skills were useful in the new era. This change in fortune alarmed investors and Prochnik's stock price fell to one-fifth of its initial value. It also led to a management shakeup, which eventually removed Barski and his assistants. Wojciech Kolignan was hired to replace Barski. Kolignan was a former Prochnik manager, who was well-known and respected in the firm for his management of its successful raincoat business and for his knowledge of the Polish fashion industry.

At the urging of prominent investors and with the aid of some consultants, Kolignan and his managers developed a coherent value-creation strategy for Prochnik. The strategy called for Prochnik to participate in two markets. First, it would produce high-end branded apparel for the Polish market. This apparel, which would include both men's and women's clothes, would be targeted at Poland's emerging professional class. Prochnik would concentrate on creating a superior brand image for its apparel and securing access to retail distribution channels. Prochnik would compete in this market by offering high-quality "upscale" products that embodied the latest fashions trends.

Prochnik's other business would be contract manufacturing ("cut-make-trim") for well-known Western apparel firms, such as Boss and Brinkmann. That is, Prochnik would manufacture apparel from their clients' designs that would then be sold in Western Europe and the United States under their clients' brand names. Prochnik would compete in this market by offering a select number of large Western clients a low-cost source of reliable manufacturing services. Prochnik's "cut-make-trim" business would help finance Prochnik's branded apparel business. (Poland's poorly-developed capital markets made external financing, such as bank loans, impractical, in the early 1990s.) In addition, the "cut-make-trim" business would give Prochnik insight into the latest Western fashion trends, trends that often caught on quickly in Poland.

In the years immediately following its privatization, Prochnik enjoyed significant success. It increased its market share, and it created an image as a high-quality, fashionable brand within the high-end Polish apparel market. By 1993, Prochnik's stock had risen to more than twice its initial offering price. However, Prochnik's prospects for continued success and future growth are uncertain. The Polish market is limited, and it is unclear whether Prochnik can market its brand's image outside Poland. Moreover, even within Poland, Prochnik is facing competition from foreign (especially German) apparel producers (including some of Prochnik's own "cut-make-trim" clients!) that are now discovering the high-end market that Prochnik targeted.

The story of Prochnik shows how knowledgeable and respected managers can foster a value-creation strategy in their firms. Prochnik's flexibility in readjusting its strategy and developing new products can also be attributed to its lack of sunk assets, such as heavy capital goods, which made asset redeployment easier in the face of environmental pressures. In more capital-intensive industries (such as the Gdansk shipyards on Poland's Baltic coast), such turnarounds were not possible.

Value Creation and the Value Chain

Value is created as goods move along the vertical chain. The vertical chain is therefore sometimes referred to as the *value chain*.[25] The value chain depicts the firm as a collection of value-creating activities, such as production operations, marketing and sales, and logistics, as Figure 12.8 shows. Each activity in the value chain can potentially add to the benefit B that consumers get from the firm's product, and each can add to the cost C that the firm incurs to produce and sell the product. Of course, the forces that influence the benefits created and cost incurred vary significantly across activities.

In practice, it is often difficult to isolate the impact that an activity has on the value that the firm creates. To do so requires estimating the incremental perceived benefit that an activity creates and the incremental cost associated with it. However, when different stages produce finished or semifinished goods that can be valued using market prices, we can estimate the incremental value that distinctive parts of the value chain create. This is called value-added analysis. The appendix to this chapter presents a fuller explanation and an example of value-added analysis.

Analyzing competitive advantage involves looking not only at the firm's value chain, but at the entire vertical chain of production, as discussed in Chapters 3 through 5. Those chapters stressed that value can be created through judicious make-or-buy decisions that are sensitive to conditions of technology (e.g., scale economies) and transactions costs (e.g., asset specificity). For example, reducing the risk of the holdup problem through vertical integration can lead to greater invest-

---

[25]The concept of the value chain was developed by Michael Porter. See chapter 2 of *Competitive Advantage*, New York: Free Press, 1985.

FIGURE 12.8
MICHAEL PORTER'S VALUE CHAIN.

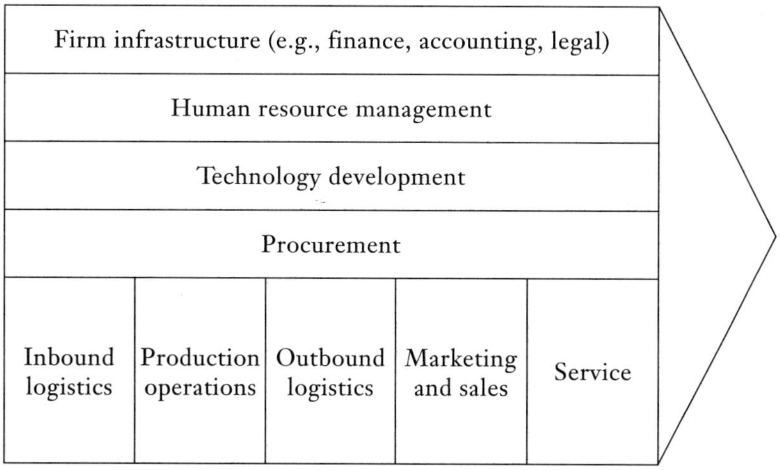

Firm infrastructure (e.g., finance, accounting, legal)
Human resource management
Technology development
Procurement

Inbound logistics	Production operations	Outbound logistics	Marketing and sales	Service

The value chain depicts the firm as a collection of value-creating activities. Porter distinguishes between five primary activities (inbound logistics, production operations, outbound logistics, marketing, and sales and service) and four support activities (firm infrastructure activities, such as finance and accounting, human resources management, technology development, and procurement).

ment in relationship-specific assets, which can often lower overall production costs. The search for competitive advantage involves reevaluating the organization of the firm's vertical chain to see if past make-or-buy decisions are still justified. If vertical integration was initially justified by high transactions costs, it may eventually become inefficient and a source of competitive disadvantage if, because of changes in technology, dedicated assets are no longer critical for production efficiency.

Value-Creation, Resources, and Capabilities

The value chain identifies the activities within the firm that create value. But a firm creates more value than its competitors only by performing some or all of these activities better than they do. To do this, the firm must possess resources and capabilities that its competitors lack; otherwise, the competitors could immediately copy any strategy for creating superior value.[26] Resources are firm-specific assets, such as patents and trademarks, brand-name reputation, installed base, organizational culture, and workers with firm-specific expertise or know-how. The brand recognition that Coca-Cola enjoys worldwide and Mattel's stock of instantly recognizable toy characters, such as Barbie, are examples of economically powerful resources. Unlike nonspecialized assets or factors of production, such as buildings, raw materials, or unskilled labor, resources cannot easily be duplicated or acquired by other firms in well-functioning markets. Resources can directly affect the abil-

---

[26]This point is developed in greater detail in Chapter 13.

ity of a firm to create more value than other firms. For example, a large installed base or an established reputation for quality may make the firm's B higher than its rivals. Resources also indirectly impact value creation because they are the basis of the firm's capabilities.

Capabilities are activities that a firm does especially well compared with other firms.[27] You might think of resources as "nouns" (they are things that firms "have") and capabilities as "verbs" (they are things that firms "do"). Capabilities might reside within particular business functions (e.g., Procter and Gamble's skills in brand promotion, Usiminas' skills in manufacturing operations, American Airlines' capabilities in yield management, or Nine West's ability to manage its sourcing and procurement functions in the fashion shoe business). Alternatively, they may be linked to particular technologies or product designs (e.g., DuPont's proficiencies in nylon, Nan Ya Plastics skills in working with polyester, or Honda's legendary skill in working with small internal combustion engines and power trains).[28] Or they might reside in the firm's ability to manage linkages between elements of the value chain or coordinate activities across it (e.g., an important element in Ford's resurgence in the mid-1980s and its ability to outperform General Motors over the past 10 years was Ford's ability to shorten the time between a product's conception and its introduction, which in turn required proficiency at managing linkages across the design, marketing, engineering, and manufacturing functions of the business).[29]

Whatever their basis, capabilities have several key common characteristics:

1. They are typically valuable across multiple products or markets.
2. They are embedded in what Richard Nelson and Sidney Winter call organizational routines—well-honed patterns of performing activities inside an organization.[30] This implies that capabilities can persist even though individuals leave the organization.
3. They are tacit; that is, they are difficult to reduce to simple algorithms or procedure guides.

Chapters 2 and 5 discussed the implication of point 1 for the vertical and horizontal boundaries of the firm. Points 2 and 3 have important implications for the sustainability of competitive advantages built upon organizational capabilities and will be developed more fully in the next chapter.

Resources and capabilities should be distinguished from key success factors.[31] Key success factors refer to the skills and assets a firm must possess to achieve profitability in a particular market. As such, they should be thought of as market-

---

[27]Other terms for this concept include distinctive competences and core competences.

[28]C. K. Prahalad and Gary Hamel emphasize this type of capability in their notion of "core competence." See "The Core Competence of the Corporation," *Harvard Business Review*, May–June 1990: pp. 79–91.

[29]This is what George Stalk, Philip Evans, and Lawrence Shulman emphasize in their notion of "capabilities." See "Competing on Capabilities: The New Rules of Corporate Strategy," *Harvard Business Review*, March–April 1992: pp. 57–69.

[30]Nelson, R. R. and S. G. Winter, *An Evolutionary Theory of Economic Change*, Cambridge, MA: Belknap, 1982.

[31]The concept of key success factors was developed by Hofer, C. and D. Schendel, *Strategy Formulation: Analytical Concepts*, St. Paul, MN: West, 1977.

level characteristics, rather than unique to individual firms. Possessing an industry's key success factors is necessary, but it is not sufficient condition for achieving competitive advantage. For example, to achieve competitive success as a distributor of athletic footwear, a firm must have the capability to develop new designs, manage a network of suppliers and distributors, and create marketing campaigns. But simply providing such services is not enough. All of the large footwear firms have them. But only a few firms, such as Nike, so excel at these activities that they can create more value than their competitors.

Resources, capabilities, and key success factors are all predictors of a firm's profitability. While the conceptual differences between them are clear, distinguishing one from the others may not be easy in particular situations. For example, a key factor may be a requirement for success for all firms in an industry, but it may also be a distinctive capability for specific firms.

The ability to manage resources, capabilities, and key success factors is also important. Just because some activity or condition can be associated with firm performance does not imply that the managers of a firm can manipulate that factor to its advantage. For example, a central location in an urban area may be the source of a retailer's competitive advantage, but the scarcity of similarly attractive plots of land limits the ability of other firms to duplicate that resource advantage. The limits to manageability are often most clear for capabilities. Because capabilities are often tacit, replicating other firms' distinctive capabilities is difficult. We will develop this point in more detail in the next chapter.

◆ ◆

EXAMPLE 12.5

MEASURING CAPABILITIES IN THE PHARMACEUTICAL INDUSTRY

Drawing on detailed quantitative and qualitative data from 10 major firms, Rebecca Henderson and Iain Cockburn attempted to measure resources and capabilities associated with new drug research in the pharmaceutical industry.[32] Though drug discovery is not the only skill that pharmaceutical firms must possess to compete effectively, it is extremely important. Henderson and Cockburn hypothesize that research productivity (measured as the number of patents obtained per research dollar invested) depends on three classes of factors: the composition of a firm's research portfolio; firm-specific scientific and medical know-how; and the firm's distinctive capabilities. The composition of the research portfolio is important because it is easier to achieve patentable discoveries in some areas than in others. For example, for the past 20 years, investments in cardiovascular drug discovery have been consistently more productive than investments in cancer research. Firm-specific know-how is critical because modern

---

[32]Henderson, R. and I. Cockburn, "Measuring Competence? Exploring Firm Effects in Pharmaceutical Research," *Strategic Management Journal*, 15, Winter 1994: pp. 63–84.

drug research requires highly skilled scientists from disciplines such as biology, biochemistry, and physiology. Henderson and Cockburn use measures, such as the firm's existing stock of patents, as proxies for idiosyncratic firm know-how.

Henderson and Cockburn also hypothesize that two capabilities are likely to be especially significant in new drug research. The first is skill at encouraging and maintaining an extensive flow of scientific information from the external environment to the firm. In pharmaceuticals much of the fundamental science that lays the groundwork for new discoveries is created outside the firm. A firm's ability to take advantage of this information is important for its success in making new drug discoveries. Henderson and Cockburn measure the extent of this capability through variables such as the firm's reliance on publication records in making promotion decisions, its proximity to major research universities, and its involvement in joint research projects with major universities.

The second capability they focus on is skill at encouraging and maintaining flow of information across disciplinary boundaries inside the firm. Successful new drug discoveries require this type of integration. For example, the commercial development of HMG CoA reductase inhibitors (drugs that inhibit cholesterol synthesis in the liver) depended on pathbreaking work at Merck on three disciplinary fronts: pharmacology, physiology, and biostatistics. Henderson and Cockburn measure this capability with variables, such as the extent to which the research in the firm was coordinated through cross-disciplinary teams and giving one person authority to allocate resources for research. The former would facilitate the flow of information across disciplines; the latter would inhibit it.

Henderson and Cockburn's study indicates that differences in firms' capabilities explain much variability in firms' research productivity. For example, a firm that rewards research publications is about 40 percent more productive than one that does not. A firm that organizes by cross-disciplinary research teams is about 25 percent more productive than one that does not. Does this mean that a firm that switches to a team-based research organization will immediately increase its output of patents per dollar by 40 percent? Probably not. This and other measures Henderson and Cockburn used were proxies for deeper resource-creation or integrative capabilities. For example, a firm that rewards publications may have an advantage at recruiting the brightest scientists. A firm that organizes by teams may have a collegial atmosphere that encourages team-based organizations. A team-based organization inside a firm that lacks in collegiality may generate far less research productivity. These observations go back to our earlier point. It is often far easier to identify distinctive capabilities once they exist than for management to create them.

Value-Creation versus Value Redistribution

The idea that competitive advantage requires a firm to create value to outperform competitors contrasts sharply with the view, implicit in much of the corporate diversification activity of the 1970s and 1980s, that a firm can succeed solely through its skills in bargaining with suppliers and buyers, or outguessing the market in acquiring undervalued firms. These skills have much more to do with redistributing existing value than creating new value. The problem with building strategy around value redistribution, as opposed to value-creation, is that the competition to redistribute value is likely to be fierce.[33] Michael Steinhardt, one of the most successful money managers ever, notes how difficult it is to outperform the market in identifying undervalued assets when he says: "Having traded for as long as I have gives me the opportunity to be 51 percent right rather than 50 percent right. Actually, it is more than a 1% edge, but it is not a big advantage like being right 80 percent of the time, or anything approaching that."[34]

Similar logic applies to the redistribution of value through skillful negotiation. Although not everyone can be a tough bargainer (there are enough tough bargainers out there), so that a firm could rarely be expected to outperform its competitors solely because it is a better at squeezing its suppliers or customers. Indeed, few firms have succeeded solely because they have been able to push around their workers, suppliers, or buyers. The same can be said for firms or individuals who attempt to redistribute surplus by taking over other firms and cutting wages or firing workers. Even notorious hardball negotiators, such as Frank Lorenzo (former CEO of Texas Air) or Albert Dunlap (former CEO of Sunbeam), find that bargaining skill alone is no guarantee of business success. If, as we would suspect, plenty of raiders and turnaround artists know how to renegotiate labor contracts and fire workers, then the contest to acquire firms and turn them around this way is essentially an auction. In the bidding to win the auction, much of the profit that is available from surplus redistribution is competed away. This would explain the findings, discussed in Chapter 6, that acquiring firms on average do not profit from unrelated acquisitions.

The Role of Industry Structure

The total value created by a firm can be written:

Value-created = Value-created by average firm in industry + differential between firm's value-created and average industry value-created

The share of the value-created that a firm retains as profit therefore depends on (a) the percentage of the value an average firm retains in its industry, and (b) the percentage of differential value-created the firm retains. Because each component is important, a firm that greatly outperforms its industry can still earn low profits in an absolute sense. For example, Nucor outperforms many other U.S. steel producers, but market economics and competitive forces within the steel industry prevent the average firm from retaining much value. Thus, even though Nucor has succeeded within its industry, it still has low profits compared with firms in other industries. Conversely, a firm can perform at its industry norm and earn high profits in an absolute sense if industry conditions soften rivalry. For example, a favorable market enables cigarette makers to re-

---

[33]See Chapter 6 for a fuller discussion of this point.

[34]This quote is taken from Stewart, G. B., *The Quest for Value*, New York: HarperBusiness, 1991.

FIGURE 12.9
DIVISION OF VALUE-CREATED IN THE PRODUCTION OF STEEL.

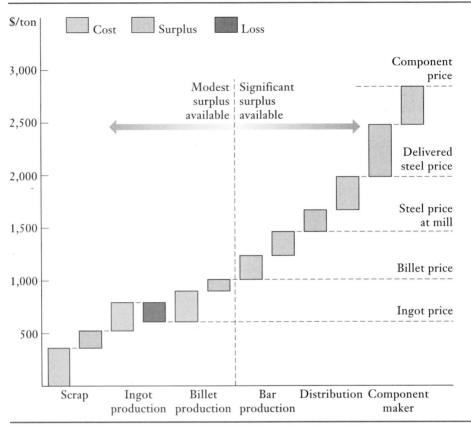

The horizontal axis in the figure shows different stages in the vertical chain for the production of steel. The vertical axis shows the price per ton of various kinds of unfinished and finished steel products. The blue blocks show the profit (per ton) earned at each stage, while the light gray blocks show the costs of production incurred at each stage, over and above the cost of purchasing the input from producers at the previous stage.
Source: Exhibit II in Hanna, A. M. and J. T. Lundquist, "Creative Strategies," *McKinsey Quarterly*, 3, 1990: pp. 56–79.

tain a large share of the value-created in their industry, so even an average firm, such as B.A.T, can be very profitable.[35]

The opportunities for retaining value-created can vary substantially along the vertical chain. This will in part be due to differences in the structure of the industry at each point along the chain. Figure 12.9 illustrates the division of

---

[35]Our analysis has glossed over an important public policy issue. We have spoken of value-created as though firms' activities created a fixed pie that is divided among consumers and firms. However, competition among firms in and of itself creates additional value. Competition drives prices down, inducing consumers already in the market to purchase more of the product and enticing new consumers into the market. Competition thus expands the number of transactions that create value. This is one reason why competition is valuable for society even though it may be undesirable for firms whose profits are dissipated as a result and justifies antitrust laws that prevent firms from colluding to restrict competition.

value-created in the production of steel.[36] Producers of scrap, ingot, and billets capture only modest portions of the overall value-created. These industries offer few opportunities for sellers to differentiate themselves. As a result, they are characterized by strong price competition and low profitability. Distributors and component producers, by contrast, capture a relatively larger proportion of value-created. This is also, in part, a consequence of the industry structure in these businesses. For example, steel distribution is essentially a regional or local market. Because operating a modern steel service center involves major economies of scale (a typical service center might take up four city blocks in each direction), barriers to entry into a local or regional market are significant. In addition, through skillful management of inventories and outbound logistics, distributors can create significant value that they share with their customers.

STRATEGIC POSITIONING: COST ADVANTAGE AND BENEFIT ADVANTAGE ◆ ◆ ◆ ◆ ◆

Competitive advantage cannot be reduced to a formula or an algorithm. Even if such formulas or algorithms could be concocted, describing them in a textbook such as this would make them valueless because they would be accessible to everyone.

But although there is no single formula for success, we can discern broad commonalities across industries in the different ways that firms position themselves to compete. For example, as discussed in the introduction, American Airlines' strategy in the airline business emphasizes frequent service; a comprehensive route structure; in-flight amenities, such as meals, "air-fones," and movies; and "extras," such as the opportunity to earn frequent-flier mileage. Southwest, by contrast, seeks to exploit its cost advantage (achieved in part, though not exclusively, through no-frills service) by offering low fares. In the delivered pizza business, Pizza Hut's strategy is built on its reputation for a quality pizza and product variety, while Little Caesar has positioned itself as the low-price alternative. In the nonprescription drug industry, Warner-Lambert and American Home Products have well-known branded products (e.g., Listerine mouthwash and Advil pain reliever) supported by extensive advertising, while Perrigo has succeeded by selling inexpensive imitations of branded products to mass merchandisers, such as Kmart, Wal-Mart, and Target, which then resell them to consumers as house brands.

These examples suggest that it is useful to distinguish between two broad approaches to achieving competitive advantage. The first is to pursue cost advantage, seeking to attain a lower C while maintaining a B that is comparable to competitors. The second is to pursue benefit advantage, seeking to offer a higher B, while maintaining a C that is comparable to competitors.[37] In this section, we discuss the economic and organizational logic of cost and benefit advantage.

---

[36]This figure is reproduced from Exhibit II in Hanna, A. M. and J. T. Lundquist, "Creative Strategies," *The McKinsey Quarterly*, 3, 1990: pp. 56–79.

[37]We discuss whether these approaches are mutually exclusive below.

The Economic Logic of Cost Advantage

A firm with a cost advantage creates more value than its competitors by offering products that have a lower cost C, with the same, or perhaps lower, perceived benefit B. But even though a firm with a cost advantage may have a lower B than its competitors, its B disadvantage must be less than its C advantage, so that its value-created, $B - C$, is greater than the competitors in its market.

This can happen in three qualitatively different ways. First, the firm can achieve benefit parity by offering the same B as its rivals: for example, by exploiting economies of scale to lower average costs relative to rivals that are producing exactly the same good, but at lower volumes. The cost advantages that Brazil's Usiminas or India's Tata Iron and Steel Company (TISCO) enjoy in the market for steel are examples of this.

Second, the firm can achieve benefit proximity, which involves offering a B that is not much less than competitors. This could occur if the firm automates processes that are better performed by hand, hires fewer skilled workers, purchases less expensive components, or maintains lower standards of quality control. Yamaha's cost advantage over traditional piano producers, such as Steinway, is a good example of this. When there is benefit proximity, the firm must underprice its rivals by more than enough to offset the lower B. Of course, this can be profitable only if the firm's cost advantage is bigger than the price differential between the firm and its competitors. If so, the firm can simultaneously increase consumer surplus and its own profit. Figure 12.10 illustrates this point. The value map depicts an industry in which all firms initially offer a product with a price-quality position at point E and an average production cost of C_E.[38] Suppose, now, one of these firms, through a combination of automation and cheaper components, can manufacture the product with a lower quality level, q_F but at a substantially lower cost, C_F. By judiciously lowering its price (e.g., to P_F), the low-cost firm can offer more consumer surplus than its competitors and thus increase its share of the market relative to rivals. Even if its competitors restored consumer surplus parity by lowering their prices to P'_E, the low-cost firm still has a higher profit margin ($P_F - C_F$ versus $P'_E - C_E$).[39]

Finally, a firm may offer a product that is qualitatively different from its rivals. Firms can sometimes build a competitive advantage by redefining the product to yield substantial differences in benefits or costs relative to how the product is traditionally defined. For example, a formerly high-margin product may be redefined to allow for economies of scale in production and distribution while still providing benefits to consumers. The Timex watch or the 19-cent Bic crystal pen are well-known examples. When a product is of much lower cost and quality than competing products, it can theoretically out-compete those products, assuming that the cost differential exceeds the quality differential. This may explain why many people continue to use the U.S. Postal Service rather than private delivery services, such as Federal Express: The cost savings are worth the lower quality for some services.

---

[38]A technical note: To keep the exposition as simple as possible, Figure 12.10 assumes that the market consists of consumers with identical preferences for product quality. Thus, we can represent the strategic position of firms in the market with reference to the indifference curve of a representative consumer in that market.

[39]Alternatively, the higher-cost firms might seek their own sources of cost advantage by copying the cost leader. We discuss the impediments to copycat strategies in Chapter 13.

FIGURE 12.10

THE ECONOMIC LOGIC OF COST ADVANTAGE.

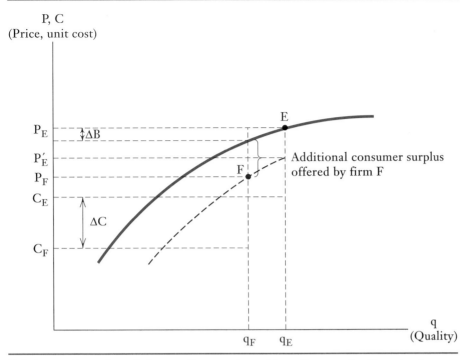

Existing producers in an industry offer a product with quality q_E, price P_E, and unit cost C_E. A new producer, firm F, can produce the product at a substantially lower cost, C_F, with only a small sacrifice in quality (q_F versus q_E). Firm F thus creates more value than existing competitors. By setting a price P_F below the solid indifference curve, firm F can share some of the additional value-created in the form of higher consumer surplus. This puts firm F on a lower indifference curve (represented by the dashed curved line). Even if existing competitors lower their prices to P'_E to restore consumer surplus parity, firm F will still enjoy the highest profit margin in the industry.

The Economic Logic of Benefit Advantage

A firm that creates a competitive advantage based on benefits creates more value than its competitors by offering a product with higher B for the same, or perhaps higher, C. A firm can exploit a benefit advantage by setting a price that allows it to offer higher consumer surplus than its rivals, while also achieving a higher profit margin. Figure 12.11 illustrates this point. Firm E sells a moderately priced product that provides a respectable quality, q_E. Its unit cost is C_E. Firm F offers a product with significantly higher quality q_F, and with unit cost C_F, it is only marginally more expensive to produce. From the value map in Figure 12.11, you can see that the additional benefit $\Delta B = B_F - B_E$ that consumers perceive from product F outweighs the extra cost of production. $\Delta C = C_F - C_E$, so firm F creates more value than firm E. Because it creates more value, firm F can "share" part of the extra value it creates with consumers by setting a price that lies below the solid indifference curve in Figure 12.11. Firm F thus offers higher consumer surplus than firm E and will gain market share at E's expense. Even if E cuts its price to restore con-

FIGURE 12.11

THE ECONOMIC LOGIC OF BENEFIT ADVANTAGE.

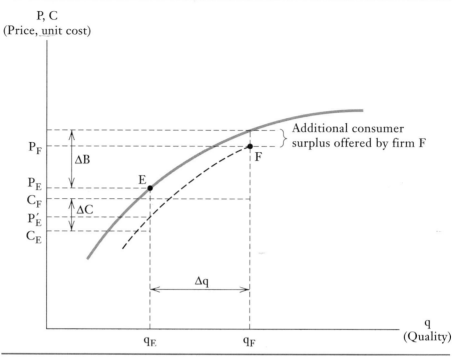

Firm E provides a moderately priced product with quality q_E, price P_E, and unit production cost C_E. Firm F offers a product with significantly higher quality q_F but which costs only a little extra to produce. The additional benefit ΔB provided by firm F more than offsets the additional cost ΔC, so F creates more value than E. By setting a price P_F that is slightly below the solid indifference curve on which firm E's price-quality position is located, firm F can "share" some of the extra value it creates with consumers in the form of higher consumer surplus and, as a result, gain market share at the expense of firm E. Even if firm F cuts price to P'_E to restore consumer surplus parity with E (thus moving to the dashed indifference curve), firm F will still earn a higher profit margin than firm E.

sumer surplus parity with F (thus, in effect, moving to the dashed indifference curve in Figure 12.11), F's profit margin will still be larger than E's.

As with cost advantage, parity and proximity can also create a benefit advantage. The firm's cost disadvantage must be small enough so that the firm's value-created, $B - C$, exceeds that of its competitors. A firm that creates a benefit advantage might achieve cost parity (same C). A good example is the Japanese auto makers in the 1980s, whose family sedans (e.g., Honda Accord) were no more costly to produce than American-made models, but offered superior performance and reliability. A successful benefit leader might instead achieve cost proximity (C not too much higher than competitors). Nordstrom, whose employees earn above average wages but provide superior service, is a good example. Finally, a firm could offer substantially higher B and C, which occurred when Eli Lilly introduced the first cephalosporin, a "magic bullet" antibiotic. Cephalosporins cost much more to produce than available substitutes, such as penicillin, but have fewer side effects and attack a broader spectrum of bacteria.

Extracting Profits from Cost and Benefit Advantage: The Importance of the Price Elasticity of Demand

A firm that creates more value than its competitors would like to keep as much as possible of that value for itself in the form of profits. However, competition limits the firm's ability to capture profits. In the simple model presented in this chapter, competition takes an especially stark form. Because we have assumed that consumers have identical preferences, if a firm provides the highest consumer surplus to one consumer, it also provides the highest consumer surplus to all consumers in the market. Competition then would resemble an auction: When a firm increases its consumer surplus "bid" slightly above competitors, it captures the entire market.[40] The auction would end only when no firm can submit a profitable consumer surplus "bid" that tops the "bids" rivals submit. This leads to two clear recipes for retaining profits for a firm that creates more value than its competitors.

- If a firm achieves a cost advantage (with no reduction in B), it can lower its price just below the unit cost of the next most efficient competitor. This makes it unprofitable for competitors to respond with price cuts of their own and thus allows the firm to capture the entire market.

- If a firm achieves a benefit advantage (with no reduction in C), it can raise its price to just below unit cost C plus the additional benefit ΔB it creates relative to the competitor with the next highest B. To top this consumer surplus "bid," a competitor would have to cut price below unit cost, which would be unprofitable. At this price, then, the firm with the benefit advantage captures the entire market.

These unrealistic recipes result because when consumers have identical preferences, an infinitesimally small decrease in price or increase in quality leads to a large shift in market share. This would not happen in a market characterized by horizontal differentiation. As we discussed in Chapter 7, horizontal differentiation arises when products possess attributes that increase B for some consumers but decrease it for others, and firms differ according to these attributes. For example, a brand's external packaging may appeal to some consumers but not appeal to others. A retailer's location may be very convenient for some shoppers, but quite inconvenient for others.[41] Some consumers may have an intense loyalty to one brand of cola that other consumers would never consider purchasing, even at very low prices.

Horizontal differentiation is likely to be strong when there are many product attributes that consumers weigh in assessing overall benefit B, and consumers disagree about the desirability of those attributes. Ready-to-eat breakfast cereals and soft drinks are businesses in which horizontal differentiation is significant. Horizontal differentiation is likely to be weak when the product is simple, and only a few easily ranked attributes matter to potential consumers. Lightbulbs and floppy disks are products for which horizontal differentiation is likely to be weak. Horizontal differentiation also tends to be weaker when business buyers rather than households purchase the good. Business buyers are often more knowledgeable and sophisticated than households because business-to-business transactions are often

---

[40]This is analogous to the Bertrand model of price competition in Chapter 7.

[41]We developed the implications of locational differences for price competition between firms in Chapter 7.

conducted by professional purchasing agents who specialize in the items they buy and often have financial incentives to seek the "best deal." Business buyers are also less likely to pay attention to a product's image.

In markets where there is horizontal differentiation, a firm's price elasticity or quality elasticity of demand will no longer be infinite. Lowering price or boosting quality will attract some consumers, but others will not switch unless the differential in price or quality is large enough. When there is horizontal differentiation, the price elasticity of demand an individual firm faces becomes a key determinant of a seller's ability to extract profits from its competitive advantage.[42] Table 12.3 summarizes how the price elasticity of demand facing a firm influences the choice between two polar strategies for exploiting competitive advantage: a margin strategy and share strategy.[43]

Consider, first, a firm that has a cost advantage. When the firm perceives a low price elasticity of demand (i.e., when consumers are not very price sensitive because of strong horizontal differentiation among competitors' products), even

TABLE 12.3
EXPLOITING A COMPETITIVE ADVANTAGE THROUGH PRICING

		Type of Advantage	
		Cost Advantage (lower C than competitors)	Benefit Advantage (higher B than competitors)
Firm's Price Elasticity of Demand	**High price elasticity of demand** (weak horizontal differentiation)	• Modest *price cuts* gain lots of market share. • Exploit advantage through higher market share than competitors. • *Share Strategy:* Underprice competitors to gain share.	• Modest *price hikes* lose lots of market share. • Exploit advantage through higher market share than competitors. • *Share Strategy:* Maintain price parity with *competitors* (let benefit advantage drive share increases).
	Low price elasticity of demand (strong horizontal differentiation)	• Big *price cuts* gain little share. • Exploit advantage through higher profit margins. • *Margin Strategy:* Maintain price parity with competitors (let lower costs drive higher margins).	• Big *price hikes* lose little share. • Exploit advantage through higher profit margins. • *Margin Strategy:* Charge price premium relative to competitors.

---

[42]This section focuses on the role of the firm-level price elasticity of demand rather than the market-level price elasticity of demand. See the Economics Primer for a discussion of the distinction between these two concepts.

[43]Table 12.3 applies to markets in which firms are "price setters" rather than markets in which firms either act as "price-takers" (as in the theory of perfect competition described in the Economics Primer) or as "quantity setters" (as in the theory of Cournot competition described in Chapter 7). The theories of perfect competition or Cournot competition apply to "commodity markets" in which competing firms produce identical products. In such markets, no individual firm determines the "market price." Therefore, the question of how a firm exploits its competitive strategy through a pricing strategy is not relevant.

deep price cuts will not increase the firm's market share much. In this case, the optimal way for a firm to exploit its cost advantage is through a *margin strategy*: The firm maintains price parity with its competitors and profits from its cost advantage primarily through high price-cost margins, rather than through higher market shares. In the health care industry, this practice is known as shadow pricing and is especially common in health insurance, where low-cost HMOs often set prices that are comparable to more costly forms of insurance. By contrast, when the firm's product has a high price elasticity of demand (i.e., when consumers are price-sensitive because horizontal differentiation is weak), modest price cuts can lead to significant increases in market share. In this case, the firm should exploit its cost advantage through a *share strategy*: The firm underprices its competitors to gain market share at their expense. In practice, the distinction between a margin strategy and a share strategy is one of degree, not kind, and firms with cost advantages will often pursue mixed strategies: cutting price to gain share, but also "banking" some of the cost advantage through higher margins. For example, using the sample of firms in the PIMS database, we found that, for the typical firm, a 10 percent reduction in unit cost relative to that of competitors translates into a 2.1 percent reduction in the firm's price relative to the prices of competitors.[44] In market environments in which the price elasticity of demand is extremely high, a firm might also be able to follow a share strategy with virtually no price cuts. When horizontal differentiation is weak, small cuts in price can achieve large increases in market share. In this case, a firm with a cost advantage can have the best of both worlds: It can significantly increase its market share while offering prices that are barely below those of its higher-cost rivals.

Table 12.3 illustrates that the logic governing the exploitation of a benefit advantage is analogous to that governing the exploitation of a cost advantage. When a firm has a benefit advantage in a market in which consumers are price sensitive, even a modest price hike could offset the firm's benefit advantage and nullify the increase in market share that the benefit advantage would otherwise lead to. In this case, the best way for the firm to exploit its benefit advantage is through a share strategy. A share strategy involves charging the same price as competitors and exploiting the firm's benefit advantage by capturing a higher market share than competitors. (The increase in market share is driven by the firm's benefit advantage.) By contrast, when consumers are not price sensitive, because horizontal differentiation is strong, large price hikes will not completely erode the market share gains that the firm's benefit advantage creates. The best way for the firm to exploit its benefit advantage is through a margin strategy: It charges a price premium relative to competitors (sacrificing some market share in the process), and exploits its advantage mainly through higher profit margins. This is the strategy Apple Computer followed before 1991. This strategy was eventually undermined when the release of Windows 3.0 in 1990 reduced the degree of horizontal differentiation between Apple PCs and IBM-compatible PCs.

Of course, other factors besides horizontal differentiation affect the relative profitability of alternative pricing strategies for exploiting a competitive advantage. For example, as Chapter 10 points out, a firm should consider the reactions of competitors before making any major pricing move. The prospect of competitor

---

[44]Besanko, D., D. Dranove, and M. Shanley, "Exploiting a Cost Advantage and Coping with a Cost Disadvantage," working paper, 1997.

reactions can alter the broad recommendations in Table 12.3. For instance, in markets with price-sensitive consumers, a share strategy of cutting price to exploit a cost advantage would be attractive if competitors' prices remained unchanged. However, it would probably be unattractive if the firm's competitors quickly matched the price cut because the net result will be lower margins with little or no net gain in the firm's market share. In this case, a margin strategy might well be a more attractive option. One way to incorporate competitor reactions into the framework in Table 12.3 is to think in terms of a firm's *perceived* price elasticity of demand: the rate of percentage change in the quantity demanded for the firm's product for every 1 percent change in price, taking into account likely pricing reactions by competitors. For example, the prospect of quick price matching by competitors will negate the market share increases that would otherwise result when the firm cuts its price and thus would tend to reduce a firm's perceived price elasticity of demand. The logic of Table 12.3 would then suggest that a margin strategy would better exploit a cost advantage than a share strategy.

Comparing Cost and Benefit Advantages

Under what circumstances is one source of advantage likely to dominate the other? Though no definitive rules can be formulated, the underlying economics of the firm's product market and the current positions of firms in the industry help make one positioning strategy more desirable than another.

Building competitive advantage on the basis of a superior cost position is likely to be relatively more attractive when:

- Economies of scale and learning economies are potentially significant, but no firm in the market is exploiting them. Strategies aimed at "growing" market share and accumulating experience will give the firm a cost advantage that its smaller, less experienced rivals cannot match. If the market is growing, however, other firms may soon gain the scale and experience necessary to achieve the same cost position. In the personal computer industry, several firms, such as Compaq and Dell, appear to have fully exploited scale economies.

- The nature of the product limits opportunities for enhancing its perceived benefit B. This might be the case for "commodities" products, such as chemicals and metals. If so, then, more opportunities for creating additional value may come from lowering C rather than from increasing B. Still, we must bear in mind that the drivers of differentiation include far more than just the physical attributes of the product and that opportunities may exist for differentiation through better postsale service, superior location, or more rapid delivery than competitors offer.[45]

- Consumers are relatively price sensitive and will not pay much of a premium for enhanced product quality, performance, or image. This would occur when most consumers are much more price sensitive than quality sensitive. Graphically, this corresponds to the case in which consumer indifference curves are relatively flat, indicating that a consumer will not pay much more for enhanced quality. Opportunities for additional value-creation are much

---

[45]See the appendix to this chapter for further discussion of benefit drivers.

more likely to arise through cost reductions than through benefit enhancements. CBIS Federal, a subsidiary of Cincinnati Bell specializing in data processing services for government agencies, failed to understand this point. According to its former chief financial officer, "The government is lower-bidder oriented; they're driven by the lowest price. But CBIS tries to distinguish itself by being the best quality provider—that created overhead that made it difficult to compete (with other vendors)."[46]

- The product is a search good rather than an experience good. A search good is one whose objective quality attributes the typical buyer can easily access at the time of purchase. Examples include office furniture and (increasingly) personal computers. An experience good is a product whose quality can be assessed only after the consumer has used it for a while. Examples include technologically complex products, such as CD players and automobiles. With search goods, the potential for differentiation lies largely in enhancing the product's observable features. But if buyers can discern among different offerings, so can competitors, which raises the risk that the enhancements will be imitated. When this is so, a firm can best create a lasting competitive advantage by keeping its costs lower than competitors, while matching their initiatives in product enhancement.

Building a competitive advantage based on superior benefits is likely to be relatively more attractive when:

- The typical consumer will pay a significant price premium for attributes that enhance B. This corresponds to the case in which the typical consumer's indifference curve is relatively steep. A firm that can differentiate its product by offering even a few additional features may command a significant price premium. Gillette counted on this effect when it launched its Mach 3 razor system in 1998. It concluded that many men would pay a premium price for blades that gave a better shave than existing cartridge or disposable razors. As a result, Gillette priced the Mach 3 blades 15 percent above its Sensor Excel blades, the highest-priced blades in the market at the time.

- Economies of scale or learning are significant, and firms are already exploiting them. In this case, opportunities for achieving a cost advantage over these larger firms are limited, and the best route toward value creation lies through horizontal differentiation—offering a product that is especially well-tailored to a particular niche of the market. Microbreweries, such as the Boston Beer Company, have attempted to build a competitive advantage in this way.

- The product is an experience good rather than a search good. In this case, differentiation can be based on image, reputation, or credibility, which are more difficult to imitate or neutralize than objective product features or performance characteristics. Bose has made major inroads in stereophonic equipment by exploiting its reputation developed through product innovations that originally appealed to a few stereophiles willing to pay $1,000 or more for high-end speakers.

---

[46]"If Cincinnati Bell's So Good, Why's the Stock So Lousy?" *Cincinnati Enquirer*, April 17, 1994, p. H2. Cincinnati Bell sold CBIS Federal in 1993.

Implications for Functional Area Strategies

While the approach the firm chooses as a basis for competitive advantage is guided by the demand and technological characteristics of the product, it guides the operating strategies of the firm's functional areas: marketing, production, engineering, and so forth. Table 12.4 contrasts the cost and benefit advantage characteristics of functional area strategies.

Product and marketing strategies in a firm seeking cost advantage will often center on standardized products that can be mass produced and easily serviced. At-

TABLE 12.4
IMPLICATIONS OF COMPETITIVE POSITIONING FOR FUNCTIONAL AREA STRATEGIES

Functional Areas	Competitive Position	
	Cost Advantage	Benefit Advantage
Product and Marketing Strategies	–standardized products –narrow price-cost margins with prices lower than competition –little or modest product promotion or advertising –modest postsale servicing or maintenance	–customized products –wide price-cost margins, with prices higher than competition –emphasis on building product, image through branding, advertising, and product promotion –extensive postsale service/maintenance –generous warranties
Production Operations Strategies	–large mass-production facilities to exploit economies of scale –capacity added behind demand to ensure full utilization –products made to inventory, with tight controls on inventory levels	–willingness to sacrifice scale in favor of customization and flexible response to unpredictable customer demand –capacity added in anticipation of demand to ensure product availability and minimize chances of stockouts –products made to order
Engineering and Design	–products designed for manufacturability	–products designed to create benefits for customers or lower their costs
Research and Development Strategies	–R&D emphasizes process innovations, rather than new products or basic research	–R&D emphasizes product innovations and basic research more than process
Human Resources/ Organizations and Control Strategies	–"traditional" managerial style, characterized by formal procedure and rigid hierarchy –tough bargaining posture with workers –tight administrative systems emphasizing cost control	–less formal managerial style, fewer formal procedures, less rigid hierarchy to promote innovation and entrepreneurship –higher than average pay to attract skilled workers

taining a benefit advantage typically requires greater attention to the breadth of product line, the size of the advertising and promotion budget, the best use of warranties, and the amount of resources dedicated to customer service than an approach emphasizing cost advantage.

In production operations, firms seeking a cost advantage will pursue economies of scale in manufacturing and logistics, as well as efficiencies in inventory management. Firms seeking a benefit advantage, on the other hand, will be more willing to forsake such advantages in the hope of earning greater revenues through higher prices. The need for additional capacity and inventory to allow flexible responses to unpredictable demand may force these firms to organize differently and incur additional costs relative to firms seeking a cost advantage.

A similar distinction is apparent with engineering and design activities. Firms seeking a cost advantage will design products to increase manufacturability or to meet a minimum set of performance standards across several markets (as with so-called global firms that produce standardized products for multinational markets). Firms seeking benefit advantage will design products to meet the needs of important customers or customer segments, even if that makes the product more difficult to manufacture and service.

With research and development activities, the differences between approaches concern both the level and type of activity. Firms pursuing a cost advantage will be more likely to rely on established and routinized technologies and thus will do less R&D than will firms pursuing a benefit advantage. When cost-oriented firms do engage in R&D, they are more likely to focus on process innovations, designed to aid manufacturability, than product innovations, which aid product differentiation.

Finally, differences in competitive approaches are often associated with differences in human resource management. Pursuing cost advantage rather than benefit advantage implies different types of jobs and workers, numbers of workers, and pay and benefits. Firms pursuing a cost advantage, especially in low-growth industries with stable technologies, have more specific and less discretionary jobs, less skilled but larger workforces, and more elaborate controls. The firm pursuing a benefit advantage, on the other hand, is more likely to delegate decision making to lower-level employees who are closer to the customer, to rely more on employee inputs into decision making, and to have more intensive, albeit less formal, supervision, due to the difficulties these firms have in identifying how jobs are done or what constitutes good performance.

Of course, the functional area strategies shown in Table 12.4 represent polar cases. The situation of a particular firm is likely to be more complicated, because it may include elements of both cost and benefit approaches. The notion that functional area strategies are linked to competitive positioning approaches is akin to the attempts of organizational theorists to link organizational configurations with product-market choices. Robert Miles and Charles Snow developed a typology of generic strategies consisting of "defenders," "prospectors," and "analyzers."[47] Firms pursuing cost and benefit advantage correspond to "defenders" and "prospectors," while the "analyzer" type is an intermediate position.

---

[47]Miles, R. and C. Snow, *Organizational Strategy, Structure, and Process*, New York: McGraw-Hill, 1978. For a related conceptual framework, see Miller, D. and P. Friesen, *Organizations: A Quantum View*, Englewood Cliffs, NJ: Prentice-Hall, 1984.

"Stuck in the Middle"

Can a firm successfully pursue both cost and benefit advantage? Michael Porter has argued that one is usually incompatible with the other. Firms that attempt to pursue both strategies simultaneously often become "stuck in the middle," providing less B than firms that have focused benefit advantage and incurring a higher C than firms that have focused on cost advantage.[48]

Porter's argument is based on a simple economic tradeoff: Higher-quality or better-performing products often cost more to produce. This is true for a variety of reasons. Producing a higher-quality product may involve more up-front design work, more expensive components, and better trained or more highly skilled labor. To the extent that benefit superiority is based on meeting customer needs, it may also require more custom building and thus a less standardized production process. Higher advertising and promotion expenditures may be needed to shape consumer perceptions about the product, and a more expensive sales force may be required if benefits are created through superior customer service.

◆ ◆

XAMPLE 12.6

Delta Airlines is Soaring Again

From 1990–1996, through recession and recovery, Delta Airlines consistently underperformed other airlines. Its profit margins were several percentage points below the industry average, and well below the most profitable carriers such as American and Southwest. In 1997, however, Delta had one of the highest profit margins in the industry. Why did Delta struggle and how did it turn itself around?

In the introduction to this chapter, we described the strategic positions of several carriers. Southwest has been highly profitable by holding costs well below industry norms and selecting routes so as to avoid competition. American Airlines is another profitable carrier. Its costs are relatively high, but it offers schedules that appeal to business travelers, with hubs in major business cities such as Chicago and Dallas. It is also the dominant American carrier flying to Central and South America. United Airlines has also done well recently. Aside from the Shuttle by United on the west coast, UAL has used a strategy similar to American's: It has relatively high costs, but it offers convenient schedules for business travelers, has strong hubs, and a dominant route structure to Asia.

Throughout most of the 1990s, Delta's costs were similar to those at American and United. But unlike those two carriers, Delta was not well-positioned to serve the lucrative business market. It has had a successful hub in Atlanta, but its other hubs are in Cincinatti and Salt Lake City, both of which lack substantial origin/destination traffic. Most significantly, Delta has lacked a "northern" hub to serve cities in the midwest and northeast. Hence, only a small percentage of business travelers have turned to Delta when selecting a carrier. Delta operates a shuttle service in the Boston–New York–Washington corridor, but this is a

---

[48]See chapter 2 of Porter, M., *Competitive Strategy*, New York: Free Press, 1980.

fiercely competitive market in which a number of carriers have failed to prosper. Finally, Delta has offered numerous flights to Europe. But this is a crowded market with fierce price competition. Delta's fares on European flights can easily be half that of American's or United's fares on comparably long trips to Latin America or Asia.

It is apparent that Delta had failed to match the strategic positioning of its most successful rivals. In some ways, Delta was "struck in the middle;" that is, its shortcomings stemmed from an effort to pursue too many strategies at once, such as its effort to serve the business market both with shuttle and full-fare service.[49] Whatever the source of its difficulties, Delta clearly needed to rethink its strategic direction.

In 1995, Delta introduced the "Leadership 7.5" plan, focusing exclusively on reducing total operating expenses. This plan was somewhat successful, but Delta also benefitted from the rebounding economy. Two years later, Delta replaced this cost-cutting plan with a strategy that seems to epitomize "stuck in the middle." The "Balanced Plan" is designed to simultaneously reduce costs and increase revenue. Despite the reservations about firms becoming stuck in the middle discussed above, so far the plan is working. Delta has reduced its costs to the point where its operating costs per available seat mile are below that of American and United. At the same time, it is boosting revenue, largely by changing its route structure. By concentrating its routes in Southeast and Florida and expanding into certain profitable routes in South America, Delta is increasingly the first choice for both tourist and business travelers to these growing regions. (Interestingly, the Operational Review in Delta's Annual Report for fiscal year 1997 does not mention the shuttle.)

It is too soon to know if Delta's strategy of maximizing $B-C$ is a permanent success. It does seem, however, that by judiciously choosing its target markets, Delta has found that it is possible to simultaneously reduce costs and increase benefits.

In practice, a firm's advantage is rarely based entirely on lower cost or superior benefits. We can cite examples of companies that seem to deliver a higher B than competitors at a lower C: Emerson Electric in air-conditioning components and Frito-Lay in snack foods are well-known examples. They suggest that the tradeoff between benefit and cost may be less strong than the preceding arguments suggest. The results of empirical studies on the tradeoff between cost and benefit strategies are also mixed. While almost all studies find visible "footprints" of benefit-based advantage and cost-based advantage, they also find that these strategies are not incompatible. For example, Danny Miller and Peter Friesen found that in consumer durables industries, firms that appeared to have achieved benefit advantages in their industries also tended to operate newer plants, had significantly better-than-average capacity utilization,

---

[49]One might argue that United has pursued a similar range of strategies, particularly with its Shuttle by United. Note that the Shuttle by United has helped it to maintain its feeder traffic for its Asian flights. Delta's east coast shuttle has not generated similar benefits for its European flights.

and had direct costs per unit that were significantly lower than the industry average. Firms that appeared to have achieved cost advantages also scored highly on measures of relative differentiation, such as product quality, and advertising and promotion expenses.[50]

From a theoretical perspective, several factors might weaken the observed tradeoff between differentiation and cost positions in an industry.

• A firm that offers high-quality products increases its market share, which then reduces average cost because of economies of scale or the experience curve. As a result, a firm might achieve both a high-quality and a low-cost position in the industry. Figure 12.12 illustrates how. By pursuing a differentiation strategy, the firm raises its average cost at each level of output, represented by an upward shift in its average costs, from AC_0 to AC_1. But differentiation also shifts the firm's demand curve rightward, from D_0 to D_1. Even if the firm raises its price, the movement to the new demand curve coupled with the fact that average cost is a decreasing function of output (reflecting economies of scale) implies that the firm's realized average cost actually goes down, from $AC_0(Q_0)$ to $AC_1(Q_1)$. Charles River Breeding Labs typified this situation in the

FIGURE 12.12

ACHIEVING BENEFIT ADVANTAGE AND COST ADVANTAGE SIMULTANEOUSLY.

A firm that achieves a benefit advantage itself shifts its demand curve rightward from D_0 to D_1 and shifts its average cost function upward from $AC_0(Q)$ to $AC_1(Q)$. Even if the firm raises its price, the movement to the new demand curve coupled with the fact that unit costs are a decreasing function of output implies that the firm's realized unit cost goes down from $AC_0(Q_0)$ to $AC_1(Q_1)$.

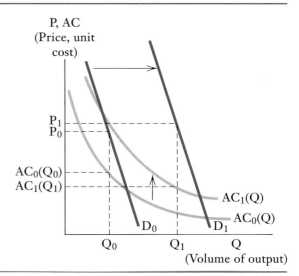

[50]Miller, D., and P. H. Friesen, "Porter's (1980) Generic Strategies and Quality: An Empirical Examination with American Data. Part I: Testing Porter," *Organization Studies*, 7, 1986: pp. 37–55. See also Phillips, L. W., D. R. Chang, and R. D. Buzzell, "Product Quality, Cost Position, and Business Performance: A Test of Some Key Hypotheses," *Journal of Marketing*, 47, Spring 1983: pp. 26–43; White, R. E., "Generic Business Strategies, Organizational Context and Performance: An Empirical Investigation," *Strategic Management Journal*, 7, 1986: pp. 217–231; Dess, G. G. and P. S. Davis, "Porter's (1980) Generic Strategies as Determinants of Strategic Group Membership and Organizational Performance," *Academy of Management Review*, 27, 1984: pp. 467–488.

1970s with its germ-free technology for raising laboratory animals.[51] The first to adopt germ-free barrier breeding technologies, Charles River Breeders became the quality leader, moved down the experience curve, and established a superior cost position relative to its nearest competitors.

- The rate at which accumulated experience reduces costs is greater for higher-quality products than for lower-quality products. The reason is that production workers must exercise more care to produce a higher-quality product, which often leads to the discovery of bugs and defects that might be overlooked in a lower-quality product.[52]

- Inefficiencies muddy the relationship between cost position and differentiation position. The argument that high quality is correlated with high costs ignores the possibility that firms may be producing inefficiently, that is, that their C is higher than it needs to be given their B. If so, then at any point in time, in most industries one might observe firms that create less B and have higher C than their more efficient counterparts. Indeed, the entire thrust of the total quality management (TQM) movement is to enable firms to improve production processes to increase B and reduce C.[53]

Figure 12.13 depicts cost and quality positions in the U.S. heavy-duty truck industry in the late 1970s.[54] If all firms were producing as efficiently as possible, but were pursuing competitive advantages that emphasized different degrees of cost and differentiation, then firms' positions would line up along the upward-sloping line that we label the efficiency frontier. The efficiency frontier shows the lowest level of cost that is attainable to achieve a given level of differentiation, given the available technology and know-how, including TQM techniques to the extent they are successful. Based on previous arguments, one might expect that the efficiency frontier would be upward sloping. Some firms, such as White Motors and International Harvester, however, have operated above the efficiency frontier. These firms delivered less quality and incurred higher costs than competitors, such as Ford and Paccar. Not surprisingly, these firms were consistently less profitable than their more efficient rivals.

What, then, can we conclude about the notion of "stuck in the middle"? To the extent that it reminds us that the pursuit of differentiation is often not costless (contrary to TQM gurus, quality is often not "free") and that a firm's competitive position should relate in an economically sensible way to its resources and distinctive competences, "stuck in the middle" is a valuable idea. However, even if there is a tradeoff between B and C, a firm need not provide the highest B or the lowest C to succeed. What matters is the magnitude of value-created, that is, $B - C$, relative to other firms. For example, Dannon in the yogurt market and Breyers in the

---

[51]"Charles River Breeding Laboratories," Harvard Business School, Case 9-376-262.

[52]Phillips, L., D. R. Chang, and R. Buzzell, "Product Quality and Business Performance: A Test of Some Key Hypotheses," *Journal of Marketing*, 47, Spring 1983: pp. 26–43.

[53]TQM is often associated with the work of W. Edwards Deming. However, Deming never used the term. TQM was the U.S. Navy's term for its quality program in the 1980s based on the philosophy and techniques summarized in Deming's book *Out of the Crisis*, Cambridge, MA: MIT Press, 1986.

[54]This figure is adapted from Hall, W. K., "Survival Strategies in a Hostile Environment," *Harvard Business Review*, September–October 1980: pp. 75–85.

FIGURE 12.13

QUALITY AND COST POSITIONS IN THE U.S. HEAVY-DUTY
TRUCK MANUFACTURING INDUSTRY IN THE LATE 1970s.

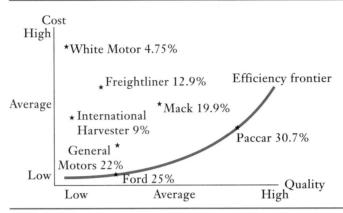

The figure depicts the cost quality positions of various competitors in the heavy truck manufacturing industry in the United States. The figure also shows each firm's return on assets for the period 1975–1979. If all firms were producing as efficiently as possible, their positions would line up along an upward-sloping efficiency frontier. The efficiency frontier indicates the lowest level of cost that is attainable to achieve a given level of quality, given the available technology and know-how. Firms that are closer to the frontier are generally more profitable than firms that are farther away.

Source: Figure adapted from Exhibit VII in Hall, W. K., "Survival Strategies in a Hostile Environment," *Harvard Business Review*, September–October 1980: pp. 75–85.

◆ ◆

XAMPLE 12.7

"TECHNOPORK"

An example of the interaction of scale economies, differentiation, and market share is occurring in the hog and pork business.[55] Through a combination of new breeding techniques, computerization, and automation, such firms as Premium Standard Farms, Tyson Foods, and Continental Grain Company can produce leaner, more consistent hogs than can small family farmers. The result is pork that is healthier, better tasting, and costs less to produce than the meat that comes from hogs bred using traditional methods. As a result of these new techniques, dubbed "technopork," agricultural economists expect the number of hog producers to decline by 50 percent in the next 10 years. The producers that will dominate the industry will probably produce hogs at a lower cost and of a higher quality than the small producers that have predominated up to now.

This rise of "technopork" can be explained in terms of Figure 12.12. The investment in land and capital equipment needed to make automated-computerized pork production pay off can be justified only if a producer can sell at

---

[55]This example draws from "Power Pork: Corporations Begin to Turn Hog Business into an Assembly Line," *Wall Street Journal*, March 28, 1994, pp. A1 and A5.

sufficient scale.[56] Tyson Foods, for example, has set a goal of achieving a 10 percent share of the U.S. hog slaughter market by the year 2000, an enormous market share in what historically has been an extremely fragmented industry. Producers like Tyson and Premium Standard may be able to achieve sufficient scale by selling at a lower price, in effect, moving down demand curve D_0 and the average cost curve AC_1. But some of the additional scale may come from the fact that leaner, more consistent hogs may stimulate the demand for pork, thereby shifting the demand curve outward from D_0 to D_1. Pork producers are counting on both effects. Tyson, for example, plans to introduce new pork products, such as breaded, stuffed, and spiced pork with flavors ranging from teriyaki to "Jamaican jerk."

ice cream business are neither the highest nor lowest quality available, but their levels of $B - C$ are high enough, so that they have long been the leaders in their product categories. Of course, if consumer tastes tend to be either extremely price sensitive or benefit conscious, then products positioned in the middle, such as Breyers, will struggle. In trying to pursue both cost and benefit objectives simultaneously, the firm may also fail to invest in developing the resources and capabilities necessary to succeed in either dimension. In these ways, Porter's admonition against getting stuck in the middle has merit.

Beyond that, however, the conditions under which the pursuit of a benefit advantage may be consistent with achieving a superior cost position arise frequently enough, so that we cannot conclude that benefit and cost advantage are generally incompatible. In addition, a firm pursuing a benefit advantage must usually achieve cost parity or cost proximity with its competitors if it is to create more value than they do. In seeking to provide more benefits, management cannot abrogate its responsibility to monitor and control costs or to continuously enhance efficiency. Similarly, since a firm pursuing a cost advantage must usually achieve benefit parity or proximity if it is to create value, it must ensure that the quantity and quality of its products is not out of line with its competitors. As always, a good grasp of the underlying economic fundamentals is critical. The pursuit of strategic positioning requires a deep understanding of how value is created. This, in turn, involves understanding what drives costs, what attributes create benefits for consumers, and how the drivers of costs and benefits vary across different segments of the market. (We discuss these subjects in the appendix to this chapter.)

TARGETING AND MARKET SEGMENTATION ◆ ◆ ◆ ◆ ◆

The pursuit of cost advantage and benefit advantage relates to the broad issue of how the firm will create value in its target markets. But choosing a firm's target markets is itself a key strategic decision, and one that often cannot be separated from its approach to value creation.

[56]If this seems like a familiar refrain, it is. This is another example of the "division of labor determines the extent of the market." See Chapter 3.

Segmentation and Targeting Strategies

A market segment refers to a group of consumers within a broader market who possess a common set of characteristics. In consumer goods markets, segmentation characteristics include demographic factors (e.g., consumers in the same age group or income class) and geography (e.g., consumers located in a particular region of the country). Segmentation in consumer goods markets might also be related to how frequently or intensively consumers use the product (e.g., heavy users versus infrequent users of a product); their depth of knowledge about the product (consumers who are knowledgeable versus consumers who are less well-informed); and their willingness to trade off quality for price. In industrial goods markets, segmentation variables include the buyer's industry; the size of the purchasing firm; the consumer segments the buyer serves; the size of a buyer's order; or the buyer's willingness to trade off price for performance, speed of delivery, and other dimensions of quality.[57] However segments are defined, buyers within segments have similar product requirements and tastes and respond to market mix variables, such as price or advertising, in much the same way, whereas consumers across segments have different needs or marketing responses.

Targeting refers to the selection of segments that the firm will serve and the development of a product line strategy in light of those segments. Targeting strategies can usefully be divided into two broad categories: focus strategies and broad coverage strategies. We discuss each in turn.

Broad Coverage Strategies

A broad coverage strategy seeks to serve all segments in the market by offering a full line of related products. Gillette follows this strategy in shaving products. It offers a full line of razors (both cartridge and disposable) for both men and women, as well as complementary products, such as shaving cream and after-shave lotions. Frito-Lay follows this strategy in snack foods, offering a full line of high calorie and "light" snacks, such as potato chips, corn chips, tortilla chips, and pretzels, as well as condiments, such as salsa, that can be eaten with those snacks. The economic logic behind a broad coverage strategy is the existence of economies of scope across product classes. These economies of scope might come from production if the products share common production facilities or components. They might also come from distribution, as Frito-Lay has done through the breadth of its product line that other manufacturers of snack foods, such as Eagle or Borden, have been unable to match. Or they might come from marketing, the way Gillette has attempted to use its brand name to convey a strong image of quality and tradition not only for its razors, but also for its shaving cream and after-shave lotion. This has allowed Gillette to establish the basis for a benefit advantage in these latter markets at a lower cost than it probably would have had to incur had it not already had an established brand equity position in razor blades.

Both Gillette and Frito-Lay are examples of broad coverage strategies that depend on products being tailored to different market segments (Gillette sells razors to men and women; Frito-Lay offers both regular and light versions of its best-selling snacks). However, broad coverage strategies might be either more or less

---

[57]See Kotler, P. *Marketing Management: Analysis, Planning, and Control* 9th ed. Englewood Cliffs, NJ: Prentice-Hall, 1997, for a fuller discussion of the dimensions of market segmentation.

customized to the firm's target segments than is true of Gillette or Frito-Lay. For example, some firms follow a "one-size-fits-all" strategy whereby a common product line is marketed to different market segments. In computer software Microsoft's major software products—Word, Excel, and PowerPoint—appeal to many kinds of users, but are not tailor-made to any particular market segment. A one-size-fits-all strategy exploits economies of scale in production to achieve a cost advantage over competitors. The opposite case would be a firm that seeks to appeal to many different market segments, but attempts to customize its product line to each of them. The economic logic of this variant of a broad based design is to create a benefit advantage in each of the segments the firm competes in by offering bundles of attributes to fit the needs of consumers in those segments. The large management consulting companies, such as McKinsey, BCG, and Booz Allen, are examples of this kind of strategy.

Focus Strategies

Under a focus strategy, a firm either offers a single product, serves a single market segment, or does both. One focus strategy is product specialization: The firm produces a single product for different market segments. In the computer industry, Cray Research only sells supercomputers, but the two main market segments that it serves (the "classic" segment consisting of universities and research labs, and the industrial segment, that is, the petroleum, automobile, and pharmaceutical industries) value different attributes and weigh price versus performance differently.

Another focus strategy is geographic specialization. Here the firm offers a variety of related products within a narrowly defined geographic market. Historically, small local breweries, such as Hudepohl in Cincinnati, illustrated this kind of focus. Hudepohl offered a full line of beers, including light, premium, and super-premium brands, but sold those beers mainly in the Cincinnati market.

A third type of focus is customer specialization. Here the firm offers related products to a particular class of customers. An example would be a firm that produces and sells industrial process control systems and related devices, such as valves, flowmeters, and recording instruments, to industries such as petroleum refiners and chemical manufacturers, that utilize this technology.

Finally, there is a niche strategy, in which a firm produces a single product for a single market segment. The PBX manufacturer InteCom (now owned by the French telecommunications equipment manufacturer Matra) sells a particular kind of PBX system to big industrial customers, such as Microsoft and General Electric, who need PBXs with more than 3,000 lines.

A focus strategy can often enable a firm to achieve economies of scale that it could not achieve if it expanded beyond the market segment or product it is concentrating on. For example, Hudepohl's strong local image ensured it a large market share in the Cincinnati area, which in turn allowed it to benefit from economies of density in distribution.[58] By expanding into markets where its key resource (its strong local brand identity) would be less valuable, Hudepohl would find it difficult to achieve those same distribution economies.

Of course, when selecting which market segments to serve, a firm must not only consider potential cost economies and demand, but also the potential for competition within the segment. In some segments, demand is only large enough for

---

[58]In the appendix to this chapter we discuss economies of density.

one or two firms. A firm may be far more profitable as a focused seller in a low-demand segment than as one of several competitors in high-demand segments. Southwest Airlines and Columbia/HCA (a for-profit hospital chain) have prospered by establishing monopoly or near-monopoly positions in small markets, while their competitive counterparts in larger markets have been less profitable. Indeed, Southwest Airlines avoids markets that would bring it into head-to-head competition with major trunk airlines. Similarly, in Japan, Kubota has dominated the agricultural machinery market. It produces lightweight, compact tractors that are especially well-suited to small Japanese farms, and because that market is limited, it faces little competition. By contrast, the U.S. tractor market is much larger and has many more competitors, including Deere & Company, Case, and Caterpillar.

CHAPTER SUMMARY

◆ A firm achieves a competitive advantage if it can earn higher rates of profitability than rival firms. A firm's profitability depends jointly on industry conditions and the amount of value the firm can create relative to its rivals.

◆ Consumer surplus is the difference between the perceived benefit B of a product and its monetary price P. A consumer will purchase a product only if its consumer surplus is positive. A consumer will purchase the product from a particular seller only if that seller offers a higher consumer surplus than rival sellers offer.

◆ A value map illustrates the competitive implications of consumer surplus. An indifference curve shows the price-quality combinations that yield the same level of consumer surplus.

◆ Value-created is the difference between the perceived benefit B and the unit cost C of the product. Equivalently, it is equal to the sum of consumer surplus and economic profit.

◆ To achieve a competitive advantage, a firm must not only create positive value, it must also create more value than rival firms. If it does so, it can outcompete other firms by offering a higher consumer surplus than rivals.

◆ The bases of competitive advantage are superior resources and organizational capabilities. Resources are firm-specific assets that other firms cannot easily acquire. Organizational capabilities refer to clusters of activities that the firm does especially well compared to rivals.

◆ Industry structure is critical in determining the share of value-created that firms capture as profit.

◆ There are two broad routes to achieving competitive advantage. The first is for the firm to achieve a cost advantage over its rivals by offering a product with a lower C for the same, or perhaps lower, B.

◆ The second is to achieve a benefit advantage over rivals by offering products with a higher B for the same, or perhaps higher C.

◆ When firms are horizontally differentiated, the price elasticity of demand strongly affects how a firm profits from a cost advantage. With a low price elasticity of demand, the firm best profits from its cost advantage through higher margins, rather than through higher market share (a margin strategy). With a high price elasticity of demand, it will underprice its competitors and will profit through higher volume (a share strategy).

◆ The price elasticity of demand determines also the profitability of a benefit advantage. With a low price elasticity of demand, the firm should charge a significant price premium relative to competitors (a margin strategy). With a high price elasticity of demand, the firm should maintain price parity with competitors and use its advantage to gain a higher market share (a share strategy).

◆ Building a competitive advantage based on superior cost position is likely to be attractive when: there are unexploited opportunities for achieving scale, scope, or learning economies; the product's nature limits opportunities for enhancing its perceived benefit; consumers are relatively price sensitive and are unwilling to pay a premium for enhanced quality or performance; and the product is a search good rather than an experience good.

◆ Building a competitive advantage based on differentiation position is likely to be attractive when: the typical consumer is willing to pay a significant price premium for attributes that enhance B; existing firms are already exploiting significant economies of scale or learning; and the product is an experience good rather than a search good.

◆ A firm is "stuck in the middle" if it pursues both a cost advantage and a benefit advantage, but achieves neither.

◆ Targeting is selecting the market segments the firm will serve and developing a product line strategy to appeal to those segments. Targeting strategies are divided into two categories: focus strategies, in which a firm concentrates on offering a single product, serving a single market segment, or both, and broad-coverage strategies, in which a firm offers a full line of related products to most or all segments of the market.

◆ When selecting a market segment to serve, the firm should consider the potential for competition. If the segment is small, the firm may face little competition and earn substantial returns.

QUESTIONS

1. How can the value chain help a firm identify its strategic position?
2. Analysts sometimes suggest that firms should outsource low value-added activities. Do you agree or disagree?
3. Two firms, Alpha and Beta, are competing in a market in which consumer preferences are identical. Alpha offers a product whose benefit B is equal to $75 per unit. Alpha's average cost C is equal to $60 per unit, while Beta's average cost is equal to $50 per unit.

   a. Which firm's product provides the greatest value created?
   b. In an industry equilibrium in which the firms achieve consumer surplus parity, by what dollar amount will the profit margin, $P - C$, of the firm that creates the greatest amount of value exceed the profit margin of the firm that creates the smaller amount of value? Compare this amount to the difference between the value-created of each firm. What explains the relationship between the difference in profit margins and the difference in value-created between the two firms?

4. Consider a market in which consumer indifference curves are relatively steep. Firms in the industry are pursuing two positioning strategies: Some firms are producing a "basic" product that provides satisfactory performance; others are producing an enhanced product that provides performance superior to that of the basic product. Consumer surplus parity currently exists in the industry. Are the prices of the basic and the enhanced product likely to be significantly different or about the same? Why? How would the answer change if consumer indifference curves were relatively flat?

5. Why would the role of the marketing department in capital-intensive industries (e.g., steel) differ from that in labor-intensive industries (e.g., athletic footwear)? How does this relate to positioning?

6. In the value-creation model presented in this chapter, it is implicitly assumed that all consumers get the identical value (e.g., identical B) from a given product. Do the main conclusions in this chapter change if consumer tastes differ, so that some get more value than others?

7. Identify one or more experience goods. Identify one or more search goods. How does the retailing of experience goods differ from the retailing of search goods? Do these differences help consumers?

8. Recall from Chapter 3 Adam Smith's dictum "The Division of Labor Is Limited by the Extent of the Market." How does market growth affect the viability of a focus strategy?

9. Firms that seek a cost advantage should adopt a learning curve strategy; firms that seek to differentiate their products should not. Comment on both of these statements.

10. Consumers often identify brand names with quality. Do you think branded products usually are of higher quality than generic products and therefore justify their higher prices? If so, why don't all generic product makers invest to establish a brand identity, thereby enabling them to raise price?

11. Industry 1 consists of four firms that sell a product that is identical in every respect except for production cost and price. Firm A's unit production costs are 10 percent less than the others, and it charges a price that is 1 percent less than the others. Industry 2 consists of four firms that sell a product that is identical in every respect except for production cost and price. Firm X's unit production cost are 10 percentiles less than the others, and it charges a price that is 8 percent less than the others. Both industries are characterized by stable demand and comparable entry barriers.

   The preceding situations have prevailed for years. The managers of these firms are very smart and are surely acting in the best interest of their owners, whose only goal is to maximize profits. Based on this information only, can you determine which industry has the higher price-cost margin (i.e., [price-unit production cost] as a percentage of price) and why?

◆ ◆ ◆ ◆ ◆ APPENDIX

Cost Drivers

Cost and consumer benefit drives value-creation. Understanding how a firm creates value and why it creates more or less value than its competitors often requires a diagnosis of cost and benefit drivers. We discuss cost drivers first.

Cost drivers explain why costs vary across firms. We discuss cost drivers in terms of average costs, rather than total costs, because a larger firm's total costs would be higher than a smaller firm's simply because it is larger.[59] We

---

[59]One way to control for the effects of size in analyzing cost difference among different size firms is to express total costs as a percentage of sales revenue. Accountants call this common-size analysis. Although useful, common-size analysis contains a potential source of confusion. To illustrate, we can write the ratio of total costs to sales revenue as $(AC \times Q) \div (P \times Q) = AC/P$, where Q denotes the volume of output per period. This expression implies that one firm's total cost-to-sales ratio might be lower than another's either because its average costs are lower or its price is higher (or both). Common-size analysis of cost advantage should account for differences in prices among firms. Such differences might be due to product quality, product mix, or geographical point of sales.

can classify cost drivers into four broad categories, each of which has several subcategories:

- Cost drivers related to firm size or scope
  - economies of scale
  - economies of scope
  - capacity utilization
- Cost drivers related to cumulative experience
  - learning curve
- Cost drivers independent of firm size, scope, or cumulative experience
  - input prices
  - location
  - economies of density
  - complexity/focus
  - process efficiency
  - discretionary policies
  - government policies
- Cost drivers related to the organization of transactions
  - organization of the vertical chain
  - agency efficiency

We will discuss each cost driver in turn.

Cost Drivers Related to Firm Size, Scope, and Cumulative Experience

Chapter 2 contains an extensive discussion of economies of scale, scope, and cumulative experience, so here we will just review the key ideas. Economies of scale exist when average costs go down as the scale of operation increases. Economies of scope exist when average costs go down as the firm produces a greater variety of goods. A paramount source of economies of scale and scope is indivisible inputs. Indivisible inputs cannot be scaled down below a certain minimum size and thus give rise to fixed costs. As the volume or variety of output increases, these fixed costs get spread out, leading to lower per-unit costs of production. In the short run, fixed costs are often spread because of greater capacity utilization. In the long run, fixed costs are spread when it becomes economical for a firm to substitute a technology with high fixed costs but low variable costs for one with low fixed costs but high variable costs. Other important sources of economies of scale are: (1) the physical properties of processing units (i.e., the cube-square rule); (2) increases in the productivity of variable inputs as volume increases (e.g., because of greater specialization of labor); (3) economies of inventory management.

Cumulative experience can reduce average costs as firms move down the learning curve. Learning economies should not, however, be confused with economies of scale that arise when the firm spreads out nonrecurring fixed costs over the volume of output it produces over time. To illustrate this distinction, consider a small producer of a specialty valve. The up-front costs of designing the valve are incurred only once. The dies and jigs used to fabricate the valve can be reused from one year to the next, so these costs are also nonrecurring. Even though the firm's annual rate of production may be small, its average cost per unit might still be low because it has produced the same model year after year.[60] Spreading nonrecurring fixed costs causes unit production costs to decrease with volume, even if the firm does not become more proficient in manufacturing the good as it accumulates experience.

Cost Drivers Independent of Firm Size, Scope, or Cumulative Experience

These factors make one firm's unit costs different from a competitor's even if their sizes and cumulative experience are the same. An important cost driver independent of scale is input prices, (e.g., wage rates, energy prices, and prices of components and raw materials). When firms in the same industry purchase their inputs in national markets, their input prices will be the same. But firms in the same industry often pay different prices for inputs. Differences in wage rates may be due to differences in the degree of unionization (e.g., large trunk airlines, such as United and American, are unionized, but many new entrants, such as Kiwi, are not). Differences in wages, the price of energy, or the price of delivered materials can also be attributed to location differences among firms.

Location can also influence costs in other ways. For example, because of weak local infrastructure and coordination problems that arose due to the distance between corporate headquarters and its production facility, the Lionel Corporation found it more expensive to produce toy trains in Tijuana, Mexico, than in Michigan, despite the large wage-rate advantage of the Mexican location.[61]

Economies of density refer to cost savings that arise with greater geographic density of customers. Economies of density can arise when a transportation network within a given geographic territory is utilized more intensively (e.g., when an airline's unit costs decline as more passengers are flown over a given route). They also arise when a geographically smaller territory generates the same volume of business as a geographically larger territory (e.g., when a beer distributor that operates in a densely populated urban area has lower unit costs than a distributor selling the same amount of beer in more sparsely populated suburbs). In both cases, the cost savings are due to an increase in density (e.g., passengers per mile, customers per square mile) rather than an increase in scope (e.g., number of routes served) or scale (e.g., volume of beer sold).

One firm may achieve lower average costs than its competitors because its production environment is less complex or more focused. A firm that uses the same factory to produce many different products may incur large costs associated with changing over machines and production lines to produce batches of the different products. It may also incur high administrative costs to track different work orders. A good example of the impact of complexity on production costs is the rail-

---

[60]Spreading nonrecurring fixed costs over time is sometimes referred to as economies of model volume. See McGee, J., "Efficiency and Economies of Size," in Goldschmidt, H. J., M. H. Mann, and F. J. Weston (eds.), *Industrial Concentration: The New Learning*, Boston: Little, Brown, 1974, pp. 55–96.

[61]"U.S. Companies are Coming Home: Costs, Quality Concerns Spell End for Offshore Operations," *Chicago Tribune*, November 22, 1987, p. F10.

road industry. Historically, the Pennsylvania and New York Central railroads had some of the highest costs in the business because they carried a much higher proportion of less-than-carload freight than railroads such as the Norfolk and Western and the Southern.[62] The Pennsylvania and the New York Central needed more classification yards, more freight terminals, and greater manpower per ton of freight than their more focused counterparts, which specialized in bulk traffic, such as coal and lumber. After the two roads merged to form the Penn Central in 1968, they were spending 15 cents for every dollar of sales revenue on yard expenses, as compared with an average of less than 10 cents per dollar of sales for all other railroads.[63]

A firm may have lower average costs than its rivals because it has been able to realize production process efficiencies that its rivals have not achieved; that is, the firm uses fewer inputs than its competitors to produce a given amount of output, or its production technology uses lower-priced inputs than those utilized by rivals. For example, in the early 1990s, Ford was using 25 percent less labor than General Motors to produce a typical vehicle. This effect is often difficult to disentangle from the learning curve, because the achievement of process efficiencies through learning-by-doing is at the heart of the learning curve. An example of a process efficiency not based on experience is the Chicago and Northwestern Railroad's (CNW) decision in the mid-1980s to reduce the crew size on its freight trains from four to three by eliminating one of the brakemen. This move allowed the CNW to become one of the lowest-cost competitors in the railroad business.

One firm may also have lower average costs than its competitors because it avoids expenses that its rivals are incurring. Its costs are lower because of discretionary factors that, at least to some extent, are within the firm's control. For example, in the tire business, Cooper Tire and Rubber generally refrains from national advertising. This results in sales and administrative expenses that are significantly lower than its competitors (e.g., in the early 1990s, Cooper's selling and general administrative expenses were about 5 percent of sales, while Goodyear's were roughly 16 percent).

Finally, a firm may have lower average costs than its rivals because of the effects of government policies. For obvious reasons, this factor affects international markets. For example, Japanese truck producers have long been at a disadvantage in selling trucks in the United States because of the steep import duty the U.S. government levies on Japanese trucks.

Cost Drivers Related to the Organization of the Transaction

Chapters 3, 4, and 5 discussed how the vertical chain can influence production costs. For transactions in which the threat of holdup is significant, in which private information can be leaked, or coordination is complicated, a firm that organizes the exchange through the market may have higher administrative and production

---

[62]Less-than-carload shipments are those that take up less than a full railroad car, and thus necessitate greater handling. The Pennsylvania's and New York Central's disadvantage was related to location. The Norfolk and Western and the Southern had lines through Appalachian coal country and could operate far more unit coal trains than the Pennsylvania and New York Central could.

[63]Daughen, J. R. and P. Binzen, *The Wreck of the Penn Central*, Boston: Little Brown, 1971, pp. 210–212.

expenses than a firm in which the same exchange is vertically integrated. In the production of men's underwear, for example, vertical integration of sewing and textile conversion operations in the same plant reduces coordination costs by improving scheduling of production runs.

One firm's costs may be higher than another's because of differential degrees of agency efficiency. A firm's internal administrative systems, organizational structure, or compensation system may make it more vulnerable to agency or influence costs than its competitors are. Paul Carroll's account of IBM's struggles in the late 1980s and early 1990s is full of examples of delays in decision making and excessive costs that arose from IBM's "contention system" that allowed executives within one business or functional area to critique ideas that came from outside their primary areas of responsibility.[64]

Agency costs often increase as the firm expands and gains more activities to coordinate internally or grows more diverse and thus creates greater conflicts in achieving coordination. The firm's agency efficiency relative to other firms can also deteriorate as its competitors adopt new and innovative internal organization that solve the same coordination problems at lower cost.

Cost Drivers, Activity-Cost Analysis, and Cost Advantage

In general, the cost of each activity in the firm's vertical chain may be influenced by a different set of cost drivers. For example, in the production of men's underwear, cumulative experience is an important cost driver in sewing but not in the more capital-intensive processes of yarn production and textile conversion. Economies of scale, by contrast, are an important cost driver in yarn production and textile conversion, but not in sewing.

Viewing firms as a collection of activities, each influenced by its own set of cost drivers, suggests that there are two major routes to achieving a cost advantage. The first is to exploit or control the key cost drivers within various activities better than competitors. The second is to fundamentally alter activities in the vertical chain. Changes in the vertical chain may be necessary due to changes in technology, which will alter the tradeoffs between outsourcing activities or performing them internally. They may also stem from changes in market conditions, which alter the prevailing costs of using the market rather than the internal organization to coordinate transactions. Altering the vertical chain is at the heart of what has come to be known as "process reengineering," a management philosophy that urges firms not to take the existing configuration of activities and processes for granted, but rather to redesign the chain of activities to maximize the value that it can deliver.[65] Classic examples of this include Federal Express, which dramatically changed the economics of small-package delivery in the 1970s by using the hub-and-spoke network; Dell, which ignored conventional wisdom in the computer business by selling personal computers directly to consumers, thereby avoiding sales force and distribution expenses; and Wal-Mart, which pioneered the use of electronic computerized inventory control systems and hub-and-spoke-based logistics systems, fundamentally changing the economics of mass-merchandising.

---

[64]Carroll, P., *Big Blues: The Unmaking of IBM*, New York: Crown, 1993.

[65]See Hammer, M. and Champy, J., *Reengineering the Corporation*, New York: Harper-Business, 1993.

Benefit Drivers

A firm creates a benefit advantage by offering a product that delivers larger perceived benefits to prospective buyers than competitors' products, that is, by offering a higher B. The perceived benefit, in turn, depends on the attributes that consumers value, as well as on those that lower the user and the transactions costs of the product. These attributes, or what we call benefit drivers, form the basis on which a firm can differentiate itself. Benefit drivers can include many things and analyzing them in any particular case involves identifying who the firm's prospective buyers are, understanding how they might use the firm's product or service, and discovering which of their needs the firm's product satisfies.

Benefit drivers can be classified along five dimensions:

- Physical characteristics of the product itself: These drivers include factors such as product performance, quality, features, aesthetics, durability, and ease of installation and operation.

- The quantity and characteristics of the services or complementary goods the firm or its dealers offer for sale: Key drivers here include postsale services, such as customer training or consulting, complementary products (e.g., spare parts) that the seller bundles with the product, product warranties or maintenance contracts, and the quality of repair or service capabilities.

- Characteristics associated with the sale or delivery of the good: Specific benefit drivers include speed and timeliness of delivery, availability and favorability of credit terms, location of the seller, and the quality of presale technical advice.

- Characteristics that shape consumers' perceptions or expectations of the product's performance or its cost to use.[66] Specific drivers include the product's reputation for performance, the seller's perceived staying power or financial stability (this would be important for industrial transactions in which the buyer anticipates an ongoing relationship with the seller), and the product's installed base (i.e., the number of consumers currently using the product; a large installed base would lead us to expect that the costs of developing product know-how will be low).

- The subjective image of the product: Image is a convenient way of referring to the constellation of psychological rewards that the consumer receives from purchasing, owning, and consuming the product. Image is driven by the impact of advertising messages, packaging, or labeling, and by the prestige of the distributors or outlets that carry the products.

Methods for Estimating and Characterizing Perceived Benefits

Unlike a firm's costs, which (at least in principle) can be tracked through its accounting system or estimated with statistical techniques, a product's perceived benefit is more difficult to estimate. Any approach for estimating and characterizing benefits has four components. First, the firm must measure the benefits provided to the consumer. Second, it must identify the relevant benefit drivers. Third,

---

[66]Michael Porter refers to these as signaling criteria. See *Competitive Advantage*, New York: Free Press, 1985, pp. 142–146.

it must estimate the magnitude of the benefit. Fourth, it must identify the willingness of consumers to trade off one driver for another. A full analysis of the techniques for estimating benefits falls within the domain of demand estimation in economics and marketing research. Four approaches might be used to estimate a firm's benefit position relative to its competitors and the importance of benefit drivers.

- Reservation price method

- Attribute rating method

- Conjoint analysis

- Hedonic pricing analysis

Reservation Price Method

Because a consumer purchases a product if and only if $B - P > 0$, it follows that the perceived benefit B represents a consumer's reservation price—the maximum monetary price the consumer will pay for a unit of the product or service. Since such an overall measure of consumer benefit is rarely available, it must be estimated from survey data or else imputed from database information on consumer choices. One approach to estimating B, then, is simply to ask consumers the highest price they would pay. Marketing survey research that precedes the introduction of new products often includes such a question. Once reservation prices have been identified, the analysis of benefit drivers can follow using the techniques discussed below.

Attribute-Rating Method

Attribute rating is a technique for estimating benefit drivers directly from survey responses and then calculating overall benefits on the basis of attribute scores. Target consumers are asked to rate products in terms of attributes. For example, for each attribute consumers might be given a fixed number of points to allocate among each product. Each attribute is then assigned an "importance weight," and relative perceived benefits are determined by calculating the weighted average of the product ratings.

Weighted scores can be divided by costs to construct "B/C ratios." Recall that a firm's strategic position is determined by the amount of $B - C$ it generates versus its competitors. As long as products have cost and or benefit proximity, the ranking of B/C ratios across firms will be similar (though not necessarily equal) to the rankings of $B - C$ differences. Thus, products with high B/C ratios will generally enjoy a superior strategic position than their lower B/C rivals.

Comparing B/C is common in public policy, where it is called "cost efficiency analysis." For example, some Canadian provinces use surveys to develop "scores" that measure the benefits of different health care treatments. They divide these scores by the costs of treatment to construct benefit-to-cost ratios, and allocate health care resources to those treatments with the highest ratios. Pharmaceutical manufacturers use similar methods in the United States to promote new products that they claim have high benefit-to-cost ratios.

However, with this approach, benefits are usually not expressed in dollars. When benefits and costs are not measured on the same scale, we cannot compute meaningful measures of $B - C$. Several sophisticated statistical procedures have been introduced to try to measure benefits, in dollars, of specific product attributes. These include hedonic pricing and conjoint analysis, which we describe below.

Hedonic Pricing

Hedonic pricing uses data about actual consumer purchases to determine the value of particular product attributes. (The term *hedonic* comes from *hedonism* and is meant to convey the idea that the pleasure or happiness a consumer derives from a good depends on the attributes that the good embodies.) For example, consumers purchase automobiles according to a variety of attributes, including horsepower, interior room, and braking capabilities. By examining how automobile prices vary with different combinations of attributes, analysts can determine how much consumers are willing to pay for each individual attribute. Hedonic pricing has been used to identify the value of innovations in automobiles and computerized axial tomography, the value of spreadsheet compatibility, and the benefits of improving job safety.[67]

Hedonic pricing requires multiple regression analysis to estimate the impact of product attributes on a product's price. The dependent variable in the regression is the product's price. The predictors are variables measuring the presence and extent of different product attributes. If you were studying the automobile market, hedonic pricing analysis could identify the extent to which a 1 percent increase in horsepower or chassis length, or the addition of side impact air bags, translates into automobile prices. This analysis generates implicit "hedonic prices" for individual product attributes.

Hedonic pricing can be an extremely powerful tool in evaluating the economic tradeoffs involved in enhancing a product. In effect, this analysis can help a firm determine the slope of the consumer indifference curves that were discussed previously. A firm considering adding additional features to a basic product or enhancing the product's performance would compare the hedonic price of the enhancement to its incremental cost. If, in the target market, the hedonic price exceeds the incremental cost, the enhancement would be worthwhile.

Conjoint Analysis

Hedonic pricing analysis uses market prices for existing combinations of product attributes. This is inadequate for studying the value of new features. To do this, market researchers use conjoint analysis. Like hedonic pricing, conjoint analysis estimates the relative benefits of different products attributes.[68] Its principal value is in estimating these benefits for hypothetical combinations of attributes. Although conjoint analysis can take several different forms, consumers are usually asked to rank a product with different features at different prices. For example, they might be asked to rank the following four "bundles": (1) a CD player without a shuffle-play feature at a price of $500; (2) the same CD player without a shuffle-play feature at a price of $600; (3) the same CD player with a shuffle-play feature,

---

[67]Zvi Griliches pioneered the development of modern hedonic price analysis. See "Hedonic Price Indexes for Automobiles: An Econometric Analysis of Quality Change," in *The Price Statistics of the Federal Government*, New York: National Bureau of Economic Research, 1961, pp. 173–196. See Trajtenberg, M., "A Penny for Your Thoughts: Patent Citations and the Value of Innovations," *RAND Journal of Economics*, 21, Spring 1990: pp. 172–187, for an application of this technique to computerized axial tomography scanners.

[68]For a review of conjoint analysis and its applications in marketing, see Green, P. E. and V. Srinivasan, "Conjoint Analysis in Marketing Research: New Development and Directions," *Journal of Marketing*, 54, October 1990: pp. 3–19.

at a price of $500; and (4) the CD player with a shuffle-play feature at a price of $600. Consumers would almost certainly rank (1) over (2) and (3) over (4). However, the choice between (1) and (4) is less clear. The proportion of consumers that ranks (4) over (1) provides information about consumers' willingness to pay for a shuffle-play feature. In a typical conjoint analysis, consumers are asked to rank many different bundles, and researchers then use regression analysis to estimate the impact of price and product features on the rankings. From this, researchers can estimate the market value of different features.

Alternatively, consumers may be asked to state how much they are willing to pay for different combinations of features. Researchers then treat the responses as if they were actual market prices and use regression techniques to estimate the value of each attribute. This approach closely mirrors hedonic pricing, except that the prices and products are hypothetical.

Value-Added Analysis

Value-added analysis is a tool for understanding where economic value is created within a firm's value chain. Consider the example of a firm that produces blue jeans. The firm sells its product to three different types of customers. It sells unlabeled jeans to manufacturers that attach their own labels and sell the jeans as house brands. It also sells jeans under its own brand name label (which it supports through extensive advertising and product promotion) to independent wholesalers, which then distribute them to retailers. Finally, it uses in-house distribution capabilities, to sell and distribute its labeled blue jeans directly to retailers. For simplicity, then, we can think of the firm's value chain as consisting of three major activities: manufacturing; brand management, which includes the marketing undertaken to support the brand; and distribution. Manufacturing creates value by transforming raw materials into finished jeans. Brand management creates value by transforming what would otherwise be no-name jeans into branded jeans with a superior image. Distribution creates value by distributing jeans that would otherwise be sold to wholesalers. Value-added analysis determines the incremental profit each of these activities creates.

Consider the information shown in Table A12.1
Note that the profit contribution is:

$$25,000 (4 - 2.50) + 70,000 (14 - 2.55) + 15,000 (18 - 2.55 - 1.80) - 800,000$$
$$= \$243,750.$$

TABLE A12.1
VOLUMES, PRICES, AND COSTS FOR A BLUE JEANS FIRM

Total quantity of blue jeans manufactured	110,000 pairs per year
Unlabeled jeans sold to private labelers	25,000 pairs per year
Labeled jeans sold to wholesalers	70,000 pairs per year
Labeled jeans, self-distributed	15,000 pairs per year
Selling price, unlabeled jeans	$4.00 per pair
Selling price, labeled jeans sold to wholesalers	$14.00 per pair
Selling price, labeled jeans, self-distributed	$18.00 per pair
Production cost per unit, unlabeled jeans	$2.50 per pair
Production cost per unit, labeled jeans	$2.55 per pair
Distribution cost per unit	$1.80 per pair
Total brand promotion and advertising expenses	$800,000 per year

The value-added analysis proceeds as follows:

- *Value added in manufacturing* = profit that would have been made if all jeans are sold unlabeled to private labelers:

$$= 110{,}000(4 - 2.50) = \$165{,}000 \text{ or } \$1.50 \text{ per pair}$$

- *Value added in brand management* = incremental profit made by selling all labeled jeans to wholesalers as opposed to selling them as unlabeled jeans to private labelers:

$$= 85{,}000[(14 - 2.55) - (4 - 2.50)] - \$800{,}000 = \$45{,}750, \text{ or } \$.54 \text{ per pair}$$

- *Value added in distribution* = incremental profit made by self distributing labeled jeans to retailers as opposed to selling them to wholesalers:

$$= 15{,}000[(18 - 2.55 - 1.80) - (14 - 2.55)] = \$33{,}000, \text{ or } \$2.20 \text{ per pair}$$

Note that the sum of the value added across the three activities is equal to the total profit contribution. This is not coincidental. It happens because value-added analysis carefully counts only the incremental profit an activity generates. Perhaps surprisingly, the analysis reveals that the highest total value added comes from manufacturing, not from branding the jeans, and the highest value added per unit comes from distribution. While branding the product and supporting it with advertising and promotion are important activities in this company, they do not contribute much to profit because they are costly compared with the benefits they generate.

SUSTAINING COMPETITIVE ADVANTAGE

13

𝒯he mid-1980s were prosperous times for Domino's Pizza.[1] Between 1982 and 1988, while industry sales grew 10 percent per year, Domino's sales increased nearly 40 percent per year, and the number of its stores increased from fewer than 500 to more than 5,000 worldwide. Domino's was, by far, the most profitable firm in the fast-food pizza business, and its success allowed Domino's founder, Tom Monaghan, to accumulate a net worth in excess of $400 million.

Domino's strategy was straightforward and simple: It offered a limited menu (2 pizza sizes and 10 toppings) to keep costs down. Focusing entirely on delivery (it offered no carry-out or eat-in pizza), Domino's guaranteed that a pizza would be delivered within 30 minutes or else the customer would get it free. This strategy drew widespread attention and praise. "Back in '85 and '86," said one pizza industry executive, "Domino's was like Superman." George Stalk and Thomas Hout, in their book *Competing Against Time*, cited Domino's (along with companies such as Sony, NEC, Matsushita, Bennetton, and Federal Express) as an excellent example of a time-based competitor.

But by the early 1990s, Domino's competitive position had significantly weakened. Starting in 1989, its revenues and profits began to decline. In 1991, the company lost money for the first time since the 1970s (almost $49 million). It lost even more money in 1992 ($64 million) and was in danger of defaulting on $200 million of debt. Domino's share of the delivered pizza market, once over 90 percent, fell to 46 percent by 1991. Once seen as one of the hottest growth companies around, Domino's attracted no serious interest when Monaghan put it up for sale in the early 1990s. Emblematic of Domino's decline was Monaghan's decision to sell the Detroit Tigers baseball club to his archrival Michael Illyich, owner of Little Caesar's Pizza.

---

[1]This example draws from Sympson, R., "Can Monaghan Deliver?" *Restaurant Business*, April 10, 1992: pp. 78–88; "New Direction for Domino's" *Advertising Age*, January 4, 1993; and Stopa, M. "Domino's Stays Focused: Delivery Niche Works for No. 2 Pizza Maker," *Crain's Detroit Business*, September, 15, 1997: p. 24.

A number of events contributed to Domino's decline. In 1986, backed with the financial resources and marketing savvy of PepsiCo, Pizza Hut had entered the delivered pizza business. Through a combination of massive spending on advertising and promotion, a reputation for superior pizza, and operating innovations, Pizza Hut increased its share of the delivered pizza market to nearly 25 percent by 1994. In 1989, Little Caesar's, which traditionally focused on the carry-out pizza market, launched a two-for-one campaign in which it cut the price of a carry-out pizza to half of what Domino's charged for a delivered pizza. And in late 1993, a St. Louis jury ordered Domino's to pay $78 million to a woman who was injured in a traffic accident involving a Domino's delivery van. Within a week of this judgment, Domino's ran ads in newspapers throughout the United States announcing the end of its famous 30-minute guarantee. After 1992, Domino's performance improved. It closed unprofitable stores and began to invest in markets outside the United States. However, due to the size of its losses in 1991 and 1992 and only modest growth in earnings since, Domino's net worth as of 1996 continued to be negative.[2] Domino's remains a significant competitor in the U.S. fast-food pizza business, but it no longer dominates that market the way it did in the early 1980s.

What happened to Domino's has also happened to many other companies: Competitive advantages that have taken years to build up are suddenly and quickly eroded by imitators who copy or improve the firm's formula for success or by innovators who neutralize the firm's advantage through new technologies, products, or ways of doing business. All this, combined with a dose of bad luck, can destroy even the top firms. Yet, while competitive advantages for many firms are fleeting, other firms seem to sustain competitive advantages year after year. Coca-Cola in soft drinks, Albertson's in grocery retailing, and Nucor in steel have consistently outperformed their competitors for nearly 20 years.[3]

Chapter 12 asked: Why do some firms outperform their industries? This chapter asks: Why do some firms persistently outperform their competitors, despite the efforts of other firms to imitate or neutralize their advantage? What, in short, makes a competitive advantage sustainable, and why?

◆ ◆ ◆ ◆ ◆ How Hard Is It to Sustain Profits?

Regardless of the competitive environment the firm is in, it is often difficult to sustain profits. Some enemies of sustainability, such as imitability and entry, are threats in all market structures. Others, such as price competition, may be greater threats in competitive markets.

---

[2]A firm will have a negative net worth if its liabilities are more than its assets. A company (like Domino's) that suffers several years of large losses, followed by moderate positive earnings thereafter, can end up with a negative worth.

[3]Between 1981 and 1981, Coca-Cola earned an average annual return in excess of its capital of about 11.07 percentage points. Over that same period, its main competitor Pepsi earned an average annual return of about 2.64 percentage points in excess of its cost of capital. Between 1978 and 1996, Albertson's earned an average annual return in excess of its cost of capital of about 4.30 percentage points, while the grocery retailing industry as a whole earned returns of 2.75 percentage points in excess of the industry average cost of capital. Between 1978 and 1996, Nucor average returns of 1.29 percentage points above its costs of capital, while the U.S. steel industry as a whole earned return 6.99 percentage points *below* the industry average cost of capital. All data for these calculations were obtained from the 1997 Performance 1000 universe of Stern Stewart & Company.

Threats to Sustainability in Competitive Markets

The theory of perfect competition is a logical starting point for our discussion of sustainability of competitive advantage. That theory—discussed in detail in the Economics Primer—has a fundamentally important implication: Opportunities for earning profit based on favorable market conditions will quickly evaporate as new entrants flow into the market, increase the supply of output, and drive price down to average cost. But just how relevant is this theory? After all, it seems to be cast in the context of special industry structure: Firms produce a homogeneous good, face identical technologies and input costs, and are so small relative to the size of the market that they act as price takers. Few industries outside of agriculture and fishing seem to be characterized by these stark conditions.

But the dynamic of perfect competition can operate under seemingly more complex conditions than the standard theory assumes. Even in industries where firms can vary the attributes of their products, potential profits can be dissipated through entry and imitation. Figure 13.1 depicts a market in which consumer benefits B are driven by a single attribute, which we call quality (denoted by q). In this market, we assume that all consumers have identical price-quality trade-offs, which, as in Chapter 12, can be represented by upward sloping indifference curves, such as I_1, I_2, and I_3. (Recall from Chapter 12, that price-quality combinations along a given indifference curve yield the same level of consumer surplus for a consumer in the target market.) Figure 13.1 also shows the efficiency frontier in this market. As discussed in Chapter 12, the efficiency frontier shows the

FIGURE 13.1
THE PERFECTLY COMPETITIVE DYNAMIC.

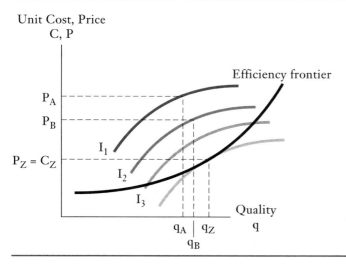

This figure depicts a market in which consumers have identical tastes, which are reflected by indifference curves, such as I_1, I_2, and I_3. The upward sloping line is the efficiency frontier for this market. A price-quality position, such as (P_A, q_A), could not be sustained when there is free entry and costless imitation. An entrant could offer a lower price and higher quality (e.g., P_B, q_B) and steal the market from incumbent firms. The perfectly competitive equilibrium occurs at price-quality combination (P_z, q_z). At this point, economic profits are zero, and no other price-quality position simultaneously results in greater consumer surplus and higher profit.

most efficient cost-quality positions that are potentially available to firms in this market. The efficiency frontier, in effect, represents a theoretical barrier that no firm can cross.

Suppose that this market is characterized by costless imitation and free entry. Because imitation is costless, existing firms and potential entrants can achieve any cost-quality position along the efficiency frontier. That is, no firm would be able to achieve higher quality at the same or lower cost as its competitors because they would instantly copy its formula for efficiency. Because of free entry, a situation in which firms offer products with quality q_A at price P_A would not persist because a new entrant could come into the market, offering the same or higher quality (e.g., q_B), undercut the price P_A (e.g., P_B), and steal the entire market from incumbent firms. Costless imitation and free entry thus imply that competitive advantage in this market cannot be sustained.

The perfectly competitive equilibrium in this market occurs at point Z, where the efficiency frontier is tangent to an indifference curve. At this equilibrium, each firm offers quality q_Z, incurs cost C_Z, charges price $P_Z = C_Z$, and earns zero economic profit. At point Z, all profitable opportunities for price-cutting, cost reduction, and quality enhancement are exhausted. Cutting price, while maintaining quality q_Z and cost C_Z, is clearly unprofitable. Moreover, profitability cannot be increased by cutting costs or enhancing quality because the alternative cost-quality positions available to a firm at Z are those along the efficiency frontier. That is, raising quality can be done only at a higher cost, while costs can be reduced only by sacrificing quality. To make a profit while operating at any cost-quality position other than Z, a firm's price P would have to exceed cost, that is, its price-quality position would have to lie above the efficiency frontier. Except for point Z, however, all such positions would lie above the consumer indifference curve through Z, which means that each would yield less consumer surplus than consumers receive at Z. Once firms reach Z, no other competitive position in this market is viable, and a competitor in this business can earn no more than zero economic profit.

EXAMPLE 13.1

AMAZON.COM VERSUS BARNESANDNOBLE.COM VERSUS . . . ?[4]

Many of you probably bought this book at your university bookstore. Some of you might have bought a used copy at a campus book exchange or from a fellow student. But you might also have bought this book without ever leaving your dorm room, apartment, or home. This is because you purchased it from an on-line book retailer, such as Amazon.com or barnesandnoble.com.

[4]This example draws from "The Other Battle over Browsers: Barnes & Noble and Other On-Line Booksellers Are Poised to Challenge Amazon.com," *New York Times*, March 3, 1998, pp. C1, C4; "The Baron of Books," *Business Week*, June 29, 1998, pp. 109–115; and "A Clash of Strategies: Amazon.com vs. Barnes & Noble," a paper prepared by Kellogg Graduate School of Management students Tracy Anderson, Valerie Castro, Dan Gordon, and Avi Tesciuba.

Until 1997, Amazon.com was the *only* on-line book retailer. Amazon.com made its first on-line sale in July 1995. Over the next three years, its sales doubled every month. Its stock price, which stood at $18 per share when it went public in May 1997, rose to $80 per share within a year.

Amazon.com creates economic value in several ways. It provides an enormous selection of titles (more than 2.5 million), ranging from *New York Times'* bestsellers to obscure, hard-to-find tomes on publishers' "back lists." Amazon offers hassle-free and safe payment by credit card, and for popular titles, customers get their books in 48 hours. Finally, Amazon.com provides powerful search capabilities, lists of related books, customized recommendations based on a customer's previous purchases, and the opportunity for customers to post personal reviews of books.

But as this chapter emphasizes, successful strategies in attractive markets almost always attract imitators. As of 1998, on-line book sales accounted for just 3 percent of overall retail book sales ($400 million out of $13 billion overall). However, industry observers and participants expect that on-line book sales will soon exceed $1 billion. Not surprisingly, then, the on-line market has attracted the attention of the world's largest book sellers. In May 1997, Barnes & Noble, the number-one book retailer in the United States, launched an on-line bookselling service, barnesandnoble.com, to compete head-to-head with Amazon.com. Barnesandnoble.com's array of services are nearly identical to Amazon.com, and the "look and feel" of its website closely resembles Amazon.com's. Barnes & Noble entered the on-line business with great fanfare: It deeply discounted the books it sold on-line (prices were 30 percent below bookstore prices); it heavily promoted its on-line service on the web and in its bookstores; and it initiated a high-profile lawsuit challenging Amazon.com's claim to be the largest bookstore on earth. (The lawsuit has since been settled.) Borders Group, the second-largest retail book chain in the United States, launched its on-line bookstore in 1998. Besides Barnes and Noble and Borders, other firms have entered the on-line bookselling market, including BuyBooks.com, Kingbooks.com, AllDirect.com, and BooksNow.com.

Whether Amazon.com will be able to maintain its dominance of the on-line book business is an interesting question. Amazon.com's founder Jeffrey Bezos says "our advantage is that we know more about e-commerce than anybody else. We've been doing it longer and we've already leveled the playing field." Other industry observers cite the intellectual caliber of Amazon.com's employees as a source of sustainable success. (Some of Amazon.com's employees are required to provide SAT scores before being hired.) And some observers claim that Amazon.com has a passion for books that competitors, such as Barnes & Noble, lack. (Barnes & Noble's chairman, Leonard Riggio, admits to reading few books, and he says that had he worked as clerk in a hardware store, rather than in a bookstore as he actually did, he would have ended up starting Home Depot rather than Barnes & Noble superstores.)

Still, e-commerce is rapidly evolving and thousands of companies are developing capabilities in this domain. One might legitimately wonder whether Amazon.com will be able to sustain its success entirely on this basis. Moreover, as we discuss in detail below, workers are a mobile resource. The employees at Amazon.com who are distinguished by their love of books or their sheer intellectual horsepower can, in principle, be hired away by competitors. The potential sources of sustainable advantage are not Amazon's employees per se. Rather, they are forces that impede mobility (e.g., employees' loyalty to Amazon.com or relationship-specific investments in human capital at Amazon.com). They are also the organizational routines that allow Amazon.com's distinctive capabilities in on-line bookselling to endure even after key employees leave the company. In addition, some of Amazon.com's imitators have important resources of their own. For example, Barnes & Noble's scale gives it bargaining clout with the major publishing houses.

The on-line bookselling business illustrates how quickly competitors can copy a brilliant business idea. Amazon.com has revolutionized how books are sold. It remains to be seen to what extent its shareholders will be able to continue to capture the profits from that revolution.

Threats to Sustainability in Monopolistically Competitive Markets

In the simple market described in the previous section, firms could differentiate themselves vertically—that is, by quality. But this did not shield them from the rigors of price competition. Because all consumers were assumed to have the same preferences, a firm that offers a price-quality combination (such as *A*) that is inferior to one offered by competitors (such as *B*) would sell nothing. A monopolistically competitive market, however, is different from the one depicted in Figure 13.1, in that sellers are usually horizontally differentiated in distinct niches (i.e., they cater to consumers with different preferences over key product attributes).[5] A seller can thus raise its price without losing all its customers—the demand curve facing each seller is downward sloping. As pointed out in the Economics Primer, when a seller faces a downward-sloping demand curve, it is optimal for it to set a price above marginal cost.

But even though a monopolistically competitive seller sets price above marginal cost, there is no guarantee that it will earn profits. The seller may be covering incremental costs, but it must also have sufficient sales volume to cover its fixed costs. However, if incumbent sellers are making profits, and there is free entry into the market, new firms will enter. By slightly differentiating themselves from incumbents, these entrants will find their own niches, but will inevitably take some business from incumbents. As discussed in Chapter 7, entry will continue in this way until incremental profits just cover fixed costs. The pizza delivery market shows how entry by differentiated sellers led to the decline of the successful incumbent. Other examples include household appliances, luxury cars, and mass market retailing. Successful incumbents in monopolistically competitive markets can do little to preserve profits unless they can deter entry. We discussed strategies for doing this in Chapter 11.

---

[5] We discuss the difference between horizontal and vertical differentiation in detail in Chapters 8 and 12.

Threats to Sustainability Under All Market Structures

Even in oligopolistic or monopolistic markets, where entry might be blockaded or deterred, a successful incumbent may not stay successful for long. One reason is that success may be due to factors that the incumbent cannot control, such as the weather or general business conditions. A March blizzard in Colorado that delays shipments of Coors beer to the West Coast will hurt Coors sales for the month, and will boost sales of competing brands, such as Budweiser and Miller. But one would not expect Coors' April sales to stay down, nor would one expect Budweiser and Miller to sustain the one-month sales increase. If, as expected, April sales revert to historical levels, we would say that profits showed *regression to the mean*. The general point about regression to the mean is this: Whenever a firm does exceedingly well, one must consider whether it benefited from unusually good luck. Conversely, an underperforming firm might have had bad luck. Since good luck is unlikely to persist (or it would not have been luck), one might expect the successful firm to be less successful and the underperforming firm to improve. The possibility of regression toward the mean means that one should not expect firms to repeat extreme performances, whether good or bad, for long.

Extremely good performance may not always be the result of good luck. As we discuss later in this chapter, firms may develop genuine advantages that are difficult for others to duplicate. Even this does not guarantee a sustainable flow of profits, however. While the advantage may be inimitable, so that the firm is protected from the forces of rivalry and entry, the firm may not be protected from powerful buyers and suppliers. Powerful buyers and suppliers can threaten firms in any market structure, but they are most likely to emerge in oligopolistic or monopolistic markets, where successful firms can earn large profits.

A good example of where supplier power has threatened sustainability is major league baseball in the United States. Thanks in part to economies of scale and an exemption from the U.S. antitrust laws, major league baseball has been a monopoly throughout the twentieth century. Even so, many team owners cannot turn a profit. One reason is the powerful Major League Baseball Player's Association, which through litigation and a series of successful job actions in the 1970s and 1980s, has elevated the average salary to more than $1 million a year. Fearful that they could no longer sustain profits in the face of ever-escalating salaries, the owners took a tough bargaining stance in 1994, which eventually led to a players' strike and the cancellation of the 1994 World Series.

Evidence: The Persistence of Profitability

If the forces threatening sustainability are pervasive, economic profits in most industries should quickly converge to zero. Entry, imitation, price cutting, and other forces would drive a firm's rate of return toward its cost of capital—the rate of return just sufficient to induce investors to provide financial capital to the firm. This, in turn, implies that profit persistence should be weak: No matter how profitable a firm is today, its profit will converge toward the perfectly competitive level. By contrast, if there are impediments to the competitive dynamic (e.g., entry barriers as discussed in Chapter 11 or barriers to imitation as we discuss later in this chapter), then profits should persist: Firms that earn above-average profits today should continue to do so in the future; low-profit firms today should remain low-profit firms in the future.

What pattern of profit persistence do we actually observe? The economist Dennis Mueller has done the most comprehensive study of profit persistence.[6] For a sample of 600 U.S. manufacturing firms for the years 1950–1972, Mueller used statistical techniques to measure profit persistence. Perhaps the easiest way to summarize Mueller's results is to imagine two groups of U.S. manufacturing firms. One group (the "high-profit" group) has an after-tax accounting return on assets (ROA) that is, on average, 100 percent greater than the accounting ROA of the typical manufacturing firm. The other group (the "low-profit" group) has an average ROA that is, on average, 100 percent less than that of the typical manufacturing firm. If the typical manufacturing firm has an ROA of 6 percent in 2000 (which is roughly the average ROA for U.S. manufacturing firms over the last 20 years), the average ROA of the high-profit group would be 12 percent, while the average ROA of the low-profit group would be 0 percent. If profit follows the pattern in Mueller's sample, by 2003 (three years later) the high-profit group's average ROA would be about 8.6 percent, and by 2010, its average ROA would stabilize at about 7.8 percent, a level 35 percent greater than that of the average manufacturing firm. Similarly, by 2003 the low-profit group's average ROA would be about 4.4 percent, and by 2010 its average ROA would stabilize at about 4.9 percent or about 19 percent less than the average manufacturing firm. Figure 13.2 shows these patterns.[7]

Mueller's results suggest that firms with abnormally high levels of profitability tend, on average, to decrease in profitability over time, while firms with abnormally low levels of profitability tend, on average, to experience increases in profitability over time. However, as Figure 13.2 illustrates, the profit rates of these two groups of firms do not converge to a common mean. Firms that start out with high profits converge, in the long run, to rates of profitability that are higher than the rates of profitability of firms that start out with low profits.[8]

Mueller's work implies that, while some forces do push markets toward the perfectly competitive outcome, other forces impede that dynamic. Michael Porter's Five Forces, summarized in Chapter 11, are an important class of such forces. Many

---

[6]Mueller, D. C., "The Persistence of Profits Above the Norm," *Economica*, 44, 1997: pp. 369–380. See also Mueller, D. C., *Profits in the Long Run*, Cambridge: Cambridge University Press, 1986.

[7]Our characterization of these patterns of profit persistence is based on the results in Table 2.2 in Mueller's book. Mueller's study is far more elaborate than we have described here. He uses regression to estimate equations that give persistence patterns for each of the 600 firms in his sample. Our grouping of firms into two groups is done to illustrate the main results.

[8]This lack of convergence may be due to different risk characteristics of the two groups. Perhaps firms in the high-profit group are riskier on average than the firms in the low-profit group, and the capital markets require a higher rate of return from them. The high-profit group may have an average risk-adjusted cost of capital of 7.8 percent, and the low-profit group may have an average rate of 4.9 percent. By the year 2010, both groups should be earning zero economic profits because their respective nominal rates of return equal their costs of capital.

In his study, Mueller tests whether there is a systematic relationship between the riskiness of firms and the level to which their profits converge in the long run. Using a variety of measures of risk, Mueller concludes that differences in risk among the firms in his sample do not account for the lack of convergence to a common mean. This suggests that the lack of convergence indicates long-run differences in economic profitability among firms, rather than differences in risk.

FIGURE 13.2
THE PERSISTENCE OF PROFITABILITY IN MUELLER'S SAMPLE.

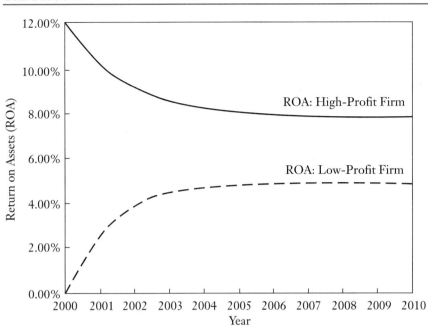

The high-profit group's average ROA starts out at 12% in 2000, and decreases over time, converging to slightly less than 8%. The low-profit group's average ROA starts at 0% in 2000, and increases over time, converging to about 4.9%. The profits of the two groups get closer over time, but do not converge toward a common mean, as the theory of perfect competition would predict.

factors, such as high entry barriers or other structural conditions that soften price competition, protect the profitability of an entire industry. We described these factors in Part Two and summarized them in Chapter 11. Here, however, we are concerned with a different class of forces: those that protect the competitive advantage of an individual firm and allow it to persistently outperform its industry. These forces are, at least in principle, distinct from Porter's Five Forces. A firm may operate in an industry with intense pricing rivalry and low entry barriers, but the sources of its competitive advantage may be so difficult to understand or to imitate that its advantage over its competitors is secure for a long time. By contrast, structural conditions in an industry may facilitate pricing coordination among firms in that industry, allowing higher-than-competitive returns, but the barriers to imitation within the industry may be so low that no firm can be more profitable than any other.

SUSTAINABLE COMPETITIVE ADVANTAGE ◆ ◆ ◆ ◆ ◆

This section discusses the economic foundations of sustainable competitive advantage. We begin by linking sustainable advantage to the concepts of resources and capabilities in Chapter 12. We then introduce the concept of an isolating mechanism and discuss its importance for sustainable advantage.

The Resource-Based Theory of the Firm

Chapter 12 defined competitive advantage as the ability of a firm to outperform its industry, that is, to earn a higher rate of profit than the industry norm. A competitive advantage is sustainable when it persists despite efforts by competitors or potential entrants to duplicate or neutralize it.[9]

As argued in Chapter 12, to achieve a competitive advantage, a firm must create more value than its competitors. A firm's ability to create superior value, in turn, depends on its stock of resources (i.e., firm-specific assets and factors of production, such as patents, brand-name reputation, installed base, and human assets) and its distinctive capabilities (i.e., activities that the firm does better than competitors) that arise from using those resources.

The link between value creation and resources and capabilities implies that for a competitive advantage to be sustainable, the market must be characterized by persistent asymmetries in terms of firms' resources and capabilities. Firms must differ from each other, and these differences must persist. Resource heterogeneity is the cornerstone of an important framework in strategy: the resource-based theory of the firm.[10] That theory points out that if all firms in a market have the same stock of resources and capabilities, no strategy for value-creation is available to one firm that would not also be available to all other firms in the market. Any other firm could immediately replicate a strategy that confers advantage. To be sustainable, a competitive advantage must thus be underpinned by resources and capabilities that are scarce and imperfectly mobile, which means that well-functioning markets for the resources and capabilities do not or cannot exist.

That a resource must be scarce to sustain a competitive advantage is obvious. Imperfect mobility is perhaps less clear. To grasp its necessity, imagine a situation in which critical resources can be bought and sold on the open market. If so, then any strategy for superior value-creation could potentially be implemented by any firm that purchased the appropriate resources. When value-creating resources are scarce, we would expect firms to bid against one another to acquire them. The additional economic profit (or, equivalently, rent) that would have resulted from the competitive advantage would then be transferred to the owner of the resources. For example, where key resources are talented employees, such as superstars in creating specialized financial derivatives, the extra-value-created would be captured by the superstar employees as higher salaries, rather than by the firm as higher profit. Moreover, in the race to acquire the value-creating resources, firms could squander the rents that the resources create in the first place. An example of

---

[9]This definition is adapted from Barney, J., "Firm Resources and Sustained Competitive Advantage," *Journal of Management*, 17, 1991: pp. 99–120.

[10]Presentations of this theory can be found in Barney, J., "Firm Resources and Sustained Competitive Advantage," *Journal of Management*, 17, 1991: pp. 99–120: Peteraf, M. A., "The Cornerstones of Competitive Advantage: A Resource-Based View," *Strategic Management Journal*, 14, 1993: pp. 179–191; Dierickx, I. and K. Cool, "Asset Stock Accumulation and Sustainability of Competitive Advantage," *Management Science*, 35, 1989: pp. 1504–1511; Grant, R. M., "The Resource-Based Theory of Competitive Advantage: Implications for Strategy Formulation," *California Management Review*, Spring 1991: p. 119–145; Wernerfelt, B., "A Resource-Based View of the Firm," *Strategic Management Journal*, 5, 1984: pp. 171–180. The pioneering work underlying the resource-based theory is Penrose, E. T., *The Theory of the Growth of the Firm*, Oxford: Blackwell, 1959.

this would be where the key resource is a potentially valuable location that can support only one retail outlet. If a retailer waited to purchase the land until the time was "just right"—the profit potential was at its height—it would probably be too late. A more forward-looking retailer would prematurely build a store before the location was ready to yield its maximal profit to preempt potential competitors from acquiring the location. This would dissipate the profitability of the location.

Why Are Resources Immobile?

Resources might be imperfectly mobile for several reasons. Many valuable resources, such as the know-how an organization has acquired through cumulative experience, or a firm's reputation for "toughness," cannot be packaged and sold in an outside market. Such assets are effectively nontradable. Other assets may be tradable, but because they are relationship-specific, they may be far more valuable inside one organization than another. This limits the incentive for parties outside the organization to bid them away. Some assets may also be cospecialized—that is, they are more valuable when used together than when separated. For example, USAirway's gates and landing slots at the Pittsburgh airport are probably far more valuable to it than they are to a potential bidder for those slots because of the strong "brand identification" USAirways has in Pittsburgh, and because prospective fliers out of Pittsburgh have built up large stocks of frequent-flier miles on USAirways.

◆ ◆

$\mathcal{E}$XAMPLE 13.2

AMERICAN VERSUS NORTHWEST IN YIELD MANAGEMENT

An example of resource mobility arose in a lawsuit involving American Airlines and Northwest Airlines.[11] The case centered on an allegation that Northwest Airlines stole valuable information related to American's yield management capabilities.

Yield management refers to a set of practices designed to maximize an airline's yield—the dollars of revenue it collects per seat mile it flies. Yield management techniques combine mathematical optimization models with forecasting techniques to help an airline determine fares, fix the number of seats it should sell in various fare categories, and adjust its inventory of seats in response to the changes in demand conditions. American Airlines has the most sophisticated yield management capabilities in the airline industry. In the early 1990s, its system was thought to have added $300 million to American's annual revenues.

By contrast, Northwest's yield management capabilities were below average. In the late 1980s, it hired a consultant to devise a mathematical model to underpin a new system. But management soon became skeptical of the consultant's efforts. The system the consultant devised was estimated to cost $30 million, but its success was uncertain. In 1990, Northwest fired the consultant.

---

[11]This example is based on the article, "Fare Game: Did Northwest Steal American' Systems? The Court Will Decide," *Wall Street Journal*, July 7, 1994, pp. A1, A8.

Northwest then tried to purchase a yield management system from American. However, in return for the system, American demanded Northwest's operating right to fly between Chicago and Tokyo, a route whose market value was estimated at between $300 to $500 million. Northwest refused to trade.

Instead, in the fall of 1990, Northwest hired John Garel, the chief of the yield management department at American. Garel then tried to lure American's best yield managers to Northwest. Out of the 38 new yield management employees hired by Northwest in 1990, 17 came from American, often with generous raises of 50 to 100 percent.

Along with hiring many of American's yield managers, Northwest also managed to acquire a diskette containing American's "spill" tables, which are a key part of mathematical models used to plan the acquisition of new aircraft. Northwest had tried to purchase the spill tables along with American's yield management system in 1990. American alleged that one of its former employees recruited by Northwest copied the diskette. Northwest also obtained internal American documents on how to improve a yield management system. One of the documents was entitled "Seminar on Demand Forecasting," which Northwest used to vastly improve its system called AIMS. American alleged that its system contains five critical techniques, all of which Northwest copied. One Northwest yield manager characterized the revision as "a heart transplant of the AIMS system."

In 1993 American sued Northwest in federal court. It sought to bar Northwest from using its revised yield management system and $50 million in damages. American also brought a suit against KLM, the Dutch airline that is Northwest's international marketing partner. According to American, Northwest passed along the internal American documents to KLM.[12]

This example illustrates that the resources that are the basis of competitive advantage can be highly mobile. This is especially true when those resources are talented individuals, but is also true when the resource is information, a technique, or formula that can be written down and copied. It is also noteworthy that Northwest was unable to capture all of the extra value that it hoped to obtain by hiring the American yield managers. Some of it had to be shared with these individuals by paying them higher salaries. This highlights a general point about competitive markets. When a scarce resource is fully mobile and is as valuable to one firm as to another, the extra profit that the firms can earn from the resource will be competed away as they bid against one another to acquire it.

Isolating Mechanisms

Scarcity and immobility of critical resources and capabilities are necessary for a competitive advantage to be sustainable, but they are not sufficient. A firm that has built a competitive advantage from a set of scarce and immobile resources may find that advantage undermined if other firms can develop their own stocks of resources and capabilities that duplicate or neutralize the source of the firm's advan-

---

[12]American's case against KLM was dismissed in 1997, but not its suit against Northwest.

tage. For example, Xerox's advantage in the plain paper copier market in the 1970s was built, in part, on superior servicing capabilities backed by a network of dealers who provided on-site service calls. Canon successfully challenged Xerox in the small copier market by building highly reliable machines that rarely broke down and did not have to be serviced as often as Xerox's. Canon's superior product neutralized Xerox's advantage and reduced the value of Xerox's servicing capabilities and its dealer network.

Richard Rumelt coined the term *isolating mechanisms* to refer to the economic forces that limit the extent to which a competitive advantage can be duplicated or neutralized through the resource creation activities of other firms.[13] Isolating mechanisms thus protect the competitive advantages of firms that are lucky enough or foresightful enough to have acquired them. Isolating mechanisms are to a firm what an entry barrier is to an industry: Just as an entry barrier impedes new entrants from coming into an industry and competing away profits from incumbent firms, isolating mechanisms prevent other firms from competing away the extra profit that a firm earns from its competitive advantage.

There are different kinds of isolating mechanisms, and different authors classify them in different ways.[14] We put them into two distinct groups:

- Impediments to imitation: These isolating mechanisms impede existing firms and potential entrants from duplicating the resources and capabilities that form the basis of the firm's advantage. For example, many firms compete in the golf club market, but few have been able to match Callaway's distinctive capabilities in designing innovative clubs and bringing them quickly to market. Clearly, impediments prevent competitors from copying the strengths of this successful firm.

- Early-mover advantages: Once a firm acquires a competitive advantage, these isolating mechanisms increase the economic power of that advantage over time. Cisco Systems, for example, dominates the market for products such as routers and switches, which link together LANs (local area networks). Its success in this business has helped establish its Cisco Internetwork Operating System (Cisco IOS) software as an industry standard. This, in turn, has a feedback effect that benefits Cisco's entire line of networking products. Perhaps not surprisingly, in the 1990s, Cisco Systems earned rates of return that vastly exceeded its cost of capital. Indeed, the 40.36 percentage point average "spread" between Cisco's annual return on capital and its cost of capital from 1992–1996 exceeded that of such notable success stories as Intel, Coca-Cola, and Microsoft.[15]

---

[13]Rumelt, R. P., "Towards a Strategic Theory of the Firm," in R. Lamb (ed.), *Competitive Strategic Management*, Englewood Cliffs, NJ: Prentice-Hall, 1984, pp. 556–570.

[14]See, for example, chapter 5 of Ghemawat, P., *Commitment: The Dynamic of Strategy*, New York: Free Press, 1991, or Yao, D., "Beyond the Reach of the Invisible Hand," *Strategic Management Journal*, 9, 1988: pp. 59–70.

[15]Between 1992 and 1996, Intel averaged a return on capital in excess of its cost of capital of 16.83 percentage points, while Coca-Cola and Microsoft averaged 21.52 and 33.54 percentage points, respectively. These data come from Stern Stewart & Company's 1997 Performance 1000 universe.

Figure 13.3 illustrates the distinction between these two classes of isolating mechanisms. In Figure 13.3*a*, all firms in an industry initially occupy the same competitive position. A "shock" then propels firm G into a position of competitive advantage over other firms in the market. "Shock" here refers to fundamental changes that lead to major shifts of competitive positions in a market. Examples of shocks are process or product innovations, discoveries of new sources of consumer value or market segments, shifts in demand or tastes, or changes in regulatory policy that enable firms to significantly shift their strategic position in a business. Isolating mechanisms that impede imitation prevent other firms from fully replicating G's advantage. This is shown in Figure 13.3*b* as the inability of other firms to match G's competitive position as time passes. Early-mover advantages work somewhat differently. Because G was the first firm to benefit from a shock, it can eventually widen its competitive advantage over other firms in the market. This is shown in Figure 13.3*c*.

If shocks are infrequent and isolating mechanisms are powerful, a firm's competitive advantage will be long-lived. Firms whose competitive advantages are protected by isolating mechanisms, Rumelt argues, may be able to take their strategies as given for a long time, while still earning higher returns than existing competitors (or new entrants that might come into the business). The companion insight is that consistently high profitability does not necessarily mean that a firm is well-managed. As Rumelt notes, "even fools can churn out good results (for a while)."

In the next two sections, we discuss impediments to imitation and early-mover advantages in greater detail.

FIGURE 13.3
IMPEDIMENTS TO IMITATION AND EARLY-MOVER ADVANTAGES.

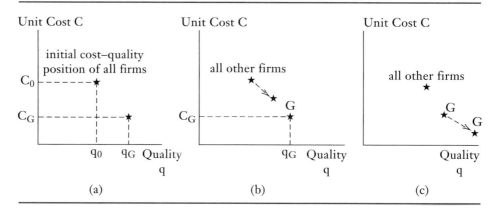

(a) The initial cost-quality position of all firms in the market is (C_0, q_0). Following a shock, firm G achieves a competitive advantage based on higher quality and lower cost.
(b) Impediments to imitation: As time passes, G's competitors may be able to reduce costs and increase quality, but they cannot duplicate G's superior cost-quality position.
(c) The dynamics of an early-mover advantage: As time passes, G's cost and quality advantage over competing firms grows more pronounced.

Impediments to Imitation

In this section, we discuss four impediments to imitation:

- Legal restrictions

- Superior access to inputs or customers

- Market size and scale economies

- Intangible barriers to imitating a firm's distinctive capabilities: causal ambiguity, dependence on historical circumstances, and social complexity

- Strategic fit

Legal Restrictions

Legal restrictions, such as patents, copyrights, and trademarks, as well as governmental control over entry into markets, through licensing, certification, or quotas on operating rights, can be powerful impediments to imitation.[16] Jeffrey Williams points out that between 1985 and 1990, patent-protected products as a group yielded higher returns on investment than any single industry in the United States.[17]

We should note that patents, copyrights, trademarks, and operating rights can be bought and sold. For example, Ted Turner has bought copyrights to old movies, such as *Gone With the Wind*, and rereleased them to theaters or showed them on his television stations. Thus, while scarce, these resources may also be highly mobile. This mobility implies that a firm that tries to secure a competitive advantage by purchase of a patent or an operating right may have to pay a competitive price to get it. If so, the purchase of the asset will be a breakeven proposition unless the buyer can deploy it in ways that other prospective purchasers cannot. This requires superior information about how to best utilize the asset or the possession of complementary resources to enhance their value relative to other firms.

We encountered this issue in Chapter 6 in our discussion of acquisition programs by diversifying firms. The evidence showing that unrelated acquisitions were generally unprofitable is consistent with the idea that buyers cannot profit from acquisitions unless they can deploy the asset in superior ways. Asset mobility also implies that the owner of the patent or operating right may be better off selling it to another firm. For example, many universities have offices that sell the patents obtained by members of their faculties. Universities realize that it makes more sense for other firms to develop marketable products. This illustrates the key point about patents and other operating rights: Once a patent or operating right is secured, its exclusivity gives it sustainable value. Whoever holds the asset holds that value. But maximizing that value is ultimately a make-or-buy decision, whose resolution rests on the principles developed in Part One of this book.

---

[16]We discuss patents, copyrights, and trademarks more fully in Chapter 11.

[17]Williams, J., "How Sustainable Is Your Advantage?" *California Management Review*, 34, 1992: pp. 1–23.

Superior Access to Inputs or Customers

A firm that can obtain high-quality or high-productivity inputs, such as raw materials or information, on more favorable terms than its competitors, will be able to sustain cost and quality advantages that competitors cannot imitate. Firms often achieve favorable access to inputs by controlling the sources of supply through ownership or long-term exclusive contracts. For example, International Nickel dominated the nickel industry for three-quarters of a century by controlling the highest grade deposits of nickel, which were concentrated in western Canada. Topps monopolized the market for baseball cards in the United States by signing every professional baseball player to a long-term contract giving Topps the exclusive right to market the player's picture on baseball cards sold with gum or candy. This network of long-term contracts, which was declared illegal in the early 1980s, blocked access by other firms to an essential input in card production—the player's picture.

The flip side of superior access to inputs is superior access to customers. A firm that secures access to the best distribution channels or the most productive retail locations will have an advantage competing for customers over rivals. A manufacturer could prevent access to retail distribution channels by insisting on exclusive dealing clauses, whereby a retailer agrees to sell only the products that manufacturer makes. Before World War II, most American automobile producers had exclusive dealing arrangements with their franchised dealers, and according to Lawrence White, this raised the barriers to entering the automobile business.[18] Most of these clauses were dropped voluntarily in the early 1950s, following antitrust decisions that seemed to threaten the Big Three's ability to maintain their exclusive dealing arrangements. Some observers speculate that the termination of these exclusive dealing requirements made it easier for Japanese manufacturers to penetrate the American market in the 1970s and 1980s.[19]

Superior access to inputs and customers may be vulnerable to changes in technologies or tastes, or to the opening up of new input or product markets. For example, International Nickel's dominance of the world nickel market ended when new high-quality nickel deposits were discovered elsewhere in the 1970s. Moreover, just as patents and trademarks can be bought and sold, so can scarce locations or contracts that give the firm control of scarce inputs or distribution channels. Thus, superior access to inputs or customers can confer sustained competitive advantage only if the firm can secure access at "below-market" prices. If, for example, a certain site is widely known to contain a high-quality supply of uranium, the price of that land would be bid up until the economic profits were transferred to the original owner, and the profitability of the firm that purchases the land would be no higher than the profitability of the losing bidders. Similarly, baseball teams, recognizing the extra revenues that result from signing a superstar, such as Ken Griffey, Jr., or Greg Maddux, will compete against one another to acquire these players, so that the original owners (Griffey Jr. or Maddux) capture the economic profit associated with their rare and valuable skills. The corollary of this logic is that control of scarce inputs or distribution channels allows a firm to earn eco-

---

[18] White, L., "The Automobile Industry," in Adams, W. (ed.), *The Structure of American Industry*, 6th ed., New York: Macmillan, 1982.

[19] See, for example, Scherer, F. M. and D. Ross, *Industrial Market Structure and Economic Performance*, 3d ed., Boston, MA: Houghton Mifflin, 1990, pp. 563–564.

nomic profits in excess of its competitors only if it acquired control of the input supply when other firms or individuals failed to recognize its value or could not exploit it.

EXAMPLE 13.3

COLA WARS: SLUGGING OUT IN VENEZUELA

The long-standing international success of Coca-Cola and Pepsi shows that a powerful brand name can confer a sustainable advantage. In recent years, there have been few credible challengers to the two leading cola makers. The reason is only partly to do with taste—many consumers believe that other colas, such as RC Cola, taste just as good as Coke or Pepsi. Competitors lack Coke and Pepsi's brand images and would need to spend huge sums in advertisements to achieve it. The owner of one potential competitor even risked his life to boost his cola's brand image. Richard Branson has twice attempted to fly around the world in a hot air balloon emblazoned with the Virgin Cola logo. Branson crashed shortly after the beginning of each flight (both crashes occurred in remote regions) and has failed to generate the publicity necessary for Virgin Cola to take off.

While Coca-Cola and Pepsi have remarkable international brand recognition, they do not share international markets equally. For example, Coca-Cola has long been the dominant cola throughout South America. The lone exception has been Venezuela, where Pepsi held an 80 percent share of the $400 million cola market until August 1996. That is when Coca-Cola struck a deal to buy half of Venezuela's largest soft drink bottler, Hit de Venezuela, from the Cisneros Group. The bottler, which changed its name to Coca-Cola y Hit, immediately switched operations to Coca-Cola, and 4,000 Pepsi trucks became Coke trucks. In a scene that could have been lifted from the movie *The Coca-Cola Kid*, Coke trucks began rolling across Venezuela, and Coke relaced Pepsi as Venezuela's dominant cola.

Coca-Cola secured its dominant market share by tying up the distribution channel. As might be expected, Coke had to pay dearly for it—an estimated $500 million for a 50 percent stake. Economic theory suggests that Coca-Cola should not have profited from this deal. After all, the source of monopoly power in this market belonged to the Cisneros Group rather than cola makers. Coca-Cola officials claimed that the benefits from the Venezuelan acquisition would accrue in the long run. A Venezuelan director stated, "We'll do whatever we have to to win this market. We don't think about today. We think about ten years from now."[20] Coca-Cola's dominance of the Venezuelan market will undoubtedly increase its cash flows over the long run. The important question was whether the present value of the cash flows from having a dominant share of the Venezuelan market exceeded what Coca-Cola paid to obtain that market share. If so, the deal created wealth for Coca-Cola's shareholders. If not, it destroyed wealth.

[20]Quoted in Beard D., "The Champ Returns," *Fort Lauderdale Sun Sentinal*, December 1, 1996, p. 1G.

Whether Coca-Cola overpaid to gain market share became moot in May 1997 when Panamco, an independent Coke bottler headquartered in Mexico, paid $1.1 billion to acquire Coca-Cola y Hit. Coca-Cola appears to have made out handsomely from these deals: It profited from the purchase and subsequent sale of Hit de Venezuela, and it still has a dominant market share in Venezuela.

Coca-Cola might have wrested control of the Venezuelan market from Pepsi, but Pepsi still possesses valuable assets in Venezuela: Pepsi's brand image and taste. (Many Venezuelans apparently prefer Pepsi's sweeter taste.) Months after Coca-Cola's takeover of the market, Venezuelans continued to express a decided preference for Pepsi—if they could find it in the stores. To exploit its assets, Pepsi signed a bottling and distribution deal with Polar, Venezuela's largest brewer. It will take some time for Polar to match Coca-Cola's bottling capacity. In the meantime, Coke and Pespi are preparing to wage an all out war over brand image and shelf space.

The winners: The Cisneros Group, Polar, and Coke. The loser: Pepsi—if Pepsi will have to spend mightily to regain its market share. One other loser: any other soft drink maker contemplating entry into the Venezuelan market. As a combined force, Coke and Pepsi are stronger today than before August 1996. As always seems to happen, Coca Cola and Pepsi might bloody themselves in the cola wars, but in doing so they gain protection from outside threats.

Market Size and Scale Economies

Imitation may also be deterred when minimum efficient scale is large relative to market demand, and a firm has secured a large share of the market. We have already discussed this situation in Chapters 2 and 11 in connection with the idea that economies of scale can limit the number of firms that can "fit" in a market and thus represent a barrier to entry. Scale economies can also discourage a smaller firm already in the market from seeking to grow larger to replicate the scale-based cost advantage of a firm that has obtained a large market share.

Figure 13.4 illustrates the logic of this isolating mechanism. Two firms, one large and one small, produce a homogeneous product, and face the same long-run average cost function. The large firm's volume of 5,000 units per year exceeds minimum efficient scale (MES), which is 4,000 units in the figure; the small firm's volume—1,000 units per year—is less than MES. If the small firm invested in additional capacity and expanded output to MES to lower its average cost, the market price would fall below the minimum of long-run average cost ($5 in the figure). The small firm would thus be unable to earn an adequate rate of return on its investment in its new plant. This illustrates that although a small firm may theoretically imitate the source of a larger firm's competitive advantage, it may nevertheless be unprofitable for it to do so.

Scale-based barriers to imitation and entry are likely to be especially powerful in markets for specialized products or services where demand is just large enough to support one large firm. This has been the case, for example, in the market for hot sauce, which has been monopolized by McIlhenny (producer of Tabasco sauce) for over a century. But a scale-based advantage can be sustainable only if demand does not grow too large; otherwise, the growth in demand will attract additional entry or induce smaller competitors to expand, allowing them to benefit

FIGURE 13.4
ECONOMIES OF SCALE AND MARKET SIZE AS AN IMPEDIMENT TO IMITATION.

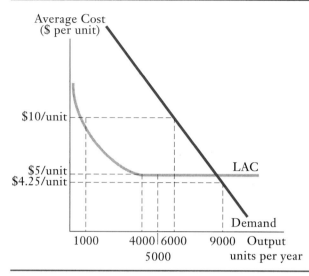

A large firm and a small firm are currently competing in a market in which the product cannot be effectively differentiated. The downward sloping straight line is the market demand curve. Production technology is characterized by economies of scale, with the long-run average cost function, LAC, declining until the minimum efficient scale of 4,000 units per year is reached. The large firm currently has a capacity of 5,000 units per year, while the small firm has a capacity of 1,000 per year. If the small firm attempted to expand capacity to 4,000 units, and both firms produced at full capacity, the market price would fall to $4.25, and at this price, the small firm would be unable to cover the costs of its investment in new plant. Thus, while the small firm could theoretically imitate the source of the large firm's cost advantage, it would be undesirable to do so.

from economies of scale. This happened in the market for table wines, as Sutter Home expanded in a growing market and virtually matched the cost advantages held by industry leaders Gallo and Taylor.

Intangible Barriers to Imitation

Legal restrictions, superior access to customers or scarce inputs, and scale economies are tangible barriers to imitation. But barriers to imitation may also be intangible, especially when the basis of the firm's advantage is distinctive organizational capabilities. We can identify these conceptually distinct intangible barriers to imitation.

- causal ambiguity

- dependence on historical circumstances

- social complexity

Causal Ambiguity   Richard Rumelt uses the term *causal ambiguity* for situations in which the causes of a firm's ability to create more value than its competitors are obscure and only imperfectly understood.[21] Causal ambiguity is a consequence of the fact that a firm's distinctive capabilities typically involve tacit knowledge. That is, capabilities are difficult to articulate as an algorithm, formula, or set of rules. Swinging a golf club in a way to hit the ball with long-range accuracy is an example of tacit knowledge: One could conceivably learn how to do it with enough practice, but it would be difficult to describe how a person should do it. Much of the know-how and collective wisdom inside an organization is of this sort. Tacit capabilities are typically developed through trial and error and refined through practice and experience; rarely are they written down or codified in procedures manuals. As a result, the firm's managers may not even be able to describe persuasively what they do better than their rivals.[22] For this reason, causal ambiguity not only may be a powerful impediment to imitation by other firms, but it may also be an important source of diseconomies of scale. For example, David Teece has pointed out that causal ambiguity might prevent the firm from translating the operational success it achieves in one of its plants to another.[23]

The tacit nature of causal ambiguity poses an additional threat. Just as superior firms may be unable to identify what they do especially well, ordinary firms may mistakenly believe that they have superior skills. Their inability to articulate their strengths may be chalked up to causal ambiguity. Absent evidence of superior skills (e.g., cost data, market research, competitive benchmarks relative to other firms, financial measures, or comments of knowledgeable observers, such as securities analysts), managers should never assume that they are more capable than competitors.

Dependence on Historical Circumstances   Competitors might also be unable to replicate the distinctive capabilities underlying a firm's competitive advantage because the distinctiveness of these capabilities is partly bound up with the history of the firm. A firm's history of strategic action comprises its unique experiences in adapting to the business environment. These experiences can make the firm uniquely capable of pursuing its own strategy and incapable of imitating the strategies of competitors. For example, in the 1960s and 1970s, Southwest Airlines was constrained by U.S. regulatory policy to operate out of secondary airports in the unregulated (and thus highly price competitive) intrastate market in Texas. The operational efficiencies and the pattern of labor relations it developed in response to these conditions may be difficult for other airlines, such as American and United, to imitate. Neither of these large carriers would be comfortable with Southwest's smaller scale of operation and historically constrained route structure.

The historical dependence of a firm's capabilities also limits its opportunities for growth. To expand much beyond its current structure, Southwest Airlines

---

[21]Rumelt, R. P., "Towards a Strategic Theory of the Firm," in R. Lamb (ed.), *Competitive Strategic Management*, Englewood Cliffs, N.J.: Prentice-Hall, 1984, pp. 556–570. See also Reed, R. and R. J. DeFillipi, "Causal Ambiguity, Barriers to Imitation and Sustainable Competitive Advantage," *Academy of Management Review*, 15, 1990: pp. 88–102.

[22]This point has been made by Polanyi, M., *The Tacit Dimension*, Garden City, NY: Anchor, 1967, and by Nelson, R. and S. Winter, *An Evolutionary Theory of Economic Change*, Cambridge, MA: Harvard University Press, 1982.

[23]Teece, D., "Applying Concepts of Economic Analysis to Strategic Management," in Harold Pennings and Associates (eds.), *Organizational Strategy and Change*, San Francisco: Jossey-Bass, 1985.

would need to develop the skills in hub-and-spoke operations and yield management that characterize large national carriers and that Southwest has little experience with. Absent distinctive capabilities for operating on a national scale, it is difficult to see how Southwest could outperform American, United, or Delta. The fate of Midway Airlines is instructive. Midway succeeded as long as it kept within its limited route structure out of Chicago's Midway airport. When it opened a hub in Philadelphia, it soon found itself at a competitive disadvantage versus other carriers and went bankrupt.

Historical dependence also implies that a firm's strategy may only be viable for a limited time. To use another airlines' example, People's Express prospered in the period immediately after deregulation through a low-price strategy based on lower labor costs. This strategy was viable, however, only as long as the major carriers were burdened by high labor costs from their union contracts. In time, these costs were reduced as more labor contracts were renegotiated. This, in turn, made it difficult for People's Express to sustain its advantage.

Social Complexity   Jay Barney has pointed out that a firm's advantage may also be imperfectly imitable because socially complex processes underlie the advantage. Socially complex phenomena include the interpersonal relations of managers in a firm and the relationship between the firm's managers and those of its suppliers and customers. Social complexity is distinct from causal ambiguity. For example, every one of Toyota's competitors may understand that an important contributor to Toyota's success is the trust that exists between it and its component suppliers. But it is difficult to create such trust, however desirable it may be.

The dependence of competitive advantage on causal ambiguity, history, and social complexity implies that major organizational change runs the risk of neglecting these factors and thus harming the firm's position. If the sources of advantage are complex and difficult to articulate, they will also be hard to consciously redesign. This may be why organizational changes, such as reengineering, are often more successful in new or "greenfield" plants than in existing ones.

Strategic Fit

Even when intangible barriers to imitation are weak (sources of a competitor's advantage are well-understood or based on easy-to-implement organizational practices), imitation might still be difficult when a firm has attained what Michael Porter calls *strategic fit*.[24] Porter argues that to succeed strategic positioning must get an entire system of activities "right." Strategic fit exists when a firm's activities form a coherent, mutually-reinforcing whole.

In Porter's view, a company like Southwest Airlines is successful, not because it performs one activity so well, but because its choices among a whole set of activities are tightly linked and reinforce one another. To illustrate, Southwest's low-cost position in the airline industry is enhanced by its ability to keep its planes in the air longer than other airlines. Its ability to offer frequent departures and its exceptional on-time performance (which gives Southwest benefit parity with competitors that offer more "frills" or better frequent-flier programs) also depends on

---

[24]The ensuing discussion of strategic fit is based on Porter, M. E., "What Is Strategy?" *Harvard Business Review*, 74, November–December 1996: pp. 61–78. The discussion of Southwest Airlines below draws from Porter's analysis of Southwest on p. 70 of this article.

its intense aircraft utilization. So how does Southwest manage to keep its planes in the air more than its competitors? One reason is that Southwest's ground logistics allow it to turn planes around in 15 minutes. But Southwest's legendary skill in turning planes around would be of little value if it operated out of congested airports, such as O'Hare in Chicago or LaGuardia in New York, where traffic delays would routinely nullify any benefit that Southwest would enjoy from loading and unloading passengers quickly. Thus, Southwest's decision to fly from satellite airports, such as Chicago's Midway, whenever possible, enhances the value of its ground logistics skills. Similarly, quick ground turnaround is far more valuable for Southwest, which operates point-to-point service, than for an airline that operates through the hub-and-spoke concept. (Hub-and-spoke airlines, such as United and American, must frequently hold a flight at the gate at a hub airport like O'Hare to collect late-arriving passengers from other flights.) Thus, its choice to provide point-to-point service also boosts the value of Southwest's skills in ground logistics. Rapid on-the-ground turnaround would be hard to attain if Southwest offered in-flight meals. (A Boeing 737 would have to be loaded with 150 to 170 fresh meals or snacks while waiting on the ground, a time-consuming activity.) Thus, its choice to provide no-frills in-flight service also makes Southwest's skills in ground logistics more valuable. Southwest's superior ground logistics are rooted in the exceptional productivity of its ground crews, which in turn is enhanced by Southwest's flexible work rules. Southwest can negotiate flexible work rules because it pays its crew members higher-than-average compensation (though not high enough to offset workers' superior productivity). Southwest's choices with respect to ground logistics, served airports, point-to-point service, in-flight services, employee work rules, and employee compensation form, in Porter's view, a coherent whole that allows Southwest to excel at creating economic value in the airline business.

Strategic fit, according to Porter, creates a powerful barrier to imitation. To successfully imitate a company whose activities are characterized by strategic fit, a rival has to align an entire system of activities. The odds of failure rise exponentially when a firm has to imitate simultaneously on multiple dimensions that must fit together in a particular way. To see why, suppose that the economic value created by a firm within a particular business depends on N discrete activities. For simplicity, imagine that a firm can either perform the activity well or poorly. Porter's notion of strategic fit is that a firm can succeed only when it performs *all* N activities well. If one firm in the market has achieved strategic fit and a prospective imitator has a 90 percent chance of performing any single activity well, its probability of successful imitation is $.90^N$. This probability diminishes rapidly as N goes up. If $N = 15$, the probability of successful imitation is just over 20 percent.

The experience of CALite, Continental's failed no-frills airline, illustrates the difficulties of imitating an entire system of activities. CALite copied some of elements of Southwest's success formula (e.g., no-frills in-flight service, no preassigned seating), but not others. For example, Continental's attempt to match Southwest's speed in ground turnaround time was done in by congestion in the airports it operated from and by its mixed fleet of jets. While Southwest passengers will often cheerfully put up with no-frills service because they know that Southwest has an impeccable on-time record, no-frills service was a disaster at CALite because of the airline's dismal on-time performance. (Passengers left their CALite flights both hungry and late!) And the cost savings from CALite's no-frills service were nullified because Continental maintained a full reservations staff for its traditional airline service and continued to pay standard travel agent commissions for CALite bookings. CALite folded after barely a year of operation, and its failure cost Continental CEO Robert Ferguson III his job.

Early-Mover Advantages

This section discusses four distinctive isolating mechanisms that fall under the heading of early-mover advantages:

- Learning curve
- Network externalities
- Reputation and buyer uncertainty
- Buyer switching costs

Learning Curve

We discuss the economies of the learning curve at length in Chapter 2. A firm that has sold higher volumes of output than its competitors in earlier periods will move farther down the learning curve and achieve lower unit costs than its rivals. Firms with the greatest cumulative experience can thus profitably "underbid" rivals for business, further increasing their cumulative volume and enhancing their cost advantage.

Network Externalities

For some products, such as computer software or consumer electronics, an individual consumer's benefit from purchasing the product is greater the more consumers currently use the product or are expected to use it in the near future. For example, the more consumers who use a particular spreadsheet, such as Microsoft's Excel, the more likely it is that books will be published giving tips about how to use it more efficiently and the greater is the chance that the user can find a friend or coworker who can help solve specific problems that arise when using the product. Economists refer to this phenomenon as a network externality: When additional consumers join the "network" of users, they create a positive "external" benefit for consumers who are already part of the network. When a network externality exists, a firm that has made more sales than its competitors in early periods and has thus developed a large installed base has an advantage when competing against firms with smaller installed bases. This further increases the firm's installed base relative to its competitors, increasing the firm's advantage even more.

eBay, the online trading community, is an example of a company that has created a sustainable advantage through network externalities. eBay was launched in 1995 by Pierre Omidyar, who created the Internet site to help his girlfriend buy and sell Pez dispensers. Early on, eBay attracted people interested in buying and selling all kinds of collectibles. Today, one can buy almost anything at eBay, including expensive jewelry, stereo equipment, baseball trading cards, and even the occasional Lexus or Ferrari (the real things, not toys!). Buyers like eBay because there are so many items for sale and because there are often several sellers of the same items. (We found four different sellers offering the 1960s yachting board game Regatta.) In addition, eBay offers buyers information about the credibility of sellers. Sellers like eBay because there are so many buyers. Thus, the sheer volume of transactions on eBay brings buyers and sellers back for more. eBay makes a small commission (2–5 percent on most transactions), but with over one million items for sale every week, this is more than enough to make eBay one of the most profitable Internet companies.

Network externalities can influence rivalry not only between firms, but also between different technologies, as illustrated by the battle between the VHS and Beta formats in video cassette recorders (VCRs). A consortium of Japanese firms led by Sony pioneered Beta-format technology. When Sony introduced its machines ahead of schedule, Victor Corporation of Japan (JVC) reacted by introducing a VHS format VCR. Though Beta-format was superior to VHS on many dimensions, Sony's high prices allowed VHS makers to capture a large share of the U.S. market. As the installed base of VHS users grew throughout the 1980s, its advantage over the Beta format became ever larger as more and more producers of videos made titles available under VHS but not under Beta. Eventually, sales of the Beta-format VCRs fell to near zero in the United States, and Beta-format tapes are no longer produced.

XAMPLE 13.4

QWERTY

You have probably noticed that the first six keys in the top row of letters on the keyboard of your personal computer are Q, W, E, R, T, and Y. This corresponds to how keys have been arranged on typewriters for over a century. But the QWERTY keyboard is not the only arrangement that could be used. Most of the world's records for speed typing have been set on typewriters that use the Dvorak Simplified Keyboard (DSK), patented in 1932 by August Dvorak and W. L. Dealey. Moreover, during the 1940s, the U.S. Navy conducted experiments that revealed that the cost of teaching a group of experienced typists to use DSK would have a payback period of 10 days due to their increased speed. Despite occasional attempts to generate interest in the Dvorak keyboard (e.g., in the 1980s, Apple equipped its Apple IIC computers with a switch that converted its keyboard from QWERTY to DSK), the QWERTY arrangement remains the industry standard.

Why? Some latter-day champions of DSK have attributed the persistence of the QWERTY keyboard to a conspiracy among members of the typewriter oligopoly to suppress an innovation that would, by making typing more efficient, decrease the demand for typists and, ultimately, typewriters. Yet, this would not explain why modern producers of computer keyboards continue to stick to QWERTY. A more plausible explanation involves network externalities. This is the explanation the economic historian Paul David gives in his entertaining analysis of "QWERTY-nomics."[25]

---

[25]The account of David's research given here draws from Paul A. David, "Clio and the Economics of QWERTY," *American Economic Review*, 75, May 1985: pp. 332–337. For further discussion, see also Paul A. David, "Understanding the Economics of QWERTY: The Necessity of History," chapter 4 in W. N. Parker (ed.), *Economic History and the Modern Economist*, New York: Basil Blackwell, 1986.

David notes that early typewriters had a serious design limitation: The printing point was located underneath the flat paper carriage. As a result, what was typed was invisible unless the typist raised the carriage to remove the paper. When an operator was typing fast, the typebars would sometimes jam; then each succeeding stroke typed the same letter onto the paper. This would be discovered only after the typist removed the paper from the carriage to see what had been printed, causing much frustration. The QWERTY keyboard evolved during the years 1867–1873 in the Milwaukee, Wisconsin, workshop of a printer and inventor named Christopher Latham Scholes, who after much experimentation, found that this arrangement minimized typebar clashes. Within a year of the licensing of Scholes' typewriter for manufacturing by E. Remington and Sons, Remington's mechanics had perfected the QWERTY keyboard. For Remington, a pleasing side benefit of the QWERTY arrangement was that the first row of the keyboard contained all of the letters a salesman would need to type out the Remington brand name, TYPEWRITER.

The next two decades witnessed tremendous technological progress in the design of typewriters. Not only were machines developed with visible printing points, but some designs did away with typebars altogether and relied on cylinders or balls for typing (anticipating the typing balls on IBM Selectrics). Much of this progress undermined the original rationale for the QWERTY keyboard.

Yet the QWERTY keyboard persisted. An important reason, David notes, was the development of "touch typing" in the late 1880s. Touch typing was originally taught on QWERTY keyboards. This created a powerful network externality that made it increasingly likely that a business would purchase a typewriter with a QWERTY keyboard, rather than one with some other arrangement. But if the savings from using alternative systems, such as DSK, were so large, why didn't businesses purchase typewriters with other keyboards and retrain their workers to use them? The answer lies in the separation of the ownership of the "hardware" (i.e., the typewriter, which was owned by the business) and the "software" (i.e., the touch-typing skill, which was "owned" by the individual worker). Few businesses would have found it worthwhile to provide their workers with a generalized skill that the workers could take elsewhere. Few individuals would have found it worthwhile to invest in developing these skills because at the turn of the century, there was virtually no market for "at-home" typewriters. With weak incentives for businesses and individuals to alter their skills, manufacturers of non-QWERTY machines found that the most profitable course of action was to become QWERTY-compatible. The development of the touch-typing know-how was thus reinforced by an increase in the installed base of QWERTY machines. By the early twentieth century, QWERTY had become the entrenched standard and has remained so, even though its original rationale has disappeared.

Reputation and Buyer Uncertainty

In the sale of experience goods—goods whose quality cannot be assessed before they are purchased and used—a firm's reputation for quality can give it a significant early-mover advantage.[26] Consumers who have had a positive experience with

---

[26]In Chapter 12 we discuss the distinction between experience goods and search goods and the implications of that distinction for competitive positioning.

a firm's brand will be reluctant to switch to competing brands if there is a chance that the competing products will not work. Buyer uncertainty coupled with reputational effects can make a firm's brand name a powerful isolating mechanism. Once the firm's reputation has been created, the firm will have an advantage competing for new customers, increasing the number of customers who have had successful trials, and thus further strengthening its reputation.

The nature of a later mover's disadvantage can be illustrated with a simple example.[27] Consider a new brand of analgesic that is competing with the brand that pioneered this product category. The pioneer entered the market at a price of $2.50, and at that price, a certain number of consumers tried its product. Suppose that the pioneer's product works, that is, it treats sinus headaches more effectively and with fewer side effects than aspirin. What price should the new brand charge? It would almost certainly have to charge less than $2.50. Why? Those consumers who purchased the analgesic from the pioneer and liked it will not switch to the newcomer if the prices are similar. Those who did not purchase it from the pioneer because they felt the price was too high would presumably be unwilling to buy it from the newcomer at the same price. And those who had not previously considered the product would presumably be drawn by the reputation of the pioneer. It follows, then, that the later mover can penetrate the market only by selling at a price below the pioneer's, even if both products are indistinguishable. If later movers fail to penetrate the market, the reputation of the early mover becomes stronger over time, as more and more consumers purchase the brand and are satisfied with it.

IBM's competitive advantage in the market for mainframes was, for years, sustained by considerations such as these. The saying, "You'll never get fired for buying an IBM," captures this point. In the 1970s, one industry expert said that it would take at least a 30 percent difference in the price-performance ratio to induce a customer to choose a competing brand over IBM.[28] IBM's reputational advantage also extended to peripheral equipment, such as tape drives. For example, Gerald Brock reports the results of an internal IBM study that revealed that 46 percent of IBM's customers would pass up a 20 percent discount from a competitor and continue to purchase equipment from IBM.[29]

Of course, the new entrant could try to overcome a pioneering brand's reputational advantage by advertising to persuade consumers that its product's benefits are superior to those of the early mover. However, this is easier said than done. Research suggests that pioneering brands profoundly influence the formation of consumer preferences.[30] If a pioneer can persuade enough consumers to try its product, consumers will consider its attributes the ideal for that type of product. To persuade consumers to switch to a new brand, they must perceive the new brand as significantly better than the pioneer brand. A good example of the per-

---

[27]The analysis in this section is based on Richard Schmalensee's paper, "Product Differentiation Advantages of Pioneering Brands," *American Economic Review*, 72, June 1982: pp. 349–365.

[28]This comes from Greer, D. F., *Industrial Organization and Public Policy*, 3d ed., New York: Macmillan, 1992, p. 141.

[29]Brock, G. W., *The U.S. Computer Industry: A Study of Market Power*, Cambridge, MA: Ballinger, 1975.

[30]See, for example, Carpenter, G. S. and K. Nakamoto, "Consumer Preference Formation and Pioneering Advantage," *Journal of Marketing Research*, August 1989: pp. 285–298.

ceptual advantage a pioneering brand enjoys is Chrysler's position in the minivan market. Chrysler introduced the first minivan in 1983. Even though Chrysler's minivans are not significantly superior or lower priced than those of Ford or GM, in the mid-1990s Chrysler made nearly two out of every three American minivans. The resilience of the Tylenol brand against competitors following its 1984 tampering crisis is another example of the advantage pioneering brands enjoy.

EXAMPLE 13.5

THE DEMISE OF THE BRAND?

The 1990s were difficult for many established brands. In the ready-to-eat cereal industry, the market share of private-label brands (i.e., cereal sold under a supermarket's label) more than doubled between 1986 and 1992. In the cigarette industry, Philip Morris' stock price dropped by nearly 25 percent when it reduced the price of its flagship brand Marlboro in response to competitive incursions by discount cigarettes (some of the most popular of which were sold by Philip Morris! See Example 9.4). More generally, research by the advertising agency BBDO suggests that nearly two-thirds of consumers around the world believe that there are "no relevant or discernable differences" among competing brands for many products.[31] Other studies have found relatively low levels of brand loyalties for such products as canned vegetables, garbage bags, blue jeans, and batteries.[32]

These examples remind us that early-mover advantages based on brand name reputation may not last forever. This is true for several reasons. First, the benefits from reputation can be overexploited. For example, managers may misjudge the relevant price elasticity of demand and price the brand too high. This happened to brands such as Kraft Singles cheeses and Pillsbury cake mixes in the early 1990s, allowing private-label brands to make inroads and undermine the perceptual advantages the established brand name enjoyed. At the same time, grocers established their own "brand names." For example, the British grocer Sainsbury's store brands from detergents to chocolates enjoy images and command prices comparable to the world's leading brands.

Second, reputation benefits may not be defensible against the efforts of buyers to appropriate them. For example, advances in information technology have increased the savvy with which supermarket chains and mass merchandisers allocate scarce shelf space. In the 1980s and 1990s, many consumer goods manufacturers responded to this increase in buyer power by reducing the relative proportion of their marketing budgets that went to advertising and increasing the proportion that went to promotions, such as shelf-space allowances (discounts in the wholesale price in return for a promise of prominent shelf space), aimed at persuading retailers to carry their products.

---

[31]This survey is reported in "Shoot Out at the Check Out," *The Economist*, June 5, 1993: pp. 69–70.

[32]See, for example, the data reported in "Brand Loyalty Is Rarely Blind Loyalty," *Wall Street Journal*, October 19, 1989, pp. B1, B8.

Third, changes in tastes, demographics, or even macroeconomic conditions can also undermine the power of an established brand name reputation. For example, marketing research suggests that higher-income people are more brand-loyal and less price-sensitive than lower-income people. The recession of the early 1990s may have weakened the power of established brands as consumer incomes declined and more consumers were tempted to shop on the basis of price, rather than reputation.

Finally, technology can weaken the advantages of established brands. Technological advances in manufacturing have raised the quality of many consumer packaged goods and have made it easier for manufacturers to extend established product lines. A third more new products were introduced in the United States in 1992 than in 1987. This proliferation may blur distinctions among competing brands, altering consumer perceptions of the differences among them, and increasing an established brand's price elasticity of demand.

$\mathcal{E}$XAMPLE 13.6

ENDOGENOUS SUNK COSTS AND SUSTAINABILITY IN FROZEN FOODS

In Chapter 2 we distinguished between exogenous and endogenous sunk costs. Exogenous sunk costs, such as the costs of building a factory, are typically associated with the technological requirements of production. These requirements are not usually associated with endogenous sunk costs, such as the costs of advertising a product to build its brand name.

As discussed previously, exogenous sunk costs can protect a scale-based cost advantage of an incumbent firm. Entrants and smaller rivals will be reluctant to sink costs into specialized production equipment and factories, knowing that the market is not large enough to support several big firms. However, as we also discussed, when the market grows, exogenous sunk costs provide less protection. When the market is big enough to support several big firms, an entrant or smaller rival might find it worthwhile to make capital investments aimed at achieving minimum efficient scale production.

Endogenous sunk costs also protect incumbents because they force entrants to make substantial investments to establish brand equity. But endogenous sunk costs differ from exogenous sunk costs in an important way: As market size grows, an incumbent firm often has an incentive to advertise even more, further strengthening the power of its brand name. The incentive to escalate advertising expenditures occurs because as the market grows, a given increase in market share (e.g., a 1 percentage point increase in share) brings in more and more revenue. It is thus increasingly valuable for an established firm to pursue this increased business through advertising. The escalation of advertising expenditures by incumbent firms makes it all the more difficult for less established rivals or new entrants to build the reputations of their brands. At the least, they have to match the escalating advertising expenditures of their established rivals. And if these established rivals benefit from economies of scale in advertising (as we discussed in Chapter 2), new entrants might have to outspend their established rivals on advertising to increase their presence in the market. Thus, when there are significant endogenous sunk costs, growth in the market can strengthen the position of incumbent firms. In this sense, the existence of endogenous sunk costs can create important early-mover advantages for firms that have been able to stake out brand name reputations early in the history of a product category. The sustained success of firms, such as Kellogg's in ready-to-eat cereal, and Anheuser-Busch in beer, that have dominated their industries for close to 50 years testifies to the economic power of endogenous sunk costs.

John Sutton finds evidence of the importance of endogenous sunk costs in creating sustainable competitive advantage in many food processing and beverage industries, including margarine, frozen foods, ready-to-eat cereal, soft drinks, and beer.[33] Sutton determines the required up-front exogenous sunk cost of a new entrant by estimating the capital a firm would need to spend to build a minimum efficient scale (MES) plant in the industries he studies. He then estimates the ratio of market size to these up-front costs determine how many firms could "fit" into the market if the only up-front costs were those associated with a minimum efficient scale plant. He finds that in the United States and other countries, one should expect to see several dozen firms in the typical food or beverage industry.

However, most food and beverage categories in the United States are not served by several dozen producers. Instead, just a few brands predominate. The U.S. frozen-food industry provides a good example. From a technological viewpoint, the MES of producing frozen foods is small. Sutton estimates that an MES plant represents less than 1 percent of the total U.S. industry size. Even so, each frozen-food submarket (e.g., frozen vegetables, frozen juice) is dominated by a small number of brands (e.g., Birds Eye, Minute Maid) that have maintained their positions for decades.

Exogenous sunk costs alone cannot account for this dominance. The explanation is that Birds Eye and Minute Maid have extremely powerful brand identities that have been reinforced over the years as these firms heavily advertise their products. Sutton observes that small and medium size firms have historically had little success in the frozen-food segments because of the substantial costs they must incur to create brand identities that are comparable to those of the industry leaders.

Sutton contrasts the history of the frozen-food category in the United States with that in the United Kingdom. In the U.K., a few supermarkets (Sainsbury's, Tesco, and Safeway) dominate. These supermarkets have established brand-name reputations of their own, reputations that cut across many food categories. With established and broad-based reputations, these grocers have had relatively low costs of establishing brand credibility in the frozen-food market. These supermarkets brands successfully compete with Minute Maid in frozen juices and Birds Eye in frozen vegetables.

The brand name reputations of the British supermarkets is so powerful that in 1997 both Sainsbury's and Tesco entered into banking. (Safeway followed in

---

[33]Sutton, J., *Sunk Costs and Market Structure*, Cambridge, MA: MIT Press, 1991.

1998.) Although many American supermarkets contain bank branches, they are operated under a bank's name, not the supermarket's. The British grocers have formed joint ventures with British banks but use the grocer's name. For example, Sainsbury's Bank is a joint venture between Sainsbury's and the Bank of Scotland. The new banks enjoyed immediate success: In its first year, Sainsbury's Bank attracted 650,000 accounts. A major worry is that the grocers might weaken their brand image. Banks, after all, must sometimes turn down loan applicants!

American grocery chains seem to be taking note from the British experience. Many have launched their own high-end private label products in hopes of establishing reputations that will give them the upper hand with branded powerhouses. Still others are teaming up with foreign private labelers whose products have already developed powerful reputations of their own. For example, the Jewel supermarket chain in Chicago and D'Agostino's in New York sell President's Choice, high-end private label products made by the Canadian supermarket chain Loblaw's.

Buyer Switching Costs

For some products, buyers incur substantial costs when they switch to another supplier. Switching costs can arise when buyers develop brand-specific know-how that is not fully transferable to substitute brands. For example, a consumer who develops extensive knowledge in using Microsoft Word would have to reinvest in the development of new know-how if he or she switched to Word Perfect. Switching costs also arise when the seller develops specific know-how about the buyer that other sellers cannot quickly replicate or provides customized after-sale services to buyers. For example, a client of a commercial bank whose managers have developed extensive knowledge of the client's business would face a switching cost if it changed banks. Finally, through coupons or "frequent-customer" points, firms can create switching costs by tying discounts to the completion of a series of transactions with customers. For example, some law firms, such as Dombroff & Gillmore of Washington, D.C., have begun to use "frequent-client" programs in pricing legal services. Customers whose billings exceed a certain amount within a given time receive credits that can be used to reduce future legal fees. The stock of these credits that a customer builds up is valuable if the customer continues to use Dombroff & Gillmore.

Switching costs can be a powerful advantage to an early mover. Suppose an established firm faces competition from a new entrant whose product provides the same quality as the established firm but requires a cost of S dollars (per unit output) to learn to use. To steal business from the early mover, the new entrant must charge a price that is at least S dollars less than the price the established brand charges.

Still, the early-mover advantage of switching costs has its limits. Although the new entrant is at a disadvantage competing for customers who have already purchased from the established firm, it is not at a disadvantage competing for new customers entering the market for the first time.[34] These customers incur a learning cost whether they purchase from the entrant or the established firm. As economists

---

[34]This, of course, abstracts from other early-mover advantages, such as network externalities or reputation, that might also protect the established firm's position.

have shown, however, an established firm might be less willing to compete on price to win these new customers than the new entrant.[35] If the established firm cuts price to attract these new customers, it reduces its profit margin on sales to its existing customers. The new entrant, which has no loyal customers, incurs no such sacrifice. The established firm's installed base of loyal customers acts like a "soft" commitment, of the kind we discussed in Chapter 9, which induces it to compete less aggressively on price than the entrant does. When this occurs, new entrants will be able to capture a disproportionate share of market demand growth over time, while the established firm's share would erode. This dynamic might explain the tremendous recent growth of the statistical software package STATA, which sells for less and enjoys higher growth than traditional market leaders, such as SAS and SPSS.

EXAMPLE 13.7

SUSTAINABILITY AT INTEL[36]

Rapid technological change or changes in customer tastes can undermine the competitive positions of longtime industrial giants like IBM. But it can also produce new successful firms that must also struggle to stay on top. A recent example is Intel.

Intel has been consistently profitable since the 1980s. In 1996, it earned net operating profits after taxes of $5.16 billion on sales of $20.8 billion, representing a 24.8 percent return on sales. Between 1987 and 1996, Intel's return on capital averaged 24.09 percent, 8 percentage points over its cost of capital of 15.98 percent.[37]

Intel's sustained success is due partly to network externalities. In 1980, IBM chose Intel's 8088 microprocessor chip to be the engine of its personal computers. With the large installed base of 8088 machines and their successors, Intel benefits from a powerful network externality: Any new chip must be compatible with the "Wintel" environment that has developed around Microsoft Windows and Intel microprocessors. The pervasiveness of the "Wintel" standard has limited the inroads made by other microprocessor manufacturers, such as Motorola and IBM, which produce chips designed for different personal computer platforms.

Intel's sustained success is also due to aggressive litigation to protect its intellectual property. Intel has been accused of fanaticism in suing any firm that

---

[35]See Klemperer, P., "Markets with Consumer Switching Costs," *Quarterly Journal of Economics*, 102, 1987: pp. 375–394, and Farrell, J. and C. Shapiro, "Dynamic Competition with Switching Costs," *RAND Journal of Economics*, 19, Spring 1988: pp. 123–137.

[36]This example draws from public sources as well as from "Intel vs. Cyrix," a paper prepared by Kellogg Graduate School of Management students David Baxter, Michael Bouhadana, Pierre Cherki, Yih-Chyuan Chiou, and Yasuhiro Kunii.

[37]Data on Intel's cost of capital and return on capital come from Stern Stewart & Company's 1997 Performance 1000 database; 1996 data on sales and profits come from Compustat.

tried to introduce a competitor for its 80X86 line of processors, which were the mainstay of DOS-based personal computers in the 1980s and early 1990s. In each case, Intel claimed that the competitor infringed Intel's patents. For example, in the mid-1980s, Intel sued NEC, charging that NEC copied Intel's "microcode"—the instructions that govern how a microprocessor reacts to electronic signals. In defending Intel's lust for litigation, CEO Andrew Grove explained, "[Property protection] is very important to us. We're basically a technology-based company. The fruits of our research and development are highly coveted." Competitors took a different view of Intel's litigious nature. Most felt that Intel filed groundless lawsuits simply to scare away competitors. Fighting lawsuits is expensive, and could deter startup firms. Advanced Micro Devices (AMD), for example, has spent over $100 million fighting Intel lawsuits (again concentrating on the use of Intel microcode).[38] In addition, the possibility of a damage award against it has limited AMD's ability to borrow money for other business expenses. AMD chairman Jerry Sanders has described Intel as the "Saddam Hussein of the semiconductor industry." Other firms that have been embroiled in patent infringement suits with Intel include Hyundai Electronics, General Instrument, Atmel, Cyrix, and NEC.

In 1994, Intel lost two key court decisions that cleared the way for more robust competition in the microprocessor market. In the first decision, a San Jose jury held that Intel could not prevent AMD from using Intel microcode. The deciding factor was a 1976 agreement between the two companies that allowed AMD to copy Intel microcode in "microcomputers."[39] The decision does not apply to other competitors. The U.S. Supreme Court, which refused to examine several lower court rulings regarding licensing arrangements with foundries (chip manufacturing plants) delivered the second setback to Intel. During the 1980s, major chip purchasers such as IBM insisted that Intel license production of chips to independent foundries to protect the purchasers against holdup by Intel. These foundries, in turn, have sold the chips to competing semiconductor makers, such as Cyrix. The court decision means that once the chips are sold, patent rights are exhausted. Firms, such as Cyrix, can now legally manufacture clones of Intel chips.

In the wake of these court decisions, AMD and Cyrix have been fighting to chip away at Intel's dominance in the market for microprocessors designed for the "Wintel" platform. Cyrix, for example, now designs and markets microprocessors that many industry observers consider superior to those of Intel. (Cyrix chips have won industry awards in recent years.) Cyrix markets its chips with nomenclature that is similar to Intel's. For instance, it uses the designation 6x86 for a chip that it markets as a faster alternative to Intel's 486 and Pentium chips.

However, Cyrix and AMD have had limited success. (In the mid-1990s, AMD, Cyrix, and other competitors accounted for just 15 percent of the microprocessor market.) This reflects another source of Intel's sustained success: its extraordinarily strong brand image. Personal computer makers, such as Dell and Compaq, are reluctant to switch from Intel microprocessors, even when price

---

[38]Slater, M., "AMD Wins Key Microcode Court Case," *Microprocessor Report*, 8, 1994: p. 10.

[39]Ibid.

differences between Intel chips and competing chips exceed 30 percent. Indeed, the "Intel Inside" logo is one of the most recognized marketing symbols in the U.S. today. Its economic power is so strong that personal computer manufacturers are willing to pay significant royalties to Intel to use the "Intel Inside" logo in their own marketing campaigns. Starting in the mid-1990s, Intel significantly increased its advertising expenditures to reinforce the power of its brand reputation. Intel has also accelerated its spending on research and development. Rather than developing microprocessor generations one at a time, as it did through the early 1990s, Intel now uses a "leapfrog" approach whereby it works on two generations of microprocessor simultaneously. These changes in how Intel competes reflects its recognition that neither network externalities nor patent protection are, by themselves, enough to sustain its competitive success. Intel must now rely on a combination of continued innovation and aggressive reinforcement of its brand reputation to outperform the crowd. The negative publicity that Intel suffered in late 1994 over flaws in its Pentium chip illustrates the challenges of this new strategic direction.

Early-Mover Advantages and Competition for Market Share

The prospect of securing an early-mover advantage often makes it valuable for a firm to capture a large share of a growing market. This suggests that although early-mover advantages may suppress competition once they are acquired, the competition for market share by firms seeking to acquire an early-mover advantage may be intense. Does the prospect of achieving early-mover advantages stimulate or suppress competition? The answer seems to depend in subtle ways on the specific early-mover advantage and the specific industry context. For example, Michael Katz and Carl Shapiro show that when network externalities exist, firms that have entered in the early stage of an industry's life cycle may be willing to set price below average variable cost to build up market share, so that they can benefit from network externalities later on.[40] On the other hand, Paul Klemperer points out that in markets with switching costs, if consumers are savvy, they will anticipate that a high-market-share firm will exploit them later on.[41] Small cuts in price today designed to attract customers who later become "captive" due to switching costs will thus not attract many consumers. As a result, each firm's demand curve early in the market will be relatively price inelastic, and firms end up setting higher prices than they would have in the absence of switching costs. The presence of switching costs may suppress competition early, as well as later, in the industry life cycle.

Early-Mover Disadvantages

Some firms pioneer a new technology or product, but fail to become the market leader. Royal Crown in diet cola and EMI with computerized axial tomography (the CAT scanner) are notable examples. This suggests that it is not

---

[40]Katz, M. L., and C. Shapiro, "Technology Adoption in the Presence of Network Externalities," *Journal of Political Economy*, 94, 1986: pp. 822–841.

[41]Klemperer, op. cit.

inevitable that early movers will achieve sustainable competitive advantage in their industries.

Early movers may fail to achieve a competitive advantage because they lack the complementary assets needed to commercialize the product.[42] This happened to EMI Ltd., a British music and electronics company perhaps best known for signing the Beatles to a record contract in the early 1960s. EMI lacked the production and marketing know-how to successfully commercialize the CAT scanner developed in its R&D laboratory, and it sold this business to GE in the late 1970s. The importance of complementary assets goes back to our discussion of the evolution of the hierarchical firm in Chapter 1. In the nineteenth century, firms that became successful early movers in their industries, such as Swift, International Harvester, and BASF, not only invested in the physical assets needed to produce their products, but also developed organizational capabilities and administrative hierarchies needed to market the product and coordinate the flow of product through the vertical chain.

Early movers may also fail to establish a competitive advantage because they "bet" on the wrong technologies or products. Thus, Wang Laboratories bet that the "office of the future" would be organized around networks of dedicated word processors. Given the uncertainty about demand or technology that exists when an early mover enters a market, these bets may be good ones, that is, the expected present value of profits exceeds the cost of entering the market. But an inherent property of decision making under uncertainty is that good decisions do not always translate into good outcomes. In the 1970s, Wang could not have known that the personal computer would destroy the market for dedicated word processors. Of course, early movers can sometimes influence how the uncertainty is resolved, as when the early mover can establish a technology standard when there are network externalities. If so, being a pioneer can be attractive, even in the face of considerable uncertainty.

But even when network externalities or learning effects are present, luck or trivial circumstances can still be important. The technology or product design that becomes the industry standard is sometimes determined by factors unrelated to the relative superiority of competing designs. For example, in the 1950s, when nuclear reactors were beginning to be built in the United States, various nuclear technologies seemed feasible: reactors cooled by light water, heavy water, gas, and liquid sodium.[43] But following the Russian's launch of the Sputnik in 1957, the priority for the U.S. government became not technological virtuosity, but quick construction of land-based reactors to preserve the U.S. lead over the Soviets in nonmilitary applications of nuclear power. Because the Navy had been using light-water designs in nuclear submarines, light-water reactors became the early favorites as the government encouraged private utilities to embark on crash programs to construct reactors. Once development began, firms moved down the learning curve for this particular technology, and by the 1960s, it had become the industry standard. This was so despite research that suggested that gas-cooled reactors might have been technologically superior.

---

[42]Teece, D., "Profiting from Technological Innovation: Implications for Integration, Collaboration, Licensing, and Public Policy," *Research Policy*, 15, 1986: pp. 285–305.

[43]This example comes from Arthur, M. B., "Positive Feedbacks in the Economy," *Scientific American*, 262, February 1990: pp. 92–99.

IMPERFECT IMITABILITY AND INDUSTRY EQUILIBRIUM

◆ ◆ ◆ ◆ ◆

In the previous section, we argued that imperfect imitation and early-mover advantages prevent the perfectly competitive dynamic from running full course. But how, specifically, would an industry equilibrium depart from the perfectly competitive model when these isolating mechanisms are at work?

Richard Rumelt and Steven Lippman point out that when there is imperfect imitability, firms in an otherwise perfectly competitive market may be able to sustain positive economic profits over long periods, but an average firm will earn below-average profits, and indeed may appear to be making negative economic profits.[44] These arguments can be illustrated with the example in Figure 13.5. The figure depicts an industry in which firms produce undifferentiated products but have different production costs. Average variable cost (AVC) and marginal cost (MC) are constant up to a capacity of 1 million units per year. We assume that this level of capacity is small relative to the overall size of the market, so the industry can accommodate many firms producing at capacity. The most efficient firms in this industry can achieve an AVC of $1 per unit. There are many potential entrants into this market, but because imitation is imperfect, not all of them can emulate those that achieve the low-cost position in the market.

The problem that each entrant faces is that before entry, it does not know what its costs will be. Accordingly, before entering the market, a prospective competitor believes that there is a 20 percent probability that its AVC will take on each of five values shown in the figure: $1, $3, $5, $7, $9. A potential entrant thus realizes that although it may be able to imitate the most efficient firms, its costs may

FIGURE 13.5
AVERAGE VARIABLE AND MARGINAL COST FUNCTIONS WITH IMPERFECT IMITABILITY.

The figure shows the different average variable cost functions (AVC) that a firm might have if it enters this market. Since AVC cost is constant up to the capacity of 1,000,000 units per year, the AVC function coincides with the marginal cost (MC) function. The firm's AVC can take on one of five values, $1, $3, $5, $7, or $9, each with equal (i.e., 20 percent) probability. The equilibrium price in this market is $6 per unit. At this price, each firm's expected economic profit is zero.

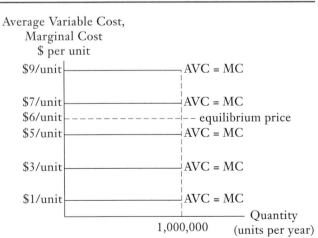

[44]Lippman, S. A. and R. P. Rumelt, "Uncertain Imitability: An Analysis of Interfirm Differences in Efficiency Under Competition," *Bell Journal of Economics*, 13, Autumn 1982: pp. 418–438.

also be higher than theirs. Suppose, finally, a firm must incur the cost of building a factory if it comes into the industry. This factory costs $36 million to build and (for simplicity) never depreciates. Investors expect a return of 5 percent on their capital, so the annualized cost of the factory is .05 × $36,000,000 = $1,800,000 or $1.8 per unit of capacity. If we suppose further that the factory represents specialized capital that can be used only in this industry, and therefore has zero scrap value, the $1.8 represents the per-unit cost of entry.

What will the equilibrium price be? Because there are many potential entrants, entry will occur as long as expected economic profit is positive, or equivalently, as long as the firm's expected operating profit (i.e., revenues minus variable costs) exceeds the costs of entry. In equilibrium, price will fall to the level at which entry is no longer attractive. Thus, at the equilibrium price, a firm's expected operating profit just equals the cost of entry. This seems straightforward, but there is one complication: Not all entrants will survive. Some will find that their AVC is greater than the price and will drop out of the market. The expected profit calculation must consider this possibility.

In this example, the price that makes a prospective entrant just indifferent between entering and not entering is $6.[45] Why? At that price, firms that learn that their AVC is $7 or $9 exit the industry because they would lose money on each unit of output they produce. These firms, in effect, earn zero operating profits, but because they have incurred the up-front entry cost, they end up net losers. A firm with an AVC of $1, $3, or $5 will produce up to its capacity, and at a price of $6, will earn a per unit operating profit of $5, $3, and $1, respectively. A potential entrant's expected operating profit per unit of capacity, when the price is $6 is thus

$$.2 \times 5 + .2 \times 3 + .2 \times 1 + .2 \times 0 + .2 \times 0 = \$1.8$$

Since this expected operating profit equals the entry costs of $1.8 per unit, a price of $6 leaves potential entrants just indifferent between entering or not. Put another way, at a price of $6, each firm's expected rate of return on its invested capital (ROIC) is equal to its cost of capital of 5 percent. This is illustrated in Table 13.1.

TABLE 13.1
SUMMARY STATISTICS FOR IMPERFECT IMITABILITY EXAMPLE

AVC	Probability	Annual Revenue@ $6/unit	Annual Total Variable Costs	Annual Operating Profit	ROIC (annual operating profits/$36 million)
$1/unit	.2	$6,000,000	$1,000,000	$5,000,000	13.89%
$3/unit	.2	$6,000,000	$3,000,000	$3,000,000	8.33%
$5/unit	.2	$6,000,000	$5,000,000	$1,000,000	2.78%
$7/unit	.2	$0	$0	$0	0%
$9/unit	.2	$0	$0	$0	0%

[45]We calculated the equilibrium price through trial and error. A systematic method exists for calculating the equilibrium price in this market, but its discussion would add little to the economic insights that this example generates.

This example illustrates Lippman and Rumelt's points. Some firms in the industry (those with AVC of $1 or $3) earn positive economic profits; that is, their ROC exceeds their cost of capital. Other firms (those with AVC of $5) fail to recover their entry cost; their return on investment is less than their cost of capital. No firm can, with certainty, match the positive economic profits of the most efficient firms. And a firm with AVC of $5 is better off remaining in the industry and earning a positive operating profit even if that profit does not fully cover the entry cost because the entry cost cannot be recovered if the firm were to exit.[46] Note also that the profit of an "average" entrant—one with AVC of $5—is less than the average profit of those firms that are active in the market.

While the numerical example is special, the insights are robust. The most efficient firms earn positive economic profits because no firm can be certain that it can imitate their competitive advantage. Average entrants earn subpar returns relative to active firms because the least efficient firms will not survive. As price declines toward the equilibrium level, these firms will exit the industry. If an average entrant survives, it will be at the bottom end of the distribution of remaining firms.[47]

The example also illustrates the distinction between *ex ante* and *ex post* economic profitability. Before entering (i.e., *ex ante*), each firm's expected economic profit is zero, that is, each firm expects to earn its 5 percent cost of capital (see Table 13.1). After entering (i.e., *ex post*), a firm's economic profit may be positive or negative; that is, a firm may earn more or less than the competitive return of 5 percent. This yields a fundamental insight: To assess the profit opportunities available in a particular business, managers should not just focus on the performance of the most successful firms. For example, the fact that some biotechnology firms (e.g., Amgen) earn annual returns on capital in excess of 50 percent does not mean a typical entrant can expect to earn this return. The average return of active firms can also be a misleading statistic of expected *ex ante* profitability. In the preceding example, the average ROC of active producers is $(13.89 + 8.33 + 2.78)/3 = 8.33$ percent, which overstates *ex ante* profitability. The reason for this is that a simple average of the profitability of active firms ignores unsuccessful firms that have lost money and exited the industry.

CHAPTER SUMMARY

◆ Under the dynamic of perfect competition, no competitive advantage will be sustainable, and the persistence of profitability over time should be weak, because most firm's profits will converge to the competitive level.

---

[46]Of course, if the firm's capital depreciated over time, then once it wears out, the firm would not reinvest if he knew that its AVC would continue to be $5. However, if reinvesting in capital gives the firm a new "draw" from the distribution of average variable costs, then at a market price of $6, the firm would be just indifferent between reinvesting and not reinvesting.

[47]We can restate this insight by drawing an analogy with a professional golf tournament. A tournament (which almost always involves four rounds of golf) typically has a "cut" after the first two rounds in which golfers with scores that place them in the bottom half of the field are not allowed to finish the tournament. Typically, golfers who achieve the average score in a tournament's first rounds just make the cut. Barring a miracle, these golfers usually end up with scores after four rounds that are at the bottom of the group of golfers who survive the "cut" and finish the tournament.

◆ Evidence suggests that the profits of high-profit firms decline over time, while those of low-profit firms rise over time. However, the profits of these groups do not converge to a common mean. This lack of convergence cannot be ascribed to differences in risk between high-profit and low-profit firms. More likely, it reflects impediments to the operation of the dynamic of perfect competition.

◆ The resource-based theory of the firm emphasizes asymmetries in the resources and capabilities of firms in the same business as the basis for sustainable competitive advantage. Resources and capabilities must be scarce and immobile—not tradable on well-functioning markets—to serve as the basis of sustainable advantage.

◆ Competitive advantages must also be protected by isolating mechanisms to be sustainable. An isolating mechanism prevents competitors from duplicating or neutralizing the source of the firm's competitive advantage. Isolating mechanisms fall into two broad classes: barriers to imitation and early-mover advantages.

◆ Specific barriers to imitation are: legal restrictions, such as patents or copyrights, that impede imitation; superior access to scarce inputs or customers; economies of scale coupled with limited market size; and intangible barriers to imitation, including causal ambiguity, dependence on historical circumstances, and social complexity.

◆ Sources of early-mover advantages include: the learning curve, network externalities, brand name reputation when buyers are uncertain about product quality, and consumer switching costs.

◆ When there are barriers to imitation, an equilibrium in a competitive market occurs at a price at which *ex ante* expected economic profits are zero. However, some firms may earn *ex post* positive economic profits. The conjunction of sunk costs and uncertainty protects these profits. No firm can be certain that it can imitate the most successful firms in the market, but a firm must incur nonrecoverable entry costs before it can learn how close it is likely to come to the efficiency of the best firms in the market.

QUESTIONS

1. "An analysis of sustainability is similar to a five-force analysis." Comment.

2. Provide an example of a firm that has co-specialized assets. Has the firm prospered from them? Why or why not?

3. Coke and Pepsi have sustained their market dominance for nearly a century. General Motors and Ford have recently been hard hit by competition. What is different about the product/market situations in these two cases that affects sustainability?

4. "Oftentimes, the achievement of a sustainable competitive advantage requires an investment and should be evaluated as such. In some cases, the benefits from the investment may not be worth the cost. Rather than trying to build a sustainable position, the firm should 'cash out,' for example, by exiting the industry, selling the assets business to another firm, or refraining from investing additional capital in the business for future growth."

   Evaluate this statement keeping a focus on two questions (a) In light of the factors that help a firm sustain a competitive advantage, explain in what sense achieving a sustainable advantage requires an "investment." (b) Can you envision circumstances under such an investment that would not be beneficial to the shareholders of the firm?

5. Do you agree or disagree with the following statements about sustaining advantage?

   a. In a market with network externalities, the product that would potentially offer consumers the highest "B-C" inevitably comes to dominate.

   b. Unusually high-performing firms may get that way either by outpositioning their competitors, belonging to high-performing industries, or both.

c. If the sunk costs of entering industry A exceed the sunk costs of entering industry B, then there will certainly be fewer firms in industry A than in industry B.

d. The Kronos Quartet (a popular classical string quartet) provides an example of co-specialized assets.

6. Which of the following circumstances are likely to create first-mover advantages?

a. Maxwell House introduces the first freeze-dried coffee.

b. A consortium of U.S. firms introduce the first high-definition television.

c. Smith Kline introduces Tagamet, the first effective medical treatment for ulcers.

d. Wal-Mart opens a store in Nome, Alaska.

7. Each of the following parts describes a firm that was an early mover in its market. In light of the information provided indicate whether the firm's position as an early mover is likely to be the basis of a sustainable competitive advantage.

a. An early mover has the greatest cumulative experience in a business in which the slope of the learning curve is 1.

b. A bank has issued the largest number of automated teller machine cards in a large urban area. Banks view their ability to offer ATM cards as an important part of their battle for depositors, and a customer's ATM card for one bank does not work on the ATM systems of competing banks.

c. A firm has a 60 percent share of T3MP, a commodity chemical used to make industrial solvents. Minimum efficient scale is thought to be 50 percent of current market demand. Recently, a change in environmental regulation has dramatically raised the price of a substitute chemical that indirectly competes with T3MP. This change undermines the market for the substitute, which is about twice the size of the market for T3MP.

8. In defending his company against allegations of anticompetitive practices, Bill Gates claimed that if someone developed an operating system for personal computers that was superior to Microsoft's Windows '95 operating system, it would quickly become the market leader, just as Gates' DOS system became the market leader in the early 1980s. Opponents countered that the market situation in the late 1990s was different than in the early 1980s, so that even a markedly superior operating system might fail to capture significant market share. Comment.

THE ORIGINS OF COMPETITIVE ADVANTAGE: INNOVATION, EVOLUTION, AND THE ENVIRONMENT

14

*P*erhaps no product so epitomizes the emergence of Japanese technological and marketing muscle on a global scale than the videocassette recorder (VCR). Chapter 13 recounts the battle that took place in the 1980s between the Beta format (pushed by Sony) and the VHS format (pushed by Victor Corporation of Japan [JVC]).[1] However, the battle to shape the future of the video recording industry began nearly 25 years earlier when the American-based Ampex Corporation invented videotape and a video recording and playback machine. Ampex translated its innovative success into a dominant position in the market for high-performance video recording systems for commercial users. Throughout the 1960s, Ampex sought to develop a cartridge-based video player and an associated video camera for the household market, and in 1970 it introduced a system known as Instavision. But Instavision was a commercial flop: It cost more than $1,500 for a cumbersome-looking video player and $500 for the camera. Two years later, Ampex abandoned the project, concentrating instead on commercial applications of video-recording technology.

Two other American entrants into the VCR-race, Cartridge Television Inc. (CTI) and RCA, also failed. CTI developed a video recording and playback machine that was included as a feature on high-end television sets manufactured by Admiral and Packard Bell. However, the product was plagued by technological glitches, and despite an agreement with Columbia and United Artists to provide films on videotape, there were not enough films to maintain consumer interest.[2] RCA, which pioneered the color television set, sought to develop a commercially viable VCR in the early 1970s. But in 1977 it too abandoned its efforts, because it

---

[1] In the early 1950s, Matsushita purchased a 50 percent ownership in then financially troubled JVC. However, JVC has generally been independently managed and has competed with Matsushita in the markets they both serve.

[2] CTI eventually went bankrupt.

could not develop an economical process for manufacturing its VCR designs and because it believed that the videodisc would become the preferred design for playing back recorded images.

While the Americans were faltering, foreign firms were succeeding. By the mid-1970s, JVC, Matsushita, Sony of Japan, and Philips of the Netherlands had all mastered the daunting technological challenges of manufacturing video recorders for a commercial market (e.g., figuring out how to compress two to four hours of videotape into a cartridge the size of a small paperback). Sony's Betamax system got an early head start after Matsushita decided to delay the production of its system, which it believed was technologically inferior to the Video Home System (VHS) being developed by JVC. Betamax developed a strong following in the high-end professional market. However, JVC set the stage for overtaking Sony in the far larger household market when it introduced a VHS machine that could record for two hours, as compared with just one hour for the Sony machines. Soon after, JVC and Matsushita convinced other consumer electronics firms, such as Thorn-EMI in the U.K., Thompson in France, and AEG-Telefunken in West Germany, to adopt the VHS model in their machines, giving VHS an edge in the race to become the technology standard. Philips, whose V2000 format was incompatible with both Sony and JVC, introduced its product a year and a half after JVC introduced VHS. Although it had managed to keep pace with its Japanese rivals in the race to develop the technology, Philips' late introduction put it at a disadvantage in the competition to accumulate an installed base of users. Eventually, Philips also began to manufacture VCRs in the VHS format.

This example shows that the origins of a firm's current marketplace success often stretch far back in time. JVC-Matsushita's success in the VCR business was shaped by decisions and commitments that those firms made 15 to 20 years before VCRs became commercially viable. This suggests that developing a competitive advantage involves looking deep into the future to anticipate unmet or even unarticulated consumer needs, betting on alternative technologies, investing in the development of new products and new capabilities to produce and deliver those products to market, and then being the first to introduce those products to the marketplace to benefit from early-mover advantages, such as network externalities or the learning curve that we discussed in Chapter 13.

This chapter studies the origins of competitive advantage. In Chapter 13 we argued that competitive advantage arises from a firm's ability to exploit market shocks and opportunities, and early-mover advantages and various barriers to imitation by other firms then protect the firm's advantage. But we did not discuss why some firms are better or luckier than others at exploiting shocks or taking advantage of opportunities. Why, for example, did Ted Turner, and not the established networks, seize the opportunity to develop a television network devoted entirely to news? Why was Honda, and not Harley-Davidson or British Triumph, able to tap into what turned out to be a large U.S. market for light- and middle-weight motorcycles? Why did JVC succeed where Ampex failed in the market for VCRs?

We divide this chapter into six main parts. The first part discusses the role of innovation and entrepreneurship in a market economy, emphasizing economist Joseph Schumpeter's notion of creative destruction and highlighting its importance for business strategy. The next part examines firms' incentives to innovate. The third part examines competition among innovators. The fourth part explores innovation from the perspective of evolutionary economics. We focus on how a firm's history and internal resources and capabilities affect its ability to innovate and develop new capabilities. The fifth part examines the relationship between the firm's local environment and its ability to gain competitive advantage. We are particularly concerned with how demand and factor market conditions, as well as the economic infrastructure in the firm's domestic market, determine competitive advantage. In the last part, we discuss the process of managing innovation inside the firm.

CREATIVE DESTRUCTION ◆ ◆ ◆ ◆ ◆

A short answer to the question, "What are the origins of competitive advantage?" is that some firms exploit opportunities for creating profitable competitive positions that other firms either ignore or cannot exploit. Seizing such opportunities is the essence of entrepreneurship. Entrepreneurship is often seen as synonymous with discovery and innovation. But, as described by the economist Joseph Schumpeter, entrepreneurship is also the ability to act on the opportunity that innovations and discoveries create:

> To undertake such new things is difficult and constitutes a distinct economic function, first, because they lie outside the routine tasks which everybody understands and secondly because the environment resists in many ways that vary, according to social conditions, from simple refusal either to finance or to buy a new thing, to physical attack on the man who tries to produce it. To act with confidence beyond the range of familiar beacons and to overcome that resistance requires aptitudes that are present in only a small fraction of the population and define the entrepreneurial type as well as the entrepreneurial function. This function does not essentially consist in either inventing anything or otherwise creating the conditions which the enterprise exploits. It consists in getting things done.[3]

Schumpeter considered capitalism to be an evolutionary process that unfolded in a characteristic pattern. Any market has periods of comparative quiet, when firms that have developed superior products, technologies, or organizational capabilities earn positive economic profits. These quiet periods are punctuated by fundamental "shocks" or "discontinuities" that destroy old sources of advantage and replace them with new ones. The entrepreneurs who exploit the opportunities these shocks create achieve positive profits during the next period of comparative quiet. Schumpeter called this evolutionary process creative destruction.

For Schumpeter, the process of creative destruction had two important implications. First, static efficiency—the optimal allocation of society's resources at a given point in time—is less important than dynamic efficiency—the achievement of long-term growth and technological improvement. Second, business strategy and market outcomes can be evaluated only in the context of creative destruction. Schumpeter criticized economists who focused exclusively on the out-

---

[3]Schumpeter, J., *Capitalism, Socialism, and Democracy*, New York: Harper & Row, 1942, p. 132.

comes of price competition when judging the social benefits of firms' performance in a market. For Schumpeter, what really counted was not price competition, but competition between new products, new technologies, and new sources of organization:

> This kind of competition is as much more effective than the other as a bombardment is in comparison with forcing a door, and so much more important that it becomes a matter of comparative indifference whether [price] competition in the ordinary sense functions more or less properly; the powerful lever that in the long run expands output and brings down prices is in any case made of other stuff.[4]

Schumpeter's ideas emphasize that the isolating mechanisms we discussed in Chapter 13 are never permanent. Competitive advantages based on inimitable resources or capabilities or early-mover advantages can eventually become obsolete as new technologies arise, tastes change, or government policy evolves. This process is depicted in Figure 14.1, which shows the hypothetical time path for profits for a firm that has achieved a sustainable advantage.

Scholars have used Schumpeter's notion of creative destruction to develop frameworks that can help managers make strategic decisions. For example,

FIGURE 14.1
HYPERCOMPETITION AND COMPETITIVE ADVANTAGE.

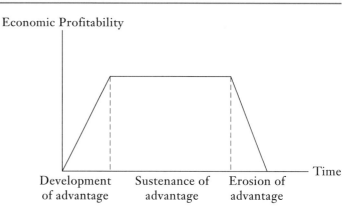

The upper diagram illustrates the dynamic of competitive advantage. Economic profits rise as the advantage is developed. They then plateau while the advantage is sustainable. Eventually the advantage is eroded, and economic profitability declines. Richard D'Aveni argues that in many markets, the period during which advantages are sustainable is shrinking. In such environments, a firm can sustain positive economic profits only by continually developing new sources of advantage, as shown in the bottom diagram.
Source: These figures are based on Figures 1–1 and 1–2 in D'Aveni, R.A., *Hypercompetition: Managing the Dynamics of Strategic Maneuvering*, New York: Free Press, 1994, pp. 8, 12.

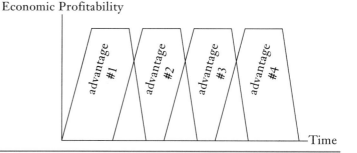

[4]Ibid., pp. 84–85.

Richard D'Aveni argues that in industries ranging from consumer electronics to airlines and computer software to snack goods, the sources of competitive advantage are being created and eroded at an increasingly rapid rate.[5] In effect, he argues that the length of the plateau in Figure 14.1 is shrinking. D'Aveni calls this phenomenon *hypercompetition* and argues that a firm's chief strategic goal should be to disrupt existing sources of advantage in its industry (including its own) and create new ones. This argument is related to the more general point that firms must create more value ("$B - C$") than do their rivals to be successful. D'Aveni reminds us that a firm that currently offers superior "$B - C$" cannot expect the status quo to last for long. Even market leaders must strive to boost "$B - C$" lest the competition overtakes them. D'Aveni cites Gillette as an example of a successful hypercompetitive firm. Indeed, Gillette recently launched the Mach 3 razor, an improvement on its market-leading Sensor.

Gary Hamel and C. K. Prahalad promote related ideas.[6] They argue that companies, such as CNN, Honda, NEC, and Sony, succeeded because of their sustained obsession with achieving global dominance in their industries. Prahalad and Hamel call this obsession *strategic intent*. The strategic intent of these companies was out of proportion to their existing resources and capabilities. Prahalad and Hamel refer to this gap between ambition and resources as *strategic stretch*. These companies had to expand and adapt their current stock of resources and create new ones. They were more concerned with "leveraging" resources than with achieving "strategic fit" between their current resources and their environment. As we discussed in Chapter 2, firms can achieve lower costs or superior quality through the economies of scope associated with leveraging resources. However, there are limits to the extent that firms can achieve economies of scope. Indeed, as Peter Kontes and Michael Mankins report in "The Dangers of Strategic Intent," most of the firms Hamel and Prahalad hold up as exemplars actually generated below average shareholder returns.[7]

The ideas of D'Aveni and Prahalad and Hamel remind us that in environments characterized by rapid technological development and fickle tastes, a firm that rests on its laurels, seeking only to harvest existing sources of advantage, can be quickly displaced by more innovative rivals. Moreover, firms may be able to create their own shocks, rather than waiting for the environment to change or for other firms to disrupt existing sources of advantage in the industry. Managers must keep this advice in perspective. Even those who have the resources may prefer not to innovate. The sunk cost effect and the replacement effect that we discuss in the next section show that it may not always pay for an established firm to match the innovative activity of its competitors. General advice can never be applied without

---

[5]D'Aveni, R., *Hypercompetition: Managing the Dynamics of Strategic Maneuvering*, New York: Free Press, 1994.

[6]Hamel, G. and C. K. Prahalad, *Competing for the Future*, Cambridge, MA: Harvard Business School Press, 1994. See also Hamel, G., and C. K. Prahalad, "Strategic Intent," *Harvard Business Review*, May–June 1989: pp. 63–76, and "Strategy as Stretch and Leverage," *Harvard Business Review*, March–April 1993: pp. 75–84.

[7]Kontes, P. and M. Mankins "The Dangers of Strategic Intent," *Marakon Associates*, April 1992.

considering the specific context in which the firm operates and the underlying economics of competitive advantage.

◆ ◆ ◆ ◆ ◆ The Incentive to Innovate

Business history contains many instances of companies with a wealth of assets—innovative products, strong reputations, deep financial resources, and powerful distribution channels—whose market position was eroded or overtaken by companies with seemingly much smaller resource bases. Xerox versus Canon in copiers, Sony versus RCA in television, and CNN versus the networks in news programming come to mind. A frequent explanation for this is that small firms are more "nimble" and less bureaucratic than large firms, and thus are more willing to innovate and break with established practices. This explanation is often expressed in familiar clichés contrasting large and small companies. The managers of large firms are "myopic" and ignore firms that come out of nowhere to challenge their dominance. Small companies are "hungry" and have the courage to pursue innovative approaches that their larger rivals lack.

Though superficially appealing, these arguments are not profound. They fail to answer a fundamental question: Assuming that their managers are rational, why would established firms be systematically less able to innovate or less willing to break with established practice than new entrants or marginal firms in an industry? Perhaps large established firms are less able to innovate due to the kinds of incentive and influence problems we described in Chapter 3. In this section we explore another possibility. Namely, under certain economic circumstances it may be rational for firms not to innovate. Two forces may make it rational for firms to refrain from innovating: (1) the sunk cost effect, and (2) the replacement effect. We also discuss a force called the efficiency effect that offsets the sunk cost and replacement effects and strengthens an established firm's incentive to innovate. We discuss each effect in detail below.

The Sunk Cost Effect

The *sunk cost effect* has to do with the asymmetry between a firm that has already made a commitment to a particular technology or product concept and one that is planning such a commitment. One result is that a profit-maximizing firm may stick with its current technology or product concept even though the profit-maximizing decision for a firm starting from scratch would be to choose a different technology or product concept. The sunk cost effect arises because a firm that has already committed to a particular technology has invested in resources and organizational capabilities that are likely to be specific to that technology and are thus less valuable if the firm switches to another technology. For an established firm, the costs associated with these investments are sunk and thus should be ignored when the firm considers whether to switch to a new technology. Ignoring these sunk costs creates an inertia that favors sticking with the current technology. By contrast, a firm that has not yet committed to a technology can compare the costs of all of the alternative technologies under consideration and is thus not biased in favor of one technology over another.

To illustrate the economics of the sunk cost effect, consider the problems of an established firm and a new entrant which are both contemplating whether to adopt a newly developed technology (denoted by a subscript N) or an established technology (denoted by a subscript O). The new technology reduces operating costs as compared with the old technology, but it entails a larger up-front investment in physical assets and know-how. For simplicity, assume that a firm's revenues are not affected by which technology it adopts. A new entrant adopts the new technology if the present value of operating costs (denoted by VC) plus up-front investment costs (denoted by I) are less than the present value of operating costs plus up-front investment costs from adopting the established technology. That is, it should adopt the new technology if

$$VC_N + I_N < VC_O + I_O$$

We can rearrange this equation as follows:

$$I_N - I_O < VC_O - VC_N$$

or

$$\Delta I < \Delta VC \qquad (15.1)$$

where $\Delta I = I_N - I_O$ and $\Delta VC = VC_O - VC_N$. This condition says that the firm will adopt the new technology if the present value of the savings in operating costs, ΔVC, from using the new technology instead of the old technology exceeds the additional investment cost, ΔI, required by the new technology. Let us assume that this condition, which we denote by (15.1), holds.

Consider, now, the problem of an established firm that has already made the investment I_O in the established technology. This investment is sunk and should be ignored when deciding whether to adopt the new technology. Suppose, further, that the established firm has benefited from accumulated experience, so its operating cost with the established technology is a fraction, αV_O (where $\alpha < 1$), of what a new entrant would hope to achieve under the established technology. The established firm goes through the same analysis as the new entrant, but gets a different condition for when adoption of the new technology is optimal:

$$VC_N - I_N < \alpha\, VC_O$$

Performing some straightforward algebraic transformations, we can express this as

$$I_N - I_O < VC_O - VC_N - (1 - \alpha)VC_O - I_O$$

or

$$\Delta I < \Delta VC - [(1 - \alpha)\, VC_O + I_O] \qquad (15.2)$$

The condition under which it pays for an established firm to adopt the new technology (denoted by [15.2]) establishes a more severe hurdle for the new technology than is the case for a new entrant. The established firm will adopt the new technology only if the additional investment cost is less than savings in operating costs less an additional amount, $[(1 - \alpha)VC_O + I_O]$ that depends on the established firm's experience advantage and the sunk costs it has already incurred. Even though condition (15.1) holds, and a new entrant adopts the new technology, condition (15.2) might not hold, and an established firm would stick with the established technology. This is the sunk cost effect.

XAMPLE 14.1

THE SUNK COST EFFECT IN STEEL:
THE ADOPTION OF THE BASIC OXYGEN FURNACE

In the early 1950s, a new steel-making technology became commercially viable: the basic oxygen furnace (BOF). The BOF reduced milling time to 40 minutes as compared with the 6 to 8 hours in the open hearth (OH) technology that had long been the industry standard. Despite the apparent superiority of BOF, few American steelmakers adopted it. Throughout the 1950s, U.S. steelmakers added nearly 50 million additional tons of OH capacity, but they did not begin to replace their OH furnaces with BOFs until the late 1960s. Meanwhile, foreign steelmakers built new plants incorporating state-of-the-art BOF technology. The cost advantage afforded by this new technology was a key reason why Japanese and Korean steelmakers penetrated the American domestic market.

Why did American steelmakers continue to invest in a seemingly inefficient technology? The standard explanation has been bad management. For example, two knowledgeable observers of the steel industry, Walter Adams and Hans Mueller, wrote:

> The most likely explanation of the hesitant adoption of the Austrian converter [i.e., the BOF] by the large American firms is that their managements were still imbued with Andrew Carnegie's motto "invention don't pay." In other words, let others assume the cost and risk of research and development, and of breaking in a new process, then we'll decide. The result was that during the 1950s, the American steel industry installed 40 million tons of melting capacity that, as *Fortune* observed, "was obsolete when it was built."[8]

Without denying the possibility of managerial myopia, there is, however, another explanation. American steel firms throughout the first half of the twentieth century had developed a considerable amount of specific know-how related to the OH technology. Their investment in this know-how was sunk: It could not be recovered if they switched to the BOF technology. This sunk investment created an asymmetry between established American firms and new Japanese firms that made it cost effective for American firms to stick with the older OH technology.

The findings of Sharon Oster's study of technology adoption in the steel industry is consistent with the hypothesis that American steel firms chose between alternative technologies based on profit-maximization criteria.[9] For example, because the BOF technology used relatively more pig iron, as opposed to scrap iron, than the OH technology, a steel plant that was located closer to sources of pig iron would save more operating costs by adopting the BOF technology. Oster found that firms that produced their own pig iron were more likely to

---

[8]Adams, W. and H. Mueller, "The Steel Industry," in Adams, W. (ed.), *The Structure of American Industry*, 7th ed., New York: Macmillan, 1986, p. 102.

[9]Oster, S., "The Diffusion of Innovation Among Steel Firms: The Basic Oxygen Furnace," *Bell Journal of Economics*, 13, Spring 1982: pp. 45–68.

adopt BOF than were firms that had to buy it from outside suppliers. More generally, Oster found that the magnitude of the savings in operating costs, ΔVC, from adopting the BOF varied considerably among firms, and that firms with larger cost savings were more likely to adopt BOF.

This is not to argue that there was not poor management in the steel industry. There almost certainly was, at least in some firms. However, we cannot attribute the lack of innovation entirely to poor management. Large sunk investments in know-how and capabilities are hard for a firm to ignore when choosing a technology. The presence of these sunk investments distinguished American producers from producers in Japan, Korea, and elsewhere who were investing in "greenfield" plants (i.e., new steelmaking facilities). Unfortunately, these differences may have planted the seeds for the competitive decline of the U.S. integrated steel sector in the 1970s and 1980s.

The Replacement Effect

Does a profit-maximizing monopolist have a stronger or weaker incentive to innovate than a new entrant? The Nobel Prize economist Kenneth Arrow pondered this question more than 30 years ago.[10] He considered the incentives for adoption of a process innovation that will lower the average variable costs of production. The innovation is drastic: Once it is adopted, producers using the older technology will not be viable competitors. Arrow compared two different scenarios: (1) the opportunity to develop the innovation is available to a firm that currently monopolizes the market using the old technology, (2) the opportunity to develop the innovation is available to a potential entrant who, if it adopts the innovation, will become the monopolist. Under which scenario, Arrow asked, is the willingness to pay to develop the innovation greatest?

Arrow concluded that assuming equal innovative capabilities, an entrant would be willing to spend more than the monopolist to develop the innovation. The intuition behind Arrow's insight is this: A successful innovation for a new entrant leads to monopoly; a successful innovation by the established firm also leads to a monopoly, but since it already had a monopoly, its gain from innovation is less than that for the potential entrant. Through innovation an entrant can replace the monopolist, but the monopolist can only replace itself. For this reason, this phenomenon is called the *replacement effect*.[11]

Arrow's insight explains why an established firm would be less willing to "stretch" itself to innovate or develop new sources of advantage than a potential entrant or a marginal firm in an industry. His logic applies not only to process innovations, but also to new product innovations.[12] Arrow's argument also shows

---

[10]Arrow, K., "Economics Welfare and the Allocation of Resources for Inventions," in Nelson, R. (ed.), *The Rate and Director of Inventive Activity*, Princeton, NJ: Princeton University Press, 1962.

[11]This term was coined by Jean Tirole. Tirole discusses the replacement effect in his book *The Theory of Industrial Organization*, Cambridge, MA: MIT Press, 1988.

[12]See, for example, Ghemawat, P., "Market Incumbency and Technological Inertia," *Marketing Science*, 10, Spring 1991: pp. 161–171.

that innovative entrants may overtake established firms, not because the latter are poorly managed or suffer disproportionately from agency costs, but because of a natural market dynamic. An established firm's success can sow the seeds of its (potential) destruction. This is not to deny that poor management, myopia, excessive risk aversion, or agency problems can hasten a dominant firm's decline. But they may not tell the entire story. Arrow's analysis is useful reminder that strategies formulated under considerable uncertainty cannot be judged solely by *ex post* outcomes.

◆ ◆

XAMPLE 14.2

INNOVATION IN THE PBX MARKET[13]

Private branch exchanges (PBXs) are dedicated switching centers that route calls from a customer's telephone to the telephone company's central exchange. Pankaj Ghemawat's study of innovation in the PBX industry illustrates a case in which the replacement and sunk cost effects shaped the incentives to innovate.

From the time PBXs were developed around the turn of the century through the late 1980s, there have been four distinct generations of PBX technology: electromechanical voice-only PBXs, electronic voice-only PBXs, voice-and-data PBXs, and voice-data-and-video PBXs. The dominant supplier of voice-only PBXs well into the 1980s was AT&T. In 1980, for example, it held 58 percent of the industry's installed base and made 46 percent of new shipments. AT&T only sold old-fashioned electromechanical PBXs, and its manufacturing costs were among the highest in the industry. Nevertheless, it was one of the most profitable producers of PBXs because its position was protected by powerful isolating mechanisms. PBXs are expensive systems meant to last for 10 to 15 years, and buyers value reliability. (Even a temporary failure of a PBX can be disastrous to a business.) Over the years, AT&T had developed a reputation for building PBXs that performed as promised, and this helped it secure both repeat and new business. AT&T also owned the wiring in its PBX installations and would not sell it to competitors. Thus, if a customer switched suppliers, the new supplier would have to rewire the customer's place of business, and this could represent about 40 percent of the cost of the new PBX. AT&T also had an important experience-based advantage: It had dealt with so many customers over the years that it could draw from an extensive information base in forecasting that buyers would need to replace existing PBX systems. The smaller, less experienced competitors in the voice-only market could not match AT&T's extensive customer knowledge and thus could not target their sales efforts as effectively as AT&T could. Finally, AT&T owned the most effective channel for distributing PBXs to final customers: the local Bell operating companies.

---

[13]This example is based on Ghemawat, P., "Market Incumbency and Technological Inertia," *Marketing Science*, 10, Spring 1991: pp. 161–171.

AT&T showed little interest in developing second-generation voice-only PBXs based on digital electronics. The leading suppliers of second-generation voice-only PBXs were Rolm, which made 10 percent of new PBX shipments in the United States in 1980, and Northern Telecom, whose 1980 share of new shipments was 8 percent. Neither these firms nor AT&T attempted to develop third-generation PBXs that integrated voice and data transmission. For example, in the early 1980s, Rolm decreased its R&D spending as a percentage of sales and concentrated instead on building an in-house sales network for selling voice-only PBXs. The pioneers of voice-and-data PBXs were marginal players in the industry or new entrants. The company that succeeded in developing a commercially successful voice-and-data PBX was InteCom, which was founded in 1978 and went public in 1982.

InteCom soon found itself in a highly competitive business with few apparent isolating mechanisms. Competing firms seeking to improve their PBX designs regularly raided design engineers, although InteCom's turnover was lower than that of many small firms due to its promise of rapid promotion and liberal stock options for its employees. Moreover, patent protection was unavailable. In 1982, InteCom held no patents and had no applications pending. Its managers estimated that any competitor could copy relevant aspects of its voice-and-data PBX design within 12 to 18 months. Yet, despite this, InteCom did not invest heavily in developing the fourth generation of PBXs: those capable of carrying not only voice and data but also video images. Instead, its strategy was to capture as much profit as it could as the first-mover in the voice-and-data segment of the PBX market and take advantage of growth opportunities that existed in this segment. The uncertain prospects for voice-data-image PBXs bolstered this inertia. InteCom's strategy succeeded, at least from the perspective of its founders. By the time it went public in 1982, InteCom's initial capital of $1.5 million had grown to over $400 million of shareholder value, of which $100 million belonged to its founders.

While the behaviors of the firms in this example are consistent with sunk cost and replacement effects, they are also consistent with other explanations of the sources and diffusion of innovations. These alternative explanations do not exclude the one we have already discussed.

The failure to develop a new generation of PBXs could stem from organizational inertia. Innovation may not be in the interest of those involved in producing the current generation of a product, and they may use their influence to impede innovation efforts by top managers. Internal resistance to change and the need for "championing" innovations are common issues in the management of innovation, and we will discuss them later in this chapter.

A reluctance to innovate could also stem from the perception that the market would not be receptive to the innovation, even though it was technically superior and feasible to produce. A common distinction in the innovation literature is between "technology push" and "demand pull" explanations.[14] In a technology push explanation, the source (or "locus") of innovation is in the firm and its prod-

---

[14]Kamien, M. I. and N. L. Schwartz, *Market Structure and Innovation*. Cambridge, UK: Cambridge University Press, 1982; Scherer, F. M., *Innovation and Growth: Schumpeterian Perspectives*, Cambridge, MA: MIT Press, 1984.

uct designers. In a demand pull explanation, the locus of innovation is the set of users outside the firm, who communicate their needs to product designers. For PBXs, the technological development of new generations made the product increasingly complex and forced users to bear more risks of failure and product obsolescence. These costs to users eventually increased the commercial viability of less sophisticated systems, such as Centrex. These systems used telephone company equipment and thus placed more of the risks of failure and obsolescence on the provider rather than the user of the product.

The Efficiency Effect

Arrow's analysis pertains to the "pure" incentive to innovate. That is, it has to do with a firm's willingness to innovate, when the innovation opportunity is not available to competitors or potential entrants. If an incumbent monopolist anticipates that potential entrants may also have an opportunity to develop the innovation, then the efficiency effect comes into play. The *efficiency effect* has to do with the fact that the benefit to a firm from being a monopolist as compared with being one of two competitors in a duopoly is greater than the benefit to a firm from being a duopolist as compared with not being in the industry at all (and thus earning no profit).[15] In other words, a monopolist usually has more to lose from another firm's entry than the entrant has to gain from entering the market. The reason is that the entrant not only takes business from the monopolist, but also tends to drive down prices. The efficiency effect makes an incumbent monopolist's incentive to innovate stronger than that of a potential entrant.[16]

In the competition between established firms and potential entrants to develop new innovations, the replacement effect, the efficiency effect, and the sunk cost effect will operate simultaneously. Which effect dominates depends on the specific conditions of the innovation competition. For example, the replacement and sunk cost effects may dominate if the chance that smaller competitors or potential entrants will develop the innovation is low. Then, the main effect of the innovation for the established firm will be to cannibalize current profits and reduce the value of established resources and organizational capabilities associated with the current technology. By contrast, the efficiency effect may dominate when the monopolist's failure to develop the innovation means that new entrants almost certainly will. In this case, a key benefit of the innovation to the established firm is to stave off the deterioration of profit that comes from additional competition

---

[15]The efficiency effect arises because competition destroys industry profitability. Thus, total industry profit if the monopolist develops the innovation will exceed total industry profit under the duopoly competition that results if the entrant develops the innovation.

[16]This assumes that the innovation will not make the established firm's competitive position nonviable if the entrant develops the innovation but the established firm does not. In a race to develop a drastic innovation that would make the current technology or product concept nonviable, an entrant's incentive to develop the innovation would be equally as strong as an incumbent's.

from firms that may develop a cost advantage or a benefit advantage over it if they successfully innovate.

INNOVATION COMPETITION ◆ ◆ ◆ ◆ ◆

Part Two emphasizes the importance of thinking about how competitors will respond when a firm develops products and chooses prices for them. It is equally critical to anticipate rivals' responses when selecting a level of investment in R&D. Even if a firm takes into account the R&D expenses necessary to produce a marketable product, the size of the target market, and the fit between the project under consideration and other projects that the firm is working on, it may still fail if it does not anticipate the possibility that other firms may innovate first.

When several firms are competing to develop the same product, the firm that does so first can gain significant advantage. The most obvious advantage is that the first innovator may be able to protect its ideas with patents and trademarks. Consider, for example, the race between Thomas Edison and Alexander Graham Bell to develop the modern telephone. Bell developed it first and claimed patent rights. Edison developed a similar prototype shortly thereafter. Bell's patent claim withstood court challenges from Edison. Because of the network externality that developed around the Bell telephone system, the patent has proved to be worth hundreds of billions of dollars.[17]

Even without the legal protection of patents and trademarks, the first innovator may gain significant early-mover advantages.[18] For example, if there are network externalities, the first innovator may gain an important head start in the race to become the technology standard. The first innovator may also benefit from the effect that its product has on consumer perceptions by being the first to market. As we discussed in Chapter 13, consumers view the attributes of pioneering brands as embodying the ideal configuration against which all other brands are benchmarked.

Still, being the first to develop a product may not be sufficient unless the firm can acquire the capabilities needed to manufacture the product and to market it. For example, biotechnology companies race each other to patent both products and the processes for making them. The California biotech firm Celtrix holds valuable patents on a cell-regulating protein that may help heal damaged cells. Though Celtrix developed the protein, Genentech won the patent for the process for producing the protein. Celtrix had to enter a joint venture arrangement on terms favorable to Genentech to get the rights to use the patented process.

Patent Races

The term *patent race* describes the battle between firms to innovate first. To develop a better understanding of the forces that drive innovation, economists have studied different models of patent races. In these models, the first firm to complete the project

---

[17]Smith, G. S., *The Anatomy of a Business Strategy: Bell, Western Electric, and the Origins of the American Telephone Industry.* Baltimore, MD: Johns Hopkins University Press, 1985, pp. 35–38, 99.

[18]In Chapter 13 we discuss early-mover advantages in detail.

"wins" the patent race and obtains exclusive rights to develop and market the product. The losing firms get nothing. While this is an extreme characterization, it does highlight the often critical advantage that goes to the first innovator, and it gives insight into how the magnitude of that advantage affects the incentives to innovate. These models also emphasize an important strategic point: Firms in a patent race must anticipate the R&D investments of competitors. Failure to do so can be costly.

Models of patent races examine the importance of uncertainty in the R&D process, the timing of R&D investments, and entry. These studies suggest that when a firm engaged in a patent race is determining whether to increase its investment in innovation, it must account for the following factors:

- How much does the investment increase its R&D productivity and thereby also increase its chances of winning the patent race? If there are diminishing returns to productivity, then increasing R&D outlays may not greatly improve the firm's chances of winning the race. If there are increasing returns, additional expenditures are usually warranted, unless they provoke competitors to increase their expenditures.

- Will other firms increase their R&D expenditures in response, thereby decreasing the firm's chances of winning the patent race? This competitive response will reduce the profitability of R&D whether it demonstrates increasing or decreasing returns.

- How many competitors are there? If there are diminishing returns to R&D, then several small R&D firms may be a bigger threat to successful innovation than a single competitor that spends the same amount of money as do all the small firms put together. If there are increasing returns, then one large firm conducting extensive R&D may be a more formidable competitor. In this case, large investments in R&D by a single firm may crowd out investments by other firms.

Choosing the Technology

Patent race models often assume that firms have a single R&D methodology, and may choose only how much to spend on it. In reality, however, firms may be able to select from a variety of methodologies. For example, while some supercomputer makers pursued vector technology that emphasized improvements in hardware, others pursued massively parallel processing that utilized improvements in software. When choosing a research methodology, firms must consider the methods their rivals are pursuing. Two dimensions of interest when choosing a methodology are (1) the riskiness of the methodology; and (2) the degree to which the success of one methodology is correlated with the success of another.

Riskiness of R&D

Research methodologies may have different completion dates. When one methodology is demonstrably faster than another, the choice is clear. But what if two methods have the same expected completion date, but the date for one is less certain than for the other? To see how competition affects the choice of methods, consider a firm choosing between two approaches to developing a new product. If either approach succeeds, and the firm is the first to develop the product, it can obtain a patent or achieve some other early-mover advantage. Approach A follows time-honored methods for R&D and is certain to be successful within two or three years. In contrast, the time frame for Approach B is relatively unproved. While it is sure eventually to bear fruit, success may come within one to four years. Both approaches distribute the time to innovation uniformly, meaning that it is equally likely to be anytime in the interval.

A monopolist will generally be indifferent between the two approaches, because both have identical expected times to development. If several firms are competing to develop the same product, however, each will wish to choose Approach B. To see why, suppose that there are four firms, and each chooses Approach A. Each firm has a .25 chance of being the first to innovate. Now suppose that one firm switches to Approach B. It has a .33 chance of innovating in less than two years, in which case it is sure to be the first. Even if it innovates after two years, it could still be the first to innovate. Thus, its chances of being first are greater than .33. Since .33 is greater than its .25 which is its chance of being first when all firms chose Approach A, the firm will prefer Approach B. A similar argument may be used to show that all firms will prefer Approach B, no matter what their competitors do.[19]

Correlated Research Strategies

The previous example assumed that Approaches A and B were independent of each other, implying that the success or failure of one approach was unrelated to the success or failure of the other. In fact, research methods may be correlated, so that if one is successful, the other is also more likely to be successful. In general, society benefits more when firms pursue uncorrelated approaches than when they pursue correlated approaches, even when some of the uncorrelated approaches have a low probability of success. The reason is that when firms take uncorrelated approaches, they increase the probability that at least one approach will be successful. But will a firm be willing to undertake a research strategy that has low probabilities for success? If many firms are performing research, the answer is yes. If all the firms pursue the same strategy, then each firm has an equal chance of success. The more firms there are, the lower the chance that any particular firm will win the patent race. A firm that pursues a strategy that is uncorrelated with the one pursued by everyone else stands to win the race if the popular approach fails. Thus, a "niche" R&D strategy can be profitable even if it has a low probability of producing an innovation, so long as the outcome is uncorrelated with the outcomes of the other firms.

EVOLUTIONARY ECONOMICS AND DYNAMIC CAPABILITIES ◆ ◆ ◆ ◆ ◆

The theories of innovation we discussed in the previous section are rooted in the tradition of neoclassical microeconomics. In these theories, firms are choosing the level of innovative activity that maximizes profits. Evolutionary economics, most commonly identified with Richard Nelson and Sidney Winter, offers a perspective on innovative activity that differs from microeconomic perspective.[20] Instead of

---

[19]Firms will generally prefer the risky approach even if there are only two competitors, with the gains from this choice becoming more transparent as the number of firms increases. See Tirole, J., *The Theory of Industrial Organization*, Cambridge, MA: MIT Press, 1988.

[20]Nelson, R. R. and S. G. Winter, *An Evolutionary Theory of Economic Change*, Cambridge, MA: Belknap Press, 1982.

viewing profit maximization as determining a firm's decisions, evolutionary economics sees those decisions determined by routines: well-practiced patterns of activity inside the firm.

A firm's routines include methods of production, hiring procedures, and policies for determining advertising expenditure. Firms do not change their routines often because getting members of an organization to alter what has worked well in the past is an "unnatural" act. As Schumpeter stressed, however, firms that stick to producing a given set of products in a particular way may not survive. A firm needs to search continuously to improve its routines. The ability of a firm to maintain and adapt the capabilities that are the basis of its competitive advantage is what David Teece, Gary Pisano, and Amy Shuen have referred to as its *dynamic capabilities*.[21] Firms with limited dynamic capabilities fail to nurture and adapt the sources of their advantage over time, and other firms eventually supplant them. Firms with strong dynamic capabilities adapt their resources and capabilities over time and take advantage of new market opportunities to create new sources of competitive advantage.

For several reasons, a firm's dynamic capabilities are inherently limited. First, learning is typically incremental rather than pathbreaking. That is, when a firm searches to improve its operations, it is nearly impossible for the firm to ignore what it has done in the past, and it is difficult for the firm to conceptualize new routines that are fundamentally different from its old ones. Thus, the search for new sources of competitive advantage is *path dependent*—it depends on the path the firm has taken in the past to get where it is now. But even small path dependencies can have important competitive consequences. A firm that has developed significant commitments to a particular way of doing business may find it hard to adapt to seemingly minor changes in technology. This is underscored in Rebecca Henderson and Kim Clark's study of the photolithographic alignment equipment industry described in Example 14.3.

A second limitation on a firm's dynamic capabilities is complementary assets. These are firm-specific assets that are valuable only in connection with a particular product, technology, or way of doing business. The development of new products or capabilities or the opening of new markets can either enhance or destroy the value of complementary assets. Microsoft's installed base in DOS was a valuable complementary asset when it developed Windows in the late 1980s. By contrast, as we discussed in Example 14.1, the development of the basic oxygen furnace in the steel industry reduced the value of American steel firms' existing capabilities in the open hearth process. A proposed change in an organizational routine that undermines the value of a complementary asset can give rise to the sunk cost effect discussed earlier, thereby reducing the likelihood that a firm will adopt the change.

Finally, "windows of opportunity" can also impede the development of dynamic capabilities. Early in a product's development, its design is typically fluid, manufacturing routines have not been developed, and capital is generally non-product specific. Firms can still experiment with competing product designs or ways of organizing production. However, as time passes, a narrow set of designs or product

---

[21]Teece, D. J., G. Pisano, and A. Shuen, "Dynamic Capabilities and Strategic Management," University of California at Berkeley, *Strategic Management Journal*, 18, August 1997: 509–534. See also Teece, D. J., R. Rumelt, G. Dosi, and S. Winter, "Understanding Corporate Coherence: Theory and Evidence," *Journal of Economic Behavior and Organization*, 23, 1994: pp. 1–30 for related ideas.

specifications often emerge as dominant. At this point, network externalities and learning curve effects take over, and it no longer becomes attractive for firms to compete with established market leaders. This implies that firms that do not adapt their existing capabilities or commit themselves to new markets when these uncertain windows of opportunity exist may find themselves eventually locked out from the market or competing at a significant disadvantage with early movers.

◆ ◆

Example 14.3

Organizational Adaptation in the Photolithographic Alignment Equipment Industry[22]

Photolithographic aligners are an important input in the production of solid-state semiconductor devices. To produce a semiconductor, small intricate patterns must be transferred to a thin wafer of material, such as silicon. This process of transfer is known as lithography. The pattern that is transferred is drawn onto a mask, which is used to block light as it falls onto a light-sensitive chemical coating placed on the wafer. A constant stream of seemingly incremental innovations in the industry has dramatically improved the performance of aligners. The industry has moved from so-called contact aligners to proximity aligners and from scanning projection to what are called "steppers." In nearly every case, new technology displaced an established firm that had invested in state-of-the-art equipment and know-how.

Kasper Instruments illustrates this dynamic. It was founded in 1968, and by 1973 had emerged as the leading supplier of contact aligners. But in the mid-1970s, the proximity alignment technique was pioneered. Unlike in contact aligning, in proximity aligning the mask and the wafer are separated during exposure. Although this distinction seems relatively minor, the two techniques involved subtle differences in design. In particular, to design a proximity aligner one must acquire the latest techniques for designing and producing the gap-setting mechanism—which determines how far apart the mask and the wafer are held during the lithography process. Incorporating the gap-setting mechanism necessitated subtle changes in integrating components of the aligner. Moving from contact aligners to proximity aligners thus entailed a significant shift in product design and production know-how.

Kasper failed to develop successful proximity aligners, mainly because of its previous success in designing contact aligners. Kasper conceived of the proximity aligner as a modified contact aligner, and saw the move into contact aligners as a routine extension of its product line. A gap-setting mechanism that had been used in its contact aligners was slightly modified for use in its proximity aligners. But Kasper's proximity aligner did not work well because the gap-setting mechanism was not accurate enough. In response to customer complaints, Kasper attributed

---

[22]This example is based on Henderson, R. and Clark K. B., "Architectural Innovation: The Reconfiguration of Existing Product Technologies and the Failure of Established Firms," *Administrative Science Quarterly*, 35, March 1990: pp. 9–30.

the problems to customers' own errors, which were the main source of malfunctions with its successful contact aligners. When Canon introduced a successful proximity aligner in the mid-1970s, Kasper failed to understand why it worked so well, and dismissed it as a mere copy of the Kasper aligner. The Kasper engineers did not consider the redesigned gap mechanism that made the Canon aligner such a significant advance to be particularly important. From 1974 on, Kasper aligners were rarely used in proximity mode, and by 1981, it had left the industry.

◆ ◆ ◆ ◆ ◆ THE ENVIRONMENT

In *The Competitive Advantage of Nations*, Michael Porter argues that competitive advantage originates in the local environment in which the firm is based. Porter noted that despite the ability of modern firms to transcend local markets, competitive advantage in particular industries was often strongly concentrated in one or two locations: The world's most successful producers of high-voltage electrical distribution equipment are in Sweden; the best producers of equipment for tunneling are Swiss; the most successful producers of large diesel trucks are American; and the leading microwave firms are Japanese.

Like Schumpeter and Nelson and Winter, Porter views competition as an evolutionary process. Firms initially gain competitive advantages by altering the basis of competition. They win not just by recognizing new markets or technologies but by moving aggressively to exploit them. They sustain their advantages by investing to improve existing sources of advantage and create new ones. A firm's home nation plays a critical role in shaping managers' perceptions about the opportunities that can be exploited; in supporting the accumulation of valuable resources and capabilities; and in creating pressures on the firm to innovate, invest, and improve.

Porter identifies four attributes in a firm's home market, which he collectively refers to as the "diamond," that promote or impede a firm's ability to achieve competitive advantage in global markets (see Figure 14.2):

Factor conditions
Demand conditions
Related supplier or support industries
Strategy, structure, and rivalry

Factor Conditions Factor conditions describe a nation's position with regard to factors of production (e.g., human resources, infrastructure) that are necessary to compete in a particular industry. Because general-purpose factors of production are often available locally or can be purchased in global markets, the most important factors of production are highly specialized to the needs of particular industries. For example, since the 1950s, Japan has had one of the highest numbers of engineering graduates per capita. This, according to Porter, has had much more to do with its success in such industries as automobiles and consumer electronics, than the low wages of its production workers.

FIGURE 14.2
THE ENVIRONMENT AND THE ORIGINS OF COMPETITIVE ADVANTAGE.

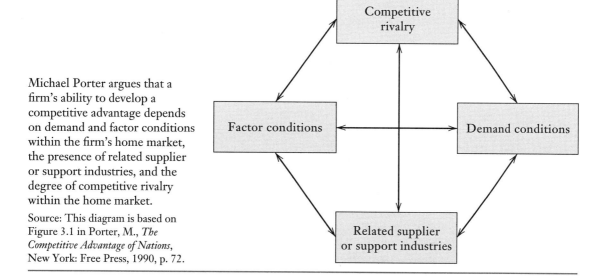

Michael Porter argues that a firm's ability to develop a competitive advantage depends on demand and factor conditions within the firm's home market, the presence of related supplier or support industries, and the degree of competitive rivalry within the home market.

Source: This diagram is based on Figure 3.1 in Porter, M., *The Competitive Advantage of Nations*, New York: Free Press, 1990, p. 72.

Demand Conditions   These include the size, growth, and character of home demand for the firm's product. Sophisticated home customers or unique local conditions stimulate firms to enhance the quality of their products and to innovate. For example, in air conditioners, Japanese firms, such as Panasonic, are known for producing small, quiet, energy-efficient window units. These product characteristics are critical in Japan where air conditioning is important (summers are hot and humid), but large, noisy units would be unacceptable because houses are small and packed closely together, and electricity is expensive.

Related and Supporting Industries   Firms that operate in a home market that has a strong base of internationally competitive supplier or support industries will be favorably positioned to achieve competitive advantage in global markets. While many inputs are mobile, and thus firms do not need geographical proximity to make exchanges, exchanging key inputs, such as scarce production know-how, does require geographical proximity. Companies with skillful home-based suppliers can be early beneficiaries of newly generated production know-how and may be able to shape innovation in supplying firms. For example, Italian shoe manufacturers have established close working relationships with leather producers that allow the shoe manufacturers to learn quickly about new textures and colors. Leather producers, in turn, learn about emerging fashion trends from the shoe manufacturers, which helps the former plan new products.

Strategy, Structure, and Rivalry   The final environmental determinant of competitive advantage, according to Porter, is the context for competition in the firm's home market. This includes local management practices, organizational structure, corporate governance, and the nature of local capital markets. For example, in Germany and Switzerland, most shares in publicly-traded firms are held by institutional investors who do not trade frequently, and capital gains are exempt from taxation. As a result, day-to-day movements in share price are not significant, which, according to Porter, creates a stronger propensity for companies in these industries to invest in research and innovation than is true of their counterparts in the United States and Britain.

Rivalry in the home market is another important part of the competitive context. According to Porter, local rivalry affects the rate of innovation in a market far more than foreign rivalry does. Although local rivalry may hold down profitability in local markets, firms that survive vigorous local competition are often more efficient and innovative than are international rivals that emerge from softer local conditions. The airline industry is a good example of this. The U.S. domestic airline industry is far more price competitive than the international industry, where entry is restricted and many flag carriers receive state subsidies. Coming out of the intensely competitive U.S. industry, U.S. airlines (such as American and United) that fly international routes are far more cost efficient and often provide better service than many of the international airlines they compete with.

As Porter points out, the role of the local environment for competitive advantage does not eliminate the need for the industry, positioning, and sustainability analyses we discussed in Chapters 7 through 13. Instead, it highlights considerations that strategy formulation usually ignores, such as the role of local competition in forging competitive strength in markets outside the firm's home country. Nor are Porter's ideas at odds with those of Nelson and Winter, who emphasize organizational factors in innovation. Many firms in favorable environments do not achieve competitive advantage, indicating that the firm's local environment is not determinative. However, Porter's framework emphasizes that firms located in unfavorable local environments face extra challenges beyond the organizational inertia and path dependence that evolutionary economics emphasizes.

ℰXAMPLE 14.4

THE RISE OF THE SWISS WATCH INDUSTRY[23]

In the eighteenth century, Britain was the largest producer of watches in the world. British master craftsman, produced nearly 200,000 watches per year by 1800, or roughly half the world's supply. Britain's dominance was the result of several factors. First, watch makers employed laborers in the British countryside, at a considerably lower wage than laborers in London would demand. More important, the watch makers benefited from the division of labor. In an eight-mile stretch from Prescot to Liverpool in northwest England, one could find cottages of springmakers, wheel cutters, dialmakers, and other specialists. Large local demand helped make this specialization possible. During the 1700s, Britain accounted for half the worldwide demand for watches. Finally, a key raw material, crucible steel, was manufactured by a British monopoly. Foreign manufacturers elsewhere did not learn how to make crucible steel until 1800.

The confluence of specialized, low-cost workers, high local demand, and access to a crucial input gave the British advantages that no other watch makers could

---

[23]This example is drawn from Landes, David, *Revolution in Time*, Cambridge, MA: Belknap Press, 1983.

match. In the mid-to-late 1700s, British watches were considered the finest in the world and commanded a premium price. But British watch makers could not keep up with world demand. They began importing watches made elsewhere and re-selling them as their own. Watch makers in Geneva benefited from this policy.

Geneva had been a center of watchmaking ever since Protestant refugees arrived from France in the mid-1500s. By the mid-1700s, Geneva was second only to Britain in watchmaking. Many watch makers whose brands still survive, including Abraham Vacheron (today Constantin Vacheron) and Czapek and Philippe (today Patek Philippe), began during this period.

The Geneva watch makers differed from their British counterparts in one key respect. The British did not have to market their product—they made high-quality watches and waited for customers to come to them. Geneva watch makers could not match the reputations of their British counterparts, and so had to become merchants as well as artisans. To keep costs down, they outsourced much of the production to workers in the nearby French and Italian Alps, at labor costs well below those in England. They also developed new markets for watches. They marketed themselves in areas such as Italy where few people wore watches. Some watch makers devoted themselves to niche markets, such as that for extremely thin watches. Others targeted cost conscious buyers. As David Landes has written, "The Swiss made watches to please their customers. The British made watches to please themselves."

In the nineteenth century, British watch makers suffered. Wars drained the British economy and dried up local demand for watches. Ill-equipped to market their watches overseas, domestic watch producers in Britain nearly disappeared. At the same time, the Swiss enjoyed growing sales and the benefits of the division of labor. The Swiss also gained access to crucible steel, by then available outside of Britain. In addition, desperate British watch makers exported uncased movements and parts, helping the Swiss match British quality. By the middle of the 19th century, Swiss watch makers were dominant. They made watches at all levels of quality, at costs below those achievable anywhere else. They tailored new product to consumer tastes. The Swiss dominated the watch industry until the mid-20th century, when the Japanese used cheap quartz movements to achieve unprecedented accuracy at remarkably low costs.

MANAGING INNOVATION   ◆ ◆ ◆ ◆ ◆

Since large firms are complex organizations whose single-minded actions cannot be taken for granted, we must consider them as vehicles for innovation and not just as inventors and users of it. How innovation occurs within firms is often as important as its results in understanding how firms create value for their customers. As Rosabeth Kanter argues, this involves seeing innovation as the process of bringing any new problem-solving idea into use.[24] This idea of organizational innovation is also developed in research on innovative cultures and internal or corporate entrepreneurship.

Corporate research and development programs have often been inflexible and unresponsive to market opportunities. This has prompted some firms to consider

---

[24]Kanter, R. M., *The Change Masters*, New York: Simon & Schuster, 1983.

alternative ways of managing their innovative processes. For example, the creation of corporate venture departments since the 1970s reflects the growing sensitivity of larger corporations to their need for mechanisms to identify and exploit opportunities for innovation beyond current products, processes, and services. Innovation outside of formal organizational mechanisms has also received attention in recent years. This work has focused on corporate entrepreneurs who push new projects forward in the face of bureaucratic obstacles.[25]

The innovation strategies of large firms need not focus solely on internal development, however. Other approaches, such as spinoffs, joint ventures, and strategic alliances, can also facilitate entry into new business areas or the development of new capabilities. One example of an interorganizational alternative to firm-based research and development is the public-private research consortium.[26] In these formal alliances, member firms pool their resources and coordinate their research activities with those of academic institutions in explicit collaboration in large-scale high-tech projects. Governments also fund these ventures as well as exempt their activities from antitrust prohibitions. While the Japanese pioneered these consortia in computer technology in the 1970s, American and European counterparts developed in the early 1980s. Perhaps the best known American consortium, MCC (Microelectronics and Computer Technology Corporation), was founded in 1982 by 16 computer and semiconductor firms. By 1993, MCC included more than 100 member firms.

In general, a firm faces a dilemma in managing its innovative activities. On the one hand, formal structure and controls are necessary to coordinate innovative activities. On the other hand, looseness and flexibility may foster innovation, creativity, and adaptiveness to changing circumstances. These competing requirements create ongoing tensions for managing innovation.

CHAPTER SUMMARY

◆ Creative destruction is the process whereby old sources of competitive advantage are destroyed and replaced with new ones. Economist Joseph Schumpeter wrote that the essence of entrepreneurship is the exploitation of the "shocks" or "discontinuities" that destroy existing sources of advantage.

◆ A dominant established firm's incentive to innovate may be weaker than that of a smaller firm or a potential entrant. The sunk cost and the replacement effect weaken the established firm's incentive to innovate. The efficiency effect, by contrast, strengthens the dominant firm's incentive to innovate as compared with a potential entrant's.

◆ The sunk cost effect describes asymmetry between a firm that has already made a commitment to a particular technology or product concept and one that is planning such a commitment. It is the phenomenon whereby a profit-maximizing firm sticks with its current technology or product concept even though the profit-maximizing decision for a firm starting from scratch would be to choose a different technology or product concept.

---

[25]Burgelman, R. A., "A Process Model of Internal Corporate Venturing in the Diversified Major Firm," *Administrative Science Quarterly*, 28, 1983: pp. 223–244; Peterson, R. A. "Entrepreneurship and Organization," in Nystrom, P. C. and W. R. Starbuck (eds.), *Handbook of Organizational Design*, vol. I, New York: Oxford University Press, 1981, pp. 65–83.

[26]Gibson, D. V. and E. M. Rodgers, *R & D Collaboration on Trial*, Cambridge, MA: Harvard Business School Press, 1994; Browning, L. D., J. M. Beyer, and J. C. Shetler, "Building Cooperation in a Competitive Industry: SEMATECH and the Semiconductor Industry," *Academy of Management Journal*, 38, 1995: pp. 113–151.

♦ When an innovation offers the prospect of the adopter becoming a monopolist, a potential entrant has a stronger incentive to develop the innovation than an incumbent monopolist. Because it already has a monopoly, the monopolist gains less from the innovation than does the potential entrant. Through innovation an entrant can replace the monopolist, but the monopolist can only replace itself. This phenomenon is called the replacement effect.

♦ The efficiency effect explains why the benefit to a firm from being a monopolist as compared with being one of two competitors in duopoly is greater than the benefit to a firm from being a duopolist as compared with not being in the industry at all (and thus earning no profit). The efficiency effect makes an incumbent monopolist's incentive to innovate stronger than a potential entrant's. The reason is that the incumbent can lose its monopoly if it does not innovate, whereas the entrant will become (at best) a duopolist if it successfully innovates.

♦ "Patent race" describes the battle between firms to innovate first. Models of patent races highlight the often critical advantage that goes to the first innovator, and give insight into how the magnitude of that advantage affects the incentives to innovate. Patent race models also emphasize an important strategic point: Firms in a patent race must anticipate the R&D investments of competitors. Failure to do so can be costly.

♦ Patent race models imply that when a firm is determining whether to increase its investment in innovation, it must account for the following factors: (i) By how much must the investment increase its R&D productivity and thereby also increase its chances of winning the patent race? (ii) Will other firms increase their R&D expenditures in response, thereby decreasing the firm's chances of winning the patent race? (iii) How many competitors are there?

♦ Evolutionary economics sees the firm decisions as determined by routines—well-practiced patterns of activity inside the firm—rather than profit maximization. At any given time, the routines of an organization determine its distinctive capabilities—those activities it can do better than other firms. Firms seldom change their routines because getting their staffs to alter what has worked well in the past is an "unnatural" act. But firms that stick to producing a given set of products in a particular way may not survive. Thus, a firm typically needs to engage in a continuous search for ways to improve its existing routines. Dynamic capabilities are a firm's ability to maintain the bases of its competitive advantage.

♦ Michael Porter argues that competitive advantage originates in a firm's local environment. He identifies four attributes in a firm's home market that promote or impede its ability to achieve competitive advantage in global markets: factors conditions; demand conditions; related supplier or support industries; and strategy, structure, and rivalry.

♦ In general, managing innovation creates a dilemma. On the one hand, formal structure and controls are needed to coordinate innovation. On the other hand, looseness and flexibility can foster innovation, creativity, and adaptiveness to changing circumstances.

QUESTIONS

1. Is the extent of creative destruction likely to differ across industries? Can the risk of creative destruction be incorporated into a five-forces analysis of an industry?

2. What is the difference between the efficiency effect and the replacement effect? Could both effects operate at the same time? If so, under what conditions would the efficiency effect be likely to dominate? Under what conditions would the replacement effect be likely to dominate?

3. What are a firm's dynamic capabilities? To what extent can managers create or "manage into existence" a firm's dynamic capabilities?

4. What is meant by the concept of path dependence? What implications does path dependence have for the ability of a firm to create new sources of competitive advantage over time?

5. How does the extent of competition in a firm's domestic market shape its ability to compete globally? Why would local rivalry have a stronger effect on the rate of innovation than foreign competition?

6. IQ Inc. currently monopolizes the market for a certain type of microprocessor, the 666. The present value of the stream of monopoly profits from this design is thought to be $500 million. Enginola (which is currently in a completely different segment of the microprocessor market from this one) and IQ are contemplating spending money to develop a superior design that will make the 666 completely obsolete. Whoever develops the design first gets the entire market. The present value of the stream of monopoly profit form the superior design is expected to be $150 million greater than the present value of the profit from the 666.

Success in developing the design is not certain, but the probability of a firm's success is directly linked to the amount of money it spends on the project (more spending on this project, greater probability of success). Moreover, the productivity of Enginola's spending on this project and IQ's spending is exactly the same: Starting from any given level of spending, an additional $1 spent by Enginola has exactly the same impact on its probability of winning. The table below illustrates this. It shows the probability of winning the race if each firm's spending equals 0, $100 million, and $200 million. The first number represents Enginola's probability of winning the race, the second is IQ's probability of winning, and the third is the probability that neither succeeds. Note: *This is not a payoff table.*

		IQ's Spending		
Enginola's Spending		0	$100 million	$200 million
	0	(0,0,1)	(0,.6,.4)	(0,.8,.2)
	$100 million	(6,0,.4)	(4,.4,.2)	(3,.6,.1)
	$200 million	(8,0,.2)	(6,.3,.1)	(5,.5,0)

Assuming that
(i) each firm makes its spending decision simultaneously and noncooperatively;
(ii) each seeks to maximize its expected profit;
(iii) neither firm faces any financial constraints,

which company, if any, has the greater incentive to spends money to win this "R&D race"? Of the effects discussed in the chapter (sunk cost effect, replacement effect, efficiency effect) which are shaping the incentives to innovate in this example?

7. In their article "Strategy as Stretch and Leverage," Gary Hamel and C. K. Prahalad argue that industry newcomers have a stronger incentive to supplant established firms from their leadership positions than established firms have to maintain their leadership positions. The reason, they argue, is that a greater gap exists between a newcomer's resources and aspirations as compared to a market leader.[27] Is Hamel and Prahalad's argument consistent with profit-maximizing behavior by both the leader and the newcomer? Is their argument consistent with ideas from evolutionary economics?

8. "Industrial or antitrust policies that result in the creation of domestic monopolies rarely result in global competitive advantage." Comment.

---

[27] Hamel, G. and C. K. Prahalad, "Strategy as Stretch and Leverage," *Harvard Business Review*, March–April 1993: pp. 75–84.

PART FOUR

INTERNAL ORGANIZATION

INCENTIVES
AND AGENCY

15

*I*n the summer of 1997, Chicago Bulls General Manager Jerry Krause negotiated a new contract for the team's leading rebounder, Dennis Rodman. The previous season had been tumultuous for Rodman. He led the National Basketball Association in rebounds per game, but he also led the league in technical fouls, disqualifications, and suspensions. Many fans felt that he was a disruptive influence in the playoffs, and when the Bulls won their fifth championship despite his erratic play, some felt that the Bulls should not re-sign him.

Jerry Krause did re-sign Rodman, offering him an incentive-filled contract. Rodman received a base salary of $4.5 million, with the potential to double to $9 million if he met certain incentives. Most of the incentives pertained to Rodman's individual performance, rather than team performance. (Rodman balked at team-based incentives, claiming that he had no control over them.) For example, the contract rewarded Rodman for rebounding. More notably, it included behavioral stipulations. Rodman stood to gain millions of dollars if he could avoid the troublemaking that led to his many disqualifications and suspensions in previous years.

No one can be certain whether the incentives were the cause of it, but Dennis Rodman was virtually a model player in 1997–1998. Not only did he dramatically cut down on his technical fouls, he was no longer one of the league leaders in this dubious category. He did not kick cameramen, head-butt referees, or do anything else to warrant a suspension. As a result, he ended up receiving most of the performance incentives in his contract. While doing so, he still led the league in rebounds and was a major reason why the Bulls remained the league's leading attraction.

Rodman's contract illustrates *agency theory*, which studies the use of financial incentives to motivate workers. In many situations, one individual or organization, known as the *principal*, delegates responsibility to another, known as the *agent*, to act on the principal's behalf. Examples of agency relationships abound. The owners of a firm may delegate managerial responsibility to a chief executive officer. The vice president of procurement may delegate purchasing decisions to a purchasing manager. A new home buyer may delegate responsibility for building the house to a general contractor. In all these situations, the principal hopes that the agent's interests are aligned with its own. But agents are often selfish. Without explicit contractual obligations, the agent may act in his or her own interest rather than further the interests of the principal.

Agents' pursuit of self-interest may undermine agency relationships. A CEO may aim for job security rather than maximizing shareholder wealth. A purchasing manager may prefer to buy supplies of inputs from longtime acquaintances rather than searching for the lowest-cost supplier. Contractors may use inferior materials to hold down their own costs.

This chapter examines the agency relationship. We will discuss why principals use agents, the opportunities for solving agency problems through contracting, the characteristics of an efficient contract for solving agency problems, and the conditions that lead to inefficiencies despite the best possible contracts. These conditions are common, so that contracts alone may not resolve many agency problems. Chapter 17 discusses a powerful alternative to contracts—"culture."

◆ ◆ ◆ ◆ ◆ THE AGENCY RELATIONSHIP

Individuals often hire others to work on their behalf. The workers do not always perform as the employer would like. Agency theory describes the opportunities and pitfalls that arise in efforts to align the interests of employers (principals) and employees (agents).

What Is an Agency Relationship?

An agency relationship exists when one individual, called the agent, acts on behalf of another, called the principal.[1] For example, the management of Toyota's Lexus division (the principal) may employ an advertising agency (the agent) to increase the demand for its line of sport utility vehicles. Such business-to-business transactions constitute an important class of agency relationships. Employer/employee relationships are another. Expert/client relationships, such as the doctor/patient relationship, represent yet a third class of agency problems.

A principal might use an agent if the principal owns some asset but lacks the skills to maximize the asset's value. Toyota may possess tools, dies, and an assembly line, for example, but it probably lacks the skills necessary to create and distribute advertisements. Patients "own" their bodies but lack the skills needed to provide proper treatment when they become seriously ill. A principal might also use an agent if the principal is resource constrained. A master chef might hire a sous chef to assist in a busy kitchen; a retailer of a popular product might award franchises if it lacks the capital to open its own stores.

The principal and agent can sometimes switch roles. Toyota could manufacture cars for the marketing firm, which would then become the retailer. This reversal of roles, in which the manufacturer becomes the agent, is not too far-fetched—firms such as Benetton and Nike are essentially marketing firms that obtain their products

---

[1]One of the first and most influential papers to describe the agency relationship in these terms is Ross, S., "The Economic Theory of Agency: The Principal's Problem," *American Economic Review*, 63, 1973: pp. 134–139.

from manufacturers that contract to produce them. In these cases, the marketing firm is the principal, because it holds the finished good and must bear the risk if it fails to sell. The manufacturing firm is the marketing firm's agent.

The Agency Contract

A contract spells out the terms of the agency relationship. The contract specifies the payments to be made by the principal to the agent, contingent on the agent taking specific actions and/or the principal observing certain outcomes. The contract may be explicit; the terms are written down and legally enforceable. An example is the contract between General Motors and workers in its Saturn division. This contract specifies bonuses to be paid out contingent on profits reported in audited accounting returns. The contract may be implicit; the terms are understood by all participants and are enforced through their desire to maintain long-term relationships and to maintain their reputations with other parties. An example is the academic tenure system. Faculty understand that they can get tenure if their research and teaching are well-regarded by their peers and their students. However, there are usually no rules specifying what constitutes tenurable performance, and the courts have allowed academic institutions great leeway in using their judgment, rather than rules spelled out in advance, as the basis for tenure decisions.

At a minimum, the contract that the principal offers the agent must satisfy two types of conditions. First, the agent must be willing to accept the contract; the contract must offer the agent the opportunity to achieve a wage at least as great as the agent's next-best alternative, or threshold wage. If the contract does not offer the threshold wage, the agent will prefer to work for someone else under other terms. During the 1980s, nurses had more opportunities to earn high incomes in relatively low-stress positions outside hospitals, such as in home health care. This raised the threshold wage hospitals had to pay to employ nurses.

Second, the agent must be willing to comply with the contract. In general, the principal would like the agent to undertake *efficient* actions, that is, actions that optimally trade-off benefits and costs and thereby afford the greatest opportunity for the principal to profit. If the agent chooses not to take the efficient actions, we say that the agent is *shirking*. A contract satisfies the *incentive compatibility constraint* if it spells out incentives that cause the agent to take efficient actions. If the contract does not satisfy this constraint, then the agent will prefer to shirk. The actions of the chief of operations at the Chicago post office in 1993–1994 gave new meaning to the term *shirking*. As part of her job, she was responsible for assigning craftsmen to do repairs and renovations. She used her authority to have her office remodeled. The project included a private bathroom and kitchen, and cost around $200,000. Her contract prevented her supervisors from taking any legal action, although she was not permitted to move into the office. The postal service (and, ultimately, postal service customers) had to bear the cost.

The First-Best Efficient Contract

What is the ideal contract from the perspective of the principal? First, the principal would like a contract that causes the agent to take efficient actions. There are potentially many such contracts, which, by definition, satisfy the incentive compatibility constraint. For example, any contract that rewards the agent sufficiently for taking the efficient action and penalizes the agent sufficiently for shirking will satisfy the incentive compatibility constraint. Of these contracts, the principal would prefer one that pays the smallest amount necessary to induce the agent to accept and abide by the contract. This contract would pay the agent's threshold wage. (The principal could not offer less than the threshold wage, or the agent would not agree to the contract.) A contract that leads the agent to take the efficient action and accept the threshold wage is *first-best efficient* for the principal.

Agency theory explains why principals are sometimes unable to develop first-best efficient contracts. To understand these problems, consider situations in which agents usually act efficiently even without elaborate contracts. There are many such situations. The owners of an airline usually expect their pilots to fly at the appropriate speed and in the right direction. Purchasers of eyeglasses can expect opticians to grind their lenses according to prescription. Purchasers of clothing expect that alterations will improve the fit. Three factors contribute to efficiency in these cases:

1. Agents do not possess hidden information. Principals know what constitutes efficient action and what outcome to expect.
2. Principals have full information about actions and/or outcomes.
3. The agents are at little risk. They know that they will get paid if they do not shirk.

Under these three conditions, agents are unlikely to shirk. Principals know what to expect, can determine if actions and/or outcomes meet expectations, and can fairly reward or penalize. At the same time, agents know that if they act efficiently, they will be rewarded. Hence, agents are unlikely to shirk.

To summarize, first-best efficient contracts are possible only when certain features are present: no hidden information, observable actions and/or outcomes, and an absence of risk. The next section details how agency problems may arise and how they can be resolved if these features are absent.

Problems in Agency Relationships

Agents do not always do what principals would like them to do. Problems can arise due to moral hazard, imperfect observability, and risk aversion. Contracts must be structured to overcome these problems.

Moral Hazard

Problems arise in agency relationships because the agent does not always prefer to take the action that the principal most prefers. We might expect this to happen as a matter of course. After all, agents and principals usually have different objectives. For example, the owners of a business may want to maximize profits, but if workers seek to minimize the chances that they will lose their jobs, they may take fewer risks than the owner might prefer. Or, workers may seek to minimize effort, thereby working less hard than the owner would prefer. The principal and agent could address such problems by agreeing to a contract that binds the agent to act in the principal's interests. But contracts are inevitably incomplete. As a result, there are opportunities for shirking, or what is often referred to as *moral hazard*.[2]

---

[2]For a rigorous mathematical treatment of the roles of moral hazard and attitudes toward risk in agency relationships, see Holmstrom, B., "Moral Hazard and Observability," *Bell Journal of Economics*, 10, Spring 1979: pp. 74–91.

Moral hazard describes selfish behavior that a contract cannot prevent. Moral hazard is closely related to the concepts of hidden action and hidden information described in Chapter 4. Recall that a hidden action cannot be costlessly observed and/or verified. If an agent's actions are hidden—if the principal cannot detect that the agent is shirking—then the principal might not be able to use a contract to rule out undesirable actions. For example, suppose that a pharmaceutical company would like an independent clinical research organization (CRO) to validate the clinical research that the CRO did for the pharmaceutical company. The pharmaceutical company could require the CRO to produce evidence of validation. But validation requires substantial physical and mental effort that the pharmaceutical company cannot easily observe. Thus, validation is a hidden action and thus is not contractible. Consequently, the CRO could shirk on validation without much risk of punishment.

An effort to control hidden action may help explain Domino's "30-minute delivery guarantee." In the early 1990s, Domino's announced, through national ads, that it would offer a $3 discount if it took more than 30 minutes to deliver a pizza. Fast delivery was a key to Domino's success. Domino's could have tried to promote fast delivery through internal monitoring—say by fining franchise owners with poor on-time performance. But Domino's could not easily verify pizza delivery times, and could not expect franchise owners to report truthfully their on-time performance to top management. But consumers could easily verify delivery times, and the guarantee gave them an incentive to report late deliveries. By offering the guarantee, Domino's used consumer monitoring where internal monitoring would not suffice.

Moral hazard may also result when the agent possesses hidden information—knowledge about the conditions of demand, technology, or cost that the principal does not have. This information is often critical for determining the agent's best course of action. By hiding some information, the agent may be able to shirk without fear of punishment. The agent uses his or her informational edge to persuade the principal to accept the chosen action as appropriate.

Hidden information helps explain why promoting research and development is an especially difficult agency problem. Innovators often have private information about the scientific merits of their ideas, and thus may know better than anyone else whether or not they are on the verge of a significant breakthrough. But when they attempt to obtain seed money for their projects, researchers have an incentive to present overly optimistic projections about the viability of their ideas. This makes it difficult for employers or other investors to determine which investors to believe and which projects to fund.

Observability

One key to preventing shirking is observability.[3] If the principal can observe actions and outcomes and the desired actions and outcomes can be spelled out in a contract that can be enforced in court, then the principal can solve the agency problem. The principal contractually requires agents to take the correct actions or achieve the desired outcomes, and punishes them if they fail to do so. Some desir-

---

[3]The seminal work on the value of information in agency relationships is Holmstrom, B., "Moral Hazard and Observability," *Bell Journal of Economics*, 10, Spring 1979: pp. 74–91. One of Holmstrom's findings is that the principal is always better off with information about the agent's performance, no matter how noisy, than with no information at all.

able actions are easy to observe and contract on. For example, people who sell their houses often require their sales agents to publish advertisements, host open houses, and show the house to a specified number of buyers. Other actions may be harder to observe. The house seller cannot easily observe the sales "pitch" and other efforts the sales agent uses. When actions are difficult to observe, contracts may stipulate pay based on observable outcomes. For example, the house owner may have agreed to pay the agent a commission contingent on the desired outcome—the timely sale of the house.

In many other agency relationships, the desired actions and outcomes are difficult both to observe and measure. If the principal cannot adequately measure the action or outcome that most interests it, it may measure another action or outcome as a proxy. A good proxy must be highly correlated with the desired measure. (Two measures are correlated when they tend to move together.) If the proxy is not correlated with the measure of interest, then the score on the proxy will be irrelevant to the score on the preferred measure. To make matters worse, the agent may try to maximize performance on the proxy measure, thereby boosting its compensation, without necessarily improving its performance on the preferred measure.

Law enforcement provides a number of examples in which the principal (i.e., taxpayers) must substitute easily measured outcomes for desired outcomes. Taxpayers would like the police to maintain safe and efficient roadways. But this is a highly subjective measure, since (a) it is difficult to know just how safe and efficient the roads would be without police, and (b) any measure of road safety and efficiency is multidimensional, combining accidents of varying severity, traffic tie-ups, and so on. This measure would also introduce unwanted risk (see below) to the pay of police, since they can only do so much to control safety. Rather than pay police based on some composite measure of roadway safety and efficiency, taxpayers have implicitly supported a system in which police are rewarded based on easily quantified measures, such as the number of speeding tickets written. Of course, this leads police to concentrate on catching speeders. While the frequency of speeding is certainly correlated with roadway safety, focusing on this particular measure may not be the best way to promote safety and efficiency. Similar issues arise in efforts to promote public safety.

$\mathcal{E}$XAMPLE 15.1

MEASURING PERFORMANCE OF HEALTH CARE ORGANIZATIONS

There is an ongoing information revolution in health care. The revolution is the result of two factors. Health care purchasers increasingly seek to spend their dollars more wisely, and reductions in computer costs lower the costs of accessing and analyzing large data sets. Purchasers use health care data to assess the performance of providers and steer patients to those providers that they believe offer the best combination of cost and quality.

To be cost-effective, purchasers must be able to measure quality. But what are the features of good-quality health care? Quality is clearly multidimensional, but most people would agree that living longer and without pain are two desirable outcomes of any treatment. Until 1984, payers had no systematic information about any dimensions related to these outcomes. One of the most widely used indicators of hospital quality, accreditation by the Joint Commission on Accreditation of Hospitals, was based on such factors as the number of fire extinguishers and the size of hallways. Patients were forced to choose their providers on the basis of this measure, as well as other easily obtainable measures, such as location and the quality of the food. In 1984, the Health Care Finance Administration started reporting hospital "inpatient mortality" rates. Many private consulting firms, such as Health Care Investment Analysts, now report similar figures. These give the probability that a patient with a given illness would die during the hospital stay. This is a better measure of quality, but it is still imperfect because patients may die after discharge. For example, a hospital may transfer dying patients to other hospitals, a hospice, or to their homes, and may thus appear to have a low inpatient mortality rate. Despite this and other problems, purchasers used mortality data because they believed it was correlated with their preferred quality measures.

As health care data grow increasingly accessible, payers are using more sophisticated quality measures. The Pennsylvania Corporate Hospital Quality Rating Project represents an effort by the University of Pennsylvania, the state government, and local business to develop a more thorough measure of hospital quality. Their measures include inpatient mortality, postoperative length of stay, and in-hospital infection rates, all of which they believe are correlated with "living longer and without pain." Purchasers in Pennsylvania can use this information to identify the best hospitals to send their enrollees to. Hospitals are using similar information to evaluate their own performance. Hospitals that score poorly may spend a little effort questioning the measures, but spend far more effort trying to score better the next time. Similar measures are being developed for physicians, and many observers believe that physicians in the future will have to provide evidence of quality to obtain staff privileges at hospitals, win contracts from Health Maintenance Organizations, and command high wages.

Employers are also interested in the quality of their managed care plans as well as their providers. The National Consortium for Quality Assurance, representing many of the largest firms in the U.S., introduced the Health Plan Employer Data and Information Set (HEDIS) in the early 1990s to measure aspects of health plan quality. HEDIS measures access and service levels of contracting providers as well as enrollee satisfaction. While HEDIS is a good start at quantifying key aspects of quality, surveys suggest that most individuals still evaluate the quality of managed care plans by asking friends and relatives for their opinions. This is ironic, because most people state they are not able to accurately judge the quality of health plans, yet they measure quality by getting the opinions of other, equally uninformed, individuals.

Piece Rate Contracts

One of the most common contracts in which pay is based on an easily observed outcome is the piece rate contract. A piece rate contract pays a fee for each unit of output, such as at Levi Strauss, where employees have historically been paid a small amount for each pair of jeans they assemble.[4] The appeal of using piece rates to motivate workers is based on a simple behavioral rule:

> When agents are paid a fixed "fee per X," where X may stand for a period of time such as an hour, or a unit of output such as pages in a report, and so on, and the fee exceeds the opportunity wage, then agents will work hard to provide X.

Thus, if Levi Strauss offers a simple fee-per-jeans contract, workers will work hard to assemble as many jeans as possible (until the fee no longer compensates for the time and energy required to work that hard). This may be exactly what Levi Strauss desires. On the other hand, the consequences of single-minded dedication to increasing output may be undesirable. For example, if workers work too fast, quality may suffer, driving down demand and possibly increasing costs due to the need to rework defective jeans. To prevent this, Levi Strauss specifies that it will not pay for defective jeans. As long as it can identify defects at relatively low cost, this type of contract should be an effective motivator.

The piece rate may encourage hard work, but it will not generally guarantee the efficient amount of effort. Consider once again the jeans assembly plant. Suppose that Levi Strauss makes a profit of $6 for each assembled pair of jeans. Suppose further that if a worker exerts effort E, the number of jeans produced per day equals .5E. It follows that the marginal contribution of each additional unit of effort to profit is $.5 \times \$6$ or $3. However, effort is costly—all else equal, most people prefer to work less hard. Specifically, suppose that the cost of effort is $Cost = E + .01E^2$. This implies that the marginal cost of effort is $1 + .02E$. The efficient level of effort would equate the marginal contribution of $3 with the marginal cost. This occurs at $E = 100$, with corresponding output of 50 pairs of jeans per day ($.5 \times E = 50$).

Suppose that the owner pays a piece rate of $4 per pair of jeans. From the worker's perspective, the marginal contribution of effort is $2 per unit of effort. Equating this to marginal cost yields an effort, $E = 50$, with corresponding output of 25 pairs of jeans per day. The worker's effort is inefficiently low because any piece rate that would leave the owner with a profit does not pay the worker the full benefit of his or her output. Alternate schemes might pay a fixed amount if the worker reaches a production goal (e.g., $500 if the worker produces 100 pairs of jeans), or penalize the worker if output is too low. These schemes have problems of their own associated with risk that we discuss later on in this chapter.

"Fee per X" contracts may encourage agents to produce too much "X." For example, stockbrokers are occasionally charged with "churning"—placing excessive buy and sell orders for their clients to increase their own commissions. In a well-known case, before 1989, Dun & Bradstreet paid commissions to salespeople whose clients increased their purchases. In 1989, disgruntled clients filed lawsuits alleging that salespeople used deceptive practices to place large orders.[5] To take another example, car owners are normally suspicious of mechanics who recommend major repairs. In another well-known case, Sears auto service centers in California were found to have prescribed unnecessary repairs. One apparent culprit was Sears' reward system— Sears paid service center managers on the basis of total volume of business.

---

[4]Interestingly, when Levi Strauss moved to a team-based compensation mechanism, productivity fell and employees complained that they were no longer paid for their performance.

[5]Roberts, J. L., "Credit Squeeze: Dun & Bradstreet Firm Faces Flap Over How It Sells Reports on Businesses," *Wall Street Journal*, March 2, 1989, p. A1.

XAMPLE 15.2

INCENTIVES AND FUND MANAGERS

Investments in mutual funds have increased dramatically in the past decade. To generate revenues, most funds collect both a fixed fee from investors for each transaction, plus a management fee that is a fixed percentage of the amount deposited. Thus, larger funds usually receive higher revenues than smaller funds. To the extent that many of the costs of managing funds are fixed—e.g., costs associated with market research and making trades—larger funds will also be more profitable. Thus, fund managers seek to maximize the amount of money investors put into the fund.

Investors, of course, tend to look for funds that generate the largest returns (and may tolerate lower returns only if there is an accompanying reduction in risk). But it is costly for investors to switch from one fund to another. These switching costs explains why Judith Chevalier and Glenn Ellison (1997) found that only the best performing funds experience above average inflows of funds, and only the worst performing funds experience above average outflows. Investors are reluctant to switch to or from "average" funds just to obtain slightly higher expected returns. Chevalier and Ellison speculate that this "s-shaped return to performance" profile (see figure 15.1 below) might create unusual incentives for fund managers to systematically seek out or avoid risky investments.[6]

FIGURE 15.1
RELATIONSHIP BETWEEN PERFORMANCE AND FLOW OF FUNDS.

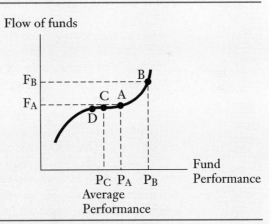

Funds flow out of the very worst funds and into the very best funds. If fund A improves its performance from P_A to P_B, it will attract funds. If its performance falls to P_C, however, the losses in funds will be minimal. Thus, the manager of fund A has an incentive to take on risk. By contrast, the manager of fund D will play it safe.

Chevalier and Ellison reason as follows. Managers of funds that are performing well, but not superlatively, will find that the gain from boosting fund performance might exceed the loss from harming performance. This is because a slight improvement in performance would place the fund among the best and generate

---

[6]Chevalier, J. and G. Ellison (1997) "Risk Taking by Mutual Funds as a Response to Incentives" *Journal of Political Economy* 105(6): 1167–1200.

a large inflow of funds. On the other hand, a small reduction in performance would not generate a substantial outflow of funds. Thus, these fund managers might make risky investments, hoping to push their fund into the top echelon. By the same token, managers of the best performing funds may want to minimize risks to assure that their funds stay in the top echelon. The incentives facing managers of underperforming funds may be analyzed in a similar way. If a fund is among the worst, its manager will take risks to try to improve performance. If a fund is merely below average, its manager may avoid risks that might plunge performance to the lowest echelon.

Chevalier and Ellison test their ideas by examining investments by mutual fund managers as the ends of fiscal years approach. They find that managers do alter their portfolio holdings in a manner consistent with theory.

Performance Standards

As discussed previously, a principal might replace a piece rate contract with one that pays a certain amount if output exceeds a certain standard. Thus far, we have assumed that the principal knows enough to set an appropriate performance standard. But what if the principal knows little about the production process or the conditions under which the agents are working? If the principal relies on the agent to help construct the standard, the agent may use hidden information to convince the principal to set a standard that is too easy to achieve. How then should the principal set the standard when it does not know how much the agents can be expected to produce?

A common performance standard is past productivity. One problem with this standard is that of "regression to the mean." Managers who have done exceedingly well in the past may be held to a high standard. But good past performance may have been partly due to good luck. Good luck is unlikely to hold for long (or it wouldn't be luck), implying that future performance may not match past performance. It may thus be unfair to hold productive workers to standards based on their own past performance. Conversely, poor performers usually suffer from at least some bad luck. Assuming that their bad luck does not hold, they might be expected to perform better the next year even if they do not work any harder, and a standard based on past performance may be too easy for them to meet.

Clever agents can also manipulate standards based on past performance. They realize that the harder they work this year, the higher will be next year's standard, a phenomenon known as the "ratchet effect."[7] Anticipation of the ratchet effect gives an agent an incentive to cut back on current effort to make future goals more reachable. For example, American auto manufacturers were accused of dragging their feet in complying with fuel emissions standards in the early 1980s. One explanation is that they feared that early compliance with the standards would lead Congress to "ratchet" the standards upward later on.[8]

---

[7]The ratchet effect has been studied by a number of scholars, including Weitzman, M., "The Ratchet Principle and Performance Incentives," *Bell Journal of Economics*, Autumn 1980: pp. 302–308 and Freixas, X., R. Guesnerie, and J. Tirole, "Planning Under Incomplete Information and the Ratchet Effect," *Review of Economic Studies*, 52, 1985: pp. 173–192.

[8]See Yao, D., "Strategic Responses to Automobile Emissions Control: A Game Theoretic Analysis," *Journal of Environmental Management and Policy*, 15, 1988: pp. 419–438.

Agents may also manipulate their recording of expenses and revenues to give the appearance of steadily improving performance. This occurred at food giant H. J. Heinz during the 1970s.[9] Managers were paid bonuses under a management incentive plan. They received points for achieving personal goals, and were expected to exceed their past year's accomplishments. Some managers manipulated payments to vendors to make it appear that their divisions had maintained growth, enabling them to receive their bonuses.

When more than one agent is performing the same task, the principal might set a relative standard, that is, evaluate agents relative to each other. This is often associated with what are known as tournaments, and is described in detail later in this chapter. Rather than evaluate agents relative to the past or to each other, the principal could employ engineering studies (e.g., time and motion studies) to objectively determine an appropriate standard.

◆ ◆

XAMPLE 15.3

INCENTIVES IN A SOCIAL SERVICE AGENCY

Some organizations do not confront market pressures. Organizations, such as public agencies, for example, are often mandated by law and continue to exist and grow without regard to their efficiency or effectiveness. However, even when an organization does not face competitive market pressures, individuals within the organization still respond to the incentives that the organization offers. Nonmarket organizations do not offer market-based incentives (such as shares of stock or performance-based pay) common in for-profit firms, but the incentives they do offer affect behavior nonetheless. Incentives in nonmarket organizations can be long-term economic rewards (such as promotions based on performance), or they can be social rewards, such as praise, citation, or formal recognition for honors (e.g., "employee of the month"). Social rewards may be used more often because of the relatively strict seniority rules in many public bureaucracies.

The Illinois Department of Children and Family Services (DCFS), the state child services agency, is a good example of the power of incentives in nonmarket organizations. DCFS has two main types of job: investigators (people who investigate reports of child abuse and determine whether the child should be removed from the home), and caseworkers (people who manage the therapy offered to the child and family once abuse has been identified). The main decision investigators must make is whether to remove a child from the home. The main decision caseworkers must make is whether to return a child to the home.

This agency lives in the public spotlight, and elected officials can prosper or suffer at the polls according to public perception of the agency's performance. The agency receives bad press when a child is hurt. On the other hand, the media tends not to report cases where children are removed from their homes with in-

---

[9]See H. J. Heinz, "The Administration of Policy (A)," Harvard Business School, Case 9-382-034.

sufficient justification. Media reports influence the budget the agency receives from the state legislature. Naturally, the legislature encourages the agency to prevent child abuse, but it is less concerned about keeping children in their homes. Primarily through punishments and reprimands (or negative social reinforcement, in the language of behavioral psychology), the agency passes this conservative bias along to its investigators and caseworkers.

For investigators, the conservative bias means that the safest decision they can make is to remove a child from the home if there is any suspicion of abuse and make the child a ward of the state. Finding that a claim of abuse is unfounded is risky: If something were to happen later to that child due to abuse or neglect, the media would blame the agency, and the investigator would be reprimanded. Removing a child from a healthy family environment may occasionally result in a lawsuit for the agency, but such lawsuits tend not to receive much media attention, and therefore rarely result in a reprimand for the investigator.

For caseworkers, the conservative bias means that the safest decision they can make is to keep a child in the system (in a foster home, for example). If a child is released from the system and is later abused again in the home, the agency will receive public censure, and the blame will trickle down to the caseworker responsible. When the decision to release a child is correct, the family does not reenter the system, and the media ignores the story.

We can conceptualize the judgments of the investigators and caseworkers using the following analysis. An investigator may make two possible judgments: Either the child is being abused (calling for removal from the home) or the child is not (which means that the child will be left in the home). Because of the agency's conservative bias, the investigators have incentives to make one type of error (False Positives) over another (Misses). It is safer for them to remove the child from the home than to risk a Miss. Caseworkers have a slightly different decision to make: It is safe to return the child to the home? Their incentives lead them to make Miss errors, rather than False Positives. That is, even when it may actually be safe to return a child to the home, they will err on the side of caution.

These two incentive systems together mean that the agency takes in far more children than it discharges: The investigators tend to let too many into the system, and the caseworkers are reluctant to let the children out of it. Over the years, this has resulted in a huge increase in agency caseloads (from 25,000 children in 1991 to over 40,000 by the mid–1990s), so that now the agency is beginning to receive media attention for failing to discharge children quickly enough. The investigators and caseworkers are each responding to the incentives the agency offered them, and their behavior is rational when judged within the boundaries of their jobs. However, perhaps in part because the agency does not face the discipline of a market environment, it offers its workers incentives to behave in a way that has dysfunctional consequences for the system as a whole.

For public bureaucracies, the media may sometimes partially correct for the lack of market competition, although this correction tends to be far from perfect. Perhaps now that the agency is receiving a different kind of attention from the media, it will change the incentives offered to investigators and caseworkers, thereby also changing their willingness to make one type of error over another. It is the incentives offered by the system, rather than abiding personal traits of workers, that are the main influence on the behavior of the agency's workers.

Performance-Based Contracts and Risk Aversion

It might seem that a principal who cannot perfectly observe effort might still be able to offer a first-best efficient contract by providing sufficient rewards for good outcomes and sufficient penalties for bad outcomes. Consider the following example. Blizzard Entertainment (BE), a developer of computer and video games (the principal), hires a small marketing firm to promote its latest game. Suppose that both BE and the marketer can observe sales, which may be either "high" or "low." If sales are high, BE will make a net profit of $300,000, not counting marketing expenses. If sales are low, its net profit will be $150,000.

The marketing firm may choose from three levels of effort. If it selects low effort, it incurs costs of $25,000, and sales will be high with probability .10. (In all cases, we assume that the costs are the marketer's opportunity costs and therefore include a reasonable rate of return.) If sales are high with probability .10, then BE's expected profits, not including marketing expenses, will be $165,000. If the marketer selects medium effort, it incurs costs of $50,000, sales are high with probability .60, and BE's expected profits are $240,000. If it selects high effort, it incurs costs of $100,000, sales are high with probability .70, and BE's expected profits are $255,000. Table 15.1 summarizes the data.

As shown in the last column of Table 15.1, the combined profits (BE software profit less marketing expense) are highest if the marketer selects medium effort. A first-best efficient contract would cause the marketer to select medium effort and pay it $50,000 to cover its costs. This contract would give BE an expected profit, after marketing expenses, of $140,000. By definition, this is BE's maximum expected profit provided that it pays the marketer enough to get it to take on the job. With this in mind, what type of contract should BE offer to the marketer?

One possibility would be to offer a *cost-based contract*, similar to those commonly used in public sector procurement for military supplies. In a cost-based contract, the principal offers to reimburse the agent for costs incurred, plus a reasonable profit margin. In this case, BE could offer to pay all reasonable costs to the marketer. Of course, this would provide the marketer with several opportunities for shirking. It could select high effort and bill BE for $100,000. BE could safeguard against this by limiting reimbursable expenses to $50,000. But then the marketer could merely go through the motions of producing a good marketing plan and still submit its bill for $50,000. Obviously, BE would prefer to tie payment to sales.

A *performance-based contract* makes payment contingent on the agent meeting some prespecified performance objectives. For example, after judiciously considering the information in Table 15.1, BE could offer to pay the marketer $70,800 if sales of the game are high and $18,800 if sales are low. What effort will the marketer select? If it selects low effort, it will receive $24,000 in expected payments

TABLE 15.1
COSTS AND PROFITS OF SOFTWARE MARKETING

Marketer Effort	Marketing Expense	Probability of High Sales	Expected BE Profits	Profit Less Marketing Expense
Low	$25,000	.10	$165,000	$140,000
Medium	$50,000	.60	$240,000	$190,000
High	$100,000	.70	$255,000	$155,000

versus $25,000 in expenses. If it selects high effort, it will receive $55,200 in expected payments versus $75,000 in expenses. If it selects medium effort, it will receive $50,000 in expected payments versus $50,000 in expenses. Hence, it will select the efficient action—medium effort.

But will the marketer agree to this contract? It might, because the contract just pays the marketer enough to cover its opportunity costs. But the answer depends on the marketer's willingness to take on risk. An agent is *risk neutral* if it is indifferent between a sure thing and a gamble of equal expected value. For example, a risk-neutral individual would be indifferent between a "safe" asset that provided a certain return of $1,000 and a "risky" asset that provided a return of $2,000 with probability .5 and $0 with a probability .5. An agent is *risk averse* if it prefers the sure thing (e.g., the "safe" asset in the previous example) to a gamble of equal expected value. An agent is risk loving if it prefers the gamble. Most individuals are risk averse, as evidenced by purchases of health and auto insurance, and other protections against financial loss.[10] This implies that all else being equal, they prefer jobs where their income is assured to jobs where they might have the same expected income but it is at risk. Risk aversion is related to the concept of diminishing marginal utility for wealth. If individuals have diminishing marginal utility for wealth, then they are willing to sacrifice more to realize their first $W than they would to gain an additional $W. Diminishing marginal utility for wealth implies risk aversion. All else equal, risk-averse individuals prefer jobs where their income is assured to jobs where they have the same expected income but their income is at risk. This implies that the principal must pay the agent to bear risk.

To identify the cost of risk bearing, suppose that the marketing firm is risk averse. We can represent this with a utility function such as $U = \sqrt{(90,000 + X)}$ where $90,000 is its guaranteed income from other business and X is its income from the BE contract. (The square root utility function implies diminishing marginal utility for wealth.) If the agent refuses to take the BE contract, its utility equals $\sqrt{90,000}$ or 300. If it accepts the contract and selects medium effort, it has a .6 chance of having an income of $110,800 and a .4 chance of having an income of $58,800. Thus, its expected total income is $90,000. Although its expected income is the same whether or not it takes the contract, that income is no longer guaranteed, and we suspect that its expected utility is less than 300. We can confirm this by direct computation. It has a .6 chance of realizing utility of $\sqrt{110,800}$ (or 332.9) and a .4 chance of realizing utility of $\sqrt{58,000}$ (or 242.5).
Hence, its expected utility would be $(.6 \times 332.9) + (.4 \times 242.5) = 296.7$. As we suspected, this is less than 300, implying that the marketer would prefer not to take the contract at all![11]

To make it worthwhile for the marketer to take the contract, BE would need to guarantee it an expected utility of at least 300. To do this, BE could offer to pay approximately $73,000 in the event that sales are high and $21,000 if sales are low. This would still be an efficient contract—the marketer will continue to prefer to select medium effort. But it is no longer first best. To induce the marketer to take

---

[10]This does imply that individuals will not gamble. Many people enjoy gambling for its own sake, such as casino gambling or playing the lottery, but risk aversion suggests that most would not risk substantial portions of their income in such endeavors.

[11]In contrast, if it selected low effort, it would have a .1 chance of realizing utility of 374.2 and a .9 chance of realizing utility of 278.4, for expected utility of 287.9.

the contract, BE must pay it $2,200 more than its costs. This additional payment necessary to get the agent to bear risk is called the *risk premium*.

The "Second-Best" Contract

We have seen that the combination of hidden information, hidden actions, and risk aversion can make it impossible for the producer to offer a first-best efficient contract. In the preceding example, the contract between Blizzard Entertainment and the marketing firm must balance two incompatible elements:

1. A cost-based contract provides the marketer with an incentive to shirk, exposing BE to excessive costs.
2. A performance-based contract imposes unwanted risk on the marketer, forcing BE to pay a risk premium in excess of expected costs.

Fortunately, BE can avoid this undesirable either-or choice by offering a risk-sharing contract that guarantees the marketer some income, but provides enough incentive so that the marketer does not shirk.

The *second-best contract*—so-called because the first-best contract that promotes efficiency without paying a risk premium is unattainable—is the risk-sharing contract that offers the best balancing act from the principal's perspective. Specifically, the second-best contract is the one that maximizes the principal's expected profit subject to the constraints that (1) the contract makes the agent's utility at least as high as it would be if the agent instead pursued its best alternative opportunity; and (2) the contract induces the agent to provide the level of effort the principal most prefers, given the need to compensate the agent to provide that effort. Because it may be costly to motivate the agent to provide effort, the principal may be content to choose a second-best contract that elicits less than the first-best efficient effort level. When this is so, the second-best contract cannot fully eliminate the agency costs associated with hidden actions.

A simple way to represent the second-best contract is as follows:

$$W = A + BX$$

where W is the agent's compensation and X is measured performance (e.g., profit, total output, or quality). The variable A represents the fixed component of the agent's compensation; the agent receives it no matter how the agent performs. The variable B represents the extent to which compensation is tied to performance. The larger is B, the more sensitive the agent's compensation is to performance. If B is relatively large, then the contract provides *higher-power performance incentives*.

The optimal value of B in the second-best contract depends on four factors already encountered, and is summarized in Table 15.2:

1. The agent's risk aversion: A high-power incentive contract will be expensive when the agent is highly risk averse because the agent will have to be given a large risk premium to compensate for the risk it will bear. In general, the more risk averse the agent, the lower the optimal value of B in the second-best contract.
2. The agent's effort aversion: An agent is effort averse if its marginal cost of effort is an increasing function of the amount of effort it provides. If the agent is highly effort averse, it takes a high-powered incentive contract (i.e., high B) to

TABLE 15.2

FACTORS AFFECTING USE OF HIGH-POWERED PERFORMANCE INCENTIVES

Factors Favoring High-Powered Performance Incentives	*Factors Favoring Low-Powered Performance Incentives*
Low-Risk Aversion	High-Risk Aversion
Low-Effort Aversion	High-Effort Aversion
High Marginal Contribution of Effort	Low Marginal Contribution of Effort
Relatively Noise-Free Performance Measures	Relatively Noisy Performance Measures

induce even a little extra effort. Even if the principal makes an offsetting reduction in A, the increase in B is costly, since it raises the required risk premium. In general, the more effort averse the agent, the lower the optimal value of B in the second-best contract.

3. The marginal contribution of effort to profitability: If additional effort does not increase the principal's profit much, then it will not be worth introducing high-powered incentives that will only increase the agent's risk. In general, the lower the marginal contribution of effort to performance, the lower the optimal value of B in the second-best contract.

4. The noisiness of the performance measure: If the performance measure is "noisy"—it does a poor job of tracking the outcome that the principal really cares about—then high-powered performance incentives will impose unwanted risk, necessitating a higher risk premium. In general, the noisier the performance measure, the lower the optimal value of B in the second-best contract.

Knowing these factors enables the principal to better tailor contracts for different workers under specific conditions. Here are two examples:

1. The profitability of local supermarkets strongly depends on store managers' staffing and pricing decisions (high marginal contribution of effort). Profits are easy to measure at the store level (relatively noise-free performance measure). These features help explain why Stop and Shop and other chains pay their local store managers on the basis of store profits and losses. By contrast, shift managers at fast-food outlets have little control over demand, pricing, and other factors that affect profits. (These are much more affected by national-level policies governing advertising and menu composition.) Although it is possible to measure the profitability of a shift, the absence of a strong link between effort and profits leads most store owners to pay their shift managers a salary.

2. The total value of the shares of publicly traded firms reflects their expected long-run profitability. Share value is not only a good measure of performance, it is also easily measured. Not surprisingly, CEOs and other top executives whose decisions are critical for long-run profitability receive large portions of their incomes in the form of stocks and stock options. Their personal wealth is thus a direct function of how their firms perform. (Not coincidentally, most CEOs are willing to work very long hours. Because they are not effort averse, high-powered incentive contracts can be very effective motivators.)

Improving the Principal's Chances: Increasing Observability

If noisy observation of actions and outcomes impedes efficiency, then the principal ought to gain by making its observations more precise. Milton Harris and Arthur Raviv have considered how the optimal contract should vary with the precision of monitoring and conclude that less-noisy performance measures lead to higher-powered incentives.[12] They analyze contracts of the form: Pay a high wage (i.e., a wage that exceeds the agent's opportunity cost) if the observed performance exceeds a threshold; dismiss the agent if it does not. They show that when monitoring grows more precise, agents are more willing to tolerate hard-edged contracts, they work harder, fewer are dismissed, and those that are retained accept a lower wage. All of these properties result from the interplay between worker risk aversion and the risk imposed by imperfect monitoring. Harris and Raviv's findings may be summarized as follows:

1. By using precise measures, the principal can reduce the risk premium that it must pay to get agents to accept the contract. This leaves the principal with a higher share of the total output that the agent produces.
2. By using precise measures, the principal can rely on performance-based incentives without exposing the agent to additional income risk. This increases the agent's output.

But even precise performance measures cannot always ensure good outcomes under performance-based incentive contracts. George Baker, Robert Gibbons, and Kevin J. Murphy suggest that objectively verifiable performance measures should be supplemented by subjective measures.[13] They argue that objective measures can be "gamed," that is, workers may devote too much time to improving their performance on these measures, to the detriment of their overall contributions to the firm. Subjective measures of performance may be a useful complement to objective measures to prevent such gamesmanship.

Limited Liability

In the Blizzard Entertainment example, the marketer stands to make money if sales are high but will lose money if sales are low. The form of this contract—the agent expects to make money if its performance is above average and pay a penalty (i.e., lose money) if its performance is below average—is characteristic of all first-best efficient contracts in which pay is based on performance. Not only must the principal pay the agent more for good outcomes than bad, to prevent shirking, the principal must also penalize the agent in the event of a bad outcome or else the expected payment by the principal will exceed the agent's opportunity cost.

But what if the agent cannot pay the penalty? We say that an agent who is unable to pay penalties has *limited liability*. When the penalty necessary to deter shirking exceeds the amount that the agent can pay, the principal may not be able to implement the first-best efficient contract. Unable to impose penalties, the principal can only induce the agent to take the efficient action by raising the pay

---

[12]Harris, M. and A. Raviv, "Optimal Incentive Contracts with Imperfect Information," *Journal of Economic Theory*, 20, 1979: pp. 231–259.

[13]Baker, G., R. Gibbons, and K. J. Murphy, "Subjective Performance Measures in Optimal Incentive Contracts," *Quarterly Journal of Economics*, 109, 1998: pp. 1125–56.

for desirable outcomes. This payment is called the *efficiency wage*, and drives up the cost of the contract, potentially well above the threshold wage.

Curt Eaton and William D. White, and Carl Shapiro and Joseph Stiglitz proposed the idea of efficiency wages to help explain why employers do not lower wages of their employees, even when many qualified job applicants are willing to work for less.[14] Their basic idea is as follows. Suppose that agents can either choose to work hard or shirk. Agents have an opportunity wage W^* that they can earn in their next-best employment opportunity, and they cannot be forced to pay a penalty to the principal. In a perfectly competitive labor market with no agency considerations, the principal would pay no more than W^* to its workers.

Now suppose a worker shirks. The principal could fire the worker, but if work can quickly be obtained elsewhere, the worker will have lost no wages and will have benefited from not having worked too hard. The principal could try to make the worker pay a fine, but many agents have limited ability to pay fines, and contracts that extract fines from fired workers are illegal. The remaining option for the principal is to make the worker want to keep the job. The principal can do this by paying a wage $W > W^*$. The principal thus "punishes" the worker who is caught shirking by forcing that worker to seek employment elsewhere at a lower wage.

Sorting

In our discussion and examples, there is a single agent, and the principal uses a contract to motivate that agent to work hard. In reality, the principal may have many agents to choose from, who may possess different abilities and motives. Some may have more skills; others may have stronger work ethics. The principal would like to attract hard-working, highly skilled agents, and may tailor the contract accordingly. When the level of wages or structure of the incentive contract systematically influences the characteristics of the agents a principal can hire, we say that sorting occurs.

Job sorting is common. Sometimes workers sort themselves according to their values. For example, Myron Roomkin and Burt Weisbrod argue that some individuals are willing to accept lower pay to work at charitable institutions, and this allows many nonprofit organizations to attract top talent without paying top salaries.[15] Workers also sort themselves by skill. Firms like Microsoft, Cray Research, and Merck are legendary for attracting the brightest talent. Some of this is due to idiosyncratic factors that are hard to duplicate; for example, computer hardware designers wanted to work with the eccentric Seymour Cray, and software designers wanted to work with Bill Gates and his staff. But the explicit and implicit reward structure of the firm can also attract the right kinds of workers.

---

[14]Eaton, B. C. and W. D. White, "Agent Compensation and the Limits of Bonding," *Economic Inquiry*, 20, July 1982: pp. 330–343; and Shapiro, C. and J. Stiglitz, "Equilibrium Unemployment as a Worker Disciplining Device," *American Economic Review*, 74, June 1984: pp. 433–444.

[15]Roomkin, M. and B. Weisbrod, "Managerial Compensation in For-profit and Nonprofit Hospitals: Is There a Difference?" Northwestern University, working paper, 1997.

How does the type of contract affect sorting? The following rules of thumb are useful:

- More able workers and risk takers prefer pay-for-performance contracts.

- Workers with low mobility are more tolerant of schemes that link pay to job tenure. As discussed in the next section, this could affect internal labor markets.

- Agents (firms or workers) with limited liability are more willing to accept contracts that provide larger rewards for success and large penalties for failure.

Managers must account for sorting when designing agency contracts. For example, universities know that tenure policies focusing exclusively on research will not only encourage existing faculty to spend most of their time doing research, but will also attract new faculty who perceive themselves to be skilled researchers. To take another example, engineering firms that do not use high-powered incentive contracts often attract risk-averse engineers, who may be content to sell existing products rather than invest the time necessary for new product development.

COMPLICATIONS TO THE AGENCY RELATIONSHIP ◆ ◆ ◆ ◆ ◆

Multiple Agents and Teams

Thus far, we have considered situations in which one principal employs one agent. In most organizations, however, several agents work simultaneously for the same principal. When this occurs, we have multiple agency.

Teams exemplify multiple agency. The decision to organize workers into teams is analyzed in Chapter 16. A critical issue of interest here is how to reward individual team members when it is only possible to measure the output of the team as a whole. This is a central problem for management, especially because workers in the 1990s have been increasingly organized into teams, and firms such as Motorola have thousands of work teams. Yet there do not appear to be easy solutions. For example a 1997 article in *USA Today* reported that the best attended session every year at the annual International Conference on Work Teams is "Why Teams Fail."[16]

The fundamental agency problem with teams is that it is difficult to provide high-powered incentives while maintaining the team concept. One approach is to treat the team as a single agent and pay it a single fee. The team then determines how to split the fee. This approach works only to the extent that the team implements a reward scheme that prevents shirking. But instead, if the team elects to share any fee equally, individual team members may choose to shirk, feeling that this will minimally affect the overall team product. Team members can prevent shirking by peer pressure or by refusing to work with shirkers on future projects.

Armen Alchian and Harold Demsetz offer another solution: Assign one team member to monitor and reward or punish the other workers.[17] They also suggest

---

[16]Newborne, Ellen "Companies Save, but Workers Pay," *USA Today*, February 25, 1997, Money, page 1B.

[17]Alchian, A. and H. Demsetz, "Production, Information Costs, and Economic Organization," *American Economic Review*, 62, 1972: pp. 777–797.

that the monitor keep any profits that are left over after paying the other team members; that is, the monitor becomes the owner of the team. This gives the monitor incentives to be vigilant and to offer fair contracts that encourage hard work while attracting good workers. But this adds to the principal's costs.

The firm might instead retain a reward structure based on individual performance. The top performers within a team might then receive more than their teammates. But this can promote unhealthy competition, not unlike the problem of influence costs described in Chapter 3. Individuals may devote more effort to improving their relative performance within the team than to the overall output of the team.

◆ ◆

$\mathcal{E}$XAMPLE 15.4

TEAM INCENTIVES AT NUCOR[18]

How does a relatively small firm in the seemingly dull business of steel manufacturing get to be profiled in leading business magazines, be the subject of a Harvard case study, and a highly regarded business trade book, and be dissected in the academically-inclined *Journal of Economics and Management Strategy*? The remarkable interest in steel maker Nucor (which we have seen before in Chapter 8) stems from its ability to consistently outperform its rivals, big and small, in a notoriously competitive industry. Nucor does it by maintaining a single-minded devotion to cost reduction, reinforced by a hard-edged incentive scheme unlike any other in its industry.

Nucor's ability to contain costs is legendary. Nucor's continuous caster (described in example 8.3) cost one-fifth as much as other casting technologies. Nucor gambled its future on the success of the technology, knowing that it needed such a cost advantage to survive. More recently, Nucor took six months and spent $25 million to build a galvanizing line. It took USX nearly two years and $50 million to build its galvanizing line. Nucor engineers are renowned for customizing lines after installation, generating further cost reductions of 10–25 percent. These examples help explain why Nucor CEO Kenneth Iverson estimates that Nucor's average costs are about 20 to 30 percent below industry norms.

Much of Nucor's success can be traced to its organizational structure and incentives. Nucor is a fairly "flat" firm, with only four levels of authority separating top management from production workers. The corporate staff of about 25 operates out of a lean office in a North Carolina strip mall. With small corporate staff, Nucor must necessarily decentralize decision making. Indeed, virtually all major decisions (except for capital expenditures, pricing, and reorganization) are made by plant managers at the plants. Nucor combines decision-making authority with high-powered financial incentives. Each plant supervisor and department

---

[18]Material for this example was drawn from Welles, E.O. "Bootstrapping for Billions," *Inc. Online*, September 1994, p. 78 and Ghemawat, P. "Competitive Advantage and Internal Organization: Nucor Revisited," *Journal of Economics and Management Strategy*, Winter 1995, 3(4): pp. 685–717.

head receives as much as 60 percent of salary based on plant performance. To facilitate information flows that aid decision making, Nucor limits the size and bureaucracy at each plant and solicits input from plant workers. (Plant workers even visit other plants to offer and obtain suggestions.)

Nucor's reliance on high-powered incentives extends to production workers, who are organized into groups of 25 to 35 that work collectively to meet production deadlines while reducing costs. Group members receive a guaranteed wage well below that paid to similar workers in competing firms. But they can receive bonuses, based on group performance, that exceed their base pay. In fact, bonus pay equals about 60 percent of total worker compensation. The result is that a worker who belongs to a high-performing group can outearn a similar worker in another firm by 20 percent or more.

Group-based incentives can fail if individual group members free-ride, especially if the outstanding performance of one group member enables the entire group to profit. It is true that Nucor rewards all members of a high-performing group even if the group's superior performance can be traced to one member. But Nucor also punishes the entire group when one member shirks. This creates intense peer pressure within groups, so that group members monitor each other's performance. It also enables Nucor to attract highly motivated workers. In many communities where it has plants, Nucor is the only employer to offer high-powered incentives to low skilled workers. Individuals who believe that they can outwork their peers are naturally attracted by the opportunity to be rewarded for their efforts. Nucor also uses psychological tests to help it identify goal-oriented self-reliant workers.

High-powered incentives can be effective during economic upturns, as all workers enjoy the financial benefits of the firm's good fortunes. But they can cause anxiety and upheaval during downturns as compensation falls. To avoid this, Nucor has sought to nurture trust between top management and workers. This results from explicit safeguards of workers' rights, such as dismissal only for just-cause, a policy of never laying workers off during a downturn, and implicit understandings between management and workers, such as the repeated investments by Nucor in plant improvement and expansion that translate into more jobs and job security, and the understanding that worker input is highly valued. As CEO Iverson states "If somebody comes up with a new idea, we seldom say no."

Multidimensional Agency

In most organizations, an agent's work for a principal has an impact on many performance dimensions simultaneously. For example, a relationship manager (RM) in a commercial bank is typically responsible for sales activity, that is, convincing a potential corporate client to do business with the RM's bank rather than another bank. But the RM is also responsible for strengthening the bank's relationship with its clients. This is why RMs are encouraged to devote effort to developing expertise in their clients' industries and why they are expected to help clients identify new financial products that could serve their future needs, even though no immediate deals result from this contact. Thus, the RM's work has an impact on two broad dimensions: sales of financial services in the current period, a dimension in which success is relatively easy to quantify; and the quality of the bank's relationship with its corporate client, a dimension in which success is harder to quantify.

Multidimensional agency refers to circumstance in which agents perform tasks that affect multiple dimensions that the principal cares about. Multidimensional agency would pose no special issues beyond those that exist in a standard agency relationship if (1) performance in each dimension could be measured equally well or (2) performing well in one dimension did not impair good performance in other dimensions. However, these conditions often do not hold. Consider, for example, a production worker who is responsible for both producing a high volume and a high quality of output. The quantity dimension is often easy to measure, but the quality dimension often is not. For example, shoddy quality may only become apparent long after the product has sold to consumers. Moreover, it is often hard simultaneously to increase both volume and quality. In many tasks, increasing the speed of one's work also increases the number of mistakes.

The inability to observe quality and the conflict between quantity and quality complicates the design of a compensation system for workers. To see why, suppose a firm used a piece-rate system to motivate its manufacturing workers. If quantity were the only dimension the firm cared about, a piece-rate system might provide acceptable incentives for workers not to shirk.[19] When quality is hard to measure, however, a piece-rate will encourage workers to cut corners on quality in order to increase their volume of output. The firm might be better off rewarding workers based on hourly wages, even though such a system might provide "lower-power" incentives for workers to produce a high volume of output.

Bengt Holmstrom and Paul Milgrom point out that multidimensional agency can explain why many contracts lack "high-power" incentive clauses.[20] They note that when an agent's actions can affect one or more important performance dimensions that cannot be measured, the optimal second-best contract will often involve paying a fixed wage and will contain no incentive provisions. Expressed in terms of the notation developed above, if the general form of the compensation contract is $W = A + BX$ (where, again, W is the agent's payment and X is the observable dimension of performance), Holmstrom and Milgrom find that $B = 0$ in the optimal second-best contract. The basic idea behind this conclusion is similar to the intuition in our piece-rate example: By rewarding an agent for doing well on an observable dimension of performance, the principal will induce the agent to over-deliver performance on that dimension but neglect performance on other, unobservable dimensions. This insight explains why you might not want to put in an incentive clause rewarding a building contractor for finishing a project on time (the contractor would cut corners to finish fast). It also explains why a medical practice might not want to reward a physician for how many patients he or she treats (the doctors will want to see many patients, leaving little time to devote to in-depth diagnosis of any one patient's malady). And it explains why a bank would not want to reward a relationship manager solely on the basis of the number of

---

[19]Though, as discussed previously, a piece-rate system will often not ensure the first-best level of effort.

[20]Holmstrom, B. and P. Milgrom, "Mulitask Principal-Agent Analyses: Incentive Contracts, Asset Ownership, and Job Design," *Journal of Law, Economics, and Organization*, 7, Spring 1991: pp. 24–52; Holmstrom, B. and P. Milgrom, "The Firm as an Incentive System," *American Economic Review*, 84, September, 1994: pp. 972–991.

deals he or she makes within a given period of time (the RM would devote inordinate time to what some commercial bankers call "grazing"—going where the grass is greenest in terms of immediate deal-making opportunities—and insufficient time developing stronger relationships with clients).

INTERNAL LABOR MARKETS   ◆ ◆ ◆ ◆ ◆

The firm is a nexus of agency problems. All workers within a firm, from top management on down, may pursue objectives that are incompatible with maximizing those of their immediate superiors, shareholders, or both. Agency problems may be less severe for some kinds of workers than for others. Peter Doeringer and Michael Piore describe some workers, such as janitors and messengers, as being in the *secondary sector* of the economy.[21] Managers can easily observe and evaluate the performance of these workers, and can easily replace them if they shirk too much. As a result, agency problems are minimal, and there are few if any pay-for-performance provisions.

Managers find it more challenging to evaluate workers in the *primary sector*, including most skilled workers and professionals. These workers make substantial contribution to profits, perform highly specialized tasks, and often work in teams. Measuring the individual outputs of these workers is both important and difficult and agency problems for these workers can be severe.

Firms frequently rely on *internal labor markets* to solve agency problems for managers and professionals in the primary sector. The internal labor market consists of an employer and a group of employees organized around a functional area (e.g., accounting), geographic area, or product. In an internal labor market, the employer relies heavily on implicit contracts to solve agency problems. Rather than specify output-based rewards, such as a fixed fee for producing a strategic plan, the employer lets its employees know that those who add value will be rewarded with opportunities for higher wages, promotion, end-of-year bonuses, stocks, and stock options.

Ideally, firms would pay their workers according to the value they create; firms do this explicitly for some workers—for example, many salespeople are paid commissions. There are several problems with paying other types of workers according to value added, however. First, firms often have difficulty determining value added. For example, how does one determine the value added of a strategic plan or of a new engineering design? Second, some workers, such as those on assembly lines, may have jobs that are easy to describe but would be costly to consistently monitor. Finally, it is sometimes difficult to precisely measure output, especially for managers and professionals. In these situations, firms must find some other mechanism to reward good work. One way they do this is by backloading compensation.

Backloading Compensation

We say that compensation is backloaded if wages are below productivity early in a worker's tenure on the job, but exceed productivity with seniority. Backloaded compensation is exemplified by the wage/tenure profile.

---

[21]Doeringer, P. and M. Piore, *Internal Labor Markets and Manpower Analysis*, Lexington, MA: D.C. Heath, 1971.

The Wage/Tenure Profile

One of the most distinctive features of internal labor markets is the sharply rising "wage/tenure" profile, as depicted in Figure 15.2.[22] At most firms, wages increase with job tenure. A simple explanation for this is provided by human capital theory. Human capital is the knowledge and skills (physical and intellectual) that an individual possesses that make him or her productive. The increasing wage/tenure profile could simply represent an increase in productivity over time. Alternatively, Gary Becker has suggested that workers might accept low wages early in their careers if they receive on-the-job training that enhances their future productivity and job opportunities.[23] This theory is consistent with the relatively low wages medical residents, law clerks, and bank trainees earn, for example.

Increases in human capital help explain part of the wage/tenure profile. But they do not explain three other important features of internal labor markets. First, until recent federal legislation made them largely illegal, many U.S. firms had mandatory retirement policies. Second, many pension plans offer a higher rate of return to employees who retire early. These two facts imply that firms appear to prefer younger workers to older workers, which contradicts the view that older workers are more productive. Finally, James Medoff and Katherine Abraham have shown that wages increase with job tenure even if performance does not.[24] This is shown in Figure 15.3. In other words, wages are backloaded, so that workers are paid less than they are worth to the firm early in their tenure and more than they are worth late in their tenure. This helps explain why firms may prefer younger workers to older workers—the firm is overpaying older workers relative to their productivity. But why do firms backload wages? The answer may be found in agency theory.

FIGURE 15.2
THE WAGE-TENURE PROFILE.

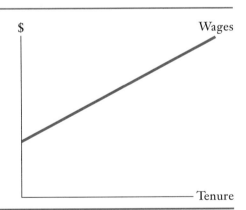

Wages tend to increase with job tenure. This may reflect increased productivity of older workers, or it may be tied to incentives.

[22]For a review of research on the wage/tenure profile, see Hutchens, R., "Seniority, Wages, and Productivity: A Turbulent Decade," *Journal of Economic Perspectives*, 3, 1989: pp. 49–64, and Carmichael, H. L., "Self-enforcing Contracts, Shirking, and Life-cycle Effects," *Journal of Economic Perspectives*, 3, 1989: pp. 65–84.

[23]Becker, G., "Investment in Human Capital: A Theoretical Analysis," *Journal of Political Economy*, 70, 1962: pp. 9–49.

[24]Medoff, J. and K. Abraham, "Experience, Performance, and Earnings," *Quarterly Journal of Economics*, 95, 1980: pp. 703–736.

FIGURE 15.3
BACKLOADED COMPENSATION.

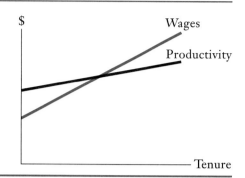

Wages tend to increase faster than productivity. For many workers, wages do not exceed productivity until they have been on the job for several years. Backloaded compensation may be useful for preventing shirking by younger workers.

Agency Explanations for Backloaded Wages

Gary Becker, George Stigler, and Edward Lazear have argued that firms may not be able to sufficiently punish workers to prevent them from shirking.[25] At most, firms can fire workers, who may then collect unemployment compensation or find another job. Firms could pay efficiency wages, but this is costly. Instead, firms may defer compensation as a kind of performance guarantee, or "bond." To receive the bond, workers must avoid getting laid off, and thus do not shirk.

A steep wage/tenure profile may also facilitate the development of firm-specific assets. Many firms train workers to perform specialized tasks—training that has little or no value should the workers leave. This training is costly for firms. In addition, the firm must tolerate low productivity by new workers until they move down the learning curve. Firms that make such investments would naturally like their workers to remain with the firm for a long time. A steep profile encourages such loyalty.

Robert Hutchens points out that workers who make firm-specific investments may be reluctant to accept a steep profile.[26] The firm could lay off the workers and thereby avoid paying wages in excess of productivity. The workers, whose skills are firm-specific, might have a difficult time finding other employment. H. Lorne Carmichael argues that firms must rely on implicit contracts and long-term relationships to convince employees to accept specific training.[27] These ideas are closely tied to the concepts developed in Chapter 17 on organizational culture.

If the wage/tenure profile serves as a carrot to reward hard work and investments in training, then increased labor market turnover may have a pernicious effect on effort. We have already discussed in Chapters 4 and 6 how these ideas have shaped thinking about the implications of corporate takeovers for the relationship between firms and workers. Recall Andrei Shleifer and Lawrence Summers' argu-

---

[25]Becker, G. and G. Stigler, "Law Enforcement and Compensation of Enforcers," *Journal of Legal Studies*, 3, 1974: pp. 1–18; Lazear, E., "Why Is There Mandatory Retirement?" *Journal of Political Economy*, 87, 1979: pp. 1261–1284.

[26]Hutchens, R., "Seniority, Wages, and Productivity: A Turbulent Decade," *Journal of Economic Perspectives*, 3, 1989: pp. 49–64.

[27]Carmichael, H. L., "Self-enforcing Contracts, Shirking, and Life-cycle Effects," *Journal of Economic Perspectives*, 3, 1989: pp. 65–84.

ment that an outside raider can abrogate implicit wage agreements. This would allow the raider to reduce the wages paid to employees with longer tenure. Since these employees' skills are firm specific, they may have to accept the lower wages. Even without takeovers, corporate restructurings and downsizing may have the same effect with alarming consequences for long-term productivity. Workers with little tenure may perceive that they are unlikely to keep their jobs long enough to climb up the wage/tenure profile. This may reduce incentives to work hard and make firm-specific investments.

EXAMPLE 15.5

ESTIMATING THE MAGNITUDE OF THE WAGE/TENURE PROFILE

Economists generally agree that wages rise significantly with seniority. They disagree, however, about the cause of this relationship. Some argue that the relationship reflects a reward for competence. In economic models that make this argument, employers retain competent workers but not incompetent ones. Rival firms can identify the workers with long tenure, infer that they must have great skill, and attempt to hire them by bidding up their wages. Other economists have suggested that the productivity of workers depends on their match to an employer. Workers with good matches have higher productivity and wages, and tend to stay on the job. Workers with poor matches will switch jobs, hoping eventually to find a good match and higher wages. Still others argue that workers improve their productivity by making firm-specific investments. Firms reward these workers with higher wages, mainly to induce them to continue making these investments.

Because wages may be related to job tenure for many reasons, it is difficult to estimate precisely the exact magnitude of this relationship. A naive researcher might obtain data about the wages and job tenure of different workers, graph wages against tenure, and conclude that the slope of the line represents the returns to tenure. But this approach would understate the true wage/tenure relationship. To see why, remember that workers may switch jobs for many reasons. Most workers who change jobs enjoy a wage increase. They have higher wages but low tenure. Including these workers in the data reduces the slope of the wage/tenure line.

To clear up the muddle, it is necessary to focus on workers who did not change jobs to increase their wages. The following example shows how this may be done. Consider two workers, Monica and Anke. Monica and Anke begin work in the same year for competing firms. After three years, Anke's firm closes, and she goes to work for Monica's firm. In this case, both workers have the same overall experience, but Anke has longer job tenure. However, there is no reason to believe that Anke is more competent than Monica, since Anke did not change jobs to secure a higher wage. A direct comparison of Anke's and Monica's wages would provide strong evidence about the magnitude of the wage/tenure profile.

Christian Dustmann and Costas Meghir recently performed an empirical analysis based on this example.[28] They obtained data for the period 1975–1990 from the German Federal Employment Office. This office collects information on wages and unemployment spells for each worker covered by the German social security system. They combined this with information about employers to identify workers who lost their jobs due to plant closures. Using sophisticated econometric techniques, they estimated that a German worker with five years tenure at a particular firm will earn 25 percent higher wages than a new worker with comparable work experience but no tenure at that firm. When they performed the "naive" estimation, they found that the return to tenure appeared to be only about half as large.

Bonuses, Promotions, and Tournaments

Most workers receive some kind of annual performance evaluation, which determines what kind of raise they will receive. The increase is generally small, however, and there may be little difference between what the best performers and average performers receive. Thus, the promise of a wage increase may not provide sufficient motivation. Many firms rely on two additional tools to motivate workers: bonuses and promotion.

Bonuses and Issuance of Stock

According to a recent report by the Hay Group, nearly all business executives (92 percent) and most managers (83 percent) are eligible for bonuses.[29] Even among entry-level professionals, more than half (56 percent) are eligible. Bonuses represent an ever-increasing percentage of total compensation. Bonuses in 1996 equaled 74 percent of base pay for executives and roughly 20 percent of base pay for managers.

Bonuses are often linked to the achievement of specific short-term *goals*, such as reducing costs, gaining new clients, or bringing new products to market. Bonuses for achieving short-term goals can be effective motivators, because the goals are usually easy to measure and the rewards for achieving them are immediate and clearly understood. It is rarer to see bonuses tied to the development of specific *skills*. Instead, most firms reward workers who develop valuable skills by increasing their base pay. This makes sense. By enhancing their skills, workers should become more productive for many years. The firm could give large lump sum bonuses to workers who enhanced their skills; the bonus would be tied to the increase in the net present value of worker productivity. Having been once rewarded for future productivity gains, however, workers might be tempted to seek other jobs, because other employers would also stand to gain from their skills. (This temptation would be minimized if the skills were firm-specific.) Thus, the firm may be better off spreading out the pay for skill enhancement over several years, for example in the form of higher base pay.

---

[28]Dustmann, C. and C. Meghir, 1997, "Seniority and Wage Growth," University College, London. Mimeo.

[29]This information was reported in *Ioma's Report on Salary Surveys*, May 1998.

Bonuses seem to offer workers greater opportunity to receive compensation for their hard work. However, even if there is no shirking, a worker may fail to achieve specific goals and therefore fail to receive a bonus. Demand for a product may dry up. Team members may not pull their own weight. Because so much is outside the control of an individual worker, the more pay is dependent on bonuses, the riskier it becomes. Despite the risk, bonuses continue to gain in popularity. One explanation is that workers are growing less risk averse. This could be occurring because more workers have spouses who also work, so that the amount of the bonus as a percentage of household income may be relatively unchanged from what it was years ago, even as the nominal size of the bonus has been increasing.

A second explanation is that firms are growing more sophisticated at measuring performance, therefore reducing the risk that a hard worker will be unfairly punished. Improvements in electronic data interfaces and activity-based accounting facilitate the measurement of individual and business unit performance, enhancing the effectiveness of bonuses as a pay-for-performance mechanism.

Executives also receive a considerable percentage of their income in the form of stocks and stock options. A 1998 survey by *Forbes* magazine of 800 U.S. CEOs found that stocks and stock options represented nearly half of their average total compensation of $2.3 million.[30] Some executives, such as Microsoft's Bill Gates, have always owned a substantial percentage of their companies. Others, such as Disney's Michael Eisner, have been awarded stocks and stock options by their boards of directors. This clearly ties compensation to the bottom line, while simultaneously exposing the CEOs to greater risk. Critics of the use of stocks and options suggest that when the overall economy is doing well, the value of stocks and options increases even for average firms. They suggest that stocks and options should only be granted for above average performance. If the economy declines, firms may need to reissue options with lower exercise prices to replace options with unrealistically high exercise prices.

Promotions

James Emshoff, an expert on corporate restructuring, observes that the hierarchical firm offers opportunities for promotion that are unavailable in "flat firms" which have few hierarchical layers.[31] The possibility of promotion is another carrot to motivate workers. There are many job levels in a typical hierarchical firm. Federal government workers progress through a series of 16 "GS" ranks, in which promotion is based on job responsibility, performance evaluation, and educational attainment. Private firms may have as many as eight job levels or more. Within each level may be several salary grades. The number of positions at each successively higher job level usually declines as one goes up the corporate ladder. George Baker, Michael Gibbs, and Bengt Holmstrom (BGH) examined the hierarchy at one firm with nearly 5,000 employees.[32] They found that there were eight levels, but that only 116 (2 percent) of the workers were in one of the top four levels.

---

[30]"Who Gets Paid What?" *"Forbes,* May 18, 1998, p. 234.

[31]Emshoff, J., "Is It Time to Create a New Theory of the Firm?" *Journal of Economics and Management Strategy,* 2, 1993: pp. 3–14.

[32]Baker, G., M. Gibbs, and B. Holmstrom, "The Wage Policy of a Firm," Harvard Business School, working paper, 1993.

XAMPLE 15.6

MOTIVATING SECONDARY SECTOR WORKERS
WITH PROMOTIONS: SERVICEMASTER

ServiceMaster Industries contracts with health care providers, schools, and industry to manage their housekeeping, foodservice, laundry, and other relatively unskilled employees. With annual revenues well in excess of $2 billion, and an annual growth rate of 10 to 20 percent, it is regarded as a remarkable and wholly unexpected success story. An important part of ServiceMaster's success is its human resources management policy.

In the 1950s, ServiceMaster recognized that hospital administrators preferred to "buy" rather than "make" management functions that involved low-level activities, such as housekeeping. ServiceMaster provided on-site management support and promised to boost productivity. Although Service-Master developed new products and techniques (including novel techniques for mopping floors), it considered its employees its greatest asset, and strove to motivate them. Employees were treated like family, and top management often devoted personal attention to the problems of lower-level workers. The company also used financial incentives, including bonuses and generous pay hikes. In addition, roughly three-fourths of the firm's associates held stock in the company.

But the greatest motivational tool at ServiceMaster is its promotion ladder. Most of ServiceMaster's managers began their careers in the secondary economy, as foodservice workers, housekeepers, and so on. Workers (known as "field managers") can advance up a career path with eight levels, from "employee" to "division manager." Promotion opportunities begin even earlier—nearly 20 percent of management trainees are hired from the ranks of support staff that Service-Master is contracted to supervise. The company's sustained growth has made the promotional ladder an effective motivating tool—workers at all levels, including those still employed by ServiceMaster's clients, perceived that they had significant opportunities for promotion as long as they work hard. ServiceMaster further rewards top workers with support for educational programs ranging from literacy training to college education. The hard work of ServiceMaster employees has made the company a huge success.

A promotional ladder can motivate workers only if they believe that the opportunities for promotion are genuine. With this in mind, ServiceMaster faces two problems as it strives to sustain its success. First, it must continue to grow to assure ever more opportunities for promotion. To maintain its growth, it has acquired lawn care and pesticide businesses and expanded overseas. But as viable growth opportunities dry up, the company will be unable to maintain its historic rate of promotion. Second, the promotional ladder ends at division manager. Workers moved up this ladder are usually unable to advance to the central office, whose employees are often recruited from business schools. ServiceMaster has been reluctant to expand the responsibilities of managers promoted through the ranks, but must still find a way to motivate them. Both of these problems may reduce the motivating force of the promotional ladder in the future.

"Promotions" usually involve movement through higher salary grades and levels. Promotions to higher grades often provide greater wage increases than are possible by achieving outstanding performance within a grade. The possibility of promotion and the attendant salary increases undoubtedly help motivate workers. In the firm that they examined, BGH confirmed that wage differences across levels served to reward ability; in other words, more highly skilled workers were rewarded through promotions up the corporate hierarchy.

Like the one studied by BGH, most firms have fewer and fewer positions as one moves up the hierarchy. This implies that not all workers at any given level will be promoted to the next level. The notion of promoting the hardest-working and most able workers has been likened to athletic tournaments, in which individuals and teams are ranked relative to other competitors.[33] Promotion tournaments work in much the same way—a worker earns rewards by outperforming coworkers and moving up the hierarchy. Tournaments can reduce shirking and attract highly skilled workers seeking rewards for their talents.

If firms could accurately evaluate individual worker performance, tournaments would be unnecessary. Firms would simply follow the contracting principals laid out earlier in this chapter. Tournaments are useful when relative performance is easier to measure than absolute performance. In a well-known application of this idea, the fictional real estate salesmen in the play *Glengarry Glen Ross* competed to see who would be among the top three in sales. The rest would be fired. This scheme rewards hard work and ability (although it does not promote teamwork!). More important, it is easier to design and implement than a scheme that rewarded each worker based on absolute performance. The latter scheme would require that the owner of the firm know how much each salesperson could be expected to sell, and then compare actual and expected sales. Actual sales are a function of effort, but also of the overall economy, of the product being sold, and of other factors beyond the control of any individual salesperson. Thus, this scheme introduces much risk. A tournament eliminates much of this risk. Firmwide fluctuations in sales affect all salespersons equally. Their relative performance remains largely a function of their own effort and ability and is therefore a less noisy measure.

Though widespread in business, tournaments have potential drawbacks. They are subject to influence costs, as workers try to convince their bosses that they deserve a high relative ranking. Workers may collude to reduce output, without any reduction in overall compensation. Even worse, they may deliberately sabotage the efforts of others. This was a frequent allegation made against premed students in the 1970s who perceived admission to medical school to be a tournament.

◆ ◆ ◆ ◆ ◆ EXECUTIVE COMPENSATION

In the second half of the 1990s, the compensation of American business executives escalated remarkably. Top executives at most American companies can now earn salaries that are hundreds of times greater than those of their lowest paid employees. Although some observers criticize these seemingly bloated salaries, others point out that they are appropriate for two reasons. First, good executives may add

---

[33]For further discussion of labor market tournaments, see Edward Lazear and Sherwin Rosen, "Rank Order Tournaments as Optimal Labor Contracts," *Journal of Political Economy*, 89, 1981: pp. 841–864.

enormous value to their firms. Second, high compensation is necessary to motivate executives.

Top management may add value to their firms in many ways. They make important strategic decisions, and help to create and oversee the organizational structure that enables workers to be productive. Few doubt that Michael Eisner's decision to reenergize Disney's animated movie division added billions to the value of Disney stock. Firms like Disney may need to offer their top managers substantial compensation to prevent them from taking jobs elsewhere. Indeed, Rachel Hayes and Scott Schaefer find evidence that the compensation of top managers does, at least in part, reflect the value that they bring to their organizations.[34] They compare the decline in shareholder value at firms whose CEOs are hired by other firms with the decline at firms whose CEOs die unexpectedly. They argue that CEOs raided by other firms are likely to have higher than average ability whereas CEOs who die unexpectedly have average ability, in expectation. They find that for the average firm in their sample, stock prices decline by $20 to $50 million more when the CEO leaves for another firm than when the CEO dies unexpectedly. They attribute this to the loss of a high ability CEO.

High compensation may not only reward executives for their high ability, it may also motivate them. If this is the case, then compensation should increase when firms do better, and decrease when firms do poorly. Michael Jensen and Kevin J. Murphy measured the relationship between executive compensation and firm performance.[35] They examined the salaries, bonuses, and stock options of CEOs as reported in *Forbes'* "Executive Compensation Surveys" from 1974 to 1986. They found that at the typical firm, the CEO's salary and bonus were not very responsive to firm performance. Specifically, they found that a CEO whose shareholders lost $400 million in a single year would earn an average of $800,000 in salary and bonus, whereas a CEO whose shareholders gained $400 million would earn $1,040,000 in salary and bonus. Thus, an $800-million swing in firm performance was associated with a $204,000 swing in salary. Jensen and Murphy question whether such an income differential can provide proper motivation. On the other hand, they found that stocks and stock options do provide some motivation. The same $800-million swing in performance was associated with a $1.2-million swing in the value of stocks and options. Finally, Jensen and Murphy found that CEOs are dismissed so infrequently that the threat of dismissal is not an important motivator.

There continues to be considerable debate about the appropriate level of executive compensation in the United States. Executives in Europe rarely receive the same level of compensation as their American counterparts. While some analysts feel that the compensation of executives in the United States is unfair, studies like Hayes/Schaefer suggest that highly skilled CEOs may add substantial value to their firms. In addition, studies such as Jensen/Murphy suggest that if anything, CEO compensation is not sufficiently tied to performance.

Prior to the stock market declines in fall 1998, American executives enjoyed the benefits of a booming stock market without appearing to face substantial

---

[34]Hayes, R. and S. Schaefer, "How Much Are Differences in Managerial Ability Worth?" *Journal of Accounting and Economics*, 27, 1999.

[35]Jensen, M. and K. J. Murphy, "Performance Pay and Top Management Incentives," *Journal of Political Economy*, 98, 1990: pp. 225–264.

downside risk. Many believe that if the CEO is largely responsible for company performance, he or she should have a personal stake in the company's gains *and* losses. Indeed, 1998 saw many CEOs take multimillion-dollar "paper losses" when their companies' stock prices declined. By early 1999, however, the market had recovered and the value of CEO stock holdings was soaring.

EXAMPLE 15.7

EXECUTIVE COMPENSATION IN JAPANESE FIRMS[36]

During the 1980s, business gurus encouraged American managers to adopt Japanese business practices. While there is no question that many Japanese firms thrived during the 1980s, it remains unclear just what made them successful. Possibilities include the engineering skills of automakers and electronics firms, the infusion of total quality management principles, the corporate cultures built on teamwork, and the cheap investment capital (attributable to high national savings rates).

Although Japanese firms have been offered up as role models for American firms, it is the Japanese firms that have struggled in recent years. In the 1990s, Japan's manufacturing sector achieved an average return on equity of roughly 5 percent, well below the U.S. average of 17 percent. As a result, many Japanese firms have begun to question some of their own management practices, including executive compensation.

Traditional Japanese compensation practices have three major features. First, pay is largely tied to seniority—there is little variation in salary as a function of performance. Second, Japanese firms focused more on market share than on profits. Third, shareholders have virtually no voice in corporate operations.

These practices stand in sharp contrast with American practices. Compensation of senior managers of American companies has increasingly been tied to divisional or corporate profitability. Many senior executives receive stock options whose values may exceed their salaries. At the same time, bonuses have become widespread throughout corporate hierarchies. Lastly, institutional shareholders have taken an active role in supervising top management and have even been instrumental in removing CEOs of poorly performing companies.

In recent years, shareholders of Japanese firms have also become more vocal. The success of Japanese firms encouraged foreign investors to take large positions in Japanese firms. (The California Public Employees' Retirement System owns nearly $6 billion in Japanese equities.) Foreign investors now own 10 percent of Japanese stocks. At the same time, Japanese pension funds and insurance companies, which also owns about 10 percent of Japanese stocks, face critical funding shortfalls. These shareholders are not content with the returns shown in recent years, and are pushing for changes. Moreover, many Japanese firms have independently recognized the need to change compensation practices.

---

[36]Much of the information in this example is drawn from Weinberg, N. "Buy Japan Now!" *Forbes* 9/8/1997, p. 78., and Brull, S. "Rohm: A Most UnJapanese Chipmaker," *Business Week* 7/21/1997 p. 324.

Changes are coming rapidly to some Japanese firms. Many have increased the link between executive pay and firm performance. For example, giant chipmaker Rohm directly calibrates salaries to performance. As a result, salaries of Rohm managers can vary as much as 50 percent depending on performance. A recent change in Japanese law permits Japanese firms to issue stock options. Almost immediately thereafter, Toyota issued stock options to its directors. (It also encouraged middle managers to buy shares of the company.) Another recent law enables shareholders to more easily buy back shares rather than leave the money in the hands of senior managers who might make unprofitable investments in pursuit of growth. Several dozen firms initiated share buybacks in the wake of this law.

Japanese firms are also introducing substantial bonus payments to top performers. Rohm offers prizes of nearly $100,000 to workers who make strong contributions to the bottom line. Computer game company Square Co. offers bonuses of up to $800,000 to developers of top-selling games.

Not all Japanese firms have been quick to adopt these changes, and many continue to be closely held by banks and other shareholders who are unlikely to pressure them for change any time soon. If the financial performance of these firms lags behind that of their competitors, we may soon see the widespread adoption of American compensation practices in Japan.

CHAPTER SUMMARY

◆ Agency theory examines the use of financial incentives to motivate workers. In an agency relationship, one individual, known as the principal, delegates responsibility to another, known as the agent, to act on his or her behalf.

◆ The principal and the agent are likely to have divergent goals. The principal would like the agent to take the most efficient action, while paying the agent a threshold wage. A contract that accomplishes this is first-best efficient. An agent who does not take the efficient action is said to be shirking.

◆ First-best efficiency is achievable if the principal can costlessly monitor the actions and/or outcomes of the agent, and the agent is not exposed to income risk.

◆ When the agent possesses hidden information or can take hidden actions, the principal must offer incentives that prevent the agent from shirking. One technique is to base rewards on easily observed outcomes that are correlated to the desired outcomes. The principal must also be concerned that the agent may manipulate information used for setting standards and evaluating performance.

◆ Piece-rate contracts are an example of a simple fee-for-X reward scheme based on easily observed outcomes. But these schemes may discourage workers from paying attention to other important outcomes that are less closely scrutinized.

◆ When the principal cannot perfectly determine effort from output, then output-based reward schemes introduce risk for the agent, who may work hard but receive a relatively low payment because of bad luck. The principal may need to increase the agent's base compensation to get a risk-averse agent to accept the risk.

◆ The second-best contract balances hard-edged incentives against the costs of exposing the agent to risk. Sometimes the principal can greatly improve performance by improving observability, rather than by altering contracts on the margin.

◆ Contracts that rely on punishments for motivation are problematic when agents have limited liability. The principal may need to increase the wage paid for favorable outcomes—that is, pay an efficiency wage—to compensate for the inability to collect from the agent in the event of an unfavorable outcome.

◆ The principal may use contracts to get workers to sort themselves by ability. More able workers are more likely to accept contracts that tie wages to performance.

◆ Firms use raises, bonuses, and promotions to motivate workers in the internal labor market. Bonuses and promotions are likely to provide stronger motivation, since raises tend to be only marginally related to performance.

◆ Wages tend to be backloaded, both to encourage loyalty and to motivate younger workers. Increases in labor market volatility may reduce the effectiveness of backloading.

◆ The incentive effects of promotions are similar to those in athletic tournaments. As workers climb the corporate ladder, opportunities for promotion diminish, but the rewards increase. Top management is further motivated by stock options whose value can exceed base salary.

QUESTIONS

1. Describe an agency relationship. Does the agent usually take the efficient action? Why or why not?

2. "Problems in agency relationships are not unlike problems in vertical chain relationships." Comment.

3. In the United States, lawyers in negligence cases are usually paid a contingency fee equal to roughly 30 percent of the total award. Lawyers in other types of cases are often paid on a hourly basis. Use agency theory to assess the merits and drawbacks of each type of fee arrangement from the client's (i.e., the principal's) perspective. Be sure to discuss incentive and sorting effects.

4. The credit card market has grown increasingly competitive. To maintain customer satisfaction, banks that issue credit cards usually provide an "800" number service center in which telephone operators handle customer inquiries, complaints, and requests for service. Some banks evaluate operators on the basis of the number of calls handled per day, while occasionally monitoring calls for courtesy and accuracy. (Banks have already determined that it is not cost-effective to do more monitoring.) Evaluate this monitoring system. What would you do differently? Consider the benefits and costs of any change you recommend.

5. Every year, the state of New York publishes rankings of surgeons based on their patients' mortality rates. It is well-known that the probability that a surgical patient dies depends both on the skill of the surgeon and the severity of the medical problem. New York tries to control for differences in severity, but lacks the data to do so effectively. Thus, it is alleged that surgeons may avoid the most severely ill patients so as to boost their ranking. Do you think that all surgeons will have the same incentives to screen their patients? How might the incentives to screen depend on the surgeon's present ranking? Do you think that the age of the surgeon might matter? Why or why not?

6. Suppose that a principal desires a worker to perform two tasks, but can only observe performance on one task. Under what conditions should the principal closely tie pay to performance on the first task?

7. School districts have debated whether to use tournaments to reward teachers. That is, only those teachers ranking near the top in performance would get bonus pay. The alternative is to tie bonus pay to some absolute measure of performance. Discuss the merits and drawbacks of each approach.

8. How can firms maintain the incentive benefits of the internal labor market in an era where employee turnover is rapidly increasing?

9. Professor Dranove's older son Daniel has a talent for making chocolate chip cookies. Each batch of cookies requires $5 worth of ingredients and one hour of Daniel's time to make. Professor Dranove can without effort, sell each batch of cookies for $25. Daniel does not mind spending one hour per week making cookies, as long as he can lick the spatula when he is finished. However, if he has to work more than one hour per week he has disutility of $5H^2$, where H is the total number of additional hours he spends making cookies. Thus, his marginal disutility of working an additional hour is $10H.

   (a) From the perspective of the Dranove family, what is the optimal number of hours Daniel should spend each week making cookies?

   (b) Suppose that Professor Dranove buys the ingredients and pays his son $10 per hour to make the cookies. How many hours will Daniel work?

   (c) What hourly rate must Professor Dranove pay his son to get him to work the optimal number of hours?

STRATEGY
AND STRUCTURE

16

Until the early 1980s, the Pepsi-Cola Company comprised three divisions that reported to corporate headquarters. Pepsi USA was largely responsible for creating marketing campaigns—the famous "Pepsi Challenge" was its brainchild. The Pepsi Bottling Group (PBG) bottled and distributed the product in local markets in which Pepsi had opted not to use independent bottlers. PBG was also responsible for local marketing campaigns, such as promotional giveaways. The Fountain Beverage Division (FBD) sold to fast-food outlets, restaurants, bars, and stadiums.

This structure caused problems. It made it difficult for Pepsi to negotiate with regional and national retailers, such as Piggly Wiggly and Wal-Mart. Pepsi USA and PBG often ran competing (and sometimes conflicting) promotional campaigns. Workers in PBG and FBD also resented the high salaries and high profiles of the Pepsi USA employees. To resolve these problems, Pepsi reorganized its beverage operations in 1988. Pepsi USA, PBG, and FBD ceased to exist. Sales and account management responsibilities were decentralized among four geographic regions. Decisions about national marketing campaigns, finance, human resources, and corporate operations, including trucking and company-owned bottlers, were centralized at headquarters and handled nationally.

But this reorganization did not solve Pepsi's coordination problems for long. Negotiations with national accounts often had to pass through several layers of management before a final decision could be reached, resulting in the loss of important accounts, notably Burger King. Conflicts between national and local promotional campaigns continued to arise. So in 1992, Pepsi reorganized again. This time, marketing and sales campaigns were further centralized, and responsibility for a given retail outlet was delegated to a single salesperson.

Throughout these two reorganizations, Pepsi enjoyed extremely popular products, a motivated workforce, and a comparatively benign competitive environment. Even so, the firm's top managers believed that these favorable factors could guarantee continued success and that to remain profitable, Pepsi needed to reorganize.

Ample general evidence supports Pepsi's view that technology, product mix, and market position do not fully account for a firm's performance. Richard Caves and David Barton found that firms in the same industry, with similar technologies and labor forces, often have substantially different levels of productivity.[1] While some of the reasons for differences in performance are idiosyncratic and do not lend themselves to general principles (e.g., the role of Bill Gates in attracting talent to Microsoft), others can be generalized. We have previously discussed, for example, the importance of appropriately applying resources and capabilities to the competitive environment. In this chapter, we consider *organizational structure*.

Organization structure describes how a firm uses a division of labor to organize tasks, specify how its staff performs tasks, and facilitate internal and external information flows. Structure also defines the nature of agency problems within the firm. A proper structure provides workers with the information, coordination, and incentives needed to properly implement strategy. In his classic set of case studies, *Strategy and Structure*, Alfred Chandler argued that the top managers of large industrial firms structured their firms to best allow them to pursue their chosen business strategy—or, simply put, that *structure follows strategy*.[2] This theme, which we believe is applicable to firms of all sizes, is the focus of our discussion.

◆ ◆ ◆ ◆ ◆ AN INTRODUCTION TO STRUCTURE

Before demonstrating the link between strategy and structure, it is helpful to introduce some basic concepts and describe the major kinds of organizational forms.

Individuals, Teams, and Hierarchies

Simple tasks performed by a small group of people can be structured in several ways:

- *Individually:* The members of the work group are paid based on individual actions and outcomes.

- *Self-managed teams:* A collection of individuals who work together to set and pursue common objectives. Individuals are rewarded, in part, on team performance.

- *Hierarchy of authority:* One member of the group specializes in monitoring and coordinating the work of the other members.

Most firms combine these structures. An employee may do some tasks individually and others in a team. The strength of hierarchical authority varies among firms, with some resembling a collection of independent workers, a common situation in professional service firms. At the other extreme, some organizations, such as police agencies, may closely resemble classic military models of command hierarchies. A work group may organize some activities around individuals and others around the group, while a supervisor may monitor the activities and outputs of both groups and individuals.

---

[1]Caves, R. and D. Barton, *Efficiency in U.S. Manufacturing Industries*, Cambridge, MA: MIT Press, 1990, pp. 1–3.

[2]Chandler, A. D., *Strategy and Structure*, Cambridge, MA: MIT Press, 1962.

The appropriateness of each task varies according to circumstances. For example, treating the workers as self-managing individuals is most appropriate when their tasks do not require coordination. When coordination is necessary, say because the work involves design attributes or relationship-specific investments, then either a team or hierarchy is more appropriate. Teams are more appropriate when individual contributions are difficult to monitor and team outcomes reflect more than the sum of individual efforts. Coordination among members of even fairly small teams can be a problem, however, as the organizational structures in Figure 16.1 illustrate.

The first structure in Figure 16.1 illustrates channels of authority and communication when members of a three-person group act as a team. Each individual must interact with each other, for a total of six interactions. In the second structure, three workers receive instructions from "supervisor" S, for a total of three interactions. In general, the number of potential interactions among n independent individuals is $n(n-1)/2$, whereas the number of interactions of among n individuals, one of whom supervises the others, is $n-1$. Hence, as n increases, the hierarchy of authority economizes on the number of interactions. This may reduce information sharing and the development of team culture, but it also reduces coordination problems. As the number of relations coordinated increases, however, individual supervisors can exhaust their coordinative abilities and go beyond their optimal *span of control*, by which we mean the number of subordinates directly reporting to a supervisor. If this occurs, a further specialization of management and the addition of more supervisors is needed. This is depicted in the third structure in Figure 16.1.[3]

Group self-management is more appropriate than a hierarchy when work outcomes benefit from frequent group interaction and group incentives (such as from information sharing or from increased motivation and group support), and when the costs of group coordination do not detract from group outcomes. Organizing by self-managing groups, however, makes it difficult to monitor and control individual out-

FIGURE 16.1
COORDINATIVE RELATIONSHIPS WITH AND WITHOUT SUPERVISORS.

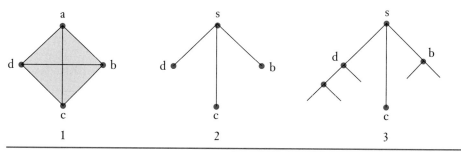

Source: Adapted from Jacquemin, 1991.

[3]For a discussion, see Jacquemin, A., *The New Industrial Organization*, Cambridge, MA: MIT Press, 1991. The issue of the optimal span of control for firms is a long-standing one in administrative research, and there is no consensus apart from the influence of such factors as the firm's size and technology, the qualifications of subordinates, or the characteristics of the market being served.

puts and align individual incentives with the firm. Armen Alchian and Harold Demsetz, whose theory of agency we discussed earlier, raise these issues about groups and hierarchies in explaining why firms exist.[4] Beyond a certain size, group self-management becomes too costly to coordinate. Some form of hierarchy is necessary to maintain and evaluate the group and reduce agency problems that occur when individuals try to influence firm decisions for their private benefit. How much control is introduced depends on the extent of agency problems and the time and effort needed to control them. These comprise the *influence* costs that we discussed earlier.[5]

Most individuals work at firms that are much bigger than the work units discussed in Example 16.1. This raises the issue of how to organize groups of work units within a larger organization. This is the problem of *complex hierarchy* that we consider next.

Complex Hierarchy

Large firms require *complex hierarchies*. By this we mean that the structure of the firm involves multiple groups and multiple levels of groupings. Complex hierarchy arises from the need not just to organize individuals into groups, but to organize groups into larger groups. Grouping in large firms quickly becomes complicated and includes two related problems:

- *departmentalization*

- *coordination of activities within and between subgroups to attain the firm's objectives*

Most attempts at organization design combine solutions to departmentalization and coordination problems under the specific conditions a firm faces.[6] We discuss each of these problems in turn.

Departmentalization

Departmentalization involves the division of the organization into formal groupings. These may be organized along a number of dimensions: tasks or functions, inputs, outputs, geography, and time of work. Departmentalization represents the choices of managers regarding the most appropriate division of labor within the firm. Examples of departments organized around common tasks or functions include accounting, marketing, and production. Examples of input- and output-based groupings include the Pepsi Bottling Group and Fountain Beverage Division that we discussed at the beginning of the chapter. Examples of departments organized around location include regional sales offices or service centers. An example of time-based groupings would be multiple shifts within a manufacturing firm.

---

[4]Alchian, A. and H. Demsetz, "Production, Information Costs, and Economic Organization," *The American Economic Review*, 62, 1972: pp. 777–795.

[5]Milgrom, P. and J. Roberts, "Bargaining Costs, Influence Costs, and the Organization of Economic Activity," in Alt, J. and K. Shepsle (eds.), *Perspectives on Positive Political Economy*, Cambridge: Cambridge University Press, 1990.

[6]The classic statement of these two problems is in March, J. and H. Simon, *Organizations*, New York: John Wiley, 1958, pp. 22–27. For a review of research on these problems, see McCann, J. and J. R. Galbraith, "Interdepartmental Relations," Nystrom, P. C. and W. H. Starbuck, *Handbook of Organizational Design*, 2, New York: Oxford University Press, 1981, pp. 60–84.

Deciding how to organize tasks within a firm reflects the choices of managers regarding what activities are be done outside the firm and their relative importance. Departmentalization is thus also associated with the choice of a firm's boundaries. For example, diversification into new businesses will be reflected in an expansion in the set of corporate divisions and groups. A decision to outsource a significant function will lead to a contraction of a firm's structure. We discussed boundary issues earlier, but the results of boundary choices will be apparent in the contours of a firm's structure. Choosing the dimensions on which to organize departments always involves tradeoffs. For example, organizing by task may lead to greater consistency in a firm's purchasing, manufacturing, and sales operations, but organizing geographically may help the firm to respond to customer demands in different locations.

In general, when selecting organizing dimensions, managers should consider economies of scale and scope, transactions costs, and agency costs. A firm should combine workers or teams into a department when their activities involve economies of scale or scope. For example, if a multiproduct firm can achieve significant scale economies in research and development, then an organizational structure that included a company-wide research department would be more efficient than dispersing R&D personnel throughout a number of independent product groups. Workers and teams should also be organized into departments when significant relationship-specific assets cut across them.

Eric Miller provides an example of this logic in his study of a small task group organization.[7] He describes the relative merits of several ways to group the tasks in a weaving mill. It is necessary to group tasks that involve treating the product with chemicals, such as bleaching and dyeing, since these require care in how they are performed and linked with other tasks. These tasks are grouped into one department, separate from those tasks, such as warping, sizing, or weaving, that do not involve chemical treatments. This grouping scheme is illustrated in Figure 16.2, along with an example of an inappropriate, or what Miller terms unnatural, grouping.

Finally, the choice of an organizing dimension has implications for agency costs in the firm, such as we discussed in Chapter 15. For example, measuring the performance of functional departments, such as finance and purchasing, can be difficult. This makes it hard to evaluate and appropriately reward the performance of department managers, which could increase agency costs inside the firm.

Coordination and Control

Once groups have been identified and organized, the interrelated problems of coordination and control arise. *Coordination* involves the flow of information to facilitate subunit decisions that are consistent with each other and with organizational objectives. *Control* involves the location of decision-making rights and rule-making authority within the hierarchy. Coordination and control involve issues of technical and agency efficiency discussed in Chapter 5. They influence technical efficiency because decision makers need access to low cost critical information, while assuring that the firm takes full advantage of economies of scale and scope in production. For example, poor coordination between the Pepsi Bottling Group and Pepsi USA resulted in technical inefficiencies when the two divisions failed to

---

[7]Miller, E. J., "Technology, Territory, and Task: The Internal Differentiation of Complex Production Systems," *Human Relations*, 1959: pp. 243–272.

FIGURE 16.2
ORGANIZING TASKS IN A WEAVING MILL.

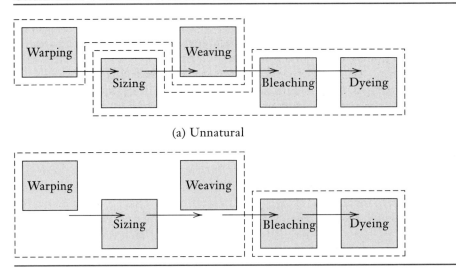

(a) Unnatural

The figure shows two ways to organize tasks in a weaving mill. The first (*a*) is deemed "unnatural" by Miller because the task sequence necessitates the unnecessary effort of shifting product back and forth between steps involving chemical treatment and steps not requiring such treatment. The process shown in (*b*) is more "natural" because it places tasks requiring chemical processing together, which avoids the need to shift product back and forth.

Source: Adapted from Miller, 1959, 257.

◆ ◆

ℰXAMPLE 16.1

THE DIVISION OF LABOR AMONG SEAMEN: 1700–1750

In his study of the organization of work for Anglo-American seamen before the American Revolution, Marcus Rediker shows how the basic approaches to task organization that we have been discussing—individual, group, and hierarchy—interacted in the daily routines of merchant ships.[8] Merchant shipping was a large industry that employed upwards of 40,000 seamen at any given time during the first half of the 18th century. Seamen formed crews of between 12 and 18 men, depending on the size of the ship and the route and purpose of the voyage. Crew "management" typically comprised the captain and his (first) mate. Larger crews had a second mate. Crews also included craftsmen, such as a carpenter, boatswain, gunner, or quartermaster (the cook was not considered a skilled worker). The rest of the crew was made up of unskilled seamen (or "common tars").

Many tasks on a ship were subject to a specialized division of labor. A crew of 12 was usually divided into five or six different ranks and an equal number of pay

[8]Rediker, M., "The Anglo-American Seaman as Collective Worker: 1700–1750," In Innes, S., ed., *Work and Labor in Early America*, Chapel Hill, NC: University of North Carolina Press, 1988, pp. 252–286.

stations, and a man's position in that ordering depended on his skills and experience. There were even two ranks for seamen—able and common—that were based on experience. A seaman's wages depended on his place within this ordering.

Along with this individual division of labor, several tasks required collective organization. For example, in loading or unloading heavy objects, such as cannon, a collective effort was needed to operate the necessary tackle and lever arrangements (such as the capstan or parbuckle). Substantial collective effort and team coordination were also needed to operate the riggings, especially during storms. Not only was collective effort necessary for a voyage to succeed, but the failure to coordinate could cause serious injury to crew members and could damage the ship's cargo. The need for precise timing of group efforts gave rise to the songs and chants often associated with life on merchant ships.

Hierarchy was also important. The captain, or master, was the direct representative of the owners of the ship (and often a partial owner himself). He had nearly complete authority on board and was responsible for navigation, securing provisions, and transacting business in port. He was also responsible for discipline and settling disputes. The mate, who was second in command, was responsible for the ship's daily operations, but had less power than the captain.

The primary unit of social organization on a ship was the watch. The crew was divided into two watches, called "starboard" and "larboard," one commanded by the captain and the other by the mate. These two units alternated around the clock in manning four-hour shifts that provided the basic cycle around which the continuity of ship operations was organized.

economize on marketing and sales efforts. On this basis, decision rights should be allocated so that individuals with the best and most timely information are empowered to make decisions.

Efficient coordination is not the only criterion for allocating decision rights. Coordination and control also affect agency efficiency because structures may differ in the opportunities they offer to decision makers to pursue personal or unit objectives that are inconsistent with the objectives of the firm. By allocating decision rights throughout a hierarchy, a firm's managers designate a legitimate basis of authority that they perceive will best support overall firm objectives. In the next chapter, we will discuss formal authority in more detail, as well as its relationship to other bases of power and influence.

There are two alternative approaches for developing coordination within firms.[9] The first emphasizes *autonomy* or *self-containment* of work units, while the second emphasizes the importance of strong *lateral relations* across work groups. When firms use autonomous work units, unit managers control information about operating decisions, and the flow of information between units is minimal. Unit

---

[9]This distinction is taken from information-processing approaches to organization design. For a review, see McCann and Galbraith, 1981. A similar distinction between informational decentralization and informational consolidation is sometimes made in economic analyses of organization structure. See Baron, D. and D. Besanko, "Information, Control, and Organizational Structure," *Journal of Economics & Management Strategy*, 1, Summer 1992: pp. 237–276.

managers provide summary financial and accounting data, including profit data when available, to headquarters. Operating information remains within the units, however.

A common example of self-containment is when a firm organizes into separate product groups, each of which contains the basic business functions of manufacturing and sales and would be capable of existing by itself in the marketplace. Managers in these groups, which are often called *profit centers*, are controlled on the basis of a target profit goal and are rewarded for meeting or exceeding the goal and punished for failing to achieve it. They have limited interactions with the other groups. Profit centers are commonly used in diversified firms, such as Procter and Gamble and Johnson and Johnson. When self-contained groups focus on other performance measures besides profit, such as cost, revenue, or investment goals, they are called *responsibility centers*. Research programs at pharmaceutical companies are examples of responsibility centers. Performance is often based on criteria indicating research productivity, such as patents and research publications.

The alternative to self-contained groupings is the development of strong lateral relations across groups. Lateral relations make sense when realizing economies of scale or scope requires close coordination of the activities of work groups. Lateral relations can be informal, such as with ad hoc or temporary teams or liaisons, or they can be formalized in the firm's structure. An example of a formal attempt to foster lateral relations is the *matrix organization*, in which employees are subject to two or more sets of managers at once. This occurs when an engineer reports both to a research and development department and a project office, or when a salesperson reports both to the head of sales for a particular product and to a regional manager. We discuss matrix organizations in more detail in the next section.

Authority within the firm is often allocated in terms of *centralization* versus *decentralization*. As some decisions come to be made at higher levels—that is, by senior managers—the firm is said to be more centralized regarding those decisions. Conversely, as certain decisions are made at lower levels, the firm becomes more decentralized regarding those decisions. Centralization and decentralization are frequently considered alternatives—a firm is either one or the other. The situation in real firms is more complicated, however. Most firms are centralized on some dimensions and decentralized on others, and characterizing a firm as centralized or decentralized is a matter of degree. For example, a firm may be decentralized in that it delegates considerable operating authority to division managers. Senior managers in that firm, however, will likely centralize the authority to review the performance of division managers and make decisions regarding their career advancement.

Types of Organizational Structures

There are four basic structures for large organizations.[10]

- The unitary *functional* structure (often called the U-form)

- The *multidivisional* structure (often called the M-form)

- The *matrix* structure

- The *network* structure

---

[10]The network structure described in the first section is an alternative that relies on external contracting relationships.

Traditional discussions of organizational structure have focused on the first three structures, which are the most widely used ones in practice. The network structure, which we briefly described in Chapter 2, represents a recent development that emphasizes contracting rather than internal organization. We describe each of the four types of structures below and depict each by a sample organization chart.

Functional Structure (U-form)

Figure 16.3 represents the unitary functional structure or U-form. The term *unitary functional* refers to the fact that in this structure a single department is responsible for each of the basic business functions (e.g., finance, marketing, production, purchasing) within the firm. A division of labor that allows for specialization of basic business tasks characterizes this structure. As a firm grows, new tasks can be added to the structure or existing departments can be subdivided. An example of a firm organized along functional lines was Cray Research around 1980, which maintained company-wide departments of finance, marketing and sales, hardware research and development, and software research and development. The component groups or units in the functional structure are called *departments*. Each department is dependent on direction from central headquarters and probably could not exist outside of the firm except as contract vendors to a firm that independently secures the other functions. Individuals grouped within a common department will share similar backgrounds, norms of behaviors, goals, and performance standards. This promotes performance within the department but renders coordination with other departments problematic. As a result, firms organized around functional lines generally centralize their strategic decision making.

The functional structure developed when firms began to grow bigger and become more specialized in the nineteenth century. From its inception, it has been a structure suited to relatively stable conditions in which operational efficiency is valued. Even so, large firms were slow to adopt the functional structure. The early growth of large firms that we discussed in Chapter 1 was characterized by loose combinations of formerly independent firms, often still run by their founders. These combinations failed to coordinate leadership, and generally did not combine work groups performing similar tasks into company-wide departments. Rather, they resembled alliances or associations of equals. (U.S. Steel looked this

FIGURE 16.3
SAMPLE CHART OF A FUNCTIONAL ORGANIZATIONAL STRUCTURE.

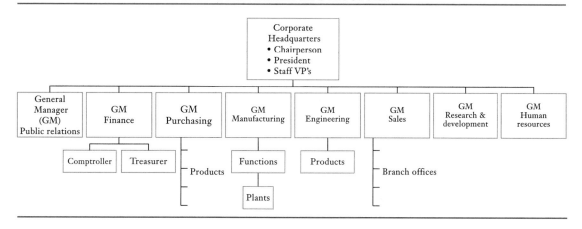

way when it became the first billion dollar firm in 1901.) This lack of coordination kept these firms from realizing potential economies of scale and scope.

Functional organization in large firms developed when managers realized that firms which rationalized their activities along functional lines could outperform those competitors that did not. The widespread adoption of the functional structure among large firms occurred during the first merger wave that took place after 1895, although Standard Oil had been rationalizing its structure along functional lines for several years.[11] A similar process of rationalization took place recently with European economic integration. Firms, such as Asea Brown Boveri (ABB) and Electrolux, are finding that success in the larger European market demands greater economies than were required for success in national markets. While the structures of these firms are more complex than were those of large firms of the last century, their corporate organization continues to include an important functional dimension.[12]

Multidivisional Structure (M-form)

Figure 16.4 shows the divisional (or multidivisional) structure. It comprises a set of autonomous divisions led by a corporate headquarters office, which is assisted by a corporate staff that provides information about the internal and external business environment. Rather than organizing by function or by task, a multidivisional structure organizes by product line, related business units, geography (e.g., by region), or by customer type (e.g., industrial versus consumer versus government

FIGURE 16.4
SAMPLE CHART OF A MULTIDIVISIONAL STRUCTURE.

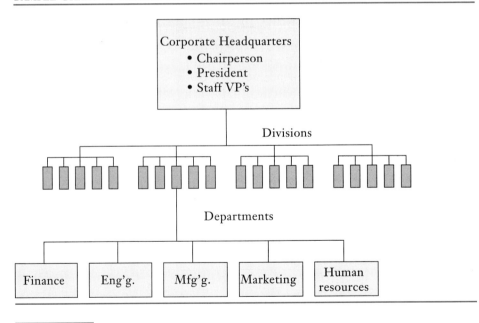

---

[11]Fligstein, N. *The Transformation of Corporate Control*, Cambridge, MA: Harvard University Press, 1990, chaps. 2 and 3.

[12]Taylor, W., "The Logic of Global Business: An Interview with ABB's Percy Barnevik," in R. Kanter, B. Stein, and T. Jick (eds.), *The Challenge of Organizational Change*, New York: Free Press, 1992, pp. 289–301.

products). *Divisions* are groupings of interrelated subunits. The subunits that comprise a division can be functionally organized departments or even other divisions that in turn could be composed of departments.

Oliver Williamson, who coined the distinction between M- and U-forms, argues the M-form develops in response to problems of inefficiency and agency that arise in the functionally organized firm as it increases in size and operating complexity. Relative to a functional structure, the M-form improves efficiency by a division of labor between strategy and operations. Division managers focus on operational issues, while strategic decisions are left to top managers. The M-form reduces agency problems because it fosters an internal capital market, in which division managers compete for discretionary corporate funds on the basis of their operating results. Corporate staff, using strategic controls, promotes corporate goals by monitoring division performance and advising managers on how to align their activities with corporate goals.

The divisional structure developed in response to problems with the functional structure in large, diversified firms. As firms diversify across geographic or product markets, they have to coordinate different functional areas within each market. For example, geographically diversified firms, such as McGaw Cellular Communications or Waste Management, run what amount to autonomous businesses in distinct geographic markets. A divisional structure organized along geographic lines allows these firms to coordinate production, distribution, and sales functions within their different markets, each of which may face unique competitive conditions.

The divisional structure also solves another problem of large organizations: the desire to reduce agency costs by closely linking individual pay to performance.[13] Authority for operating decisions is generally decentralized to division managers, who are held accountable for their divisions' performance. A simple example of this occurs in retailing. In a chain of retailers, such as Piggly Wiggly or Macy's Department Stores, each store is, in effect, its own division, with profits calculated on a store-by-store basis. This provides top management with a simple measure of store performance, which they can then use to evaluate individual store managers and reward good performance.

As we discussed in Chapter 15, the lower the "white noise" or "measurement error" in the performance measure used in pay-for-performance schemes the less susceptible it is to covert manipulation by managers, and the more effective the pay-for-performance scheme will be in motivating managerial effort and reducing agency costs. The divisional structure clearly measures how much the performance of each division contributes to overall corporate success: divisional profits and losses. Equally clear and non-manipulable measures of the contribution of departmental performance to overall corporate success are often unavailable, which is why functional structures have tended to focus on efficiency rather than on profitability.[14] This could change, however, with the development of modern activity-

---

[13]Chapter 15 discusses pay-for-performance in greater detail.

[14]Besanko, D., Regibeau, P. and K. E. Rockett. "A Multi-Task Principal-Agent Approach to Organizational Form," unpublished mimeo, Northwestern University, Department of Management and Strategy, January 1988. The authors model the relationship between incentives and organization structures and generally support the value of the divisional form. The only exception occurs if there are significant asymmetries between functional area contributions to organizational success and cross-product externalities within functions. In such a situation, organizing by function may be superior to a product organization.

based accounting systems that enable top management to evaluate middle managers in complex environments. If so, it may weaken an agency justification for a divisional structure.

Divisions are often subdivided into functional areas. For example, each of the regional divisions of Waste Management has marketing, service, and finance departments. A functional organization can also be analyzed and reorganized along divisional lines. For example, IBM recently reorganized its sales organization from a geographic to an industry-focused structure. The rationales for these subdivisions are as stated earlier—to take advantage of economies of scope, monitoring, and evaluation, at lower, albeit more appropriate levels of the organization.

Matrix Structure

Figure 16.5 illustrates the matrix structure: the firm is organized along multiple dimensions at once (usually two). Any particular combination of dimensions may be used. For example, matrix structures can include product groups and functional departments or two different types of divisions (such as geographic and client divisions). Individuals working at the intersections of the matrix (usually middle managers), report information to two hierarchies and have two bosses. For example, the Pepsi matrix that was created in the late 1980s was organized along geographic and functional lines. Area manufacturing managers simultaneously reported to re-

FIGURE 16.5
A MATRIX ORGANIZATION STRUCTURE WITH PROJECT
AND FUNCTION DIMENSIONS.

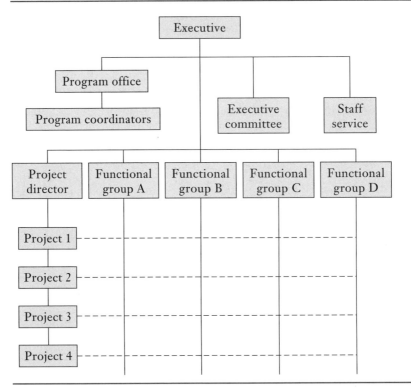

Source: Adapted from McCann and Galbraith, 1980.

gional general managers (geographic-based divisions) and a national senior vice president for operations (functional-based divisions). Although the matrix may extend throughout the entire firm, some level within the firm is often organized according to a matrix, while the rest of the organization is not. Thus, Pepsi's national marketing group has remained outside of the matrix. At the same time, area-manufacturing managers reported to two bosses. Individuals reporting to these area managers, however, had just one boss and thus were not part of the matrix.

A matrix structure is valuable when economies of scale or scope or agency considerations provide a compelling rationale for organizing along more than one dimension simultaneously. For example, Pepsi believed that national coordination of manufacturing helped achieve scale economies in production, justifying organization along functional lines, while regional coordination increased Pepsi's effectiveness in negotiating with large purchasers, justifying organization along geographic lines.

A matrix structure also allows the organization to economize on scarce human resources. For example, a firm that produces industrial controls for continuous-flow manufacturing environments (oil refining, chemical processing, flour milling) may find that a structure using product groups based on customer type, (e.g., an oil industry group or a chemical industry group) maximizes the effectiveness of its product development, marketing, and servicing efforts. To develop new applications for existing products and designs for new products, however, a firm's chemical and electrical engineers must develop enough firm-specific, product-specific, and customer-specific know-how to be most productive. Because recruiting and training good engineers is costly and because the engineers benefit from interaction and collaboration with one another, it may be neither possible nor desirable for the firm to maintain a separate engineering department within each product group. A matrix structure in which engineers are part of a company-wide engineering department but also report to individual product groups may allow the firm to economize on scarce human resources while also encouraging its engineers to develop product-specific and customer-specific know-how.

A disadvantage of a matrix structure is that employees can find themselves torn between two lines of authority. For example, if a conflict develops in a matrix between the demands of an area manager and a product manager over a salesman's obligations toward a major client, the hierarchy does not dictate which manager would prevail, since they share the same level within the firm. This would not happen in functional or divisional organizations. Settling a conflict such as this would require discussion and negotiation between affected individuals on the merits of each case.

Matrix or Division? A Model of Optimal Structure

The potential for conflicts with managers in balancing the demands of matrix dimensions raises the issue of when a matrix structure is preferable to another form of divisional organization. David Baron and David Besanko developed an economic model of shared incentive authority to address this question. They focus on firms that face organizing demands on both product and geographic dimensions.[15] The optimal structure to use emerges from the interplay of spillovers within product lines and within geographies and the interrelationships among multiple activities that local units perform.

---

[15]Baron, D. P. and D. Besanko. "Shared Incentive Authority and the Organization of the Firm," unpublished mimeo, Northwestern University, Department of Management and Strategy, July 1997.

Baron and Besanko see two considerations driving the choice of a structure. The first is whether demand-enhancing activities, such as advertising or product promotion, and cost-reducing activities, such as downsizing or production rationalization, are profit complements or substitutes. Demand-enhancing and cost-reducing activities are complements when an increase in the level of one activity increases the marginal profitability of the other. For example, this would occur when managers redesign their products and in the process reduce their defect rates. Demand-enhancing and cost-reducing activities are substitutes when an increase in the level of one activity reduces the marginal profitability of the other. This would occur when managers allocate scarce resources (e.g., managerial attention to control costs) to some products at the expense of others.

The second consideration driving a choice of structure is whether spillovers of know-how in different activities are positively or negatively correlated. Spillovers refer to the transfer of knowledge within the firm that occurs when a given activity is performed. The spillovers that are available to a firm in a given situation depend on the firm's capabilities at that time. Spillovers in two activities are positively correlated if they both primarily benefit a single dimension. For example, this would occur if the introduction of a new product in one market helps the firm produce or sell the product in other markets. They are negatively correlated if spillovers in one activity benefit one dimension (e.g., products) while spillovers in a second activity benefit the other dimension (e.g., geography).

The general problem corporate management faces in a decentralized multiproduct, multilocation firm is to shape the incentives for local managers so that they perform appropriately on both product and geographic dimensions. Doing this counteracts the free rider problem that arises when local managers fail to internalize the benefits that their activities generate for the rest of the firm. The choice of an appropriate organization design can shape local managers' incentives to perform optimally.

From their model, Baron and Besanko identify the conditions in which a matrix structure is never optimal and those conditions in which a matrix can be optimal. A matrix will never be optimal when spillovers are positively correlated and activities are profit complements. When activities are profit complements but spillovers are negatively correlated, a matrix may be optimal if spillovers do not disproportionately favor one dimension over another. If activities are profit substitutes and spillovers are positively correlated, then a matrix can be optimal if the activities are strong substitutes. Otherwise, a product or geographic structure is optimal. Finally, if spillovers are negatively correlated and activities are profit substitutes, a matrix will be optimal if spillovers are strongly product-specific in one activity and strongly specific to geography in the other activity.

To see whether a global firm acted consistently with their model, Baron and Besanko, looked in depth at how Citibank reorganized as it adopted a global approach to its business that required a balance between product and local market demands.[16] They examined the formation of the Global Relationship Bank (GRB) in 1994 and the creation of the Global Markets unit in 1997 to bridge between the GRB and Emerging Market units within Citibank. They concluded that Citibank's reorganizations were consistent with a need to balance customer and geographic orientations within a global framework.

---

[16]Baron, D. P. and D. Besanko, "Strategy, Organization, and Incentives: Global Banking at Citicorp," unpublished mimeo, Northwestern University, Department of Management and Strategy, April 1998.

◆ ◆

XAMPLE 16.2

ABB'S MATRIX ORGANIZATION[17]

Asea Brown Boveri (ABB) is a large global producer of heavy capital equipment, such as turbine generators and railway engines. It was formed in 1988 when ASEA of Sweden merged with Brown Boveri of Switzerland.

Soon after the merger, ABB's senior management concluded that to be more responsive to customer needs in different parts of the world, ABB's organization would have to be decentralized and made flexible to local conditions. ABB was thus reorganized. The reorganization resulted in a matrix structure in which ABB's 1,300 local business units (e.g., its railway engine division in Norway) were organized along two dimensions: products and geography. On the product dimension, ABB created 65 business areas (BAs), each responsible for one of ABB's product lines. On the geography dimension, ABB created country-wide organizations. At the intersection of a matrix were local business units, each responsible for a particular product line within a particular country. The head of each local unit was subject to "dual reporting." That is, the manager for a particular product line in a given country would report to both the worldwide business area manager for that product line and to the head of the country-wide organization for that country.

Some of the immediate successes that arose from ABB's restructuring were reductions in manufacturing costs through rationalizing production operations and improving new product development through better targeting of R&D funding. The BAs organized themselves according to a "lead center" concept. Under this concept, for each product line, one location was chosen to provide worldwide product leadership and support. All R&D and process improvement efforts were concentrated in this location, from which successful strategies were transferred to other locations. Each lead center became the single source for the collective knowledge within each of ABB's product lines.

ABB's matrix structure also encouraged healthy competition among the various geographic units that made up a BA. The units that provided the most efficient manufacturing facilities were retained to cater to the BA's worldwide requirements. These plants were then expanded to achieve global scale production levels, thereby giving them scale efficiencies. This helped the company become the leader in almost all the product groups it competed in. Inefficient plants were with shut down or sold.

ABB encountered one serious problem with its matrix structure, however. Because the structure essentially requires multiple reporting, important decisions had to be taken by multi-member teams from all over the world. This slowed down decision making. To overcome this, ABB embarked on an ambitious internal mail and information system based on Lotus Notes. This system allowed managers to freely communicate, exchange files and data, and thus make decisions more quickly. With over 70,000 users around the world, ABB's Lotus notes network became a backbone for reporting and decision making within the organization.

---

[17]We would like to thank Suresh Krishna for developing this example.

Network Structure

Figure 16.6 represents the network structure. The basic unit of design in the network structure is the worker, rather than the specified job or task. Workers, either singly or in combination, can contribute to multiple organizational tasks or can be reconfigured and recombined as the tasks of the organization change.

Work groups in a network are organized into crosscutting teams on the basis of task, geography, or customer base, but relationships between work groups are governed more by the often changing implicit and explicit requirements of common tasks than by the formal lines of authority that characterize other structures.[18] A network is preferable to other structures when the substantial coordination costs of employing it are less than the gains in technical efficiency. The Japanese *keiretsu* structure that we discussed in Chapter 5 is a variety of the network structure in which informal ties between member firms facilitate coordination and reduce agency problems. The fluid interrelationships among firms in the biotechnology industry provide an example of network structures that facilitate information flows among high technology companies. Such flows are necessary because the technologies of these firms can have broad applications that include such diverse areas as pharmaceuticals, seeds, and beer. Several observers have seen these networks as a principal reason for the historically high levels of new product development in this industry.[19]

◆ ◆ ◆ ◆ ◆ CONTINGENCY THEORY

The optimal organizational structure for a firm depends on the circumstances it faces. For example, a functional structure may work well for a manufacturer of supercomputers, such as Cray Research, but would probably work poorly for a

FIGURE 16.6
THE SPIDER'S WEB ORGANIZATION—AN EXAMPLE OF A NETWORK.

The figure shows a network organization structure based on communications patterns.

Source: Adapted from J. B. Quinn, *Intelligent Enterprise*, 1992, pp. 120–129.

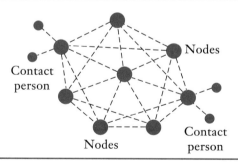

Nodes

Contact person

Nodes

Contact person

---

[18]For an extended discussion of the network organization, see Baker, W. E., "The Network Organization in Theory and Practice," in Nohria, N. and R. G. Eccles, *Networks and Organizations*, Boston, MA: Harvard Business School Press, 1992, pp. 397–429.

[19]For recent studies of interfirm networks that focus on Japanese and biotechnology examples, see Nohria, N. and R. G. Eccles (eds.), *Networks and Organizations*, Boston, MA: Harvard Business School Press, 1992, pp. 309–394. Also see Mizruchi, M. and Schwartz, M. (eds.), *Intercorporate Relations*, Cambridge, UK: Cambridge University Press, 1987. For a general approach to network analysis that includes relations within and between firms, see Burt, R. S., *Structural Holes*, Cambridge, MA: Harvard University Press, 1992.

super-regional bank, such as Banc One. The idea that there is no uniformly "best" structure for all firms in all circumstances is known as *contingency theory*. Contingency theory, which is primarily associated with organizational behavior rather than economics, has focused on three factors that may affect the relative efficiency of different structures:

- Technology and task interdependence

- Information flows

- The tension between differentiation and integration

We discuss each of these factors below.

Technology and Task Interdependence

Contingency theory argues that as the characteristics of the firm's technology change, the firm's structure will also change to accommodate new coordination needs. For example, if a firm's technology changed to permit increased production volume and more routine handling of raw materials, its coordination needs would also change. As a result, its structure would need to change to accommodate the increased volume of activities that the firm would have to perform and the increased number of decisions that it would have to make. This might require creating a new division with responsibilities in purchasing.

James Thompson points out that technology determines the degree of *task interdependence*, which is the extent to which two or more positions depend on each other to do their own work.[20] Thompson defines three modes of task interdependence: reciprocal, sequential, and pooled. *Reciprocal interdependence* exists when two or more workers or work groups depend on each other to do their work. *Sequential interdependence* exists between two or more positions when one depends on the outcomes of the others, but not vice versa. Finally, *pooled interdependence* exists when two or more positions are not directly dependent on each other, but are associated through their independent contributions to the success of the firm.

Organization design is a successive grouping of positions to coordinate activities and use shared resources efficiently. Coordination needs imply that positions that are reciprocally interdependent should be grouped together first. Positions that are sequentially dependent, for example positions at different points of a firm's value chain, may be grouped together in a separate unit or in separate units linked by formalized relationships. Finally, positions having pooled interdependence need only be linked by a common affiliation with the firm.

As technology changes, so will the nature of task interdependence, thus also changing the appropriate structure of the firm. Advances in computers and telecommunications have weakened reciprocal and sequential interdependence among many positions and significantly reduced the costs of coordinating activities among individuals and groups. For example, using faxes, personal computers, and "group-ware" computer software, engineers and product specialists located on different continents can coordinate the design of a new product without ever

---

[20]Thompson, J. D., *Organizations in Action*, New York: McGraw-Hill, 1967.

meeting face to face. This would not have been possible 20 years ago. This reduction in the costs of coordination reduces the need for members of a team to be in the same part of the firm's formal organization. It also may eliminate the need for them to be part of the same firm.

Improving Information Processing

Jay Galbraith presents a contingency-based argument for organization design based on considerations of information processing.[21] Galbraith argues that work groups can normally operate independently and can manage themselves, according to work rules that become routine over time. Administrative hierarchy (i.e., bosses, supervisors, and so forth) develops, according to Galbraith, to handle "exceptions": decisions that cannot easily be made by applying standard organizational routines. Successively higher levels of organization are needed to handle more difficult exceptions. Decisions that reach the top of an organization are presumably the most difficult and least routine of all the decisions the firm faces—that is, strategic decisions.

Galbraith's argument implies that changes in structure come about in response to changes in the amount, complexity, or speed of information processing that a firm must undertake to make decisions. As work groups are forced to process more information or act more quickly, existing organizational routines become strained. For example, marketing decisions that may have been fairly routine in an industry characterized by stable demand, high entry barriers, and a few well-known domestic competitors become less routine as the market becomes more globalized or as changes in technology destroy entry barriers. Effective pricing and promotion decisions may now require keeping track of unfamiliar foreign competitors and monitoring demand conditions in an increasingly segmented market. This might easily overwhelm standard operating procedures that were developed in a simpler, more stable era.

Luis Garicano formally models the influence of information processing on organization design and achieves a result consistent with Galbraith's work. He proposes a production function that requires time and knowledge as inputs about production problems and in which problems differ according to their difficulty and the frequency with which they occur. Workers in this setting can acquire and communicate knowledge about solutions to problems. He finds that an optimal organization design involves dividing workers into production workers and problems solvers who specialize in dealing with more difficult and/or infrequent problems. His results are consistent with a pyramidal structure in which the human capital of workers increases as the number of workers at a level decreases. His results also imply that a decrease in the cost of acquiring or transmitting knowledge increases the average span of control and may reduce or increase the number of organizational levels in the firm through scale effects.

The reorganization of Pepsi in 1988 illustrates how demands for faster information processing driven by changes in the external business environment can overwhelm a hierarchy. For Pepsi, a key change was the emergence of large re-

---

[21]Galbraith, J. R. and R. K. Kazanjian, *Strategy Implementation: The Role of Structure and Process*, 2d ed. St. Paul, MN: West Publishing, 1986.

gional supermarket chains. These often operated in territories that encompassed several different regional offices within the Pepsi Bottling Group, while Pepsi's existing structure gave nobody region-wide authority over pricing. When faced with requests for promotions or special pricing deals by a supermarket chain, executives at Pepsi often disagreed over the appropriate strategy to follow. Their disputes were then funneled up the hierarchy to Roger Enrico, then the head of Pepsi USA, who was forced to become involved in region-level pricing and promotion decisions. Not surprisingly, this impaired Pepsi's ability to respond and put it at a competitive disadvantage in a market that demands nimble marketing responses to fast-changing circumstances. Part of the reason Pepsi chose a geographically oriented matrix structure when it reorganized was to clarify the lines of authority in pricing and promotion decisions. The new structure created the position of area general manager, who had final authority for operational decisions (including pricing and promotions) within areas that were roughly the size of the territories of the large supermarket chains.

Instead of changing its formal organizational structure, a firm could respond to demands for more complex or faster information processing by making other structural changes, involving positions with responsibilities that cut across the established hierarchy. Creating cross-functional teams (i.e., teams that coordinate different functions and whose members are drawn from and knowledgeable about these functions), would be an example of such a change. Incorporating cross-cutting positions or teams into a structure increases the amount of information flowing to individuals throughout the organization and thus adds a lateral dimension to organization structure.

Arthur Stinchcombe emphasizes the role of organizational structure in promoting more efficient *information retrieval*.[22] He argues that firms should be structured to facilitate the efficient retrieval of information. For example, a pharmaceutical firm might want an independent R&D department capable of rapid interaction with medical school faculty, an important source of new product development. Different levels of structure can deal with different informational needs. For example, information about labor costs or demand may be highly local. If local work groups control these factors, they will have the proper incentives to gather information. Dealing with federal regulations, however, should be the responsibility of a broader work group.

Stinchcombe also argues that firms should internalize activities (rather than rely on market coordination) when information from them is critical. It is important for firms to be "where the news breaks, whenever it breaks," since rapid information processing facilitates effective adjustments. This is related to Kenneth Arrow's argument (discussed in Chapter 5) that firms may integrate upstream to obtain better information about input availability and prices.[23] Of course, as innovations in computer technologies, telecommunications, and financial markets reduce the costs to firms of information gathering, this has become less important in choosing an organizational structure.

---

[22]Stinchcombe, A. L., *Information and Organizations*, Berkeley, CA: University of California Press, 1990.

[23]Arrow, K., "Vertical Integration and Communication," *Bell Journal of Economics*, 6, Spring 1975: pp. 173–182.

❖ ❖

*E*XAMPLE 16.3

ORGANIZATIONAL STRUCTURE AT AT&T

Robert Garnet examined the growth of the Bell System between 1876 and 1909, during the early years of the firm when neither its monopoly status nor even its corporate survival could be taken for granted.[24] Garnet's study illustrates the relationship between a firm's structure and contingency factors, such as size and market turbulence.

One conclusion of contingency theory is that as the volume of its activities increases, a firm will have to reorganize to meet the increased informational demands. AT&T faced this situation during these years. Between 1885 and 1920, the Bell System went from fewer than 2,000 central offices with 25,000 employees to nearly 6,000 offices and 240,000 employees. In the aftermath of this growth, Bell needed substantial reorganization.

Contingency theory also argues that as the environment becomes more volatile, for example, because of increased competition, a firm would need to reorganize to promote rapid processing of information. AT&T faced increased competition during this period. Its initial patents expired in 1894, after which new competitors entered local telephone markets.

The changes made by AT&T in its organization structure are consistent with contingency explanations. When the firm was first consolidated around 1880, it was a loose affiliation of Bell Company interests and licenses, held together not by formal structure, but by the terms of licenses and by partial equity ownership of licenses by the Bell Company. By 1884, this structure had become inefficient, and attempts were made to tighten leases, improve accounting controls, and consolidate the firm. Despite these efforts, the company's earnings declined.

By 1890, the first significant organization structure was proposed, largely along territorial lines. Corporate accounting procedures were also revised in 1891. Another major reorganization occurred at AT&T in 1909, this time focusing on operating companies that were organized on state lines and that were subject to overall control by AT&T corporate headquarters.[25] Each operating company was internally organized along functional lines. This reorganization occurred, coincidentally, at the lowest ebb of corporate performance before the Kingsbury Commitment, a 1913 agreement between AT&T and the U.S. Department of Justice that secured the firm's dominant market position in exchange for a commitment to allow competitors to interconnect with the AT&T system. Figure 16.7 shows this reorganization of the Bell Companies. AT&T corporate headquarters was also reorganized on functional lines in 1912. These reorganizations are consistent with a contingency view. The functional structure improved

---

[24]Garnet, R. W., *The Telephone Enterprise: The Evolution of the Bell System's Horizontal Structure, 1876–1909*, Baltimore, MD: The Johns Hopkins University Press, 1985.

[25]A state basis for defining operating companies rather than some other geographic criterion was necessary because state governments were regulating telephone companies. Management responses that differed from one state to another were needed.

FIGURE 16.7
FUNCTIONAL ORGANIZATION—BELL TELEPHONE COMPANIES.

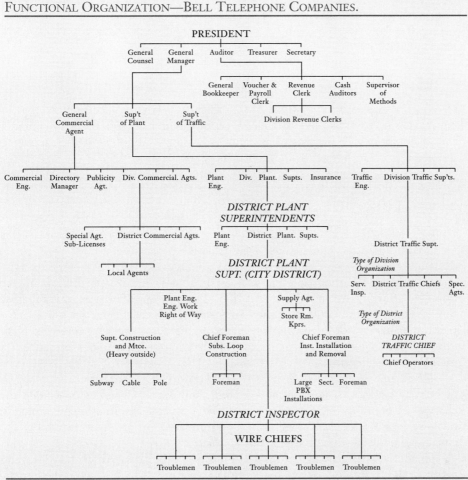

Source: AT&T, Historical Archives, *Application of Some General Principles of Organization* (New York, 1909).

the operating companies' ability to handle the increased volume of operations that developed during this period. The new headquarters structure fostered a division of labor between operating companies and headquarters and allowed the firm to expand as the Bell system grew.

Balancing Differentiation and Integration

Paul Lawrence and Jay Lorsch note a tension in complex organizations between the benefits of creating independent specialized work groups, what they refer to as *differentiation*, and the need to integrate these groups into a corporate whole.[26]

---

[26]Lawrence, P. R. and J. W. Lorsch, *Organization and Environment*, Boston: Harvard Business School Press, 1986.

In designing a structure, managers must balance differentiation and integration. An organizational structure may fail to sufficiently differentiate a firm's activities, such as when a firm groups different products in the same division and uses a common incentive scheme for all product managers regardless of their product's market environment.

It is also possible to differentiate too much, as when several groups in a firm are given responsibility for complementary marketing decisions. Differentiation should be deemphasized when the distribution of resources and information between work groups is not distinct. More integrated planning, decision making, and control are necessary to help the managers of the firm act in a unified manner, so that they "speak with one voice" as much as possible and not allow their pursuit of individual goals to detract from the firm's overall performance.

◆ ◆ ◆ ◆ ◆ STRUCTURE FOLLOWS STRATEGY

Understanding the relationship between structure and contingency factors, such as technology and external demands for information processing, is a necessary part of explaining how a firm organizes. Knowing possible contingency factors for a firm is not sufficient for understanding structural choices, however, because many factors may affect a firm in a given situation. The appropriate organizational structure depends on the context of the firm's strategy, in particular on those factors that top managers consider most important. In his classic work, *Strategy and Structure*, Alfred Chandler first articulated how firms' strategic choices influence how their structures develop.[27]

Based on case studies of firms, such as DuPont, General Motors, Standard Oil of New Jersey (which later became Exxon), and Sears, Chandler concluded that changes in organization structure were driven by changes in strategy, which, in turn, were associated with changes in the external conditions firms faced. Put succinctly, Chandler's thesis is that *structure follows strategy*.

Chandler's basic argument runs as follows. In the late 19th century, developments in the technological and market infrastructures (which we describe in detail in Chapter 1) created opportunities for achieving unprecedented economies of scale and scope in various industries, such as tobacco, chemicals, light and heavy machinery, and meatpacking. Firms such as American Tobacco, DuPont, McCormick Harvesting Machine Company (which became International Harvester), and Swift, responded by investing in large-scale production facilities and internalizing activities, such as sales and distribution, that independent companies had previously performed for them. They also quickly invested in the development of managerial hierarchies. The first organizational structure typically employed by these early hierarchical firms was the U-form. This structure allowed firms to develop a specialization of labor that facilitated the achievement of economies of scale in manufacturing, marketing, and distribution.

The firms that were the first in their industries to invest in large-scale production facilities and develop managerial hierarchies expanded rapidly and often dominated their industries. But most of the early growth of these firms was within a single line of business or occurred within a single market. Shortly after 1900, however, this began to change. Some firms, such as Singer and International Harvester, aggressively expanded overseas. Indeed, by 1914, the largest commercial

---

[27]Chandler, A. D., *Strategy and Structure*, Cambridge, MA: MIT Press, 1962.

EXAMPLE 16.4

STRATEGY, STRUCTURE, AND THE ATTEMPTED MERGER BETWEEN THE UNIVERSITY OF CHICAGO HOSPITAL AND MICHAEL REESE HOSPITAL

The idea that strategy follows structure has implications for mergers between firms that have pursued different strategies. In melding two such organizations together, issues relating to the control of assets and resources frequently arise. As we saw earlier, the allocation of rights of control of assets is a key determinant of how efficiently a vertical chain or a partnership of two organizations performs. Inside an organization, structure determines the basic rights to control the firm's assets. Thus, organizational structure can critically affect the success of a merger.

The attempted merger between the University of Chicago Hospital and the Michael Reese Hospital provides an example in which control of assets and resources was a key issue in the attempted integration of the two organizations. The University of Chicago Hospital is on the campus of a leading research university, which led the hospital to pursue a strategy based on a reputation for providing state-of-the-art medicine. Indeed, advertisements for the hospital celebrated the research accomplishments of its medical staff. Consistent with this strategy, most physicians had faculty appointments in the university's medical school, and faculty were evaluated on the basis of their research. Physician salaries were based more on their academic standing than on the patient revenues they brought to the hospital.

The University of Chicago Hospital's nearest competitor on the city's south side was the Michael Reese Hospital. This hospital also had a long history of quality care, with special emphases on community service and close relationships between medical staff and patients. The medical staff was organized according to a traditional scheme—staff members were identified by clinical areas, but billed patients for their services independently of the hospital's billings. In other words, physicians were rewarded exclusively for providing patient care.

The two hospitals sought to merge in 1985. The merger would allow them to consolidate and reallocate some services and possibly avoid price and nonprice competition in the markets they both served. Anticipating the potential for conflict between medical staffs over resource control and authority to set policy, the two hospitals attempted to negotiate an organizational structure before they merged. As it turned out, they could not develop an agreeable structure to manage their surgical departments as an integrated unit. University physicians refused to be evaluated on the basis of clinical care, while Reese physicians refused to be thought of as research faculty. Unable to coordinate this vital area and fearful that economies in surgery would not be realized, the hospitals called off the merger.

enterprises in Russia were Singer and International Harvester.[28] Other firms, such as DuPont and Procter and Gamble, diversified their product lines. This shift in strategy revealed serious shortcomings in the U-form. According to Chandler, the

---

[28]Chandler, A. D., *Scale and Scope: The Dynamics of Industrial Capitalism*, Cambridge, MA: Harvard University Press, 1990, p. 200.

attempt by the top management of the newly diversified firms to monitor functional departments in the U-form structure led to administrative overload and searches for alternative organizational structures.

The multidivisional structure, or M-form, that emerged in the United States after 1920 was a response to the limitations of the U-form in diversified firms. The M-form removed top managers from involvement in the operational details of functional departments, allowing them to specialize in strategic decisions and long-range planning. Division managers monitored the operational activities of the functional departments that reported to them and were rewarded on the basis of divisional performance. As we discussed earlier, divisional contributions to overall corporate success are easier to measure than functional-area contributions. Thus, running divisions as profit centers and basing rewards for division managers on divisional profit-and-loss statements are effective ways to motivate divisional managers.

While corporate structures have evolved since the days of the M-form, the principle that structure follows strategy still applies. The network structure of the well-known clothing manufacturer Benetton provides a clear example. Benetton's generic strategy is to differentiate itself from its competitors based on unique color combinations and bold designs. Its formal structure is functional, although it outsources many of its traditional functions. The organization operates not just through internal coordination, but through active external coordination of a network of suppliers and distributors. Top management maintains direct lines of communication with storeowners to exchange information about customer demands. Benetton also works with several suppliers who can rapidly fill orders for undyed wool and cotton sweaters. Benetton's network structure, built around functional areas, enables it to rapidly tailor its product line to meet ever-changing consumer tastes.

EXAMPLE 16.5

SAMSUNG: REINVENTING A CORPORATION[29]

Major environmental shifts often force firms to reassess strategies and restructure their organizations. The Samsung business group provides an example of how to reinvent a corporation when faced with the hostile market forces that Asian firms must increasingly endure. Samsung was founded in 1938 as a general trading store, exporting fruit and dried fish to Japanese-occupied Manchuria. It has since become the largest South Korean business group, or *chaebol*, at $54 billion in sales in 1995. Samsung operates in such diverse industries as aerospace, chemicals, and finance, but is best known as the world's largest maker of leading-edge computer memory chips.

---

[29]This example is based on materials from four sources: "Samsung's Radical Shakeup," *Business Week*, February 28, 1994: pp. 74–76; "Samsung: Korea's Great Hope for High Tech," *Business Week*, February 3, 1992: 44–45; "Good to Be Big, Better to Be Good," *The Economist*, August 18, 1990: 7–10; "Samsung: South Korea Marches to Its Own Drummer," *Forbes*, May 16, 1988: 84–89.

Samsung's rise to prominence, however, was based on strong support from the Korean government, inexpensive labor, and an authoritarian culture. As a result, Samsung's strategy from the 1960s until the mid-1980s was based on using cheap labor to produce lower-quality products at low prices. By also producing large volumes, Samsung reaped economies of scale and thus captured comfortable margins, which also enabled them to enter a variety of businesses with great success.

In the late 1980s, however, a combination of factors impaired Samsung's historical sources of competitive advantage and caused its managers to reevaluate strategies that had brought the company such success for over two decades. South Korean wages began to rise and workers began to unionize and strike, causing labor instability. Samsung does not have unions because it pays high wages. Even so, the general labor climate has become less friendly. The value of the South Korean currency, the won, had also appreciated, making South Korean exports more expensive. In addition, increased global competition has further eroded Samsung's competitive positioning.

In response, Chairman Lee Kun-Hee has launched a sweeping remake of Samsung's culture, including a restructuring of operations. Lee has radically decentralized decision making and encouraged individuality in a company that was known for its rigid hierarchy and subservience to authority. Managers who are not able to assume such responsibility are fired. To encourage individuality, Lee has initiated training programs and other innovative techniques. For instance, each year Samsung sends 400 managers abroad, fully subsidized, for 12 months to do whatever they want. The only requirement is that when they return, they must show proficiency in the host country's language and culture.

In addition to reinventing the culture at Samsung, Lee has consolidated groups that are in related businesses and has specialized in more capital- and technology-intensive industries. Samsung has also tried to shift from being a low-quality, low-cost producer to producing higher-quality goods. Lee wants to continue to pursue high-quality, high-tech markets and compete on an equal basis with leading American, Japanese, and European firms.

This shift in culture and operations has forced Samsung to be at the leading edge in innovation and productivity. The firm traditionally adopted its technology from more advanced firms, but Lee instituted massive R&D spending to make Samsung more self-sufficient. Further, Lee has automated plants and even moved some plants to Mexico to save labor costs. Samsung has transformed itself in response to major changes in both global markets and South Korea. One sign that Lee's programs are working is that Samsung recently won IBM's seal of approval as a supplier, resolving many doubts about its ability to provide quality products. A bigger test, however, will be how Samsung survives the East Asian currency crisis that began in 1997 and has seriously affected the South Korean economy.

A similar network structured developed in SAP AG, a German firm that is one of the world's largest software producers and the leading producer of real-time, integrated applications software for client-server computing. The company has grown rapidly (sales revenues grew nearly 400 percent between 1991 and 1995 to (DM) 2.7 billion), while its founders have been intent on SAP remaining largely a product development firm with a flat organization structure. To this end, SAP managers decided not to significantly expand into related, but different lines of business, such as training and implementation consulting, even though meeting customer needs during implementation would be critical to successful expansion. To accomplish these objectives, SAP has developed a network organization of partners, who perform 80 to 90 percent of the consulting implementation business generated by SAP products. Partners range from major consulting firms, such as Andersen Consulting and CSC Index, to hardware manufacturers, such as IBM, HP, and Sun, to software and chip manufacturers, such as Oracle, Microsoft, and Intel. Relationship managers for these partnerships play an important role in SAP's corporate structure.

Strategy, Structure, and the Multinational Firm

The idea that structure follows strategy has been applied to firms that compete internationally.[30] As multidivisional firms became larger, they were more likely to expand their operations overseas. These firms initially created "international divisions" to manage their foreign activities. As foreign business grew, however, this structure increasingly failed to coordinate foreign operations that, in effect, duplicated the activities of the domestic firm in multiple markets. This led to reorganization into multinational firms, characterized by separate divisions for different countries (or regions, if national markets were sufficiently similar or if the volume of business in a particular area was small).

Growing multinationals faced pressures for coordination across countries and specialization within countries, especially firms with technologies that permitted substantial scale and scope economies. This led to global strategies that viewed the world as the firm's market. Firms that pursued this strategy reorganized to promote scale economies in global production and distribution. The final step in the development of these firms in the international arena occurred when headquarters learned to balance responsiveness to local conditions with centralization to achieve global economies. This transnational strategy is associated with flexible organizations that combine matrix and network structures.

Structure, Strategy, and Decision Making

Thomas Hammond argues that structure influences strategy because critical knowledge and decision-making capabilities in large firms are dispersed throughout the firm rather than concentrated in top managers.[31] This means that a firm's structure determines how and in what order lower-level decision makers come together to contribute their information to corporate decisions. Structure sets the agenda for top managers in making strategic decisions, since it determines which

---

[30]For examples of these applications, see Stopford, J. and L. Wells, *Managing the Multinational Enterprise*, London: Longmans, 1972; Yoshihara, H. "Towards a Comprehensive Concept of Strategic Adaptive Behavior of Firms," in Ansoff, H. I., Declerck, R. P., and R. L. Hayes (eds.), *From Strategic Planning to Strategic Management*, New York: John Wiley, 1976, pp. 103–124; and Galbraith, J. R. and R. K. Kazanjian, *Strategy Implementation*, 2d., St. Paul, MN: West Publishing, 1986, pp. 128–144.

[31]Hammond, T. H., "Structure, Strategy, and the Agenda of the Firm," presented at the Fundamental Issues in Strategy Conference, Napa, CA, November 29–December 1, 1990.

XAMPLE 16.6

TRANSNATIONAL STRATEGY AND ORGANIZATION STRUCTURE AT SMITHKLINE-BEECHAM[32]

SmithKline-Beecham, a transnational pharmaceutical firm that was created in 1989 by the merger of the American firm SmithKline-Beckman and the British firm Beecham, illustrates the interaction of strategy and structure in global markets. A merger with Beecham was attractive to SmithKline for several reasons. SmithKline depended on a few products (primarily the ulcer drug Tagamet) for much of its sales. It was vulnerable to losing market share to generic drugs, and was open to a takeover because it had overdiversified. Moreover, SmithKline-Beckman and Beecham had several complementary product lines. Beecham was strong in consumer health products and self-medications, while SmithKline was stronger in prescription drugs. The two firms also had potential synergies in their scientific competences and new product development schedules. This merger created a firm with a combined annual research and development budget of over $750 million. Finally, the firms had complementary geographic markets: Beecham was strong in Europe; SmithKline in the United States and Japan.

SmithKline might have been able to expand into new products and markets and develop additional scientific competences either through internal development or through hybrid organizational arrangements, such as strategic alliances and joint ventures.[33] But its managers felt that internal product development and market expansion would have been too slow to be of much practical value in the increasingly competitive global pharmaceuticals market. And while it did experiment with strategic alliances and joint ventures, SmithKline found both experiences to be unsatisfactory. Alliances were too loose to provide incentives for the allied firms to cooperate with each other, and the autonomy of the partners in their joint ventures led to governance and incentive problems.

Given the complex synergies that motivated the merger, determining an organizational structure for the combined firm was a significant issue. Henry Wendt, the CEO after the merger, summed up the problem: "neither form of organization structure (product or geography) simultaneously captures the kinds of global-local synergies of skills, scale, and scope now considered necessary by aggressive transnational companies." SmithKline-Beecham eventually adopted a "flexible matrix" structure that comprised "modified matrix-based multifunctional teams." This structure combines both centralized functional structures with local autonomy. The flexible matrix emphasized strong local management teams, with responsibility for customer-focused functions, including sales, marketing, and product design. In addition to local decision-making autonomy, the structure allows global efficiencies to be pursued at the corporate level by functional groups, such as manufacturing, information technologies, and research and development.

---

[32]This example is based on material in Wendt, H., *Global Embrace*, New York: Harper-Business, 1993, chaps. 2 and 6.

[33]Strategic alliances and joint ventures are discussed in Chapter 5.

options are considered for a decision, which options are to be compared, and in what order comparisons are to be made.

Organizational structure can also bias the information that flows up through the hierarchy to top managers. The perspectives of lower-level decision makers may be systematically biased according to the requirements of their positions within the firm's structure. For example, manufacturing, sales, and research personnel often differ in their time frames (e.g., short-run versus long-run orientations) and their responsibilities to the organization.[34] This means that top managers bear the additional burden of compensating for lower-level biases.

Hammond argues that organizational structure determines which decision options firms consider and the criteria by which they evaluate them. The options that managers consider must be based in part on the current activities of the firm and on information about current product market conditions and profit possibilities. For most firms, this information comes from lower-level individuals in the firm by way of the firm's structure. Different structures present different sets of options to executives. For example, it will be difficult to develop a strategy emphasizing mergers and acquisitions in a firm that has not organized its product lines into separate business units that can be bought and sold.

Structure also influences how strategies are implemented by providing rules for resolving disputes. The means for dispute resolution provided by a given structure may be consistent or inconsistent with the requirements of the firm's strategy. For example, if a strategy requires that employees perform their tasks and represent themselves to customers consistently, then disputes among employees should be referred up the hierarchy, so that a consistent approach to problems can be developed. A structure that provides incentives to employees to use the hierarchy for resolving disputes would be consistent with this strategy. On the other hand, if a strategy required the timely use of localized knowledge by employees, then approaches that consistently referred problems up the hierarchy to superiors would be inconsistent with the strategy and would probably increase the firm's implementation costs.

A firm's structure also influences what information reaches top managers about strategy implementation. If top managers delegate much of their decision making to lower-level individuals, then they will learn about implementation primarily from the conflicts that are referred to them for resolution. If the firm's structure is biased to prevent certain types of conflicts from being referred upward, the information that managers receive will also be biased.

The overall message of these perspectives is that organizational structure can bias in various ways the information or set of decisions that reach the top of the hierarchy. Gary Miller argues that an exclusive reliance on formal hierarchy, administrative controls, or incentive systems is likely to be self-defeating. An optimal piece-rate system, for example, will always tempt managers to cheat and raise performance standards to obtain more from employees. An optimal group incentive system will likewise tempt members to take advantage of the work of others.

---

[34] This point about position-based bias is well-established in organizational analysis. For example, see Barnard, C., *The Functions of the Executive*, Cambridge, MA: Harvard, 1938; Cyert, R. and J. March, *A Behavioral Theory of the Firm*, Englewood Cliffs, NJ: Prentice-Hall, 1963; Lawrence, P. and J. Lorsch, *Organization and Environment*, Boston, MA: Harvard Business School Press, 1986.

While formal hierarchy may improve on transactions costs in the marketplace (as discussed in Chapter 3), it generates its own dilemmas for managers. Miller suggests that hierarchy and administrative controls must be supplemented by informal ways of achieving the cooperation of managers and subordinates, such as leadership and culture.[35]

Structure as Routine and Heuristic

Richard Nelson and Sidney Winter, proponents of "evolutionary economics," view the actions of firms as the result of a complex set of behavior patterns, or *routines*.[36] These routines evolve as the firm develops in response to changes in it's external environment. Routines simplify the complexity of the information a firm receives from its environment and constitute its "learning by doing." As the firm encounters problems, it experiments by varying current routines until it obtains a satisfactory result. When that occurs, the organization "remembers" the solution by continuing to perform the routine in the future. In this sense, an organization's routines form the basis of its distinctive competencies. A firm's routines can also concern conflict resolution and governance. As the firm develops, it also encounters problems with conflict resolution, incentives and motivation, and control. Satisfactory solutions to these problems are retained in routines, while unsatisfactory activities are eventually changed. Thus routines represent "truces" among contending parties within the firm.

Nelson and Winter offer two views of the strategy-structure relationship that differ from Chandler. The first is a "bottom-up" view, in which strategy and structure evolve from local interactions of the firm with its environment rather than from top managers formulating and implementating a comprehensive reorganization. This suggests that the relationship of the firm to its environment, as well as the current patterns of interpersonal relationships generally referred to as the firm's "structure," are both the cumulative result of a long series of adaptations to environmental stimuli.

A second view of the strategy-structure relationship that Nelson and Winter present considers how managers make decisions. Strategy and structure are examples of high-level *heuristics*: principles or guideposts that reduce the average time spent by decision makers in addressing difficult and unusual problems. In this sense, strategy is a set of principles or decision guidelines that managers use to foster a firm's survival and profitability. Similarly, structure is a set of principles or decision guidelines for coordinating a firm's actors in a manner consistent with its activities in the environment. A heuristic view of strategy and structure is not consistent with a comprehensive optimizing view of top management decision making, however. In making strategic decisions, top managers will be bound by their routines and will either maintain prior decisions or incrementally modify them. Large-scale strategic change by firms will be rare, as will comprehensive reorganizations. Current decisions about strategy and structure will be heavily constrained by past decisions.

---

[35]Miller, G. J., *Managerial Dilemmas*, Cambridge, UK: Cambridge University Press, 1992, chaps. 10 and 11.

[36]Nelson, R. R. and S. G. Winter, *An Evolutionary Theory of Economic Change*, Cambridge, MA: Belknap, 1982.

CHAPTER SUMMARY

◆ Organizational structure refers to the general and persistent patterns by which firms organize tasks, people in tasks, and information flows.

◆ If a firm's strategy is to be carried out, or *implemented*, individuals working within the firm must know about the strategy and its operational details. A firm's structure reflects the ways in which the firm solves problems of information and coordination on a regular basis.

◆ Problems of incentives and controls complicate the problem of coordinating cooperative agents to carry out the firm's strategy.

◆ Simple tasks performed by small work groups can be structured in three ways: (1) *Individually:* members of the work group are treated as if they were independent and receive incentives based on individual actions and outcomes; (2) *Self-managed teams:* a collection of individuals, each member of which works with others to set and pursue common objectives, with individuals rewarded, in part, on the basis of group performance; and (3) *Hierarchy of authority:* one member of the group monitors and coordinates the work of the other members.

◆ Large firms often require *complex hierarchies*, by which is meant a structure that involves multiple groups and multiple levels of groupings. Complex hierarchy arises when there is a need to organize simple work groups together into larger groups.

◆ Complex hierarchy involves two related problems: (1) *departmentalization* and (2) *coordination of activities within and between subgroups to attain the firm's objectives.*

◆ Departmentalization identifies formal groupings within the organization. These groups may be organized along a number of different dimensions: common tasks or functions, inputs, outputs, geographic location, and time of work.

◆ Once groups have been identified and organized, problems of coordination and control arise. *Coordination* involves the flow of information to facilitate subunit decisions that are consistent with each other and with organizational objectives. *Control* involves the location of decision-making rights and rule-making authority within the hierarchy.

◆ There are two alternative approaches for developing coordination within firms. The first emphasizes *autonomy* or *self-containment* of work units, while the second emphasizes the importance of strong *lateral relations* across work groups.

◆ The allocation of authority within the firm is typically considered in terms of *centralization* versus *decentralization*. As decisions are made at higher levels, the firm is said to be more centralized regarding those decisions. Conversely, as certain decisions are made at lower levels, the firm is more decentralized regarding those decisions.

◆ Four basic types of structure for large organizations can be identified: (1) the unitary *functional* structure (often called the U-form); (2) the *multidivisional* structure (often called the M-form); (3) the *matrix* structure; and (4) the *network* structure.

◆ The functional structure, or U-form, allows a specialization of labor to gain economies of scale in manufacturing, marketing, and distribution.

◆ The multidivisional structure, or M-form, creates a division of labor between top managers and division managers that removes top managers from involvement in the operational details of functional departments and allows them to specialize in strategic decisions and long-range planning. Division managers in the M-form firm monitor the operational activities of the functional departments and are rewarded on the basis of divisional performance.

◆ While corporate structures have evolved since the days of the M-form, the principle that structure follows strategy still applies for more complex structures, such as matrices or networks.

◆ The best organizational structure for a particular firm depends on the specific circumstances it faces. The notion that there is no uniformly "best" organizational structure for all firms in all circumstances is known as *contingency theory*.

◆ Contingency theory has focused on three factors that affect the relative efficiency of different structures: (1) technology and task interdependence; (2) information flows; and (3) the tension between differentiation and integration.

◆ Contingency factors are not sufficient for understanding a firm's structure, however, because many plausible contingencies may affect a firm in a given situation. The firm's strategy determines the organizational structure that is appropriate for it.

◆ The thesis that structure follows strategy has been applied to firms that compete internationally. Multinationals have discovered the need to balance responsiveness to local conditions with centralization to achieve global economies. This is the transnational strategy, and it is becoming associated with flexible organizations that combine matrix and network structures.

QUESTIONS

1. A team of eight individuals must fold, stuff, seal, and stamp 250 preaddressed envelopes. Offer some suggestions for organizing this team. Would your suggestions differ if, instead of envelopes, the team was responsible for assembling 250 personal computers? Why?

2. Consider a firm whose competitive advantage is built almost entirely on its ability to achieve economies of scale in producing small electric motors that are used by the firm to make hair dryers, fans, vacuum cleaners, and food processors. Should this firm be organized on a multidivisional basis by product (hair dryer division, food processor division, etc.) or should it be organized functionally (marketing, manufacturing, finance, etc.)?

3 What types of structures would a firm consider if it was greatly expanding its global operations?

4. Procter and Gamble is one of the largest consumer product companies in the world. The company is organized along both product and country lines. For a specific product, such as dish soap, each country manager may select product characteristics, price, and marketing strategy. This decentralized structure has enabled P&G to be successful in many parts of the world, including Europe, where P&G's brands frequently outperform locally produced brands. As trade barriers in Europe disappear, do you think that P&G will need to move to a more centralized structure?

5. In the 1980s, Sears acquired several financial services firms, including Allstate Insurance and Dean Witter Brokerage Services. Sears kept these businesses as largely autonomous divisions. By 1994, the strategy had failed and Sears had divested all of its financial services holdings. Bearing in mind the dictum that structure follows strategy, identify the strategy that Sears had in mind when it acquired these businesses, and recommend a structure that might have led to better results.

5. Matrix organizations first sprang up in businesses that worked on scientific and engineering projects for narrow customer groups. Examples include Fluor, which built oil refineries in Saudi Arabia, and TRW, which supplied aerospace equipment to NASA. What do you suppose the dimensions of the matrix would be in such firms? Why would these companies develop such a complex structure?

7. It is sometimes argued that a matrix organization can serve as a mechanism for achieving *strategic fit*—the achievements of synergies across related business units resulting in a combined performance that is greater than units could achieve if they operated independently. Explain how a matrix organization could result in the achievement of strategic fit.

POWER AND CULTURE

<u>17</u>

*M*ichael Eisner, chairman and CEO of The Walt Disney Company, is justly credited with its turnaround and resurgence, which began with his ascendance to the top job in 1984 and continued in the 1990s. Growth under Eisner was astonishing. Disney's share price rose 1400% over 10 years, from a value of $3 in December 1983 to $42 in December 1993. Sales grew at an annual rate of over 21%, from $1.3 billion in 1983 to $7.5 billion in 1992, while net income increased at an annual rate of 27 percent over the same period, from $93 million to $817 million. In a decade of restructurings and layoffs, total Disney employees rose from 30,000 in 1983 to 58,000 in 1992. This growth and profitability were based on a strategic reorientation of Disney that included a reemphasis on theme parks, enhanced video marketing for the Disney film library, and a rebirth of animated feature films, with such successes as *The Little Mermaid, Beauty and the Beast, Aladdin*, and *The Lion King*. Eisner's strategy also included new ventures in cable television, TV production, the retailing of Disney merchandise, and even professional sports teams (the Anaheim Mighty Ducks hockey team). There is no doubt that Eisner is the ruler of the Magic Kingdom, and represents the firm to investors and the public.

However, 1994 was not an entertaining year for Eisner and Disney. Part of Eisner's troubles certainly stemmed from the continuing poor performance of Euro Disney, which lost nearly a billion dollars in 1993 and for which Disney took a $350 million charge. (In 1997 it began to turn a profit.) The most noteworthy difficulties in 1994, however centered on Eisner himself and on conflicts within his management team over succession and power. To start with, Disney's president and chief operating officer, Frank Wells, died in a helicopter crash. Then, the poor performance of Disney's nonanimated features led Eisner to fire Ricardo Mestres, head of Disney's Hollywood pictures unit. Following that, Eisner himself had emergency bypass surgery. Finally, investors were unsure about Disney's possible ventures into telecommunications. Eisner had opposed such ventures earlier in 1994, but then had supported them. Disney's future direction was unclear.

In this context Eisner announced the resignation of Jeffrey Katzenberg, chairman of the Walt Disney Studios. Katzenberg had come to Disney with Eisner from Paramount in 1984 and his unit was responsible for Disney's immensely successful animated feature films. According to news reports, the resignation reflected Katzenberg's dissatisfaction at not getting the number-two position at Disney, which had been vacant since the death of Frank Wells. Katzenberg signaled his intention to leave if passed over for promotion in September 1993, when he waived substantial Disney stock options ($100 million), so that he could leave the studio within the year if he wished, well in advance of his contract terms.

Rather than fill the number-two position, Eisner announced a sweeping reorganization of Disney's filmed entertainment businesses into two groups. The first would deal with television and telecommunications services and would be headed by Richard Frank, who had been president of the Walt Disney studios since 1985. The second would concentrate on the production and distribution of motion pictures and would be headed by Joe Roth, head of Caravan Pictures, a Disney Studios unit.

Observers uniformly took Katzenberg's resignation to mean that Eisner did not want to share decision-making power at the top of Disney, even if it also meant the loss of Mr. Katzenberg. One Disney insider was quoted as saying, "I guess Eisner has to be a one-man show." Katzenberg, on the other hand, felt he had earned the right to have more participation in Disney's direction and was resolved to leave if he could not obtain it. He also sought a more independent relationship with his longtime mentor Eisner.

What is power and how do CEOs, such as Eisner, gain it? How did Eisner's strong reputation for success enhance his power? What was the nature of the corporate culture at Disney under Eisner? How did Eisner build that culture? To what extent do Disney traditions either enhance Eisner's prospects for future success or limit his strategic options? These questions raise issues about the nature of power and culture within large firms. These are the issues of interest in this chapter, which considers the topics of power and corporate culture.

◆ ◆ ◆ ◆ ◆ POWER AND CULTURE IN COMPLEX ORGANIZATIONS

As we have emphasized throughout this book, the modern firm represents a complex division of labor across several dimensions of activity. The firm links a variety of activities together both horizontally and on the vertical chain. Each business unit can comprise a variety of divisions, departments, and other subunits. These groupings *within* business units are complicated by groupings *among* business units, which range from larger divisions to more complex matrix relationships. Furthermore, individuals within the firm maintain extensive relationships with outsiders, including buyers, suppliers, competitors, media, and regulators.

Firms embody a complex array of goals and subgoals in the pursuit of which individuals link their individual activities and rewards to those of the groups and subunits to which they belong and ultimately to the firm. The performance of individual employees thus ultimately determines the overall performance of the firm. The uncertain environment in which firms operate, along with the complexity of the firm's goal and reward structures, however, makes conflicts among individuals over what goals to pursue as well as how and when to pursue them very likely. In these conditions, an individual may be tempted to pursue his or her own goals, even to the detriment of the firm, provided the incentive to do it is sufficiently high. One would like to think that a control system could be designed to integrate individual behaviors into unified organizational action, but that seems impossible.

The conditions that give rise to market failures (and thus to internal organization in the first place) also work to frustrate hierarchical control and guarantee that conflicts among employees over which tasks to perform and how to perform them are unlikely to be resolved solely through formal controls. This is because employees are able to act without being observed by managers and managers receive insufficient information to assess whether employees have acted appropriately. These are the problems of hidden action and hidden information that were discussed in Chapters 3 and 15, and together, they allow ample room for opportunistic behavior by employees. In addition, an effective control system needs to both ensure that employees are working toward goals that are consistent with those of management and allow employees to make their best choices in performing their specific tasks. This balance has proven difficult to accomplish.

Organization structure represents the formal and contractual allocation of decision-making rights within firms, while organization controls comprise those explicit and contractable incentive arrangements that firms make with their employees. Yet there are many activities and interactions within organizations that must occur outside the scope of formal structure and controls. It is in this context of chronic goal conflict in situations where contracts are difficult to fashion that power and culture are important. While structure and controls provide the formal rules and guidelines within which a firm functions, power and culture create an atmosphere that enables employees to work together toward common goals in ways that the formal rules might otherwise frustrate. Unless employees have contracts that define their duties, they are obliged to act in the way their superiors mandate. Superiors use employees' desire for praise, money, and promotion to induce them to obey. Managers could also induce compliance in other employees through control of the resources they need to do their jobs.

Culture, on the other hand, is a set of collectively held values, beliefs, and norms of behavior that unites individual employees to act together to achieve the firm's goals. As David Kreps explains, "culture . . . gives hierarchical inferiors an idea *ex ante* how the firm will "react" to circumstances as they arise—in a very strong sense, it gives identity to the organization."[1] While power and culture are interrelated, we discuss them separately in the remainder of the chapter.

POWER

◆ ◆ ◆ ◆ ◆

Because power and related terms are so widely used by both academics and business practitioners, the meanings associated with them are potentially confusing. We take power to be an individual's ability to accomplish his or her goals by using resources obtained through *noncontractual exchange relationships* with other actors. By this, we mean exchanges of goods, services, or promises on terms that are diffuse or implicit and not enforceable in court. For example, someone in need of

---

[1] Kreps, D. M., "Corporate Culture and Economic Theory," in Alt, J. and K. Shepsle (eds.), *Perspectives on Positive Political Economy*, Cambridge, UK: Cambridge University, 1990.

emergency assistance may receive help from an individual and have little to offer that individual in return at the moment. The individual providing assistance may never have need of a reciprocation in kind. Nevertheless, there may still be an exchange, one of assistance now in exchange for an implied promise of assistance in return should it be needed. The terms of the agreement are not specified, since it is not known how the favor can best be returned. In addition, a failure to provide future assistance when requested would not give cause to legal action, since there was no contract. Still, it is reasonable to think of such an arrangement as an exchange, one whose obligations many people would fulfill.

This is not the same as authority, which stems from the explicit contractual decision-making rights a firm grants to an individual. A powerful manager may exercise his or her power by redirecting the activities of other actors away from their immediate goals and toward accomplishing the manager's own goals. In this sense, power is the ability to get things done. Influence, a related term, refers to the exercise or use of power in a given situation by an individual rather than the individual's overall power or his or her general ability to get things done. The influence a person has over others is an effect of his or her power.

Power exists at many levels in a firm. Individual managers, for example, may be powerful relative to their peers on the management team. For example, the power of the CEO relative to the board of directors is critical for allocating key resources. It is also common to discuss power at the level of departments or groups. In universities, for example, academic departments continually vie for budgetary resources and view their success in obtaining such resources as tangible evidence of their power, which may stem from their popularity with students, from the research productivity of their faculty, or from securing government and foundation grants. Finally, firms can exercise power in their product markets, in other factor markets (such as with raw material or labor suppliers), or in relations with groups that operate in the firm's environment. A powerful firm like Disney, for example, may obtain a more favorable distribution of a new animated film than would a rival movie studio. Disney would also have power in negotiations with toy manufacturers seeking to develop products based on Disney characters.

The Sources of Power

Power is often exerted in an economic market, as when a firm with a patent for a new drug uses its market power to set a high price-cost margin. Our interest here is in power that cannot be exerted in the market (i.e., that cannot be easily priced). Individuals attain this power when they possess resources that others value but are not readily tradable. Examples include Michael Eisner's power to veto a new film project or an academic dean's power to permit new courses. What are the sources of such power? Answering this involves two questions. First, what types of resources can provide power to actors? Second, under what conditions does possessing a resource give its holder power?

John French and Bertram Raven identify five bases of power: legitimate power; reward power; coercive power; expert power; and referent power.[2] *Legiti-*

---

[2]French, J. R. P., Jr. and B. Raven, "The Bases of Social Power," in Cartwright, D. (ed.), *Studies in Social Power*, Ann Arbor: University of Michigan, Institute for Social Research, 1959.

mate (or formal) power is based on the formal authority one receives from the firm. By legitimate, we mean that an individual has a right to expect compliance from others and that others in the firm will generally defer to that individual on certain decisions. This area of deference is what Chester Barnard refers to as the "zone of indifference."[3] *Reward power and coercive (or punishment) power* are the flip sides of the same coin. Coercive power is the power to punish. If you do not do what I want, I have the power to punish you. Reward power is more positive: I will do what you tell me to because you have the power to reward me when I comply with your demands. *Expert power* stems from the possession of specialized knowledge that is valued by other actors, especially knowledge that can solve problems. Finally, *referent power* accrues to those whom others admire as role models, charismatic leaders for example.

While formal and coercive authority dominates some organizations (i.e., military units, prisons) and is important in most, power based on formal authority has clear limits in business firms and other voluntary organizations. Managers' authority must be considered legitimate by their subordinates. This legitimacy must rest on more than formal rank. Two factors can minimize managers' formal authority. First, the division of labor within the firm means that managers must delegate authority to subordinates. Second, there are limits to managers' ability to oversee subordinates. Given these limitations, compliance based on formal authority alone may evaporate once the manager moves on to other tasks and ceases observing subordinates directly—as must inevitably happen. Managers thus depend on subordinates as much as subordinates depend on managers. John Kotter, who bases his work on that of French and Raven, argues that successful managers need to build several bases of power of the kinds discussed earlier, especially referent and expert power, whose effects are more persistent than formal authority.[4]

Power can also be based on image or reputation. An individual with a well-known history of winning will have a reputation for power that could lead potential adversaries to comply with his or her demands without a struggle. Similarly, acknowledged expertise is usually based on previous accomplishments and ability at solving problems in the past. Otherwise, there is no reason to expect an individual to repeat past successes and therefore no reason to defer (or delegate power) to that person. Power stemming from a long string of successes may be put at risk by a significant or poorly timed failure. At Disney, the coincidence of poor results from Euro Disney, the death of Frank Wells, and Michael Eisner's heart surgery, which all occurred in a short period of time, made more than a few analysts ambivalent about Disney's future, especially the long-run strength of its management team.

Power is not only rooted in individuals, however, but can also stem from the interactions of individuals within and between firms, and from the control of information and resources in these interactions. Power can stem from such relational characteristics as:

1. the dependence of an actor on others in a set of interrelated jobs and tasks (e.g., when one actor depends on the work of another, but not vice versa)

[3]Barnard, C., *The Function of the Executive*, Cambridge, MA: Harvard University Press, 1938, pp. 167–171.

[4]Kotter, J., "Power, Dependence, and Effective Management," *Harvard Business Review*, July–August 1977: pp. 125–136.

2. the centrality of an actor within an organization's communication network
3. the degree to which the individual is substitutable in a relationship
4. the dependence of a firm, or a unit within a firm, on the ability of key individuals to cope with uncertainties that affect performance.

We develop these points in the next section.

Example 17.1

The Sources of Presidential Power

One of the most famous studies of the bases of power was *Presidential Power*, Richard Neustadt's 1960 examination of how Franklin Roosevelt, Harry Truman, and Dwight Eisenhower dealt with power and influence during their administrations. The book was widely read at the beginning of the Kennedy administration and has remained important to sitting Presidents, their staffs, and policy analysts.[5]

The issue of most importance to Neustadt is the conflict between the image of the president as powerful and the reality of the presidency as institutionally weak. Presidential power does not consist of the president taking direct action on some front, such as Truman's recall of General Douglas MacArthur or his seizure of the steel mills in 1952, or Eisenhower's decision to send troops to Little Rock, Arkansas in 1957, to assist in desegregation. These command decisions were more exceptions than typical uses of power. Nor did any of them solve the president's policy problems. Instead, they used up scarce presidential power and, at best, allowed the president and others involved in the situation more time to search for a lasting solution. Neustadt suggests that decisions made by command or fiat are more likely to be evidence of a lack of power than of its effective use. In a given situation, however, there may have been no other choice than to command. For example, whatever problems Truman encountered in recalling MacArthur, the cost of not recalling him and thus allowing civilian authority to be flouted would probably have been higher.

Presidential power is the ability to influence the people who make and implement government policies. It has three sources. The first comprises the bargaining advantages that come with the office that enable the president to persuade others to work in his interest—the formal powers and authority of the president. The second source of presidential power is professional reputation, which comprises the expectations of professional politicians, bureaucrats, and others in the political community regarding the president's power and his willingness to use it. This is related to the president's ability to control the votes of Congress on key issues. Once the president loses control of a majority in Congress, he cannot guarantee that his programs will be enacted, and he loses power. A third source of presidential power is his prestige among the public, specifically how the political community assesses his support among different constituencies and the consequences to politicians of failure to support the president.

---

[5]The material for this example is taken from Neustadt's 1990 revision. See Neustadt, R. E., *Presidential Power and the Modern Presidents* (New York: Free Press, 1990).

Although the global political situation facing the president of the United States is different from those facing firms, Neustadt's three sources are consistent with those that we discussed above. The formal powers of the job, whether stemming from the Constitution, laws, or customs, along with the institutional routines that have grown up around it, provide a basis for power for incumbents, a basis that can be used well or poorly. Professional reputation in a firm refers to how observers expect the powerholder to act in a given situation, based on accumulated experience with the powerholder. Finally, prestige for politicians is analogous to control over critical resources. For the president and professional politicians, that resource is public sentiment that translates into votes in elections.

Looking back to 1990, in light of the six presidents who had served since *Presidential Power* was first published, Neustadt saw little reason to change his fundamental conclusions. For example, the experience of Nixon and Watergate, on the one hand, and Johnson and Vietnam, on the other, showed the importance of credibility and perceived legitimacy for both public prestige and professional reputation. Similarly, while Neustadt still emphasizes the importance of political skills for the president, the experiences of Johnson and Nixon also emphasize the relevance of individual temperament for success in office. The president needs to be patient enough to tolerate a complex political system that rarely allows him to successfully implement major policy initiatives immediately.

Neustadt still sees political skills and experience as crucial for success in office. (The presidency is no place for amateurs.) Political skills and experience, however, while necessary to success in the presidency, are not sufficient. Both Nixon and Johnson were highly experienced in elective office and possessed formidable political skills, yet their sense of power led both of them to support policies that ultimately dissipated their power and impaired their effectiveness.

SOCIAL EXCHANGE AND RESOURCE DEPENDENCE ◆ ◆ ◆ ◆ ◆

The most common view of power in organizations is based on the idea of *social exchange*. By social exchange, we mean a transfer between two or more parties of resources, or rights to control resources, that occurs outside the terms of a market context.[6] Power arises from persistent inequalities in the terms of repetitive social exchanges between two individuals.

To illustrate how power arises in social exchanges, suppose that A and B are exchange partners (individuals or firms). If an acceptable exchange occurs between them, the transaction is complete. Suppose, however, that they cannot complete an exchange (or series of exchanges) in a mutually acceptable manner, and that, as a result, A provides more of value to B than B can provide to A in return. B, in effect, "owes" A the deficit of the exchange. Note that this is not a formal debt, and A cannot sue B to recover the deficit. Over time, this deficit may be made up in

---

[6]For the principles of social exchange, see Coleman, J. S., *Foundations of Social Theory*, Cambridge, MA: Belknap, 1990, chap. 2.

other exchanges, the nature of which are not specified in advance. As B's deficit to A increases, B is said to be increasingly dependent on A. A is said to have power over B to the extent that B is dependent on A (i.e., A has the opportunity to obtain B's resources at A's discretion to satisfy A's own objectives). The dependence of B upon A is mitigated to the extent that A depends upon B for some other matter or in some other set of exchanges. If there was such an interdependence, then neither A nor B would be dependent on the other, since the deficits of one exchange would cancel out those of the other exchange. These two aspects of an exchange view of power—power and dependence—can be summed up as follows. The power of A over B (P_{AB}) is equal to B's dependence on A (D_{BA}). The net power of A over B is given by ($P_{AB} - P_{BA} = D_{BA} - D_{AB}$).

How does this view of social exchanges differ from the economic exchanges that individuals or firms make and with which we have been concerned in other chapters? If both parties agree to participate, why are power relationships any different from other exchanges? In voluntary exchanges, why would an actor like B choose to become dependent on another actor like A and presumably commit future resources to A's discretion? Why would A provide resources in the present in return for the uncertain future obligations of B? After all, despite B's "debt," A cannot use formal means, such as the courts, to force compensation from B.

One could argue that an individual enters into a dependence relation because he or she lacks a better alternative. The resources controlled by the other party may be important to the future of the firm, there may be no clear substitutes or alternative sources, and/or it may be too costly to write a formal contract. This is the *resource dependence* view of power, expressed by Jeffrey Pfeffer.[7] In this view, individuals and firms seek to gain power by reducing their dependence on other actors, while increasing the dependence of other actors on them. This is analogous to the efforts by firms to avoid supplier power by securing multiple supply channels and to achieve market power by selling to customers who have few alternatives. Pfeffer also suggests that firms avoid dependence on suppliers of critical inputs by relying on long-term contracting or vertical integration. Absent coordination or transaction costs, however, this is not a viable solution, because suppliers will insist on a premium price for relinquishing their power.

Resource dependence helps explain why firms benefit from asymmetric social exchange, but does not explain why individuals are willing to give up resources today in exchange for an uncertain exercise of power in the future. One explanation is that, on the merits of the exchange itself, it is beneficial to the actor providing resources to trust that the other party will reciprocate. Once trust has been established by several interactions, then similar social exchanges will seem less risky. A will not distrust B's willingness to reciprocate because B needs what A is providing on a continuing basis. Conversely, A may value what it expects B to provide so highly that A is willing to tolerate the chance that B will not reciprocate in the future. The willingness of an actor to provide resources in exchange for unspecified future consideration may also be based on more generally held societal norms of reciprocity or trustworthiness.

---

[7] Pfeffer, J., *Managing with Power: Politics and Influence in Organizations*, Boston, MA: Harvard Business School Press, 1992; Pfeffer, J., *Power in Organizations*, Marshfield, MA: Pitman, 1981; Pfeffer, J. and Salancik, G., *The External Control of Organizations: A Resource Dependence Perspective*, New York: Harper & Row, 1978.

Along with the idea that actors will work to reduce their dependency on other actors, the resource dependence view also has implications about which individuals within a firm are likely to attain power. Specifically, individuals who control critical resources will accumulate power. Those individuals who help the firm cope with problems that pose major threats to it will come to exercise the most power within the firm. Examples of this can be seen in firms where members of a critical occupational or professional group gain control (petroleum engineers in oil companies), where individuals with links to key regulators or stakeholders gain control (lawyers in regulated businesses, such as public utilities), or where individuals who possess unique skills gain control (surgeons in some teaching hospitals).[8]

To analyze power and use it to make decisions, one must first be able identity it (or its absence). The task of measuring power, however, has several problems attached to it. Identifying the relevant actors involved in an exchange is often difficult. Assessing the relative power of actors is also difficult, because such assessments are often based on self-reports, and individuals with power may want to understate their positions, while individuals without power may want to overstate their positions. It is also unlikely that all individuals contacted will be equally knowledgeable about the actual power distribution in the firm. There are also difficulties about how to interpret observed unequal relationships.

Can one use the resource dependence view of power to identify actual power relationships among individuals or firms? The answer is generally no. That one party provides resources but apparently receives nothing immediate in return does not imply that the party either has power or is dependent. The actor providing resources while seemingly receiving nothing in return may already be powerful and thus will benefit from the dependence of the other party. That same actor could also be dependent, however, and is providing resources to a more powerful actor while seemingly receiving much less in return. Finally, there may simply be no power relationship between the actors, indicating that they do not expect to be dependent on each other or to be compensated in power terms for the exchange of resources.

Edward Laumann and David Knoke developed what they term *resource deployment* and *resource mobilization* perspectives on power to clarify the ambivalence of an observed uneven exchange.[9] A resource deployment strategy (RDS) looks at power from the standpoint of the actor providing resources, while the resource mobilization strategy (RMS) looks at power from the standpoint of the recipient of resources. RDS considers that power comes from getting others to employ your resources on your behalf (i.e., that you control their behavior). RMS, on the other hand, considers power to be the ability to obtain resources from other actors that you can employ while pursuing your goals (i.e., that you control their resources and not their behavior). A thorough analysis of resource dependence relationships in a situation requires a comparison of the results of both models over the set of situations of interest to identify which model provides the best explanation for different situations.

---

[8]This variant of the resource dependence approach is the "strategic contingencies" view of power. See Hickson, D. J., C. R. Hinings, C. A. Lee, R. E. Schneck, and J. M. Pennings, "A Strategic Contingencies Theory of Intraorganizational Power," *Administrative Science Quarterly*, 16, 1971: pp. 216–229.

[9]Laumann, E. O. and D. Knoke, *The Organizational State*, Madison, WI: University of Wisconsin Press, 1987.

Power and Transactions Costs

Recall from Chapters 3 and 4 that transactions costs are the costs of using the firm or the market as a mode of economic coordination. As market-related transactions costs increase, it becomes more desirable to use the firm rather than the market. Conversely, as bureaucratic dysfunctions and influence costs increase within firms, it becomes increasingly reasonable to either reorganize the firm or else use the market more. The conditions that give rise to high transaction costs in the market-place are precisely those situations in which we are most likely to see power relations associated with resource dependencies. The reason is simple. Transactions costs arise in complex situations that contracts cannot easily govern. In these situations, the development and exercise of power are most important.

To see the relationship between power and transactions-cost arguments, consider the holdup problem discussed in Chapter 3. There, asset specificity prevents the owner of an asset from redeploying it for other uses. Inefficiencies arise due to underinvestment in relationship-specific assets. When it is costly to craft contingent claims contracts to govern exchanges, the solution to the holdup problem may be to vertically integrate or otherwise reorganize to reduce dependence on a given seller. In this sense, the implications of resource dependence and transactions-cost arguments are similar.

Resource dependence and transactions-costs arguments differ in two ways. First, resource dependence assumes that actors are myopic and thus that parties to a transactions fail to anticipate transactions-cost problems and arrange appropriate safeguards. This means that dependency problems are generally unanticipated and unwanted. Transactions-cost arguments do not assume that actors are myopic and recognize that contracting arrangements are chosen after carefully considering the hazards and safeguards of different arrangements. A second difference is that resource dependence arguments focus on contracting problems associated with specific assets and neglect the evidence that specific assets are often selected despite transactions costs, due to their productive benefits.[10]

Vertical integration does not solve the holdup problem by eliminating asset specificity, however. Instead, it relies on powerful managers to craft governance mechanisms that assure parties to an exchange within the firm that they will be compensated for their investments. In this way, powerful managers provide the assurances to individuals that market contracts cannot provide.

How power is exercised in the firm is critical, because of the persistence of bureaucratic rigidities and their associated influence costs. Formal control and budgetary systems are likely to be incomplete in practice and thus will not remedy problems of hidden information and hidden action within firms. This means that many of the dependency problems experienced in imperfect market exchanges may also be experienced inside the firm. For example, holdup may occur within firms if the effective control of sunk assets depends on the cooperation of interdependent employees who are not linked together by a common source of authority. An upstream unit that provides a critical component (e.g., a microprocessor with several applications) to another unit may also provide that same component to other branches of the firm or to outside buyers. If one of the downstream units is critically dependent on it and does not have ready access to alternative sources, the upstream

---

[10]These arguments are presented in Williamson, O. E., *The Mechanism of Governance*, Oxford, UK: Oxford University Press, 1996, pp. 238–239.

unit may be in a position to hold it up, even though they are in the same firm, due to the discretion of the supplier and the vulnerability of the buyer. Clearly, a powerful manager who can punish holdup activities by subordinates can improve intrafirm efficiency. But hidden information and hidden action may allow the upstream unit to disguise its holdup activities, thereby limiting the manager's power.

If resource dependence and transactions-cost explanations are related, then we would expect to see an association between the degree of dependence among industries that buy or sell from each other and the extent of merger and acquisition activity among them. There should be more mergers where firms in one industry are relatively dependent on the sales to or purchases from firms in another industry than in a situation in which there was not a relative dependence on transactions with another industry. In the former situation, a powerful manager may be needed to assure effective exchanges, given market imperfections. In the latter, however, mutual interdependence would assure effective exchanges in the market. Menachem Brenner and Zur Shapira investigated this question, using input-output data from the U.S. Federal Trade Commission.[11] Their results were largely consistent with a resource-dependence explanation. Mutual interdependence across industries was inversely related to the proportion of vertical mergers involving those industries, while dependence was positively related. Their results were evident for both upstream and downstream relations between industries, but were stronger for downstream relations. Vertical mergers appeared to be motivated by the need to control critical resource relationships.

Michel Crozier provides an example of power gained by control over key information in his case study of a French cigarette firm.[12] The firm was a government-controlled monopoly, with a stable competitive environment and stable demand. The only contingency that the managers of the firm faced in meeting production schedules was to keep their machines operating without breakdowns. The firm's maintenance workers had come to control access to knowledge of how to keep the machines operating through their tradition of training new engineers verbally, rather than with standardized documentation. Over the years, the original documentation for the machines had disappeared. These workers thus gained considerable power relative to management and other workers, such as machine operators. The power of the maintenance workers and technical engineers in the factory was not unlimited, however. Plant managers could recommend that the plant be retooled. If this happened, then new machines would replace the old ones, and managers would have full documentation about the machines. This would eliminate both sources of power of the maintenance engineers. This situation resulted in a rough power equilibrium within the plant.

Structural Views of Power

Although power ultimately stems from control of scarce resources, it may be embodied in the structure of a firm. Those who occupy certain critical locations within a structure have more power. For example, Jeffrey Katzenberg's position as head of

---

[11]Brenner, M. and Z. Shapira, "Environmental Uncertainty as Determining Merger Activity," chap. 3, in W. Goldberg (ed.), *Mergers*, New York: Nichols Publishing Co., 1983: pp. 51–65.

[12]Crozier, M., *The Bureaucratic Phenomenon*, Chicago: University of Chicago Press, 1964, pp. 61–142.

the Walt Disney Studios most likely gave him more power within the Disney organization than the heads of other business units Disney possessed. Several types of structure can provide power to well-situated members. Often the most powerful individuals in a firm will occupy key positions in multiple structures. For example, Michael Eisner presumably has more power at Disney by virtue of his being chairman and CEO than he would have if he occupied only one of these positions.

Within the structure of authority that characterizes most firms, designated managers will have authority over others by virtue of their position. The most common example of this is the military, where troops in uniform salute all superior officers. Individuals in positions of authority can expect their subordinates to comply with their directives within a generally defined sphere of action. In effect, employees agree to acknowledge the decision-making authority of superiors on matters within their jurisdiction. Within their domain of authority, managers will receive some benefit of the doubt from employees regarding a manager's right to make a decision. This is the basis of their formal or "position power" within firms, which they receive by virtue of their location in the firm's structure.

Structure can also mean the information network operating within a firm or the informal social relationships that develop among the firm's employees, customers, suppliers, and other stakeholders during their interactions. These networks can both support and impede the exercise of power in firms. As we have already discussed, having a prominent position within informal networks can give an individual referent power that will enhance his or her formal authority and make it easier to influence organizational outcomes. Informal organizational networks can also allow opposition to mobilize, spread gossip, and strengthen resistance to change.

If information on key developments, such as in the marketplace or with regulators, is critical for firm performance and a particular individual is in a position to regulate that flow of information from the market into the firm, that individual will control a critical resource for the firm and accrue power from that control. For example, Thomas Whisler studied decisions in insurance companies about the introduction of computers and the adoption of management information systems. He found considerable conflict about issues of where in the organization the computers would be located, whose budget would be charged, and who would control the computers. He attributed this conflict to the recognition by managers of the power that would accrue to whoever gained control over the information system of the firm.[13] As with other types of power, the information provided by a key individual must be both important to the firm and the individual difficult to replace before control of that information leads to power. The individual must be indispensable. If the firm has other means to obtain the information or gain access to key constituencies, then the location of an individual in an informational or social network will not be influential.

Ronald Burt provides a general version of structural power in his theory of structural holes.[14] A *structural hole* is a relationship in a social network in which one actor is the critical link between individuals or entire groups of actors. To associate with each other, these individuals or groups must go through the actor who

[13]Whisler, T., *Information Technology and Organizational Change*, Belmont, CA: Wadsworth, 1970.

[14]Burt, R. S., *Structural Holes: The Social Structure of Competition*, Cambridge, MA: Harvard University Press, 1992.

spans the structural hole. The presence of a structural hole allows the individual who can span the hole to use the control of information or resource flows as a source of power. The elimination of a structural hole, such as when representatives of the two previously separate groups begin interacting on their own, eliminates the dependence of the two groups on the focal individual and thus also his or her power. Structural holes are generic features of networks, whether the networks comprise individuals or organizations. The potential for power from spanning a structural hole is applicable to most types of networks, including market networks, formally defined networks within a firm, or informal networks that span the formal boundaries of firms, voluntary organizations, or government agencies.

Providing a valued relationship between two unconnected parties (actors or groups of actors) provides a basis for power to individuals employing what Burt calls a *tertius gaudens* (happy third) strategy. The tertius is the "third who benefits," and the strategy involves spanning a structural hole and bargaining with the parties on either side for the most favorable terms. There are two kinds of tertius strategies. The first occurs when an actor is the third between two parties in the same relationship, such as being the broker in a buyer-seller relationship. The second occurs when an actor is the third between two parties in two or more relations with conflicting demands. An example of this would be parties working on different projects who must compete for scarce time with their manager. A tertius strategy creates power for an actor through control of the movement of information between contacts on either side of the relationship, making this strategy a general example of resource dependence in social networks.

Roberto Fernandez and Roger Gould apply ideas of structural holes in their study of the influence of brokerage positions in decision making on national health policy.[15] Brokers span structural holes in that they permit communication between actors who do not regularly communicate with each other. In national health policy, brokers add value, and thus potentially accrue power, in two ways. First, the sheer number of actors involved in health policy formation makes it unlikely that any actor will be able to regularly maintain contacts with all other actors. Brokers can provide established channels for communications. Second, particular policy issues may present temporary opportunities for coordination to a given pair of actors who might otherwise never communicate with each other. Brokers can recognize and bring about such opportunities for productive contact.

Fernandez and Gould examine whether and under what conditions the occupancy of five types of brokerage positions provides an actor with influence. They found that occupancy of brokerage positions was generally associated with a reputation for having influence. To gain this influence, however, actors also had to be perceived as neutral in the decision-making process. Given the contentiousness of health policy debates and the expectation among interest groups of government neutrality on political matters, this is a reasonable result. Exceptions to this general finding occurred when it was reasonable for the government to take a stand, for example, when the government was contracting with outside vendors. Overall, these results imply a paradox of power that is based on spanning gaps in social networks—spanning structural holes appears to augment power, so long as one does not use that power overtly to pursue one's individual interests.

---

[15]Fernandez, R. M. and Gould, R. V., "A Dilemma of State Power: Brokerage and Influence in the National Health Policy Domain," *American Journal of Sociology*, 99, May 1994: pp. 1455–91.

Do Successful Organizations Need Powerful Managers?

It is tempting to claim that an organization must have powerful managers to succeed. After all, power represents the means to get things done in a firm. Unless employee relationships can be completely governed by incentive contracts, a manager must have power to be successful. The implications of power for firm performance are not unambiguously positive, however. A manager might use power for personal interests that significantly diverge from those of the firm. The results may be counterproductive for the manager and harmful for the firm.

Even the most powerful manager in a firm is someone else's agent. The CEO is the agent of the shareholders, by way of the board of directors. In the presence of agency costs arising from hidden actions, hidden information, and related problems, a powerful manager may divert information and resources toward personal goals. For example, a powerful financial management team within a firm may push for a merger to increase their team's influence on corporate policy, rather than for sound business reasons. The effects of this abuse of power can be critical for a firm in a changing business environment. The financial management team may have risen to power when restructuring was vital to the firm's success and the team provided the skills needed to implement it effectively. If R&D is now more important to the firm than financial prowess, then the financial management team may trade on its status and organizational position to divert resources away from R&D and toward mergers, merely to hold on to power.

Clearly, power is a two-edged sword, whose effects can be positive or negative for firms. We expect that the accumulation of power will be helpful or harmful according to the following conditions:

Accumulation of power is helpful when

1. there are high agency costs between managers and lower-level workers
2. the firm's environment is relatively stable

Accumulation of power is harmful when

1. there are high agency costs between levels of upper management
2. the firm's environment is relatively unstable

A good example of the dangers of power is provided by the Chernobyl nuclear power plant accident in 1986.[16] P. S. Neporozhny, the Soviet Minister of Energy and Electrification until 1985, wielded great power in overseeing the entire nuclear power program. This power grew not from his scientific knowledge or engineering expertise (he was decidedly ill-informed about the intricacies of nuclear reactors and their differences from other sources of power), but from his position in the Soviet government and, presumably, his bureaucratic skills. While the position of energy minister was initially unimportant, it became more significant with the growth of nuclear power. Neporozhny used his power to prevent higher officials (i.e., his principals) from learning about accidents and other deficiencies in the nuclear program. He thus lessened the incentives of government managers to expend resources on reactor safety, which exacerbated the safety problem in the Soviet nuclear power program.

His successors continued this policy of secrecy and it was still in force when the Chernobyl reactor erupted. This prevented Soviet leaders from correctly eval-

---

[16]The information in this example comes from Medvedev, G., *The Truth About Chernobyl*, New York: Basic Books, 1991. Medvedev was the senior government investigator of Chernobyl, and his book summarizes the findings of the investigation.

uating the disaster and delayed effective responses to it. From this example, we see that high agency costs at the upper levels of management, combined with rapidly changing technology, allowed individuals to attain power who were not sufficiently informed to effectively oversee the nuclear energy program. The subsequent abuse of power by these individuals led to the worst nuclear accident in history. The Soviet government learned little from Chernobyl regarding the abuses of power that secrecy can foster. Fewer than three months after the accident, new government instructions forbade public discussions of Chernobyl by government officials with the press, radio, or television.

XAMPLE 17.2

POWER AND POOR PERFORMANCE: THE CASE OF THE 1957 MERCURY

While power may be useful in getting things done, it can also be dysfunctional if it helps the wrong programs to be accomplished—that is, if it is used to circumvent the checks and balances that are necessary to evaluate the market feasibility and cost effectiveness of any effort. An example of this occurred with the development of the 1957 Mercury. Called the "Turnpike Cruiser" by Ford managers and a "steel cartoon" by its critics, the model was introduced to great fanfare, but failed to make good on its high costs and lofty sales projections. Overall, Ford lost an estimated $369 on every 1957 Mercury it sold, and the car proved a harbinger of even greater problems that came with the now infamous Edsel. In his group history of the careers of the "Whiz Kids" at Ford, John Byrne provides an example of the functions and dysfunctions of power in the career of one of the Whiz Kids responsible for the new Mercury, Francis "Jack" Reith.[17]

Reith had a number of power bases from which to push the development of the new Mercury. First, he was a dynamic and almost charismatic leader, who drove his subordinates, but inspired considerable admiration in the process. He was also highly intelligent and effective at persuading others to follow his direction. Reith had a considerable track record since he joined Ford in 1946. Most recently, he had received credit for the successful turnaround and sale of Ford's subsidiary in France. On the basis of this success, Reith enjoyed the support of his superiors, Lewis Crusoe and Henry Ford II. He also gained standing from his association with the Whiz Kids, who had nearly all distinguished themselves at Ford and who were clearly recognized as a group as well as individually. Finally, Reith had position power, in that he was promoted to the head of the Mercury division, once his 1957 plan had been approved.

---

[17]Byrne, J. A., *The Whiz Kids* (New York: Currency Doubleday, 1993). The Whiz Kids were a group of academics and operations analysts, including Reith, Charles Thorton, Robert McNamara, and Arjay Miller, who distinguished themselves in operations analysis for the Army Air Force in World War II and later joined the management of Ford as a group in early 1946. Most rose to senior positions within Ford and two, McNamara and Miller, rose to its presidency.

Reith saw the 1957 Mercury as part of a larger plan by which Ford could contend with General Motors for leadership in automobiles through a major expansion of an existing make (Mercury) and the introduction of an entirely new one (the Edsel). Reith's boss, Lewis Crusoe, promised him his support (and the top job) at Mercury, if the plan could be approved by the board of directors. In preparing for that board meeting, Reith used all of his bases of power effectively.

He was perhaps too effective. There were doubts about the initiative in several quarters. The plan promised too much (a 54 % sales increase). It required a larger expansion of the dealer network than Ford had ever anticipated. The projected expenses of the project were staggering and, in effect, required a large increase in market share to justify the project. As one executive remembered, ". . . the numbers were totally unrealistic. They had to be. It was the only way to justify the plan." (Byrne, p. 225). The estimated price for the project was equal to the company's total profit before taxes the previous year ($485 million).

These doubts were not raised, however, because Reith's colleagues, whose job it was to ask difficult questions about projects, failed to do so in this case, out of deference to their friend. When questions were raised, Reith and Crusoe jointly overpowered the opposition. Much of this persuasion was based on fear intimidation and concern for the career consequences of resistance. The rational analysis that the Whiz Kids introduced to Ford was forgotten.

The failure of the car, which ended Reith's career at Ford, was due in part to the flawed decision processes described above that allowed Reith to push through his initiative at the expense of critical analysis. Reith and his managers, however, also failed to pay attention to market research, which indicated increased consumer interest in safety and descreased interest in the stylistic flourishes that characterized the car. Instead, the 1957 Mercury was based on managerial intuitions about consumer preferences for stylish cars rather than on data. The car also suffered from numerous quality and safety problems. In making this error, however, Reith was not alone. 1957 was a strong year for the Volkswagen, a small simple car that focused on economy. It was also the first year in which consumer's interest in automobile safety and quality increased. Many managers in Detroit missed this shift in the market, which would lead to further problems for the industry in the 1960s and 1970s.

◆ ◆

EXAMPLE 17.3

POWER SHIFTS IN THE NEWSPAPER BUSINESS

Power conflicts are often sharpest during periods of pronounced environmental change, which shifts the control over the key contingencies facing firms from one group to another, without altering formal power, as expressed by the organizational structure of the firm. New groups claim more decision-making rights as a result of the influence they wield in the future of the firm. Established groups, however, can resist claims for influence by new groups through their control over the firm's formal authority structure.

The newspaper business has seen increased conflicts in the past two decades between the marketing and related functions of the business, on the one hand, and the editorial function, on the other. Newspapers have always gained revenues through subscription and newsstand sales, along with the sale of advertising, and incur significant costs in paper and supplies, editorial expenses, printing, and distribution. There is also a traditionally strong role for an independent editorial function in newspapers that relies on constitutional guarantees of freedom of the press, stresses the public interest, and is characterized by a critical and at times adversarial role versus business, government, or other large interests. While there has long been tension between a newspaper's editorial and business functions, the tradition in large newspapers is to balance the two, while preserving the independence of the editorial function. This was known in the industry as "the separation of church and state." Thus until the 1980s, the *Chicago Tribune* maintained separate elevators in its headquarters for editorial and noneditorial staff.[18]

This balance has been disrupted because several factors have greatly increased the competitiveness of the business environment for newspapers. Advances in satellite, cable, and data-processing technologies have changed what used to be separate industries, such as newspapers, magazines, television, radio, movies, and computers, into a much larger and less defined information-processing sector. Newspapers are no longer the only, or even the principal source of news for readers. They are also no longer the only, or the most appropriate medium for their traditional advertisers, who can now choose among online services, cable television, broadcast television and radio, and direct mail as alternative media for their advertising expenditures. In their traditional functions of providing printed information and advertising to readers, newspapers have never had a more competitive environment.

At the same time, the ownership of newspapers has increasingly come under control of concentrated investor groups that are strongly motivated to maximize profitability. The traditional owner-publishers who controlled large urban daily newspapers in this century, with names like Hearst, Pulitzer, Bingham, and McCormick, have increasingly given up their control to newspaper groups (also called chains), such as Gannett or Knight-Ridder. The number of newspaper groups grew from 13 in 1910 to 155 in 1980, while during that period, the percentage of newspapers owned by the groups grew from 3 percent to 65 percent. This concentration of ownership has continued through the 1980s, and today few major newspapers remain independent. The largest of these corporate groups have diversified beyond newspapers and are now multimedia corporations that manage a wide range of broadcast and information business, from books and magazines, on the one hand, to cable television, satellite operations, network programming, radio, and interactive media, on the other.[19]

---

[18]Squires, J. D., *Read All About It! The Corporate Takeover of America's Newspapers* (New York: Times Books, 1994), pp. 72–73.

[19]For more details on newspaper groups, see Krieg, A., *Spiked: How Chain Management Corrupted America's Oldest Newspaper* (Old Saybrook, CT: Peregrine Press, 1987), Chapter 3; Mayer, M., *Making News* (Boston, MA: Harvard Business School Press), Chapter 5; Squires, J. D., *Read All About It! The Corporate Takeover of America's Newspapers* (New York: Times Books, 1994).

While newspapers have generally been profitable business, these new owners have been more strongly motivated to maximize their profitability than previous owner-publishers were. As a result, the balance of power between business and editorial functions within papers has shifted, with business functions coming to hold more power. This is apparent in conflicts between business and editorial staff on issues where the professional interests of the two diverge.

One area where such conflicts emerge is investigative journalism, where the interests of good business and good journalism may conflict if key community advertisers are targets of inquiry. Andrew Krieg details an example of this in his book on the acquisition in 1979 of the *Hartford Courant* by the Times–Mirror group.[20] In 1983, the paper mounted an exploratory investigation of workplace hazards and illnesses, as well as the processes by which these hazards were regulated and how workers were treated after they became ill and filed workers' compensation claims. The investigation reached a number of disturbing conclusions about workplace hazards and how insurance companies handled claims. The problem with this story was that Hartford is known as "the insurance city," in part because fourteen major insurers are headquartered there. In addition, one of Connecticut's largest private employers, United Technologies, was also headquartered in Hartford and was criticized in the story.

After a year of preparation, the story was cancelled (or "spiked") by a new editor appointed by the Times–Mirror chain. He claimed that the story was boring and poorly written and would not interest readers. Subsequently, a greatly reduced "human interest" version of the story, one that omitted critical references to insurers and United Technologies, was run in a night edition. Krieg's response to the alleged flaws in the story is to note that much of the story was subsequently published elsewhere, to wide acclaim. The clear interpretation that Krieg gives to the cancellation and subsequent dilution of the story is that it was due to the perceived threat the story posed to the insurance companies and the business community, upon whose advertising the paper depended for three quarters of its revenues.

The Decision to Allocate Formal Power to Individuals

Thus far, our discussion of power has skirted a critical managerial issue: Why should the firm grant formal authority to individuals who already wield great power by virtue of their control over key resources? When should power not be allocated to such individuals? To begin to answer these questions, we should recall the transactions-cost rationales for why firms exist at all that we discussed in Chapters 3 and 4. The choice of internalizing decisions is made in part because transactions-costs make dispute resolution in markets too costly. Firms internalize decisions when fiat and administrative discretion are more efficient ways of settling disputes. However, this does not indicate who should be allowed to exercise that discretion and authority. The question is who should receive formal power in the firm.

---

[20]Kreig, A., *Spiked: How Chain Management Corrupted America's Oldest Newspaper*, Chapter 11.

A first part of the answer is that *knowledgeable* individuals should receive power. If formal power is to be used effectively, then its holders should be informed about the policies they will need to approve and the disputes they will have to resolve. The importance of knowledge as a basis for position authority and power has been recognized since the earliest writings on bureaucratic organizations. For example, knowledge, in terms of both technical expertise and about the organization, was a critical aspect of Max Weber's theory of bureaucracy, which was essential for the development of modern organization theory.[21]

It may be argued that the holder of formal power on an issue need not be the most knowledgeable individual in the firm on that issue. Indeed, in some settings (e.g., research laboratories) it would be inefficient to make the best scientist the manager, because that individual would be most useful to the firm as a generator of knowledge rather than a resolver of disputes. Even so, that scientist's manager should know enough science to evaluate performance and allocate resources.

A second basis for allocating formal authority concerns the motivations and interests of the managers who would receive power. A manager must not only be knowledgeable, but must also have the same interests as the firm. Otherwise, the firm will become vulnerable to holdup by the very person whose responsibility was to reduce transactions-cost problems through internal decision making. Holdup would occur when the firm makes relationship-specific investments with managers whose interests are likely to diverge from the firm if noncontractible contingencies arise, as suggested by the Grossman-Hart argument that we discussed in Chapter 4. The ownership of the specialized human capital that managers provide to the firm cannot be fully transferred, which would leave managers with the opportunity to hold up the firm. This is less of a problem when the interests of managers are tied to those of the firm, such as through substantial bonuses that are linked to firm performance.

If the wielders of power in the firm control critical resources, then the firm is also vulnerable if they leave, especially to join the competition. This implies that power should go to individuals who are relatively likely to stay with the firm. Excessive turnover of key decision makers not only takes critical knowledge out of the firm, but also paralyzes its strategic decision making. Julio Rotemberg argues that firms actually prefer to give decision makers power rather than higher wages as a way of reducing turnover. Power may be thought of as a firm-specific asset—the worker may get better pay elsewhere, but might not achieve comparable levels of power and influence.[22]

The firm must solve the problem of allocating formal power to individual managers. The "best" match of individuals and formal powers is likely to be a matter of balancing, in response to changes in the firm's environment and in the people holding power. This may be why the management shuffles at Disney that we mentioned at the beginning of this chapter received such attention. The allocation of power to managers is a fundamental task of management and is intimately connected with the direction that the firm takes and how successful it is.

---

[21]Weber, M., *Economy and Society*, Vol. 1, Berkeley, CA: University of California Press, 1978, pp. 212–226.

[22]Rotemberg, J. J., "Power in Profit-Maximizing Organizations," *Journal of Economics and Management Strategy*, 2, 1993: pp. 165–198.

◆ ◆ ◆ ◆ ◆ CULTURE

According to many students of business strategy, the profitability of firms is only partly linked to technical and agency efficiency, competitive strategy, and positioning. It is also a function of the firm's *culture*. Concepts related to culture are frequently employed to explain such anomalies as the persistent high performance of some firms versus their competitors or why otherwise comparable firms in different countries or geographic regions seem to perform so differently. Although the basis of corporate culture research stems from some classic case studies of firms and public sector organizations, the popularity of such books as *In Search of Excellence*, by Tom Peters and Robert Waterman and *Theory Z*, by William Ouchi, has also sparked interest in corporate cultures, especially as traditionally successful large firms were hurt by foreign (and especially Japanese) competition.

What Is Corporate Culture?

By *corporate culture*, we mean a set of values, beliefs, and norms of behavior shared by members of a firm that influences individual employee preferences and behaviors. Culture also refers to the material products or behavior that provide evidence of collective values and norms, such as symbols, art, ritual practices, or other social constructions, that members of the firm use to reinforce their sense of belonging to a common culture. The underlying values, beliefs, and norms that are the basis of culture are difficult to observe and measure, however. A more operational view, which also suits our interest in culture's economic implications, is that culture represents the behavioral guideposts in a firm that are not spelled out by contract but that nonetheless constrain and inform the firm's managers and employees.

There is great disagreement regarding the definition and scope of culture. Moreover, different departments within a firm may have different cultures. In addition, a firm's culture may appear to be diverse, reflecting the culture of the various countries in which its product divisions are located. While there may be such a thing as a firm culture, distinguishing its effects from those of other cultures may be difficult. What appears to be a firm's culture in a given situation may actually be the result of an overlapping of national culture, local culture, firm culture, subunit culture, and group culture. For example, David Landes has argued the importance of national culture in explaining differences in economic performance between nations, and by implication differences in the performance of firms from those nations.[23] While culture may be broad in scope, we are interested in those aspects of it that can potentially influence a firm's economic performance. In addition, while it may be difficult in a large firm to identify a single culture that embraces all its members, we are interested in that culture (or subcultures) that is most prevalent among the firm's decision makers, since it will have the most economic significance.

Culture and Performance

An obvious concern for general managers is whether an organization's culture affects its performance. It is difficult to directly link the two. Culture may be associated with high performance without necessarily causing that performance. For

---

[23]Landes, D. S., *The Wealth and Poverty of Nations*, New York: W. W. Norton, 1998.

example, IBM, until it experienced problems in the late 1980s, was seen as having a strong culture, combining customer service, employee development, and professional standards, that contributed to its success. However, IBM's persistently high earnings, as well as its competitive practices, may have provided an environment in which a strong culture could develop and persist. It is unclear whether the culture caused the firm's high performance or vice versa.

Jay Barney identifies the conditions under which culture can be a source of sustained competitive advantage.[24] First, the culture must be valuable for the firm. This is critical, and we discuss it below. To be a source of sustained competitive advantage, corporate culture must also be particular to the firm. If the culture is common to most firms in the market, so that it reflects the influence of the national or regional culture, then it is unlikely to lead to a relative competitive advantage, since most firms in the industry or sector will share the same cultural attributes. Finally, culture must be inimitable. If a firm's culture is easy to imitate, other firms will begin to emulate it, which will soon nullify the advantage it gave the firm that first developed it. That organizational cultures can be described by researchers does not render them imitable. The influence of the culture on the firm is likely to rest on tacit factors that are not easily described and that represent the accumulated history of the firm much better than a simple description does. The complexity that would make a culture difficult for others to imitate will also make it difficult for managers to modify the culture of their firms to significantly improve performance. Barney even suggests a trade-off between the degree to which a culture is manipulable and the amount of sustained value that a firm can obtain from it. A culture that is manipulable is not likely to be linked to the fundamental resource commitments of the firm, which form the basis for sustained competitive advantage. Rather, it is more likely to be common to several firms and imitable and hence less valuable.

Culture creates value for firms in three principal ways. First, culture reduces information-processing demands on individuals within the firm, allowing them to better focus on their activities. Second, it complements formal control systems and thus reduces the costs of monitoring individuals within the firm. Third, it shapes the preferences of individuals toward a common set of goals. It thus reduces negotiation and bargaining costs within the firm and fosters cooperation. We discuss these value-creating properties of culture in more detail below.

Culture Simplifies Information Processing

A culture's values, norms of activity, and accompanying signals can focus the activities of employees on a limited set of arrangements. This frees employees from the need to continually negotiate what their tasks will be within the firm. A strong culture may thus reduce the costs of decision making and permit a specialization of effort. It allows individuals to share both experiences about what they have done and expectations about their work, and thus reduces uncertainty. This affects both the content of actions (certain product definitions over others, certain levels of riskiness in advertising and new product development versus others) and the forms of interactions among employees, customers, and stakeholders, including appro-

---

[24]Barney, J. B., "Organizational Culture: Can It Be a Source of Sustained Competitive Advantage?" *Academy of Management Review*, 11, 1986: pp. 656–665; for the general criteria, see Porter, M., *Competitive Strategy*, New York: Free Press, 1980.

priate language, rules for transactions, and other matters. Culture can thus focus activities and increase a firm's technical efficiency.

An example of how culture can help reduce uncertainty and focus activities is the case of Cray Research.[25] Founded by Seymour Cray in 1976, Cray became well known for its innovations in the development of supercomputers. The culture of the firm was an important part of its reputation. This culture stressed innovation and strong employee commitment, using the accomplishments and activities of Cray himself as focal points and examples. Starting in 1978, however, Cray grew at a phenomenal rate. Had its culture not been strong, it could probably not have absorbed this growth and remained prosperous. Without a strong culture, the coordination costs of the workforce alone might have overwhelmed the ability of Cray managers to adapt to change. The number of Cray employees, for example, grew five times between 1978 and 1983, from 321 to 1,551. During that same period, total revenue grew from $17 million to nearly $170 million. However, the structure of the firm remained fairly simple and nonbureaucratic, and decision making remained decentralized in small work groups. Without a central focus for managers and employees, the complexity of managing such an enterprise in such an unstructured manner would have posed major problems for Cray executives.

Culture Complements Formal Controls

Culture, as a set of collective values and behavioral norms can serve a control function within organizations. Culture controls the activities of employees on the basis of their attachment to the firm rather than on the basis of incentives and monitoring. Individuals who value belonging to the culture will align their individual goals and behaviors to those of the firm. If culture serves this function in a firm, then individual activities will be controlled more efficiently than they will be through formal control systems, since individuals will control themselves and monitoring costs will be reduced. If a firm's culture is strong, by which we mean it is intensely held by most employees, it may be more effective at controlling employees than a formal control system would be. The combination of motivated self-control, informal monitoring by coworkers, and the lack of specificity of organizational norms means that individuals are more likely to be compliant than they would be if controlled by formal systems that allow for more opportunistic behaviors because all formal control systems are incomplete.

William Ouchi has written on culture as an alternative control system to bureaucratic or market models of control.[26] Ouchi introduces the idea of *clan control*, by which he means control through an internal system of organizational norms and values. This model of control forms the basis for Ouchi's analysis of the differences between Western and Japanese firms. Clan control is characterized by moderate to low specialization of organizational roles and tasks, long-term employment in the organization, individual self-motivation and responsibility, and collective decision making. This type of control is distinguished from *bureaucratic control*, which is characterized by much greater specialization of organizational roles and tasks,

---

[25]Information in this example comes from *Cray Research, Inc.* (HBS #385-011).

[26]Ouchi, W. G., "Markets, Bureaucracies, and Clans," *Administrative Science Quarterly*, 1980: pp. 129–140; Ouchi, W. G. and B. Johnson, "Types of Organizational Control and their Relationship to Emotional Well Being," *Administrative Science Quarterly*, 1978: pp. 293–317; Ouchi, W. G., *Theory Z*, Reading, MA: Addison-Wesley, 1981.

short-term employment, individual responsibility, and individual decision making. Both are distinguished from *market control*, control on the basis of price in a market.

Ouchi's framework is useful in distinguishing how culture, as a means of control, is different from rules and regulations in an authority system, on the one hand, and from market prices, on the other. In this sense, the framework provides a set of *ideal types*. However, Japanese firms may not be as different from Western firms as Ouchi suggests, and clan control may be too diffuse, unless it is supplemented by other controls. James Lincoln and Arne Kalleberg suggest that the clan control of Japanese firms is better explained by the skill of these firms' managers at fostering consent and loyalty from individual workers through job guarantees, worker participation in decisions, welfare services, and needs-based compensation than by the power of overarching cultural values. While culture may affect organizational practices, management practices, such as those of Japanese firms, also influence the dominant values of the firm.[27]

Most firms, however, will make use of some combination of the control techniques that Ouchi describes. Very competitive marketplaces, like the Chicago Board of Trade, will also be governed by an extensive set of rules, as well as by a long history and set of traditions. Bureaucratic organizations may use market-based controls within their structures, such as a profit-center system (explained in Chapter 16), but can also be governed by strong cultural norms. It is difficult to envision a clan organization for a firm that would not involve some formal organization and controls and that would exempt the firm from the demands of the product markets in which it competed. High-performing firms are likely to have all three types.

Culture Facilitates Cooperation and Reduces Bargaining Costs

Gary Miller has examined the complex relationship between culture and organizations, in which culture mitigates the detrimental effects of power dynamics within firms by creating "mutually-reinforcing" norms within the organization that permit mutually beneficial cooperative activities to emerge that would not be likely among self-interested actors outside the organization. Miller builds on the work of David Kreps, who examines the problems of securing cooperative outcomes in repeated games. Both Miller and Kreps are interested in the implications of a result called the *folk theorem*.[28]

The folk theorem concerns the possibilities for achieving an equilibrium result in repeated play of games, such as the prisoner's dilemma (discussed in the Primer). Its general result is that many Nash equilibria are possible in infinitely repeated games. Not only are many equilibria possible, but these solutions do not need to be cooperative. Indeed some can be conflictual, combining expectations of opportunistic behavior with threats of strong retaliation if the other player responds inappropriately.

The implications of this result for cooperation within organizations are important, once it is realized that attempting to arrive at a cooperative organizational arrangement by means of contracts, incentives, and monitoring is directly analo-

---

[27]Lincoln, J. R. and A. L. Kalleberg, *Culture, Control, and Commitment*, Cambridge, UK: Cambridge University Press, 1990, chap. 1.

[28]Miller, G. J., *The Political Economy of Hierarchy*, Cambridge, UK: Cambridge University Press, 1992, chap. 10; Kreps, D. M., *A Course in Microeconomic Theory*, Princeton, NJ: Princeton University Press, 1990, chap. 14.

gous to solving a complicated repeated game situation. The result of the folk theorem implies that it may not be possible to arrive with certainty at a cooperative organizational arrangement—cooperation is only one of many possible arrangements. In addition, even if cooperation was possible, the costs of reaching it, in terms of the haggling costs involved in choosing one arrangement over other possible ones, are likely to be high.

Miller takes this point and argues that any attempt to solve organization problems through contracts, incentives, and formal controls, is likely to entail large influence costs, due to hidden action, and hidden information. The problem with hierarchical organization is that, while it mitigates transactions costs associated with market coordination of economic activity, it creates dilemmas of its own. These dilemmas cannot be resolved by recourse to formal governance mechanisms or by increased controls over employees. Building on ideas of Kreps, Bengt Holmstrom, and others, Miller argues that any hierarchical organization will have serious principal-agent problems built into its structure. A "machine" model of organization is likely to self-destruct.

Most real organizations appear to arrive at some acceptable organizational arrangements, despite these bargaining problems. To account for this, Kreps suggests that norms and social conventions may provide a focus for actors around which a consensus can form. This set of norms and conventions on behavior is the organization's culture. Kreps defines corporate culture as "the means by which a principle [of group decision making] is communicated to hierarchical inferiors . . ." It says "how things are done and how they are meant to be done" in the firm.

Miller argues that a firm's culture resolves these problems if its norms stress cooperation and not conflict. A cooperative culture modifies individual expectations and preferences and allows actors to expect cooperation from others in the organization. If the content of the culture is noncooperative, however, it will not serve this function. These mutually reinforcing overarching values and norms allow firms to fashion solutions to agency problems that would not be possible in a market.

Miller is ambiguous about the ability of management to intentionally influence a firm's culture. On the one hand, he argues that managers can exercise leadership that fosters cooperation rather than conflict among employees. On the other hand, a cooperative culture is also likely to be fragile, so that attempts to modify it to gain advantage could backfire and result in employees becoming noncooperative.

◆ ◆

XAMPLE 17.4

CORPORATE CULTURE AT 3M[29]

The 3M corporation has become known for a nearly endless array of useful products that builds on the firm's strength in adhesive chemistry. *Scotch tape* and *Post-it* note pads are just two of the best-known 3M products, which have

---

[29]The materials for this example came from stories in *Minneapolis/St. Paul* magazine (July 1992); and *Corporate Report Minnesota* (June 1990).

ranged from health care products, such as the bioelectronic ear, to copy machine. In developing these products, 3M also became known for its innovative culture and was featured in such books as *In Search of Excellence*. This innovative culture is not an accident or a byproduct of prior successes and a technological base. It sterns from the way 3M managers, from the top of the firm down to the smallest venture teams, have encouraged innovation and protected risk-takers.

Innovation has been a consistent priority for 3M's top management. Louis Lehr, who was chairman of the board and CEO of 3M from 1980 to 1986, provides a good example of this emphasis. During his tenure as CEO, while the firm basked in its reputation for innovation, Lehr commissioned an internal survey to identify the actual levels of innovation in the firm. He found that, while many employees took pride in the firm's reputation, others in the finance, warehousing, and sales/marketing departments believed that innovation and entrepreneurship at 3M were largely confined to the laboratory areas.

In response, Lehr established a task force to let employees know that everyone in the firm could be entrepreneurial and to establish such innovative practices as quality circles throughout the firm. Lehr saw that resting on the appearance of being entrepreneurial was not sufficient. Employees throughout the firm needed to know that they were expected to think and behave differently and that 3M would support them in doing so.

Innovation is also built into the 3M corporate planning and control systems. A standard goal in long-term plans of business unit managers, for example, is that after five years, 25 percent of a unit's sales must come from new products. The results of these programs are apparent in the 2,500 new products that the firm introduces each year.

The stimulation of innovative and risk-taking activities has also become part of the general management style at 3M. In evaluations, risk-takers are favored over risk-avoiders. Successful individuals and teams receive firm-wide recognition, as well as opportunities to work on new projects. Dual personnel tracks allow technical specialists to progress in their project careers without necessarily having to move into management. Managers acting as project sponsors are urged to "smooth the way" for innovators, by providing resources and rewards, removing organizational obstacles to projects, and protecting innovators from the usual penalties for failure.

Innovation not only comes from management, but from contacts with product users. Innovative firms keep in active contact with users and avoid the NIH (not invented here) syndrome that can impede innovation. At 3M, managers are pushed to incorporate market-based strategic analyses into their project planning. One of 3M's core product groups, *Scotchlite* Brand Reflective Materials, developed in this way over 50 years ago, when feedback from government customers identified a need for increasing the visibility of highway signs after dark. It is not clear how much of 3M's success is "caused" by its innovative culture. Many of the firm's products, such as *Scotch tape* and *Scotchguard*, were accidental discoveries. However, the 3M culture does seem to try to increase the firm's ability both to generate innovative trials and to ensure that 3M can develop and commercialize those discoveries that do occur.

Culture, Inertia, and Poor Performance

Culture can also impair firm performance. Examples of an apparent negative association between culture and performance are nearly as common as those showing a positive one. In fact, sometimes the same firm provides examples of both. For example, IBM was seen as recently as 1986 as a powerful exemplar firm that was admired for its management depth and corporate culture. Yet less than 10 years later, obituaries were being written for IBM and its inertial culture.

If culture is related to firm performance, it is because the fundamental alignment of the firm and its environment is a positive one, in that the firm has made investments and oriented its business toward a set of technological, competitive, and regulatory conditions that affect the firm's operations in anticipated ways. In making their investments, the firm managers must also have correctly anticipated how the conditions facing the firm affect its operations. Another way to say this is to adopt the contingency logic discussed in Chapter 16. When the firm's strategy "fits" with the demands of its environment, then culture can support the direction of the firm and make it even more efficient. This need for fit involves not only the conflict reducing function of culture but also the values espoused by a culture. For example, a cultural misfit would occur when the values of a firm culture stressed routines, efficiency, and stability while the firm's environment had changed in ways that require innovative, entrepreneurial, and flexible responses from the firm.

The negative influence of culture on performance becomes important when the environmental situation a firm faces changes and makes significant demands on it to adapt to survive. Then, the conditions making culture a source of sustained advantage that were raised by Barney will make culture a source of persistent poor performance. In an unfavorable business environment, in particular, the unmanageability of culture will become a source of inertia or a barrier to change. It will also become apparent in maladaptive decisions by managers that seek to forestall change instead of addressing environmental problems. This inertia may occur for several reasons. Executives with long tenure in the firm may have learned their jobs during prosperous times and may be poorly equipped to handle change. The power bases within a firm may allow threatened parties in the firm to block change. The terms of managers and board members, the rules by which they are chosen, and the procedures by which they operate may be designed with a conservative bias that frustrates change. This could occur, for example, as a result of staggered and lengthy terms for the board.

$\mathcal{E}$XAMPLE 17.5

CORPORATE CULTURE AND INERTIA AT ICI

Andrew Pettigrew provides an example of how cultural inertia can stymie organizational adaptation in his case studies of Imperial Chemical Industries (ICI), the leading British chemical manufacturer.[30] In 1973, ICI was the largest manufac-

---

[30]Pettigrew, A. M., *The Awakening Giant: Continuity and Change at ICI* (Oxford, UK: Blackwell, 1985), Chapter 10, pp. 376–437; Pettigrew, A. M., "Examining Change in the Long-Term Context of Culture and Politics," Chapter 11 in Johannes M. Pennings and Associates, *Organizational Strategy and Change* (San Francisco: Jossey–Bass, 1985), pp. 269–318.

turing firm in Great Britain. It had possessed a strong and homogenous culture for the nearly fifty years it had existed. Sales growth in 1972 was strong in chemicals, at twice the national growth rate for manufacturing. ICI had also been successful at new product development, with half of its 1972 sales coming from products that had not been on the market in 1957.

Strong threats to ICI's continued success developed in its business environment in the 1970s. These threats included overcapacity in its core businesses, threats of both inflation and recession in the British domestic economy, and import threats from Europe and North America. These pressures substantially affected ICI's profitability in 1980, when its profit totals and profitability ratios were halved. Several years of consistently poor performance followed. In the five years between 1977 and 1982, ICI cut its domestic workforce by nearly one third.

Individuals within top management had been recommending changes in the structure and governance system of ICI to allow it to better adapt to changed economic and political conditions since at least 1967, when they were raised by a single individual during a board election and ignored. A board committee on the need for reorganization had been set up in 1973 and issued a report calling for extensive organizational changes within ICI. The report encountered extreme political opposition from the start and, in the words of an executive director, "sank at the first shot." These calls for reorganization and strategic change were not adopted by ICI until 1983, when the firm had already experienced several years of poor performance.

Pettigrew's analysis of this history highlights the culture of conservatism and "smoothing" of problems that dominated ICI at this time. These aspects of its culture were functional during prosperous and stable times, but were dysfunctional during environmental shifts. Individuals who had benefited from the prior success of the firm were able to block initiatives, while external stimuli that could move management to action, such as poor performance, were not forthcoming until 1980. As management and board members changed during the 1970s, however, the culture also changed, so that management became more receptive to new ideas. Despite the best efforts of the individuals who saw the need for change, however, the culture constrained the firm and kept its managers from deciding upon change until conditions were present. The culture of ICI, which had benefited the firm during its first fifty years, kept it from adapting in the late 1970s.

Culture and Power

We have considered culture and power as two important aspects of firm behavior that are not governed by contract. Power concerns the ability to get things done by controlling critical resources, while culture involves the ability of the firm's general normative orientation to direct the behaviors of its employees and keep their activities within generally accepted bounds. While we have discussed them separately, culture and power may interact in most firms. How might culture and political relationships interact on a given issue? Does culture enhance the influence of powerful individuals or limit it? Can individuals in the firm manage or shape culture, or at least its consequences? Researchers have offered different answers to these questions. Jeffrey Pfeffer argues that power and culture are alternate means of getting things done in organizations. Of the two, power is the more useful, since it is less costly to maintain and less fragile than culture. Andrew Pettigrew views power and culture as complementary sources of influence. Managers can control the symbolic resources of the organization and thus can influence how the values of the firm can be used to support their personal interests. Gary Miller also links power and culture, with managerial leadership and culture as possible substitutes for organizational processes based on power relationships.

XAMPLE 17.6

POLITICS, CULTURE, AND CORPORATE GOVERNANCE

Analyses of laws governing corporate governance in such areas as the board of directors, executive pay, and tender offers, have emphasized how management practices contribute to the efficiency of firms by attenuating principal-agent problems and reducing their costs for owners. Because of this, corporate law has been seen as the set of governance principles that has evolved over years of corporate trials and that constitutes the starting point in determining how firms govern themselves.[31] Gerald Davis and Tracy Thompson argue that economic explanations are incomplete and neglect the influence on governance changes of actors in the political and cultural environment of the firm.[32] The political environment is important because the laws and regulations governing corporate activities, while of economic significance, are the products of political bodies, such as legislatures and regulatory agencies. The cultural environment is important because the attitudes and values of the general public on a given issue can be a source of legitimacy for political actors and will thus influence how they regulate firms.

Davis and Thompson provide an example of the importance of explanations incorporating power and culture in their discussion of the controversy in the early 1990s over "runaway executive pay." On its economic merits alone, it appeared that shareholders had at best weak incentives to pursue the issue. While the average U.S. CEO made 85 times the pay of a typical factory worker (versus 17 times in Japan), the dollar amounts that were paid to these executives were so small, relative to the overall value of the firm, that they had little or no effect on corporate performance. (There would still have been no effect if overpaid executives had given back their entire salaries to their firms.) While it was plausible that linking executive pay to corporate performance would help the firm's share price, it was far from clear that this actually happened. Regardless of its economic merits, however, the issue of CEO pay took on national political significance, in that it received extensive media coverage, many politicians

---

[31]See Easterbrook, F. H. and D. R. Fischel, *The Economic Structure of Corporate Law* (Cambridge, MA: Harvard University Press, 1991) for the most forceful statement of this position.

[32]Davis, G. F. and T. A. Thompson, "A Social Movement Perspective on Corporate Control," *Administrative Science Quarterly* (forthcoming).

raised the issue, and several pieces of legislation limiting executive pay were introduced in Congress.

Shareholder activist groups and institutional investors were more interested in changing the proxy rules of firms—the mechanisms by which shareholders vote on the management of the firm—than in fighting over CEO pay. They had been stymied at reforming proxy rules, however, because these had traditionally been the province of state governments, where pro-business interests were better organized. In fact, 40 states had passed significant antitakeover legislation in the 1980s, including Delaware, where most major firms were incorporated.

Shareholder activist and institutional investors seized upon the political attention given to the CEO pay issue at the national level (that of the SEC), where they were relatively better organized and prepared to lobby. They pursued proxy reform indirectly, through a focus on CEO pay as one instance of a broader failure of management accountability. The apparent affront to national values and sensitivities caused by excessive CEO pay gave activists the opportunity to move proxy reform from the state government level, where they had little power, to the SEC, where they enjoyed greater power. This allowed the SEC to take up proxy reform at a national level. By the end of 1992, this campaign had succeeded in expanding the power of large shareholders, as evidenced by their greater participation and influence in corporate governance. This influence extended down from the national political domain to individual firms. Negative publicity and pressure on such large firms as ITT, W. R. Grace, and Ryder led to changes in executive compensation systems that more tightly linked pay to corporate performance.

Changes in the firm's larger political and cultural context also affect the incentives that top managers employ. As the incentives and compensation of top managers are better aligned to firm performance, follow-up changes in the rest of the firm may involve substantial reorganization, decentralization of decision-making, and the increased use of market-based performance incentives. These changes, in turn, will prompt changes in norms and values, leading the firm to develop a culture aligned to shareholder value. Michael Useem describes how these changes affected the cultures inside firms and how managers in firms that realigned themselves towards shareholder value used their control over organizational architecture, symbols, and vocabulary to support realignment.[33]

Some firms resist reorganization, and a near-crisis atmosphere develops among employees. In these situations, culture is inertial rather than supportive of change. Other firms react much more positively. The 1990 reorganization of Hewlett-Packard both maintained the firm's culture and improved shareholder value. While the reorganization required the elimination of thousands of positions in a firm that had prided itself on not laying-off employees, the aggressive management approach of CEO John Young managed to retain the firm's innovative culture and to significantly increase performance.[34]

[33]Useem, M., *Executive Defense: Shareholder Power and Corporate Reorganization* (Cambridge, MA: Harvard University Press, 1993), Chapter 3.

[34]Yoder, S. K., "A 1990 Reorganization at Hewlett-Packard Is Already Paying Off." *The Wall Street Journal*, July 22, 1992: A-1; A-10.

EXAMPLE 17.7

POWER, CULTURE, AND RESISTANCE TO CHANGE

The inertial effects of culture are often observed in resistance to major organizational changes. Resistance appears to managers as a collective response to change that is seen as incorrect or illegitimate, which can occur in a firm that is reorganizing, or during the course of a merger and subsequent consolidation. There is also an individual aspect of resistance to change, however, which stems from a change that is threatening to one's job or one's situation in the firm. It is also ultimately individuals who resist changes and who must be informed about the change and why resistance is detrimental. This suggests the importance of informal networks in the firm as the paths through which resistance develops. It also suggests that individuals occupying key positions in those networks will be able to influence the extent of resistance to change that occurs.

Rene Torenvlied and Gina Velner studied the relationship between informal networks and resistance to change in the introduction of ISO (International Organization for Standardization) quality standards in a small Dutch transport company.[35] They considered three different explanations for resistance: legitimacy, job satisfaction, and formal position. They also considered three types of network relationships: instrumental relations and job advice, authority and hierarchy and intimate relations and trust.

Torenvlied and Velner found that trust relations were important in understanding resistance. A lack of trust was positively associated with high levels of resistance, while trust contributed to confidence in the future and eased concerns about the change. They also found a U-shaped association between resistance and the number of trusting relations an individual took part in. Moderate numbers of trust relationships were associated with low resistance, while few or many trust relationships were associated with high resistance.

Most importantly, there were also significant network effects in understanding resistance. The lower one's position in the hierarchy, the less resistance was encountered. Critical to the acceptance of the new standards was the trust that employees placed in three intermediate and well-liked members of the firm. Their acceptance of the change influenced many other employees to reduce their resistance.

CHAPTER SUMMARY

◆ *Power* is an individual's ability to accomplish his or her goals by means of resources obtained through *noncontractual exchange relationships* with other actors.

◆ There are five general bases of power: legitimate power, reward power, coercive power, expert power, and referent power. Power can also be based on image or reputation.

---

[35]Torenvlied, R. and G. Velner, "Informal Networks and Resistance to Organizational Change: The Introduction of Quality Standards in a Transport Company," *Computational & Mathematical Organization Theory*, Vol 4, No. 2, 1998: pp. 165–188.

◆ The most common view of power is based on *social exchange*—a transfer between two or more parties of resources, or rights to control resources, outside of a market context.

◆ In the *resource dependence* view of power, individuals and firms seek to gain power by reducing their dependence on other actors, while building the dependence of other actors on them through the control of critical resources.

◆ The conditions that give rise to high transaction costs in the marketplace are the same as those that give rise to power relations associated with resource dependencies.

◆ Power is also embodied in the structure of a firm. Particular positions give their holders more power than others have.

◆ Power can help or hurt a firm's performance. Power is helpful when there are high agency costs between managers and lower-level workers and when the firm's business environment is stable. Power is harmful when there are high agency costs between levels of upper management and when the firm's environment is relatively unstable.

◆ Formal power should be allocated to individual managers on the basis of the value they create for the firm, the costs of replacing them, and the likelihood that they will tend to act in a manner consistent with the firm's objectives rather than in conflict with those objectives.

◆ *Culture* is a set of collectively held values, beliefs, and norms of behavior among members of a firm that influences individual employee preferences and behaviors on the job.

◆ To help sustain a firm's competitive advantage, culture must be valuable, rare, and inimitable by competitors.

◆ A culture's values, norms of activity, and accompanying signals can focus the activities of employees on a limited set of task and governance arrangements. This frees employees from the need to continually renegotiate their tasks within the firm, which reduces the costs of making decisions and permits a better specialization of effort.

◆ Culture, as a set of collective values and behavioral norms, can serve a control function within firms by controlling the activities of employees on the basis of their attachment to the firm, rather than on the basis of individual incentives and monitoring.

◆ Culture mitigates the detrimental effects of power dynamics within firms by creating "mutually-reinforcing" norms that permit the emergence of mutually beneficial cooperative activities that would not be likely among self-interested individuals in the marketplace.

◆ When a firm's strategy "fits" with the demands of its environment, then its culture supports the direction of the firm and makes it even more efficient. When the environment changes, however, and requires firms to adapt to changes, culture is more likely to be inertial and lead to maladaptive firm behavior.

QUESTIONS

1. How does the resource-dependence view of power differ from the perspective of transactions-cost economics? In what situations would their predictions about economic transactions be similar; in which situations would they be different?

2. If agents are risk neutral and have unlimited liability, and the principal can find an objective measure that is correlated with performance, then a principal can write first-best efficient contracts. Does this imply that the principal can ignore culture and power?

3. How does the exercise of power and culture within an organization expose agents to risk? Which method, incentives, power, or culture, do you think is most effective at motivating risk-averse workers?

4. Is formal authority different from other sources of power?

5. How might a favorable location within the interpersonal networks of a firm help an individual acquire and maintain additional bases of power?

6. Social-exchange views of power tend to emphasize individual abilities to make decisions and prevail in conflicts. How might power also be associated with an individual's ability to not make decisions and to avoid conflict?

7. Discuss structural holes in the context of value creation and value extraction. Use these ideas to identify some of the skills necessary to be a financially successful general manager.

8. How can there several different cultures with the same firm? If this situation occurs, what are its implications for the relationship between culture and performances?

9. Why is culture generally inertial in its effects on firms? Why is a firm's culture difficult to engineer or change?

10. How can powerful individuals influence a firm's culture?

STRATEGY AND THE GENERAL MANAGER

18

INTRODUCTION

"The last thing IBM needs right now is vision."—Louis Gerstner, CEO of IBM

"It's an accountant's answer, not a leader's."—Robert Galbreath of Philip Crosby Associates, commenting on Gerstner's statement.

"Being a visionary is trivial. Being a CEO is hard. All you have to do to be a visionary is to give the old 'MIPS to the moon' speech. That's different from being the CEO of a company and seeing where the profits are."—Bill Gates, CEO of Microsoft[1]

What is the role of the CEO? Is the CEO a problem solver or a visionary? We believe that a successful manager must be both. Managers must manage a firm's internal and external relations, but must also establish a profitable and defensible position in fierce markets. Bill Gates has skillfully managed vertical relations, market competition, and innovation within Microsoft. But he also had the vision from the beginning to understand that a large installed base of DOS-based personal computers would create a network externality permitting DOS to become the industry standard and Gates to become a multibillionaire (although we doubt he used the term *network externality*). While most general managers (GMs) will not realize the same financial rewards as Gates, they will face similar short- and long-term strategic problems. This chapter describes the many tasks general managers confront and the different decision-making roles that they have to perform.

The GM has comprehensive decision-making responsibilities for his or her unit at some level within the firm. CEOs and presidents are general managers, as

---

[1]Miller, M. and L. Hays, "Gerstner's Nonvision for IBM Raises a Management Issue," *Wall Street Journal*, July 29, 1993, p. 131.

are those in charge of divisions or product groups. General managers may also be located at lower levels within the firm, such as at a plant or a local sales office. For example, John Kotter found seven types of general management positions in his comparative case studies of managers, ranging from corporate CEOs to division managers to operations and product market managers in profit centers.[2] While a firm's GM is a single individual, a top management team often exercises general management responsibilities for the firm.

The GM position has interested business observers ever since the development of the first large firms. Alfred Chandler notes that the first references to managers appeared in the early journals of railroad engineers, reflecting the role of the railroads in fostering modern firms. As large firms developed around 1900, the general manager became a critical asset that enabled administrative expertise to diminish the risks of marketplace decisions. Managers became the "visible hand" that replaced the "invisible hand" of the market in making decisions for the firm.[3]

As managers became more important within firms, interest in managers grew among observers, students, and even critics of business. General management classes in leadership and business policy have been important in MBA curricula since the first MBA programs were developed shortly after 1900. Classic essays and prescriptions on the general manager, by such authors as Chester Barnard, Philip Selznick, and Alfred Sloan, remain in print today.[4] Even critics of the large corporation, in a tradition that began with the work of Adolphe Berle and Gardiner Means, have focused on the increasing power and importance of managers, coupled with their lack of accountability to shareholders, as threats to social and economic stability.[5] The link between the general manager and the firm's strategy has persisted in current research. This is due in part to the enormous influence of the Business Policy group at the Harvard Business School, which developed the concept of strategy as a "simple practitioner's theory" of general management (i.e., strategy is synonymous with what general managers do).[6]

While there has been much interest in studying them, we still know little about general managers, leadership, and related issues. Theories of management have been superficial and prescriptive, while evidence on managerial behaviors has been both sparse and difficult to interpret, due to the lack of developed theory. For example, Warren Bennis, in reviewing research on strategy and leadership, concludes that "never have so many laboured so long to say so little".[7] Only recently have researchers obtained sufficient data to begin explaining managerial behavior.

---

[2]Kotter, J., *The General Managers*, New York: Free Press, 1982, pp. 22–27.

[3]Chandler, A., *The Visible Hand*, Cambridge, MA: Belknap, 1979.

[4]Barnard, C., *The Functions of the Executive*, Cambridge, MA: Belknap, 1938; Selznick, P., *Leadership and Administration*, Berkeley, University of California Press, 1957; Sloan, A., *My Years with General Motors*, Garden City, NY: Doubleday, 1964.

[5]Berle, A. and G. Means, *The Modern Corporation and Private Property*, New York: Macmillan, 1932.

[6]See Bower, J., C. Bartlett, C. Christensen, A. Pearson, and K. Andrews, *Business Policy: Text and Cases*, 7th ed., Homewood, IL: Irwin, 1991, p. ix.

[7]Bennis, W. and B. Nanus, *Leaders: The Strategies for Taking Charge*, New York: Harper & Row, 1985, p. 4.

WHAT DO GENERAL MANAGERS DO? ◆ ◆ ◆ ◆ ◆

At the conclusion of a book on the economic principles underlying strategic decisions, it is reasonable to ask if there are any principles to offer regarding the tasks and roles of the individuals who make strategic decisions—the general managers of a firm and its business units. If the general manager's tasks could be simply mapped onto the economic decisions the firm requires, then understanding the GM position would not be difficult. There would also be little to say above and beyond what we have already discussed in earlier chapters. Problems with the GM position arise because a manager must make whole sets of decisions simultaneously. This complicates our view of the position and motivates our search for managerial roles.

In discussing GMs, it is tempting to assume that lone general managers at the top of their respective hierarchies control firms and their business units. We do so only for analytic simplicity. Before continuing our discussion, we must note that, in reality, top management teams that collectively perform the tasks we ascribe to GMs often run firms. Employing a top management team allows for a full delineation of top management roles (and the tensions among them) without placing all complex top management decisions on a single individual. Research on top management teams has been growing, and its findings parallel those of studies of general managers.[8] In addition, understanding top management teams requires understanding the behavioral processes by which these teams operate, dividing up managerial responsibilities, communicating, settling disputes, and the like.[9]

In the remainder of this chapter, we discuss the tasks and roles of general managers. We then consider the many tensions among these roles that make the GM position so difficult. We conclude by noting that, just as the definition of the firm changes in response to history and changing business conditions, so also the definition of the GM also evolves and does not describe the same combination of tasks from one era to the next.

Case Studies of General Managers

Henry Mintzberg's case studies were among the first to show how the behavior of managers differed from both common perceptions and general prescriptions. He found that, rather than being reflective and systematic, the behavior of effective managers was characterized by brevity of interactions, discontinuity of action, and a general lack of reflection. Similarly, rather than favoring written, aggregated, and well-analyzed quantitative information, managers tended to strongly prefer informal, disaggregated, and verbal media for communicating and obtaining information. Mintzberg was one of the first to show that the management profession was a craft rather than a science.[10]

---

[8]Hambrick, D. C., "Top Management Groups: A Conceptual Integration and Reconsideration of the 'Team' Label," in B. M. Staw and L. L. Cummings (eds.), *Research in Organizational Behavior*, 16, 1994: pp. 171–214.

[9]For a review, see Hambrick, D. C., Nadler, D. A., and M. L. Tushman (eds.), *Navigating Change: How CEO's Top Teams, and Boards Steer Transformation*, Boston, MA: Harvard University Press, 1998, sec. II.

[10]Mintzberg, H., *The Nature of Managerial Work*, New York: Harper & Row, 1973; For a shorter summary, see Mintzberg, H., "The Manager's Job: Folklore and Fact," *Harvard Business Review*, July–August 1975: pp. 49–61.

While much of a manager's work is routine, it tends not to be written down and standardized. Rather, managers organize their work according to more informal roles and rely on intuition and judgment to make their decisions. Managerial roles include: interpersonal roles, such as being a leader; informational roles, such as being the spokesman for the firm or one of its units; and decisional roles, such as being a negotiator or someone who handles disturbances.

John Kotter's case studies of GMs have shown the variety of ways in which individual general managers adjust to the fluid surroundings in which they must accomplish their tasks.[11] He comes to three general conclusions. First, effective managers build agendas for their businesses and then work to accomplish them. This is a more fluid process than the stereotype of managerial goal-setting implies. While managers are rational, they are also flexible in how they pursue their goals and opportunistic in taking advantage of situations that permit progress toward goals.

Kotter also finds that effective general managers build extensive interpersonal networks to get the information necessary to accomplish their agendas. Viewing managers as key players in dense interpersonal networks is reasonable, given the internal complexity of large firms, the range of supplier and product markets these firms serve, and the types of decisions that managers have to make. This view of GMs as builders of relationship networks has been further developed by John Gabarro, who studies how successful GMs develop as they begin their tenure within a firm, and Hermine Ibarra, who considers the characteristics of successful GM networking strategies.[12] It is also consistent with the structural hole argument of Ron Burt (discussed in Chapter 17) that managers gain power by occupying critical network positions.

Finally, Kotter finds that managerial effectiveness is cumulative and reflects the experience of managers honing their skills in specific firms. While it may be possible to identify a set of generic management skills, a manager's value to his or her firm depends on how those skills are developed within specific decision contexts. In addition, critical interpersonal networks take time to develop. For example, knowledge of the key decision makers or new product development practices in one firm will be less valuable if the manager possessing that knowledge moves to another employer. If management capability is an asset for firms, it is a highly firm-specific asset that develops over time. This goes against the conventional wisdom taught in many MBA programs that management skills are generic and highly portable from firm to firm. Leader tenure in position and with a given organization is important for political as well as business leaders for similar reasons.[13]

The Roles of the General Manager

In addition to the fluid view of managerial tasks developed by Mintzberg, Kotter, and others, we can ascribe basic substantive roles to any GM. These roles are in-

[11]Kotter, J., *The General Managers*, New York: Free Press, 1982, pp. 60–79.

[12]Gabarro, J. J., "When a New Manager Takes Change," *Harvard Business Review*, May–June 1985: pp. 110–123; Ibarra, H., "Structural Alignments, Individual Strategies, and Managerial Action: Elements Toward a Network Theory of Getting Things Done," in Nohria, N. and R. G. Eccles (eds.), *Networks and Organizations: Structure, Form, and Action*, Boston, MA: Harvard Business School Press, 1992, chap. 6.

[13]Bienen, H. S. and N. van de Walle, *Of Time and Power: Leadership Duration in the Modern World*, Stanford, CA: Stanford University Press, 1991.

terrelated and stem from the basic decisions that GMs and their teams make. The GM is an *entrepreneur* and *value creator*, in that it is managers who make and change the fundamental position of the firm in its product markets, as well as commit the necessary resources to create value in a given position. The GM is also an *organizer/implementor*, who establishes a division of labor in the firm and coordinates the allocation of decision-making rights with the requirements of the firm's strategy. Related to this role, the GM is a *contractor*, who balances inducements and contributions in formal agreements with employees, buyers, suppliers, and other key contributors to firm action. Since there are limits to the possibilities for contracting within the firm, the GM also must be a *facilitator*, who uses interpersonal skills and power to build relationships and secure agreement even in the absence of formal contracts. Along with coordinating action within the firm, the GM is also a *competitor*, who adapts the firm's activities to those of other firms in the industry. Finally, the GM must be an *adapter*, who readjusts the firm's assets and commitments in response to significant changes in business conditions that affect the firm and threaten its profitability. We discuss each of these managerial roles in detail below.

The General Manager as Value Creator/Entrepreneur

Many managerial decisions follow from the long-lasting choices the firm makes about how best to use its resources to create and sustain economic value. The managerial role of defining the firm and how it creates and sustains value is analogous to the entrepreneurial function of management addressed by Alfred Chandler, Henry Mintzberg, and others as the central creative task that managers perform. Just as entrepreneurs choose where to commit the capital of their investors and how best to manage those investments, so GMs choose how best to commit the capital of owners and position the firm in its product markets to create value on a sustained basis. The sheer size of large firms ensures that GMs will make many of these important decisions that define the boundaries of the firm and its value-creation opportunities. The large amount of fixed strategy-specific assets these decisions require ensures that the decisions made by GMs in this role will commit the firm to a strategic position with long-term implications for firm performance.

While the value-creator/entrepreneur role is critical for the firm, many GMs find at the time they assume their positions that they are already committed to an extensive set of value-creation opportunities, by virtue of their firm's history, sunk investments, and long-term relationships. Large manufacturing plants, once built, cannot be readily adjusted to meet new market demands. Long-term labor agreements can constrain the human resource flexibility of firms for years. This is not a problem in stable and/or regulated environments. If competitive conditions change unexpectedly, however, firms may be vulnerable to competitors that are not constrained by prior investments and commitments. This suggests that GMs may face serious constraints in defining how their firm creates value.

While these constraints may limit a manager's freedom to create new strategies, they do not render the value-creation function altogether moot. Rather, the constraints that GMs face increase the pressures on them to identify and exploit opportunities for value creation within their firms and within their market relationships. Indeed, it is when environmental constraints seem highest, such as in a competitive market, that it is most important to find opportunities for value creation. Perhaps the greatest opportunities for contemporary managers lie in these marginal opportunities for value creation. Observers of GMs, such as James Brian

Quinn, Charles Lindblom, H. Edward Wrapp, and others, argue that opportunities for value creation tend to be incremental rather than broad and that GMs tend not to spend much time on broad policy decisions.[14]

The General Manager as Organizer/Implementor

GMs also organize their firms and implement their strategic choices. Chandler's dictum that structure follows strategy (discussed in Chapter 16) implies this. This role is also suggested by the implications of strategic choices for specific functional areas within the firm. This is behind approaches to "generic strategies," in which the implementation decisions of managers need to be consistent with the overall strategic choices of the firm.[15] As we discussed in Chapter 11, for example, a choice of a competitive position highlighting cost advantage will be associated with such implementation choices as standardized products, mass production facilities, and a traditional management style. A position favoring differentiation advantage, however, will be associated with customized products, tradeoffs between scale and flexibility in production, and a less formal management style.

The organizer/implementor role involves several generic decisions. The first is how best to coordinate information and resource flows within the firm around its strategy. This is akin to Galbraith's idea of organizational design based on efficient information processing (discussed in Chapter 16). This role also involves decisions regarding which organizing dimensions are most important, which types of activities need the most coordination, which coordination takes priority, and how to resolve coordination conflicts. Another aspect of this role is delegation, specifically deciding who should have decision-making rights over which of the firm's decisions.

Decisions concerning organization and implementation are not just derivative from the firm's strategy, however. Implementation decisions often require information that is not available until after strategic decisions have been made. This can involve highly contingent matchings of people and organizational resources that force managers to link the content of a strategy with specific situational conditions and requirements. The failure to make these decisions appropriately may lead to more than suboptimizing performance by the firm for a given strategy. Implementation mistakes could threaten the entire value of the strategy. Merger integration is a situation in which the costs of implementation failures can be very high.[16] For example, a merger whose strategy was predicated on specialized human capital in the acquired firm could be implemented in ways that alienate key individuals and even drive them away from the firm. Incomplete or haphazard changes in incentive systems could do this.

The choices that managers make in implementing their strategies also commit the firm to courses of action that will be difficult to alter. Implementation can promote inertia through large investments in sunk assets, training and human re-

---

[14]Quinn, J. B., *Strategies for Change: Logical Incrementalism*, Homewood, IL: Irwin, 1980; Lindblom, C., "The Science of Muddling Through," *Public Administration Review*, Spring 1959: pp. 79–88; Wrapp, H. E., "Good Managers Don't Make Policy Decisions," *Harvard Business Review*, September/October 1967: pp. 91–99.

[15]Miles, R. E. and C. C. Snow, *Organizational Strategy, Structure, and Process*, New York: McGraw-Hill, 1978.

[16]Haspeslagh, P. C. and D. B. Jemison, *Managing Acquisitions*, New York: Free Press, 1991, pp. 122–137.

source development, or critical relationships with other actors that impede the firm's flexibility and responsiveness to environmental changes. Implementation choices also constrain the future strategic choices of the general manager, such that the firm's future strategy will be determined in part from its current implementation activities.

The General Manager as Contractor

Managers are contractors, both inside and outside the firm. Contracting was the starting point for our discussion of the vertical boundaries of the firm from a transactions-costs perspective in Chapter 2. As the transactions costs of securing activities through the market increase, it becomes increasingly worthwhile to internalize these activities inside the firm, because of asset specificity and market imperfections. Based on our consideration of incentives and controls in Chapter 15, we can conclude that, to the extent possible, managers should act as contractors and try to accomplish their ends both within and outside the firm on the basis of contingent claims contracts. In dealing with employees and other stakeholders, a contracting perspective is also relevant, even if most employees do not work with an explicit employment contract. This is because interactions akin to contract negotiation can occur in a wide range of relationships. We discussed this in Chapter 17 in terms of social exchange and power-dependence relationships. In all these situations, the managerial role of contractor is clear—to get the best deal and spell out the terms of an agreement as completely as possible.

While the contracting role of GMs is clearly important to the firm in its external dealings with other firms and organizations, the management literature has underemphasized the importance of contracting within the firm. Indeed, as we discuss below, the other means by which managers accomplish their objectives within firms, such as power, culture, and leadership, make sense largely as options to employ for situations and activities for which contracts cannot be fashioned at all or only with excessive costs. Chester Barnard, in his classic, *The Functions of the Executive*, used the contractor role in his inducements/contributions framework for understanding executive action.[17] Gordon Donaldson and Jay Lorsch also employ the contractor role in their analysis of how top managers balance the demands of stakeholders from product, capital, and labor markets to maintain the independence of the top management team.[18]

The General Manager as Powerholder

As we discussed in Chapter 17, activities occur within the firm that cannot be fully specified and for which cost-effective contracts cannot be easily developed. These activities can nonetheless be important to the firm. In these situations, power can be understood as the ability of individuals to mobilize resources to accomplish their goals through noncontractual asymmetric relationships. In pursuing their objectives for the firm and/or their units, managers also need to develop new bases of power and use them to complement their formal authority and their contracting activities and to secure the cooperation of all the parties necessary for an activity to succeed.

---

[17]Barnard, C., *The Functions of the Executive*, Cambridge, MA: Belknap, 1938.

[18]Donaldson, G. and J. Lorsch, *Decision Making at the Top*, New York: Harper & Row, 1983, pp. 32–48, 160.

While power is important for the job performance and career growth of managers, we also need to consider the costs to the firm of their using power. The goals of managers will only rarely be fully aligned with those of the firm, and conflicts will often arise among managers who implement different aspects of a firm's strategy. In such situations, the use of power by a manager may hinder firm performance by impeding the achievements of other managers, even while it aids firm performance through the activities of the powerful manager. Even if the exercise of power does not impede the achievement of others' goals, the immediate exercise of power itself will be costly. In addition, GMs are not immune from the temptation to pursue personal goals, even at the expense of the firm's goals. In such circumstances, power will detract from firm performance. The overall costs of using power and its net effect on firm performance will be clear only in specific situations.

The General Manager as Facilitator

GMs often need the cooperation of others, yet cannot either contract for that cooperation or bring their power and influence to bear. One example of this would be when one manager needs the cooperation of another manager with comparable authority in the firm. Other examples would occur when the success of an activity depends on efforts by crucial employees, but where the manager cannot monitor what the employees actually do, where the employees can legitimately refuse to provide such effort, and where the manager cannot provide sufficient tangible incentives to the employees. In these situations, the GM's role is to persuade and shape the impressions and preferences of others to increase the chances of obtaining their cooperation. These activities are often associated with building an organization culture.

Benjamin Hermalin considers facilitation in terms of two problems that any manager faces in securing cooperation from others.[19] First, a manager must convince potential followers that it is in their interest to follow him—that they will gain from cooperating with him and contributing to unit performance. This involves transmitting more information to potential followers than they already possess. Second, a manager must convince followers that they are not being misled, that is, that the leader is telling them the truth. Potential followers may believe that a manager has an incentive to mislead them to get them to work harder.

There are two ways to convince them that they are not being misled. The first is to lead by example. A manager could work long hours and thus convince others that it is worthwhile for them to do so too. The second way is by sacrifice. A manager may offer gifts or other side payments to potential followers to gain their cooperation. This sacrifice is convincing not because of the worth of the side payments to their recipients but because the payments signal the manager's true beliefs regarding the value of an activity. Hermalin models this choice between leading by example and leading by sacrifice and finds that leading by example is the best way of signaling the quality of information to potential followers. Leading by sacrifice may still be necessary if leading by example is not possible.

GMs also facilitate cooperation by building relationships with key individuals inside their firms and within their larger business environments. If a manager is

---

[19]Hermalin, B. E., "Toward an Economic Theory of Leadership: Leading by Example," forthcoming in *American Economic Review*.

embedded within a network of valued relationships, then he or she will be able to resolve disputes over particular transactions more easily because the parties probably value maintaining this long-term relationship more than the gains they might obtain from a particular transaction. John Kotter sees relationship-building as a central activity of general managers. In emerging or newly deregulated markets, relationships may be crucial for strategic success because the legal and institutional infrastructure may not have developed sufficiently to permit the cost-effective governance of particular transactions. In Eastern European countries, such as Poland, Hungary, and the Czech Republic, for example, concepts of contract and fiduciary obligation are still underdeveloped. Western firms entering these markets need to do so on the basis of longstanding relationships with government and business leaders rather than on specific guarantees that may not be maintained in a contracting dispute. This means that the firms that are first to enter these markets have the potential to build first-mover advantages through relationships with key actors.[20]

Gary Miller advances this culture- and relationship-building view of how managers facilitate cooperation as a complement to their use of incentives, controls, and formal structure.[21] By engaging in these nonpecuniary motivational activities, managers shape employee expectations of how activities within the firm will be conducted, how managers will work with employees, how disputes will be resolved, and other issues. In shaping these expectations, managers limit the range of activities open to employees and reduce the chances for noncooperative norms to develop within the firm.

Robert Eccles and Nitin Nohria take this role of shaping expectations within the firm further by arguing that a fundamental management task is to craft a rhetoric that directs and motivates individuals in the firm to act.[22] To them, it is the manager's job to fashion a language within the firm that encourages individuals to cooperate and act productively. This occurs from building individual and collective identities, rationalizing action in terms of identities, and defining performance in terms that best explain past results and motivate future behaviors. This perspective is consistent with studies of managerial behavior, such as Kotter's, that show that managers spend most of their days talking. This view of the GM's role in crafting rhetoric can be taken to extremes in situations in which firms face strongly contradictory demands from various environmental stakeholders or when demands to rationalize activities conflict with the activities that firms need to pursue to be efficient. Nils Brunsson provides case examples of how conflicting political demands on firms can cause GMs to promote systematic hypocrisy, in an attempt to rationalize irreconcilable demands.[23]

---

[20]For more detail on these issues, see Buckley, P. J. and P. N. Ghauri (eds.), *The Economics of Change in East and Central Europe*, London: Academic Press, 1994.

[21]Miller, G. J., "Managerial Dilemmas: Political Leadership in Hierarchies," in Cook, K. S. and M. Levi (eds.), *The Limits of Rationality*, Chicago: University of Chicago Press, 1990.

[22]Eccles, R. G. and N. Nohria, *Beyond the Hype: Rediscovering the Essence of Management*, Boston, MA: Harvard Business School Press, 1992.

[23]Brunsson, N., *The Organization of Hypocrisy: Talk, Decisions, and Actions in Organizations*, Chicester, UK: John Wiley, 1989.

The General Manager as Competitor

As the manager of a business unit that competes in a market, the GM must adjust the activities of his or her unit to take into account the activities of competitors who are trying to gain a competitive advantage. At a minimum, GMs must understand the nature of competition in their markets. They must gather and analyze information about competitors, anticipate their reactions to proposed moves, and decide how and to what extent to communicate with them and how best to modify their unit's strategic activities on the basis of expected interactions. Interactions with competitors can be direct or indirect and can be as limited as evaluating their observed activities without any explicit, implicit, or tacit collusion. The activities associated with this role typically occur during product market interactions, but can involve other areas of firm action, such as at trade association meetings.

The General Manager as Adapter

Managers' decisions are often time, condition, and strategy specific. What appears to be a reasonable investment may prove less desirable as conditions change. Significant changes in the business environment may lead GMs to reassess their basic decisions regarding the horizontal and vertical boundaries of the firm. For example, this could occur as managers in basic metals industries, such as steel and aluminum, discover that the market conditions that made extensive vertical integration reasonable during the early history of these industries have changed. Vertically integrated firms may now be inertial and unresponsive to conditions in world metals markets that have become more competitive.

If fundamental change occurs, then the firm needs to change itself significantly to survive in its new situation. This can occur by directing discretionary resources. More often, however, major change requires making new, costly, and risky sunk investments and changing relationships and assets to which the firm may be committed from past investments. Such fundamental reorientation may be possible (the example of Disney comes to mind), but it is likely to be painful, as whole categories of assets and employees that were valuable under one set of conditions lose value and must be let go.

The GM will not only need to decide whether a fundamental reorientation and restructuring is necessary, but will also need to facilitate the cooperation of the firm's employees and stakeholders if the reorientation is to be effective.[24] Those workers who remain after their firm restructures itself will often find that their position in the firm has been greatly altered. Workers who are now critical to the value-creation activities of the firm may find their positions enhanced. Other workers, however, will find themselves increasingly relegated to a peripheral and tenuous role in the firm and will see themselves as increasingly vulnerable to future cutbacks and restructurings.[25]

---

[24]Tichy, N. M. and M. A. Devanna, *The Transformational Leader*, New York: John Wiley, 1990.

[25]Arthur, M. B., and D. M. Rousseau (eds.), *The Boundaryless Career*, New York: Oxford University Press, 1996; Donaldson, G., *Corporate Restructuring: Managing the Change Process from Within*, Boston, MA: Harvard Business School Press, 1994; Useem, M., *Executive Defense: Shareholder Power and Corporate Reorganization*, Cambridge, MA: Harvard University Press, 1993.

The Tensions of Managerial Work

Some of the managerial roles discussed earlier are inherent in the managerial activities of a firm at any given time. The tensions among many of these roles are also inherent, however, and may pose different problems for managers in a given situation. These tensions can be managed but probably never totally eliminated. Given that these tensions concern fundamental managerial roles, eliminating them would likely produce inferior decisions by GMs.

A first tension concerns the degrees of routine in different parts of a manager's tasks. Some parts of the firm can be routinely managed, with clear goals, tasks, and outcomes, an effective incentive system, and ample information flows. The job of the GM for these tasks is to administer clearly defined systems. For other decisions, however, the task is harder. For example, GMs may have difficulty integrating disparate functions at the firm level because these functions differ in their tasks, their goals, their time span for results, and even the complexity of their language.

The problem of managing individuals from manufacturing, sales, and research and development (R&D) under a single set of policies and procedures provides a classic example of this tension. While each function may be manageable and possess characteristics with sufficient routines to allow the development of administrative procedures, the functions differ in which of their characteristics are manageable and what values to attach to a given set of results. While manufacturing has a well-defined set of tasks, a short-term time frame, and unambiguous results, R&D has less defined tasks, a long-term time frame, and more ambiguous (although potentially more valuable) results. The sales function differs from both manufacturing and R&D on these dimensions. It has a longer time frame than manufacturing but a shorter one than R&D. It has less ambiguous results than R&D, but is also less clear than manufacturing on the most efficient means to achieve its goals. To be effective, the GM must both administer each function and integrate the functions, so that the firm can coordinate how its product reaches its customers and how it develops new products. This integration function is often less routine and more sporadic, reactive, and unpredictable than the administrative tasks associated with each function. Yet the GM must perform both types of tasks.

In addition to routine and nonroutine internal tasks, the GM also faces a market at some level and must respond to unpredictable market demands, as would any other market participant. Marketplace demands become further complicated if the GM has to jump additional internal hurdles set by the firm's capital budgeting and planning systems. The policy instituted by General Electric under Jack Welch, that business units be number one or two in their respective markets or risk being sold off, is an example of how corporate management can attempt to intensify the market pressures that GMs face and thus motivate them to greater effort.

Corporate-level GMs face their own variant of this tension with their subsidiary managers. On the one hand, if they fail to intervene with divisions, they risk being seen as unnecessary and ineffective. If divisions do not need corporate guidance, then what purpose does corporate management serve? On the other hand, intervening with divisional management may harm corporate performance by hurting the ability of divisions to respond to markets. Corporate GMs also face their own integration problems in getting staff units to work together for the firm rather than to justify particular projects or groups.[26]

While some parts of the GM's tasks appear ordered, the overall demands of this job make it appear disorganized and reactive. Nowhere is this tension for GMs between routine and disorder more apparent than in formal strategic planning processes, such as those popularized by General Electric, that attempt to make strategic decision making more routine and to control the most nonroutine aspects of the business environment. Henry Mintzberg emphasizes this tension in his critique of strategic planning systems.[27]

A second tension that the GM faces stems from the need to adopt different (and potentially conflicting) perspectives, according to the particular managerial role that he or she is playing. For example, relative to the board of directors and the shareholders, the GM is an agent whose ultimate objective is to maximize shareholder value. However, the GM can also act like a principal in relationships with employees and in contractual relationships with actors outside the firm.

This tension in the GM's role relative to owners and other stakeholders is recognized in writings about top managers. Gordon Donaldson and Jay Lorsch, in their study of top management decisions, show how the GM can perceive owners as but one of the many stakeholder constituencies that must be accommodated when managing the firm.[28] Chester Barnard's inducement-contribution framework also suggests that owners, as suppliers of capital, are one group among several stakeholders of the firm and that the firm's success depends on balancing the demands of many different stakeholders.[29] David Hickson and his colleagues document how strategic decisions are characterized by the involvement of numerous parties inside and outside firms. The more parties involved, the greater the likelihood of serious conflicts of interest among them.[30]

A third tension is between the GM's implementor and adapter roles. As discussed in Chapter 8, implementing a firm's strategy often requires investments in sunk strategic assets that commit the firm to a long-term course of action. Commitment, however, presumes some stability in the firm's strategic environment, so that it can persist in its strategic activities long enough to recoup its investments. Managers are all too aware, however, that the business environment can change and that their firms need to be flexible enough to respond to these changes. The firm's strategy often conflicts with the need to respond to environmental pressures and uncertainties.

This tension between commitment and flexibility is apparent in the work of Gary Hamel and C. K. Prahalad.[31] On the one hand, Hamel and Prahalad focus on

---

[26]Goold, M., Campbell, A., and M. Alexander, *Corporate-Level Strategy: Creating Value in the Multibusiness Company*, New York: John Wiley, 1994, chaps. 5–8.

[27]Mintzberg, H., *The Rise and Fall of Strategic Planning*, New York: Free Press, 1994, pp. 380–396.

[28]Donaldson, G. and J. Lorsch, *Decision Making at the Top*, New York: Harper & Row, 1983.

[29]Barnard, C., *The Function of the Executive*, Cambridge, MA: Belknap, 1938.

[30]Hickson, D. J., R. J. Butler, D. Cray, G. R. Mallory, and D. C. Wilson, *Top Decisions: Strategic Decision Making in Organizations*, San Francisco, CA: Jossey-Bass, 1986, pp. 42–54.

[31]Hamel, G. and C. K. Prahalad, *Competing for the Future*, Boston, MA: Harvard Business School Press, 1994.

the need to build a *strategic intent*, by which they mean a fundamental focus of a firm's strategy that commits it well beyond its current resource profile. On the other hand, a firm can become inflexible and overfocused on a particular strategy. Firms need to achieve what Hamel and Prahalad describe as *strategic stretch*, which involves a focused view of strategy that combines commitment to firm intentions with the flexibility to change with circumstances.

An example of this tension between commitment and flexibility would be the situation faced by Western capital-intensive firms in seeking to develop their businesses in emerging markets. On the one hand, these firms work hard to commit resources to a new market, to gain first-mover advantages and a position that will allow them to prosper once the market develops. On the other hand, the political and economic instability of emerging markets makes firms hesitate before committing their resources. Firms that handle this tension well do so by combining sunk investments in physical capital with risk pooling of capital providers, careful contracting with host nations, and the creation of options for future investments to hedge against current commitments. These steps are part of the emerging markets strategy of Ameritech, a U.S. telecommunications firm, and show how to effectively manage this tension.

For GMs in charge of subunits within the firm, a further tension exists between firm and subunit objectives. A division of labor inside the firm that creates subunits runs the risk that managers of those units will work to maximize subunit performance at the expense of overall firm profitability. For multidivisional firms, the delegation of operational authority to divisional managers compounds the problem. This means that for product market decisions, the divisional GM is independent, while still remaining just one component of corporate profit objectives. These tensions can become particularly acute when, as in corporate portfolio strategies, the division manager may be called upon to limit the expansion of his or her own division to cross-subsidize the activities of other divisions.[32]

Changing Definitions of Managerial Work

While in many important ways, we think that managers act according to general principles that remain applicable over time, they make decisions in a changing context, which we discussed in Chapter 1. Their decisions regarding the definition of the firm and its strategic choices so change the firm and how it operates that the nature of managerial work itself changes. The nature of managerial work is defined by the nature of the firms in which managers work.[33] Since the nature of the firm has changed greatly over the last century, it is not surprising that the nature of the GM's job has also changed, no doubt frustrating the efforts of observers who seek to neatly characterize it. Writings about GMs have frequently emphasized the changing nature of managerial work, to the point where the rhetoric of change has become part of a manager's tasks, even when a manager is working in a period of relative stability rather than one of dramatic change.[34]

---

[32]Hrebiniak, L. and W. Joyce, *Implementing Strategy*, New York: Macmillan, 1984.

[33]Leavy, B. and D. Wilson, *Strategy and Leadership*, London, UK: Routledge, 1994.

[34]Eccles, R. and N. Nohria, *Beyond the Hype: Rediscovering the Essence of Management*, Boston: Harvard Business School Press, 1992, chap. 1.

When managers first became prominent, large vertically and horizontally integrated firms were new and had developed in response to the inability of existing markets to handle the requirements of firms that had to produce and distribute large volume production to a mass market. Under these conditions, the manager was seen as a visible hand that substituted for the market and whose job required much more administration than market coordination. As firms grew larger and more diverse, however, they became more difficult to coordinate. Firms responded by introducing the M-form, whose structure included decentralized decision making, profit-based controls of business unit managers, and a division of labor between corporate and divisional managers. These changes exacerbated the already difficult problems of coordination across business units and among corporate GMs and introduced market-based decision-making criteria into managers' behavior.

General views of managerial tasks and roles have tended to develop in firms in industrialized economies and then diffuse to firms in less developed economies. This diffusion has tended to follow the diffusion of industrial techniques and other managerial innovations, such as the M-form structure. As these general models of management have diffused to new settings, they have often become adapted to the social and cultural conditions of those settings. Mauro Guillen showed how this diffusion occurred as "scientific management" doctrines developed in the United States diffused to European economies, including Great Britain, Germany, and Spain.[35]

As conditions changed again in the 1990s, with the global expansion of firms, the general increase in rivalry in many industries, and changes in telecommunications and data processing that have made it possible to communicate more quickly with more people, the tasks of managers have changed further. Christopher Bartlett and Sumantra Ghoshal see these changes in terms of a shift from corporate strategy to corporate purpose.[36] By corporate purpose, Bartlett and Ghoshal mean that managers must increasingly integrate strategy and operations at much lower levels within the firm than had previously been the case. This approach combines managerial roles of value creation, implementation, and facilitation in ways that were less common in the strategy-structure approach to managing the multidivisional firm. Instilling a corporate purpose ensures that lower-level managers, who increasingly work in diverse markets around the globe, can effectively address local market issues and remain linked to corporate objectives. By internalizing corporate purpose in its employees, firms can achieve a degree of integration that would not be possible under more formalized integration approaches.

Changes in business conditions that require adaptation by managers are often limited to particular sectors or geographic areas. In deregulated industries, managers are being forced to obtain market-related skills, as traditional restrictions on entry are eliminated and new rivals emerge. In different geographic areas, political changes are forcing similar adjustments by managers. Changes in Eastern Europe, following the fall of communism in 1989, provide a good example of this. In these countries, business and governmental infrastructures were obsolete and unsuitable for current economic conditions. This has prompted large-scale experimentation throughout the region, both in the governmental sphere, where formerly state-

---

[35]Guillen, M. F., *Models of Management: Work, Authority, and Organization in a Comparative Perspective*, Chicago: University of Chicago Press, 1994.

[36]Bartlett, C. A. and S. Ghoshal, "Changing the Role of Top Management; Beyond Strategy to Purpose," *Harvard Business Review*, November–December 1994: pp. 79–88.

owned enterprises are being privatized and a commercial and legal infrastructure is being developed, and in the new private sector, where new forms of organization in manufacturing, distribution, and human resources are developing.[37] While culture and history may affect managerial needs in these emerging markets, such as with the bureaucratic culture developed under 50 years of communism, the problems of management development in these areas are similar in many ways to the general managerial challenges facing Western firms today.

General management roles are also being shaped by the changing demographic profile of the workforce in industrialized nations. The aging of the baby-boom generation, the increased entry of women into the workforce, and related factors, have made it more difficult for firms to employ the incentives and controls that had been effective with managers after World War II. Good managers are increasingly turning down promotions, transfers, and increased responsibilities in an effort to balance work and family issues. These issues are requiring firms to provide child care and related services if they hope to retain the talented managers who are a critical resource for their success.[38]

CHAPTER SUMMARY

◆ The general manager (GM) is both a problem solver and a visionary. As a problem solver, the GM defines and manages the boundaries of the firm, sets a competitive strategy, and oversees the firm's internal incentives, culture, and structure. As a visionary, the GM identifies a sustainable position for long-term success.

◆ General managers use both formal and informal means to accomplish objectives. While relying on qualitative analyses as much or more than quantitative analyses, they also rely on formal agendas and information networks.

◆ The general manager may play one or more of several roles: entrepreneurial, organizer/implementer, contractor, facilitator, competitor, and adapter. Tensions arise when these roles require conflicting actions.

◆ General managers have had to change their roles in response to changing technological, regulatory, and competitive conditions.

---

[37]Buckley, P. J. and P. N. Ghauri (eds.), *The Economics of Change in East and Central Europe*, London, UK: Academic Press, 1994.

[38]For an excellent discussion of these issues, see Bailyn, L., *Breaking the Mold: Woman, Men, and Time in the New Corporate World*, New York: Free Press, 1993; also see Arthur, M. B. and D. M. Rousseau (eds.), *The Boundaryless Career: A New Employment Principle for a New Organizational Era*, New York: Oxford University Press, 1996.

GLOSSARY

activity-cost analysis   A method of assigning costs that views the firm as a set of value-creating activities and then assigns costs accordingly, Templates such as Porter's value chain or the McKinsey Business System Framework can be used to identify the relevant activities for this analysis

agency costs   Costs associated with slack effort by employees and the costs of administrative controls designed to deter slack effort

agency theory   A theory that examines the use of financial incentives to motivate workers

agent   One to whom responsibility has been delegated

applied research   Applies principles from basic research to specific products with the goal of bringing a product to the market

arm's-length market transaction   A market transaction in which autonomous parties exchange goods or services with no formal agreement that the relationship will continue in the future

autonomous work units   Business units in which the unit managers control information about operating decisions, and in which the flow of information between units is minimal

backloaded wages   Wages which are below productivity early in the employee–employer relationship, but which exceed productivity with seniority

backward integration   An organizational arrangement, in which a downstream firm owns the assets of an upstream firm, so that the downstream firm has control over both operating decisions

barriers to entry   Factors that allow incumbent firms to earn positive economic profits by making it unprofitable for newcomers to enter the industry

basic research   Theoretical models and preliminary studies designed to further understanding of scientific principles rather than to facilitate design or development of a specific product

benefit drivers   Attributes of a product that form the basis on which a firm can differentiate itself, including: the physical characteristics of the product itself; the quality and characteristics of the services or complementary goods the firm or its dealers offer for sale; characteristics associated with the sale or delivery of the good; characteristics that shape consumers' perceptions or expectations of the product's performance or its cost in use; and the subjective image of the product

blockaded entry   A condition where the incumbent need not undertake any entry-deterring strategies to deter entry

bounded rationality   Limits on the capacity of individuals to process information, deal with complexity, and pursue rational aims

broad coverage strategy   A targeting strategy that is aimed at serving all segments in the market by offering a full line of related products

bureaucratic control   Control that is characterized by much greater specialization of organizational roles and tasks, short-term employment, individual responsibility, and individual decision making

buyer power   The ability of individual customers to negotiate purchase prices that extract profits from sellers

capabilities   Clusters of activities that a firm does especially well in comparison with other firms

causal ambiguity   A term coined by Richard Rumelt to refer to situations in which the causes of a firm's ability to create more value than its competitors are obscure and only imperfectly understood

clan control   An idea, developed by William Ouchi, which means control through a system of organizational norms and values

competitive advantage   The ability of a firm to outperform its industry, that is, to earn a higher rate of profit than the industry norm

conjoint analysis   A set of statistical tools used by market researchers to estimate the relative benefits of different product attributes

constant returns to scale   Indicates that average costs remain unchanged with respect to output

consumer surplus   The perceived benefit of a product per unit consumed minus the product's monetary price

contingency theory   An idea which posits that there is no uniformly "best" organizational structure for all firms in all circumstances; Contingency theory has focused on three factors that may affect the relative efficiency of different structures: (1) technology and task interdependence, (2) information flows, and (3) the tension between differentiation and integration

control   The location of decision-making rights and rule-making authority within a hierarchy

conversion cost   The sum of direct labor plus manufacturing overhead

cooperative pricing   Refers to situations in which firms are able to sustain prices in excess of those that would arise in a noncooperative single-shot price or quantity-setting game

coordination   The flow of information within an organization to facilitate subunit decisions that are consistent with each other and with organizational objectives

corporate culture   A set of collectively held values, beliefs, and norms of behavior among members of a firm that influences individual employee preferences and behaviors

cospecialized assets   Assets that are more valuable when used together than when separated

cost-based contract   A contract in which an agent is reimbursed for the costs deemed appropriate for producing the desired outcome, plus some prenegotiated profit margin

cost advantage   One of the major strategies to achieve a competitive advantage; When pursuing a cost advantage, firms seek to attain lower costs while maintaining a perceived benefit that is comparable to competitors

cost drivers   The basic economic forces that cause costs to vary across different organizations

cost of capital   The rate of return just sufficient to induce investors to provide financial capital to the firm

cross-price elasticity of demand   Given two products x and y, the cross-price elasticity of demand measures the percentage change in demand for good y that results from a 1 percent change in the price of good x

customer specialization   A targeting strategy in which the firm offers a variety of related products to a particular class of consumers

departmentalization   The division of an organization into formal groupings

deterred entry   Occurs when an incumbent can keep an entrant out by employing an entry-deterring strategy

differentiation advantage   One of the major strategies to achieve competitive advantage; When pursuing a differentiation advantage, firms seek to offer a higher perceived benefit, while maintaining costs that are comparable to competitors

direct labor costs   The costs of labor that are physically traceable to the production of the finished goods

direct materials costs   The costs of all materials and components that can be physically traced to the finished goods

diseconomies of scale   Indicates that average costs increase as output increases

dominant strategy   A strategy that is the best decision for the firm, no matter what decision its competitor makes

double marginalization   An inefficiency in a vertical relationship in which upstream and downstream firms both equate marginal benefit to marginal cost, but would be jointly better off by equating combined marginal revenue to combined marginal cost

due diligence   A detailed analysis of the financial and managerial consequences of a merger; The analysis relies primarily on accounting data provided by the merging firms

dynamic efficiency   The achievement of long-term growth and technological improvement

economic profit   A concept that represents the difference between the profits earned by investing resources in a particular activity, and the profits that could have been earned by investing the same resources in the most lucrative alternative activity

economies of density   Cost savings that arise with a greater geographic density of consumers

economies of scale   Indicates that average costs decrease as output increases

economies of scope   Cost savings which the firm achieves as it increases the variety of activities it performs, such as the variety of goods it produces

efficiency effect   Refers to the fact that the benefit to a firm from being a monopolist as compared with being one of two competitors in a duopoly is greater than the benefit to a firm from being a duopolist as compared with not being in the industry at all

efficiency frontier   Shows the lowest level of cost that is attainable to achieve a given level of differentiation, given the available technology

efficiency wage   A wage payment made to an agent which exceeds his opportunity cost of working. The extra payment is made to discourage the agent from shirking

endogenous fixed costs   A concept, developed by John Sutton, which refers to fixed expenditures that are not necessitated by production considerations; Examples include research and development and advertising expenses

exclusive dealing   A practice whereby a retailer agrees to sell only the products made by one manufacturer

experience good   A product whose quality can be assessed only after the consumer has used it for a while

experience goods   Goods whose quality cannot be assessed before they are purchased and used

expert power   Power that stems from the possession of specialized knowledge that is valued by some other actor or by the organization as a whole

five-forces analysis   A method, developed by Michael Porter, which systematically and comprehensively applies economic tools to analyze an industry in depth; The five forces are

internal rivalry, entry, substitute and complement products, supplier power, and buyer power

fixed costs   Costs that must be expended regardless of total output

focal point   A strategy so compelling that it would be natural for a firm to expect all others to adopt it

focus strategy   A targeting strategy that concentrates either on offering a single product or serving a single market segment or both

folk theorem   An idea that concerns the possibilities for achieving an equilibrium result in repeated play of games, such as the prisoner's dilemma; Its general result is that many Nash equilibria are possible in infinitely repeated games

forward integration   An organization arrangement, in which an upstream firm owns the assets of a downstream firm, so that the upstream firm has control over both operating decisions

game theory   The branch of economics concerned with the analysis of optimal decision making when all decision makers are presumed to be rational, and each is attempting to anticipate the likely actions and reactions of its competitors

general administrative expenses   Salaries of plant managers, security personnel, personnel administrators, cost accountants, and supervisors

geographic specialization   A targeting strategy in which the firm offers a variety of related products within a narrowly defined geographic market

Herfindahl index   The sum of the squared market shares of all the firms in a market

hierarchy of authority   An organizational arrangement in which one member of a group specializes in monitoring and coordinating the work of the other members

holdup problem   A problem that arises when a party in a contractual relationship exploits the other party's vulnerability due to relationship-specific assets; For example, a seller might attempt to exploit a buyer who is dependent on the seller by claiming that production costs have risen and demanding that the price be renegotiated upward

horizontal differentiation   Differences between products that increase perceived benefit for some consumers but decrease it for others

human capital theory   A theory, developed by Gary Becker, which suggests that workers might accept very low wages early in their careers if they receive on-the-job training that enhances their productivity and job opportunities later on

indifference curve   The set of price-quality combinations that yields the same consumer surplus to an individual

indirect labor costs   Salaries of production workers whose efforts usually are not directly traceable to the finished good, including personnel, quality-control workers, and inspectors

indirect manufacturing costs   *See manufacturing overhead*

influence costs   A concept, developed by Paul Milgrom and John Roberts, which denotes the costs of activities aimed at influencing the distribution of benefits inside an organization

internal labor market   An employer and a group of employees organized around a functional area, geographic area, or product

internal rivalry   Competition for share by firms within a market

isolating mechanisms   A term coined by Richard Rumelt which refers to economic forces that limit the extent to which a competitive advantage can be duplicated or neutralized through the resource-creation activities of other firms

joint venture   A particular type of strategic alliance in which two or more firms create, and jointly own, a new independent organization

key success factors   The skills and assets a firm must possess to achieve profitability in a given market

learn-to-burn ratio   The ratio of the "learn rate"—the rate at which new information is received by a firm that allows it to adjust its strategic choices, and the "burn rate"—the rate at which a firm is investing in sunk assets to support its strategy

learning curve   An idea that refers to the cost advantages that flow from accumulating experience and know-how

legitimate power   Formal authority one receives by occupying a high-ranking position

limit pricing   The practice whereby an incumbent firm can discourage entry by charging a low price before entry occurs

M-form   *See multidivisional structure*

make-or-buy decision   The decision of a firm whether to perform an upstream, downstream, or professional supporting activity itself or to purchase it from an independent firm

manufacturing overhead   All the costs associated with manufacturing other than direct labor and indirect materials

marginal cost   Refers to the rate of change of total cost with respect to output

market control   Control on the basis of price in a market

market definition   The process of identifying the market or markets in which a firm competes

market for corporate control   An idea, first proposed by Henry Manne, which states that control of corporations is a valuable asset that exists independently of economies of scale and scope; If this is so, then a market for this control exists and operates such that the main purpose of a merger is to replace one management team with another

market segment   A group of consumers within a broader market who possess a common set of characteristics

market structure   The number and size distribution of the firms in a market

materials overhead   The costs of indirect materials (supplies, such as glue or solder, that are used in small quantities in many products); also includes the costs related to the procurement and movement of materials, such as the salaries of purchasing, receiving, and stockroom personnel

matrix organization   An organizational form in which employees are subject to two or more sets of managers at once

minimum efficient scale   The smallest level of output at which economies of scale are exhausted

monopolistic competition   A theory of competition for markets in which there are many sellers and each seller is slightly differentiated from the rest

monopsonist   A firm that faces little or no competition in one of its input markets

moral hazard   Opportunities for shirking due to hidden action or hidden information which cannot be prevented by contracts

most favored customer clause   A provision in a sales contract that promises a buyer that it will pay the lowest price the seller charges

multidivisional structure   An organizational form that is comprised of a set of autonomous divisions led by a corporate headquarters office, assisted by a corporate staff that provides information about the internal and external business environment; Rather than organizing by function or by task, a multidivisional structure organizes by product line, related business units, or customer type

multiplant economies of scope   Economies of scope that arise when a firm diversifies into several products at one or more plants

N-firm concentration ratio The combined market share of the N largest firms in a market

Nash equilibrium Indicates an outcome of a game where each player is doing the best it can, given the strategies of all of the other players

natural monopoly A market in which there is insufficient demand for more than one firm to reach minimum efficient scale

net present value (of an investment) The present value of the cash flows the investment generates minus the cost of the investment

network externality Refers to a situation where, when additional consumers join a "network" or users, they create a positive external benefit for consumers who are already part of the network

network structure An organizational form in which work groups may be organized by function, geography, or customer base, but where relationships between work groups are governed more by often-changing implicit and explicit requirements of common tasks than by the formal lines of authority that characterize other structures

niche strategy A targeting strategy in which the firm produces a single product for a single market segment

numbers-equivalent The number of equal-sized firms that can generate a given Herfindahl index in a market; The numbers-equivalent is also equivalent to the reciprocal of the Herfindahl index

oligopoly A market in which the actions of individual firms materially affect industry price levels

opportunity cost A concept which states that the economic cost of deploying resources in a particular activity is the value of the best foregone alternative use of those resources

option value The expected net present value that arises when a firm leaves itself with options that allow it to better tailor its decision making to the underlying circumstances it faces

own-price elasticity of demand The percentage change in a firm's sales that results from a 1 percent change in price

patent race A term used to characterize the battle between firms to innovate first

perceived benefit The perceived gross benefit of a product minus the user cost of the product and minus any purchasing and transactions costs

percentage contribution margin The ratio of profit per unit to revenue per unit on additional units sold

perfectly contestable market A market in which a monopolist cannot raise price above competitive levels because of concern over possible entry

performance standard The output that a hardworking agent can be expected to produce

perpetuity A level cash flow received each year forever

piece-rate contract A contract that pays a fee for each unit of output

predatory act A strategy that increases profits by deterring entry or promoting exit by competitors

predatory pricing The practice of setting a price with the objective of driving new entrants or existing firms out of business

price elasticity of demand The percentage change in quantity demanded brought about by a 1 percent change in price

prime cost The sum of direct labor and direct materials costs

principal One who delegates responsibility to another, known as the agent

process reengineering A management philosophy which advocates that firms should not take the existing configuration of activities and processes for granted, but rather should start from scratch and redesign the chain of activities to maximize the value that can be delivered

product life cycle A model developed by the Boston Consulting Group in which demand for a product is low when it is introduced, then enters a phase in which demand grows rapidly, and later levels off as the product matures

product performance characteristics Attributes of a product that describe what the product does for consumers

product specialization A targeting strategy in which the firm concentrates on producing a single type of product for a variety of market segments

profit center A product group which contains the basic business functions of manufacturing and sales and which would be capable of existing by itself in the marketplace; Managers in these groups are controlled on the basis of a target profit goal and are rewarded for meeting or exceeding the goal and are punished for failing to achieve it

quasi-rent An amount equal to the difference between (a) the revenue a seller would actually receive if its deal with a buyer were consummated according to the original terms of the implicit or explicit contract, and (b) the revenue the seller must receive to be induced not to exit the relationship after it has made its relationship-specific investments

referent power   Power that accrues to those who have earned the admiration of others

regression analysis   A statistical technique for estimating how one or more factors affect some variable of interest

related acquisition   A purchase of one firm by another, where both firms are active in similiar lines of business

relationship-specific asset   An investment made to support a given transaction

rent   An amount equal to the difference between the revenue a seller receives in a transaction and the minimum amount it must receive to make it worthwhile for it to enter into a relationship with the buyer

replacement effect   A phenomenon whereby, despite equal innovative capabilities, an entrant is willing to spend more to develop an innovation; The reasoning behind this phenomenon is that through innovation the entrant can potentially replace the monopolist in the industry; however the monopolist can only "replace" itself

resale price maintenance   A pricing practice that allows manufacturers to dictate the retail prices for their products

reservation price   The maximum monetary price the consumer is willing to pay for a unit of a product or service

residual rights of control   All rights of control that are not explicitly stipulated in a contract

resource-based theory of the firm   A framework used in strategy based on resource heterogeneity; It posits that for a competitive advantage to be sustainable, it must be underpinned by resource capabilities that are scarce and imperfectly mobile, which means that well-functioning markets for the resources and capabilities do not or cannot exist

resource dependence   A view of power, developed by Jeffrey Pfeffer, in which individuals and firms seek to gain power by reducing their dependence on other actors, while increasing the dependence of other actors on them

resource deployment strategy   A perspective on power, developed by Edward Laumann and David Knoke, which looks at power from the standpoint of the actor providing resources

resource mobilization strategy   A perspective on power, developed by Edward Laumann and David Knoke, which looks at power from the standpoint of the recipient of resources

resources   Firm-specific assets such as patents and trademarks, brand-name reputation, installed base, and organizational culture; Resources can directly affect the ability of a firm to create more value than other firms, and can also indirectly impact value-creation because they serve as the basis of the firm's capabilities

responsibility center   A self-contained group that focuses on other performance measures besides profit, such as cost, revenue, or investment goals

risk-sharing contract   A contract that guarantees an agent some payment, but provides enough incentive so that the agent does not shirk

risk averse   Describes an agent who prefers a sure thing to a gamble of equal expected value

risk neutral   Describes an agent who is indifferent between a sure thing and a gamble of equal expected value

risk premium   An extra payment above and beyond the expected outcome of a gamble which must be offered to a risk-averse individual to willingly accept the gamble

search goods   Goods whose quality is relatively easy to evaluate before purchase

second-best contract   A contract that maximizes the principal's expected profit subject to the constraints that (1) the contract makes the agent's utility at least as high as it would be if the agent instead pursued its best alternative opportunity; and (2) the contract induces the agent to provide the level of effort the principal most prefers, given the need to compensate the agent to provide that effort

self-managed team   A collection of individuals, each member of which works with others to set and pursue some common set of objectives

short run   The period of time in which the firm cannot adjust the size of its production facilities

social exchange   A transfer between two or more parties of resources, or rights to control resources, that occurs outside the terms of a market context

soft commitment   A commitment made by a firm such that, no matter what its competitors do, the firm will behave less aggressively than if it had not made the commitment; Thus, in a Cournot game a soft commitment will cause the firm to produce relatively less output, while in a Bertrand game a soft commitment will induce the firm to charge a higher price than if it had not made the commitment

sorting   Describes a situation where the level of wages or structure of an incentive contract systematically influences the characteristics of the agents a principal can hire

span of control   The number of subordinates reporting to a supervisor

stakeholders Shareholders, employees, and others with a stake in the firm

static efficiency The optimal allocation of society's resources at a given point in time

strategic alliance An agreement between two or more firms to collaborate on a project or to share information or productive resources

strategic commitments Decisions that have long-term impacts and that are difficult to reverse

strategic complements Two or more products whose reaction functions are upward sloping with respect to the actions taken by one another

strategic group A set of firms within an industry that are similar to one another and different from firms outside the group on one or more key dimensions of their strategy

strategic intent An idea, developed by Gary Hamel and C. K. Prahalad, which means a fundamental focus of a firm's strategy that commits it well beyond its current resource profile

strategic stretch An idea, developed by Gary Hamel and C. K. Prahalad, which combines commitment to the firm's ambitions with the flexibility to change with circumstances

strategic substitutes Two or more products whose reaction functions are downward sloping with respect to the actions taken by one another

structural hole A relationship in a social network in which one actor is the critical link between individuals or entire groups; The presence of a structural hole allows the individual who can span the hole to use the control of information or resource flows to his or her own advantage

stuck in the middle The idea—argued by Michael Porter—that firms which attempt to pursue both a cost advantage and differentiation advantage simultaneously will be ineffective, providing both a lower perceived benefit to consumers than those firms that pursued a differentiation advantage and incurring higher costs than those that pursued a cost advantage

structure (of a market) The number and characteristics of the firms that compete within a market

subgame perfect Nash equilibrium An outcome of a game where each player chooses an optimal action at each stage in the game that it might conceivably reach and believes that all other players will behave in the same way

sunk cost effect A phenomenon whereby a profit-maximizing firm sticks with its current technology or product concept even though the profit-maximizing decision for a firm starting from scratch would be to choose a different technology or product concept

sunk costs Costs that have already been incurred and cannot be recovered

supplier power The ability of input suppliers to negotiate prices that extract profits from their customers

sustainable competitive advantage A competitive advantage that persists despite efforts by competitors or potential entrants to duplicate or neutralize it

switching costs Refers to costs incurred by buyers when they switch to a different supplier

tactical decisions Decisions that are easily reversed and where impact persists only in the short run

tapered integration A mixture of vertical integration and market exchange in which a manufacturer produces some quantity of an input itself and purchases the remaining portion from independent firms

targeting Refers to the selection of segments that the firm will serve and the development of a product line strategy in light of those segments

task interdependence The extent to which two or more positions depend on each other to do their own work

throughput The movement of inputs and outputs through a production process

tit-for-tat strategy A policy in which a firm is prepared to match whatever change in strategy a competitor makes

total cost function Represents the relationship between total cost and output, assuming that the firm produces in the most efficient manner possible given its current technological capabilities

total quality management A management philosophy which teaches that firms can lower their costs and maintain or increase quality by improving the efficiency of their production processes

tough commitment A commitment made by a firm such that, no matter what its competitors do, the firm will behave more aggressively than if it had not made the commitment; Thus, in a Cournot game a tough commitment will cause the firm to produce relatively more output, while in a Bertrand game a tough commitment will induce the firm to charge a lower price than if it had not made the commitment

tournament   Competition among workers to outperform one another to earn rewards and move up the hierarchy of the firm; Arises when individuals are ranked relative to one another and when the hardest-working and most able workers are promoted

transactions costs   A concept, developed by Ronald Coase, which denotes the costs to using the market—such as costs of organizing and transacting exchanges—which can be eliminated by using the firm

transfer price   An internal price between divisions of a vertically integrated firm

U-form   *See unitary functional structure*

uniform delivered pricing   A single delivered price that a seller quotes for all buyers and in which the seller absorbs any freight charges itself

uniform FOB pricing   A price that a seller quotes for pickup at the seller's loading dock, and the buyer absorbs the freight charges for shipping from the seller's plant to the buyer's plant

unitary functional structure   An organizational form in which there is a single department responsible for each of the basic business functions within the firm; This structure is characterized by a division of labor that allows for specialization of the basic tasks that a business performs; Each department depends on direction from central headquarters and probably could not exist autonomously outside the firm except as contract vendors to a firm that independently secures the other functions

unrelated acquisition   A purchase of one firm by another, where the two firms are active in different lines of business

user cost   The costs of installing, learning how to use, operating, maintaining, and eventually disposing of a product

value-added analysis   The process of using market prices of finished and semifinished goods to estimate the incremental value-created by distinctive parts of the value chain

value-created   The difference between the value that resides in a finished good and the value that is sacrificed to produce the finished good

value chain   A concept, developed by Michael Porter, which describes the activities within firms and across firms that add value along the way to the ultimate transacted good or service

variable costs   Costs, such as direct labor and commissions to salespeople, which increase as output increases

vertical chain   The process that begins with the acquisition of raw materials and ends with the distribution and sale of finished goods

vertical differentiation   Distinction of a product that makes it better than the products of competitors

vertically integrated firm   A hierarchical firm that performs many of the steps in the vertical chain itself

NAME INDEX

SUBJECT INDEX